SHOOTING
VICTORIA

SHOOTING VICTORIA

MADNESS, MAYHEM,
and the REBIRTH of the
BRITISH MONARCHY

PAUL THOMAS MURPHY

First published in 2012 by Pegasus Books

This edition first published in the UK in 2012 by Head of Zeus Ltd

Copyright © 2012 Paul Thomas Murphy

Interior design by Maria Fernandez

9 7 5 3 1 2 4 6 8

A CIP catalogue record for this book is available from the British Library.

ISBN (hardback): 9781781851272
ISBN (export trade paperback): 9781781854334
ISBN (eBook): 9781781851982
ISBN (paperback): 9781781851975

Printed in Germany

Head of Zeus Ltd
Clerkenwell House
45-47 Clerkenwell Green,
London EC1R 0HT

WWW.HEADOFZEUS.COM

To Walter and Olive Murphy

Contents

PREFACE   *ix*

Part One
YOUNG ENGLAND

1. Wedding Portrait   3
2. Bravos   30
3. If It Please Providence, I Shall Escape   52
4. That Is All I Shall Say at Present   65
5. Going to See a Man Hanged   78
6. Guilty, He Being at the Time Insane   102
7. Bedlam   123

Part Two
THE GAUNTLET

8. Most Desperate Offenders   133
9. Royal Theatre   153
10. A Thorough Scamp   171
11. Powder and Wadding   191
12. Hunchbacked Little Miscreant   207
13. Tory Spies   236

Part Three
EXHIBITIONS

14. Birthday   255
15. The Man from Adare   269
16. Cut and Thrust   293
17. The Most Disgraceful and Cowardly Thing
       That Has Ever Been Done   315
18. Great Exhibition   344

Part Four
TRIUMPH

19. What Does She Do with It?   353
20. Leap Day   376
21. Out of the Country   402
22. Blue   420
23. Worth Being Shot At   451
24. Special Verdict   471

epilogue
JUBILEE   493

Citations   521
Works Cited   641
Index   659

PREFACE

S hooting Victoria is the narrative history of the seven boys and men who, driven by a variety of inner demons, attacked Queen Victoria on eight separate occasions between 1840 and 1882. And as all but one of her seven would-be assassins attacked her publicly with pistols, *Shooting* Victoria—in the most obvious sense of that action— befits the title of this book.

Actually, however, I had a very different notion of "shooting" as I came up with this title, as well as the overall range and shape of this book. I was, rather, inspired by the title and contents of a frantic and fiery mid-Victorian essay written by the great sage and prophet of the era, Thomas Carlyle. In 1867 Carlyle was alone, his wife Jane having died the year before. He was in the twilight of his career, his greatest works behind him. And he was steeped in despair, certain that his society had erred greatly from the true path. He had become a voice—a strident and powerful one—in the Victorian wilderness. In August 1867, Carlyle responded with horror and loathing to the great national event of that year, if not of the entire era: the passage of the Second Reform Act, which in a stroke doubled the British electorate and greatly increased the voting power of the urban working class—the great "leap in the dark," as Prime Minister Lord Derby put it. Carlyle, who despised democracy as an ideology that rendered any man equal to another—"Judas Iscariot to Jesus Christ . . . and Bedlam and Gehenna equal to the New Jerusalem"—could only see out-and-out disaster as the immediate consequence of the Act's passage, a national smash-up that he likened to being carried in a boat through the rapids and over a mighty waterfall. The title of his essay is "Shooting Niagara: And After?"—a title that balances nicely Carlyle's dual concern with the disaster itself, and with the consequences of that disaster.

And after? Carlyle could see light after the coming darkness, restoration after the imminent collapse. His faith in his fellow human beings to do right may have diminished over the years. But his belief in an order-loving, chaos-abhorring divinity remained unshaken, and Carlyle proclaimed with certainty that a new and greater social order lay ahead—a new order that would come that much more quickly because of his own society's foolhardy and impetuous actions.

Shooting Victoria, as one would shoot rapids and plunge over the falls: taking on the Queen with a single, desperate, life-changing and world-changing action, leaping into the chaos with no way of knowing or telling what the consequences might be—*shooting* in this sense more precisely sums up the shape and movement of this narrative, with its dual focus on the disasters themselves, and the consequences of those disasters. For the consequences of the eight attempts unite seven separate stories into one grand epic. As each epic has a hero, so does *Shooting Victoria*: the Queen herself. For it was the Queen who repeatedly wrestled out of the chaos forced upon her by her would-be assassins a new and a greater order. Victoria, with unerring instinct and sheer gutsiness, converted each episode of near-tragedy into one of triumphant renewal for her monarchy, each time managing to strengthen the bond between herself and her subjects. *Shooting Victoria* thus documents the important if unwitting parts the Queen's seven assailants played in the great love story between Victoria and the Victorians. Their seven stories have, until now, never been brought together in one book. Victoria's story, on the other hand, has been told innumerable times; no woman of modern times has been more written about. And yet I believe that *Shooting Victoria*, in presenting Victoria's life for the first time in the context of the attempts upon her life, does contribute something new to our understanding of this truly great queen: Victoria, it becomes clear, was a canny politician who inherited a tainted monarchy and made it her life's work to create anew the stable, modern monarchy that endures to this day. *Shooting Victoria* traces that course to its triumphant conclusion: a turbulent ride down the rapids—and, I hope, an exhilarating one.

Victoria's seven would-be assassins were all shooting stars: they came from nowhere, burst into the light of public attention for a short time following their attempts, and disappeared back into obscurity, all of them living on, anonymously, for years after their attempts. Penetrating the obscurity of their lives before and after their attempts, therefore, presented quite a challenge and involved a great deal of digging through records in England, Australia, and in the United States. Without a great deal of help with these, I could not have written this book. Much of my research I conducted in Colorado, and I am greatly indebted to the staff at Norlin Library, University of Colorado—and especially Norlin's Interlibrary Loan department—for bringing the world of the seven to me in Boulder. I am grateful as well to the amazingly efficient staffs of the British Newspaper Library at Colindale, and the Public Record Office at Kew. Thanks to Colin Gale at the Bethlem Royal Hospital Archives and Museum, and Mark Stevens at the Berkshire Record Office, who enthusiastically provided insight about the Bethlem and Broadmoor Hospital records for Edward Oxford and Roderick Maclean. Thank you to Ruth Roberts, who provided valuable information on Robert Pate, and to Beatrice Behlen, archivist at the Museum of London, who allowed me the wonderful opportunity to hold and examine Victoria's curious chain-mail parasol.

I'm grateful as well to Pam Clark and the diligent and efficient archival staff at Windsor, and for the kind permission of Her Majesty Queen Elizabeth II to quote material from the Royal Archives. I cannot let this acknowledgement pass, by the way, without noting that Queen Elizabeth showed a great deal of her great-great-grandmother's pluck, and her own instinctive faith in the goodwill of her subjects, when on 13 June 1981 seventeen-year-old Marcus Sergeant fired six blanks at her while she was Trooping the Colour on the Mall, not far from Buckingham Palace. The Queen stopped to calm her horse, and, as Victoria would have done, rode on, refusing absolutely to seek safety or curtail her participation in the ceremony.

I owe thanks as well to those in Australia who assisted me in fleshing out the antipodean afterlives of the five of the seven who were transported—or transported themselves—to Australia in the wake of their attempts. Jenny Sinclair freely shared her abundant knowledge of Edward Oxford's fascinating later life in Melbourne under the alias of John Freeman—knowledge that she is putting to good use in a forthcoming book on the subject. And Carole Riley did a truly amazing job at uncovering the story of Arthur O'Connor's decades in Sydney asylums under the alias George Morton.

I cannot adequately express my gratitude to my good friends in London, who made each research journey to England a joy, and who have been the strongest supporters of this project from the very start. Thanks to Peter Burgess, Tracy Ward, Steve Terrey, Michael Guilfoyle, Nana Anto-Awuakye, John Watts, and—especially—Steve and Nina Button and Linda Gough. Thanks to Charlie Olsen, my agent at Inkwell; his unflagging enthusiasm sustained mine. Claiborne Hancock and the folks at Pegasus have been a pleasure to work with. Thank you Paul Levitt and Elissa Guralnick for giving me whatever ability to write I now have. And thank you Lawrence Goldman for teaching me to think about history. Finally, I am infinitely grateful to my wife Tory Tuttle, who read and commented upon every page of this book before anyone else did, and who for years now has patiently put up with my freeform articulations of the undigested results of my research—enduring all of that chaos before it was wrestled into some kind of order. Thank you. Love you.

"It is worth being shot at to see how much one is loved"
—Queen Victoria, 1882

"Don't know what I want, but I know how to get it"
—John Lydon, 1976

Part One

YOUNG ENGLAND

one

WEDDING PORTRAIT

O n the morning of 4 May 1840, Edward Oxford stepped out of his lodgings in West Place, West Square, at the Lambeth border of Southwark, and set off eastwards into the heart of that densely populated, proletarian district south of the Thames. He was eighteen, though his diminutive stature and baby face made him look much younger. He was—unusually for him—suddenly prosperous, with £5 in his pocket. And, for the first time in ages, he was free: unemployed by choice, and finally able to pursue the ambition that had been driving him for some time. He set off into what Charles Dickens called the "ganglion" of Southwark's twisted streets, his destination a small general goods store on Blackfriars Road.

Behind him lay one of the very rare green expanses within the gritty boroughs of Lambeth and Southwark. West Square, where Oxford, quitting his job in the West End, had moved four days before to be with his mother, his sister, and her husband, was one of the very few gardened squares on that side of the river. The square was meticulously maintained and gave this neighborhood an unusual air of gentility. And directly to the west of the square, a stone's throw away, a bucolic English-style garden relieved the area from the surrounding urban sprawl. This greenery, however, was not part of a public park—no such thing existed in Southwark at the time—but rather the connected grounds of two institutions. Directly adjacent to West Square stood the Bridewell House of Occupation, a home and school to indigent children. And behind this rose the cupola of an immense neoclassical building: Bethlem Hospital for the Insane.

Southwark had been for the last twenty-five years the latest location of Bedlam, or Bethlem Hospital, which had held many of London's insane since the fourteenth century. Behind Bethlem's walls operated a carefully structured world within a world designed to deal with different degrees and classifications of insanity. And, at the extremities of the hospital, segregated from the rest of the hospital and, with high walls, from the world outside, lay the feature that made Bethlem unique: it housed England's only purpose-built facility for the criminally insane. Communication between the worlds inside and outside the asylum was largely restricted to sound: the occasional shrieks of the patients might have carried as far as West Square; the clanking and clattering of industrial South London must have intruded upon the disturbed thoughts of the patients.

But on this day, if Edward Oxford was even aware of Bethlem's world within a world, he was headed away from it, literally and figuratively. He had his entire life largely kept himself—his dreams and his plans—to himself. Today, however, that would change. Today, Oxford would take a major step toward recognition by all of London—by the world. Today, he would buy his guns.

Back in his room at West Square, Oxford kept a locked box. When, five weeks later, the police smashed its lock and opened it, they found the cache of a secret society: a uniform of sorts—a crepe cap tied off with two red bows—and, neatly written on two sheets of foolscap, a document listing the rules and regulations of an organization optimistically named "Young England."* The documents revealed Young England to be a highly disciplined insurrectionary body. All members were expected to adopt an alias and to be well armed and prepared for covert military action: "every member shall be provided with a brace of pistols, a sword, a rifle, and a dagger; the two latter to be kept at the committee room." Every member, as well, was expected when necessary to be a master of disguise—ready to play "the labourer, the mechanic, and the gentleman." And, apparently for mutual recognition on the day of the insurrection, every member was to keep "a black crape cap, to cover his face, with the marks of distinction outside." These marks of distinction denoted rank in the organization, and the two red bows on Oxford's cap made him a captain, a position of true command, as captains were members "who can procure an hundred men." Oxford had chosen the rather transparent alias of "Oxonian," one of the four captains named in this document.

It was, on paper, an organization of over four hundred armed members. And when this document became public, many believed Oxford to be a part of a wide-ranging conspiracy to overthrow the Queen's government. But Young England was entirely Oxford's own creation, and this manifesto, though signed by a fictitious secretary Smith, was in Oxford's own handwriting. His hundred troops and the generals existed only in his own mind. This fantasy was to Oxford a compelling—now, controlling—one, for that fantasy gave him a stature wholly denied him in everyday life, as well as a profound sense of self-worth and purpose in a life that heretofore lacked both.

---

* "Young England" happens to be the same name that young Benjamin Disraeli and his companions would choose for their quasi-feudalistic movement within the Tory party, two years after this. The correspondence is almost certainly a complete coincidence, unless one of the Tory Young Englanders recalled news accounts of Oxford's society when formulating his own.

He was in the process of creating and collecting the props with which to support this fantasy. He had the cap. The sword would come. Today he would buy what he needed most to perform fully the role of a Captain of Young England: a matching brace of pistols. The shop selling the pistols was a short walk through Southwark, up the London Road, past the obelisk at St. George's Circle and the philanthropic institutions for the blind and for repentant prostitutes. Oxford likely knew nothing of what went on inside these places, but he did know the streets and the shops of Southwark well. Although he had just moved in with his family, he had lived here as a child, attending school in Lambeth; and, until the age of fourteen, he assisted his mother with a coffee shop she had run on the Waterloo Road. Oxford slipped into the human press traveling up Blackfriars Road, the bustling thoroughfare leading to Blackfriars Bridge and to the City, and ducked into Hayes's general goods store.

He wanted guns that would make an impression, that befit the important plans of Captain Oxford. Style was everything to Oxford, accuracy secondary. Hayes had exactly what he needed: a pair of dueling pistols with handsomely carved stocks. These pistols incorporated the very latest advance in firearms—the percussive cap. For the past two hundred years, most firearms had been flintlocks, on which a snapping, grinding flint would ignite loose powder, which ignited the powder in the barrel of the gun, firing the ball. By the 1830s, and because of refinements in percussive gunpowder—that is, gunpowder that would explode not upon ignition, but upon impact—flintlocks became increasingly obsolete, more and more likely to be found in pawnshops. Newer, flintless pistols fired when a cocked hammer engaged and struck a percussive cap. Like flintlocks, however, these percussive pistols were muzzle-loaded. The pistols Oxford was buying could each be fired only once; to fire again, he would have to reload powder, wadding, and ball through the front of the gun, and replace the percussive cap.

Although dueling was technically illegal, the practice was carried on, Wimbledon Common being a favorite venue. Indeed, just two months before, Prince Louis Napoleon, then in exile in London, was involved in a duel there with his cousin, the Comte Léon—a contest broken up before it started by Inspector Pearce of the Metropolitan Police (whom Oxford would soon meet). Dueling pistols, then, were still available for purchase. But these particular pistols hardly suited the purpose of the duelist, unless that purpose was to miss: they were not weapons of quality. They were priced at two guineas, or 42 shillings—overpriced, according to one gunmaker, who later valued them at less than 30 shillings. Certainly, there were cheaper pistols to be had, but a guinea apiece hardly suggested fine workmanship. Experts would later describe them as "coarsely and roughly finished," designed more for show than effect. They were manufactured in Birmingham, the center of the British firearms industry at the time, but they bore no maker's mark—an obvious sign of their shoddiness. When Charles Dickens later described Oxford's pistols as "Brummagem firearms," he intended to emphasize their utter worthlessness as weapons, virtually guaranteed to miss their targets. Oxford was certainly no expert on firearms, but he must have had some sense of the limitations of these pistols when he asked the young clerk assisting him how far a bullet would carry from them: twenty or thirty yards, he was told.

That was enough for his purpose. What was important was that he look the part: Captain Oxonian, standing steadily as he took one shot, and then another; like a duelist, a highwayman, a bravo—a dashing, handsome, romantic figure, a gentleman worthy of the world's attention. The guns were perfect for that effect. And they were guns that he could afford. With typical Victorian haggling, he bargained down the price of the pistols from 2 guineas (or £2 and 2 shillings) to £2. With the two shillings he saved, he bought a powder-flask and two bags for the pistols. The clerk took Oxford's money and entered the transaction on a slate, which his employer, Mr. Hayes, logged into his account book the next day.

Oxford made his way back past the obelisk and through the warren of side streets, to 6 West Square. Though the lodgings, kept by Mrs. Packman, were new to Oxford, his mother, his sister, and his brother-in-law had been living there for some time. Their choice of residence suggests a position of some comfort in the upper ranks of the working class, at least. A clergyman lived there, as did some of the professionals who staffed Bethlem. Oxford's mother, Hannah, had attempted a number of businesses of her own—a public house, a coffee shop—but all had eventually failed. Others in her family were more successful, however, and helpful to her: she apparently supported herself with a legacy. Oxford's brother-in-law, William Phelps, husband of his older sister, Susannah, was a baker who worked at a local soda-water factory but was on the verge of a major career change: he was days away from joining the Metropolitan Police. Oxford's family, then, fit the upscale proletarian precincts of West Street. Oxford himself, however, was far less comfortably situated. He had engaged with Mrs. Packman for a separate room, and for a separate rent. Oxford had no legacy, and no employment. The rent would quickly prove too much for him to pay, and he would very soon fall into arrears.

Oxford found his mother Hannah at home and lost no time showing her his pistols. While she knew nothing of his locked box of secrets, she did know of his childhood obsession with gunpowder and weaponry, remembering his fascination with toy cannons and remembering the arm injury he suffered as a boy, nearly blowing himself up while playing with fire and gunpowder, burning his eyebrows off and keeping him up for two nights screaming with pain. She knew, as well, that her child ached to be somebody. He had often spun out for her grandiose plans to rise in the world. A favorite dream of his came straight out of Captain Marryat's then-popular novels—the very sort of fiction Oxford loved to read. He would join the Royal Navy and move quickly up the ranks. "He said he would allow me half his pay," Hannah would later say in court, "and how proud I should be of my son when I saw his name in the papers, Admiral Sir Edward Oxford!" All he needed to realize that ambition, he told her, would be a midshipman's place, which he could obtain for £50. He had begged her to return to her family in Birmingham to get it for him. On this day, he proudly showed her his pistols as a sign of his higher stature and a promise of his coming renown.

She was not pleased. Her son had just given up his job as a barman at the Hog in the Pound, a popular public house on Oxford Street across the river. Hannah had been exhorting him to find a job since he moved in, but he made it clear to her that he was in no hurry to do that: "He said nothing was stirring, and he should rather wait till a good place offered itself than answer advertisements." And now he had wasted a huge portion of his £5—a full quarter's pay for a barman—on these pistols. "How could you think of laying your money out in such folly!" she cried out, exasperated. Oxford, humiliated, lied to her. He had not paid for these new pistols, he explained; he was simply holding them for a friend.

And then, as often happened, the shame and inadequacy he felt turned to a blind rage, the sort of rage that had previously manifested itself in his breaking anything that he could grab hold of. His mother simply could not understand how important these pistols were to him, could not understand that he was not just a barman and was not destined to live a barman's life. He was not a servant; he was *Oxonian*, Captain of Young England!

He raised one of the pistols and pointed it, cocked, at his mother's face.

That same day—4 May 1840—a diminutive young woman sat quietly a mile and a half across the River Thames in her home in the very greenest part of London, while an artist sketched her face. Queen Victoria was only two years older than Edward Oxford, a few weeks away from her twenty-first birthday. For the last three years she had sat on the British throne. The artist was her current favorite, George Hayter, who, as her official portrait painter, had depicted many of the important events in her short life. He had, at the request of her Uncle Leopold, painted her when she was a thirteen-year-old princess and heir apparent. He had painted her with her court in full pomp at her 1838 coronation. And, most famously, he had in 1838 depicted her as every inch a queen, yet very much an innocent, in her state portrait: she sits, enthroned and crowned, in a flowing, virginal white dress bedecked with the heavy robes of state, gazing to the side and upwards beyond her scepter with a hint of a wide-eyed surprise interrupting her placidity, as if she contemplated the many coming years of her reign with wonder and confidence.

And now, Hayter was sketching her for another commemoration of an important event in her reign—indeed, a turning point: Victoria's marriage to Albert of Saxe-Coburg and Gotha, which had taken place just three months before. Hayter was this time intent on capturing a very different Victoria than he had in the state portrait. In the finished wedding portrait, Victoria and Albert stand together, surrounded by and yet apart from the crowd. Victoria is dressed in white satin, a circlet of white flowers in her hair; Albert is dressed in the brilliant red uniform of a British field marshal. To Victoria's other side stands her beaming uncle, the Duke of Sussex, who gave her away, and to Albert's side stands Victoria's mother (and his aunt), the Duchess of Kent, staring intently forward. The rest of the guests form a semicircle around the wedding party, the men generally in red uniforms and the women in white, imperfectly reflecting the colors of the royal couple: Victoria and Albert literally shine in the spotlight created by the rays of the sun as they pour through an upper window of the Chapel Royal of the Palace of St. James. Victoria's expression is very much as it was in the state portrait, gazing upward in surprise and wonder. But the object of her gaze has changed completely: instead of contemplating an unseen and solitary future, it is Albert alone who is the object of her attention.

Victoria was in love with Albert, deeply and wholly, and she had no doubt whatsoever that the marriage to him was good, and right, not only for herself but for the nation as well, elevating her and it into something greater. The day after her wedding, she wrote from Windsor to her (and Albert's) Uncle Leopold, to proclaim as much:

> I write to you from here the happiest, happiest Being that ever existed. Really, I do not think it possible for any one in the world to be happier, or as happy as I am. He is an Angel, and his kindness and affection for me is really touching. To look in those dear eyes, and that dear sunny face, is enough to make me adore him. What I can do to make him happy will be my greatest delight. Independent of my great personal happiness, the reception we both met with yesterday was the most gratifying and enthusiastic I ever experienced; there was no end of the crowds in London, and all along the road.

Her new attachment, however, did not come without its confusions and potential problems. Albert was her husband and, by the domestic ideals of the time, her master, but she was Queen, with a powerful and jealous sense of her royal prerogative, as well as the firm resolve of her royal uncles and her grandfather, George III. Albert, too, could be inflexible about principle. How much authority would he have over her? What authority would he bring to the monarchy? Could he rule the household while she ruled the nation? These were questions that the young couple was to wrestle with, at times with great tension, over the coming years.

On this day, Albert was away, at the Royal Dockyard at Woolwich, reviewing the Royal Artillery, leaving Victoria alone with Hayter. The subject for which she was posing offered the perfect occasion to consider how much things had changed over the past three years—and how much she had changed since she became Queen. Now, Albert was everything to her; but on the day she came to the throne, Victoria finally knew what it was to be *alone*, and she relished the feeling. Victoria's childhood had been an unceasing struggle for personal autonomy and, with the death of her uncle King William IV, she had finally achieved it. Her childhood experience had instilled within her a hardened resolve that she would keep the monarchy entirely to herself.

She had been locked in that bitter battle for autonomy since before she could remember, and it had rendered her privileged childhood utterly miserable. Her father, the Duke of Kent, had died when she was eight months old, leaving her in a direct line of succession to the throne. If her three uncles George IV, Frederick Duke of York, and William Duke of Clarence did not bear any legitimate children, she would become Queen. Victoria's widowed mother, Victoria of Saxe-Coburg, Duchess of Kent, inherited her husband's debts along with the general disdain her royal brothers-in-law had shown him: she was a foreigner and an outsider, and very much wished to return to Saxe-Coburg. Her brother Leopold persuaded her not to for her daughter's sake. She stayed, and found much needed support in the man the Duke of Kent called "my very intelligent factotum," Sir John Conroy, late captain of His Majesty's army. Before long, Conroy, wildly ambitious, deeply unscrupulous, and with the tongue of an Iago, had rendered the Duchess wholly dependent upon him. As time passed, the likelihood of Victoria's becoming queen grew. George IV would never have another child with his estranged wife, Caroline, and was unlikely to remarry. The Duke of York resolved to remain unmarried and, in any case, died in 1828. The Duke of Clarence—who had ten illegitimate children—rested all of his hopes of an heir in his wife, Adelaide, who seemed unable to produce anything but stillbirths or sickly infants who soon died. George and William were by now old men, quite likely to die before Victoria had attained her majority. To Conroy, then, a glittering political prospect became more and more likely: he could rule Britain through the Duchess, who would almost certainly become Regent. That prospect became even more likely when, soon after the Duke of Clarence became King William

IV in 1830, the Duchess of Kent was legally designated Regent in the event that William died before Victoria's majority.

In order to realize his dream of power, however, Conroy needed to monitor, manipulate, and control Victoria, rendering her wholly dependent upon her mother. He created, to this end, a carefully-thought-out plan for the sensitive child's upbringing that was nothing less than an oppressive internment. The Duchess would have complete control over Victoria's acquaintances, her finances, her whereabouts, and her course of study. Moreover, Victoria would be presented to the public as a complete contrast to her royal uncles: as young and virtuous in comparison to them, who with their mistresses and their excesses epitomized aging vice, the moral darkness of an earlier age. The contrast was a political as well as a moral one: Victoria's uncles were, for the most part, uncompromising Tories, while the Duchess sympathized with the Whigs. Conroy devised to present Victoria as the embodiment of a new hope and a new age.

This system under which Victoria suffered became known as the "Kensington System." Conroy and the Duchess hand-picked Victoria's teachers, companions, and observers. Their choice for Victoria's governess turned out to be a grievous disappointment to them: the Hanoverian Baroness Lehzen. As Victoria grew, she and Lehzen formed an emotional bond that triumphed over Conroy's colder manipulation: Lehzen became totally devoted to the child—at times, it seemed to Victoria, her sole ally in her struggle against her mother and Conroy. For companions, Conroy imposed his two daughters upon her; Victoria despised them. A later companion forced upon her was the Duchess's Lady-in-Waiting, Lady Flora Hastings, thirteen years older than the Princess. Victoria was never allowed to be alone; she slept in a small bed in her mother's room, and could not walk down a flight of stairs without taking the hand of another. Victoria would have no money of her own; when, as Victoria approached her eighteenth birthday, the King attempted to put £10,000 a year "entirely in her power and disposal," the Duchess responded with rage, on Conroy's advice drafting a letter rejecting the offer, which she forced Victoria to copy and send to the king. ("Victoria has not written that letter," William realized.)

When Victoria was thirteen, Conroy began to build Victoria's image—in part, at the expense of her uncles'—in a new way: he sent her out on a number of "journeys" throughout the country. Conroy proposed to have her interact with the British public on all levels. Victoria visited towns and traveled throughout England, with all the trappings of royal visits—crowds of well-wishers, welcoming bands, floral decorations, addresses to and from the Princess and the Duchess—and in one case a royal salute by cannon, a practice King William quickly put a stop to. Conroy hoped to provide a connection between Victoria and the people—a connection between public and monarch that had largely been severed over the past few decades, with the madness and isolation of George III and the notorious disdain to the public shown by George IV as Regent and as King. Her predecessor, William IV, began his reign by resisting this seclusion, habitually strolling through the streets of London and mingling with passersby. The tension between monarch and public over the passing of the Reform Bill of 1832, however, encouraged William, too, to isolate himself from the public for the rest of his reign.

These journeys taught Victoria much more about her country and its people than she could learn in the isolation of her Kensington Palace classroom. She was able to experience first-hand the wide social range of the 1830s, from the fox-hunting and country-house world of the gentry in whose homes she stayed, to the middle-class ceremonial of the towns, to the hard social reality of the poor tossed in the tempest of industrial upheaval. Victoria began her lifelong journaling during the first of these journeys, and, in one of her earliest entries, she writes of the mining district outside of Birmingham:

> We just passed through a town where all coal mines are
> and you see the fire glimmer at a distance in the engines
> in many places. The men, women, children, country and

houses are all black. . . . The country is very desolate every where; there are coals about, and the grass is quite blasted and black. I just now see an extraordinary building flaming with fire. The country continues black, engines flaming, coals, in abundance, every where, smoking and burning coal heaps, intermingled with wretched huts and carts and little ragged children.

A perceptive observer, Victoria as Queen always demonstrated her greatest empathy for her subjects when she could be among them.

Victoria did not like the journeys; she suffered from bad health for much of these years, and found them extremely fatiguing. Though she was affectionate and inquisitive, her sensitivity and shyness rendered the progressions painful. It certainly did not help that Conroy maintained an oppressive control over her every movement. However selfish and despicable Conroy was in thrusting the young girl before the public, however, he taught her the key lesson for creating and preserving popularity for the tainted monarchy she would inherit: a regular, open, and completely trusting interaction with every level of her public. Encouraging her daughter to embark on a tour in 1835, the Duchess of Kent revealed more, perhaps, than she realized: "it is of the greatest consequence that you should be seen, that you should know your country, and be acquainted with, and be known by all classes."

Victoria's uncle William resented the journeys immensely, knowing very well that their object was to separate in the public eye the young child from the old man. He resented as well Conroy's and the Duchess's removing the child from Court whenever possible: William and his wife Adelaide had a great deal of affection for Victoria (and she for them), but Conroy intended his Kensington System to strain the relationship between present and future monarch—and it did. Matters came to a head at the King's seventy-fifth birthday party, at which the seventeen-year-old

Victoria and her mother were guests, along with Lord Adolphus Fitzclarence, one of William's many bastard sons, who recorded the scene. William turned venomously upon the Duchess, chastising her publicly for isolating the Princess from him—and vowing to ruin the Duchess's and Conroy's plans:

> I trust in God that my life may be spared for nine months longer, after which period, in the event of my death, no Regency would take place. I should then have the satisfaction of leaving the royal authority to the personal exercise of that Young Lady (pointing to the P[rince]ss), the Heiress presumptive of the Crown, and not in the hands of a person now near me, who is surrounded by evil advisers and who is herself incompetent to act with propriety in the station in which She would be placed.

The King was as good as his word: he lived for a month after Victoria's eighteenth birthday. As it became clear to Conroy that there would be no regency, he attempted desperately to maintain his hold over the Princess beyond her majority by forcing her to take him on as her confidential private secretary. Both Conroy and the Duchess browbeat Victoria, their efforts growing in intensity as William grew more and more ill in the weeks after Victoria's birthday. Victoria, supported by her staunch ally Lehzen, as well as by another supporter sent her by her uncle Leopold—Baron Stockmar—stood her ground.

On 20 June 1837, William died, and with him died the oppressive Kensington System. When, that morning, the Lord Chamberlain and Archbishop of Canterbury came to Victoria with the announcement of her accession—when, soon after, she met the Prime Minister, Lord Melbourne—when she then saw the Privy Council, she did all, as she pointedly notes in her journal, *"alone."* By the end of her first day as Queen, she had removed her bed from her mother's room and had dismissed Conroy from her household.

With her mother (and her mother's comptroller) relegated to a distant suite in Buckingham Palace, the young Victoria reigned according to her own will and her own whims. Her beloved Lehzen, whose loyalty to the Queen's interests was beyond question, now occupied her mother's former position: Lehzen and the Queen had adjoining bedrooms. And in political and social matters, the Queen very quickly developed a very close bond with her prime minister, Lord Melbourne, who succeeded where Conroy failed because his personality was antithetical to Conroy's: warm and affectionate, rather than cold and overbearing; a considerate and thoughtful adviser, not an impulsive tyrant. When Victoria took the throne, Melbourne was everything the politically inexperienced Queen could want in her most trusted advisor: a canny political operative with a wealth of political wisdom, able to guide her through the confusions of political etiquette and party strife. She depended upon him from the first day, when, meeting with the Privy Council for the first time, she looked over to him for cues about her behavior. Her dependence grew in the first years of her monarchy, and her affection for him grew apace—as did his for her. Melbourne spent much of his time over the next few years as a fixture of her domestic world: dining regularly at the Palace, playing chess and cards with the Queen's ladies during the evenings; riding with the Queen in Hyde Park in the afternoons. All this time, he contributed to her political education and, as their friendship developed, so Victoria developed a political outlook that reflected her mentor's: Melbourne was a Whig, of course. Victoria, the daughter of one of the few Whigs among the royal Dukes, and who grew up in a Whig atmosphere—the Duchess of Kent being at the center of the Whig opposition of the past few years—had always seen herself a Whig. But Melbourne's Whiggism was a distinct variety: Melbourne was hardly a reformer, and his government sought no major changes, indeed seeing resistance to change, and to any parliamentary struggle, as a positive end in itself. Moreover, Melbourne demonstrated to the Queen an innate cynicism in their everyday conversation that she found charming, recording in her journal with approval his cutting comments about women, about the poor, about the Irish. She drank in his adherence to *laissez-faire* economics, any violation of which—say, to improve the dire lot of the overworked factory child—was anathema. Surrounded by her Whig ladies in waiting, and in constant communication with her Prime Minister, Victoria became a thorough political partisan in her first years: a Whig, or more accurately a Melbournian.

Her first year, from ascension to coronation, had been a giddy one, in which the nation seemed to share her joy in emerging into a new world—free of the old uncles, the unsullied reign of a young woman. Her eldest surviving uncle, Ernest, Duke of Cumberland, had left Britain to take up the throne of Hanover, which, as a woman, Victoria was denied by Salic Law. Good riddance to him; he was the most reactionary of all her uncles: one of his first acts at Hanover was to abolish its constitution. The fact that he was Victoria's heir only served to cause the overwhelming majority of her subjects to wish her a long life, and a fruitful one in every respect. Her popularity during this time was unparalleled, and Parliament testified in its own way to this royal excitement by voting the Queen £200,000 for her coronation, fully four times what had been spent on the coronation of William IV. It was very much a public affair, designed to represent her physical contact with her people, foregoing a closed coronation banquet (as had been the tradition before William IV) for a state procession through the streets of London. The procession echoed Princess Victoria's journeys on a much larger scale, and once again brought home to Victoria the fundamental role that simply being among her subjects would play in the success of her reign:

> It was a fine day, and the crowds of people exceeded what
> I have ever seen; many as there were on the day I went
> to the City, it was nothing, nothing to the multitudes,
> the millions of my loyal subjects, who were assembled

in every spot to witness the Procession. Their good humour and excessive loyalty was beyond everything, and I really cannot say how proud I feel to be the Queen of such a Nation.

That idyllic relationship could not last forever, of course; and in 1839, in the second year of Victoria's reign, she was personally and politically disturbed by two interrelated scandals at court, as her adamant partisanship and her innate stubbornness together worked to diminish her popularity.

From the start, Victoria preferred to surround herself with sympathetic and loyal ladies—which, in her mind, meant Whig ladies. With Melbourne's encouragement and in the face of Tory protests, she kept her household free of Tories. One exception to this—one that Victoria had little control over—was the Duchess of Kent's Tory lady-in-waiting, the now 32-year-old Lady Flora Hastings, whom Conroy had attempted to impose upon the Princess as a companion years before. Though the Duchess was relegated to a distant part of the Palace, and Conroy effectively banished from the royal presence, Lady Flora Hastings was by her position a part of Court life—and therefore a living reminder to the Queen of the despised Kensington System. Moreover, there were rumors at court that Hastings and Conroy were romantically involved. In January 1839, Lady Flora returned to Court from home (sharing a carriage on the way with Conroy) with a protuberance of her stomach that clearly suggested to Victoria, Lehzen, and the ladies of the bedchamber that she was pregnant. Who exactly started this rumor is unknown, but Victoria was certainly one of the first to think so, recording in her journal her (and Lehzen's) certainty not only that Hastings was *with child!!*" but that "the horrid cause of all this is the Monster & Demon Incarnate"—Conroy.

Lady Flora was not pregnant. She was ill, with a growth on her liver that would, in a few months, kill her. She had the Duchess of

Kent's (and the Queen's) physician, Sir James Clark, examine her, fully clothed; he prescribed rhubarb pills and a liniment, and was himself suspicious that she was pregnant. As suspicions grew, and as the moral welfare of the younger ladies in waiting was apparently being challenged in such a brazen fashion, the senior ladies in waiting—with the encouragement of Baroness Lehzen—took steps to force Lady Flora to prove her innocence, informing the Duchess that Lady Flora was no longer welcome at court unless she did so. The next day, Lady Flora consented to be examined under her clothes by Sir James Clark and another physician, Sir Charles Clark. The Doctors Clark examined her and issued a vindication: Lady Flora, they declared, was a virgin. Victoria immediately wrote her a note of apology.

The matter, however, did not end there. Both Doctors Clark still had their suspicions, and the day after the examination they brought them to Melbourne. Yes, they were sure that Lady Flora was a virgin. Nevertheless, they thought, she still might be pregnant—such a thing had been known to happen. Melbourne clung to this cynical theory of virgin pregnancy, and so did Victoria, writing to her mother that Sir Charles Clark "had said that though she is a virgin still that it might be possible and one could not tell if such things could not happen. There was an enlargement in the womb like a child." The poisonous atmosphere only grew, and so did the rumors; soon, the press was involved, generally very unsympathetic to the Queen. Flora Hastings wrote frank accounts of her plight to her influential Tory relatives, who relayed details to the press. Soon there was a call for an investigation: Who had started this insidious rumor? Lehzen was the primary suspect, and Victoria could not help but think herself the victim of a campaign to remove her closest companion from her Court. (Her fears were only strengthened by the suspicion that Conroy was behind much of the press's clamor.) At the end of March, one of Lady Flora's letters, blaming "a foreign lady"— Lehzen, obviously—appeared in the *Examiner*: the entire affair, according to Lady Flora, was a Whig plot to discredit herself and the Duchess of Kent.

By May, Lady Flora was gravely ill, but forced herself to go out into public, to dispel any rumors about her immorality. She was cheered, while Victoria found herself and Melbourne were hissed when in public—riding in Hyde Park, and at Ascot, where she was additionally mortified by cries of "Mrs. Melbourne." Melbourne and Victoria held to their suspicions until very close to the end, laughing in early June at the excuse that illness was keeping Lady Flora from Court. When Victoria visited her in person at the end of the month, however, her suspicions were gone: Lady Flora was obviously dying. She died on 5 July 1839. A post-mortem revealed that she had of course never been pregnant. With Lady Flora's death, the newspaper attacks on the Queen redoubled, and her public image was seriously compromised. In accord with the tradition of the time, she sent her empty carriage to Lady Flora's funeral: some threw rocks at it.

In the midst of the Flora Hastings affair came another crisis, of shorter duration in itself, but of longer-lasting consequence. Melbourne's government existed by virtue of a tiny majority; it was sure to fall at any time. In early May 1839, it did, when radicals and Tories combined to defeat the government's motion to impose Parliamentary control over Jamaica. Victoria was thrown into a "state of agony, grief and despair," both at the prospect at losing her Melbourne—whom she would obviously prefer to have as her minister forever—and at the unpleasant prospect of working with his successor. Sir Robert Peel was "stiff" and "close," according to Melbourne. In her first interview with Peel, Victoria found him a complete contrast to Melbourne: he was cold and inflexible— someone, apparently, cut from the Conroy cloth.

Melbourne advised her fully during the negotiations for a new government, and did her a great disservice by appealing to her fierce Whig partisanship, encouraging her to make no changes whatsoever in her household, "except those who are engaged in

Politics," by which he meant those male members of her household who were also members of Parliament. Conroy had imposed her companions on her; she should not let Peel do the same. And Melbourne had assured her that by precedent, queens had the power of choice over their ladies. Peel disagreed, holding that precedent—the constitution of the households of earlier queens—did not apply in this case for the simple reason that Victoria was a reigning queen, and for the monarch to surround herself completely with Whig ladies—who, after all, amounted in a sense to her most intimate advisors—during a time of Tory government would signify to the world that the Queen had no confidence whatsoever in that government. Victoria and Peel reached an impasse: unless she replaced the Mistress of the Robes, and some senior Ladies of the Bedchamber, with Tories, he simply could not form a government. Victoria was adamant: as she wrote in her Journal,

> Sir Robert said, "Now, about the Ladies," upon which I said I could not give up any of my Ladies, and never had imagined such a thing. He asked if I meant to retain all. "All," I said. "The Mistress of the Robes and the Ladies of the Bedchamber?" I replied, "All."

Melbourne met with Whig leaders and—encouraged by the Queen's stalwart accounts to Melbourne of her interviews with Peel—agreed to form another ministry. The Queen, then, held her ground and kept her Ladies and her beloved Melbourne—for another two years, as it turned out; Melbourne was still her Prime Minister as she sat for Mr. Hayden on this day in May. She would later admit that her partisanship was a mistake, but for now she was happy at the outcome, even though what became known as the Bedchamber Crisis further tarnished her public image and perpetuated a weak, unpopular, do-nothing Parliament.

Criticism of the Queen from the Flora Hastings scandal continued into the fall of 1839. But by that time, Victoria found a complete distraction from the scandal: her cousin Albert came to England.

During the first two years of her reign, Victoria, freed from Conroy's oppression and intoxicated with the autonomy that came with the throne, buttressed with the affectionate support of Lehzen and by "dear" Lord Melbourne, was cool to the idea of marriage, and indeed had made up her mind to delay marriage by two or three years. Her sentiments shifted in an instant, however, when she stood at the top of the staircase on the evening of 10 October 1839 to welcome her cousin from Coburg. She had met him three years before, as Princess, when a number of her cousins had been brought before her for her consideration. He had been shorter, stockier—a boy, then: now, he was tall, very handsome—a man, and in an instant, he was the paragon of men to her. "It was with some emotion that I beheld Albert—who is *beautiful*," she wrote; she was in love with an intensity far greater than she would ever feel for any other mortal. She was, she felt from the start, unworthy of his greatness, and her new object in life was, as she put it, to "strive to make him feel as little as possible the great sacrifice he has made." Over the next three days, she sent encouraging messages to him, via Lehzen; on the 15th, she proposed to him. (*Her* proposing to *him* was a bit awkward, of course, but, as she was monarch and he was not, she realized it had to be that way: though overwhelmed by love for him, she could never, and would never, forget the prerogatives and responsibilities of her position.)

Albert accepted, the more enthusiastically as he too had very quickly developed a genuine affection for his cousin. His own emotions aside, he was eager to accept her hand; since the time he was an infant, he had been groomed by his family to be consort to Victoria. His cosmopolitan and rigorous education, coupled with his innate and powerful sense of duty, prepared him for this, and for nothing besides this. Indeed, he had caught wind of the Queen's plan to delay the marriage, and had come to England with the intention of putting an end to that notion, one way or another.

The simple sight of him convinced Victoria that her marriage to Albert—and marriage quickly—was her destiny.

He was a happy choice, in almost every respect. He grew up in a bitter, broken home—a place of mutual adultery, separation, and divorce—and he was at a very young age separated from his mother. His father was the ugly, dissipated, indebted Duke of Coburg, and his brother Ernest promised in every way to follow in the footsteps of his father. Albert hardly seemed to be related to them: he was fair (while they were dark), he was sober, studious, with a zealous sense of duty and a deeply held belief that a good life was one of good works. He was, in short, more a Victorian than Victoria was. And he was *hers*, Victoria felt, with the sense that this was too good to be true. Life at court quickly shifted so that now Albert and Victoria shared the spot at the center: he prominently rode beside her in her cavalcades and at a military review. They lunched several times a week with the Duchess. Albert, of course, was the Duchess's nephew, and the engagement itself began to lift Victoria's relation with her mother out of the depths into which it had dropped. Both Victoria and Albert, however, had decided that the Duchess would have to move out of the Palace when they married, and this—very much contrary to the Duchess's own expectation and desire—would create new tensions between Victoria and her mother. (The Duchess did indeed move out of the Palace two months after the wedding, and moved into a private residence in Belgrave Square.) For the most part, Victoria and Albert spent the first few days of their betrothal surprising one another, becoming familiar with one another's bodies: holding hands, embracing, kissing. Albert quickly took upon himself what had been Lehzen's task of warming the Queen's tiny hands with his own. He also found his place beside her while she worked, but in a way that made it clear to both that the political responsibilities were very much Victoria's: "I signed some papers and warrants etc.," she wrote in her Journal, "and he was so kind as to dry them with blotting paper for me."

By the time Albert left the Court, on 14 November, in order to spend two months in Germany before the wedding, the two were very much one.

The ambiguous nature of Albert's role in national affairs, however, placed public and private strains on the relationship. There was, first of all, the question of the Prince's allowance. Traditionally, male or female spouses of the reigning monarch were awarded £50,000 a year; Queen Anne's, George II's, and George III's spouses got that amount, as did Uncle Leopold when he married Charlotte, daughter and Heir Apparent of George IV. Leopold, however, hardly helped the Prince's cause: after Charlotte died in childbirth in 1817, Leopold continued to receive his allowance, until he gave it up in 1831 to become King of the Belgians: a huge public expenditure in return for no public duty. The British public knew very little about Albert at the end of 1839, but it did tend to see him as a penniless German princeling who had surely made an excellent financial move by this betrothal. A broadsheet of the time expressed the following unflattering and cynical sentiments:

Here comes the bridegroom of Victoria's choice,
The nominee of Lehzen's vulgar voice;
He comes to take "for better or worse"
England's fat Queen and England's fatter purse.

Melbourne had promised the Queen an allowance of £50,000 for Albert, but he was of course the head of a weak government, existing during a time of economic and political difficulty; Tories and Radicals turned down that sum, and instead awarded an allowance of £30,000. Victoria raged against the "vile, confounded, infernal Tories," and particularly against that "nasty wretch" Peel, who had spoken in favor of the bill. Albert was far more complacent with the vote, regretting only that it would lessen his ability to do good to poor artists and intellectuals.

Then, there was the question of Albert's precedence: a serious question, given the many official appearances that Albert would be expected to make, with and without the Queen, over the next decades. Victoria felt deeply that her husband should take precedence over all except for herself, as monarch: take precedence, in particular, over her living royal uncles. While her uncles Cambridge and Sussex at first agreed with her, her wicked uncle Cumberland would have none of it—and he bullied his royal brothers into taking his side. The Tories, and particularly the Duke of Wellington, also objected—holding that the consort had precedence over all except the monarch and princes of the Royal Blood. Victoria responded with partisan, Jacobean rage: "this wicked old foolish Duke, these confounded Tories, oh! May they be well punished for this outrageous insult! I cried with rage. . . . Poor dear Albert, how cruelly are they ill-using that dearest Angel! Monsters! You Tories shall be punished. Revenge! Revenge!"

That Victoria fumed about Albert's rank might suggest that she foresaw that Albert, after the marriage, would be her political equal. But nothing could be further from the truth. Two disagreements that the two had, in making arrangements for the wedding and their life together, demonstrate clearly that Victoria saw the business of ruling as belonging to her alone. When Albert suggested that the two spend at least a week after the wedding away from business, on a true honeymoon, Victoria responded patronizingly to him, in a way that made it clear that there were strict political limits to their shared life: "You forget, my dearest Love, that I am the Sovereign, and that business can stop and wait for nothing. Parliament is sitting, and something occurs almost every day, for which I may be required, and it is quite impossible for me to be absent from London; therefore, two or three days is already a long time to be absent. I am never easy a moment, if I am not on the spot, and see and hear what is going on. . . ."

Just as serious was the question of the composition of Albert's household. Victoria, with the support of Lord Melbourne, believed that Albert's household staff should, in composition, politically reflect her own staff; anything less would suggest a political difference among the couple—and could even suggest a political opposition within the Court. That meant a fully Whig household, of course; Melbourne attempted to soften the effect by appointing "non-political" Whigs—that is, Whigs not currently serving in Parliament. And he suggested as Albert's private secretary his own secretary, George Anson. Albert disagreed with Melbourne completely. He already saw himself as a stranger in a fairly strange land, and would very much have preferred to surround himself with a number of old (and of course German) acquaintances. Moreover, he disagreed vehemently with his betrothed and her prime minister on principle: he had already seen the reputation-damaging effect of the Bedchamber Crisis, and held as a bedrock belief that the monarch and the monarchy must remain above party. It would be a principle that would eventually triumph and reshape Victoria's reign and every reign that followed hers. But now, Albert was powerless: "As to your wish about your gentlemen, my dear Albert, I must tell you quite honestly that it will not do," Victoria wrote him. Anson became Albert's secretary, and Victoria made it clear that her political autonomy in the marriage was to be total.

Albert returned to England on the 8th of February, after a horrendous sea crossing—and to enthusiastic crowds from Dover to Buckingham Palace. Cheering crowds were always to be a barometer indication of the health of the relationship between monarch and public, and she was well aware of the crowds during and after her wedding, as promising a marriage and a reign that was blessed. "I never saw such crowds of people," Victoria wrote, as she had seen in the park between Buckingham Palace and the Chapel Royal at St. James. And then the glorious ceremony, less glorious to Victoria because of the red, gold, and white trappings of the ceremony (with which Hayter was faithfully festooning his state painting) than because of the perfect man with whom she was exchanging solemn vows. Victoria was in ecstasy about the match in every respect, including the physical. Victoria was neither a prude, as traditional-ists have it, or an erotic firecracker, as the revisionists do. But she was an extremely affectionate and physical being, and she was a woman extremely attracted to male beauty, truly believing Albert to be the most beautiful man, physically, she had ever seen. Her joyful journal entries after her marriage express repeated awe at Albert's body. The morning after the wedding, she waxed ecstatic about Albert's—throat: "He does look so beautiful in his shirt only, with his beautiful throat seen . . . He had a black velvet jacket on, without any neckcloth on, and looked more beautiful than it is possible for me to say."

After their marriage, unanswered questions about Albert's role in the monarchy continued to strain their relationship. Socially, he and the Queen were one: riding together in the afternoons, cheered at the theatre or dancing together in the evenings. But for someone raised for duty, eager to take on the responsibilities of government, Albert was thwarted at every turn. He still helped the Queen with the blotting paper when she signed official documents, but that was as close as he got to them. He was not allowed to see the contents of the state boxes. When Victoria saw her ministers, she saw them alone—as she had, on principle, from the first day of her reign. Even the running of the household was closed to him: all of Victoria's personal expenses were handled not by the Prince, but by Lehzen. Indeed, Lehzen's deep personal loyalty to Victoria now acted as a gall to the Prince: something that he saw as standing between the two of them. By May, he was writing complainingly to a friend that he was "the husband, not the master of the house."

He did find ways to take on a greater role in the monarchy. For one thing, there were the personal appearances as Victoria's repre-sentative; this was the reason he was in Woolwich now. He would soon be involved in non-partisan, charitable organizations: he had accepted the presidency of the Anti-Slavery Society; he was slated to give his first public speech in England for that organization on the first of June. And, of course, there was the coming event that would change the nation and reform his relationship with Victoria: within weeks of the wedding, Victoria knew she was pregnant; now, at three months, her "interesting condition" was becoming more obvious to the world, and certainly to the perceptive artist who sketched her.

At six that evening, Albert returned to her. Before she married, Victoria had regularly exercised on horseback, but soon after her marriage—and perhaps because of her pregnancy—she stopped, preferring to take her airings with her husband, in an open carriage. While in residence in London, the two regularly rode out in the late afternoons; their rides regularly reported in the Court Circular, published in every newspaper. Their rides were regular enough so that crowds outside the Palace gathered to cheer them. This evening was no exception: soon after Albert's return, the two emerged, accompanied by their equerries, for their regular airing up Constitution Hill and in Hyde Park.

two

BRAVOS

Hannah Oxford did not know, and would never know, whether the pistol her son had thrust into her face was loaded or not. But she had seen this sort of violent and irrational behavior many times before—from Edward, and from Edward's father (also named Edward) before him. The elder Edward Oxford's behavior suggested what we would diagnose today as extreme bipolarity: he cycled regularly between episodes of frantic mania, followed by tremendous bouts of depression. More than once, neighbors discovered him riding indoors on horseback, and at another time throwing his entire dinner ("both meat and vegetables") out the window. When Edward was an infant, he sold every stick of furniture in his house without telling his wife, and decamped to Dublin to spend the money. He repeatedly threatened to harm himself, and at least twice attempted to kill himself with an overdose of laudanum.

His marriage to Hannah was a nightmare. As their son was to do, he threatened her with pistols. He abused her mentally, threw things at her, regularly beat her. The two had met when they were both twenty, in the Birmingham public-house that Hannah's father owned. From the start, the elder Oxford intimidated her. Their six-week courtship—if courtship is the proper term for the torment Hannah experienced—consisted of his beating down her will: he repeatedly and unsuccessfully pressed her to marry him, and "on those occasions," according to Hannah, "he would pull a razor out of his side pocket, and bare his throat, saying he would cut his throat in my presence if I refused him." Eventually, he showed her a double-barreled pistol and threatened to blow her and then his brains out if she refused him. She accepted.

Oxford's father was, by profession, a gold-chaser, or engraver—a highly skilled and remunerative craft, one that earned him £20 for a good week—the same amount his son later earned in a year. According to his wife, he was skillful and quick, "the best workman in Birmingham." He was, however, an outsider. He was reportedly ethnically distinct: the son or grandson of a black father.* (Hannah Oxford, however, denied this.) Moreover, the man's inner demons destroyed any hope of worldly success, and any hope of a successful marriage. On the day before their wedding, Hannah confronted him with a letter she had received, detailing his bad character. He responded by pulling a large roll of banknotes from his pocket and setting them afire. Intimidated again, Hannah married him.

Her husband's abuse only increased with time. He tormented his wife when she was pregnant with Edward's older brother: starving her, throwing things at her, making faces at her: "jumping about like a baboon, and imitating their grimaces." This sort of behavior to a pregnant woman would strike most Victorians as particularly

---

* "The prisoner's father was a mulatto, and his grandfather was a black." *Morning Chronicle* 12 June 1840, 7; "Oxford's great grandfather was a black man, but how he came to England none of the family can tell, which is no doubt extraordinary. . . ." *Caledonian Mercury*, 18 June 1840, 4.

ominous, as many at the time believed that a woman's extreme emotional shock during pregnancy could physically and mentally imprint itself upon the child. The superstition is perhaps best remembered today in the celebrated case of Joseph Merrick, popularly and cruelly known as the Elephant Man, whose deformities, his mother believed, were a direct result of her stumbling into the path of a parading elephant while she was pregnant.

Oxford's brother was born, in the terminology of the day, an idiot, and died at two. When Hannah was pregnant with Edward, his father repeated his abusive behavior: the grimaces, the threats—and the physical abuse: he knocked Hannah unconscious with a quart pot, and a local surgeon treated her frequently at this time for head injuries. Hannah herself believed her husband's abuse the cause of her son Edward's eccentricity, claiming that his torment "had an effect upon her then situation by means of that species of secret sympathy of which there are many instances, and communicated to the unborn child the insanity with which the father was afflicted."

Edward was born on 9 April 1822, and, whether because of upbringing, or genetics, or even "secret sympathy," his behavior eerily reflected his father's. Edward for the first years of his life was a witness to his father's excesses—though, by all accounts, father and son got on very well. After years of abuse, when Edward was five or six, Hannah finally separated from her husband. Oxford Senior died in 1829, on the 10th of June—a date that his son knew about and remembered: a date, perhaps, very much on his mind when he was living at West Place.

From an early age, Edward had fits of unprovoked, maniacal laughter. Hannah later admitted that she attempted to cure him of this by beating him. Edward's fits were extremely disruptive; Hannah supported herself in her widowhood first with a pastry shop, and then with a coffee-and-tea shop, both of which failed—because of young Edward, according to Hannah: "my customers complained of his conduct" of "crying out and bawling aloud," she claimed, "and I lost my business." Edward would have episodes of near-catatonia, and episodes of motiveless, violent rage, in which he would "knock and destroy anything he might have in his hand." His fits were often directed against strangers, as when he positioned himself in the upper room of his house and rained household goods on the heads of passersby. "He was once taken to the station house for this," said his mother, "and he did not seem conscious of having done wrong." Another time, he was brought to the station house for leaping onto the back of the carriage of a woman he did not know, simply to torment her. Edward proved to be too much for his mother to handle, and she left much of his upbringing to others: he lived with his uncle Edward Marklew, Hannah's brother, and with his maternal grandfather for some time; he stayed with a neighbor, George Sandon, for about a year; he boarded at schools in Birmingham and South London. His odd behavior continued at all of these places. Sandon recalled that he constantly beat other children, "very severely." Sandon also remembered his "habit of throwing things out of the up-stairs upon children below." And there were his laughing and crying fits. "When I asked him why he did so," according to Sandon, "he gave me no straightforward answer, but ran out, which I thought was very singular for a boy of eight years of age." Not surprisingly, as a boy, Oxford had very few friends.

Coming from a family of publicans on his mother's side, Edward was "brought up to the bar," as he later joked, at the age of four- teen, working for his aunt Clarinda Powell at the King's Head, in Hounslow, southwest of the metropolis. He proved to be a gener- ally capable (though at times scatterbrained) employee. Still, he continued to attract trouble. He was arrested after a scuffle with a neighbor—he struck the man on the head with a chisel, was brought before a magistrate, and found guilty of assault. At the time, his aunt Clarinda defended him. But she certainly had serious doubts about the boy's sanity. He seemed incapable of empathy. When, for example, Oxford overheard a customer at the King's

Head speak to his aunt Clarinda about the vicious assault he had suffered the night before, he could only laugh and "jeer" at the injuries the man had received. As he had done when he assisted his mother, Oxford tended to unnerve customers and cost his aunt business: his aunt remembered one time, when she was ill, leaving Edward to run a busy bar. At ten o'clock, hours before closing time, he methodically shut off every gas jet in the house, plunging the crowded pub into complete darkness. "He could not account why he did so," she claimed. "I was obligated to come down from a sick bed, at the risk of my life, to soothe him." The King's Head closed eleven months after Oxford's arrival.

Oxford then—without his aunt's reference, she later made clear—sought employment in London, and worked for the next three years in three public houses, located ever closer to the heart of the metropolis: first, the Shepherd and Flock, on Marylebone High Street, then the Hat and Feathers, in Camberwell, and finally at the Hog in the Pound, at the intersection of Oxford and Bond Streets. He held the position of barman at these pubs, and, not surprisingly for someone who created the rank-obsessive organization of Young England, he was obsessive about his place in the public house hierarchy: as he would later protest, not a lowly potboy, but the man who drew pints, poured spirits, and oversaw the till. As a barman, he earned something around £20 a year, or approximately eight shillings a week. That pay would put him on a level with the poorest of the poor as described by social investigator Henry Mayhew in his revelatory *London Labour and the London Poor*. But of course Oxford had one great advantage over the street-folk described in that work: free room and board. His wages, then, were not terrible—but would never give him the wealth or independence that befitted a Captain of Young England.

Edward Oxford's London employers generally considered him a capable and efficient worker, though they, as well as their employees and customers, could not help but be baffled and disconcerted by his eccentric behavior. The inexplicable, maniacal laughter continued. He would fall into deep self-absorbed trances, spells of heated internal dialogue, activity visible to onlookers only in the resultant bursts of heightened emotion. A reporter at the *Morning Chronicle* described one such episode, at the Shepherd and Flock:

> When not engaged in his business and while sitting down in front of the bar he has been observed by Mr. Minton and the barmaid, a respectable young woman named Evans, to be for a few minutes absorbed in deep thought, and, then, without any apparent cause he would burst into tears, and conceal his face with his hands, when on being spoken to and asked what had affected him, he would stare at the inquirer, and, suddenly starting up, give way to a fit of laughter, and proceed with his employment as usual.

Mary Ann Forman, a barwoman at the Shepherd and Flock, recalled his "strange ways": "laughing and crying when he made a mistake, and then he hardly knew what he was about." John Tedman, an Inspector with the Metropolitan Police and a regular at the Shepherd and Flock, often came upon the boy crying, laughing hysterically for no reason, or sullenly silent, and noted as well his propensity for violence. He concluded quite simply that Oxford was an idiot and persuaded Mr. Minton, landlord of the Shepherd and Flock, to turn him away. Oxford moved on from the Shepherd and Flock to another pub, the Hat and Feathers, taking one great prize with him: to his fortune, Mrs. Minton had died while he was there, and in accordance with the custom of the day, Mr. Minton purchased full mourning dress for all of his employees; Oxford thus had a suit of clothing that suggested a respectability above his station.

Trouble seemed to follow him; he tended to work for a few months at each place, impressing upon customers and co-workers alike his oddities. His employment at the Hat and Feathers lasted six months. From there, Oxford moved to the Hog in the Pound on Oxford Street. Mr. Robinson, the landlord there, had to let him go after a single quarter. "I gave him warning because he was always laughing," Robinson claimed. "When I reprimanded him for it he still kept laughing. This often took place, and I suffered inconvenience from his conduct. Some of my customers were offended with it." Robinson must have been particularly mortified when his wife's falling down a flight of stairs provided Oxford with another occasion for an uncontrollable fit of laughter.

When Robinson sacked him, on April 30th, 1840, he provided him with a quarter's wages—the £5 with which he bought his pistols, four days later.

Oxford now had £3, no job, and time: five weeks, to think, to read, and consciously to transform himself into a marksman and a gentleman of affairs: someone with mysterious connections with illustrious figures, caught up in a complicated political conspiracy. He aimed to make Young England credible to the nation. He settled into a routine at West Place. Oxford's mother Hannah had stayed with Oxford for only a week after he had threatened her, at which point she decamped for Birmingham and an extended stay with her relatives there. Whether she had planned on this trip before Oxford's arrival, or whether his own behavior motivated her to leave is not known—but certainly, he could not have been easy to live with: he is known to have threatened her with a pistol again, and struck her in the face, during their few days together. With Hannah gone, Oxford's sister Susannah Phelps became the primary witness to his behavior and the primary object of his torment; as he had done with his mother, he often thrust his pistols into her face, once waking her in this way. Despite this, she later claimed that his regular and virtuous routine demonstrated his innocence of conspiracy: he spent his days at home, took his meals with his remaining family, abstained from drinking, and though he did leave the house regularly—setting out in the late afternoon—he was always home by ten or eleven at the latest: regular hours, she thought, that would not be conducive to membership of Young England, which she was sure must be a society whose meetings were conducted in hidden places in the depths of the night.

Despite later public opinion which held Oxford to be an idiot, he was actually an avid reader and spent much of his time this month intent upon his books, flying into a rage if his sister interrupted him. His favorite novels were sea tales, tales that would certainly feed his ambition to become Admiral Sir Edward Oxford: he read James Fenimore Cooper's *The Pilot*, and the far less-known and much more lurid *Black Pirate*, a book that suggests Oxford's love of pedestrian sentiment and high melodrama: of the stuff in other words that popular publishers of penny dreadfuls would be churning out *en masse* within the next few years to the general disapproval of polite society.

Two other books that Oxford read were recently published, highly popular, and highly controversial: Charles Dickens's *Oliver Twist* and William Harrison Ainsworth's *Jack Sheppard*. Both novels after their initial success attracted criticism amounting to opprobrium from a number of critics, who lumped them together as "Newgate novels," and held that by glorifying criminals, they would lead impressionable young readers into lives of vice: Dickens, by rendering the criminal entertaining, and Ainsworth, even worse, by rendering it heroic. Oxford was exactly the sort of impressionable youth critics thought these books would corrupt.

Oxford clearly found true inspiration in the other book he read while at West Place. *The Bravo of Venice*, a German novella written nearly fifty years before, anticipates Newgate novels in its obsession with criminals. The protagonist begins as a nobody and rises to become one of the "two greatest men in Venice"—the other being the Doge. He rises by becoming King of Assassins—though at the end of the story we learn he has actually killed no one. *The Bravo of Venice*, in other words, valorizes the fake assassin. At the heart of the novel is a scene eerily similar to the one that Edward Oxford would publicly enact in a few weeks, when the Bravo presents a gun loaded with powder, but without bullets, to the face of his ruler. The novel features a secret society of assassins which has its secret meeting place, its own weaponry, its disguises, and its regalia, similar to that which Oxford delineates in his rules for Young England.

Oxford spent his time at home writing, as well. Indulging, perhaps, a quickly developing millennial obsession, he copied, according to his sister, passages from the Bible. And at some point three letters addressed to Edward Oxford became a part of his secret collection of documents, regalia, and weapons. The letters are dated and signed, each one appearing to have been sent to Oxford at his three previous places of employment during the past year. None of the letters appears to have been sent, however: none is postmarked. And each of the letters, though signed by "A. W. Smith," the fictitious secretary to the fictitious Young England, is almost certainly written in Oxford's own hand. He could have written them at any time over the past year—could even have written them on or around the dates written on each one. It is, on the other hand, quite possible that he composed them, as he composed his rules and regulations for Young England, during his five weeks of leisure, as a part of his endeavor to recreate himself and to present himself to the world, when the time came, as a man with a history of covert political involvement, with a *bona fide* political motive for assassination.

The first letter is dated from a year before, May 16th, 1839, addressed to Oxford at Mr. Minton's Shepherd and Flock public house in Marylebone. It depicts Oxford as a new but promising member of the organization, beginning to learn the ropes:

> Young England—Sir,—Our commander-in-chief was
> very glad to find that you answered his questions in such
> a straight-forward manner. You will be wanted to attend
> on the 21st of this month, as we expect one of the country

agents to town on business of importance. Be sure and attend. A. W. Smith, Secretary. P.S.—You must not take any notice of the boy, nor ask him any questions.

The detail about the boy is a nice poetic touch, stressing the cloak-and-dagger nature of Young England, and suggesting an intersection between Oxford's mundane, cover existence as a barman, and his secret existence as a Captain (or soon-to-be Captain) in Young England.

The second letter, addressed to Oxford at Mr. Parr's Hat and Feathers, and dated 14 November, suggests Oxford, through his great talents, is rising to stardom in his secret society. It also demonstrates Oxford's literary side, as he—with a novelist's touch—invents a melodramatic scene in an attempt to root his imaginary organization in the real world:

> Young England—Sir, I am very glad to hear that you improve so much in your speeches. Your speech the last time you were here was beautiful. There was another one introduced last night, by Lieutenant Mars, a fine, tall, gentlemanly-looking fellow, and it is said that he is a military officer; but his name has not yet transpired. Soon after he was introduced, we were alarmed by a violent knocking at the door. In an instant our faces were covered, we cocked our pistols, and with drawn swords stood waiting to receive the enemy. While one stood over the fire with the papers, another stood with lighted torch to fire the house. We then sent the old woman to open the door, and it proved to be some little boys who knocked at the door and ran away. You must attend on Wednesday next. A. W. Smith, Secretary.

Oxford's third letter connected his virtual secret society with actual political currents of 1840, and with actual political fears. This is the letter that Oxford surely expected would strike terror into millions of hearts once it became public. Dated a month before (3 April 1840) and addressed to Mr. Robinson's Hog in the Pound, it makes clear that things are quickly building to a climax among the conspirators, to the point that Oxford would have to risk his position as barman to play the role of conspirator:

> Young England—Sir,—You are requested to attend to night, as there is an extraordinary meeting to be holden, in consequence of having received some communications of an important nature from Hanover. You must attend; and if your master will not give you leave, you must come in defiance of him. A. W. Smith, Secretary.

It is the reference to Hanover that would have been chilling to any British reader in the spring of 1840. Hanover suggested Queen Victoria's Uncle Ernest, without question the most wicked, the most feared, and the most reviled of George III's sons. He was, in the minds of many, a murderer, thought to have slit the throat in 1810 of his servant. (In reality the servant attacked Cumberland before killing himself.) In politics, he was an ultra-Tory reactionary, the enemy, in a progressive age, to every progressive cause, and a particularly virulent enemy to the Reform Bill of 1832. In religion he was an extremist as well: the Grand Master of the ultra-protestant Orange Lodges, the fiercely anti-Catholic Protestant fraternal organizations. He had a following—of the distinctly conspiratorial kind—and in the minds of many he had ambition and an agenda that could not be contained by the lesser throne of Hanover. And now only the young Queen and her unborn child stood between him and the throne. Upon the death of William IV in 1837, many feared that Ernest and his Orange supporters would rise up and declare for him rather than his niece. That did not happen.

But what didn't happen in 1837 could happen in 1840, with an assassin's bullet.

While Oxford spent much of his time over these few weeks in quiet seclusion, his explosive side frequently needed an outlet as well. Thus his aggression toward his mother and sister. Besides this, Susannah was a frequent witness to his habit of firing his pistols—loaded with powder, but most likely without ball—into the garden from out of the back windows of his lodgings. His family later claimed that he never fired out his own windows in the front of the house, into the Square—but Oxford himself later claimed that he fired to scare old women on the street. (Apparently, his landlady, Mrs. Packman, being extremely hard of hearing, was not disturbed by the shooting.) The explosive crack of his pistols certainly startled the inhabitants of number 6, and many others in the environs of West Square, and quite likely carried beyond the square, beyond the home for Indigent Children, past the grounds of Bethlem Hospital, and into the various airing yards of the asylum's inmates. It is an intriguing possibility, then, that the echoes of Oxford's shots might have further disturbed the thoughts of one of Bethlem's oldest and longest-detained residents, and might have reminded that man of two shots that he had fired from his own pistols, forty years before.

James Hadfield was, as a young man, a soldier in King George III's army, who in 1793 had fought in the war against France that erupted after the execution of Louis XVI. At the battle of Lincelles* that year while serving in the bodyguard of the George III's second son, the Duke of York, Hadfield suffered severe saber-wounds to the head. The damage was apparently psychological as well as physical, and Hadfield was soon discharged from the army because of insanity. He moved to London, became a maker of silver spoons,

---

* Roubaix, according to the *Oxford Dictionary of National Biography* (Eigen).

and brooded about the special role he felt destined to play in what he knew was an imminent cosmic struggle. His apocalyptic beliefs intensified when he by chance fell in with a messianic shoemaker and religious ranter, Bannister Truelock, who convinced Hadfield that the assassination of George III would bring about the end of kings and the end of time. Hadfield by this time considered himself a latter-day messiah who must sacrifice himself to save mankind. He bought a brace of pistols in May 1800 and wandered through London, wondering whether to kill himself to hasten the apocalypse, but held back, fearing eternal damnation. He then hit upon a plan that would bring about the end of kings and bring about the self-sacrifice he needed: he would shoot George III in a public place, and would then happily be torn apart by the crowd. On 15 May, then, Hadfield bought a second-row seat for a performance of Colley Cibber's *She Would and She Would Not*, a performance at Drury Lane Theatre which he knew the Royal Family would be attending. When the King entered and came to the front of the box to acknowledge the cheering of the audience, Hadfield stood upon his seat, leveled one of his pistols at the King, and fired. The pistol's two slugs missed the King's head by inches, lodging in a pillar near the ceiling of the box. George reacted with notable calm, displaying, according to the *Times*, "that serenity and firmness of character which belong to a virtuous mind"; he put his family at ease, and they stayed to watch the entire performance. Hadfield, meanwhile, was seized and taken to a music room adjoining the stage, where he was questioned by the police, by the proprietor of the theatre (and the great dramatist) Richard Brinsley Sheridan, and—in an emotional reunion, on Hadfield's part—by his former commanding officer, the Duke of York. He claimed that he had missed the King on purpose, wanting only to be torn apart himself, and darkly hinted at the coming chaos: "it was not over yet—there was a great deal more and worse to be done."

Hadfield was tried a month later. He was charged with High Treason, and by the law of the time that meant that he was entitled to the best counsel in the land, at the expense of the state. And he got just that in Thomas Erskine. Erskine mounted an insanity defense, in the face of the contemporary legal concept of that defense which held insanity to be complete derangement, and an insane man thus unable to plan a criminal act or understand its consequences. Hadfield had planned his attempt carefully—buying the gun, manufacturing his own slugs, choosing a seat at the theatre with an ideal vantage from which to shoot the King. And he arguably knew very well the consequences of his action; he hoped he could cause enough of an uproar in order to bring about his own death. Erskine argued that a man suffering from a powerful delusion might appear sane in most ways, and yet still commit an insane act. He brought forth a number of witnesses to testify to the eccentricity of Hadfield's behavior—behavior that included an attempt to kill his infant son days before the attempt on the King. And he brought forth medical witnesses to testify both to the severity of Hadfield's head wounds, and to the obvious insanity he demonstrated in his behavior. Chief Justice Kenyon, long before Erskine called all of his witnesses, stopped the trial, persuaded the Attorney General, John Mitford, to agree that Hadfield was obviously deranged, and directed the jury to return a verdict of not guilty on the grounds of insanity, which they dutifully did.

Hadfield, however, was not free. The Chief Justice, the Attorney General, and Hadfield's own counsel agreed that Hadfield must be further confined, Erskine stating "most undoubtedly the safety of the community, and of all mankind, requires that this unfortunate man should be taken care of." He was returned to Newgate. Four days after his trial, Mitford introduced a bill in Parliament to deal with Hadfield and those like him. The Safe Custody of Insane Persons Charged with Offences Bill empowered courts to detain those acquitted of a crime on the grounds of insanity at the pleasure of the monarch. The act was retroactive; Hadfield's legal acquittal resulted in a lifetime of mental confinement. He was conveyed to Bethlem Hospital, which in 1800 was located not in Southwark, but in Moorfields, north of the river. He escaped in 1802, but was quickly caught in Dover, attempting to flee to France, and sent not back to Bethlem but to Newgate Prison for fourteen years. When arrangements were being made to move Bethlem from Moorfields to Southwark, the government requested that Bethlem establish special sections for female and male criminal lunatics; the governors of the Hospital agreed, and Hadfield was one of the first sent to the new building, in 1816. There he grew old, "grumbling and discontented," clearly chafing under a lifetime of imprisonment, and petitioning repeatedly for release. He had renewed hopes for his freedom when Victoria came to the throne, and he asked her to recognize his sanity and his service to the nation and make him a Chelsea Pensioner. But it was Victoria's pleasure, as it had been her grandfather's and her uncles', to detain him.

By the time, then, that Oxford was disturbing the neighborhood and the lunatics, both criminal and non-criminal, with his pistol-shots, Hadfield was old, hopeless, and ill of tuberculosis, having "no desire to again mix with the world."

Within weeks, Oxford would meet the old man.

For more than a month after buying his pistols, Oxford invariably spent the early part of his days at home, leaving the house in mid- or late afternoons, returning in the evening. His first destination was usually Lovett's coffee shop on the London Road, two blocks away from West Square, between the obelisk at St. George's Circus and the snarl of streets leading from Elephant and Castle. At Lovett's, Oxford had access to London's newspapers. He scanned the employment columns of the *Morning Advertiser*, apparently having not given up the possibility of seeking employment in yet another public house. He could follow the movements of the Queen, set out in the Court Circular, published in a number of newspapers. He also was able to follow the latest news, and therefore, with the rest of the nation, he must have been captivated by the breaking news of one of the most sensational murders to occur during Victoria's reign.

In the very early morning of 6 May 1840 (two days after Oxford bought his pistols), sounds of alarm burst out in the aristocratic neighborhood of 14 Norfolk Street, tucked between Park Lane and Park Street, within sight of the northeast corner of Hyde Park. It was the home of 72-year-old Lord William Russell, great-uncle of Lord John Russell, who was at the time the Colonial Secretary in Her Majesty's government. Upon rising that morning, Lord Russell's housemaid had discovered signs of disorder throughout the house. In the drawing room, Lord William's writing desk had been smashed open. By the street door, several of his possessions were found wrapped in cloth. In the kitchen, drawers were forced open and plate was missing. The housemaid hurried to the attic to wake the cook, who, in turn, sent her to wake the valet, in the next room; she did so, oddly finding the man almost fully dressed. Housemaid and valet—a man by the name of François Benjamin Courvoisier—surveyed the kitchen, concluded that a burglary had occurred, and rushed upstairs to check upon their master. They discovered Russell's corpse, his throat slit from ear to ear: his carotid artery and jugular vein severed. Russell's right thumb, as well, was nearly cut away from the rest of his hand. Though his blood had not spurted widely, as might be expected with a wound of this kind, he had bled copiously: blood was pooled deeply around his head, and had dripped through in a puddle under the bed. The servants sent immediately for the police.

While the scene pointed at first to a botched and somehow interrupted burglary, the police quickly began to doubt that this was the case. No one had seen or heard any intruders the night before (though a neighbor did claim to hear groans emanating from Lord Williams's room, during the night). Marks on the back door suggested that it had been violently forced open. But it became clear to the police that the door had been forced from the inside, where several bolts had already been drawn. Moreover, any intruders exiting from this door would have to scale a high wall to escape the property, a wall thoroughly whitewashed, which would have shown marks of intrusion; it did not. A careful search showed no marks of forced entry whatsoever outside the back door. It was highly unlikely that anyone had used this door for entry or escape, and much more likely that someone had doctored the door to create the appearance of a burglary. By the time of the inquest, the police had concluded that this was an inside job, with particular suspicion falling on Courvoisier, a native of Switzerland who had only been in service with Russell for five weeks. Courvoisier's odd behavior had attracted attention: besides the fact that he was inexplicably nearly dressed upon being woken, he displayed a great deal of anxiety during the search, and continually "kept running and drinking water." His reaction to the crime, as well, demonstrated a shocking lack of empathy for the victim. One of the police on the case, Inspector John Tedman—the same John Tedman, incidentally, who had witnessed Oxford's odd behavior at the Shepherd and Flock—was from the start suspicious of the valet, noting Courvoisier's self-centered reaction to the crime: "this is a shocking job; I shall lose my place and lose my character." And then there was Courvoisier's suspicious wealth: he had in his room a banknote and change amounting to six sovereigns; asked where he obtained the note, he claimed he got it in making change for his master. Most damning at all, a chisel had been found among Courvoisier's possessions, and the chisel exactly fit marks left when the kitchen drawers had been forced.

The police hoped that the murderer had not yet removed the stolen items from the house. The items actually stolen were few, and were small—larger items of far greater value in Russell's room were, surprisingly, left alone. Besides the plate from which Russell had eaten the night of his death, and various items of cutlery, there were banknotes, coins, and rings taken from the fingers of the dead man. The police tore up floorboards and baseboards. On Friday, they made the discovery that led to Courvoisier's arrest: behind the skirting-board in the butler's pantry, a room that was for Courvoisier's use alone, workmen found two banknotes—for £5 and £10—and much of Russell's stolen jewelry. Courvoisier was held in his room under close observation until Sunday, when he was conveyed to Tothill Fields prison. After repeated examination of the crime at Bow Street, he was at the end of May committed to Newgate, to be tried at the Old Bailey on the 18th of June.

This news of the murder electrified Mayfair—the *Times* reported that the carriages of the fashionable clogged the area for days. While murder and burglary were far from uncommon in London in 1840, this particular murder trumped others in terms of public fascination, playing on a host of British fears. For one thing, the crime took place in the most fashionable neighborhood in the metropolis, and the victim was an aristocrat, the brother of the fifth Duke of Bedford, and the uncle of a leading Whig politician of the day, Sir John Russell, the future prime minister. Then there was the terrifying thrill that accompanied the growing realization that Russell had been slaughtered by his own servant. The *Times* noticed the growing fear, not that the criminal could strike again—he couldn't, of course—but that this type of crime could happen again, anywhere: that all masters and mistresses were vulnerable to their servants. As the *Times* noted, "the excitement produced in high life by the dreadful event is almost unprecedented, and the feeling of apprehension for personal safety increases every hour, particularly among those of the nobility and gentry who live in comparative seclusion." For a middle and upper class already threatened in 1840 with the specter of mass insurrection demonstrated by reports of increasingly militant activity by the working-class radicals of the Chartist movement, this reminder that the potentially dangerous working class inhabited their very homes turned an individual tragedy into general cause for alarm. More than this, the realization that the murderer was a foreigner added to the general sense of terror. Courvoisier's Swiss ethnicity and the fact that he was only five weeks in Russell's service were mentioned repeatedly in reports: both facts clearly worked against him.

On the day that Inspector Tedman arrested Courvoisier, another officer of the Metropolitan Police, Sergeant Charles Otway, was in

Gravesend, hoping to arrest another criminal, one who had captured the attention of the British public two months before. On 17 March, the body of John Templeman was discovered in his home in Islington. Templeman was an old man who made a modest living from renting a couple of properties; he was generally known to be a miser and was rumored to have hidden a large amount of money in his house. His hands and his eyes had been bound; his head had been beaten severely, and several of his teeth had been forcibly extracted. Obviously, he had been the victim of a burglary, his attacker or attackers apparently attempting to torture out of him the hiding place of his fortune. Three people were quickly under suspicion and quickly arrested for the crime: a married couple, John and Mary Ann Jarvis, who were neighbors to Templeton, and their close acquaintance, Richard Gould, who as it happens was (unlike Oxford) actually a potboy, though at that moment out of work. The Jarvises were aware that Templeton had taken in some cash soon before the crime, and Gould had boasted to others that he was about to free himself from poverty by robbing an old man who was known to wave a £50 note about. He had also asked two comrades if they could provide him with a "screw" and a "darkey"—a lockpick and a bull's-eye lantern (one that could be covered and thus darkened). The Jarvises, who may have been complicit with Gould in other ways—Mary Ann was Richard Gould's lover—were soon cleared in this case. But Gould was caught in possession of bloody clothing, and several pounds in coin were found at his premises, secured in one of his stockings and hidden in the privy. He was brought to trial on 14 April. His attorney was able to suggest that those testifying against Gould were not credible and indeed more suspicious than he was, and he established that no physical evidence connected Gould with the crime scene. The jury very quickly returned a verdict of not guilty, and Gould was freed.

The police, however, were convinced that they had found their man. Learning in May that Gould was about to sail for Sydney, the Superintendent of A Division sent Sergeant Otway to Gravesend with a warrant for Gould's arrest: he could not be tried again for murder, but the warrant was for burglary. Otway confronted Gould not with the warrant, but with an offer: the Home Office, he told Gould, was offering £200 to anyone who could give information on the case. Thinking that his acquittal protected him from any prosecution, Gould told Otway that he and the Jarvises committed the crime together: Mrs. Jarvis acting as a lookout, and Mr. Jarvis murdering Templeman before Gould's eyes. Quite simply, Otway entrapped Gould, and he was later censured for his action by the courts and by the police. More than this, Gould's testimony appeared to the police self-serving and inaccurate; the Jarvises had nothing to do with the murder, and had already been cleared after repeated examination. Among his lies, however, Gould revealed a number of details that the police were able to corroborate: in particular, that he had thrown the "darkey" or dark lantern that he had used in committing the crime into a pond behind the house in which he was living. The police searched the pond, and were able to find not only the lantern, but a chisel which corresponded exactly to marks made on drawers forced in Templeman's house. If, because of entrapment, his confession to Otway could not be admitted in trial, this hard evidence could: Gould was rearrested, and sent to Newgate for trial at the Old Bailey on the charge of burglary.

Oxford would soon meet Courvoisier, and Gould as well.

As Oxford sipped his coffee and perused the newspapers at Lovett's, other customers must surely have noticed the handles of his two pistols, bursting out from his bulging pockets. They were hard to miss: a servant at West Place noticed them, and so did the landlady, who commented to Mrs. Oxford on her son's want of economy: what use had he of *two* guns, after all? The locks of the pistols—carefully protected with rags between hammer and percussive caps, to prevent Oxford from shooting himself in the foot—rubbed so relentlessly against the Gambroon fabric of his trousers as to create a noticeably worn patch within a few weeks. Oxford's life in public centered upon his guns; he haunted London's shooting galleries for hours each day. He shot regularly at a local one, attached to the baths on Westminster Bridge, and frequented as well William Green's "pistol-repository and shooting gallery" in Leicester Square. He also reportedly shot at a gallery elsewhere in the West End, as well as one in the Strand. He might have spent some of his time at these places flourishing the scimitar-shaped sword he had obtained during these weeks—but he certainly spent most of his time practicing marksmanship, with his own pistols and with the gallery's rifles. His habit, it seems, was to spend a shilling each visit, for a few shots with pistol and with rifle. He claimed that he was a better shot with rifle than with pistol, but apparently was a fairly miserable shot with either: at one point he bet that he could hit within six inches of his target—and he lost. "He was more fit to shoot at a haystack than at the target," noted one companion. Oxford apparently did not mind the terrible shooting; more important to him, his restless perambulations to a number of galleries suggest, was to be *seen* shooting, to mingle with all varieties of men: "he associated," as the *Morning Chronicle* put it, "alternatively with the higher and lower classes of society."

As May became June, Oxford began to vary his trips to the shooting galleries with trips to his old haunts, looking up his few old friends and hobnobbing with his former workmates. His only friend from childhood—the only person who visited him in his home, according to Oxford's sister—was a butcher's son, John Lenton. The two were together a great deal at this time, Oxford sharing his obsession with his pistols with the boy: coaxing him into accompanying him to the Lambeth shooting gallery to see him take six shots at a target, and later boasting to him that he had since been to a "much better" gallery across the river. He looked up his old places of employment as well, bringing another well-dressed acquaintance (very likely Lenton) to the Shepherd and Flock, and at another time returning to the Hog in the Pound to seek out a more recent friend he had made, a boy by the name of Thomas Lawrence, a Bond Street perfumer's assistant and a regular at that pub.

With another motive than friendship in mind, Oxford sought out an old schoolmate and neighbor. J. J. Gray worked in the shop of his father, an oilman (or grocer) at 10 Westminster Bridge Road, Lambeth, a few houses down from lodgings that Edward had lived in with his mother eight or nine years before. The shop stood close to the south bank of the Thames, in the shadows of Astley's equestrian theatre. On the 3rd of June, Oxford went there to make a final necessary purchase. Gray recognized Oxford the moment he entered the shop, but had no interest whatsoever in renewing whatever relationship once existed between them, and pretended not to know him. Oxford was persistent, asking him if he had ever heard of anyone named Oxford—and revealing himself as the Oxford with whom Gray had attended school. The conversation then turned to guns. Oxford needed more percussion caps and gunpowder for his pistols. Gray had both; Oxford drew one of his ubiquitous pistols from his pocket, and the two tested if the cap fit. It did, and Oxford bought fifty. Gray's shop only sold gunpowder in a large canister, too large for Oxford, who only wanted a quarter-pound. Gray recommended a gunsmith just across the river.

Leaving Gray's shop, Oxford crossed Westminster Bridge, passed the newly rising Houses of Parliament,* and to Parliament Street, where he waited while the proprietor molded him two dozen bullets, and sold him a quarter-pound of gunpowder.

He was ready.

---

* The Houses of Parliament had burned down six years before; rebuilding had just commenced.

three

IF IT PLEASE PROVIDENCE, I SHALL ESCAPE

Wednesday the 10th of June 1840 was fine and bright: perfect weather for an outing in Hyde Park. Edward Oxford dined with his sister early in the afternoon. His mother was still with her family in Birmingham; his brother-in-law was at work at the soda manufacturer. Perhaps Edward and Susannah talked about their father; it was his birthday that day. When they were done, Edward geared himself up just as he had over the past few weeks: he carefully placed his two pistols, loaded with powder and wadding, in his gray Gambroon trousers, and carefully placed red rags between hammer and cap. He also equipped himself with a knife. He was off to the shooting gallery, he told his sister—and on the way he would buy some linen for shirts, and some tea from Mr. Twining's shop in the Strand.

He stopped first at Lovett's, to take coffee and glance at the newspapers, as usual. If he followed habit and looked over the employment advertisements, he did so ironically; he knew now that pulling pints of ale was not in his future. He might have glanced at the Court Circular, to reassure himself that the Queen was in residence and following the usual routine. She was. Yesterday, she had met with her aunt Adelaide, the Queen Dowager; she had gone for an airing with Albert late in the afternoon; in the evening, she and Albert had attended the opera—Rossini's *Barber of Seville*—with her half-brother, the Prince of Leiningen. Lovett, the proprietor, saw Oxford sitting there, but didn't see the pistols bulging in his pockets: Oxford's coat hid them. Oxford left, abruptly, without paying. He would never be coming back.

Oxford doubled back past his home and past Bethlem, up Westminster Bridge Road, across the river and past Parliament and Whitehall, into the green heart of the metropolis: St. James's Park, Pall Mall, and the Gates of Buckingham Palace, with Green Park and Constitution Hill in the distance. He joined the crowd milling about the Marble Arch—then in its original position as the front gate to Buckingham Palace*—everyone there hoping to catch a glimpse of the Queen or her Consort. Albert had left the Palace in the morning, visiting, as he had a month before, Woolwich Dockyard. The Queen was scheduled to go with him, and a royal salute had been planned, but on this morning she felt ill—quite possibly from morning sickness—so she stayed, and Albert went as her representative.

Albert was taking his first steps into public life. He had chaired, and given his brief speech to, the Anti-Slavery Society nine days before; writing it in German, translating it with Victoria's help, and practicing it repeatedly and nervously before her. In the end,

---

* The Marble Arch would be moved to its present location outside Hyde Park in 1851, when its openings were deemed simply too small to allow the passage of the state coach.

Exeter Hall was filled beyond its capacity of four thousand, and Albert's slightly accented words were received with "tremendous applause." Albert made a great success of his trip to Woolwich, as well: three thousand inhabitants of the town were on hand to cheer his coming. With his genuine interest in industry and manufacture—an interest that only grew with time, and would lead to the enormously successful Great Exhibition, in 1851—Albert was fascinated by the construction of a new warship, the 120-gun HMS *Trafalgar*, speaking with laborers and watching them at work. After an "elegant *dejeuné*" with the supervisor of the yard, he left to the "three hearty cheers" of the workmen, and was now riding in a carriage back to the Palace. The Queen had spent a quiet day in the Palace, her only engagement seeing Lord Melbourne in the morning; she awaited Albert's return so that the two could go for their daily airing in Hyde Park. Oxford was there to see Albert's carriage sweep up the Mall and through the palace gates. He knew who was in the carriage, and knew from whence it had come.

At around four o'clock, Oxford walked around to the north side of the Palace, a couple hundred yards up Constitution Hill. Invariably, when they took their regular airing, Victoria and Albert left the front gates of the Palace, turned sharply left, and traveled up the Hill, with the walls to the Palace gardens on their left, and the palings to Green Park on their right, in order to reach Hyde Park. The crowd was not as numerous on the hill as it was at the gate. Oxford paced back and forth beside the road, his hands inside his jacket, each gripping a pistol up under his armpits, giving him a bulging breast and a Napoleonic stoop. A number of bystanders saw him in this curious pose, but apparently thought little of it; they, like he, were focused on the gate down the Hill, from which they expected the little Queen and her Consort would soon emerge.

At six, the gates opened and the procession emerged: two outriders, the Prince and the Queen in a droshky, a very low carriage that rendered the royal couple sitting alone fully visible to all. Two pair of horses pulled the carriage; riders sat upon the horses on the left side, responsive to Albert's commands. Two equerries followed behind. The procession trotted out of the front gate of the Palace and up Constitution Hill, joined by many of the crowd at the gate, who were eager to lengthen their view of the royal couple. Few saw Oxford as the carriage approached—although one witness watched the odd, pacing figure, and watched Oxford stare at the carriage and "give a nod with his head sneeringly." Among those on the path that day was the young artist-to-be John Everett Millais, then just eleven, and only months away from being the youngest student ever accepted to the Royal Academy Schools. He was there with his father and his older brother, John. The boys doffed their caps to the royal couple, and were delighted to see the Queen bow to them in response.

At that moment, Albert saw a "little mean looking man" six paces away from him, holding something that the Prince couldn't quite make out: it was Oxford, pointing his pistol at the two, and in a dueler's stance, firing a shot with a thunderous report that riveted the attention of all. Victoria, according to the Prince, was looking the other way at a horse and was stunned, with no idea why her ears were ringing. (She later told Lehzen that she thought someone was shooting birds in the park.) "I seized Victoria's hands," Albert wrote later, "and asked if the fright had not shaken her, but she laughed at the thing. I then looked again at the man, who was still standing in the same place, his arms crossed, and a pistol in each hand." The carriage moved on several yards, and then stopped. Oxford looked around him to see the impression he was making and then turned back to the Queen and the Prince. He drew the pistol in his left hand from his coat, and adopted the highwayman's pose he had been practicing for weeks, steadying his left hand on his right forearm, and taking careful aim at the Queen.

If he had expected the royal reaction to be sublime terror, he was mistaken. Victoria had not yet realized what the noise was, and Albert, writing to his (and Victoria's) grandmother after the shooting, claimed that Oxford's "attitude was so affected and theatrical it quite amused me." Oxford later declared that he was equally amused with Albert, stating "when I fired the first pistol, Albert was about to jump from the carriage and put his foot out, but when he saw me present the second pistol, he immediately drew back." Oxford cried out, "I have another here." Now, the Queen saw Oxford and crouched, pulling Albert down with her, thinking to herself "if it please Providence, I shall escape." Oxford fired a second time.

For an instant, silence; the carriage had stopped, and the crowd and the royal couple took a moment to register what had just happened. Then, shouts and screams. Oxford's position made obvious by the smoke of the exploding percussion cap, the crowd converged upon him, some crying "Kill him!" The equerries and postilions stopped, and awaited a command. The Queen spoke to Albert, who called out to the postilions to drive on, and they did.

Victoria's whispered command turned near-tragedy into overwhelming personal triumph. The decision to move forward—on to Hyde Park and the completion of their ride—and not to follow the instinctive impulse to go back and seek safety in the palace, was entirely Victoria's, with her husband's full agreement. The royal couple was surrounded by an escort of equerries, and the Metropolitan Police had stationed a number of officers at and around the Palace, three of whom ran immediately to Oxford at the sound of the first shot. But the royal couple had nothing like the police protection offered the monarch and other heads of state today, in which at the first inkling of an assassination attempt the protectors take charge and take steps to isolate their charges.

On the contrary, Victoria and Albert chose, for the next hour and then for the next few days, to expose themselves fully to her public. In doing so, she and Albert signified that absolute trust existed between them and their subjects, and demonstrated their belief that no would-be assassin could come between them. As Albert told his grandmother, he and Victoria decided to ride on in public "to show her public that we had not, on account of what

happened, lost all confidence in them." In return, they were showered with an immense and spontaneous outpouring of loyalty and
affection, and enjoyed several days of national thanksgiving for
the preservation of the monarchy—and the preservation of *this*
monarch, and her husband and unborn child. In an instant, Lady
Flora Hastings and the Bedchamber Crisis, and all suspicions about
her German husband, were forgotten. Victoria's personal courage
and her unerring sense of her relationship with her people were
responsible for it all.

As she and Albert rushed toward Hyde Park, Victoria decided to
alter her route. The news of the shooting, she knew, would travel
with electric speed. Since very soon the Duchess of Kent in her
mansion in Belgrave Square would hear the story, Victoria decided
that she would personally tell her mother what had happened.
Before they had reached the top of the hill, then, she again spoke
to Albert; he directed the postilions to proceed at the usual pace
through the Wellington Arch at the entrance of Hyde Park, and
then veer south down Grosvenor Place to the Duchess's residence,
Ingestre House. They remained there until seven, and then set out
to complete their turn around the Park.

By this time, Oxford's attempt was the single topic of conversation throughout London, and the Park had filled with Londoners
of all social classes, the elite on horseback, all others on foot. The
Queen's aunt, the Duchess of Cambridge, was there with her children, as was Prince Louis Napoleon. All hoped to get a glimpse of
the Prince and the Queen; all were by now aware of her "interesting
condition," and all (including, initially, Albert) were concerned
that the shock of the attempt had had an effect upon the child; all
yearned to demonstrate their loyalty and sympathy. The *Times*
describes the joyous and spontaneous ceremony that followed:

> . . . the apprehensions of the bystanders were in some
> degree relieved by seeing the Royal carriage containing
> the Queen and Prince Albert return along the drive

towards the palace at about 7 o'clock. The carriage was attended by a great crowd of noblemen and gentlemen on horseback who had heard of the atrocious attempt in Hyde Park, and on seeing the carriage return accompanied it to the Palace gates, and testified their delight and satisfaction at the escape of her majesty and the prince by taking off their hats and cheering the Royal couple as they passed along. The joy of the populace was also expressed by long and loud huzzahs, and indeed the enthusiastic reception of her Majesty and the Prince by the assembled crowd must have been highly gratifying to them both. Her Majesty, as might well be supposed, appeared extremely pale from the effects of the alarm she had experienced, but, notwithstanding the state of her feelings, she seemed fully sensible of the attachment evinced to her Royal consort and herself by repeatedly smiling and bowing to the crowd in acknowledgement of their loyalty and affection.

In everyone's mind—all, that is, except for Oxford's—both the Queen and the Prince had shown an amazing amount of courage under fire. Once inside the Palace and in private, Victoria and Albert were able give in to the powerful emotions they had been experiencing during the shooting. By one account, Victoria burst into tears; by another, Albert held her and kissed her repeatedly, "praising her courage and self-possession." Before long, they gathered themselves for their next audience: Victoria's royal relatives and London's leading politicians—Melbourne, Peel, John Russell, the Home Secretary Lord Normanby, on hearing of the shooting, had rushed to the Palace to see them. Victoria quickly rallied, and soon went to dinner "perfectly recovered."

While Victoria and Albert moved forward to their triumphant procession, Oxford experienced his own procession—a hostile and derisory one. Bystanders began rushing toward Oxford before his second shot, and the first to reach him were Joshua Lowe, a spectacle-maker, and his nephew Albert, who had been running beside the royal carriage as it made its way up Constitution Hill. Joshua seized Oxford, while Albert disarmed him. Now holding both pistols, Albert Lowe appeared to be the shooter, and William Clayton, a cabinetmaker, fell upon him, calling him a "confounded rascal" while struggling for the pistols, succeeding in wrestling one of them away. This annoyed Oxford; it took attention away from himself. "I am the man who fired; it was me," he cried out. Then, it seemed to Oxford, everyone who could grabbed hold of him: "in an instant several persons seized me by the skirts of the coat, some took hold of my trousers, others twisted their hand into my handkerchief, and all within reach of me had me by the collar. Some could not get to my coat, and being resolved to have some share in the apprehension, seized me by the shirt-collar." The restraint, Oxford later claimed, was completely unnecessary, "as I had no intention to run away."

Three policemen from A Division—the police administrative district that covered Buckingham Palace and provided protection to the royal family—came running: George Brown and Charles Smith, who had been on duty at the Palace, and William Smith, patrolling Green Park, who jumped the palings separating the park from the road, cutting his hand in the process. They came upon a growing and quite angry crowd—an "immense assemblage," according to the *Times*, which could only with "the greatest difficulty" be prevented from executing summary judgment upon Oxford. The police, Oxford, and the crowd, with a great deal of "hooting and execration," proceeded to the A Division station house, which stood at the other end of St. James's Park on Gardiner Street, between Parliament and Whitehall.

En route, Oxford took the opportunity to drop a hint that he was part of a larger conspiracy. The Lowes were suspicious of William Clayton, who still held one of Oxford's pistols, and who appeared to them to be protecting Oxford by challenging Albert Lowe. Joshua warned his nephew: "Look out, Albert. I dare say he has some friends." Oxford, obviously thinking not of Clayton but of Young England, agreed: "You are right, I have." The police took note of this remark.

Halfway to the station house, someone in the crowd articulated the question that would become a central one in Oxford's trial: Were there bullets in his pistols? To this Oxford answered, according to P.C. Brown, "if the ball had come in contact with your head you would have known it." Despite the fact that the conditional nature of his remark disqualifies it as any sort of confession, the police clearly understood him to mean that his pistols were loaded. And that is likely the impression Oxford wanted to give. Indeed, at the station Oxford was asked, before a number of witnesses, whether the guns were loaded, and Oxford admitted that they were.

When they reached the station house, P.C. William Smith, not quite sure whether Clayton was a hero or an accomplice, took him as well as Oxford into custody; he was searched and locked in a cell before he was released. Oxford was searched: in his pocket were his knife, the key to his box at home, and half a crown—two shillings and sixpence—in change. The police also took note of the wear above his trouser pockets, obviously caused by the constant friction of the pistols against the fabric. Oxford was questioned by the constable on duty, James Partridge, and freely revealed his name, his age, his address, and his occupation: "a servant out of place."

All accounts of Oxford's behavior at A Division station house suggest he was having the time of his life. Everyone around him was paying the most careful attention to his every utterance: he had suddenly become a person of great importance. The *Times* noted one interchange at the station house that captures Oxford's giddy mood. When asked his profession, he joked "I have been brought up to the bar." A lawyer, then? "No, to the bar, to draw porter." When asking what that meant, exactly, his questioner struck a nerve: "Are you a potboy?" "No," Oxford replied. "I'm above that."

His elaborate plan to represent himself as a Captain of Young England seemed to be working. In the evening, the Superintendent of A Division dispatched officers to search his room at West Place; soon they would find his box of secrets. Important people from the government and the Queen's Household were gathering to interview him. Lord Uxbridge, the Lord Chamberlain, hurried over from the Palace to learn about Oxford. Oxford was apparently delighted to see him, and asked whether the Queen was hurt. Uxbridge rebuked him for his effrontery in asking. Oxford, nonplussed, chatted amicably with him, hoping again to promote his tale of conspiracy: he had been practicing his shooting for over a month, he told Uxbridge, ever since someone had given him the pistols on the third of May, and had given him more besides: money—with the promise of much more, "as much more as he pleased." Uxbridge, understanding Oxford's implication, told him "you have now filled your engagement." "No, I have not," Oxford replied. "You have, as far as the attempt goes," Uxbridge said.

As it happens, Oxford had shot at the Queen and had been arrested in A Division of the Metropolitan Police, the division operating out of the buildings at the edge of Whitehall abutting Scotland Yard. While Scotland Yard is now associated with the detective branch of the Metropolitan Police, in 1840 the Metropolitan Police technically had no detective branch. In forming the Metropolitan Police in 1829, Home Secretary Robert Peel had deliberately established that force as fully preventative, and not as investigative or detective: government spies in plain clothes were seen as something unpleasantly European—particularly French—and certainly un-British; Peel sensed that the British public was not yet ready for such a force. Moreover, there was an effective detective service in 1829: the Bow Street Runners, serving not the Commissioners of the Police, but of the London magistrates. Reforms of the year before—1839—under Home Secretary John Russell, had led to the elimination of that group, and no official detective force now existed in the metropolis. By 1840, however, the two commissioners of the Metropolitan Police had come to look upon A Division as the special division of the force, and used its officers to reinforce other divisions, when necessary, to serve special functions outside of London—90 officers and Superintendent May traveling to Birmingham, for example, to battle militant Chartists in the Bull Ring Riots a year before. Moreover, the commissioners looked upon the higher officers of A Division as their eyes and ears, and asked them—Inspector Nicholas Pearce, a former Bow Street Runner, in particular—to undertake investigative duties across London and beyond. Thus, Pearce (with the assistance of Sergeant Otway) raced across London to prevent the duel between Louis Napoleon and the Comte Léon. Thus, Pearce took charge of several murder investigations outside A District—including the Courvoisier case—and one outside London completely. Thus, Sergeant Otway traveled to Gravesend to rearrest Gould. The station house at Gardiner Lane was, then, the location of London's unofficial detective branch, and several officers jumped into detective action soon after Oxford's arrival at the station.

Inspector Hughes and Sergeant Otway were the ones dispatched to West Place, and they arrived so quickly that the news of the shooting had not yet crossed the river to that part of Southwark. They found the landlady, Mrs. Packman, there with her sister. They broke the news to the women with great delicacy, Sgt. Otway first making sure Mrs. Packman was not Oxford's mother before telling her that Oxford had shot at the Queen. Mrs. Packman immediately told Oxford's sister Susannah, who, devastated by the news, immediately ran to her husband at the soda factory. The two policemen made a search of Oxford's room and quickly came upon his locked box. Not finding the key, they obtained a hammer and chisel from Mrs. Packman and smashed the lock. There, they found all Oxford's evidence of Young England—sword and scabbard, crepe cap with two red bows, bullet mold, some loose bullets, gunpowder—and a red pocket book, "which contained a memorandum," as well as other papers—Oxford's created letters, as well as the rules and regulations of the organization. Hughes and Otway clearly understood the documents to be important evidence.

They brought the evidence back to the station house, and Inspector Hughes described his findings to Lord Uxbridge and other members of the Royal Household. They tried one of the confiscated bullets in Oxford's pistols; it fitted perfectly. Inspector Hughes spoke of the rules and regulations of Young England, and there was no doubt in his mind that Oxford was indeed a member of a larger conspiracy. Then Oxford was brought from his cell and confronted with this evidence. He had meant to destroy the papers, he claimed. He did not deny that all that they had found was his, or that he was a member of Young England. He would not, however, tell them where the society met, or give the names of any other members.

Although reporters now clamoring at the station house for news weren't given full details about Young England from Oxford's documents, they were told enough to have a good idea about the size of Oxford's imagined conspiracy, about its structure, and about its political loyalties: the information from the third letter that news had arrived from Hanover was released to a reporter, and was in the newspapers the next morning. Victoria's wicked uncle was thus quickly connected to Oxford's crime.

Some time after Hughes returned to the station, Fox Maule, Undersecretary at the Home Office, arrived to coordinate Oxford's government examination. With Superintendent May he interviewed Oxford in his cell for some time: Oxford after this interview would greet Maule as a particularly close acquaintance. Maule likely imparted to Oxford the delightful news that he would be examined at the Home Office to ascertain whether there was enough evidence to try him for High Treason. Oxford spoke glibly to these two, as well as to the officers of A Division and his many visitors that night—expressing republican sentiments to some; suggesting at one time that he thought it wrong that England was ruled by a woman.

While Oxford regaled his audience with dark hints of reactionary conspiracy, at all gatherings throughout the metropolis—at dances and dinners, the theatre and the Opera—the attempt was on everyone's tongue. At Almack's Assembly Rooms, a venue traditionally limited to the elite of London society, a sense of melancholy prevailed: first, Lord William Russell murdered in his bedroom, and now the Queen and Prince Consort shot at: who among the aristocracy was safe? Elsewhere, the mood was more celebratory: rousing versions of "God Save the Queen" were sung; improvised speeches of horror at the attempt and joy at its failure were given. "Our theatres begin the thanksgiving," one reporter wrote, "to be completed in our churches."

By all accounts, Oxford slept very soundly that night, and the next morning complimented the police on the comfort of their accommodation.

four

THIS IS ALL I SHALL SAY
AT PRESENT

Whether Oxford's pistols had been loaded with ball or not quickly became the central question to those investigating the crime. A successful prosecution for High Treason depended upon proof that Oxford had done more than startle the Queen with smoke and noise—that he had aimed and fired a bullet at her. Oxford was asked whether his guns had been loaded so many times in the hours after his arrest that he eventually refused to answer.

Immediately after Victoria and Albert drove from the scene of the shooting, all bystanders not mobbing Oxford and hauling him to the station house hastened to scrutinize the wall to the Palace gardens, hoping to find Oxford's bullets themselves or any marks they left. The Millais family was among them, and, years later, William Millais (John's brother) claimed that two bullet marks were clearly visible, marks that disappeared over the next few days, as gawkers poked new marks into the walls with their walking-sticks and umbrellas.* No bullets were found, however. Soon after Oxford's arrest, a large detail of officers was dispatched to the wall with birch brooms and barrows, to sweep up all the dirt beneath the walls and convey it to the station house for careful sifting. They toiled until eleven that night and for much of the next day, finding nothing. The next evening, two boys claimed to have found a ball in a place the police had already carefully scrutinized—but the police soon discovered the ball was too large for Oxford's pistol; someone, it seems, was attempting to assist the police by planting evidence against Oxford. By Friday, police attention shifted from the wall to the gardens on the other side, on the theory that Oxford had shot high and over the wall. No balls were ever found there, either.

There was never any question in the minds of Victoria and Albert, however: they had been shot at, at dangerously close range—from six paces away, according to Albert—and it was a miracle that the Queen had not been hit. "It seems the pistols were loaded," Victoria wrote in her journal, "so our escape is indeed providential." Albert was too surprised to notice the trajectory of Oxford's first shot, but claimed that he saw that of the second—with a certainty that transcended the actual evidence: "The ball must have passed just above [the Queen's] head," he wrote to his grandmother, "to judge from the place where it was found sticking in an opposite wall." The royal couple were as certain about the shooter as they were about the lethality of his shots: he was not mad, certainly, but "quiet and composed"—a villain who deserved punishment.

On Thursday morning, two angry and curious crowds gathered, one outside of the A Division station house on Gardiner Street, and the other, a short distance away, in front of the Home Office, at

---

* The Millais' brush with Edward Oxford obviously became an important part of their family mythology, and, as family myths will do, this one inflated with time: In his later account of the attempt, William Millais claimed that his father had personally seized Oxford and held him until the police came. No contemporary account of the shooting supports this story.

Whitehall, where Oxford was to be examined. To avoid a confrontation with the crowd, the police decided to hustle Oxford out the back
door. As he emerged from his cell between Inspectors Hughes and
Pearce, he saw, for the first time since he had left West Place after
dinner the day before, his sister Susannah, accompanied by their
uncle, Edward Marklew. Susannah had been desperately applying
to see him since his arrest, but his family's requests to see him were
denied. Upon seeing her brother, Susannah shrieked "there he is!"
and nearly fainted. After learning of the shooting, and after fetching
her husband William from the soda factory, Susannah had written
her mother in Birmingham with the news and then she sought her
Uncle Edward's assistance. Edward Marklew, as Hannah's brother,
was naturally a publican, landlord of the Ship, in the City. His assistance so far had been tireless and wholly ineffective. He had tried
to obtain legal counsel for his nephew, but the solicitor he contacted
refused, claiming to be too busy with the prosecution of the two
sensational legal cases of the day: Courvoisier's and Gould's. Marklew
had then applied at the Home Office for Oxford to have some sort
of an adviser during the coming examination: if not a solicitor, then
he himself asked to attend. He was turned down flat; Oxford, at this
stage, would have to represent himself.

Susannah's letter to her mother in Birmingham would arrive
later that day, but the police were faster; Sergeant Otway had taken
the seven o'clock train from Euston Station to Birmingham, one of
the first intercity train routes in Britain. He found Hannah among
her relatives. Hannah received the news badly, responding with a
hysterical fit, by one account, and fainting, by another. She would
take the afternoon train to London and be there by the evening.

Inspectors Pearce and Hughes bundled Oxford past his sister and
uncle, out the back of the station, where the three jogged through
the Horse Guards' parade ground and into the back entrance to the
Home Office, at Whitehall. Oxford ran, without handcuffs, and in
a jocular mood. He was clearly enormously excited at the prospect
of his examination by all the leading Whig politicians: Melbourne,

Russell, Palmerston, and the rest would be giving him their focused attention: he had wanted to make a noise—and the examination proved to him that he had done exactly that. If he had known of his uncle Marklew's attempts to find him counsel, he would certainly have disapproved. He had, at that moment, no desire to let anyone speak for him, and no desire to be found innocent. If his pistols had indeed been empty, he preferred everyone not to know that, seeing him instead as a dangerous conspirator with high if mysterious political connections. He was placed to wait in a room adjoining the room where depositions were to be taken, and a reporter, seeing him there, noted his self-centered pleasure: "he paced up and down the room with perfect self-possession, and an air of consequence and satisfaction, as if he felt pleased to find himself an object of so much interest."

At eleven, Oxford was examined first by the Home Secretary and his undersecretaries, Phillipps and Maule; Normanby then decided upon a fuller examination by a larger body, at two o'clock. The ministers discussed the constitution of that larger body. Precedent was unclear as to whether the Privy Council or the Cabinet should examine the evidence. In the end, they decided upon the Cabinet. One of that body, John Cam Hobhouse, recorded his less than impressed opinion of Oxford in his diary. "He was young," Hobhouse wrote,

> . . . and under the middle size, neatly made, with a darkish olive complexion.* He had black eyes and eye-

---

* Oxford's darkness—and his sister's, as grandchildren or great-grandchildren of a black man, was noted by the newspapers of the day, but only incidentally. When, however, the American abolitionist William Lloyd Garrison, arriving late on a ship for the Anti-Slavery Conference that Prince Albert chaired, read an account of the shooting to his fellow passengers, he claimed his British auditors went wild when they learned Oxford was a man of color: "they yelled like so many fiends broke loose from the bottomless pit . . . swore that Oxford 'ought to be strung up, without judge or jury, and cut in pieces,' in true Lynch-law style—the whole 'nigger race' made to suffer for so foul an act, ay, and all those who are disposed to act as their advocates! I have seldom seen so horrid an exhibition of fiendish exultation and murderous malignity" (Garrison 2:364).

brows, dark chestnut hair. He had not a bad expression, but with a curl on his lips, as if suppressing a smile or sneer. He was dressed as became his condition, which, we were told, was that of a barman at a pothouse. There was nothing displeasing in his look or manner, until he spoke, when his pert audacity and his insolent careless-ness gave him the air of a ruffian.

Maule orchestrated the examination to convince those assembled that Oxford was the shooter, and his pistols were loaded. Establishing the first point was simple: several witnesses stated that, without any doubt, they had seen Oxford shoot; three of these testified as to Oxford's incriminating statement, upon his capture, that he had done the shooting. Establishing that the pistols had been loaded was more difficult, as no ball had been found despite an intensive search. One witness, however, claimed that the ball "passed directly before my face," with a whizzing sound, and another that he had seen a mark left by one of the balls on the wall.

Oxford was given the opportunity to question each of the wit-nesses, and his questions—punctuated by his uncanny bursts of laughter—did little to further his case, and nothing in particular to challenge the flimsy evidence that his pistols had been loaded. Rather, he quibbled about details: some witnesses claimed that he had shot his two pistols with his two hands, some that he shot both using one hand; one witness claimed that he was between five and eight yards away from the royal carriage when he shot the second time, another that he was thirty yards away. Allowed to make a final statement, Oxford reiterated these discrepancies, and couldn't resist impugning Albert's reported courage, claiming that he jumped up at the sound of the first pistol and shrank back at the sight of the second. "Then," Oxford said, "I fired the second pistol. This is all I shall say at present."

Nothing Oxford did or said affected the cabinet's decision, and he was bound over for trial on the charge of High Treason. Home

Secretary Normanby drew up a warrant for Governor William Wadham Cope of Newgate Prison to take in Oxford as soon as he could be transferred from the Home Office. Oxford was removed, still apparently in good spirits. If he had considered the government's line of questioning more closely, however, he might have been more concerned. Although Inspector Hughes did tell the Cabinet about Oxford's box of secrets, that was as far as any reference to Young England went. The police still took the conspiracy theory very seriously: they had gotten it into their heads that the handwriting on all of Oxford's documents was not actually Oxford's, and considered it possible, at the very least, that another person might have encouraged Oxford to shoot the Queen—a Truelock to Oxford's Hadfield. But the government was not interested in establishing Oxford as a conspirator. Already, the image that Oxford had worked so hard to create—the myth of the valiant Bravo—was on the decline. The caricature of the foolish potboy was on the ascent.

Outside of the examination room, Oxford once again saw his family: Susannah, flanked by her husband William and uncle Edward. This time, Oxford was able to embrace his sister. Her distress was palpable and infectious, and Oxford began to cry. The police separated the two forcibly. Oxford did however manage to recover his highwayman's mien for one act of gallantry before leaving for Newgate, laughing and flourishing his hat to some girls in the building's lobby. At a few minutes before six, Hughes and Pearce clapped a cap on Oxford's head to disguise him, and put him in a coach for the journey up the Strand, Fleet Street, and Ludgate Hill, up Old Bailey to the door of Newgate Prison, where he was taken into custody by Governor Cope.

With the shooter safely shut away in the decaying bowels of Newgate Prison, Oxford's motive became the focus of discussion, and rumors connecting others with the crime began to fly. One of these held that the letters E R were stamped on Oxford's pistols or his pistol case—suggesting Oxford was acting on the orders of

Ernestus Rex, the King of Hanover. And while many (Baron Stockmar and Albert's personal secretary George Anson among them) could not believe that Hanover was directly involved, many took seriously the possibility that "Young England" was real: a reactionary, ultra-Tory movement bent on destroying the British constitution (as Uncle Ernest had abolished the Hanoverian one) and bringing absolutist government to Britain. Daniel O'Connell, the defender of Irish Catholics, was not alone in holding this view, but was its strongest articulator, seeing in the threat of Victoria's death a particular danger to her Irish subjects. Ten days after the shooting, in a letter addressed to the people of Ireland, O'Connell railed against the "underlings of that Orange-Tory faction which naturally detests the virtues of our beloved Queen." If Victoria had died, O'Connell thundered,

> I shudder even to think of the scenes that would have followed. I have no doubt that the Tory party in England would submit to be converted into another Hanover. They would sacrifice to the last remnant all constitutional liberty for the sake of enjoying irresponsible power. The gratification of trampling upon Ireland and the Irish would amply repay that worthless faction for the loss of any vain boast of ancient freedom.

O'Connell was convinced that Oxford had had assistance: how else, he argued, could this potboy obtain respectable clothing, serviceable pistols, and the training to use them? One persistent rumor in support of this theory held that a respectable, older man had stood near Oxford as the Queen's carriage approached, and gave him the signal to fire.

Other rumors held Oxford to be a creature of the left, not the right. After all, in the years leading up to 1840, the greatest threat to the constitution through political violence came from the working-class Chartist movement, a movement that had only grown stronger with the weakened economy of the early 1840s, a movement whose agitation had burst into violence in July of the year before, when the national convention of Chartists in Birmingham devolved into riots, violence that culminated in an attempted insurrection in Newport in November. Oxford's Birmingham working-class origins helped fuel this theory. The *Northern Star*, the leading Chartist newspaper, attempted energetically to dispel the rumor that "the diabolical deed was a premeditated act of a band of Chartists"—floating the counter-rumor that Oxford had acted in collusion with the police.

Most concluded that Oxford was a pathetic madman, and that shooting at the young and innocent Queen offered on the face of it solid evidence for his insanity. Even then, however, he may not have acted alone: rumors persisted (helped by reports of police investigations) that the Young England documents were not written in his hand, and that he was the "tool" of a "designing villain"—one either taking political advantage of Oxford's insanity, or perhaps someone equally deranged. Oxford's own mother for a time believed that some malefactor must have goaded her son into this act.

Victoria however, simply could not accept the idea that Oxford was a part of conspiracy of any stripe, for in accepting such a belief, she would have to acknowledge a life-threatening opposition to her among a portion of the British public, and thus relinquish the trust she had in her people, and lose the absolute trust she was certain they had in her. Trust in her subjects was instinct to her, and that instinct ruled her actions after Oxford's attempt, though she would be shaken, after every attempt to follow. Oxford was an aberration, apart from and antithetical to her public, and she refused to allow him to change her relationship with them. In shooting at her, Oxford forced the nation to contemplate what might have been. The *Morning Chronicle* stated that had Oxford succeeded, "We should have been at this moment the vassals of a now foreign potentate. We should have been breathing in the dominions of King ERNEST of Hanover! . . . The oppressor would soon have been abroad, and close on his track the insurgent whom the oppressor makes and infuriates." Victoria, in response to Oxford's threat, over the next few days provided the public with every opportunity to celebrate what was. After the worst had almost happened, she demonstrated to the nation that *nothing* had happened. She refused to hide or allow any visible sign of heightened security. She and Albert repeatedly exposed themselves to danger, to show that no such danger existed. In this way Victoria successfully (and virtually singlehandedly) converted an act of public discord into a new concord.

And the public responded enthusiastically, realizing that it had dodged a bullet just as its monarch had: if she labored to demonstrate her trust for them, they demonstrated their trust in her and their personal joy in her preservation. Throughout the country, organizations submitted addresses to the Queen protesting their loyalty and deploring Oxford's act. Theatres altered their programs to honor the Queen. At Her Majesty's Theatre, the night after the attempt, the entire troupe assembled for the opening curtain. "The effect was electrical; and the 'God Save the Queen' that broke forth was responded to by enthusiastic shouts of approbation from her Majesty's lieges." At Drury Lane Theatre, a lead singer, "to the warmest welcome and applause," sang a revised version that reflected the recent event: "God *Saved* the Queen." And at dinner at the Middle Temple on Thursday, when the usually "unostentatious" toast to the Queen was made, "one simultaneous burst of cheering arose, and then the members . . . gave a round of nine times nine in loyal testimony of their heartfelt pleasure for the escape of the Queen from the shot of the assassin." A similar scene occurred at Gray's Inn, the enthusiasm there helped along by a much larger allowance of wine than usual.

And Londoners, in huge numbers, gathered about the Palace over the next few days, both to see the scene of the crime and to have "oracular demonstration of the well-being of their Sovereign."

Constitution Hill was of course thronged, as all there exchanged the latest news and rumors, and all gathered around to hear the accounts of several witnesses (and, surely, several pretend witnesses) to Oxford's attempt. The wall to the Palace gardens was a particular focus of attention, as everyone (including the Dukes of Cambridge and Wellington) squeezed in between the police officers, still busy seeking, in vain, balls from Oxford's pistols.

On the day after the shooting, at about ten o'clock, much of the crowd shifted to the gates of the Palace, where a new show was beginning. The appropriate time for visiting the Palace had arrived, and a seemingly unceasing stream of carriages drove up throughout the morning and afternoon, filled with aristocracy and gentry who came to leave their cards, to sign the Palace register, and to inquire after the health of the Queen. (They were invariably and reassuringly told that she suffered from no ill effects whatsoever.) It was an unprecedented show of loyalty to the Queen by the social elite. Among these carriages were those of Victoria's family, of members of the Queen's government, of a number of foreign ministers and high church officials; throughout the day Victoria and Albert met personally with these.

By the afternoon, Victoria somehow made it clear to the masses outside that she and Albert would take their usual airing by carriage.

The Queen and the Prince were careful to give this ride the appearance of all their other rides: they would have the same number of attendants they had had the day before—two outriders ahead, two equerries behind—in the same low, very exposed carriage, and without any discernible increase in police presence (although most certainly the officers of A Division were on their guard). Soon after six, the outriders trotted through the gates and Victoria and Albert emerged into a deafening sea of humanity that "all but impeded the progress of the royal party." The Queen bowed repeatedly, and Albert doffed his hat. A spontaneous procession of riders formed behind the royal carriage and followed in a parade up Constitution Hill and to Hyde Park. A reporter from the *Times* was waiting there, and described the scene:

> The loyalty of the English was never more finely exhib-
> ited than it was during the afternoon of yesterday. . . .
> About 6 o'clock it was evident that the Royal party
> were approaching, and upon one of the Royal outriders
> appearing through the gateway leading from Constitu-
> tion-hill to Piccadilly, the cheers within the park were
> plainly heard. In an instant after an open carriage and
> four was driven through the archway containing Her
> Majesty and her Royal Consort, followed by a numerous
> cavalcade of ladies and gentlemen. The cheers of a vast
> assemblage of British subjects instantly burst forth with
> an animation and sincerity we have seldom witnessed—
> every hat was waved, and every heart seemed gladly to
> beat on seeing their Sovereign apparently in good health
> and spirits still among them. From the highest to the
> lowest there seemed to be but one feeling, and we can
> hardly imagine a much greater punishment of the wretch
> whose attempt was so providentially frustrated than to
> have seen how joyous the multitude were that his effort
> was not successful. Both the Queen and Prince looked
> exceedingly well. They drove twice round the Park—on
> the first occasion being loudly cheered all the way round,
> and on the second having every hat raised to them. The
> scene was one of deep and affecting interest.

On the next day, Friday, the Queen and Albert were prevented from riding as both Houses of Parliament paraded from West-minster to the Palace to present a congratulatory address. Three to four thousand spectators gathered before the Palace gates, and a substantial detachment of police from A Division was needed to clear a space before the Marble Arch. The Members set out from

Parliament in a parade of 190 carriages, the first of which reached the Palace gates before the last had left Westminster. The Commons arrived formally dressed: in court clothing, or, if they had them, full regimentals, red and blue Windsor uniforms, or uniforms of deputy lord-lieutenants; members of the bar wore wigs and gowns. The Speaker, who led the procession, wore the state robes. "Never on any previous occasion in our recollection," stated the *Times*, "has such a brilliant array of the Commons of England attended the presentation of an address to the throne." The Lords—in their various formal uniforms—followed behind the Commons, in order of ascending hierarchy: barons first, then bishops, earls, marquises, dukes—and finally Victoria's uncles Cambridge and Sussex, and the Lord Chancellor in his state carriage. It was a formal display of Parliamentary unanimity and a complete repudiation of the partisanship the Queen had herself shown months before in wishing to exclude the Tories from her wedding. The crowd outside the Palace, on the other hand, displayed a strong sense of party spirit, showing its hostility to the beleaguered Whig government: Lord Melbourne, on leaving the Palace, was hissed "loud and deep," while the Duke of Wellington was cheered, and Robert Peel's carriage was followed and "cheered until out of sight." That the crowds could hiss the Queen's ministry while cheering the monarch reveals a sea change in attitude toward the Queen: she was no longer "Mrs. Melbourne," a Whig Queen: she had turned away from the partisanship she, and her uncles and grandfather before her, had always exhibited. Victoria was anticipating Albert's ideal of a neutral monarchy— before Albert had had a chance to promote it.

Saturday and Sunday were quieter days, though the crowds continued to assemble, and the royal couple continued to ride in public. On Monday, however, Westminster once again burst into celebration, as Victoria and Albert departed Buckingham Palace by carriage for Windsor. Inhabitants of every suburb and village on the route—Kensington, Hammersmith, Brentford, Hounslow, Colnbrook, and Windsor itself—set out flags, pealed church bells, and assembled along the route to cheer the Queen's cortege. She and Albert set out with Albert's brother Ernest in one carriage, followed by three others. The crowds assembled on Constitution Hill were said to match in number those who had assembled for the Queen's coronation; they made the route nearly impassable. And the crush of well-wishers was equally great at Kensington. Victoria ordered her postilions to drive slowly through it all, as she and Albert, as exposed as ever, bowed from the Marble Arch to Windsor. "The reception of the royal party from the assembled thousands was," according to one reporter, "the most enthusiastic we have ever witnessed."

five

GOING TO SEE A MAN HANGED

T he abuse she had received at the hands of her husband, as well as years of difficult parenting, and more than one failed business, had rendered Hannah Oxford a fragile, highly-strung woman; her family doctor, James Fernandez Clarke, went so far as to claim she was "most eccentric, if not insane." After recovering from the initial shock of her son's arrest, however, she developed an iron and indefatigable resolve to save him from the death penalty at any cost; it was she more than any other who laid the groundwork for Edward's legal defense. Arriving in London from Birmingham on the day after his arrest and not knowing that her son had been transferred to Newgate, Hannah rushed from Euston Station to the A Division police station. She had at this time heard enough about Young England to believe that her son must have been a pawn serving the interests of others, as he could not have come up with the plan to assassinate the Queen on his own. She was certain that if she could speak with him—alone—he would reveal his accomplices to her. At A Division, she learned that since Oxford was to face trial for High Treason, she could not visit him at Newgate without first obtaining an order from the Home Office. The next day, Friday, accompanied by her daughter and her brother Edward Marklew, Hannah spoke with the permanent undersecretary there, Samuel March Phillipps, and received qualified permission to see her son: of the family, only she could speak with him, and would have to do so in the presence of Newgate's governor. From Whitehall, the family rushed to Newgate, and arrived at six in the evening— to find the governor gone, and the jailer on duty refusing them admittance until the next morning.

Before returning to the prison on Saturday, Hannah and Edward Marklew retained a solicitor for Edward. William Corne Humphreys agreed to take on the case, and accompanied the family to Newgate to consult with him.

Oxford was cheerful when he entered Newgate on Thursday evening. He might be shut away in London's most notorious lockup, but he was still an object of public fascination, and like his celebrated predecessor, Jack Sheppard, if he could not see the world, the world could see him, and they came: the undersecretaries at the Home Office, Maule and Phillipps, visited him there, and a number of London aldermen, some of whom were magistrates at the Central Criminal Court, spent a great deal of time with him—at least as much out of sheer curiosity as in any official capacity. With these aldermen—James Harmer, Sir Peter Laurie, and Sir George Carroll among them—Oxford showed signs of his former giddy volubility, proudly recounting the story of his attempt—an account that was changing: when Alderman Laurie asked him whether he had balls in his pistols, Oxford denied it outright, and laughed derisively. Oxford's openness about his actions, as well as his complete unconcern for their consequences, led the aldermen to conclude him insane.

When his illustrious visitors departed, however, Oxford was left alone with guards who were strictly ordered to discuss nothing with him beyond his immediate needs, and he began to show signs of depression and anxiety; reverting to fits of crying, and developing the odd habit of whistling to mask his distress. To Governor Cope and the prison chaplain, James Carver, he revealed his depression, acknowledging he cared little that he had thrown his own life away, but that he was terrified that he had "sacrificed" his mother's life as well.

Oxford had announced to the aldermen that he had decided to act as his own counsel during the trial, a fact that they had reported to Governor Cope, so that Cope issued an order prohibiting any interview with a lawyer. When William Corne Humphreys accompanied the Oxfords to Newgate, then, on Saturday 13 June, he never saw Edward. Humphreys was livid, concluding that the aldermen— Alderman Harmer, in particular—had encouraged Oxford to refuse legal assistance. Because of this "extraordinary interference," he refused to have anything further to do with Oxford's case. With Governor Cope as a witness, but otherwise alone, Hannah had a "heart-rending" conversation with her son, during which he made a last-gasp attempt to promote his conspiracy theory: "there are others in it," he told her.

That was the last time Oxford endeavored to implicate others, and the last time his mother gave any credence to the notion: neither mentioned the idea again. His sister Susannah, who had more closely than anyone else watched Oxford's movements over the past month, was certain that there was no Young England, and apparently was able to convince her mother. The police on the other hand continued to take the possibility of a conspiracy seriously, and busily collected writing samples from the residents of West Place. By the time of Oxford's trial, however, the police too had given up their theory of a conspiracy, and could offer no evidence of one.

Indeed, Oxford's defense at trial largely took shape in the days after the shooting, and Oxford's mother contributed greatly not simply to the formulation of that defense but to its promulgation. She spoke to anyone who would listen about the family madness, and the newspapers eagerly reiterated her stories to a public hungry to know everything about the boy. Her words helped shift public opinion about Oxford from sinister desperado to pitiful victim of hereditary mental illness. Speaking two days after the shooting to the *Morning Chronicle*, she promoted just this image:

> The unhappy parent of Oxford states that her husband died about twelve years since, and that during his life-time he evinced great irritability which left little doubt of the occasional unsoundness of his mind. Upon one occasion, in a fit of excitement, he cut the bedclothes up into shreds, and on another he rode into the sitting-room on horseback. She says that at times she is afflicted with nervous delusions, and she describes her son as an inoffensive and affectionate child, and declares her belief that he committed the act in a boyish frolic, and that there were no balls in the pistols at the time. The pistols, [s]he says, he brought home about a month ago, and one morning he held one of them (empty) to her head, and threatened her in a joke, which exceedingly alarmed her.

And at Newgate the next day, Hannah spoke with the aldermen who surrounded her son, telling them of her deceased husband's insanity and abuse: offering to show Sir Peter Laurie the scar where Edward Senior had fractured her skull; Laurie declined to look, concluding that Hannah was "decidedly mad"; he had no doubt that her son was mad as well.

To create a defense for her son, then, Hannah had not only to engage a solicitor, but a medical specialist to organize a case for the boy's insanity. She and her brother found a solicitor in the East End. Jabez Pelham, who had a practice off Ratcliffe Highway, was at first hesitant to take on the case, having heard that Humphreys was already engaged, but after consulting with that solicitor, agreed to do so. Edward Marklew and a number of his acquaintances agreed to pay his fees.* Upon being engaged on Tuesday the 16th, Pelham attempted to interview Oxford at Newgate, but as Oxford still refused counsel, Governor Cope prevented any meeting. Overnight, however, Oxford changed his mind, and Pelham was able to see him the next morning. Oxford proposed to Pelham that they defend his action as a foolish lark. Pelham, on the other hand, quickly resolved that the defense would prove a case "if not of positive insanity, at least of monomania, which will entitle him to the merciful consideration of the Court and jury."

For a medical specialist, Hannah consulted the family doctor who deemed her "eccentric, if not insane." She could not have made a better choice. James Fernandez Clarke had treated her for years, knew Edward, and had for some time been concerned about his mental state; indeed, the instant he had learned that Oxford had been arrested, he exclaimed "the boy is mad. I am not surprised." Clarke was, moreover, an editor of the *Lancet*, the leading medical magazine of the day, and thus was personally acquainted with England's greatest medical minds. He agreed to assist with the case, and met with Pelham to work out the specifics. Pelham had, in the meantime, engaged a lawyer to argue Oxford's defense at trial: J. Sydney Taylor, a highly reputable barrister and well-known journalist, adamant in his opposition to the death penalty and willing to pursue any legal remedy to keep Oxford from the noose. Consulting with Taylor, Clarke suggested three eminent doctors besides himself who might be willing to testify to Oxford's insanity.

In 1840, psychological science was still largely anatomical science, and the psychologist, or in the terminology of the day the mad-doctor, was at best a specialized physician. General physicians were usually considered competent, and often called upon,

---

* It was a promise that Edward Marklew apparently reneged upon; in January 1841, Jabez Pelham appeared in court as an insolvent debtor, citing, among other debts owed him, £510 due from Hannah Oxford for the defense of her son (*Times* 29 Jan. 1841, 7).

to treat the mental illnesses of their patients. Clarke, himself no mad-doctor, certainly considered himself well qualified to make an expert diagnosis of Oxford's psychological state. And of the three doctors he recommended to Oxford's defense, two—Drs. Hodgkin and Chowne, of Charing Cross Hospital—were pathologists and anatomists, specialists in physical disorder. Only one of those he recommended was truly a specialist in mental illness. This was Dr. John Conolly, at the time the most popular psychologist in Britain. Conolly had become superintendent of Hanwell Asylum in Middlesex the year before, and had quickly enforced a program of treatment that prohibited any restraint of patients: a revolutionary treatment, but one that, within a few years, would become the norm. Conolly's fame rested upon this system, and upon the side career he was beginning to adopt as an expert psychological witness. Critics claimed that he was able to testify to madness in any situation. Conolly's reputation made him, to Clarke, the "most important" of the witnesses. All agreed to testify, and Hannah added two more to the list: John Birt Davis and William Henry Partridge, Birmingham doctors who could testify as to the insanity of Oxford's father and grandfather.

Pelham decided to supplement this medical testimony with a barrage of witnesses—as many as 110 people, from Birmingham and elsewhere—who had witnessed three generations of Oxford family madness. And he commissioned Hannah to subpoena many of them. A week after she had arrived in London, then, Hannah Oxford took the four o'clock train to Birmingham on this mission. And on the same day—just a day after he first met with his solicitor—Oxford demonstrated that he, too, was willing to support an insanity plea. He sent Pelham a letter:

Newgate, June 18, 1840.
My dear Sir,—Have the goodness to write to Lord Normanby and ask him to let me have some books to read—such as "Jack the Giant Killer," "Jack and the

Beanstalk," "Jack and his Eleven Wives," "My little Tom Thumb," "The Arabian Nights' entertainments," and all such books from such celebrated authors. And ask him, as a prisoner of war, whether I may not be allowed on a parole of *honour*, and on what grounds, ask him, dar (sic) he detain one of her Majesty's subjects.

I remain respectfully,
Edward Oxford
To Mr. Pelham, solicitor, Gravel-lane, London.

Oxford was far more literate, and much more cognizant of British legal process, than he made himself out to be here. He was, to put it in Victorian terms, shamming, trying too hard to appear insane: he almost certainly realized that this letter would find its way into the newspapers—as it did—and reinforce the public perception that he was an idiot. Benjamin Disraeli, reading this letter in the newspapers, saw not idiocy but canniness in Oxford's words, writing to his wife that the letter suggests "that P[rince] Albt is an ogre and the Q[uee]n an ogress"—and by implication, that Oxford is Jack, the humble but heroic fairy-tale slayer of giants. This may have not been what Oxford intended, but it is an interpretation that surely would have pleased him immensely.

Oxford likely had another motive in writing this letter: he almost certainly felt he was fading from the spotlight he so craved. Victoria's intensified love affair with her public continued: two days before, she and Albert had attended the races at Ascot to immense crowds (many who had come to see her more than the races) and "deafening cheers from every part of the course." The hissing she had experienced there a year before, in the midst of the Flora Hastings scandal, was forgotten. But Oxford was shut away, and he had been, since his arrest, sharing prison space and newspaper columns with other criminal celebrities. On this particular day, one of his criminal colleagues was stealing public attention. As Disraeli put it, "all the world is talking about Courvoisier, and very little of the quasi Regicide." This day, 18 June, was the first day of Courvoisier's trial for murder.

For his first couple of days in Newgate, Oxford inhabited an ordinary cell among the general population. (Within a couple of days, however, because the elevated charge of High Treason demanded a more careful monitoring, Oxford was moved into a condemned cell, a larger cell created a few years before by knocking down the wall dividing two smaller cells. These cells were furnished with a bench and table so that jailers could comfortably observe, and if necessary prevent the suicide of, condemned prisoners.) From the start, then, Oxford was in contact with François Benjamin Courvoisier. Whether he mingled at first with Newgate's other notorious inmate, Richard Gould, is another question. Gould, with another inmate who had achieved some amount of public attention at the time—Samuel Bailey, a seaman who had attempted to murder his captain with an axe—had, two weeks before, attempted to break out of the prison. The two removed the bars of a window to Gould's cell and descended an improvised rope into a courtyard. At that point, they realized they had no way of ascending to the roof and escaping and, after a frustrated night in the open, they clambered back into their cells. Evidence of their attempt was discovered, and they were locked up more securely. If Gould was at first removed from Oxford's presence, though, joint appearances at the Central Criminal Court would soon bring them together.*

On the first day of his trial, Courvoisier had genuine and warranted hopes of acquittal. The evidence against him was circumstantial and incomplete: prosecutors, for one thing, were unable to

---

* Oxford, Courvoisier, Gould, and Bailey formed such a notorious quartet at Newgate that a request was made to Sir Peter Laurie, alderman and official of the prison, to take plaster casts of the heads of the four. He refused, arguing that this sort of thing was done only *after* criminals were tried and found guilty (*Morning Chronicle* 17 June 1840, 3).

account for all of the goods stolen from Sir William Russell, despite keeping Courvoisier under close watch from the morning the body was discovered. His lead counsel, Charles Phillips, intended to suggest to the jury that Russell's other servants could just as easily have committed the murder, and intended to suggest as well—with strong evidence—that the police had botched the case, tampering and planting evidence. Phillips's aggressive cross-examination on the first day of trial of Courvoisier's fellow servant Sarah Manser indicated this intention.

On the second day of the trial, however, Phillips's strategy collapsed. The evening before, a witness, Charlotte Piolaine, came forward with new evidence. Piolaine was the wife of the proprietor of a rundown French hotel in Leicester Square at which Courvoisier had worked four years previously. He had come to her some time before the murder with a package that he asked her to hold for a few days. When she read in a French-language newspaper of the murder and of police interest in the missing loot, she gathered a few witnesses, engaged a solicitor, and opened the package. It contained, among other items, silverware stamped with the Bedford crest. Piolaine was brought to Newgate, and was able to pick out Courvoisier from a number of prisoners in the yard as the one who had given her the package. The prosecution thus had compelling proof that Courvoisier had stolen from Lord William—though not proof that he had killed the man.

Courvoisier, aware of this new evidence, called his two lawyers to the dock the next morning. As Phillips remembers it, the following stunning exchange took place:

> Up to this morning I believed most firmly in his innocence, and so did many others as well as myself. "I have sent for you, gentlemen," he said, "to tell you that I committed the murder!" When I could speak, which was not immediately, I said, "Of course, then you are going to plead guilty?" "No, sir," was the reply, "I expect you to

defend me to the utmost." We returned to our seats. My position at this moment was, I believe, without parallel in the annals of the profession.

Phillips's first instinct was to drop the case altogether. He consulted, however, with the associate judge for the trial, who recommended that he continue to defend Courvoisier, "and to use all fair arguments arising on the evidence." Phillips's plan to throw suspicion on the other servants, then, was now off limits; he would have to limit his defense to throwing doubt on the evidence implicating his client: in particular, he questioned Inspector Tedman's finding of a pair of bloody gloves in a trunk the police had thoroughly examined days before, finding nothing. He also attempted to discredit Mme. Piolaine's evidence by suggesting that her hotel was nothing but a sordid gaming-den. In the end, the circumstantial evidence was too strong.* Courvoisier was found guilty and sentenced to hang on the 6th of July, outside Newgate's debtor's door, and then to be buried within the precincts of the prison. He was removed from the courtroom by a passageway to the prison and placed in the condemned cell neighboring Oxford's. There, he immediately attempted to kill himself by forcing a towel down his throat.

For Edward Oxford, whose level of happiness correlated exactly with the amount of attention he received, the morning of 22 June was a time of pure joy, as he and a more doleful Richard Gould stood in the dock of the Old Bailey, in the place that Courvoisier had been sentenced to death two days before. Oxford could hardly contain himself, and grinned "and with difficulty restrained his propensity to laughter" to see a courtroom packed full with an

---

* Later, when news of Courvoisier's confession came out, Phillips was savaged in the press for defending a man he knew to be guilty, especially by attempting to place blame for the murder on others. He was forced to defend himself from this charge for years after the trial (Costigan 324).

audience eager to witness his and Gould's trials. Gould chose to act as his own counsel; he pleaded not guilty and sat to await his trial. Oxford pled not guilty, and sat with his solicitor, Pelham, while his barrister, Sydney Taylor, presented an affidavit from Pelham and Hannah Oxford requesting a delay until the next sessions. They gave a number of reasons for their request—a delay would give the public time to cool down, for one thing, and would allow the defense reasonable time to formulate their response to prosecution witnesses. Their primary need for delay, however, was to allow Hannah to complete her mission and subpoena witnesses to Oxford and his forebears' insanity. The Attorney General, Sir John Campbell, who would lead the prosecution, attacked every point in the affidavit save one—the most important one: he would agree to a delay so that Oxford's defense could adequately prepare a case for insanity. Campbell "should be extremely sorry, when the case came before the jury, that it should be charged against the Attorney General of the day by any future historian that he had followed the example of a former Attorney General, who had hurried on the trial of Bellingham for shooting Mr. Perceval, although it was stated on affidavit that evidence would be brought forward to prove that he was insane."

Campbell was referring to the only assassination of a British prime minister in history. On 11 May 1812, John Bellingham, who some years before had suffered abysmal treatment in Russian prisons for crimes he was certain he did not commit, and who had been repeatedly denied help or redress from the British government during and after his time in Russia, decided that his only recourse was to kill the head of government, Spencer Perceval. He obtained a pair of pocket pistols and had a tailor alter his coat lining so that he could conceal them. He waited for Perceval to appear in the lobby of the House of Commons and shot him through the heart. Perceval died within minutes. Bellingham was tried for murder four days later. His counsel pleaded energetically for a delay; he could, given time, offer testimony from several persons outside of

London that Bellingham had been insane for years. The application was denied outright.

Bellingham in his defense gave a touching narrative of his travails in Russia, and a convincing account of the insensitivity of his own government toward him. And his counsel brought up three witnesses from London who testified to his eccentricities, though all agreed, on cross-examination, that he had never been to their knowledge restrained for insanity, and that he was always in command of his business affairs. The judge, in summing up, pointed out that no personal injury could warrant taking the law into one's own hands. Bellingham was found guilty and hanged on the next Monday morning—a week to the day after he shot Spencer Perceval.

Lord Chief Justice Tindal agreed to avoid such an appearance of undue haste in Oxford's case, and set his trial for the next sessions, on 9 July. The hearing was brief, but for as long as it lasted Oxford had the time of his life. He exclaimed to Pelham, "did you see how I was noticed!—what a noise my case seems to make." Pelham attempted to distract him from reveling in his celebrity, but to no avail; Oxford insisted that his solicitor identify all of the "lords and gentlemen" who had come to see him. He asked in particular about a gentleman with black whiskers who was watching him: it was, Pelham told him, the Duke of Brunswick, who, deposed in a public uprising and exiled, had plenty of time on his hands to view British criminal trials. "What, a Duke come to see me?" said Oxford. "I am glad of that. Will there be any more dukes present at the trial?" (Pelham predicted that it would not be likely.) Oxford also nodded to Fox Maule as to a friend. "He was very anxious to know if he was 'cried out' in the streets; if his likeness was taken, and what was said of him by the French newspapers . . . he frequently rubbed his hands and exclaimed, with great self-satisfaction, 'nothing else will be talked of but me for a long time. What a great character I shall be!'"

Many of his supposed friends the aldermen were in court as well, but it was just as well for them that his trial was delayed, for later the same day, they proceeded with pomp and solemnity, in the company of over 150 London officials, to Buckingham Palace and to Ingestre House, to present their addresses of congratulations to the Queen and Prince, and then to the Duchess of Kent.

Oxford would have been disappointed to know that the Duke of Brunswick might have been more interested in Richard Gould's impending trial than Oxford's, having attended Gould's earlier examination for burglary. But Gould was likely much less impressed by his august presence; he was focused instead upon mounting his own defense. His counsel in his previous trial—for murder, and not for burglary, the charge in this trial—had done an excellent job of attacking the credibility of many of the witnesses and much of the evidence against his client. Gould endeavored this time to do the same thing, without success: his attempts only earned the laughter of the court. The prosecution refrained from introducing the tainted confession Sergeant Otway had elicited from Gould, but Gould introduced it anyway, hoping to elicit sympathy from the jury that a policeman would thus entrap a drunken man into falsely implicating others. The prosecution did, however, introduce as compelling evidence the fruit of that confession—the bull's-eye lantern, fished out of the pond behind the house where Gould was staying. The couple with whom Gould was living both identified the lantern as having been taken from them, and connected Gould with its disappearance. The two also established that Gould, impoverished before the burglary, was now flush with cash: he had used some to buy new shoes, and the bulk of the money was found bound up in one of Gould's stockings.

The jury returned after fifteen minutes and pronounced Gould guilty of burglary. Baron James Parke, the presiding judge, noted his and the Lord Chief Justice's full agreement with the verdict, and told Gould that no one was fooled by his earlier acquittal: he was a murderer as well as a burglar. Parke threw the book at Gould: transportation for life to a penal colony, "there to pass the remainder of his existence in hopeless slavery, poverty and misery of the worst description." Delighted spectators applauded the verdict as Gould, emotionless, was led from the courtroom. Two weeks later, Gould was, in a sense, back where he had started before Sergeant Otway entrapped him: on a ship bound for Sydney, New South Wales. Now, though, he sat in chains on the convict ship *Eden* and faced a far different future.

As Oxford awaited his trial, Courvoisier in the neighboring condemned cell offered him ample opportunity for diversion. Courvoisier had developed, since his condemnation, a pressing need to confess, and he did so repeatedly and fervently, apparently to anyone who would listen to him or would act as witness to his written statements. He wrote at least four confessions. The first of these, written on the same day Oxford and Gould appeared in court, set out in very specific detail events surrounding the murder. Courvoisier's lawyer and Governor Cope witnessed the confession, and sent it on to the Home Office (from where it soon found its way into the newspapers). Very many of the details of this confession, it quickly became clear, were false; Courvoisier lied, for one thing, in claiming that Lord William Russell had surprised him in his burglary of the house, and that was what convinced him on the spur of the moment to murder the old man. The evidence of the case made it clear that his murder was premeditated, not impulsive. Why did he lie? He could have done so to reduce his culpability. Courvoisier was most certainly aware that the overwhelming majority of death sentences—over 95% of them—were commuted to lesser sentences in his day; a well-publicized confession that somehow mitigated his guilt might do the trick.

In later confessions, he continued to provide careful (and sometimes contradictory) details, all suggest a variety of mitigating factors. In his third confession—a spiritual biography of sorts, written in French—he claimed that he had been influenced to the deed by bad reading:

> I read a book containing the history of thieves and murderers, being under the dominion of Satan I read it with

pleasure, I did not think that it would be a great sin to place myself among them. On the contrary, I admired their skill and their valour. I was particularly struck with the history of a young man who was born of very respectable parents, and who had spent his property in gaming and debauchery, and afterwards went from place to place stealing all he could. I admired his cunning, instead of feeling horrified at it; and now I reap but too well the fruit of those papers and books which I had too long suffered to supplant devotional works.

Courvoisier's suggestion that low literature can create thieves and murderers was the popular theory at the heart of the criticism of the Newgate novel, and indeed, the story got about that Ainsworth's *Jack Sheppard* had turned Courvoisier evil, compelling Ainsworth to write to the newspapers contradicting "this false and injurious statement." The connection between Courvoisier and the Newgate novel and the resulting furor, was enough to kill the subgenre.

There was another culprit in this confession—Satan, whose hold on Courvoisier became even stronger in his fourth confession, in which Courvoisier represented the murder of Russell as a cosmic battle. As he stood above the sleeping man:

> . . . the evil disposition of my heart did not allow me to repent. I turned up my coat and shirt-sleeve, and came near to the bed on the side of the window. There I heard a cry of my conscience, telling me, "Thou art doing wrong"; but I hardened myself against this voice, and threw myself on my victim, and murdered him with the knife I was holding in my right hand.

If Courvoisier expected his sentence to be commuted by the Queen's government, however, he was disappointed: a servant slaughtering his master in such a cold-blooded manner was beyond their ability to forgive. (The fact that he was a foreigner killing a member of one of the best-known aristocratic families in England certainly didn't help.) Courvoisier's zealous religiosity during his last days, however, had all the signs of a genuine religious conversion, and the genuine hope that faith would save him in the next life, if not in this one. Courvoisier spent most of his last days in fervent prayer, often in the company of James Carver, Newgate's chaplain, and M. Baup, the Swiss minister of a nearby French church.

In the sermon traditionally spoken before a condemned man, given the day before Courvoisier's execution, Reverend Carver promised him the "pardon and peace" that God offered to every repentant sinner. The chapel at Newgate was filled to overflowing. The sheriffs, besieged by applications, gave out tickets and opened a gallery that had been closed for the past fifteen years. Courvoisier—his coffin placed in front of him—attended to the sermon with "sorrow and contrition," and demonstrated great agitation at every reference to his crime. Edward Oxford sat directly behind him, flanked by two jailers. He, too, appeared to enter into the solemnity of the occasion, showing a "decent seriousness." But, just for a moment, his vainglory got the better of him. When the chaplain offered up a prayer for the Queen, Oxford couldn't help it: he looked up, and around the chapel, with a foolish grin on his face.

Though resigned to die, Courvoisier had not completely resigned himself to strangle on a rope before the eyes of thousands, and plotted to take his own life by binding up an arm with a strip of cloth and cutting a vein with a sharpened fragment of wood that he had secreted in his mattress. His plan was discovered and foiled when he was forced to strip completely before going to sleep.

He was to be hanged at the customary time of 8:00 the next day. He was woken at four the next morning, as he had requested, and for two hours he quietly wrote final letters to his family. At six, the ritual of execution began, as Courvoisier was joined by a sheriff, by

Carver, and by his Swiss minister Baup; they prayed until 7:30, and Courvoisier "fervently" took the sacrament of communion.

If Oxford was not awoken early that morning by the clankings of cell doors or the fervency of prayer, then his sleep would certainly have been disrupted by the growing activity outside the prison. Crowds had been assembling since the night before, to reserve the best vantage point to see Courvoisier hanged: these were a celebratory bunch, mostly rowdy youths, and the local gin shops remained open all night to cater to them. In the early hours of the morning, the scaffold was wheeled into place outside Newgate's debtor's door and hammered into place. The bulk of the crowd began arriving after dawn. Charles Dickens and William Makepeace Thackeray, apart from one another, were among this crowd. Both were, in 1840, staunch opponents of the death penalty, and both were to find their views strengthened considerably by what they were about to witness. Thackeray, recording his impressions of the event in his essay "Going to See a Man Hanged," noted the great social and moral diversity of the spectators: from the immoral—the young blackguards and their prostitute girlfriends at the front of the crowd, as well as the upper-class dandies and "Mohawks" who had retained window seats above the mass and who entertained themselves by spraying those below with brandy-and-water—to the respectable: the tradesmen and tradesmen's families, and the bulk of the working-class spectators, whom Thackeray, standing squeezed among them, deemed "extraordinarily gentle and good-humoured." Pickpockets were at work, as were broadsheet-sellers: Courvoisier was a popular subject for these; as many as 1.6 million would be sold. The crowds, as the hour of execution approached, filled Old Bailey and Giltspur streets and overflowed to Ludgate Hill to the south and Smithfield to the north. The *Times* conservatively estimated 20,000 were there; Thackeray reported 40,000. Places in the windows of the houses surrounding the scaffold were going for three guineas, and for two sovereigns one could obtain treacherous places on the house-roofs: places for those "with less money to spare, but more nerve."

After Courvoisier had taken communion, William Calcraft entered the cell. Calcraft had been Newgate's executioner since 1829, and was to continue in that position until 1874: a long if not illustrious career. Calcraft was well aware that this was bound to be a highly profitable day for him. For his earliest hangings he was paid a guinea per hanging; in time, he would earn £10 a body. He would also be given Courvoisier's hanging-rope and his effects, including his clothing. He could sell the former, cut into little pieces, as souvenirs—and Courvoisier's notoriety would guarantee a high selling price for these. He could also sell the clothes to Madame Tussaud's waxworks; Courvoisier would soon be a star attraction in Madame's Chamber of Horrors.

Calcraft drew from a black bag a rope with which he pinioned Courvoisier's arms before him. At a few minutes before eight, the procession left the condemned cell, Carver in front, reading the burial service.

The procession stopped in Newgate's press yard—so-called not because of any journalistic connection, but because this was the area in which, until as late as 1772, prisoners who refused to plead were crushed with stones until they spoke or died. On this day, a number of esteemed guests had assembled in the yard; they had paid for the privilege of watching Courvoisier in his last moments, as his leg-irons were stricken off and he was led to the scaffold. (Afterwards, they would have a hearty breakfast with Governor Cope.) Among this group was the celebrated actor Charles Kean. Kean's father Edmund, the even more celebrated actor, had come to Newgate twenty years before to witness the ultimate moments of Arthur Thistlewood and his fellow conspirators, sentenced to hanging and decapitation for plotting to assassinate the cabinet: Kean wished to broaden his education as an actor. His son, one assumes, was at Newgate on this day for the same reason.

At 7:55, the prison bell tolled; with an "immense sway and movement," the entire crowd uncovered their heads, and, according to Thackeray, "a great murmur arose, more awful, *bizarre*, and indescribable than any sound I had ever before heard." After a suspenseful pause, Courvoisier emerged, with the sheriffs and the hangman. He showed, by all accounts, a preternatural calmness; his only agitation, beyond an imploring look around at the immense crowd, was a clasping and unclasping of his bound hands. The crowd replied in kind to him: after a few yells of execration, they remained silent. He strode to the middle of the platform, under the beam, where Calcraft quickly slipped a hood over his head, adjusted the noose, stepped back, and pulled the lever that shot back the bolt. Courvoisier dropped.

William Calcraft was renowned as a bungler famous for his "short drops," in which the hanged man, only dropping a few inches, would not suffer a broken neck and would thus slowly strangle to death, Calcraft often helping with this process by racing under the scaffolding and pulling on the legs of the dangling man. To be fair to Calcraft, however, the short drop was the norm in 1840. Long drops of several feet, designed to break the neck—drops which could go horribly wrong in their own way—were not a feature of Newgate hangings until the 1880s; and broken necks and quick, painless deaths were not considered by all at the time to be good hangings. According to the *Times*, however, Courvoisier's death—perhaps with Calcraft's help under the scaffolding—was relatively benign: "He died without any violent struggle. In two minutes after he had fallen, his legs were twice slightly convulsed, but no further motion was observable, excepting that his raised arms, gradually losing their vitality, sank down from their own lifeless weight."

Both Dickens and Thackeray were sickened by the scene. Dickens saw the only the lowest form of humanity: "nothing but ribaldry, debauchery, levity, drunkenness, and flaunting vice in fifty other shapes. I should have deemed it impossible that I could have ever felt any large assemblage of my fellow-creatures to be so odious." Thackeray couldn't watch. For weeks after the hanging, however, he suffered, and he wrote eloquently upon the human degradation effected by public hanging, not the degradation of the masses, as Dickens saw it, but the degradation of himself:

> I fully confess that I came away down Snow Hill that morning with a disgust for murder, but it was for *the murder I saw done.* . . . I feel myself ashamed and degraded at the brutal curiosity which took me to that brutal sight; and I pray to Almighty God to cause this disgraceful sin to pass from among us, and to cleanse our land of blood.

After hanging for an hour, Courvoisier's body was placed in the coffin, and brought back into the prison. A medical officer examined the body and proclaimed it lifeless. A death mask was taken of his face. One cast from that mask remained at the Governor's office; another was exhibited at Madame Tussaud's: a hauntingly angelic-looking 23-year-old, displayed until well into the twentieth century.

In the afternoon, Courvoisier's body was buried in a passageway to the Old Bailey.

Of Courvoisier, Gould, and Oxford, only Oxford remained, and in the relative silence of his condemned cell he must, on this day, have given some thought to his own possible fate: a guilty verdict for High Treason entailed hanging, decapitation, and quartering. If there was any vainglory left in the boy, after his committal to Newgate, the events of this day must have eradicated it.

Not long before his trial, Oxford was visited by an Italian artist from Manchester; he had come to take a plaster cast of his head and face. The operation was conducted as quietly as possible; Governor Cope later denied knowing about it, as did the aldermen, who found the situation disgraceful. Nor was his family consulted: Hannah, on learning of this visit, became hysterical. Knowing that Newgate made and kept plaster casts of condemned felons like Courvoisier after their deaths, she assumed that the Home Secretary had ordered the cast of her son, and that his execution was thus inevitable.

It was not Normanby's power at work here, but Madame Tussaud's, and by September she was able to advertise proudly in the newspapers:

> The LUNATIC EDWARD OXFORD.—Madame TUS-SAUD and SONS respectfully announce that they have added a full-length model of OXFORD (taken from life) to their Exhibition, representing him in the act of attempting the life of Her Majesty Queen Victoria. Likewise the Models of Gould and Courvoisier.

Madame Tussaud was not the only one fascinated by Oxford's head. At one o'clock the afternoon before the trial, James Fernandez Clarke and two of his hand-picked team of medical experts—Chowne and Conolly, accompanied by Oxford's solicitor, Pelham—took a carriage to Newgate with an order from the Home Secretary in hand, to examine Oxford and decide whether he was insane. Actually, they all had for the most part made up their minds. From their later testimony, it is clear that the newspaper reports had convinced them that his motiveless act, his inviting capture, and his statements after the fact all pointed to insanity. When Clarke went to Hanwell to speak with Conolly, Conolly said "I cannot believe that the prisoner is responsible for his actions. There is an entire want of motive, and, from what I have heard of his conduct since his committal, I feel convinced that a plea of insanity can be maintained." "Of course," he added, "I can only satisfy myself on this point by seeing and carefully examining him." Conolly came to Newgate to reinforce his conclusion, not to draw one.

At the prison, Governor Cope, still taking his position of gatekeeper very seriously, at first refused the doctors admittance.

George Maule,* who as Solicitor of the Treasury was responsible for putting together the prosecution's case in the trial, was with Cope when the doctors arrived, and it was likely Maule who ordered Cope not to admit the medical experts for the defense unless they were accompanied by the prosecution's expert. That expert, Charles Aston Key, a highly reputed surgeon at Guy's Hospital, was not called as a witness at Oxford's trial, but he attended, and advised the prosecution in cross-examining the defense's expert witnesses. Cope immediately sent a messenger to Key's house, but he was out, and no one knew when he would return. After nearly two hours in the governor's office, Clarke pointed out the obvious to Cope: the doctors had a government order to see Oxford; the trial was the next day; if Cope continued to deny them access, he would be denying Oxford a fair trial. Cope and Maule relented, Maule accompanying the doctors in Key's place.

Oxford exhibited to his guests the same clear and straightforward method of answering questions he had shown to the police when he was captured. While this manner had then impressed the police with a firm sense of his sanity, the doctors drew the opposite conclusion. To them, Oxford's demonstration of cool, rational behavior, when he was caught apparently red-handed, imprisoned for High Treason, and faced a possible death sentence, was in itself a sure sign of the deepest insanity. Showing no agitation whatsoever convinced at least Dr. Chowne that the boy was missing normal brain function: was, in a word, an imbecile.

John Conolly was a true believer in what was, at the time, considered by many to be the reputable study of phrenology— the sub-science which held to the oversimple premise that brain size and brain shape determined human behavior, and that the skull, conforming to the size and shape of the brain, could thus be examined to provide clues to an individual's psychological makeup.

---

* Not to be confused with the Undersecretary for the Home Department, Fox Maule.

After Clarke introduced Conolly to Oxford, then, he was soon probing the boy's skull and, not surprisingly, he quickly found the evidence he needed to support his diagnosis: a sunken spot at the upper part of Oxford's forehead that suggested to him a missing part of the brain: a sure sign of idiocy. "This youth," Conolly told Clarke, "cannot with such a configuration be entirely right."

While Oxford seemed eager to answer the doctors' questions, Conolly and the others found his answers unsound in more than one respect. For one thing, Oxford consistently demonstrated a lack of affect. When they reminded him that his family would suffer if he were convicted, he seemed not to care. When told he had committed a great crime, in shooting at the Queen, he seemed not to understand, replying "that he might as well shoot her as any one else." Moreover, in some of his answers he demonstrated illogic. It is hard, though, not to get a sense that he was trying too hard to appear insane with some of his replies. For instance, when Chowne, obviously hoping for an agitated reaction, reminded Oxford that he'd be decapitated if found guilty, Oxford, perhaps with Courvoisier's execution fresh in his mind, and certainly remembering the Italian artist from Manchester, replied calmly that "he had been decapitated in fact a week before, for he had a cast taken of his head." The doctors, concerned that Oxford might be faking madness, sought evidence besides his speech for insanity. For Conolly, it was the abnormal shape of his skull. For Chowne, it was his walk: "I told him to get up and walk about the room, and the brisk manner in which he walked proved to me he was not acting a part, for I think if he had been he would not have walked so much at his ease."

One question that Oxford did answer clearly directly demonstrates that he was aware of what his defense was to be, and that he fully intended to cooperate: there had been no bullets in his pistols, he stubbornly maintained, even when the doctors suggested to him that there had been.

The doctors walked away resolved to testify that he was insane. "We held a consultation after the interview," Clarke states, "and we all felt convinced that we could justly uphold the plea of insanity, notwithstanding the opposition we contemplated from the Government." They expected a fight.

They got one.

six

GUILTY, HE BEING AT THE TIME INSANE

The courtroom was packed on the first day of Oxford's trial. The sheriffs, however, had just had good practice with handling the crowds at the Courvoisier trial, and they adopted the same procedure with this one: they gave out a limited number of tickets and restricted access to all avenues leading to the courtroom.

At a quarter to ten, Oxford was called to appear, and every eye in the courtroom turned to the dock. He emerged after a few seconds, at first dejected: but he looked out over a sea of bewigged magistrates and barristers, and at the roomful of notables, and was heartened. His solicitor Jabez Pelham's prediction to him at his arraignment turned out to be true: there were no more Dukes present than there had been then. But the Duke of Brunswick was again a spectator, as were the Earls of Errol, Colchester, and

Uxbridge, as well as a Baron and a Count, and a scattering of Lords and Honorables. The Lady Mayoress of London and a retinue of "elegantly-dressed ladies" occupied a box usually reserved for the county magistracy. Undersecretary Fox Maule, Oxford's seeming friend, and his wife were among the first to arrive. Oxford's expression of dejection changed to a silly-looking smile of bafflement, excitement, and curiosity. He would for most of the trial exhibit a *nonchalance* that, for many, confirmed his lack of reason. Rather than pay attention to the proceedings, he was captivated much more by the herbs strewn before him, "picking, rubbing, and smelling" them for the next two days. These herbs, particularly malodorous rue, had been placed before the dock at every Old Bailey session for ninety years, ever since a prisoner suffering from gaol-fever—the various contagions consequent to the seriously overcrowded prison—had infected and killed a judge, an alderman, and a number of jurymen and witnesses. They had been strewn thereafter not simply to mask the stink of prisoners, but in an attempt to sanitize the noxious miasma that inmates at Newgate were considered to be emitting. Oxford likely had no idea that the herbs stigmatized him. But they did provide him with a welcome distraction.

To defend Oxford, Pelham had engaged John Sydney Taylor and William Bodkin, both highly respectable advocates and philanthropists, both strongly committed to a number of reformist causes. Taylor, who led the defense, was a founding member of the Society for the Abolition of Capital Punishment, and fought passionately for that cause in the columns of the *Morning Herald*. At the time of this trial, however, Taylor's poor health seriously undermined his energetic advocacy; he had for some time been battling against a mysterious and malignant disease. At age forty-four he was dying, and would be dead in a year.

In terms of legal reputation, however, Bodkin and Taylor could not hold a candle to their opposition. Leading the prosecution were the attorney general, John Campbell, and the solicitor general, Thomas Wilde. Campbell, who would handle opening arguments, had a reputation for aggressive advocacy in his writing, his politics, and in the courtroom. His assertiveness and ambition had made him a number of enemies, including, as it happened, the presiding judge in this case, Lord Denman. His superb analytical mind, however, was obvious to all. Thomas Wilde, who would handle the prosecution's closing, had admitted liabilities in his presentation of a case—he had a flat voice and a monotonous delivery—but he made up for these with an astute command of legal niceties and tactics. Both Campbell and Wilde would one day sit on the woolsack as Lords Chancellor. The two had four prosecutors assisting them. Foremost among these was Sir Frederick Pollock, the conservative predecessor to Campbell as attorney general, whose presence on the prosecution made clear that Whig government and Tory opposition were united in desiring a guilty verdict.

There were three judges presiding over the case. At their head was Baron Denman, who, as Lord Chief Justice of the Queen's Bench, was the second-ranking judge in the country, after the Lord Chancellor. Denman was thought not to have one of the greatest legal minds of his day, but was renowned for his impartiality and courtesy—as the "personification of judicial dignity." Joining him on the bench were Sir Edward Hall Alderson and Sir John Patteson. The trial was to raise a number of puzzling legal questions, and—as Denman himself was to make clear—was to create a number of important precedents. These three judges would show themselves very much aware of the important issues, if not always clear on how to deal with them.

At ten, the judges entered, and the clerk read the charge of High Treason against Oxford: he "did compass, imagine, and intend to bring and put our said lady the Queen to death." And to do it, he "maliciously and traitorously did shoot off and discharge a certain pistol . . . being loaded with gunpowder and a certain bullet . . . with intent thereby and therewith maliciously and traitorously to shoot, assassinate, kill, and put to death our said lady the Queen." In order to prove Oxford guilty, then, the prosecution had to convince a jury that there were bullets in Oxford's pistols, even though no bullets were ever found.

Oxford pleaded not guilty to the charge, in a "distinct and firm tone." The jury was then sworn in with no challenges on either side.

In his opening, the Attorney General anticipated and countered the defense's two-pronged defense, first that the guns were not loaded; and second, if that didn't work, that Oxford was insane. Oxford's pistols *were* loaded, Campbell insisted, and a great deal of evidence supported that claim. Oxford had, in the days before the shooting, sought to buy bullets. He had used bullets in shooting galleries across London. He had, on the night before the shooting, showed off his loaded pistol. On the day of the shooting, eyewitnesses had heard the whizzing of bullets. And while the prosecution was to bring forward two witnesses who would testify that certain marks on the palace wall were likely caused by bullets, Campbell was less certain about the validity of that evidence: he was sure that the bullets passed over the wall, and were lost there. Moreover, Oxford's words proved that he had fired live ammunition. When, after the shooting, one bystander, William Clayton, accused another bystander, Joshua Lowe, of shooting, Oxford stated "It was I"—admitting, according to Campbell, to the act of firing bullets. In custody, he had asked "Is the Queen hurt?"—an absurd question, if Oxford had done nothing to hurt her. And when at the station house he was asked if his guns were loaded, he had answered that they were.

As to Oxford's supposed insanity, Campbell delved into legal precedence, citing a number of legal views on insanity and citing four previous criminal cases—including Hadfield's—to argue for a very high bar in proving insanity. Legal minds agreed, he claimed, that in order for an insanity defense to succeed, one must establish that the defendant was wholly insane at the time; partial insanity was not enough. Only "total alienation of the mind, or total madness, excuses the guilt of felony or treason." And legally, total madness involves a complete inability to distinguish between right and wrong: to acquit a defendant on the grounds of insanity, "it must be shown that at the very time, the particular time, when the offence charged was committed, he was not an accountable being; that he was then labouring under some delusion, that he could not distinguish right from wrong, and that he was unconscious of committing any offence." In all of the four legal cases Campbell cited, the defendants demonstrated mental aberration; in one of them, there was a clear history of insanity in the family. But in three of the four, the defendants were found guilty because it could not be shown that they were totally deranged and incapable of distinguishing between right and wrong at the time of their criminal act. Only Hadfield was acquitted. But, Campbell claimed, Oxford was no Hadfield. Hadfield suffered a head wound that discernibly affected his sanity. He suffered delusions, and his behavior became increasingly irrational to the point that, soon before his attack on King George, he attempted to murder the son he loved: thus, his insanity was manifest to all at the time of the shooting.

Campbell claimed that Oxford was *not* manifestly deranged—not even partially insane—at the moment of the shooting. Anticipating the defense's many witnesses, Campbell questioned their relevance: while Oxford may have exhibited bizarre behavior throughout his life—while he might be the son and grandson of unbalanced men—that evidence could not establish his total derangement on 10 June. No one ever sought his committal for madness then, or before; rather, he was a capable employee. In support of this line of argument, Campbell pointed out that Oxford was not a "potboy," as was popularly thought, but a "publican"—rare recognition of his superior stature that must have pleased Oxford. Moreover, his signed statement after his examination before the Cabinet, coolly admitting to the shooting, demonstrated conclusively that Oxford was very much aware of what he had done.

The prosecution's witnesses both placed Oxford at the scene and testified that his pistols were loaded. The defense conceded the first point, but argued that his guns were not loaded at all. That Oxford often shot live ammunition at targets before the attempt hardly proved the pistols were loaded on the day of the shooting. Oxford's own claims after his arrest that his pistols were loaded, given his manifestly vainglorious attempt to promote himself as an adherent of Young England, were dubious. The testimony by two witnesses that bullets had made marks on the wall of the Palace gardens was undercut by the Attorney General's opinion that Oxford's bullets had carried over that wall. And the two witnesses who swore that they heard the whizzing of a bullet seemed quite confused in their testimony. The defense, in cross-examination, let pass the fact that it would be virtually impossible to hear the whizzing of a ball immediately after a gun's violent explosion. There was hardly any need to bring this up: both witnesses seemed hopelessly confused about the difference between seeing and hearing a shot. Thus Samuel Perks's (or Parkes's) testimony: "the report of the pistol attracted my attention, and I had a distinct whizzing or buzzing before my eyes, between my face and the carriage." The other witness to the shot, Elizabeth Stockeley, was even more confused about what she saw and what she heard:

> . . . it was the second flash which appeared to come over the Queen's head, and it came close past me; the flash did—it seemed something that whizzed past my ear, as I stood; it seemed like something quick passing my ear, but what I could not say . . .
>   Q. What do you mean by the flash? A. The light and the smoke—I cannot explain what it was that whizzed by my ear—it was my right ear.

As for testimony that Oxford was sane at the time of the shooting, the prosecution refrained from presenting a single witness to counter the many witnesses the defense planned to call to demonstrate Oxford's insanity. They had such a witness available to them: Charles Aston Key, the surgeon who had declined to examine Oxford with the defense's medical witnesses, was present and offering advice to the prosecution. But the prosecution had no intention of having anyone testify to Oxford's sanity. They certainly preferred to prove the boy guilty of High Treason: the formidable prosecutorial team demonstrated that. Executing Oxford would have a highly desirable value in deterring future would-be Oxfords from threatening the Queen. But they surely knew that their evidence that Oxford's pistols were loaded was weak, and thus they could lose the case. Moreover, asking the jury to convict him of a capital crime—one for which the penalty was hanging, drawing, and quartering—was always a risky proposition. The public's perception of Oxford by the time of the trial had shifted: while he was once the desperate and malevolent bravo, he had become a rather pathetic boy who craved attention. The jury might acquit Oxford just to save him from the excessive punishment of an excruciating death.

Oxford's insanity defense offered the government a third option. While each defense strategy—proving unloaded guns, or proving insanity—would result in Oxford's acquittal, the consequence of acquittal for unloaded guns differed dramatically from the consequence of an acquittal for insanity. If Taylor and Bodkin succeeded in proving that Oxford had no balls in his pistols, he would walk from the Old Bailey a free man. If, on the other hand, he was acquitted on the ground of insanity, he would be subject to confinement at the Queen's pleasure—confinement that could last for decades, if not a lifetime, as happened in the case of James Hadfield.

The prosecution recognized that Oxford's defense counsel could be *too successful*: they could earn Oxford an acquittal and see him in effect confined for life. That fact shaped Oxford's prosecution. Campbell, Wilde, and the other prosecutors promoted, as energetically as they could, the case that the pistols were loaded. But they offered next to nothing to prove that he was sane. Indeed, they actually helped promote the notion that he might be insane. In his opening, Campbell read Oxford's Young England papers to the jury in full: all the rules and regulations, as well as Oxford's three letters. Moreover, during testimony the prosecution asked Samuel Hughes, the policeman who discovered and broke open Oxford's box of secrets, to read all of the documents in full a second time. Campbell offered no explanation for these documents. He had no intention of suggesting that Young England was real; both prosecution and defense agreed that the organization was a figment of Oxford's imagination. The prosecution, in other words, introduced the very evidence that Oxford's defense would claim to make the strongest case for his insanity.

When Sydney Taylor rose to address the jury, he had good reason to be confident in his client's acquittal, given the weakness of the government's claim that the guns were loaded. If Taylor had simply reviewed the evidence and rested the defense's case, it is more than likely that the jury could not conclude beyond a reasonable doubt that Oxford shot at the Queen, and Oxford would be free. Oxford, however, had without question disturbed the Queen's peace, and a jury might just convict him, bullets or no bullets. Taylor and Bodkin, then, hoping for absolute acquittal, but wishing in any case to save Oxford's life, divided the defense into two completely distinct parts: *first*, he had not committed High Treason at all—but *second*, only if the jury decided that the act was High Treason, then Oxford was insane and not responsible for that act. And in his opening, Taylor carefully instructed the jury to keep their decisions separate: if they found that Oxford had never shot bullets at the Queen, then the question of his sanity or insanity was not relevant to the case at all.

Taylor then reviewed the weaknesses of the government's case. The evidence, he claimed, actually worked to prove that the guns were not loaded: "the suggestion of the ball having passed over the wall was negatived by the witnesses; but the evidence which tended to show that it had struck against the walls was perfectly inconclusive." Oxford's alleged boast after his arrest that his pistols were loaded counted for little—simply an extension of the vain-glory he exhibited in foolishly but harmlessly pointed a bullet-less pistol at the Queen. And in asking whether the Queen was hurt, Oxford might have been wondering whether he had caused her mental alarm. Taylor then turned to the evidence for Oxford's insanity, and questioned the Attorney General's conception that insanity must be total, without motive, premeditation, or plan, in order to acquit. All of George III's assailants, he argued, were deemed to be insane and yet showed some signs of rational thought. Margaret Nicholson, who in 1786 attempted to stab the King when he reached out to take a petition from her, showed premeditation in drawing up a blank petition for the King and inscribing it in the accepted form. Moreover, she was able to speak coherently at her examination.* A second, seemingly coherent assailant who threw a stone at the King's carriage was similarly committed. And Had-field most certainly had motivation for his shooting: he was deeply dissatisfied to be discharged from the army on the pension of 4d. a day. Moreover, he showed "premeditation and contrivance" in concealing his weapon upon entering the Drury Lane Theatre.

Oxford, Taylor pointed out, was born into a family with a long history of mental illness; his grandfather, John Oxford, was once restrained in a strait-waistcoat, and died in a lunatic asylum. And if his father was not confined for his bizarre acts—well, he should have been. Oxford was of an age, Taylor claimed, when latent mental illness generally manifested itself, and it certainly had done so in Oxford's case: the Young England papers, written in Oxford's hand, and the "creations of his own foolish fancy," "furnished the strongest evidence against the prisoner in proof of his insanity." He showed, moreover, no rational motive in shooting at the Queen,

---

* Nicholson spent 42 years in Bethlem, first in its Moorfield location, where she was a star attraction when Bethlem was itself a major tourist destination, and then, more secluded, in the women's criminal wing of the Southwark location. She died on 14 May 1828 (Andrews *et al*. 390-91;Eigen).

and, having shot at her, he made no attempt whatsoever to flee. Obviously he was mad. The jury would delight the Queen by finding him so: "the mind of Her Majesty would be relieved from the unpleasant impression that any one of her subjects could be found guilty of imagining and compassing her death."

Having thus demolished the image of bravado that Oxford had so carefully constructed for himself, Taylor and Bodkin called to the stand twenty-eight witnesses, twenty-six of whom provided evidence as to the derangement of three generations of Oxfords. Notable among these witnesses were several long-suffering Oxford women: his grandmother and her cousin, his mother, sister, and two aunts spoke of enduring the abuse of Oxford men for more than forty years. Uncles Edward and Charles (the latter a Birmingham publican), landlords and a landlady, teachers, employers, workmates, and Inspector Tedman, all confirmed these women's claims, and contributed a host of their own. Witnesses testified that Oxford's grandfather often thought he was St. Paul or the Pope, and testified to his capacity for "indecent behavior" and his proclivity to violent rages when he would smash everything in sight, and which resulted in episodes of restraint and confinement: with cords, in a strait-waistcoat, at Petworth Bridewell. Oxford's father, they testified, inherited his father's manic propensity to destroy. The jury learned of his inappropriate behavior—burning money, riding horses in the parlor—and learned of his horrible abuse, most of it directed at his wife Hannah. Hannah Oxford, testifying during the evening of the first day of the trial, offered up a particularly lengthy litany of sorrows imposed upon her first by her husband, and then by her son. Oxford's father "delighted in annoying and teasing me," she claimed, and told of his bullying her into marriage, his starving her, and his relentlessly beating her: kicking her, once fracturing her skull and nearly killing her, and at another time, when she was pregnant with Edward, smashing a quart-pot over her head, and after he was born, plunging a file into her breast while he was suckling. He abandoned her, only to return and further abuse her. He dramatically threatened suicide before her, and at least twice made the attempt. And through it all, he was utterly indifferent to her and to her suffering.

Her son, she claimed, shared his father's "fractious" nature, and showed the same violent rages, and showed, as well, a disturbing habit from infancy of maniacal motiveless laughter, mixed in with inconsolable crying—behavior she had tried to control with beatings, with locking Edward in the cellar—but which she could not control, behavior that lost her customers, ruined her businesses, and forced her to send him away. Hannah then brought the abuse up to date, telling the jury of his rages at West Place two months before, culminating in his punching her violently in the face and bloodying her nose the day before she left for Birmingham.

Hannah finished her testimony at eight o'clock in the evening, and when Taylor called another witness, Campbell interrupted: did they intend to call many more witnesses? Taylor and Bodkin said that they were. The Chief Justice then adjourned the trial for the night; Oxford was removed from the bar and brought back to his cell, and the jurors sequestered.

The trial resumed promptly at nine the next morning, with a multitude of witnesses to bolster the insanity defense. Every oddity, it seemed, of Oxford's life was presented to the jury: his assaults on strangers and schoolfellows; his scrapes with the police as he harassed a woman in her carriage, or as he assaulted a neighbor; his frightening the customers in his aunt Clarinda's public house by shutting off the gas—and his pleasure in the suffering of others. At times, witnesses seemed to stretch to find anything that would support the notion that Oxford was, in the word nearly all of them used, "unsound." Thus Emily Chittenden, a nursemaid who worked with Oxford at the Hog in the Pound, and for whom he obviously had some sort of affection, testified about a letter that Oxford sent her at the end of May. The contents she apparently considered unimportant, but the address she thought "extraordinary":

> Fly, postman, with this letter bound,
> To a place they call the Pig in the Pound;
> To Miss Chittenden there convey it,
> And with "speedility" obey it.
> Remember, my blade,
> The postage is paid.

And if bad verse could be offered as a sign of insanity, so could bad reading: and as the controversy about the Newgate novel reached its zenith outside the courtroom, Oxford's sister Susannah connected him with that apparently degrading literature, revealing that he had recently read, among other books, *Oliver Twist* and—worse—*Jack Sheppard*. Oxford's eerie lifelong habit of uncontrollable laughing ran through almost all of the eyewitness accounts: hilarity often leading to fits of sobbing, all generally without discernible motive.

Oxford was thus for hours enlightened as to how all who knew him viewed him. No one saw him as gallant Oxonian, a bravo, or even as a respectable barman: to all—family, friends, Emily Chittenden—he was unsound, annoying, ill. Confronting this horror was enough to shake him from his silly smile, and when he heard his last employer, Newman Robinson, speak of his laughing uncontrollably—to the point where his customers were offended, to the point that Robinson had to give Oxford notice—Oxford broke, bursting into tears and weeping bitterly.

To pull together the mass of anecdotal evidence with an expert diagnosis of insanity, Taylor and Bodkin brought forward the three doctors who had examined Oxford two days before, as well as three more. The very notion of an expert medical witness at the time was highly controversial. Passing judgment on the moral aberration of a defendant was, in the minds of most legal authorities of the time, the province of the jury, not of any witness: judging good or evil behavior was a legal and not a medical issue. To be sure, several medical witnesses had testified in Hadfield's case forty years before, leading to a directed verdict of not guilty on the ground of insanity. But Hadfield had a discernible head injury, while Oxford did not: the doctors in Hadfield's case offered physiological testimony, while the doctors in Oxford's case offered abstract psychological judgments. Taylor had attempted in his opening statement to justify the need for such expert judgments: there was such a thing as a partial insanity, he pointed out, something that could be at times invisible to the world (and to a jury), but could be clear to the trained mind of the physician. In seeking the professional opinion of six doctors, only one of whom had known Oxford for some time, the defense was challenging legal precedent—and the judges would not let new precedent be established without a struggle.

It was the first doctor to testify who bore the brunt of the judges' attack. John Birt Davis, one of the many witnesses called to London from Birmingham, was actually called to the stand as an eyewitness, not an expert witness. He was in 1840 a leading citizen of Birmingham: magistrate and coroner, as well as a highly respected physician. In 1824, however, he was at the start of his career, and had been called to treat Edward's father after he attempted suicide by drinking laudanum. As an eyewitness, Davis had little to offer: he claimed he did not know enough to form any opinion about Oxford's father's state of mind, and that he had not ever seen Edward after the boy had turned two. Bodkin therefore shifted the questioning to his professional opinion of the state of Oxford's mind: "Assuming the facts which have been given in evidence to be true—I mean the facts with respect to insanity affecting the prisoner—looking to the manner in which the crime was committed, and the whole circumstances of the transaction, what is your opinion to the state of the prisoner's mind?"

The Attorney General objected vociferously to this question, and the judges supported him. Lord Chief Justice Denman was adamant:

judging the state of the prisoner's mind must be left to the jury. Taylor disputed this: insanity was a medical question, and he had every right to "take the opinion of a medical man upon that evidence." No, Denman responded: that would be like "asking the witness to pronounce a verdict for the jury." Bodkin then altered and re-altered his question, trying to find a way to admit Davis's opinion that Oxford was insane. The judges thwarted his every attempt. In the end, Bodkin was forced to render his question completely hypothetical:

> Mr. BODKIN . . .—Supposing a person in the middle of the day, and without any suggested motive, was to fire a loaded pistol at Her Majesty passing along the road in a carriage, and that such person afterwards remained on the spot, declaring that he was the person who had fired— nay, even took pains to have it known, and that afterwards he entered freely into discussion, and answered questions put to him on the subject, would you refer such conduct to a sound or unsound state of mind?
>
> Sir F. POLLOCK asked the Court if it thought this was a medical question. He did not object.
>
> Lord DENMAN.—It may be put . . .
>
> Witness.—If I heard these facts stated, I should conclude that the party must be mad. . . .
>
> Mr. BODKIN.—Supposing, if in addition to the facts and circumstances already mentioned, it was shown that immediately before the transaction, the party had written papers such as those found in the prisoner's box, and which you heard read yesterday, would they serve to strengthen or otherwise the inference you have drawn[?]
>
> Witness.—It would greatly strengthen it.

The doctors who followed Davis found that he had made their path easier. The second doctor to testify, William Henry Partridge, also from Birmingham, had apparently no personal knowledge of

Oxford, and only testified briefly about treating his mother's head injuries. The next doctor was Thomas Hodgkin, the Quaker social activist and specialist in morbid anatomy (and incidentally, the one who first studied the symptoms of the disease that bears his name). There is nothing in Hodgkin's testimony that suggests he had personally known or examined Oxford before the trial. Sydney Taylor began his questioning guardedly, asking Hodgkin a hypothetical question similar to that asked Davis. Hodgkin quickly connected the hypotheticals with the boy in the dock, and proceeded to diagnose his illness: "If all the appearances described were exhibited by the prisoner, and coexisted in him, I should conclude that he was insane, because such a form of insanity has been recognized. It is called by Le Marc, a French writer, *lesion de la volonté*, or morbid propensity." Such an illness would likely not be apparent to the layman, and would necessitate an expert medical witness to consider the evidence and guide the jury to an accurate conclusion about sanity or insanity. This was exactly the breach of precedent that the Judges had attacked in their curtailing of Davis's testimony, and the Chief Justice was not going to let Hodgkin's assumption of authority pass without question:

> Lord DENMAN.—Do you consider that a medical man has more means of judging with respect to such a subject than other persons?
> Witness.—I do; because I think that medical men have better opportunities for judging with respect to the disease of insanity than others.

Hodgkin's testimony stood.

Testifying immediately after Hodgkin, John Conolly—the only one of the doctors testifying who was renowned for his work with the insane—offered a diagnosis of Oxford which made clear his opinion that specialists have a superior ability to judge moral and mental aberration: "I am a physician to the Hanwell Lunatic Asylum, and have at present 850 patients under my care, and I have considerable experience in disorders of the mind. I had some conversation with the prisoner at the bar, and, in my opinion, he is a person of unsound mind." Neither the prosecution nor the bench, in their questions to him, suggested any reservations about his authority.

Dr. Chowne, next to testify, further created precedent for the physician's authority by combining the specific knowledge of the case exhibited by Conolly with the technical knowledge of mental illness shown by Hodgkin. The facts of the crime convinced Chowne that Oxford was insane, and his short interview with the boy confirmed him in his opinion. He diagnosed a "lesion of the will," or moral insanity, combined with imbecility. According to Chowne, lesion of the will is often a partial insanity, in the sense that sufferers can "perform the duties of life with accuracy." He thus challenged Campbell's claim that an insanity defense depended upon proof of complete derangement.

The Oxford family's doctor James Fernandez Clarke was the defense's last witness. He had nothing to say about lesion of the will; Oxford, he claimed, based upon his longstanding experience with the family, was an imbecile, the son of an unsound father. Oxford's madness manifested itself most apparently in his "involuntary laughter, which is seldom found in sane persons," and, as is typical of hereditary insanity, "which breaks out in open acts of violence and disease generally exhibits itself at the period of puberty, between fourteen and twenty years of age, according to the French writer Esquirol."

The prosecution sought to chip away at the claims of the defense witnesses, attempting to establish that Oxford's grandfather and father were not as demented as Taylor and Bodkin tried to make them out to be, that Oxford had occupied a number of positions of responsibility, and that no one had ever as much as considered restraining or committing him for insanity. Solicitor General Sir Thomas Wilde, summing up the prosecution's case, reiterated these claims, and attempted again to define insanity in a case of High Treason as entailing total derangement—something that Oxford simply did not suffer. Indeed, Wilde alone argued that Oxford was actually quite intelligent. Oxford was not at all insane, according to Wilde—he was driven instead by the quite rational desire to be someone: to attain notoriety. His actions culminating in the shooting demonstrated a concerted and clever effort to attain that desire. Considered in this light, the Young England papers demonstrate not Oxford's delusion, but the products of his canny and methodical plot to delude the nation: "There was nothing of imbecility about them; they were written probably, he might say certainly, to produce deception, not that the writer himself was deceived, but that he wished to deceive others."

Wilde questioned the doctors' conclusions, claiming that the grounds for their pronouncements that the boy was insane were thin, based on a hasty examination which gave them nothing that allowed them a solid conclusion of insanity. The doctors, he claimed—quite correctly, at least in the cases of Clarke and Conolly—"went to Newgate with minds prepared to see a madman, with the previous statements of the prisoner's mother and friends incorporated in their minds, and racking their brains to find some rash or inconsistent act in the prisoner's conduct during a period of eighteen years." Significantly, however, Wilde did not question the doctors' sense of special expertise in testifying directly upon Oxford's mental state.

After Wilde spoke, Lord Chief Justice Denman instructed the jury, emphatically reiterating Sydney Taylor's point about the specific sequence of decisions they had to make: first, decide whether the pistols were loaded—and then, *only if they were*, decide whether Oxford was responsible for his actions: "These questions," he told the jury, "are perfectly separate in themselves." In speaking of the testimony of the doctors, he made it clear that the expert medical witness occupied a legitimate place in English jurisprudence. Dr. Conolly, he said, "a gentleman who it must be presumed was familiar with the treatment in cases of insanity, and must be an extremely good judge, has given his opinion, and the jury would give that weight they think due to it." He similarly commended the testimony of Chowne and Clarke.

When he finished, it was evening: Oxford had endured two days of depressing testimony from both sides. As far as his drive for notoriety went, he must have realized that no matter what the verdict, he had lost: after this trial, if he were to be remembered at all, it would be as a pitiful, unsound potboy. A sentence of death might redeem him somewhat. But he was terrified at the prospect of a guilty verdict and Courvoisier's fate. He nervously turned to Governor Cope, who stood beside the dock, watching over him, and said, of the jury, "they are against me, all of them . . . I didn't like that Solicitor General's speech at all; he pitched it very strong against me, and I think they'll hang me."

The jury retired, and in their deliberations obviously made little attempt to separate the two major questions of the trial. When an hour later they returned to the court, their verdict was a hopeless muddle: "We find the prisoner, Edward Oxford, guilty of discharging the contents of the two pistols, but whether or not they were loaded with ball has not been satisfactorily proved to us, he being of unsound state of mind at the time."

There was an immediate uproar. Attorney General Campbell recognized immediately that the jury had in essence acquitted Oxford twice—by not actually committing the crime, *and* by reason of insanity; it was very much in the government's interest to have Oxford adjudged acquitted for the second reason. He therefore jumped up "with prompt dexterity" and shouted that as the jury had declared Oxford insane, he was subject to the provisions of the Safe Custody of Insane Persons Act*—passed after the Hadfield trial, and responsible for Hadfield's forty years' confinement. Oxford was, in other words, to be detained at the Queen's pleasure.

Taylor objected to this. The jury had clearly decided that reasonable doubt existed that the guns were loaded; therefore, Oxford was acquitted outright—on lack of evidence, not because of insanity—and was a free man.

---

* 40 Geo. 3. c. 94.

But, Campbell rejoined, Oxford *was* found guilty of discharging his pistols, and that, compounded with his insanity, was enough for the government to detain him.

This Taylor "strenuously denied." The indictment clearly held that Oxford had fired "leaden bullets." The jury declared that this fact was not proved. Oxford was therefore free.

Not quite, claimed Campbell. The jury showed confusion about the first part of the verdict; but they were perfectly clear about the second: Oxford was insane. Moreover, the jury had been called upon to answer two questions, and surely their answer to the second was germane to the sentence.

Taylor angrily accused Campbell of rewording an act of Parliament in order to suit the purposes of the Crown. The jury had not found Oxford guilty of any offense, "and in a prosecution of this kind, where the prisoner's life was at stake, it was not fitting on the part of the Attorney General to stand up and endeavour to visit the prisoner with perpetual imprisonment when the jury found him not guilty."

At this point, Taylor and Bodkin were the ones legally on solid ground: no matter what else the jury claimed, it was clear that they were not convinced that Oxford's guns had been loaded. Dr. Clarke, commenting on the trial, considered that if Taylor had pressed the issue, he could have won a full acquittal for his client. But, claimed Clarke, Taylor was a sick man, and, at this crucial moment of the trial, lacked the stamina to defend Oxford adequately.*

Chief Justice Denman intervened. "The jury," he said, "were in a mistake." They had muddled the verdict: they did not state clearly whether the guns were loaded at the time of the crime. Apparently Denman made a liberal interpretation of the very first part of the jury's verdict, seeing in the fact that Oxford "was guilty of discharging the contents of two pistols" the conclusion that he had fired bullets, a

---

* Clarke says nothing about Bodkin's efforts, and indeed seems to have forgotten Bodkin's existence in the trial.

conclusion contradicted by the subsequent words of the verdict. They hadn't made up their minds, and the only thing to be done was for the jury to return to deliberation and decide that point.

But they *had* made up their minds. They could not say whether Oxford fired ammunition, claimed the jury's foreman, "because there was no satisfactory evidence produced before them to show that the pistols were loaded with bullets."

A spirited discussion followed, the specifics of which are lost to history because not one of the stenographers in court (and there were several) recorded it. One imagines Taylor and Bodkin passionately arguing that the jury could not say with certainty that the guns were loaded—a clear verdict of "not guilty" in an English courtroom; Campbell and Wilde, equally strenuously noting that the jury had made its verdict of insanity clear; and Denman and the other justices maintaining that the jury simply had not returned a clear verdict, and therefore needed to go back and get it right. In the end, of course, the justices prevailed, and the jury again left the courtroom.

In their absence, the defense, the prosecution, and the bench argued about what would happen to Oxford if the jury acquitted him on the evidence, as it seemed to be doing. Campbell thought the prospect "monstrous" that Oxford might be "let loose upon society to endanger the life of Her Majesty or her subjects," and asked that Oxford's insanity be taken into consideration regardless of the rest of the verdict; he wanted, in other words, the state to have power over him even if he didn't actually shoot bullets at the Queen. Taylor and Bodkin were of course dead set against this, and found support from all three justices, Baron Alderson pointing out the obvious flaw to Campbell's argument—"The construction you contend for would lead to this, that if a man were charged with an offence, and the jury thought that no offence had been committed at all, yet he must be handed over to the mercy of the Crown perhaps for his life." Campbell persevered: "If no evidence of insanity had been given, then the prisoner would have been entitled to his discharge; but if a prisoner sets up the defence of insanity he does it at the peril of the finding of the jury." In other words, Taylor and Bodkin had indeed argued their case too well: their case for insanity was too successful to be ignored.

The jury returned after an hour with a verdict at least as muddled as their first one: "Guilty, he being at the time insane." But by law no one could be simultaneously found insane and guilty of a crime. This time, however, the judges did not send the jury back, but asked them to revise their verdict on the spot:

> Mr. Baron ALDERSON.—Then, you find the prisoner guilty but for his insanity.
> The Foreman.—We do, my Lord.
> Lord DENMAN.—The Court asked you this question— "Do you acquit the prisoner on the ground of insanity?
> The Foreman.—Yes, my Lord, that is our intention.
> Lord DENMAN.—Then the verdict will stand thus— "Not guilty on the ground of insanity."

By this verdict, Oxford was liable to a lifetime of confinement. Campbell quickly proclaimed that Oxford should "be confined in strict custody during Her Majesty's pleasure." Lord Denman agreed—"That is a matter of course." Taylor and Bodkin said nothing.

As his fate was being decided—and relieved of any fear of execution—Oxford returned to a state of complacent vacancy. He likely did not care whether he was freed or sent to Bethlem. But he was very likely unaware of one detail of the Safe Custody of Insane Persons Act: it made no provision whatsoever for a release in the event of a cure. Oxford was to be held at the Queen's pleasure, and if all the mad-doctors in the world were to claim the boy perfectly sane, it just might please the Queen and her government to keep him confined—forever. Time, Oxford was soon to discover, had become his enemy.

seven

BEDLAM

O xford remained in custody at Newgate for a week, until an order arrived from the Home Office for his transfer to Bethlem. Now that the threat of death was removed, he was visibly more cheerful. Keeping watch over him now was a single jailer, who had been released from the order to limit his conversation; both he and Oxford lost their reserve, and talked. Oxford's mother, his sister, and his uncles Edward and Charles visited him, and he now spoke at length about his attempt, regaling his hearers with the details of the shooting as if it were a great adventure story, a bravo's exploit.

On 18 July, Governor Cope received the order from the Home Office for an immediate transfer. He personally went to Oxford's cell and told him to get ready; the two would go to Bethlem together. Oxford "did not betray the slightest emotion" upon hearing that the time had come, apparently accepting the possibility of a lifetime of confinement at the asylum, even if he hadn't accepted the possibility of his own insanity.

Cope and Oxford climbed into a hackney-coach for the trip south of the Thames. The coach traveled toward Ludgate Hill, away from the looming walls of Newgate, and then down to the Thames on Bridge Street, and over Blackfriars Bridge, leaving behind the London of the Queen—of Whitehall and St. James, Buckingham Palace and the expansive parks—as Oxford returned to the neighborhoods of his childhood: gritty Southwark and Lambeth. He would never again cross the river. As he passed down bustling Blackfriars Road, if he wasn't too absorbed in friendly chatter with Governor Cope, he might have noticed in passing Hayes's general goods store, where he had bought his "Brummagem" pistols. (The pistols were now the property of the state. Albert would show them to the Queen, and for decades it was thought that one of them ended up in Scotland Yard's Crime Museum.[*]) The coach continued to St. George's Fields, past the ornate charitable institutions there, and down Lambeth Road. If Oxford had any sense of nostalgia about the few last weeks he spent with his family, he very likely craned his neck there, looking back as the coach passed St. George's Road; he could just catch a glimpse of West Square. The carriage then pulled up before Bethlem.

Governor and prisoner ascended the stairs and passed the tall Ionic columns of the portico, topped by a small cupola. (The distinctive towering dome of the hospital, still visible today in the truncated building's present incarnation as the Imperial War Museum, was added four years after this.) Inside, Cope relinquished authority over Oxford to those at the hospital. No record was made of his admittance, but certainly he was examined as to the nature of his illness, and then likely bathed. Though during his trial the medical witnesses had diagnosed Oxford with everything from congenital imbecility to "moral insanity" and "lesion of the will," the doctor at Bethlem

---

[*] But it did not. An inquiry to the curator of the Museum by the author, listing specific descriptive details about the pistols Oxford used, resulted in the hasty removal of a pistol exhibited for decades as Oxford's, since that pistol clearly did not resemble either of Oxford's.

very likely concluded none of these things, but rather concluded he was about to send a sane man into indefinite confinement in the male criminal lunatics' wing. A medical record from 1864 when Oxford was transferred from Bethlem to Broadmoor notes that the medical staff "had always considered him sane."

Oxford was taken into the wards, escorted down a long corridor to the right—the male patients' wing—and further escorted down another corridor, a darker one, in which signs of confinement—cells and heavily barred windows—were much more evident: he was now in the ward for male criminal lunatics. He was shown his cell. He would be locked in there at eight o'clock every night, until eight the next morning. He would spend the coming years largely cut off from the outside world. Visitation with relatives was allowed once a month, and his mother could only see him behind bars, several yards away from her, so far away she could hardly hear him. And for the first years of his confinement, he was prohibited from reading newspapers. Oxford's social world, then, was almost entirely restricted to his fellow lunatics, and during the day, he could interact with them as much as he liked. For a time, he chose not to, at all: Sir Peter Laurie, an alderman as well as a governor of Bethlem, informed his mother that he had a "repugnance to mingle" with them and refused to leave his room. Later accounts of his commitment, however, note his gregariousness. One other inmate was notorious for his aloofness, one who had no friends, and "could not be prevailed upon for some years to walk about with or join the other patients": an old man with a very discernible wound to the head. James Hadfield, whose own shooting resulted in the Act of Parliament that led to Oxford's own indefinite detainment at Bethlem, was now sixty-eight or sixty-nine years old. He had, according to a witness seventeen years before, long since stopped showing any symptoms of insanity. He was sick with tuberculosis, and he was desperately tired of his confinement for the last forty years at the pleasure of three kings and a queen: "the loss of liberty," he claimed, "was worse than death."

For six months, the two would inhabit the criminal lunatics ward together. It is not known if Oxford's natural glibness returned to him in time, and triumphed over Hadfield's world-weariness. But it is tempting to think that the two looked into each other's eyes, and spoke, driven by professional curiosity, perhaps—or because they were the only living members of that most exclusive group: would-be British regicides: Oxford with the fresher memory, and yet relating it in a way that made him out to be the hero, and Hadfield, more bewildered, haltingly remembering that violent night in the Drury Lane Theatre, forty years before.

Hadfield died on 23 January 1841. Oxford lived on, a resident of the criminal lunatics' wing for over two decades, until that wing closed down upon the opening of Broadmoor Asylum, an entire hospital devoted to the confinement and care of the criminally insane. Oxford happened to be one of the very last male patients to make the trip, by train, from London to Crowthorne (and Broadmoor). Soon after, Bethlem's criminal buildings were demolished. Between them, then, Hadfield and Oxford witnessed the entire history of Bethlem's criminal lunatics' wing.

Confined to Bethlem, Oxford was soon largely forgotten as a living being, remaining forever the pitiful potboy, recalled to public consciousness every time one of Oxford's six successors made his attempt at the Queen. Nevertheless, the *tableau vivant* he had burned into the British consciousness, of a young man shooting point-blank at the young, pregnant Queen and her even younger husband—the incident Oxford had instigated with his startling action, and the royal couple had completed with their sublime reaction—had long-lasting consequences for the British monarchy. In that instant, the Queen was, politically, born again, the embarrassing and partisan fits and starts of her early reign suddenly forgotten. Mrs. Melbourne, the royal Whig, was a creature of the past. Now Victoria was Queen of all, and Albert's wife. Albert became, with the shooting, more than the adventurer with the foreign accent, but a hero worthy of his cousin's hand. By seeking their safety among their people, and not within Buckingham Palace, the royal couple had demonstrated to the nation the Queen's fitness to rule, and the Prince's fitness to assist. The House of Saxe-Coburg Gotha gained, after Oxford's shooting, a permanent ascendancy over the House of Hanover. That bugbear King Ernest, and Victoria's other uncles Suffolk and Cambridge, were suddenly just a part of the extended royal family, peripheral in the public eye to the Queen, her Consort, and their children to come. Oxford had unwittingly ushered in the Victorian age.

A week before Oxford's trial, Melbourne approached the Queen with the delicate issue that had been on the minds of everyone since the shooting: it was quite possible that the Queen could die, leaving an infant child as her heir. A Regency Bill was in order, such as the one created ten years before, when Victoria became Heir Apparent, and which held her mother, the Duchess of Kent, sole regent in the event of her King William's death. In the present situation, the only question was whether Albert would be sole regent if Victoria died, or whether he would serve in a Council of Regency with others—Victoria's royal uncles. Baron Stockmar was convinced that Albert as sole Regent would be by far the superior arrangement. Seeking to ensure that a Regency bill to that effect would pass with overwhelming bipartisan support, he set out to negotiate with Tory leaders. He feared that Albert would face great obstacles: "I don't hide from myself that there will be all manner of objections, such as his youth, his want of acquaintance with the country and its institutions, &c., and that the Dukes of Cumberland, Cambridge, and Sussex, not wishing to be passed over, will endeavour to put a spoke in the wheel, the former by means of the ultra-Tories, the latter by means of the ultra-Liberals."

Stockmar needn't have worried. He was able to ensure that the Tory opposition would side with Melbourne's government in overwhelmingly supporting the Bill, but Albert had already laid the groundwork, making it clear from before the marriage that he preferred that the monarch (and her Consort) be above party, and culture positive relationships with both sides. He had done his best since the marriage to do exactly that. Stockmar and Melbourne had no problems convincing both Peel and Wellington that Albert should be sole Regent; both claimed that this was their position exactly. In the end, there was only a single dissenter in all of Parliament to the Bill—Victoria's Uncle Augustus, the Duke of Sussex. Sussex stood before the House of Lords on 21 July, proclaiming himself to be personally disinterested in the Bill, but to have questions about it: it did not, for one thing, make provision for the possible incapacity of the Regent. Moreover, it did not impose any restriction upon the possible alienation of the regent from the best interests of Britain: Albert could marry again, and might marry a foreigner! Indeed, Albert was a foreigner himself, and not as bound to the nation's interests as a native would be. Sussex suggested Parliament make provision for a successor-regent in the contingency of Albert's incapacity or inadequacy. He was not, he proclaimed, attempting to elevate himself in any way: the country was well aware of his complete lack of self-interest or ambition. But he was very careful to point out to the Peers that he was the closest heir to the throne actually residing in England.

His self-interest and ambition were palpable to all. Baron Cottenham, the Lord Chancellor, in responding to his speech, reassured him that he had every right to be concerned about the Regency, as a member of the royal family; then, he quickly demolished his concerns. Provision for a successor to Albert as Regent could easily be made once Albert became Regent. And the fear of Albert's marrying a foreigner who could unduly influence the monarchy was simply not justified, as it had been with the Duchess of Kent (which was why in the 1830 Regency Bill, she had been forbidden from marrying a foreign prince without the consent of Parliament): Albert would be a *male* regent and was thus—an irony, given his current situation—above the undue influence of a spouse. The bill quickly sailed through both houses without further objection and became law before Oxford was three weeks in Bethlem. Lord Melbourne attributed the great success of the bill to Albert alone, and certainly Albert's endearing himself to the Tories had everything to do with the Bill's easy passage. "Three months ago," Melbourne told Victoria, "they would not have done it for him. It is entirely his own character."

Albert was jubilant, seeing the bill as "an affair of the greatest importance to me" and writing to his brother Ernest "I am to be Regent—*alone*—Regent, without a Council." As designated Regent, Albert had not gained a whit of actual power: all was Victoria's, until her death. But symbolically, everything had changed. As King Leopold wrote to Albert's private secretary, George Anson, the bill "had helped the Prince immensely, the country thereby demonstrating the great confidence they placed in the uprightness of his character." While in the public eye he ranked second only to Victoria, he still faced a battle with Victoria's uncles and aunts for precedence within the Kingdom. And he still faced a long wrangle with Baroness Lehzen and her cabal for political and domestic influence with his wife. But now, time was entirely on his side.

Charles Dickens took an obvious interest in the Oxford case. He was in 1840 mulling over what became his 1841 novel *Barnaby Rudge*, a novel centered upon three troubled young men, at least one of which—the vainglorious apprentice Sim Tappertit—bears more than a slight resemblance to Oxford. Within two days of Oxford's attempt, Dickens realized that the mischief that the boy had caused would not end with his sentencing. He wrote to his friend John Forster "It's a great pity they couldn't suffocate that boy, master Oxford, and say no more about it. To have put him quietly between two featherbeds would have stopped his heroic speeches, and dulled the sound of his glory very much. As it is, she will have to run the gauntlet of many a fool and madman, some of whom may perchance be better shots and use other than Brummagem firearms."

The fools and madmen would not be long in coming.

Part Two

THE GAUNTLET

eight

MOST DESPERATE OFFENDERS

Well over twenty thousand Londoners had gathered outside Newgate on Monday morning, 23 May 1842, again to see a man hanged. Eager to get a view, the crowd began forming on Sunday night; as usual, the best seats in the windows and rooftops surrounding houses had been snapped up by the wealthy: the *Times* reported one nobleman, a true connoisseur of hangings, who had attended the last four or five of them (including Courvoisier's) and who paid a high premium of £14 for a window seat this time. At six in the morning, this nobleman would have seen seething below him the largest crowd to gather outside of Newgate for decades—larger than the crowd that had seen Courvoisier die two years before—a solid mass stretching out of sight down the four streets that formed a cross, with the scaffold at the crux. Somewhere among that mass stood a swarthy, good-looking, twenty-year-old man by the name of John Francis.

The police, well aware that this hanging would attract crowds, were taking no chances: two hundred City and Metropolitan police were stationed between scaffold and spectators. If they were concerned that the audience might rush the scaffold out of sympathy with the condemned man, they need not have worried. Crowds at public executions could be fickle, capable of awe-stricken silence in the face of imminent death, as they were with Courvoisier, or, when they considered the death sentence unfair, hostile to the state— or to the state's most visible representative, the executioner. But John Francis and the suffocating mass all around him were of one mind about this monster: they were ready to welcome his death with howls of execration, or with grim satisfaction and genuine relief. For Daniel Good had, for the last six weeks, captivated and affronted them, both by committing one of the goriest murders of the nineteenth century, and by escaping for ten days the detection of an increasingly anxious metropolis and of an increasingly embarrassed Metropolitan Police force. Lord Chief Justice Denman anticipated the mood of this crowd when in sentencing Good to death, ten days before, he had told him "you will leave the world unrespected and unpitied by any one." This crowd had come to see, in Denman's words, "a good deed done."

It was a pair of trousers that had done Good in. He was a coachman when he wasn't engaging in his dual passions of larceny and bigamy. He worked at the southwestern edge of the metropolis, in Putney, near Richmond, out of the stables of the expansive estate of Queely (or Quelaz) Shiell, who had made his fortune as the largest slaveholder on the West Indian island of Montserrat. On the evening of a fine day, 6 April 1842, Good and his ten-year-old son, Daniel, were returning to Putney on Shiell's pony-chaise from Woolwich, where Good had been courting Susan Butcher, his latest romantic interest. An hour after sunset, father and son pulled up to Collingbourne's pawnshop on Wandsworth High Street. There, Good bought on credit a pair of breeches, and there, on exiting, according to vigilant shopboy Samuel Dagnall, Good snatched up a pair of trousers, secreted them beneath the flaps of his greatcoat, hurried to the carriage, and slipped both breeches and trousers beneath the chaise-seat upon which his son sat. When Colling-bourne, alerted to the theft, confronted Good, Good denied the charge indignantly and drove off. Collingbourne quickly fetched a local policeman, PC William Gardiner, who enlisted the aid of Dagnall and a boy from the shop next door, Robert Speed, and proceeded to Shiell's stables. There, they found Good more concil-iatory; he was more than willing to return to Wandsworth to pay Collingbourne for the breeches—but the trousers, he would not admit to taking. Gardiner insisted upon searching the chaise. Good had no objection. Gardiner found nothing there, and extended his search to the chaise-house and its stables and harness room. When Gardiner moved to search another stable, Good planted his back against the door and refused entry: he would, he said, rather return to Wandsworth and settle the matter.

The commotion attracted Thomas Houghton, Shiell's bailiff and head gardener, who had an antipathy for Good (which Good heartily returned) and authority over him: Houghton agreed to the search. The six (Gardiner, Houghton, Dagnall, Speed, Good, and Good's son) entered the stables. Gardiner asked Speed to keep a close watch on Good, and asked Dagnall to hold a lantern while he scrutinized every stall, hayrick, and cornbin. Good's anxiety grew as the search continued, and he pleaded that they return to Wandsworth. As Gardiner searched a cornbin, he saw Good enter the fourth stall and begin to move hay. Snarling that he did not need Good's assistance, Gardiner shooed him away to the doorway of the stable and the scrutiny of Speed, while he, and Dagnall with the lantern, entered the stall. Gardiner moved two hay-bales and some loose straw underneath, when he saw what he thought was a plucked goose and cried out "My God, what's this?"

Speed, across the room, turned away from Good to see what Gardiner saw—and Daniel Good bolted, slamming the stable door to, locking it, throwing the key and a lantern into a hedge, and lighting out across the fields, trapping Gardiner, Houghton, the shopboys, and his own son. Robert Speed picked up a two-pronged hayfork and attempted unsuccessfully to force the door. The group then went back to the fourth stable, to see exactly what they had found. It was flesh—a human being, Gardiner cried.

Robert Speed denied this, reached out, and turned the thing over. It was the trunk of a woman, head and limbs partially sliced and partially hacked off. It had been gutted—sliced in a ghastly cross vertically from sternum to pubis, and horizontally around the top of the pelvis, in a single cut from one side of the backbone around to the other. All of the lower organs were removed, including the uterus, which made it impossible for surgeons later examining the body to say for certain whether this woman had been pregnant—though they speculated that she had been, from the size and condition of her breasts.

With an energy redoubled by horror, the party made another attempt to force the door, and succeeded. Good was now fifteen minutes gone. Gardiner sent Samuel Dagnall to the station house in Wandsworth to fetch help, give a description of Good, and raise the alarm, sending him any policemen he met along the way. A policeman arrived in twenty minutes; Gardiner sent him to Putney to fetch more police. Another arrived in half an hour; Gardiner sent him, as well, to Wandsworth, to fetch the Superintendent of V Division, Thomas Bicknell. When Bicknell arrived to take command, it was past 11:30, the stable was filled with police, and Good was two and a half hours away from Putney Park Lane. The police made little attempt to pursue him beyond the neighborhood, focusing instead upon the crime scene. There, they found an abundance of evidence. One officer, Sergeant Palmer, opened the door to the adjoining harness room and was nearly knocked over by the overpowering stench: in the fireplace, beneath an abundance of coal and wood set to create an intense fire, he and others after him found a number of charred, and recognizably human, bone fragments. Others found a bloody knife and axe, and two bloody fragments of a woman's petticoat, "violently torn asunder."

In a very short time, the police had all the evidence they needed to convict Good. Within two days, they had identified the victim. They had connected Good—and only Good—to the murder. They had recovered the woman's many belongings—including the clothing she had been wearing on the day she disappeared—and were able to trace all of it to Good. They had a solid case—but they had let their man slip away.

What the police did not realize this night is that they had with them on Shiell's estate the key to apprehending Good quickly. Ten-year-old Daniel Good had been with his father for the last three days, and before that had lived for over two years with Jane Jones—known to all as Jane Good—in a basement kitchen on South Street, Manchester Square, in Marylebone. At his father's wishes— and from genuine affection—the boy faithfully called this woman "mother," while his father referred to the woman as the boy's aunt. The Sunday before, on Good's orders, an anxious Jane Jones had left the boy to sleep with a neighbor while she went to visit Good in Putney. She never returned. The next day, Good fetched the boy out of his school and told him that his aunt had found employment in the country—the boy wouldn't see her for another six months. He then took the boy to Putney, and gave him over to the supervision of others while he disappeared for long hours, night and day. On the day of the discovery in the stables, the boy had traveled with his father in Shiell's chaise across the south of London to Woolwich, where he met the woman his father had recently proposed to, Susan Butcher. He saw his father make a gift to the young woman: a gown, a shawl, a fur tippet, a pair of gloves, a pair of boots, and, in a hatbox, a blue bonnet. The boy recognized the clothing: it was what "mother" had been wearing on the day she disappeared. The Goods then took Susan Butcher for a ride in the chaise through Greenwich to a public house in New Cross: at his father's request, Butcher wore mother's bonnet. Aunt was gone, his father told him at that time.

He was now to call Susan Butcher "mother." The boy waited outside the pub while father and Susan drank gin and water. Leaving Susan Butcher to catch a train, father and son and drove across southern London in the growing darkness to the pawnshop on Wandsworth High Street. From there they returned to Shiell's stables, and to the search for the trousers—which were never found, and which the boy swore his father never took. Young Daniel Good then witnessed his father's flight, and the discovery of the trunk—which he first thought was the body of a pig. Knowing all that he knew, young Daniel Good's confusion must have been short-lived—he must have come, before anyone else, to the horrifying conclusion that this body was mother's. Moreover, he knew the address where his father was most likely to be found.

Young Daniel apparently disclosed that address to one of the policemen investigating the stables. And the police discovered that Good was headed in the direction of the city: Sergeant Palmer, investigating the fields around the stable, found a broken paling on a fence, and beyond this, footsteps headed northeast. The Metropolitan Police were adept, through an established system of "route-papers," at communicating information about breaking crimes and fleeing criminals to all metropolitan station houses and to all active officers in a matter of hours. And Superintendent Bicknell indeed ordered a description of Good sent to every division: "V division, April 6, 1842.—Absconded, about half-past 9 o'clock, from Mr. Shiell's, Putney-park-lane, Daniel Good, the coachman, an Irishman, about 40 years of age, 5 feet 6 inches high, very dark complexion, dressed in a dark frock-coat, drab breeches and gaiters, and a black hat. He is suspected of having murdered a female, the body having been found in the stable." If Bicknell had heard of the South Street address from young Daniel Good, he did not think it fit to include it.

If Bicknell had broadcasted Jane Jones's address, Good would certainly have been caught, for it was indeed to 18 South Street that the murderer fled that night, dashing through the toll gate at

Putney Bridge (according to local legend, he tossed the gatekeeper his coachman's coat as he flew by), running most of the seven miles before taking a cab to Marylebone, arriving around midnight without a key, breaking into the room with a screwdriver he borrowed from a nearby pub. He remained there, unbothered by the police until morning, not sleeping but bundling up all of Jane Jones's possessions. In the meantime, at 3 A.M., Inspector Bicknell's route paper had arrived at the station house of D Division, which covered Manchester Square. There, the officer on duty, Inspector Tedman—the very same John Tedman who had observed Edward Oxford so carefully at the Shepherd and Flock three years before—erred greatly by neglecting to convey Good's description to patrolling officers until the next patrol arrived for duty at 6 A.M. Had he conveyed Bicknell's information earlier, a policeman who had at 5 A.M. witnessed Good hailing a cab, filling it with bundles and a box, and clapping a bed onto the roof, would certainly have arrested him on the spot. (Tedman was suspended from the force for several weeks because of this mistake.) Good escaped and made his way east to Spitalfields, where he sought out his actual wife, Molly Good, whom he had abandoned a good two decades before. God had directed him back to her, he told the delighted woman. Together, Daniel and Molly pawned and sold most of Jane Jones's worldly goods.

The police, and the press, were able to trace Good's movements to this point. But they were always a step behind him, and the trail went cold at Spitalfields. The newspapers soon excoriated the police for their lack of diligence in catching the murderer. After Good disappeared, the *Times* reported the public sense of "unmitigated indignation" against the police, and thundered "Nine days have now elapsed since the discovery of the above most inhuman murder, and the perpetrator of the horrid deed is still, we regret to state, at large. Surely the public had a right to expect better things from the metropolitan police—a force so great in numerical strength, and maintained at so heavy a cost to the country." The problem was a systemic one: "The conduct of the metropolitan police in the present case . . . is marked with a looseness and want of decision which proves that unless a decided change is made in the present system, it is idle to expect that it can be an efficient detective police, and that the most desperate offender may escape with impunity." Without a detective branch—in other words, without a set of officers trained and experienced in the ways of the criminal mind, in an intimate knowledge of the criminal underworld, and with the authority to coordinate action across divisional lines in order to *investigate* crimes, rather than simply prevent them—the police would continue to suffer embarrassments. Typical of the problem was Inspector Tedman, as well as Inspector M'Gill of the Holborn division. M'Gill successfully tracked Good to Spitalfields, and rather than enlist the local police in apprehending Good, he confronted Molly directly, broadcasting to the neighborhood that Good was wanted. Believing Molly's lie that she hadn't seen Good, M'Gill returned to Holborn to write up his report. "Thus," the *Times* blasted, "the circumstance soon got circulation through the neighbourhood, and thus the chances of detection were considerably lessened, as there are unfortunately in that particular locality a class of persons who would do their utmost to protect an offender, no matter what the enormity of his crime may be, and prevent his being brought to justice."

The *Times* was right. There was, at the time, no formal detective branch of the Metropolitan Police. There were, however, the special "active officers" of A Division, particularly Nicholas Pearce, whom commissioners Rowan and Mayne quickly assigned to the case—but not quickly enough; Pearce knew that the best lead to capturing Good had been his wife Molly, and he was enraged by M'Gill's hamfisted intrusion, which stymied his investigation. This tiny and unofficial detective force, therefore, was neither known to the public nor adequate to capture Good. The popular anxiety caused by a monster at large, and the subsequent call by the newspapers for immediate reform, made it clear to the Commissioners that, in the public mind, the fear of violent crime now outweighed the fear of continental-style espionage. It was time to create a detective branch.

Ten days after the discovery of Jane Jones's body, Good was captured. He had bought himself a laborer's fustian outfit and a bricklayer's hod, and escaped south to Tonbridge, in Kent. There he found work building houses springing up beside the new railway. Thomas Rose, a fellow laborer, recognized him. By a remarkable coincidence, Rose had been a constable in V Division—the division covering Roehampton—where Rose knew Good well. Rose reported his suspicions to the railway police; Good was, in quick succession, arrested, transferred to Bow Street, examined, clapped into Newgate, tried, and sentenced to death.

If the Commissioners needed further evidence that London was in need of a formal detective branch, they soon had it; while Good sulked in Newgate, awaiting trial, a petty criminal in the northern outskirts of the metropolis demonstrated to all the weakness of a wholly uniformed and largely unarmed police force.

Thomas Cooper, a morose 23-year-old who had an obsession with guns, a pathological hatred of the police, and a powerful suicidal urge, had launched a personal crime wave north of Highbury. Equipped with a couple of formidable flintlock horse pistols—but no horse—Cooper fancied himself a highwayman and had taken to brutally mugging passersby on the semi-rural roads of Hornsey. The superintendent of this police division—N division—had assigned extra officers to patrol the area. On the afternoon of 5 May, one of these officers, Charles Moss, was watching carefully a gentleman who ostentatiously exhibited a heavily ornamented watch chain, expecting that this man might encourage his own mugging. Moss then spotted Cooper lurking behind the gentleman. Cooper, perceiving Moss in his police uniform, ducked behind a hedge, where Moss found him, his two pistols lying on the ground beside him. When Moss attempted to take Cooper into custody,

Cooper sprang up and pointed one of the pistols at Moss's head. Moss defensively stooped and raised his left arm as Cooper fired a bullet point-blank through that limb. He then shifted his pistols and pulled the trigger again: the hammer clicked—a misfire. Moss then grappled with Cooper with his one good arm as long as he could; Cooper pushed him away, retreated a few steps, and growled at him: if Moss tried to follow him, or raise an alarm, he would shoot him dead. Moss of course raised an alarm, crying out "Murder!" Cooper then pulled a carving-knife from his coat, menaced the officer, turned, and fled across the fields. Moss followed him as far as he was able, but soon collapsed from loss of blood. But he had raised the hue and cry; a waiter from a nearby inn and another policeman soon ran up to him, and continued the chase. Had Cooper run north, he would have found cover in nearby woods, but he headed south, toward the city, making himself visible to all at some distance, while the alarm traveled faster than Cooper did. A number of men joined in a surreal chase, during which Cooper was always visible, but always out of reach: he outmatched his pursuers in leaping hedges and fences, and thus found time to pause, both to reload his pistols (using grass instead of wadding to hold his bullets in place), and apparently to gulp down a vial of poison—a mixture of arsenic and laudanum that he had been holding for some time. (This slow-acting poison did not kill him, but in time, and for the rest of his short life, it debilitated him.) As he lost some pursuers, he gained even more. After zig-zagging for a couple miles and reaching Highbury, Cooper managed to run into one of the few cul-de-sacs in the area, with a dozen or more men on his heels, including a journeyman baker, Charles Mott, and yet another police constable, Timothy Daly. One pursuer took up a brick, and another—probably Mott—a stick, but Cooper was the only one with pistols, and he used them to keep his pursuers at bay for some time. Daly challenged him—"I don't think those pistols are loaded," he called out, to which Cooper promised to shoot the first man who tried to take him. While Cooper glanced from side to side at those grouped around him, the baker, Mott, lunged toward him; he tripped while doing so, and Cooper fired his left pistol, wounding him in the shoulder. Cooper then turned, took deliberate aim at Daly with his right hand, and shot him through the stomach; Daly reeled half a circle and fell dead. The crowd then seized and bound Cooper.

Cooper was well known to the police of N Division, having appeared repeatedly at police court both for assault and for robbery. He was once taken up with his mother for stealing a gown; this charge was unfounded, but he was so angry at the treatment of his mother by the arresting officer, Inspector Penny, that Cooper assaulted Penny brutally, earning himself a month's imprisonment. Ever since, he had harbored a special enmity toward Penny, and, in custody, he only regretted killing Daly instead of Penny. Nonetheless, he seemed pleased to have killed a policeman: it served him right. Witnesses testified that he'd several times stated "I shall never be happy until I am the death of one of them."

The result of this pursuit was messy: one policeman was dead, and another policeman, as well as a civilian, seriously wounded. Cooper was a sociopath, well known to the police; detectives on the case, in plain clothes—and perhaps armed—would likely have brought about a happier outcome. Commissioners Rowan and Mayne had a second impetus for formally instituting a detective branch.

They would soon have a third, occasioned by the swarthy and good-looking young man standing outside Newgate waiting for Good to be hanged.

Thomas Cooper, occasionally sullen and occasionally violent in custody, was remanded to Newgate to be tried for the murder of Timothy Daly. He would have been tried in the same session as Good, except that his lawyer had successfully pleaded for more time to track down witnesses who could testify to his insanity. When Daniel Good was led to his execution, then, Cooper listened to the sounds of another man's execution from his Newgate cell, as Edward Oxford had heard Courvoisier's two years before.

For days, all of those surrounding the condemned man—the sheriffs, prison ordinary Carver, Governor Cope—persistently exhorted Good to confess to his crimes. They failed: unlike Courvoisier, who couldn't confess enough, Good went to his death denying he had committed any crime. He stuck to the same story he had blurted out the moment his sentence of death was spoken. Susan Butcher, he claimed, was the cause of all his troubles. Jane Jones, on discovering Good's relationship with Butcher, despaired and killed herself. Good decided the body needed to be disposed of, and so he enlisted the help of an itinerant match-seller from the neighborhood of Brompton, a man whom no one else ever saw: this helpful gentleman, for a guinea, chopped up the body and burned up the limbs since they were too heavy to carry away; he was supposed to return to Roehampton to finish the job, but never did. According to this story, Good was guilty neither of murder nor of dismemberment: "I never touched the body of the woman, alive or dead! So help me God!" he cried to anyone who would listen. No one believed him, but Good stuck to this story with a religious intensity, dividing his moments before his walk to the scaffold between protesting his innocence vehemently and bestowing passionate blessings on all around him.

The hangman Calcraft stood apart from the rest; he was not concerned with Good's soul—only with his body; in the minute before Good's final walk, he removed his neckerchief and turned down his collar. The party then set out, Good with a firm step, loudly begging God to save his soul. He climbed, unassisted, the steps of the scaffold to the thunderous noise of an enraged mob, with their "hideous yells" and "long-continued execrations." Calcraft slipped the noose around his neck and prepared to slip a black hood over his head. "Stop! Stop!" Good cried, wanting to address the crowd. It was not in a mood to listen. Calcraft told him he'd be better off listening to Reverend Carver's prayers, slipped on the hood, and drew the bolt. It was one of Calcraft's short drops, and Good struggled violently before dying.

It was, as Denman predicted, a good deed done: so the now-dispersing crowd thought, anyway, including the good-looking, swarthy young man named John Francis. When the pressing humanity lessened to the point that Francis could move, he set out with a feeling of moral edification up Skinner Street and Holborn Hill, toward the neighborhood in Marylebone, where he shared a room with his good friend William Elam. He made his way to the Caledonian Coffee House, on Mortimer Street, where he spent hours every day, where he had first met Elam, and where he had become well acquainted with many others. A number of his friends were here this morning, some, certainly, returning from Good's execution. Francis was in a gregarious mood: he joked about the hanging over his coffee. It was a damned good job that Good was executed, he told his friends. Hanging "was much too good for such a fellow."

Francis had every reason to be high-spirited and morally complacent; the contrast between that monster Good and himself must have seemed absolute. Good had rendered himself a pariah in the eyes of all Englishmen. Francis had been for weeks following in the newspapers Good's downward trajectory, and had witnessed his last step into well-deserved oblivion. Good was nothing, while his own moral and economic stock was rising. He was poised to rise above the social status of a craftsman that his father, a stage carpenter at Covent Garden Theatre, had occupied for decades, a life that his father had attempted to force upon him by apprenticing him to the theatre. He had left that all behind, and yearned for middle-class respectability, as the owner of well-appointed tobacconist's business. Later this day he was to take a lease on a shop and parlor at 63 Mortimer Street. He had already engaged for his name to be painted on the door, for business cards to be printed, and for delivery of tobacconists' supplies; these would arrive on Wednesday. Good had fallen. Francis was confident that he would ascend.

Young John Francis had grown up in the heart of the teeming metropolis, at the busy intersection of Tottenham Court Road and Oxford Street. His parents still lived there with his sisters Mary and Jane. Though he lived in the center of the civilized world, Francis's own existence was strictly circumscribed. When he first began work, he traveled each day to Covent Garden, a few streets southeast, closer to the river. Then, just a few months before Good's execution, he had a violent altercation with his father, and he fled his home. He moved into a nearby room on Great Titchfield Street, James Foster, a tailor, as his landlord and Elam as his roommate. He attempted—feebly, it seems—to survive as a journeyman carpenter in the adjoining neighborhood of Paddington, around the fairly newly built terminus for the Great Western Railway. Since then, he had lived within shouting distance of his family but could have been an ocean away, for all they knew about his life. He might have dropped in on them occasionally—his father mentioned that he came for Sunday dinner—but he was a cipher to them: they did not know where he lived, what he did, what company he kept. He was too proud to tell them that he was finding few jobs and was almost out of money, having been too poor for the last three months to pay rent for his room.

A few months before, it seemed certain that he would follow in his father's footsteps. John Francis Senior was a fixture at Covent Garden, working as carpenter and machinist there for a quarter-century. He was a close and long-standing friend of the head machinist, Henry Sloman, who had been a witness to the marriage of John Francis Sr. and Elizabeth, Francis's mother, in 1817. John Francis Jr. had been born in November 1822, and likely experienced his father's theatrical world at close hand, from backstage—perhaps witnessing as a child the slapstick antics of Grimaldi, the sublime acting of Kean, the dazzling virtuosity of Paganini, or, more recently, the seductive dancing of young Lola Montez. The census of 1841 lists John Francis Sr. as a carpenter, and his son as an apprentice carpenter—an apprentice, in other words, at Covent

Garden. John Jr. showed talent. And in 1841, there were few places in the world where a talented young stage carpenter would be able to culture his talents better than Covent Garden Theatre.

Covent Garden in the early 1840s was one of London's three patent theatres, all under royal license with exclusive rights to perform serious drama. Because of the patent, John Francis Senior saw himself as, in a sense, a servant to the Queen: when, in coming weeks, he had occasion to write to Victoria, he presented himself as "one of the Artisans of Your Majesty's Theatre Royal Covent Garden . . . for more than 23 years." The idea was not completely absurd: the Queen was a true lover of drama, and a frequent play-goer in the early years of her reign, and thus a frequent witness to the work of the Francises and their colleagues. Covent Garden's stage crew was expected to perform miracles daily. The theatre was immense, seating upwards of three thousand playgoers, and for years the various proprietors of the theatre faced a losing battle to fill those seats. Their strategy, invariably, was to provide everything for everyone, presenting variety, quality, and quantity, night after night. The plays of Shakespeare were, of course, staples, but the theatre provided the gamut of performance: contemporary drama, melodrama, farce, opera, dance, pantomime, "extravaganzas," and musical and animal acts. A ticket for an evening's performance would buy admission to not one show, but two or more: Congreve's *School for Scandal* might be followed by the pantomime *Guy Earl of Warwick or Harlequin and the Dun Cow*, Douglas Jerrold's comedy *Bubbles of the Day* by an elaborated version of Milton's masque *Comus*, Mozart's *Marriage of Figaro* by Planché's fairy tale *White Cat*. Victoria and Albert had seen all these shows in the early months of 1842.

Covent Garden Theatre had been for the last few years conducted by a series of renowned actor-managers. Francis and son worked under the most famous actor of the day, William Charles Mac-ready, who in his two seasons at Covent Garden—1837 through

1839—introduced a number of productions of Shakespeare which were extremely well received, but which did not turn a profit. He left to manage Drury Lane, and was succeeded by the celebrated comic couple, Madame Lucia Vestris and Charles James Mathews. Vestris and Mathews kept the theatre going, with more success than their predecessors, for three seasons. The key to their relative success was spectacle. They employed well over a hundred men (including twenty-six carpenters) to deal with creating props and machinery—and to shift scenery and to deploy special effects during performances. The results could be stunning. In honor of the marriage of Victoria and Albert, for example, Vestris and Mathews produced J. R. Planché's *The Fortunate Isles*, a sumptuous masque with breathtaking transformations to represent all of English history, culminating, according to a review, in the rising of a hymeneal altar, heraldic cupids flying about the air, and a "Star of Brunswick" rising out of the ocean, "which opens as it enlarges, and discovers the word 'Victoria' in brilliant letters, surrounded by smaller revolving stars." Then there was their production of *A Midsummer Night's Dream*: the first performance in London in which Mendelssohn's famous music was employed, and the first in which an actress played the role of Oberon, King of the Fairies: Madame Vestris, renowned for her beautiful legs and for displaying them in breeches roles, was responsible for that innovation. The play was a hit largely because of its showstopping finale, in which fairies as blue and yellow lights burst from the stage and filled the theatre—floating among the galleries, flying through the air.

Not surprisingly, it is with pantomime that the stage crew at Covent Garden showed off its most amazing effects, and where an aspiring stage carpenter and machinist could best demonstrate his talent. Indeed, young John Francis was specifically noted for his cleverness in the construction of pantomime tricks. The one Christmas pantomime at Covent Garden with which Francis was certainly involved, *The Castle of Otranto or, Harlequin and the Giant Helmet*, was arguably the most mechanically laden pantomime of all time—a "machinist's Sabbath," according to one historian, a pantomime possibly even *written* by a Covent Garden machinist to show off his crew's talents. The pantomime essentially ditched the frenetic human interaction which, when the clown Joseph Grimaldi ruled the pantomime stage two decades before, was crucial to the genre. Instead, in this production, machinery took the starring role. *The Castle of Otranto*, a burlesque of Horace Walpole's gothic novel, brought to life a monstrous, robotic giant, of a size too immense to completely fit in the playhouse's sizeable stage, and thus appearing in parts: in one scene, a giant head rolls its eyes, smiles, and thumbs its nose; in another, immense arms converge from the wings upon human actors, clutching, lifting, shaking, and then dropping them; or, in the climactic scene, a gigantic arm rises from the stage, drew a sword, and hacked down a life-sized castle tower.

One can imagine young John Francis, not only helping to design this immense and complicated machinery, but also, lithe and quick-witted, clambering into the stage machinery in order to operate it. On a February night in 1841 he performed before the Queen, who stayed to watch the pantomime after viewing all of *A Midsummer Night's Dream*. For all the effort of Francis and his fellow machinists, the Queen very likely was not amused; she was truly eclectic in her love of performance, but of all forms of entertainment, she liked pantomime least—noting in her journal after one that it was "noisy and nonsensical as usual."

Francis seemed to have the skill to continue in the theatre for as long as his father had. But after his quarrel with his father at the end of 1841, he turned his back on Covent Garden and on his family. Francis's move, as it happens, was a prescient one, for, a few months after he left, the Vestris-Mathews management had collapsed, and the pair had finished their third season in serious arrears. Charles James Mathews was arrested for debt and had spent the two weeks before Good's execution at Queen's Bench Prison. Covent Garden never completely survived as a full-fledged theatre after this season; successive managers experienced even greater losses, and after extensive renovations, the theatre finally found success opening in 1847 as an opera house—which it is today.

Why did Francis quit? Perhaps he suffered under the oppression of too many employers—his own father, Sloman the head machinist, George Bartley the stage manager, Vestris and Mathews—and perhaps, in Francis's mind, the Queen. Perhaps the demands on his time—hours of preparation every day, followed by five hours of frantic scene-shifting—were simply too great for someone of Francis's character: Robert Gibbs, the proprietor of the Caledonian Coffee House, who had endless opportunities to observe him, considered him "idle and reckless." Perhaps, despite his talent at carpentry, his interests lay elsewhere: he wrote poetry, for one thing, and preferred musing over coffee to seeking work. Perhaps he simply considered that carpentry would never provide him with the wealth he dreamed of.

His actions a year before had demonstrated his discontent with the life he was living. On 14 July 1841, between Covent Garden seasons, Francis was arrested on suspicion of stealing more than thirty-two sovereigns from an 85-year-old man he had met at a coffee house. While visiting the man in his lodgings, Francis excused himself to wash his hands; the old man later discovered the money gone from a box in his bedroom. Francis was jailed for three days, until the charge was dismissed for lack of evidence. The officer who arrested him, Inspector Maclean of the City police, was certain that he had committed the robbery, but a search of his room at his family's home turned up nothing.

The episode could not have improved relations with his family; now, on this day—23 May 1842—as he prepared to open his tobacconist's shop to make his fortune, he knew he could not look to them for support. Charles Johns, an outfitter of chemists and tobacconists, would in two days, on Wednesday, be delivering a full inventory to Francis's shop, and he would be expecting full payment on delivery. Francis thus needed hundreds of pounds, but he had nothing; he would need to sell much of the stock before he could hope to pay for it. To fill his shop, then, he had lied to Johns outright, presenting himself as a young man with great expectations. He told Johns that his grandmother had recently died, and that once the executors to her will signed off on the necessary documents, he would be in possession of several thousand pounds. Johns, amazingly, believed Francis, and drew up the agreement. The goods would arrive on Wednesday—when Francis would have to come up with a further excuse to delay payment.

On Wednesday morning, Johns's men drew up in a cab to 63 Mortimer Street and unloaded into the shop all that Francis needed to commence business: bundles of Havana cigars (and imitation Havanas), bales of loose Virginia and Middle Eastern tobacco, packages of snuff; clay and meerschaum pipes—perhaps even a hookah or two—and very likely canisters of a patent medicinal snuff popular in 1842: "Grimstone's Eye Snuff," promising "cataract, inflammations, and all other diseases of the eye and head completely eradicated, glasses left off after using them 20 years, and the breath rendered impervious to contagion." With the stock laid in and his name on the door, Francis commenced selling—or, at least, commenced waiting for custom. Few, if anyone, came in on that day. Francis's friends at the coffee house, and the youth he slept next to, William Elam, were startled by Francis's sudden foray into keeping shop, and dubious about his prospects; but until this moment, it must have seemed so simple to Francis: take in stock, sell it at a profit, replenish the stock, sell that—and in time make his fortune. Now, he realized that success would take time—time that he did not have.

Charles Johns was the one certain visitor to Francis's shop on this day; he came for his payment. Francis fended him off: the executors of his grandmother's will were being difficult, delaying on signing off on his inheritance. They had promised, however, to call on him at the shop at noon tomorrow—Thursday; they would then comply the terms of the will, and give him his thousands, after which Francis could pay Johns immediately.

Again, remarkably, Johns agreed to wait. When he returned to Francis's lonely shop at noon Thursday, however, he returned with a companion, ready to confiscate all of the shop's contents. Francis had another excuse ready. The executors were creating problems; he now knew that his grandmother's thousands would not be soon forthcoming, and that he could not hope to discharge his debt completely. He proposed instead a renegotiation of the deal: by the next day—Friday—he would borrow £10 from "the old man" and with that, make a payment on the whole; he would pay the rest in installments.

And Johns agreed one more time to wait a day—or, quite possibly, he walked out of the shop on Thursday fully intending to bring a larger crew to clean it out on Friday.

Francis knew that he could no longer stall with excuses. He had to come up the cash overnight. He also knew that coming up with £10 honestly was impossible. The proceeds of the shop so far had amounted to a few coppers. The "old man" might have enough money, but Francis could not—would not—go to him now. And he must have been aware of the skepticism about his project shown by his friends and his roommate. He could not hope to borrow £10 from them for this. He felt cornered and desperate. To gain his future of respectability and riches, he would have to commit one—just one—despicable act of robbery.

Francis was, according to those who knew him, "good-tempered" and "inoffensive," a sober lad, patron of coffee houses—not public houses or gin palaces—who came to his meals regularly and did not stay out late at night. On this Thursday night, then, he likely dined with the Fosters at the usual time and climbed early into bed next to William Elam, ready for a full day's work on Friday. And he must have done his best to appear untroubled, even cheerful, for he would not want anyone at the house on Great Titchfield Street to know of his desperate resolve.

nine

ROYAL THEATRE

O n that same Thursday night, 26 May 1842, Queen Victoria, Prince Albert, and their household set out from
Buckingham Palace in six carriages for the short drive down the
Mall, past St. James's and the gentlemen's clubs on Pall Mall to
the Queen's favorite theatre: Her Majesty's, Haymarket. Usually,
that theatre housed the Italian Opera, just reaching the peak of its
season with performances of Donizetti's *Lucia di Lammermoor*
and *Lucrezia Borgia*. Tonight, however, the royal couple had not
come to hear the soprano Persiani or the celebrated tenor Mario
sing. Tonight, Victoria and Albert were themselves to be the star
attractions, performing before a packed house.

Just before 10:30, the carriages drew up to the entrance on
Charles Street reserved exclusively for the Queen's use. Victoria
and Albert, with their visiting uncle Count Mensdorff-Pouilly,
descended from the last carriage to meet the Count's four sons,
who had emerged from the carriage in front of them. Together

they entered the theatre and waited a few moments for the Duchess of Kent and her suite to arrive. They ascended to the royal box, which had on this night been converted into an antechamber that opened through a scarlet curtain to a magnificent, white and gold Corinthian-pillared royal pavilion—draped with crimson damask, lined with glowing velvet, trimmed with gold lace—extending into the center of the theatre. As they came into view, the sounds of a thousand humming voices and one of two full orchestras suddenly hushed, and a "simultaneous sensation of delight" thrilled the audience. Victoria looked down and around to see Her Majesty's Theatre magically transformed. The pit was covered over and raised to the level of the stage, forming an enormous ballroom floor. The walls around the boxes and the stage were festooned with the richest of fabrics—silks, satins, and velvets—in a rainbow of colors. Suits of armor and displays of weaponry brought in from the Tower of London by royal command ranged the stage and bedecked the walls. Extra gas chandeliers had been rigged up inside and outside the pavilion to illuminate the house and the royal party in particular. Gazing from floor below to boxes above, Victoria saw a "perfect crush": 2,300 of her subjects, the men in their nattiest suits and uniforms, the women in brilliant new dresses of the finest silk.

For a few moments, there was a quiet confusion; no one quite knew whether the etiquette of the situation called for acknowledging the royal presence. Then both orchestras struck up the National Anthem, and all doubt was removed; the crowd burst into cheers.

It was the beginning of a triumphant evening for Victoria, the second ball she had thrown this month, in which she demanded that her wealthiest subjects display shameless, highly conspicuous consumption. Admission to this ball had been pricey: a guinea to join the crowd on the ballroom floor; five guineas to let the best boxes; five shillings apiece to observe the finery from the upper gallery. Anyone able to afford tickets and appropriate *couture* was welcome. The draw, of course, was the spectacle of the splendidly dressed royal couple, appearing as it were both in state and on stage, greeting notables and condescending to observe the festivities from their elevated state and station.

Two weeks before this ball, the British nobility had had their chance to display their wealth when the Queen threw at Buckingham Palace a glorious, invitation-only *masque* or costume ball, an event which the papers of the day unanimously deemed the social event of the century. The theme was medieval. Albert came elaborately dressed and bejeweled as Edward III, the hero-king of the Hundred Years' War, and Victoria came as his faithful (and fertile) queen, Philippa. Others masqueraded as monarchs and courtiers of all of Europe, and beyond: elaborately attired as French, Germans, and Spaniards, *Cosaques* and Saracens, Highlanders, Knights Templars, and Hungarians. The elite among the guests were organized into various *quadrilles* representing each foreign court. They assembled in the Palace's lower rooms and were led by heralds up the throne room, where they passed before Victoria and Albert, made obeisance to the couple, sitting above them on elaborate gothic-revival thrones, and danced in accordance with the nations they represented. The latest in Victorian technology—530 jets of naphthalized gas— spotlit the thrones and drew all eyes to the royal couple.

The aristocracy had strained to outdo one another in preparing for this ball. They bought up the metropolis's supply of the finest embroidered silk, the prescribed fabric for the occasion, as well as the costliest furs—miniver, ermine, sable—to create outrageously expensive costumes, which they embellished with their family jewels. The gold lace of Albert's tunic was edged with 1,200 pearls, and Victoria wore a pendant stomacher valued at 60,000 pounds, but the Duchess of Sutherland outdid them both, wearing jewels valued at an astronomical hundred thousand pounds. Those who did not own, rented, emptying the shelves of London's finest jewelers, paying hundreds of pounds for one night's security.

The newspapers played to the public's wild anticipation and ensured that they were able to savor every detail, dwelling for weeks with awe and careful calculation on the lavish specifics of the royal and aristocratic outfits. As it happens, the balls coincided with a startling innovation in the press: on 14 May 1842, the *Illustrated London News*—the first fully illustrated newsmagazine— published its very first issue, and its first full layout covered the *bal masque*. In a sense, Britain experienced its first multimedia event—and hailed its first media monarch.

The contrast between these highly publicized, opulent *haute monde* fantasies and the hard reality of life in Britain during this year could not but strike everyone forcefully. This was *1842*, after all, the hungriest year of the "Hungry Forties": the year of the worst industrial recession of the nineteenth century. A series of bad harvests, dating back to the thirties, had raised food prices and the overall cost of living. The Corn Laws, which guaranteed high tariffs on foreign grain, helped keep those prices up. A nationwide economic slowdown hit everywhere, but hit the northern industrial towns particularly hard, leading there to massive unemployment and depressed wages for those who could still find work. Crime rates and pauperism skyrocketed.

Chartism, the working-class political movement which had come to life in the first year of Victoria's reign, reached a peak in membership and agitation in this year. On 2 May, just ten days before the *bal masque*, the Chartists had, with banners and bands and great hope, trundled an immense petition through the crowd-lined streets of London to Parliament. The petition, signed by 3,317,752—well over a tenth of the entire population of Britain—was too large to fit through the members' entrance, and so was brought in pieces into the chamber, where it lay in a massive 671-pound pile on the floor. In their petition, the Chartists claimed that the current misery facing working people was the direct consequence of a corrupt Parliament that acted solely in the interest of the upper classes, a corruption they claimed could only end with working-class participation in government. The petition lashed out at the (to the Chartists) obscene gap in income between

rich and poor, targeting the Queen in particular: "whilst your peti-
tioners have learned that her Majesty receives daily for her private
use the sum of 164*l*. 17*s*. 10*d*., they have also ascertained that many
thousands of the families of labourers are only in receipt of 3¾*d*.
per head per day." A motion to have six Chartists speak at the bar
of the Commons about the sufferings of the poor was soundly
defeated, and the petition itself was never considered. This crushing
of hopes, coupled with sheer hunger, bore bitter fruit: by the time
the Queen attended the ball at Her Majesty's, riots were already
erupting in the Midlands and the North. The Queen's government
was about to confront a long, hot summer of violent agitation.

Also during this month of May 1842, Parliament released its
first report on the employment of children, over two thousand
pages with illustrations, spelling out in sickening detail the dire
physical and moral conditions that children as young as six faced
in Britain's mines: half or fully naked creatures laboring as many
as sixteen hours a day, often in utter darkness, chained with "dog-
belts" to coal carts, crawling up and down two-foot-high passages
for hours, subject to the physical and at times sexual abuse of adult
miners. The newspapers culled the reports and presented to their
readers the darkest, most painful details, in articles in the same
newspapers that detailed the luxurious ball-costumes of the rich.
The "Condition of England Question," in the parlance of the day,
was never more apparent, and never more pressing.

The popular satirical magazine *Punch* bitterly contrasted the
"purple dress" of the reveling rich with the "cere-cloth" or shroud
of the destitute. And the Chartist newspaper *Northern Star* scath-
ingly compared Victoria to Rome's most vicious emperor: "The
most detested tyrant whose deeds history hands down to posterity,
set fire to Rome that he might enjoy the sight of a city in conflagration, and while the flames were raging, he amused himself by
playing on the violin. We know of no nearer approximation to the
unmatched cruelty of the monster Nero, than the conduct of the
British Court and aristocracy, in thus reveling amidst the most

superfluous waste, while the more humble of their countrymen are doomed to starve for bread, by the laws these same Nobility have framed for their own advantage."

Victoria, however, did not plan these balls simply to escape the hard reality her subjects faced. Rather, she was attempting to confront the Condition of England Question directly, attempting to aid the most miserable of the poor by encouraging luxurious consumption, to reawaken dormant industry by creating need.

She wished to assist one particular industry with these balls. For years—long before the present recession—the silk-weaving trade of Spitalfields had become synonymous with London's most grinding poverty. The weavers had once been among the aristocracy of labor, but the economic forces unleashed by the Industrial Revolution had strangled their trade nearly to the point of extinction. Competition, for one thing, was killing the weavers: they had once enjoyed protection in the form of a tariff against foreign goods, but this had been revoked in the 1820s, and imports of cheaper French silks, generally acknowledged to be the finest in Europe, cut into their trade, as did rougher silks woven on the handlooms of northern England, cheaper because weavers there could survive upon a lower wage. And mechanized looms were beginning to match in quality the work of Spitalfields handlooms. The present recession, and the subsequent drop in demand for the weavers' luxury product, had simply made a bad situation worse. Charles Dickens a few years later described the under- and unemployed weavers of Spitalfields as "sallow" and "unshorn," living a miserable existence in London's most densely populated neighborhood, suffering from the highest mortality rate: Spitalfields, he claimed, "is now the grave of modern Manufacturing London."

The Queen hoped to set the Spitalfields handlooms clacking away again by requiring that the costumes, the dresses, and the waistcoats for the ball be spun exclusively from Spitalfields silk. It was a plan that speaks volumes about the Queen's—and Prince Albert's—political and social sensibilities. They both genuinely cared about the sufferings of the poor: for Albert, in particular, improving the lot of the poor was becoming a mission. But they were hardly egalitarians; their ideal society depended on strict social demarcation. The pleasure of the rich would enable the content—and busy—life of the laborer.

In the short term, the Queen's plan worked. In April and May of this year, the Spitalfields weavers had as much work as they could handle. But in the long term, nothing could halt the decline of that pre-modern industry. Dickens knew that the effect was as a drop in a bucket: "the weavers dine for a day or two, and, the ball over, they relapse into prowling about the streets, leaning against posts, and brooding on door-steps." The organizers of the ball at Her Majesty's Theatre hoped for a more lasting support for the weavers: a school of design for their children built on the ball's proceeds—but the school was to fail. Improving the dismal economy of 1842 depended on more than a party or two, however extravagant.

Despite the limited economic impact of the balls, Victoria scored a symbolic *coup* with them, demonstrating with an enormous amount of publicity that her own interests were completely inter-twined with the interests of her people. As the *Times* put it, the ball at the theatre was an occasion in which the Queen associated "publicly and personally with her subjects in promoting a common object." And Victoria was fortunate in having a government and prime minister to aid her in achieving her object. Robert Peel had taken office the previous August, and, since then, Victoria was slowly warming to the man she had found so "insufferably cold and officious" during the bedchamber crisis. Albert was very largely responsible for the change; it was Albert, fearing a repeat of the crisis, who had, with the help of his secretary, George Anson, smoothed Peel's path to power, negotiating an amicable solution to the problem of the Queen's ladies: Peel would make his suggestions, but the Queen would make the appointments.

Albert found a kindred spirit in Peel. Both men were generally perceived as haughty and aloof in public, but both were actually deeply shy, their shyness born of the unshakable sense that they were outsiders in British society. Albert was a foreigner in a society ever conscious of its own national superiority, and Peel was the son of a manufacturer amongst a class-conscious elite. Albert discovered in Peel a guide and mentor; indeed, in Peel he discovered one of the two Britons he could honestly call a friend. (Anson was the other.) Peel offered Albert an entry into public affairs: as one of his first acts as Prime Minister, Peel appointed Albert president of the Fine Arts Commission. Victoria later said that Albert found a "second father" in Peel—and, she might have added, a better one. Peel in return found in Albert a path to the good graces of the Queen. And as Victoria began more and more to adopt Albert's political perspective, her respect for Peel would grow—would, indeed, grow considerably with the events of the coming weeks.

There was a world of difference between Victoria's old prime minister and her new one. Her beloved Lord Melbourne, for all his avuncular warmth and charm, was a complete cynic who believed poverty an inescapable reality in society, and therefore impossible to manage effectively through legislation. He practiced a negative *laissez-faire* in his government, rarely concerning himself with the political affairs of his ministers, and putting off dealing with problems whenever he could. He once told Victoria "all depends on the urgency of a thing. If a thing is very urgent, you can always find time for it; but if a thing can be put off, well then you put it off." Melbourne was the last Georgian prime minister, yearning for a country and a way of life that was quickly passing. Peel, on the other hand, was the first modern PM, always looking forward, fully aware that the momentous material developments of his time forced equally momentous social change; he came into office committed to reform. Certainly, the leader of the Tories was no radical: he was a social conservative and a true believer in the class hierarchy, dead set against the Reform Bill of 1832, for example, which extended the franchise to the middle class. He certainly had no objection to the privilege and luxury of the rich; he attended the *bal masque,* dressed as a figure from a van Dyck painting. Nevertheless—and despite his perpetually icy demeanor—he was an empathetic humanist and a committed social activist. That commitment drove him while in the Home Office in the 1820s to simplify the criminal codes and to form the Metropolitan Police. And now he was seeking to legislate social change through a budget that was nothing short of revolutionary. He proposed the introduction of the first-ever income tax in peacetime—a tax of seven percent, to be levied on all incomes over 150 pounds. Moreover, he proposed massive overall tariff reduction. Together, these changes would have the effect of limiting indirect taxation, which burdened all including the poor, and making up for the loss of revenues by taxing the middle and wealthier classes. It was a budget informed by his growing belief in free trade, calculated not simply to redistribute wealth—but to *create* wealth.

On this Thursday night at Her Majesty's Theatre, positioned directly above the pit, Victoria had the best view in the house of the energetic dancers below. A barrier had been erected beyond the pavilion's base to allow space for a chosen few to trip out waltzes and quadrilles before their monarch. The crowd, however, watched not the dancers but the royal pavilion, as with "mute up-gazing curiosity" they observed Victoria perform the rituals of state, alternating between observing her subjects with greeting their special guests: the Queen's uncle Cambridge and his family, the Lady Patronesses of the ball, and the Duke of Wellington.

All of it—the court ceremony, the omnipresent silk and satin, the crush of spectators in this very theatre—all of it must have seemed familiar to Victoria. It had all happened five years before, at the beginning of June 1837—a week after her eighteenth birthday. This place was the King's Theatre, then, for William IV was suffering through the last month of his reign. The Spitalfields weavers were then as now experiencing horrible destitution, and to aid them William and his queen Adelaide had come up with the idea of a ball, everyone attending in Spitalfields silk. Then, too, the pit was covered over, the walls were festooned with multicolored, shiny Spitalfields fabric, decorated with arms and armor. Adelaide and William were expected to be the guests of honor, but William was dying (and would die in three weeks), so Victoria took his place, arriving amid "deafening plaudits" to play the same role that she played on this night. But if the similarities between that night and this were striking to Victoria, so were the differences. Five years before, she was accompanied by her mother and attended to by John Conroy and Lady Flora Hastings; her uncle the Duke of Cumberland was seen to be "very constant in his attention" to his Royal niece. Cumberland was now king in Hanover, his despotic ways finding much greater favor among the Hanoverians than among the British. Flora Hastings was of course dead, and Conroy—an exile in Berkshire—as good as dead to Victoria. Her mother of course was still at her side—but the tenor of their relationship had changed beyond recognition: now, Victoria was in control. And Victoria's world had changed absolutely, because of the man who was *not* there five years before, but who stood beside her now, towering over her in his Field Marshal's uniform dripping with five orders of knighthood, his power implicit in the enormous jackboots he wore (attire that the more proper of the ladies in attendance considered not quite *de rigueur* for the ballroom): Victoria's all-in-all, her Albert.

From the moment she beheld him from the steps of Buckingham Palace in 1839, Victoria's love for Albert was a fact, and she would never stop loving him until the day of her death. Nevertheless, Albert had suffered greatly during the first two years of their marriage, struggling to establish himself socially and politically in the face of Victoria's tenacious conviction that she would rule *alone*: that Albert would be her lover and husband, but never be the master of the Royal Household and never play a role in politics. He had scored a victory with the Regency Bill—but it was a victory more symbolic than actual, where gaining power depended upon

Victoria's death. To become powerful in the Royal Household and in affairs of state, Albert had to change Victoria's mind about her own self-sufficiency. And to do that, he faced two obstacles, two people who jealously guarded their own influence over Victoria and promoted Albert's exclusion from power: Victoria's political mentor and chief political adviser, Lord Melbourne, and her chief confidante, with full sway over household affairs, Baroness Lehzen.

Of the two, Melbourne had been the easier to deal with. His genial hegemony over her political affairs was necessary to Victoria when, throwing off Conroy's and her mother's oppressive influence, she first became queen. Melbourne's influence over her weakened considerably when she fell in love with Albert, and weakened further as she learned of, and fell in love with, his mind and his ways. During the first months of their marriage, Victoria, to Albert's great frustration, preferred to meet with her ministers alone, keep to herself the key to the government dispatches, and spend her evenings with Albert, wishing to talk about anything but politics. Albert refused to humor her in this way. By the end of 1841, she regularly used the term "we" in setting out her opinions—not a haughty royal we, but rather a simple acknowledgment that she and Albert were politically of one mind. When their daughter Victoria, the Princess Royal, was born on 22 November 1840 (with Albert— unusual for the time—in the room), the Prince hurried from Victoria's side to lead the Privy Council in her stead. Victoria found him indispensable in dealing with government business during her confinement and recovery, and, soon after Vicky's birth, she entrusted Albert with the keys to the boxes containing Cabinet and confidential documents. He became, according to his own secretary Anson, "in fact, tho' not in name, Her Majesty's Private Secretary." At both Buckingham Palace and Windsor by this time, their desks were joined so that they could work as one.

Party politics completed the process of Melbourne's removal. In June 1841, the Whig government lost a vote of no confidence by a single vote and Melbourne called for elections. The results were a disaster for the Whigs: the Tories gained fifty seats, and Peel took Melbourne's place. With Peel's coming, Albert and Victoria became full political partners. He attended all ministerial meetings, read his wife's correspondence, and conducted an extensive political correspondence of his own.

Lehzen might have been a far less significant opponent on a national scale, but she proved to be a much trickier and tenacious one. For two years, she and Albert warred with one another, covertly and overtly, with ferocious intensity. If Lehzen at first welcomed a Coburg consort for Victoria, she quickly and accurately saw him as an enormous threat to her privileged position in Victoria's court. In the dark days of the Kensington regime, Lehzen was Victoria's sole ally, and the grateful Queen repaid her loyalty by giving to her complete control over her daily affairs—writing Victoria's correspondence, holding the keys and the Privy Purse, acting as go-between in dealings with the Queen's household officers. And when Princess Vicky was born, Victoria naturally gave Lehzen—once her own governess—oversight of the nursery. Lehzen fiercely resisted every attempt by Albert to take control of his household as an attack on her own prerogatives. Less than two weeks after Oxford's attempt, for example, Albert confronted Lehzen, through Anson, about not reporting to him that a certain Captain Childers was stalking the Queen with "mad professions of love." Lehzen resisted Albert's intrusion, telling Anson that Albert had once told her to leave the Palace, but "he had no power to turn her out of the Queen's house." Albert, to her mind, had no power whatsoever over palace affairs: "the Queen would brook no interference with the exercise of her powers of which she was *most jealous.*" Albert responded to Lehzen's opposition with an obsessive bitterness and loathing. She was to him *"die Blaste"*— the hag, the "Yellow Lady" (a reference to her jaundice), "a crazy, stupid intriguer, obsessed with the lust of power, who regards herself as a demi-God." Albert considered her the single cause of every dysfunction in the royal household, including all tension between him and Victoria. Certainly, she took advantage of her position as *confidante* to pour poison in Victoria's ear about Albert; Anson noted her "pointing out and exaggerating every little fault of the Prince, constantly misrepresenting him, constantly trying to undermine him in the Queen's affections and making herself appear a martyr."

Once again, time—and biology—were Albert's allies as Victoria's dependency upon Albert as husband and father grew. During her first pregnancy, Albert attended upon her constantly and arranged for her obstetrician. After Vicky was born, he read to Victoria and wrote for her—and carried her from bed to sofa, and back. Lehzen found herself increasingly shut out.

An assault of sorts upon the Queen, occurring less than two weeks after Vicky's birth, resulted in a considerable jump in Albert's influence over the household. On the evening of 3 December 1840, palace servants were startled to discover an unkempt young man hiding under a sofa in the Queen's dressing room—a sofa upon which just hours before the Queen had been sitting. The boy— Edward Jones—had been roaming the palace for two days, from kitchens to royal apartments. He claimed that he "sat upon the throne, saw the Queen, and heard the Princess Royal . . . squall." Jones had broken into the Palace two years before, but then the Queen was at Windsor. This time, the breach in security—literally trespassing under the Queen's nose—caused a public sensation, and Jones—dubbed "the Boy Jones" (or "In-I-go Jones")—became a nine-day's comic wonder in the Sunday papers and in *Punch*: the epitome of enormous if inappropriate ambition.

In the palace, though, no one was laughing. Baron Stockmar, in a memorandum he wrote for Albert on the deplorable state of the Royal Household, attributed Jones's intrusion to "the absence of system, which leaves the palace without any responsible authority." And indeed the Palaces were in a state of sometimes quaint but more usually maddening dysfunction—working according to an archaic structure that would have been familiar to Henry VIII.

Servants worked under one of three masters—the Lord Chamberlain, the Lord Steward, and the Master of the Horse—who rarely supervised directly or coordinated their servants' duties with one another. The results were predictably chaotic. The Lord Chamberlain's servants, for instance, were in charge of cleaning windows inside the palace, while the Master of the Horse's servants cleaned the outside—and palace windows were consequently never quite clean. The Lord Steward's servants laid fuel in fireplaces; the Lord Chamberlain's servants actually lit fires—and rooms thus remained cold. Repairs were subject to a byzantine process of signature and countersignature—and thus many palace fixtures, once broken, remained broken. Servants, largely unsupervised, were often less than diligent. Moreover, archaic expenses drained money from the royal purse; servants, for example, regularly sold off the day's unused candles for their own profit. Albert, in going over Palace expenditures, discovered a weekly charge of 35 shillings for guards at Windsor who hadn't actually served since George III's day—and now going into the pocket of a half-pay officer who did nothing. Jones's intrusion gave Albert the excuse that he needed to commence the long process of Palace reform, centralizing authority in the position of a single Master of the Household. Lehzen's influence over the household faded further.

Albert's genuine fears about the health of his children led to the final explosion. The royal couple's second child, Bertie—the future Edward VII—was born on 9 November 1841, the first Prince of Wales born in eighty years. The public was jubilant, not least because the specter of that reactionary, constitution-busting bogeyman, Victoria's uncle Cumberland, ever taking the British throne now faded into near-nothingness. Victoria herself, however, slipped into a serious post-partum depression, of which Lehzen attempted to take advantage: she "lets no opportunity of creating mischief and difficulty escape her," Anson wrote. Attempting to raise her spirits, Albert took Victoria away to Claremont in the countryside, leaving the children at Windsor. Within four days,

Stockmar called them back; the Princess Royal was seriously ill—thin, pale, and feverish.

Albert was livid. All connected with the children—their nurse Mrs. Southey, Dr. Clark, the Queen herself—he considered responsible, but that meddling *Blaste* was at the bottom it all: "All the disagreeableness I suffer," he wrote, "comes from one and the same person." He and Victoria had the worst argument of their married lives, the Queen accusing Albert of wishing to kill their children, and screaming that she wished they had never married. Albert stormed off, and the couple continued their argument through missives sent to Stockmar. In one of these, Albert enclosed a ferocious note to Victoria: "Dr. Clark has mismanaged the child and poisoned her with calomel and you have starved her. I shall have nothing more to do with it; take the child away and do as you like and if she dies you will have it on her conscience." He had reached the breaking point; as he told Stockmar "the welfare of my children and Victoria's existence as sovereign are too sacred for me not to die fighting rather than yield them as prey to Lehzen."

The Queen gave way. Albert was to have total control of the nursery and their children's upbringing. He quickly replaced Mrs. Southey with Lady Lyttelton, the Queen's Lady of the Bedchamber, who adored the Prince. Lehzen was now in an internal exile, inhabiting a room in the Palace but removed from Victoria's daily life. Significantly, she did not attend the *bal masque*, or this ball at Her Majesty's. By the end of the coming summer, realizing that the Queen had no need for her anymore, she would retire to a small house in Hanover. Albert had successfully become everything a man could be to Victoria. Her esteem for him could only grow if he could become superhuman—godlike—in her eyes.

For two hours that night at Her Majesty's Theatre, the Queen and Albert performed on their pavilion stage. One reporter empathized with the fatigue Victoria must feel, when she and her court had to rise, turn, and curtsey with the arrival of every one of her many honored guests. Soon after midnight she rose and curtseyed to the crowd. The two bands struck up the national anthem, and "amidst loud cheering and clapping of hands" the royal party returned to their carriages and to the Palace. Once the royal couple left, the crowd thinned, giving room to all on the floor to dance, which they did until the early hours, caring for the destitute weavers by forgetting about them. Those last to leave could not have gotten to bed before dawn, not long before respectable shopkeepers like John Francis woke to the new day.

Francis continued to play the charade that it was just another day of business, setting out early to open his shop. He waited in the aromatic stillness until he knew William Elam had risen and set out for his own place of work. Then, he shut up shop and returned to Titchfield Street, crept up the two flights to his room, and broke open a locked box containing all of his roommate's possessions. If he expected to find the full ten pounds there, he was disappointed: Elam's box contained less than half of that, four pounds and ten shillings in gold. It would have to do—or it wouldn't. He returned to his shop to wait for Johns.

When the door with his name on it opened, however, he looked up not to see Johns, but instead his landlord, Mr. Foster, angrily bearing down upon him. William Elam had returned to his room at Great Titchfield Street, discovered that his box had been rifled, and reported the theft immediately to Foster, who had seen Francis's return and suspected him immediately. Francis knew why Foster had come, though he attempted to appear unconcerned.

"What have you been about?" Foster asked him. "I suppose you know what I have come here for?"

"Oh," said Francis, "I suppose you want the money." He pulled the gold from his pocket and gave it to Foster. Foster had always had a good opinion of Francis, but in an instant that was destroyed. He told Francis never to return to his home again. Francis, however, had boxes containing all his possessions at Foster's: what about those? he asked. Foster refused to hand them over, thinking that they might contain evidence of other crimes Francis had committed. He left Francis alone to contemplate the impending ruination of his business.

Johns, again accompanied, came later that day. Francis gave up, telling him at last that he could not pay a penny. Johns and his men then emptied the shop: trundling cigars, tobacco, snuff, pipes, Grimstone's Eye Snuff into a cab, leaving Francis with nothing but the lingering odor of tobacco, a few coppers, and his name on the door to a room he had almost certainly not paid for. His great project had ended, and he had lost everything—all his clothes (besides those on his back), his carpentry tools, his poetry, his room, and his friends, gone. In the afternoon, he closed up shop, and walked out and away from this neighborhood forever.

He set out south, down past Buckingham Palace, Green Park, and St. James's, to Tothill Street, to the pawn shop of a Mr. Ravenor. There, he told the clerk he wanted to buy a pistol—a cheap one. The clerk, James Street, found two for him to look at. Both were old—older and in far worse shape than the pistols Oxford had bought: flintlocks missing flints, and with rusted screw barrels, which, when new, could be removed with a key for more effective loading. Each was missing its key, however, and could only be loaded through the barrel. Francis chose the smaller of the two, one seven inches long. Well aware of its low value, he offered three shillings for it. Street wanted more, but quickly agreed to Francis's price. Francis paid with his small change: three fourpenny pieces, a sixpence, and the rest in pennies, halfpennies, and farthings. "It appeared to be all he had in the world," Street later told police.

Not quite. Francis still had two purchases to make. He struck out north, toward Whitehall, and within minutes entered a small oilman's shop on Charles Street. He needed a flint. The clerk told him they rarely sold flints, but he looked anyway, and found one among some old stock. Francis showed him the pistol; the clerk noticed it had no leather to tie a flint on, rooted around his shop until he found a strip, and with it tied the flint to the pistol. He also noticed that the pistol seemed to have no trigger, but Francis pulled back the cock, and the trigger sprang out. Francis paid for the flint with two halfpennies.

He made one more purchase later that night; the police later found a shopkeeper across town who thought—but could not swear—that Francis bought gunpowder from him. The location of his shop, deep in Marylebone, makes this unlikely, but Francis clearly did buy gunpowder someplace—a small quantity, but enough to load the pistol through its muzzle. While the police learned about all of these purchases, however, they could never prove that Francis bought a bullet for his pistol, although they made an exhaustive attempt to do just that.

To sleep, and to hide away until Sunday, Francis found shelter at yet another coffee house: St. Ann's, at the very end of Oxford Street. Since this place was just doors away from his parents' home, he likely knew the owner, Mr. Goodman, and possibly was able to defer his payment for a little time. A little time was all he needed. This was one Sunday when he would not be returning home for dinner; his family never knew how close Francis was to them as he lay low and awaited his opportunity.

ten

A Thorough Scamp

It was easy, in 1842, to catch sight of the Queen on Sundays while she was in residence at Buckingham Palace, since she regularly attended service at the Chapel Royal at St. James's Palace. It was of course the shortest of walks from Buckingham Palace to St. James's—less than a quarter-mile—but the Queen rode from palace to palace with her household, in a series of carriages. On either side of the Mall, under the shade of the magnificent elm trees, bystanders watched the short parade come, and, after the service, return. While Victoria and Albert attended the sermon of the Bishop of Norwich at the Chapel Royal during the early afternoon of Sunday 29 May, a crowd outside awaited their return to Buckingham Palace. Among that crowd, standing on the Mall directly across from the southeastern entrance to Green Park, stood a sixteen-year-old boy by the name of George Pearson. Pearson had only recently arrived in London from Suffolk to work at his brother's printing business as a wood engraver. This Sunday he was exploring the wonders of the metropolis and had come to St. James's to see the greatest wonder of all, the Queen.

Pearson was a shy boy and betrayed that shyness with an acute stammer, one that amounted to verbal paralysis when he felt fear or stress. It was two in the afternoon when the crowd stirred upon seeing the activity on Stable Yard Road. The train of closed carriages emerged from there, turned right for the Palace, and approached the boy. The crowd cheered, all eyes fixed on the last carriage, the one carrying the royal couple. Albert sat to the right, Pearson's side, with his equerry Colonel Wylde riding beside him; Victoria's equerry Colonel Arbuthnot rode apace on the Queen's side. Victoria bowed to those on her side of the Mall while Albert acknowledged those around Pearson. They passed Pearson and trotted on. He turned to watch the backs of the footmen standing on the back of the Queen's carriage.

He froze. Three or four yards in front of his eyes, a dark-complexioned youth, his back against the rails of St. James's Park, stood with arm extended, clutching a small pistol and pointing it toward the carriage. The youth didn't fire, Pearson thought.* He seemed confused and angry with himself as he returned the pistol to the breast of his black surtout coat. Pearson heard him mutter "They may take me if they like, I don't care—I was a fool not to shoot." For some moments—as long as a minute or two—the two young men stood still, indecisively. Then John Francis crossed the Mall and disappeared through the gate and into Green Park.

Pearson, immobilized by agitation, watched him go, wondering whether what he had seen was a joke, and wondering if he had really seen what he thought he had: no one else in the now-dispersing crowd seemed to. But then he saw next to him a tall, white-whiskered old man, whose startled face showed he had obviously witnessed what Pearson had. "What a remarkable thing it was!"

---

* According to another witness, the youth did pull the trigger, but the pistol misfired; see page 175.

he said to Pearson: he "never knew such a thing in his life!" Then, he turned and slowly walked away, toward Piccadilly. Pearson quietly followed him: perhaps the man was on his way to report the attempt to the police, in which case Pearson too should come forward as a witness. The old man walked on, Pearson following, to St. James's Street, where he stopped and turned to the boy, again commenting on the remarkable scene the two had just witnessed. He then asked the boy for his name and address; Pearson haltingly articulated them, and the old man carefully wrote them down. The two then walked together down Piccadilly. The man turned and left Pearson on the corner of Duke Street. Pearson watched him amble slowly away—and never saw him again. In the coming days, the police (with Pearson's help) exerted an enormous amount of energy attempting to find the old gentleman—to no avail. The gentleman, whoever he was, must have had the questionable pleasure of reading about himself in the newspapers a few days later, when he was excoriated for not raising an alarm or reporting the crime.

Pearson continued on east, to his brother's home in Holborn. He assumed that the old man was reporting the attempt to the police, and supposed that the police might come to him soon. They never came. When he spoke with his brother, he was calmer, able to tell him what he had witnessed without his stammer defeating him.

George's brother, Matthew Flinders Pearson, was a good fifteen years older than he, and a respectable businessman in Holborn. He was genuinely alarmed by his brother's account, and knew that they could not leave reporting the crime to the old gentleman, or wait for the police to come. Indeed, he mistrusted the very idea of reporting to the police, considering it unlikely that they would give the tale of a semi-articulate country boy much credence, and fearing the consequences of public alarm: he considered that the attempt should be kept as secret as possible. That need for secrecy was the opinion shared by everyone who learned of the attempt in the next twenty-four hours. Matthew decided therefore to report the attempt to a political authority, and the brothers Pearson set off on an odyssey that would bring them overnight to the presence of the highest powers in the kingdom.

Matthew brought George to a Holborn friend he knew to be politically inclined. Thomas Dousbery, a boot and shoe retailer, dabbled in radical thought and was the secretary of the Cordwainer's benevolent fund; he was acquainted with a number of political figures, and he would surely know what to do. With Matthew translating, George haltingly told Dousbery his story. Dousbery believed George's account demanded serious attention, and recommended the three speak with the most highly placed city official he knew: Alderman Sir Peter Laurie—the same Sir Peter who had taken such an interest in Oxford's case, and, incidentally, was still taking an interest in his official capacity as President of Bethlem Hospital. Dousbery was sure that Laurie trusted in him, and would not see Pearson's account as a "trumped up tale."

At six that evening, then, Dousbery and the Pearsons were received by Laurie at his ornate mansion on aristocratic Park Square: surroundings guaranteed to overawe young Pearson and hopelessly tie his tongue: He stammered so badly, Laurie wrote in his diary, "that his brother who was with him had to repeat a statement he had made to him when he was not excited or afraid." Laurie considered that Pearson should take his account straight to Buckingham Palace. He doubted the discretion of the police and the Tory Home Secretary, James Graham, believing that if Pearson went there his account was likely to make "noise" and to become public. Best to speak with a royal official. Laurie therefore wrote them a letter of introduction to Charles Augustus Murray, the Master of the Queen's Household—a letter which Laurie, a man well known for his egotism, later claimed saved the Queen's life.

From Laurie's mansion adjacent to Regent's Park, the three hurried south to Buckingham Palace to find themselves stymied by royal protocol. Upon presenting their letter at the door, they were curtly informed that Murray had just sat down to dinner at the Queen's table, and could not—"on any pretence"—be spoken with until bed time. Rather than wait until then, and rather than argue that the matter was of sufficient importance to interrupt Murray, they decided to bring the letter to Murray in the morning, and returned to Holborn. The Queen, they thought, would have to wait to hear about her assailant.

Victoria, however, already knew. For besides George Pearson and the mysterious old man, there was one other witness to Francis's attempt: Prince Albert. Albert, watching the crowd from his carriage, had seen the "little swarthy ill-looking rascal" aim the flintlock at his face, and had spent the entire afternoon certain that he had nearly been killed. He wrote about the assault to his father the next day:

> . . . when we were nearly opposite Stafford House, I saw a man step out from the crowd and present a pistol full at me. He was some two paces from us. I heard the trigger snap, but it must have missed fire. I turned to Victoria, who was seated on my right, and asked her, "Did you hear that?" She had been bowing to the people on the right, and had observed nothing. I said, "I may be mistaken, but I am sure I saw some one take aim at us."

As far as Albert was concerned, the swarthy ill-looking rascal was aiming directly at him and not at the Queen; Victoria later wrote to her Uncle Leopold "Thank God, my angel is also well; but he says that had the man fired on Sunday, he must have been hit in the head."

Albert was deeply distressed after this attempt—distressed at the attempt itself, and at the amazing fact that no one around him had seen what he had. He asked his footmen if they had noticed anyone stretch a hand toward the carriage. (He didn't mention the pistol, thinking that best be kept secret.) They had seen nothing. He then ran out onto the palace balcony to see if there was a commotion on the Mall: surely, if anyone else had seen the assailant, there would be an outcry, and hundreds would have converged on the perpetrator. But all was quiet; the crowd had dispersed, "satisfied with having seen the Queen." Albert then spoke with the Queen's equerry, Colonel Arbuthnot—who, riding on the Queen's side of the carriage, also saw nothing. Albert, wishing Arbuthnot to maintain "profound secrecy," asked him to communicate what had happened to four people only: the two Commissioners of the police; the Home Secretary, James Graham; and the Prime Minister, Robert Peel.

Upon hearing of the attempt, Peel rushed to the Palace and listened to Albert's tale as the two walked in the palace gardens. With a member of the police, Peel took down Albert's statement in writing, taking special note of Albert's description of Francis. He then acquainted the Home Secretary with the situation. Sir James Graham walked to Scotland Yard to call on the elder and the more military of the two police commissioners, Colonel Charles Rowan: from the start, Graham envisioned something like a military operation to catch the would-be assassin. Rowan was out, but he returned between five and six and hurried around the building to the Home Office, where Graham showed him Albert's statement. Both men then reported to the Palace. Peel was there, and the Prime Minister and the Home Secretary left Rowan to confer with the Prince. The three agreed that they should limit the knowledge of the assault to a very few—the Prince, Peel, Graham, Rowan, the two equerries, and the two police inspectors attached to the Palace—while at the same time launching a major police operation to catch the assailant. The Queen in the meantime would not present herself as a target by going out in her carriage until she absolutely had to—that is, not for three days, until Wednesday, when she was to attend a royal levee at the Throne Room at St. James's. That was the plan that Rowan took from the Palace, anyway. Whether Peel, Graham, and particularly Albert were fully aware of the same plan, agreed upon in two separate conversations, is unclear. And the Queen herself had not agreed to anything. The subsequent confusion put Victoria in grave danger.

Rowan left Buckingham Palace at 7:30, quite possibly crossing paths obliviously with the Pearsons and Dousbery on their way in. At Scotland Yard, Rowan established a plan to capture the assailant. Rowan believed that, failing in his first attempt, the assailant would likely soon show up in the neighborhood of the palace hoping for another opportunity to shoot at the Queen. He thought he had three days to work with. Rowan thus ordered his detective (in all but name) Inspector Pearce to join the inspectors assigned to the Palace and patrol Green and St. James's parks in plain clothes, watching for anyone who fit the description Albert had given.

The next morning at nine, the Pearsons and Dousbery came to Buckingham Palace to call on the Master of the Household. This time Murray saw them, and patiently listened to the boy's excruciatingly drawn-out tale. Murray, with less of a sense of imminent danger than Laurie had shown, or perhaps an awareness of Sir James's work schedule at the Home Office, wrote the three a letter for Graham and told them to call on the Home Secretary that afternoon between two and three. He then brought the Prince the welcome news that his story was corroborated: "There was no longer any doubt," Albert wrote with relief to his father.

At two on Monday afternoon, then, a good twenty-four hours after the attempt, George Pearson was finally able to tell his story to the police, the Home Secretary calling in Colonel Rowan to take the boy's statement. George Pearson's tale did not come more easily with the retelling, his stammer if anything worse in the magisterial precincts of Whitehall. "I was present," Rowan wrote with exasperation, "during a very long Examination of the Lad who saw the pistol presented made tediously long by the impediment in his speech."

Rowan too must have been relieved to have corroboration for Albert's story. But the fact that it was a sixteen-year-old from Holborn who witnessed the attempt, and that the story had already been told a number of times, to a number of people, concerned him. Surely it would not be long until the story got out and spread through the metropolis like wildfire. If the attempted assassin learned that he had been spotted, he would likely run for cover and might never be caught. Rowan, then, decided to intensify the search. He ordered his clerks to write up "as many written descriptions of the offender to be made out as there are entrances with St. James Park"—seventeen in all. Seventeen plain-clothed officers, each equipped with a bulletin, would stand, one at each gate, ready to seize anyone meeting the assailant's description. Rowan and Graham agreed that it was not necessary to tell these officers—or any of the other officers on patrol in the parks—*why* this man was wanted; besides the four inspectors, no police officer was told about the attempt on the Queen, or that her life was now in danger. For almost all of the police in the parks on this day, therefore, the mission was to protect St. James's Park, not to protect their monarch.

It then struck Rowan that George Pearson—who had stammered out his story and returned to Holborn—would be, as an eyewitness, of immeasurable help to the police. He sent Inspector Pearce to fetch him and accompany him around the parks.

Rowan operated under two assumptions in setting out his orders. First, he considered that the assassin would return to the exact scene of his first attempt, hoping to find the Queen there. In other words, Rowan thought it more likely that Francis would return to St. James's Park than that he would look for his opportunity in Green Park. True, he had directed officers on patrol to search both parks—but the dragnet he had established at St. James's had no counterpart at Green Park. Second, he had left the Palace the night before certain that Victoria would refrain from her afternoon ride for two days. He had not heard Victoria's own opinion, assuming that her husband and ministers would of course know what she wanted to do.

Rowan was wrong, utterly wrong, in both assumptions.

Victoria was unnerved by the attempt of the day before, and especially by the thought that one of her subjects, still at large, apparently sought to kill her. But she knew instinctively that hiding in the Palace and letting one misfit intrude between her and her subjects, for days or longer, was not an option. Better to take on the threat directly than live under its shadow. She told Albert's secretary, George Anson, that she had had for some time a premonition that such a "mad attempt" would be made. It would be a relief to scotch the problem, by flushing out the shooter. Albert noted that, upon confirmation of Sunday's attempt, "we were naturally very much agitated, Victoria very nervous and unwell." He indeed claims that a doctor recommended she deal with her agitation by going out. But that doctor (likely Dr. Clark) had no knowledge of the attempt, and it is not at all likely he recommended the Queen deal with her nerves by placing herself in the line of fire. It was Victoria who made the decision. She simply refused, under any circumstances, to jeopardize her well-cultured relationship with the public—one that depended upon her regularly going among her subjects. She had inherited a tarnished monarchy, her predecessors—through illness, disdain, or reclusiveness—secluding themselves from the public, inviting at best the apathy, and at worst the active dislike of the people. Victoria, as Princess and as Queen, had actively resisted seclusion, and had enhanced the reputation of the monarchy simply by demonstrating an absolute trust of her good relationship with her people. She refused to let any ill- or good-looking boy challenge that. Her openness signified a sea change in royal style—a sense of daily responsibility to the public that defines the British monarchy today. The public *expected* her to ride among them. She would not disappoint them. As for Albert, if he had known of the plan to keep the Queen at home, he now forgot or ignored it, and concurred with his wife's decision. They were determined to go out, he wrote to his father, "for we should have to *shut* ourselves up for months, had we settled not to go out, so long as the miscreant was at large." Victoria rode out, she informed her Uncle Leopold, because she honestly felt she had no other option.

She would, however, take precautions. While continuing to keep yesterday's attempt from the household, she made it clear that her ladies in waiting would not be needed or welcomed on this ride. "I must expose the lives of my gentlemen," she wrote to her uncle, "but I will not those of my ladies." Her lady in waiting, Lady Portman, and her maids of honor, Matilda Paget and Georgiana Liddell, waited in vain that afternoon to be called; Liddell, thus shunned, stalked off to grumble in the palace gardens. The gentlemen whose lives Victoria exposed were her and Albert's equerries, Colonels Arbuthnot and Wylde, whom she instructed to ride as close to the open carriage as possible, in order to shield them from any bullets. She also ordered her postilion to drive the horses faster. Moreover, she and Albert possessed a touching faith in the police whom they had unknowingly misled: they knew that there were plenty of police in plain clothes in the parks: they were on the lookout for the assailant, and, as Albert thought, "would seize him on the least imprudence or carelessness on his part."

Albert—who knew from his experience on Sunday that he was in as much danger as his wife—was the first to leave the Palace. He had an appointment at Somerset House, in one of his first official positions: as Lord Warden of the Stannaries. It was just the sort of involvement in political affairs that Albert craved; he wouldn't miss it for anything. At 3:00, he set out from the Palace. He returned before six—surely scrutinizing the assembling crowds more carefully than usual.

The weather was superb that evening, the sun still fairly high in the late May sky, when the carriage, preceded by outriders, followed by grooms, clattered out of the Palace gates. Racing up Constitution Hill, Victoria and Albert must have remembered Oxford's attempt, two years before, at this very spot. As they sped by, their equerries crowding so closely to them as to almost touch the sides of the carriage, the royal couple refrained from their usual greetings to the public, instead glancing around anxiously, watching for a pistol, straining to hear a shot. (Later, Victoria's visiting Uncle Mensdorff helpfully told her "one is sure not to have been hit when one hears the report, as one never hears it when one is hit.") "Looking out for such a man was not *des plus agreables*," Victoria wrote. Albert concurred: "You may imagine that our minds were not very easy. We looked behind every tree, and I cast my eyes round in search of the rascal's face." They sped up the hill and into Hyde Park without incident, and began to relax, finding comfort in the stunning weather and the appreciative "hosts of people on foot." They rode into the suburbs as far north as Hampstead before turning back for the Palace.

Meanwhile back at Green Park on Constitution Hill, standing near a pump directly across the road from where Edward Oxford had fired his pistols, William Trounce, one of the many plainclothes constables patrolling the parks from A Division, thought he had found his man. He had been observing the youth for some time. The youth matched the description of the assailant. He stood alone. And he had been behaving strangely—pacing agitatedly about the pump. He realized Trounce was watching him, and resented it: "I had seen the prisoner half an hour before this," Trounce later told authorities, "and when I looked at him he appeared to go behind the tree, as if to conceal himself"—peering out furtively, hoping in vain that the constable would lose interest in him. He only succeeded in increasing Trounce's suspicion. Trounce was right: he *was* observing John Francis, who, his pistol concealed in the breast of his coat, was waiting for the return of the royal couple. But Trounce, curiously, did nothing to detain Francis; he simply continued to observe him. True, Francis had done nothing wrong—yet. And while Trounce had been given a description of Francis, he had absolutely no idea that Francis had made an attempt on the Queen the day before, and thus had no idea that Francis posed a threat today to the royal couple, whose carriage was now rushing through the gate at Hyde Park and racing down Constitution Hill.

The carriage had been proceeding at the fast clip of eleven miles an hour, according to Victoria's equerry Arbuthnot. But Arbuthnot, feeling in his gut that something was wrong as they approached Constitution Hill, rode up to the postilion and demanded he ride even faster until they reached the Palace gates. Trounce turned away from Francis, who now stood a yard downhill and behind him, in order to catch sight of the quickly approaching carriage, rushing up to a point six feet away from him. (He was later to speculate that the speed of the carriage saved the Queen's life.) Trounce now faced a dilemma. He had been a policeman for two years, but had only been with A Division for a month, and was unfamiliar with royal protection and etiquette. How was a police officer observing a suspect supposed to respond to the royal presence?

Trounce in that instant opted for loyalty over security. He stood at attention and smartly saluted the Queen as she passed.

The explosion in Trounce's ear completely disconcerted him for a moment. Then, turning, he saw to his horror Francis, his left hand resting on the pump, his right hand steady on his left, still pointing the discharged flintlock at where the Queen had been: a "theatrical attitude," according to one of many witnesses who now focused absolutely upon him. Colonel Arbuthnot cried out "secure him!" but Trounce already had Francis by the collar with one hand, and had Francis's pistol in the other. The policeman was mortified by the fact that he had allowed Francis to get off a shot: "I did not intend to make any delay in seizing the Prisoner. . . . It was not as if I had seen him fire the Pistol—I could have then laid hold of him sooner, or if I had known he was going to fire it. . . ." he later sputtered guiltily in a police report.

The carriage moved on, Arbuthnot pulling up for a moment to see Francis captured before rejoining the Queen. Wylde meanwhile galloped from Albert's side toward Francis. Albert and Victoria, looking behind them, glimpsed a number of bystanders converging on Francis, before they turned and galloped through the Marble Arch and into the Palace yard.

A private in the Scots Fusilier Guards, Henry Allen, was the first to join Trounce in securing Francis. Allen had seen the flash from the pistol and heard the shot: there was a sharpness to the sound that convinced him that the pistol had indeed been loaded.

Other witnesses—Colonel Arbuthnot in particular—agreed that the pistol's report was sharp and loud, the sign "of a pistol well loaded and rammed." Victoria, on the other hand, was certain that the shot was not loud at all—certainly, less loud than when Oxford had shot at her. She would not even have noticed it, she claimed, if she hadn't actually been expecting to hear it at some point during the ride. The *sound* of the shot became a central question at Francis's trial, sound suggesting substance—a loaded weapon. Another important question was where the bullet—if there was one—went. Albert was sure Francis aimed low, the bullet going under the carriage; others claimed it went above; one of the Queen's grooms, riding behind her, thought Francis actually aimed not at the Queen, but at the hind wheel of her carriage. In any case, a bullet was never found.

Inspector James Russell—who, as one of the inspectors assigned to palace duty, was one of the very few in the park that day who had actually known the Queen's life was in danger—ran up to Trounce and the others securing Francis. Trounce handed Russell the pistol; it was warm, suggesting recent discharge. The group marched Francis to the Porter's Lodge of the palace. There, he was searched: a little notebook, a key or two, a penny—and a small amount of gunpowder, screwed up in a piece of paper: enough to recharge his pistol. But he did not have any bullets. Wylde attempted to question him, but Francis remained sullen, silent and frightened—Wylde observed the quiver in his lips. Within minutes, they led Francis across the palace to the equerries' entrance, bundled him into a cab, drove him to the Gardiner Lane station, and shut him in the cell Oxford had occupied two years before. Meanwhile, two more carriages sped from the Palace—to inform the House of Commons and the House of Lords about the attempt.

At Gardiner Lane, Francis lost his anonymity. Two ex-colleagues from Covent Garden had coincidentally come to Green Park that evening and had witnessed the shooting. The two compared notes. One of these two, Mark Russell, nearly sure that the young man he had seen was John Francis Senior's son, hurried to Gardiner Lane, where he identified Francis positively and provided police with the whereabouts of Francis's father. Inspector Pearce was quickly dispatched to fetch him. Francis admitted his identity.

Word of Francis's capture was sent around the building to Colonel Rowan, still in the process of giving orders to find the assailant of the day before; he was shocked to learn that the Queen had gone out at all, let alone that she was shot at.

The news quickly crossed the street and disrupted Parliament. In the Lords, the news was brought to the Duke of Wellington, then Leader of the House of Lords in Peel's government. Without a word, Wellington started up and rushed from the chamber, followed by the Lord Chancellor and a number of other peers; business was immediately suspended. In the Commons, the news could not have come at a more dramatic moment: the third (and final) reading of Peel's income-tax bill had just been proposed. The Home Secretary, hearing the news, called Peel from the house to tell him. Although Peel of course knew that an assailant was at large, he, like Rowan, thought that the Queen would be safe in the Palace all day and was shocked by the news. He returned to the House, which now, catching wind of the attempt, was in a state of "much inattention and confusion." Peel interrupted a hapless M.P. attempting to continue the debate, and, in a voice in which his "excitement well nigh overpowered his utterance," he informed the House of the attempt, the Queen's providential escape, and the capture of the would-be assassin, calling for immediate adjournment. Lord John Russell seconded, the motion passed, and Peel rushed from the House.

He crossed over to Whitehall and to the Home Office, where a number of Privy Councilors—most, but not all, with the Government—were assembling for an immediate examination of Francis. Francis, like Oxford, would have his moment when the highest of the land focused their attention upon him exclusively. Besides the Prime Minister himself, the Duke of Wellington was there, as well as the Home, Foreign, and Colonial Secretaries and the Chancellor of the Exchequer. Also in attendance was Prince Albert (who had been made a member of the Privy Council just before his marriage to Victoria), who thus was able to take a closer and longer look at the youth who aimed a pistol at his head. He was not impressed: "He is not out of his mind, but a thorough scamp. His answers are coarse and witty. He tries to make fun of his judges . . . a wretched creature. I hope his trial will be conducted with the greatest strictness."

Francis was examined from eight to ten that evening; witnesses quickly established that he had indeed pointed a gun at the royal carriage on two occasions. As Albert observed, Francis acted during his examination to some extent as Oxford had—with a braggadocio born of the sense of importance the Privy Council gave him simply by paying attention to him: a coolness, calmness, and firmness that astonished the Council. But in another way, he acted very differently than Oxford: there was little madness, and much method, in the questions he was allowed to make in cross-examining the witnesses. He was already looking forward to his trial and attempting to minimize his actions to something less than High Treason. To Colonel Arbuthnot, he asked "whether he thought he intended to shoot the queen, or whether it was done in a frolic." ("I cannot say," Arbuthnot answered.)

After the examination, Francis was bundled out the back entrance and conveyed to Tothill Fields for the night. At the prison, he divulged his name and address, and grew socially indignant when someone asked whether it was true that his father was a "scene-shifter" at Covent Garden. "Scene-shifter! No, he's a stage carpenter." He was, as policy dictated, stripped naked and bathed.

The next day, he was brought back to Whitehall at noon to finish his examination. There, young, stuttering George Pearson, brought by the police to Tothill Fields to pick Francis out from among a crowd of prisoners, was able to positively identify Francis as the Queen's assailant on Sunday. The Council charged Francis with High Treason and sent him in a hackney cab to Newgate. His night in jail, and the capital charge leveled against him, had apparently had a sobering effect: the crowd assembled outside the Home Office saw him lean back in the vehicle and pull his hat over his brow, seeming to "wish to shrink from public gaze."

The news of Francis's attempt spread quickly to become "the all engrossing topic of conversation amongst all classes"—a "ferment . . . not to be done justice to in description." As they had two years before, the population of the metropolis erupted into a celebration of the monarchy and of Victoria: a celebration completely spontaneous, and yet now beginning to take on the sanctity of tradition. Victoria did not ride to her mother's home this time, instead sending her Uncle Mensdorff to inform her about the attempt; the Duchess hurried back with her brother-in-law to the Palace, where, bursting into tears, she fell upon Victoria, who calmly caressed and reassured her. Again, her relatives, leading politicians and diplomats, the Archbishop of Canterbury, all rushed to the Palace while the crowds swelled outside. Robert Peel belied his usual coolness in an emotional meeting with the Queen. Many of the gentry, in full evening dress, stopped at the palace on their way to parties and the theatres to sign the registry and tender their congratulations. At all the theatres, patrons and performers alike gave vent to tumultuous cheering and displays of "unmixed joy." At Covent Garden—Francis's theatre—the German Opera was performing; Madame Schodel and the sublimely voiced bass, Herr Staudigl, sang every verse of the national anthem to "loud plaudits"—an excellent rendition, according to a reporter for the *Morning Chronicle*— "making allowance for the foreign accent of the vocalists."

The next day was an impromptu holiday for Londoners of every class. The crowds began to form anew by 8:00—around the Palace, and at Whitehall, where Francis was to return to complete his examination by the Privy Council. At the more polite hour of ten, the carriages of the elite began arriving at the Palace, in a throng that continued all morning and into the late afternoon. By that time, the crowd lining Constitution Hill and assembled in Hyde Park had grown to a crushing volume, thousands of the Queen's subjects certain that she and Albert would ride and all desiring to be a part of that triumphal procession. That she would ride again was never a question to the Queen. It was inconceivable to her that Francis, like Oxford, was anything but an aberration. "When her Majesty goes abroad among the people for the purpose of taking recreation or exercise," John Russell said in Parliament that afternoon, "there is not one among her subjects who has less reason to fear an enemy in any single individual of the millions who constitute her subjects." That Victoria and Albert agreed with him without reservation was demonstrated by the fact that they had allowed Lady Lyttelton to take the Princess Royal and the infant Prince of Wales on an airing that morning in a coach and four.

And at around 4:30, the gates opened; several outriders in scarlet livery trotted out, and, with their guest the Duke of Saxe-Meiningen, followed by the five Counts Mensdorff, Victoria and Albert rode triumphantly into their public. They rode into an increasingly thicker crowd as they approached the Wellington Arch: "the crowd of spectators was so great," wrote one anxious reporter, "that it was miraculous that some serious accidents did not occur." In Hyde Park, they were slowed to a near standstill by the horses and carriages of the nobility. Again, the royal couple witnessed the completely spontaneous and yet entirely ordered jubilation and homage of all classes; the Queen was said to be overcome by the sight.

That evening, the Queen returned to her favorite theatre—the Italian Opera at Her Majesty's—with Albert and the ubiquitous Mensdorffs. They arrived just after the national anthem was sung and the opera had begun. The full house greeted Victoria with thunderous huzzahs, waving hats and handkerchiefs, refusing to let the opera proceed until they had sung the anthem again, bursting into applause at the end of every line, and screaming "deafening acclamations" at the song's command "Scatter her enemies." The crowd, unfortunately, were unable to transfer an iota of their enthusiasm for the Queen to the opera itself, a production of Mercadante's *Elena da Feltre,* called by a critic an "abortion" and "utterly worthless and common-place." The crowd responded to the opera with apathy, when not actually hissing. Again, the royal couple were the star performers at Her Majesty's.

In the House of Commons earlier that afternoon, Robert Peel, in agreeing to a joint Parliamentary address to the Queen, revealed for the first time news of Francis's first attack on Sunday, and that the Queen—in Peel's words, "relying with confidence in the generous loyalty of her people with a determination not to be confined as a prisoner in her own palace"—had ridden on Monday with a full awareness of the threat against her. Peel also praised the Queen's consideration for her ladies, in refusing to subject them to the danger that she willingly faced. (Lady Portman's brother in the House of Commons, and her husband in the House of Lords, emotionally concurred.) With the dissemination of that news, the spontaneous celebration took on a different tenor. Albert's secretary Anson noted the difference, writing in his journal that "the feeling now was of a deeper cast" than it had been after Oxford's attempt. Over the next days, newspaper editors and speakers at hundreds of congratulatory meetings across the country waxed enthusiastically about Victoria's chivalric heroism: her calmness and resolution; her "kindness . . . consideration . . . generosity." A poem in Wednesday's *Times* held Victoria "A King in courage, though by sex a Queen/Our lion-hearted monarch. . . ." A writer in the *Morning Chronicle* wrote "we feel sure that it is no flattery to say that a finer instance of mingled heroism and generosity than this would be difficult to find; and it will deepen, if possible, the affection and the admiration so universally felt for her Majesty's character by her subjects."

The Queen, it seemed, could do no wrong. Few considered (publicly, anyway) the Queen's facing the bullet of an assailant with no more than the bodies of her equerry and his horse to protect her to be an astoundingly foolhardy risk. The clearheaded Charles Greville, writing privately in his diary, was one of the few at the time to see it that way: her action he thought "very brave, but imprudent. It would have been better to stay at home, or go to Claremont, and let the police look for the man, or to have taken some precautionary measures."

Commissioner Charles Rowan could not have agreed more with Greville: it was his understanding that the queen *would* be prudent and stay at home, while the police went about weeding out the shooter. He was well aware of how close a call this attempt had been, and knew that if Francis had succeeded, his police would have suffered the opprobrium of the public and the wrath of the government. Trounce's nearly fatal salute demonstrated the danger of trusting royal protection to officers untrained for the job. But more than this, the miscommunication between the Palace, the Home Office, and Scotland Yard made it clear to Rowan that threats against the Queen could not be dealt with on the spur of the moment. The newspapers were not slow to take to task the police and the government for offering the Queen so little protection. The *Globe*, for instance, held that "the Queen's bravery is more impressive when contrasted with the ministers' apathy" and thundered in particular at Home Secretary Graham's "unaccountable disregard" for the Queen's safety, given that he knew about the threat the day before she rode on Monday: no precautions seem to have been taken, such as the posting of extra police on the Queen's route. This was not completely fair, but Rowan was well aware that the police should have and could have done better. First Good, then Cooper, and now Francis: three high-profile cases that exposed all the weaknesses of a police force committed to prevention and not detection of crime. The department had to change. For years Rowan's younger and in effect junior co-commissioner Richard Mayne had favored a detective branch, and had quietly been acting unofficially in creating one, setting aside one officer in each division, for example, to trace stolen goods, and creating "special officers" whose duties included plainclothes work and detection. But Waterloo veteran Charles Rowan, the prime mover behind the military structure of the police when the department was formed in 1829, had long resisted any official action. No longer. Rowan now threw his influence and energy behind its official establishment.

Within two weeks of Francis's attempt, on 14 June, the Commissioners forwarded a memorandum to Graham at the Home Office. Their proposal was a modest one, calling for two detective inspectors and eight detective sergeants, all to be stationed at Scotland Yard and to be paid slightly more than their uniformed counterparts. Two days later, Graham replied through his permanent undersecretary. He was interested. But he had some questions. What was the cost to be—and where was the money to come from? And how were the ten detectives (in a city, by the way, of two million) to keep themselves busy when their detective services were not needed?

Rowan and Mayne responded quickly. The cost was to be less than £1,000 a year, to be drawn out of the general police funds. And, when they were not actively pursuing a case, detectives would keep busy by penetrating and exploring the criminal underworld—gaining that omniscient knowledge of crime and criminals that Charles Dickens, who later became the most enthusiastic and vocal fan of the detective branch, declared to be one of their strongest assets.

On the twentieth, Graham agreed to their proposal, but reduced the number of sergeants from eight to six. The commissioners had created a detective branch in all of six days.

Filling the positions was quickly done, as well; Mayne had probably long had a list in mind for this occasion. The experienced Pearce was to take charge as Senior Inspector; his junior colleague was to be John Haynes from P Division. Pearce's aide, Sgt. Thornton, was to take the lead among the six sergeants.

eleven

POWDER AND WADDING

John Francis's family was devastated by the news that their son and brother had shot at the Queen. His delicate mother, Elizabeth, "was seized with the most alarming illness" upon hearing the news, her husband fearing for her life. Her precarious state did not prevent the police from searching their Tottenham Court lodgings the night of and day after Francis's capture, searching for evidence of an accomplice. (They found nothing.) It was up to John Francis Senior to follow his son from the Home Office to prison, and to hire a solicitor.

Francis himself attempted in Newgate to project the sense that his act had been little more than a frolic, but the persistence with which he repeatedly claimed "there was no ball in the pistol; it only flashed in the pan" to warders, to the governor, to reporters, belied his anxiety about the enormity of the penalty he faced, if not of the crime itself. Still, he was hopeful: surely, everyone knew he could not have harmed the Queen, since his gun was not loaded?

The fact that this was the second attempt on the Queen's life in as many years made the motivation of these young assailants an urgent question. Many were completely perplexed: Victoria's youth, her virtue, her gender should guarantee her freedom from any attempt on her life. But a consensus was building. The reports of Oxford's comfortable confinement were well known, and appeared to most to be a reward of sorts, as freedom from the hardship of poverty and "the disagreeable condition of perpetually collecting pewter pots." It seemed obvious that Francis wished for what Oxford had—a life of ease at the Queen's pleasure. The crowd that formed outside Buckingham Palace on the night of the attempt agreed, claiming (according to an eavesdropping policeman) that "his only motive could be like Oxford to ensure a situation for life." On hearing of Francis's attempt, Oxford himself claimed that "If they had hanged me, there would have been nothing of the kind again." But there was more to it than this. The instant fame he gained from the attempt was just as important to Oxford as it was to his imitator, Francis. A writer in the *Examiner* described the thrill that these boys experienced in being charged and tried for High Treason. The procedure "flatters the diseased appetite for *éclat* and notoriety which prompted Oxford's attempt, and has probably also been one of the motives of Francis— messengers hurrying hither and thither in search of Ministers—the pomp and circumstance of examination before the Privy Council, instead of the quiet undramatic course of an examination in the nearest dingy police-office before the sort of magistrate who is the habitual terror of the sort of prisoner." As long as assailants were treated as the chief players in "State pageants," this sort of crime would happen again; the law as it stood was an encouragement, not a deterrent, to the crime.

But that was the law; the government had no other option than to try Francis for High Treason. His trial was scheduled for Friday 17 June. Thomas Cooper, now in Newgate's infirmary suffering from the effects of the poison he had taken, would face trial the next day, the eighteenth.

Both Francis's defense and his prosecution prepared their cases with Oxford's trial in mind. Francis's barrister William Clarkson, a hardheaded, "rough, bluff, testy personage," had no intention of mounting an insanity defense. Public anger at Oxford's sentence, rekindled by Francis's attempt, made it unlikely that any jury would acquit Francis for that reason, even if the defense could succeed at the difficult task of finding witnesses to testify to mad behavior on Francis's part. Moreover, Oxford's acquittal for insanity had ironically resulted in what amounted to imprisonment for life. If Sydney Taylor had forgone an insanity plea and simply argued that Oxford's pistols were not loaded, Oxford would almost certainly have walked from the Old Bailey a free man. Taylor's two-pronged defense only confused the jury and resulted in a muddled verdict. In Francis's case, there was no substantial evidence that his flintlock was loaded. Clarkson would concede that Francis bought a gun, that he pulled it out on the Mall on Sunday, and that he presented it and fired it, without ball, on Constitution Hill on Monday. He would produce no witnesses to counter these facts; rather, he would oppose the prosecution's attempts to suggest that the gun was loaded. If Francis had no bullets in his gun, Clarkson would argue, he could not have intended to harm the Queen. Therefore, Francis's public disturbance was certainly illegal, and prosecutable as a lesser charge, but it did not amount to High Treason. His entire case, then, would hinge upon the claim that Francis had had only powder and wadding in his pistol.

The prosecution was formidable, composed of Attorney General Frederick Pollock (who had helped prosecute Oxford), Solicitor General William Webb Follett, and three others. They must have been delighted to learn that Clarkson had no intention of arguing insanity. Two years before, an insanity verdict and detention at the Queen's pleasure seemed a victory of sorts for the government. But the general sense that Oxford had improved his life by committal to Bethlem, and the prevailing belief that his committal positively incited malcontents to attack the Queen, would now render that outcome the worst of defeats.

They were well aware that the weak link to their case was a lack of hard proof that Francis's gun had been loaded. Despite their strenuous efforts, the police had not found any shopkeeper in London who had sold Francis bullets. No spent bullet was found after the attempt, and even though Francis had fired at the Queen from seven feet away, no bullet had done damage to her, her equerry, his horse, or her carriage. They planned two strategies to deal with this weak link. First they would introduce evidence that the *sound* of Francis's shot suggested that his gun was loaded. Second, they would argue that it was not at all necessary to prove that Francis's gun was loaded: even if it wasn't, he was *still* guilty of High Treason.

To this end, the government very carefully articulated the indictment against Francis, breaking it down into eight counts. Four held that Francis did "compass, imagine, devise, and intend" to kill the Queen; four held that he endangered her life. And each of these charges consisted of four counts—differing in degree, but still amounting to High Treason. Count 1 held that Francis's gun contained gunpowder and a bullet; count 2 held that it contained gunpowder and "certain other destructive materials and substances unknown"; count 3 held that Francis fired a loaded pistol; and count 4 held that Francis simply fired a pistol. Arguably, by that last count, Francis could be found guilty for High Treason simply by firing an unloaded weapon at the Queen. Clarkson's strategy was to argue that the evidence did not reach the high bar set for High Treason. The prosecution's strategy was to lower the bar.

John Francis was placed in the dock of the Old Bailey on the morning of 18 June, well dressed in a black suit, to viewers discernibly handsome—and deeply anxious. Two weeks of jailers' and visitors' disappointingly impassive responses to his claims that his gun was unloaded, and that he had no intention to harm the Queen, had destroyed the "most perfect *sang froid*" with which he had entered Newgate. And since there was to be no insanity defense, he knew he would not be sharing Oxford's enviable fate, whatever happened. Outside, huge crowds pressed to enter the courtroom. But the sheriffs only admitted those with written orders: the room was full but not uncomfortably so. Francis was far less concerned than Oxford had been at the quality of his audience: his attention from the start was fixed on his own barrister, William Clarkson, on the three judges above him, led by Nicholas Conyngham Tindal, Chief Justice of the Court of Common Pleas, and upon the five prosecutors who sought his life. He bowed respectfully to the court, and was read the elaborate charges against him. "Not Guilty," he said, in a low voice.

Attorney General Pollock laid out the prosecution's case. After describing the assault and praising the Queen's bravery, he focused on the fact that no bullet was found. Was that really surprising? Any number of materials could substitute for a lead bullet, he argued: "A child's marble—why, gentlemen, the very gravel path he was treading might have furnished him with a stone smooth or angular, quite adequate to the purpose in view." Demanding the proof that a bullet existed to prove an attack, moreover, defied simple common sense. "Why, gentlemen," he said to the jury, "put the case for yourself; make it for a moment your own. If at some distance from a wife or sister of your own you were to perceive a stranger deliberately aim firearms at the object of your regard, and were to see that succeeded by the discharge of a pistol or a gun, and you had to advance to seize the assassin, as you would deem him, and he were to turn round and quietly say, 'Before you take me into custody I beg you will show that I had a bullet in that pistol I have just discharged,' what would you think?" They had the evidence of the act—and the act itself demonstrated his intent to harm the Queen.

Then came the witnesses, who established that Francis bought gun, flint, and powder, and that he was the one on Constitution Hill who fired a pistol at the Queen's carriage as it drove by. None of this evidence was surprising. But one witness was. Young George Pearson, brought forward as the only witness who could testify to

Francis's first attempt, astonished all who had heard him stutter badly through his account two weeks before: now he spoke fluidly, unhaltingly: for the last two weeks he had been taken in hand by a creator and purveyor of a treatment for stammering, Thomas Hunt, and apparently cured.*

The defense contested nothing, except for any testimony suggesting that Francis fired directly at the Queen, or that his gun was loaded. In response to two witnesses who claimed the former, Clarkson called a witness from the prosecution's list who maintained Francis had aimed at the hind wheels of the Queen's carriage. When the second witness, Henry Allen of the Coldstream Guards (the soldier who grabbed Francis immediately after Trounce did) pronounced his opinion that the sound of Francis's shot was consistent with a loaded gun ("a piece fired off with ball sounds somewhat sharper than blank cartridge"), Clarkson in cross-examination chipped away at his ballistics expertise: he was a private; he had been in the army for only a year and on drill for three or four months; he was a tailor before he joined the army. When Chief Justice Tindal recalled the first witness, the Queen's Equerry Arbuthnot, to establish that he, too, thought the pistol was loaded, Clarkson pressed him to the point of retraction: it may or may not have been loaded, but in any case the powder was "well rammed down."

At this point, the Chief Justice introduced an idea that essentially destroyed Francis's defense. "Now," he asked Arbuthnot, "what I want to know is, whether a pistol fired from the spot where the prisoner stood, if only loaded with wadding, would cause injury to the Queen?" Arbuthnot's "decided opinion" was that it would. Attorney General Pollock quickly took the hint, and elicited from another military witness—Albert's equerry, Colonel Wylde—the possible fatal properties of paper wadding, fired at very close range: "At seven to nine feet the wadding of the pistol would wound the

---

* It was perhaps Hunt's most celebrated case, and within a week he was advertising his success in the *Times*, to drum up business.

skin or any exposed part, such as the face, or set fire to the dress."
Clarkson must have realized to his growing dismay that his central
claim—that the gun was empty *except* for powder and wadding—
would quite possibly not win this case.

Clarkson called no witnesses of his own. He argued that all of the
facts established by the prosecution indeed established that a crime
had taken place—but not the crime with which he was charged.
Edward Oxford's motive was to gratify "morbid feeling and wretched
vanity" by attaining notoriety. He became "ten times better off than
he was before he committed the act." Isn't it likely that Francis had no
intention whatsoever to harm the Queen, but rather "hoped to render
himself notorious in the eyes of the people, and to make himself an
important personage, and also to better his condition?" Certainly,
he deserved punishment for that—but punishment in another court,
under another charge: his act did not amount to High Treason. As
for the notion of lethal wadding, Clarkson had nothing to say beyond
the nebulous, baffled, and baffling "I know that the books state, and
so do my learned friends, that you must give evidence of the pistols
being loaded beyond powder and wadding."

The Solicitor General, responding to Clarkson's speech, argued
that it was impossible to be certain about motives in this case. It was
necessary to consider the act itself. And everything about Francis's
act suggested an attempt to harm the Queen.

Judge Tindal, in summing up, returned to the wadding, pro-
nouncing that its existence in the pistol alone was enough to establish guilt. ". . . though there were no ball or destructive materials,"
he instructed the jury, "yet there might have been powder and wadding, which being fired off so close to the Royal person must have
been intended to do bodily harm as the necessary consequence." If
the jury believed this to be the case, then they must find Francis
guilty on the third count. Twice more before finishing his summation, Tindal brought up the wadding.

He finished at 4:29. The jury conferred for a moment and asked
leave to discuss the verdict in private. They withdrew; Francis was

removed from the court. Clarkson then objected vociferously to Tindal's instructions to the jury, and his repeated emphasis upon the wadding. The charge against Francis was that he attacked the Queen intending to endanger her life: and the fact that there was a piece of paper to hold the powder in Francis's pistol surely did not suggest that intent.

The jury returned half an hour later, and Francis was brought back, breathing heavily and "very much agitated." They had a verdict—and, like Oxford's verdict, it was muddled. The foreman said "we find the prisoner Guilty on the second and third counts. We think there is a doubt on the first. . . ." The second count suggested (if it didn't explicitly hold) that there was something more than powder and wadding in the pistol. The third did not. The initial verdict, then, pointed to some disagreement or confusion on the part of the jury. Judge Tindal thus pressed the foreman for clarity. Did the jury find the prisoner guilty on the first count? No. On the second? Yes. "You think the pistol was loaded with something more than the wadding—with some other destructive substance?" "Yes, my Lord." The verdict was recorded: guilty of High Treason—specifically of firing a pistol containing "destructive materials and substances" at the Queen. That verdict, according to a court reporter, "rendered Mr. Clarkson's objection immaterial." Not quite. Whether all of the jury agreed on both the second and third counts is unclear. And what the "destructive materials" besides wadding might be, and what evidence led the jury to that conclusion, is hard to imagine. Quite possibly, the paper stuffed in his flintlock ensured Francis's guilt.

The Clerk of the Arraigns spoke. "John Francis, you stand convicted of high treason: what have you to say why the court should not give you judgment to die according to the law?" Pale and quivering, Francis said nothing. He waited in agonized silence for a few minutes while black caps were fetched and placed on the judges' heads. Tindal then pronounced Francis's guilt, and passed sentence: ". . . that you, John Francis, be taken hence to the place from whence you came, and that you be drawn from thence on a hurdle to the place of execution, and there hanged by the neck until you are dead; that afterwards your head be severed from your body, and your body divided into four quarters, and be disposed of as Her Majesty may think fit, and may the Lord God Almighty have mercy on your soul!"

The usher's "Amen" rang out like a death knell.

Francis sobbed convulsively, fell back in a faint into the arms of his jailers, and was dragged from the court.

The next morning was Thomas Cooper's turn at the bar. This time, there was no clamor to obtain a seat, the public seemingly sated with sensational trials. Or, perhaps, this one did not promise to be quite as sensational as Good's or Francis's. To a reporter for the *Morning Chronicle*, the relatively empty courtroom presented a clear sign of a jaded population, which "seems to require stimulants of an extraordinary nature to arouse it. . . . Poor Daly was only shot. *He was not cut up!*"

At ten, Judges Patteson and Gurney, who had assisted Judge Tindal the day before, took their places on the bench. Cooper was immediately brought into the dock. Still suffering the effects of his self-administered arsenic and laudanum, he was allowed to sit in a chair. He appeared at the same time ferocious, brutal, and idiotic: unable or unwilling to follow the events of the next thirteen hours.

His barrister, Sidney Calder Horry, held a bad hand, and he knew it. The prosecution—led by Mr. Bodkin*—would be offering up a host of eyewitnesses to the shootings of Moss and Mott and the killing of Daly. As far as he could see, the only way to avoid the death penalty was with a desperate attempt to prove Cooper insane. Hadfield's and Oxford's trials, which Horry was to cite often this day, would provide the model; he would make use of medical

---

* Bodkin had, two years before, helped prosecute Courvoisier and helped defend Oxford.

witnesses to suggest insanity, and introduce family members, neighbors, and acquaintances to testify to Cooper's lifetime of odd behavior. But Cooper was no Hadfield or Oxford. This trial played out as a ludicrous parody of those two.

The prosecution's witnesses methodically established all of Cooper's actions on the fifth of May, from his confrontation with Moss to his eventual apprehension, bringing forth no fewer than seven eyewitnesses to establish that he wounded Mott and killed Daly. Horry largely refrained from challenging any of this evidence. When, however, Edward Drury, the surgeon who examined Daly's body at the scene of his death, came to the stand, Horry launched into an energetic cross-examination—concerning not the state of Daly's body, but rather the state of his client's mind. Would a person who exhibited continual wakefulness have an affected brain? Or a person who showed no pain when his arm was scalded with boiling water? What about a person with a ravenous appetite, or filthy habits—or who claimed he was King Richard at times, and Dick Turpin at others—or who claimed he "should have his father up out of his grave, as there was no use in his lying there": was such a person mad? Drury resisted stating that any of these symptoms signified insanity, but did concede that all of them together might suggest unsoundness. Nevertheless, his unshakeable opinion was that Cooper was sane.

Having thus used Drury to lay the groundwork for his plea as best he could, Horry sought to establish that everything about Cooper—his actions of shooting policemen and refusing to give up when cornered on the day Daly died, his lack of empathy for his mother, his love of pistols, as well as his insomnia, ravenousness, and filthiness—pointed to his derangement. Cooper's odd behavior had all begun with a bout of "putrid fever" at twenty months old, after which he was never the same. Cooper's mother Isabella was the central witness to her son's insanity: under questioning, she dutifully and suspiciously ticked off every single symptom that Horry had brought out in questioning Drury. Neighbors, and

Cooper's two brothers, were brought forward apparently to corroborate Isabella Cooper's testimony. They could do little more than establish that Cooper was pathologically suicidal, and that he had the economically questionable habit of taking apart and putting together clocks and watches—his brother James claiming that "he once bought a silver watch for 14s., and picked it to pieces. He then sold it for 7s., which he gave for a metal one. He picked that to pieces also, put it together again, and sold it for 1s."

The prosecution was well prepared to respond to the claim of insanity by establishing that Cooper's behavior was simply criminal, not lunatic. They called forth a number of witnesses to establish Cooper's brutal criminal acts, and called a number of policemen, all well acquainted with Cooper, and including the hated Inspector Penny, to vouch for his sanity. The parish beadle, the jailer at Clerkenwell Police Court, and Governor Cope of Newgate did the same. Two medical witnesses who had examined Cooper in Newgate took the stand; both judged him perfectly sane. The first of these witnesses, Mr. Fisher, revealed that he examined Cooper in the presence of two other medical gentlemen, obviously specialists that the defense had asked examine Cooper. They were tellingly absent at this trial, and Horry was left without a specialist to advocate the insanity plea. He was thus forced, in his closing statement, to discredit the medical gentlemen. They did not examine Cooper long enough, he argued. They neglected to speak with members of Cooper's family. Most remarkable of all: the "regimen and restraint" of Newgate had had a deeply therapeutic effect on his client, *restoring* Cooper's sanity by the time he was examined.

Justice Patteson, summing up, claimed that the facts of the shootings were established beyond dispute, and so restricted his comments to the insanity defense. He reminded the jury that in the case of that plea, the burden of proof lay with the defense: "every person who had arrived at the age of discretion must be considered sane until he was proved to be otherwise." The question in this case was simply whether at the time of the shooting Cooper knew that he was doing wrong. If he did, the jury must find him guilty; if he did not, they must acquit him.

The jury had little to discuss. They huddled for a moment in the jury box and then pronounced Cooper guilty. The two judges put on their black caps (this time, apparently, close at hand). Debilitated or not, Cooper was ordered to stand while Patteson pronounced the sentence, and he rose with a "savage scowl." While Patteson catalogued his crimes, Cooper's mind wandered; he turned to look at his nemesis, Inspector Penny, sitting with other witnesses tantalizingly close to the dock. He suddenly lunged at Penny, and shook his fist at the officer as the jailers on either side pulled him back.

"You had better listen to me. You had better listen to me, prisoner, instead of shaking your fist at any one there," Justice Patteson said. He then exhorted him to use his little time remaining to come to a better state of mind, and pronounced sentence: to be taken to the place of public execution, hung by the neck until dead, and buried, as Courvoisier and Good had been, in the bowels of Newgate. "And may the Lord have mercy on your soul."

With the usher's "Amen," Cooper burst into a frenzied rage and tried to tear an inkwell out of the bar of the dock. Failing in this, he instead again shook his fist and hurled threats of vengeance against all the witnesses; the two turnkeys dragged him toward the underground passage and to his death watch at Newgate.

Francis and Cooper thus faced a similar fate—but in different ways. John Francis was ruined; his grand plans to make something of himself had come to this: absolute disgrace, almost certain death, and the possible mutilation of his corpse, if that was the pleasure of the Queen and her advisers. When returned to his cell after his trial, he collapsed into a seat, moaning and weeping, wailing once again that he had not meant to kill or injure the Queen: he just wanted the notoriety that Oxford had gotten by seeming to shoot at her. James Carver, the prison chaplain, attended to him, helpfully exhorting Francis to prepare for death: the public was "exasperated against him," and the newspapers accurately trumpeted that opinion. As if in concurrence, the *Times* on the next day ran an editorial that predicted, based on Justice Tindal's "grave and solemn" way of passing verdict, that Francis would indeed be executed. He deserved it, for his "cold-blooded cruelty" in attacking the Queen. Even if his pistol was unloaded, he deserved to die, as an example to others, and for the "shock to all good" in his act.

And yet, reports about Francis and his behavior that trickled out of Newgate over the next few days portrayed a pitiful boy rather than a depraved would-be killer. When—covering his face with shame— he spoke with his father the day after the trial, he claimed he never meant to harm the Queen, that he knew "there could be no pretence for entertaining a single thought to her prejudice or against her sacred person." The reporter for the *Morning Chronicle* reporting this scene held that Francis was weak-minded and impressionable: the "noise" of Oxford's attempt, the "ridiculous sympathy" many had for Oxford, and the recent reports of his comfortable life at Bethlem were simply too much for Francis to resist.

He reportedly became a model prisoner after the trial, remarkable for his mildness and humility and his attentiveness to Rev. Mr. Carver's ministrations.

Thomas Cooper's behavior, on the other hand, acted as a foil to Francis's. Cooper expected no reprieve; he wished death to come as soon as possible. After all, he had wanted to die many times before this. Like Francis, Cooper was meekly attentive to the chaplain. In his absence, however, Cooper generally reverted to his natural state of rage, sputtering curses and threats of violence against the Metropolitan Police. His only regret was that he could not hurt them or the witnesses against him. He would go to his unmarked grave hating life and hating them. The public, reading reports of the two, were clearly getting the sense that there was a good thief and a bad one in Newgate.

On the Thursday after the trials, the sheriffs announced the date for both executions: 4 July—eleven days away. Francis received the news with "heart-rending despair." His family, in the meantime, worked to save his life. John Francis Senior sent his petition for clemency to the Queen via Home Secretary Graham, protesting his utter devotion and loyalty, noting his years of servitude to Victoria at Covent Garden, hinting that his wife's tenuous hold on life depended completely upon the survival of her son, and arguing—in the face of the verdict in his son's trial—that the pistol was not loaded, and that his son had no intention of hurting the Queen. Francis's sister Jane wrote her own petition, and sought a different avenue to the Queen: poignantly, but with no knowledge of the recent seismic shifts in influence at the Palace, she sent hers through Baroness Lehzen. In it she repeatedly begged the Queen to consider Francis's afflicted family, and humbly submitted that Francis had never intended to harm the Queen. At least three other groups drew up petitions to Graham or the Queen. The Queen sent the ones she received to the Home Office: her government would decide Francis's fate.

Almost certainly against Cooper's wishes, his mother drew up a petition for her son as well, pleading for a delay in the execution to further examine her son for evidence of insanity. Thirty neighbors signed the petition, claiming that they were willing to testify to Cooper's insanity, but were not able to attend the trial. She delivered this to the Home Secretary on Thursday the twenty-third; two days later, she had her answer from the undersecretary: "I am directed to express to you [Graham's] regret that there is no sufficient ground to justify him consistently with his public duty in advising her Majesty to comply with the prayer thereof."

Cooper's fate, then, was sealed, but the fact that there was no response yet to any of the petitions for Francis augured well for him. Still, nothing was decided for another week, and on the last day of June, when Francis met with his family for the last time before the execution date, it might have been the last time ever. It was a scene of "a most distressing character," according to a witness.

Unbeknownst to them, however, his fate had been decided. Two days earlier, the judges in his case had met, made their decision, and sent it on to the cabinet, which made theirs. On Saturday 1 July, Peel reported the decision to Prince Albert: Francis's sentence would be commuted to transportation for life, at hard labor. He was to serve in the colony's harshest penal colony. It was all the Francises could hope for. Others wondered whether the commutation was a mercy at all. The young poet Elizabeth Barrett, for one, thought not. "Norfolk Island is scarcely safety*—prolonged agony it certainly is," she wrote to a friend.

Victoria and Albert had softened their attitude toward Francis in the month since the shooting, coming to the conclusion that his pistols were not loaded: "the feeling that he is to be executed is very painful to me," Victoria wrote in her journal. And when she learned of the commutation she wrote "I of course am glad." But, she added, "Albert & I are of the same opinion, that the law ought to be changed, & more security afforded to me." The death penalty seemed an excessive punishment for Oxford's or Francis's assaults—and transportation for life (or, for that matter, commitment to Bethlem) had dubious deterrent value. What they needed was a new law, specifically designed for Oxford's and Francis's crime—with a penalty befitting the crime, one that would shame the offender, not give him the dubious elevation of national notoriety.

Robert Peel agreed, and set out to create such a law.

Peel and his cabinet resolved to remove Francis from England as quickly as possible. A convict ship, the *Marquis of Hastings*, had arrived in Portsmouth on 24 June to take on convicts for the voyage around Cape Hope and to Van Diemen's Land. Francis would be on that ship. He remained in Newgate long enough to hear the

---

*   Francis actually was transported to Port Arthur, Van Diemen's Land, and not to Norfolk Island.

ominous sermon in the prison chapel on the eve of Cooper's execution. He remained in his cell on Monday 4 July while Cooper was hanged. Two days later, on the sixth, he was clapped in heavy irons and one of Newgate's chief jailers conveyed him by the South-western Railway to Gosport. On the eighteenth, he embarked. "The opinion is that he will not long survive the hardships consequent on the fulfillment of his sentence," wrote a writer in the *Examiner*. Francis was to prove that writer wrong.

The authorities had removed him as quickly as they could. But Francis had not even left Newgate before he learned that another had eclipsed his notoriety as the Queen's latest assailant.

twelve

HUNCHBACKED LITTLE
MISCREANT

The young man—the boy—stood under the elms close to where John Francis had stood five weeks before. It was around noontime on the hot sunny Sunday of 3 July 1842, and he had positioned himself behind and apart from the crowd of high-spirited Londoners who had assembled on either side of the Mall, two or three deep, to view the Queen's cortège make its usual Sunday trip from Buckingham Palace to St. James's and the Chapel Royal. He must have looked like a fool in his dark, oversized coat, but he had to keep it on for two reasons: he was homeless, carrying all his possessions on his back; and he needed it to conceal the small flintlock pistol at his breast. He was sweating, he was dirty; he smelled. He hardly saw himself as a human being. John William Bean Junior was seventeen and tired to death of his life.

The world found him repulsive. His vertebrae, devastated by disease—perhaps extrapulmonary tuberculosis—curved in an S and slumped into a conspicuous hump over his right shoulder. His head hung at little more than four feet off the ground—if that. His arms were atrophied sticks, his hands those of a young child. When he walked, his twisted body lurched in the direction of his hump. His eyes sunk into his head. His expression was permanently careworn and weary. As a final indignity, God or happenstance had marred his face with a scar or a blotch about his nose.

It is possible that but for his scoliotic spine, he would not be a dwarf at all.* The world did not make such fine distinctions; to anyone who stared at him, he was a hunchbacked dwarf and a freak. Literary hunchbacks and dwarves were prevalent in the popular culture of the early 1840s, shaping and reflecting popular attitudes toward people like him. First, there was Quasimodo, the pitiful and repulsive Pope of Fools out of Victor Hugo's *Notre-Dame de Paris*, a book as popular with the British as with the French since its first English translation came out nine years before. Quasimodo's greatest folly was to believe that others could love him in spite of his deformity; he paid with his life for that belief. More recently—just last year, in fact—Charles Dickens had endowed the villain of his *The Old Curiosity Shop*, the dwarf Daniel Quilp, with every imaginable evil: he is a bitter, wife-beating, pedophiliac sociopath. Quilp's supernatural vitality, crammed into a too-small body, curdles into ceaseless misanthropic rage. He is antithetical in every way besides size to the virtuous, loving and beloved heroine

---

* On the other hand, he might have been unnaturally short even without the spinal curvature. Estimates of John Bean's height varied considerably—from 3'6" to 5'6". The most careful estimate may have been by an eyewitness to Bean's naked body, who claimed Bean's scoliosis rendered his height 3'6" when he would otherwise stand at 4'6", making him a hunchback *and* a dwarf, in the cruel vernacular of the day.

ABOVE: *The Marriage of Queen Victoria and Prince Albert, 10 February 1840,* by George Hayter. Three months after the wedding, as Victoria posed for this painting, Edward Oxford bought the pistols with which he shot at the royal couple. Courtesy of The Royal Collection © 2012, Her Majesty Queen Elizabeth II. RIGHT: A portrait of Edward Oxford from *Bell's New Weekly Messenger,* 12 July 1840. As crude as it is, the illustration well captures Oxford's pretensions to a higher status and his desperate resolve to "make a noise" in the world by whatever means.

EDWARD OXFORD,
TRIED AT THE CENTRAL CRIMINAL COURT
FOR SHOOTING AT
THE QUEEN AND PRINCE ALBERT,
IN St. JAMES'S PARK.

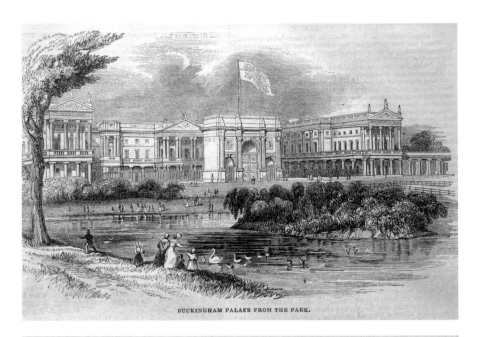

BUCKINGHAM PALACE FROM THE PARK.

OXFORD'S ATTEMPT TO ASSASSINATE THE QUEEN AND PRINCE ALBERT.
On Constitution Hill, Wednesday Evening, June 10 1840.

Published by T. Lyne, 8 Paternoster Row, June 17, 1840.

ABOVE: Buckingham Palace as it appeared in 1842. The now-familiar east façade had not yet been built, and the Marble Arch, not yet moved to the corner of Hyde Park, still served as the main gate. All but one of the attempts on the Queen took place near Buckingham Palace. From the *Illustrated London News*. BELOW: Oxford's attempt, 10 June 1840, on Constitution Hill: Oxford was a "little mean looking man," according to Prince Albert.

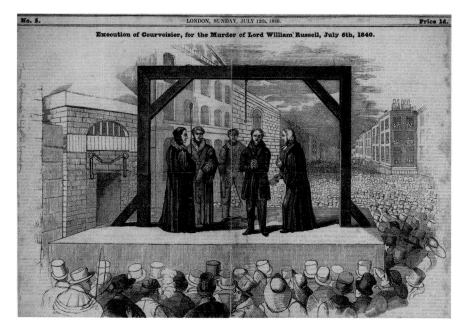

Execution of Courvoisier, for the Murder of Lord William Russell, July 6th, 1840.

ABOVE: The execution of François Benjamin Courvoisier for the murder of Lord William Russell, 6 July 1840. While Courvoisier was hanged outside Newgate Prison, Edward Oxford occupied a cell within, awaiting his trial for treason. The print conveys some idea of the many thousands who came to watch Courvoisier die. Two years later, John Francis would stand in an even larger crowd to witness the execution of Daniel Good. From *Tom Spring's Life in London*. BELOW: *Queen Victoria and Prince Albert at the Bal Costumé of 12 May 1842,* by Edwin Landseer. The royal couple held the ball during that impoverished year in order to ameliorate poverty, but many found their conspicuous display of wealth disturbing. Less than three weeks after the Ball, John Francis made his two attempts. Courtesy of The Royal Collection ©2012, Her Majesty Queen Elizabeth II.

THE PRISONER BEAN.
BY THE OBSERVER'S OWN CORRESPONDENT.

TOP: John Francis's second attempt and capture, 30 May 1842, from *Illustrated London News*. Grabbing him is P.C. Trounce (wearing the Metropolitan Police uniform of the day). Trounce's decision to salute the Queen allowed Francis the opportunity to get off a shot—although whether he fired a bullet or just wadding became a central question at his trial. BOTTOM: The police roundup of hunchbacked dwarves in the wake of John William Bean's attempt of 3 July 1842, as depicted in *Punch* magazine, in which Punch himself is among those captured.

TOP: Victoria's first Prime Minister William Lamb, 2nd Viscount Melbourne, with whom she shared a close bond at the time of Edward Oxford's attempt. Courtesy of the National Portrait Gallery, London BOTTOM: Robert Peel, Victoria's second Prime Minister. The Queen's initial repulsion to Peel had under Albert's influence changed to respect and affection by 1842, the year of Francis's and Bean's attempts. Courtesy of the National Portrait Gallery, London.

William Ewart Gladstone, the prime minister Victoria most despised, and the one who did the most to strengthen her monarchy. Courtesy of the National Portrait Gallery, London.

RIGHT: Lord John Russell, prime minister at the time of Hamilton's and Pate's attempts in 1849 and 1850. Courtesy of the National Portrait Gallery, London. BELOW: Henry John Temple, 3rd Viscount Palmerston, who as Foreign Secretary drove Victoria and Albert to a state of distraction. Palmerston's stunning speech in the 1850 Don Pacifico debate, given two days before Robert Pate struck the Queen, saved his career and confirmed him as the most popular politician of the day. Courtesy of the National Portrait Gallery, London.

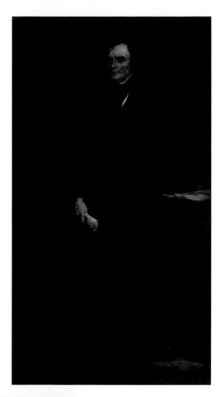

The Opening of the Great Exhibition by Queen Victoria on 1 May 1851, by Henry Courtney Selous. Victoria proclaimed this day the greatest of her life. She stands with Albert and her two eldest children, diplomats and dignitaries arrayed before them. Foremost in the group on the right is He-Sing, owner of a Chinese junk, and Victoria's benign assailant on this day. Courtesy of the Victoria and Albert Museum.

of the book, Little Nell.* And then there was that timeless comic monstrosity, that mixture of clownishness, viciousness, and irrepressible energy—Punch. The hunchbacked puppet had been the king of British street performance for nearly two hundred years, but less than a year before, he had been resurrected and revitalized as the acerbic star of the extremely popular humor magazine *Punch*, always laughing at British society from his perspective as an outsider. Hunchbacks, dwarves—hunchbacked dwarves: they were laughable, or pitiful, or repulsive as freaks—but in any case they were *other*, never quite human. John William Bean was physically and mentally debilitated by his differences. "I shall never be otherwise than I am," the seventeen-year-old had said more than once in despair to his father. "I shall resemble no man, and yet I am fast approaching to manhood."

He had lived in the neighborhood of Clerkenwell. His father, John William Bean Senior, was (as Edward Oxford's father had been) a gold-chaser, and he encouraged his son to become his apprentice. John Bean tried and kept trying to succeed at that profession, but the painstaking work was simply too exhausting for his pitiful limbs. He sought easier occupations, but his apprenticeship to a cheesemonger resulted in failure, as did a job as an errand boy at Her Majesty's Stationery Office. Most recently, he had been working Sundays for a news vendor, Mr. Hilton. That job had suited him the best, for, besides the short hours, Hilton allowed him to read in the afternoon the Sunday papers he sold in the morning. Two months before, he had come across in this way several articles on Edward Oxford, exposing his life of ease in Bethlem: a pint of wine to drink a day! A personal tutor to teach him German and French! He had spoken both to Mr. Hilton and his father about

---

* Interestingly, *The Old Curiosity Shop* may be the one work of literature to contain a portrait of one of Victoria's would-be assassins: in chapter 28 the illustrator of that novel, Hablôt K. Browne—"Phiz"—anachronistically but unmistakably places a beerpot- and flintlock-toting Edward Oxford among Mrs. Jarley's waxwork figures (Dickens, *Old Curiosity Shop* 284).

these stories. They were nonsense, both men rightly told him. But Bean could not shake the belief that Oxford's catered confinement was a great improvement over his own wearisome freedom.

Life at home was an ever-increasing torment to him. He knew that his parents loved him in spite of his deformity. But he suffered greatly from the insults and disrespect of his younger brothers. Their four healthy bodies alone were a reproach to him. As his own torso continued to collapse into itself, they grew taller and stronger; by now, even nine-year-old Henry likely looked down on him in every way. John Bean's eighteenth birthday was days away. He was sure now that he would not mark that day at home: not in the face of their derision.

And so he had run away from home three weeks before this Sunday, two weeks after Francis's attempt. His mother fell ill with worry; his father frantically took a full description of the boy to Clerkenwell police station and pressed them to find him. They did nothing. Four days later, Bean's employer Mr. Hilton spotted the boy lurking outside his business and persuaded him to return home. He went, knowing that his return was a temporary one, an opportunity to plan more carefully his escape from this miserable life.

The newspapers that came out on the day he returned home were filled with news of Francis's trial and condemnation. Bean then could not but realize that if he followed through with the plan he was now formulating, he might face the gallows rather than a comfortable bed at Bethlem. This did little to deter him. Three days later, he bought his pistol from a neighbor, Mr. Bird. His father was later surprised that he had found the money, but discovered that he had sold off his meager collection of books, including his Bible, to get it. It was an old and rusty pocket flintlock, probably not worth the three shillings he paid. Mr. Bird assumed that the boy had bought it as a toy and was surprised when Bean came back to his shop three times, complaining that it did not work. After fending the boy off twice, Bird charged him a penny to replace the useless flint that Bean had thrown away. Bird noticed Bean's "childish glee" upon seeing the new flint strike sparks, and the flash in the pan when Bird instructed him how to fire it. Bean then brought the pistol to a neighbor to clean it, but he was unable to unscrew the pistol's rusty barrel and returned it to Bean unfixed. Later, when Bean had primed the gun, loaded it with coarse powder he had bought elsewhere, rammed down with wadding and, inexplicably, a few fragments of a clay smoking-pipe, he could not get the pistol to work. He would have to hope for better results when they mattered. The next day, he ran away again.

That had been a week ago. He again lived on the streets, sleeping where he could—in abandoned houses, in fields—on the outskirts of Islington, and spending his days roaming the metropolis, earning a pittance at street errands: a few pennies for holding two horses for one gentleman, and a few more on Hungerford Pier fetching a glass of ale for another. He was as unsuccessful at street work as at any other occupation; he had survived last week on only eight pence. One of those pennies he used, the day after he absconded, to post a letter to his parents:

> June 28, 1842
> Dear Father and Mother,
>   Thinking you may feel surprised at my prolonged absence, I write these few lines to acquaint you I am seeking employment, which if I do not obtain I will not be dishonest though I may be desperate. It is useless to seek for me. Please give my love to [my] brothers, though they never used me as such. I have very little more to say, except remember me to my aunt and uncle; thank them for what they have done for me. I should have written sooner, but I did not like. Hoping you will excuse this scribbling, and think no more of me. I am your unhappy, but disobedient son, J. B.

For the last three days he haunted the parks around Buckingham Palace, waiting for his opportunity to present his pistol at the Queen. Somehow, she managed to elude him. She and Albert had not taken an airing in all that time; both were busy entertaining their guests, Victoria's favorite Uncle Leopold and his wife Louise, King and Queen of the Belgians. The four had come and gone from the palace: to visit the Duchess of Gloucester Thursday for an evening of *tableaux vivants*, to visit Adelaide the Queen Dowager Friday afternoon. And Albert had managed to get out for a ride without his wife on Saturday. All these comings and goings were unpredictable and Bean had missed them. Today would be different.

Given the examples of Oxford and Francis, Bean had a good idea about the possible consequences of his act. He was ready for anything. Death—suicide by Queen—either at the gallows or at the hands of an angry crowd: that would be welcome, as would be confinement at the Queen's pleasure, with Oxford, wine, and tutors. Last night, a new possibility had become apparent when the evening papers reported the commutation of Francis's sentence. Transportation and a lifetime of hard labor would likely have seemed the worst possible outcome to Bean, well aware of his pitiful lack of stamina. Even that did not deter him; anything was better than the life he lived.

The crowd quickened; heads turned left to watch two scarlet-liveried outriders and then three carriages and two equerries clatter out of the gates of the Palace. The carriages were all covered landaus, as was usually the case when Victoria and Albert rode to the Chapel Royal. The Queen and Albert, Bean and everyone else knew, were in the third carriage. Leopold rode with them. (The Queen of the Belgians, a Roman Catholic, remained behind at the Palace, taking visitors.) As the outriders approached, Bean elbowed his way through the crowd to the edge of the Mall, coming up against a boy to his right. If he had looked in that direction, he would have been disgusted. The boy was a year younger than Bean, "genteel-looking," of normal size and stature, and very nattily dressed: a dark frock coat, white trousers with Wellington boots, a blue silk waistcoat and crimson silk neckerchief, his collar, by one account, "turned down *á la Byron*": in other words a swell, a toff, everything that John William Bean was not and never would be. His name was Charles Edward Dassett; he was a shopboy in his father's art-supply business. He had come through the parks from his home in Portman Square with his brother and his uncle to see the Queen.

The crowd cheered the passing carriages. Their windows were down because of the heat, allowing just a glimpse of the royal party—some could see the light blue or maybe pale green bonnet of the Queen. As the rear wheels of the last carriage rushed past, John Bean pulled his cocked flintlock from his coat, held it at arm's length, and pulled the trigger.

The hammer snapped down but the explosion did not come, and the royal party rode on, oblivious, toward the stable yard of St. James's. Suddenly Bean felt a pull, felt pain, and lurched right. He turned to see Dassett's large hand clutching his small wrist, and looked up to see the boy's eyes. They displayed an odd combination of shock—and amusement.

While the rest of the crowd had focused only upon the royal carriages, Charles Dassett had watched Bean push his way through the crowd, present his pistol, and pull the trigger. He clearly saw the hammer drop and heard the click. In an instant he grabbed Bean's shooting hand and in the same instant deduced Bean's motivation. He turned to his brother. "Look here, Fred," he exclaimed, "this chap is going to have a pop at the Queen—I think he wants to be provided for for life." He then turned back to Bean and relieved him of his pistol. People began to gather around the boys. Dassett pondered the pistol with amusement, turning it over and over, almost playfully, exhibiting it to the growing group of onlookers. It seemed to them to be some sort of joke; Dassett laughed, and so did they.

Dassett looked around to find a policeman to take charge of Bean and his pistol. There were plenty about. Perhaps in official response to Francis's first attempt while the Queen rode to the chapel, a number of A Division officers were stationed along the route to protect the Queen's *cortége*. Across the Mall and in front of St. James's, Dassett saw two of them. With his brother and uncle and the ever-growing crowd, he crossed over, tugging at a slightly resisting Bean. ("He did not walk so fast as my brother wished," said Frederick Dassett: "he *is* a cripple.") Dassett "certainly appeared to me," one member of the crowd later said, "to be disposed to excite the mob as he walked for a considerable distance laughing with a Pistol in his hand." And indeed the crowd was amused by it all, thinking that the poor deformed lad had acted in fun—and thinking that the boy Dassett was taking the game too far. It was a hoax, some shouted—the gun wasn't loaded! Others called out to Dassett to give the boy back his pistol, and to let him go. One helpfully suggested that Bean take his pistol back: "put it into your pocket and run away with it."

At the gate leading to the Chapel Royal, Dassett presented pistol and Bean to P.C. Thomas Hearn, explaining what had happened. Hearn—who had been on the force for only three months—laughed out loud: this did not amount to a charge, he said. He walked away. Behind Hearn was another officer, P.C. William Claxton—who also refused to take Bean in charge. "Pooh, pooh, it's all nonsense," he laughed, following Hearn and disappearing.

Meanwhile, up Constitution Hill, P.C. James Partridge, an officer with much more experience on the force and particularly with guarding the Queen,* spotted the growing crowd outside St. James's Palace with alarm—and immediately ran toward it. Dassett was moving in the opposite direction, looking for yet another officer, with Bean still in his grasp. The crowd numbered at least three hundred people and was growing fast; the word that another attempt had been made was spreading, and "large numbers actually clambered the sharp-pointed railings" of St. James's Park to catch a

---

* Partridge was the officer on duty two years before when Edward Oxford was brought to A Division station house.

glimpse of the perpetrator. Confusion and hostility grew as well: wasn't the boy holding the gun the assailant? Who was the poor hunchback he was holding? John William Bean, sensing opportunity, politely asked Dassett whether he might have his gun back. Dassett ignored him. The crowd roiled as the curious pushed toward the center and as the angry pushed to separate Dassett and Bean. Dassett was forced to let go of Bean—"otherwise my arm would have been broken." Since he held the gun, the crowd stayed with him. Bean slipped away, past the running P.C. Partridge and into Green Park, heading north—heading homewards.

The mob now had at its gravitational center a confused boy with a gun—*his* gun, obviously. Bean was quickly forgotten and the crowd turned on Dassett as the Queen's assailant. Partridge forced his way to the center of the now-ugly mass, saw the boy with the gun outside the Chapel, and drew the obvious conclusion. Dassett attempted to explain, but Partridge dismissed Dassett's story of the hunchbacked dwarf as "shamming," relieved him of the pistol (which he wisely slipped into his pocket) and took the boy into custody.

While John William Bean escaped, then, a noisy mass proceeded up the Mall, across the Horse Guards Parade outside Whitehall, and to Gardiner Street station: Partridge (joined by Inspector George Martin, who took custody of the pistol), Charles Dassett, his brother and his uncle, and at least six hundred of the Queen's loyal subjects,[*] heaping angry execrations upon the perplexed sixteen-year-old.

Robert Peel was out of town on this day, at the estate of his Secretary of War, Henry Hardinge. Home Secretary James Graham, who had learned from Commissioner Rowan of the attempt within minutes of Bean's arrival at the station, headed the government examination of the incident. After the experience of the two previous attempts on the Queen, Graham like Peel was convinced

---

[*]   Three thousand, according to the *Times*.

that the elevated process of a Privy Council examination served if anything as an incentive to miscreants like Oxford, Francis, and Bean. But Bean's attempt on the Queen could still be construed as High Treason, and therefore Graham summoned the Privy Council (or at least what there was of it in or near town on this summer Sunday) at 4:30 that afternoon. In the intervening hours, the station house was again besieged by the curious and the concerned. One of the first there was Daniel O'Connell, who, though he led the charge in 1842 to repeal the Act of Union between Ireland and Great Britain, was second to none in demonstrations of personal loyalty to the Queen. Inside the station, meanwhile, a clearer sense of what had happened on the Mall emerged. A number of witnesses—the Dassetts, their uncle John Janes, and several who had seen Charles Dassett seize Bean, as well as the embarrassed constables Hearn and Claxton—convinced the police that Dassett's tale of a hunchbacked dwarf was not an invention, and that the true perpetrator was at large. By the time that the Council examined witnesses, then, Charles Edward Dassett had become the hero of the day; Graham personally complimented him after his testimony for his meritorious behavior. Hearn and Claxton, on the other hand, were severely reprimanded, and told to consider themselves suspended. (Within a day, they were to be dismissed from the force.)

The inquiry concluded at 8:00, to be resumed upon the capture of the assailant. By this time, the police—suffering yet another public embarrassment, thanks to Hearn and Claxton—were eager to find the culprit quickly. In this, they were assisted greatly by Bean's unusual appearance: a hunchback should be easy to find. A Division quickly broadcast to all the station houses in the metropolis by route paper a description to be read to all officers before they began their shifts, one that more accurately caught Bean's spinal deformity than his limited height:

A Station, Gardener's Lane, Sunday, July 3, Quarter-past 6 P.M.

Description of a boy who presented a pistol at the Queen's carriage in the mall of St. James's park this morning.

He is about 16 or 18 years of age, five feet six inches high, thin made, short neck, and humped back, walks a little on one side, long sickly pale face, light hair, and dressed in a very long surtout coat, of a dark brown or dark colour, which appeared much too large for him, a dark cloth cap, his nose marked with a scar or a black patch, and he has altogether a dirty appearance.

The police will make every exertion to apprehend this boy, and convey him immediately to this station.

William Haining, Inspector.

The description led to one of the most ludicrous episodes in the history of police profiling. Suddenly, it was open season on London's hunchbacks. Constables fanned out across their districts and hauled into their station houses every person who remotely matched the route-paper description, zealously competing with one another for the *coup* of bringing in the Queen's assailant. One of the first to be taken was a cabman in Somers Town, whom somebody someplace remembered had been outspoken in his admiration for John Francis. This young cabman, a hunchback with a splotch on his face, and the oddly near-familiar name of John Oxman,* was tricked by an officer of S Division to come to that station house; a reporter there who had never seen the suspect but had heard witness descriptions of him identified the "exceedingly agitated and flushed" boy as the assailant. Oxman was bundled off to A Division early enough so that some newspapers the next day were able to report the certain capture of the assailant. At Smithfield, an inspector was particularly enthusiastic, rounding up two brothers

---

* The inclusion in the 1851 census of a 27-year-old cabman by the name of John Oxman suggests that this seeming alias was nothing of the kind.

with severe spinal deformity, and then an entire afflicted family. In another instance, a hunchbacked man was walking down the road dividing E and F Divisions, when he was spotted simultaneously by two officers on either side of the street; both rushed to grab him, each crying that he had seen the man first. They finally negotiated a settlement, together hauling the man to A Division station house, where he was quickly let go. Scores, at least, of hunchbacks spent that Sunday evening in a police cell. The *Illustrated London News* noted that "during the twelve hours for which the majesty of British justice was distanced by that crooked piece of malignity . . . the number of little deformed men 'detained,' to use a mild phrase, was astonishing. Before one station-house, a whole regiment of these unfortunate individuals was paraded." *Punch* caught the absurdity of the moment with a cartoon depicting a parade of stalwart policemen collaring in both hands a scowling set of hunchbacked dwarves, among them a sorry-looking Punch himself.

It was G Division in Clerkenwell, and Thomas Cooper's nemesis Inspector Penny, who took the prize. When Penny read the route paper to officers just beginning evening duty, one of them, P.C. Henry Webb, lingered after muster and reminded Penny that the description in the route paper matched the description a distraught John William Bean Senior had given the police nearly three weeks before of his son. Penny then sent Webb to 14 St. James's buildings, Rosamon Street, to find out whether Bean's parents had heard any news of the runaway. At ten that evening, Webb knocked on the Beans' door; John Bean Junior, to his surprise, opened the door himself. His state of undress, in Victorian terms—no coat, waistcoat, or cap—suggested he had settled back in some time before. Webb asked him where his father and mother were; he did not know, he said—father might be at the public house. Webb duped Bean into putting on coat and cap and following him, either by asking his help in finding his father, or in telling him he had to come to the station house because he had run away. When Webb touched Bean's shoulder, he realized the boy was trembling uncontrollably.

As they left the house, Bean's alarmed mother, Sally, came upon them. Webb allayed her fears by telling her that he was taking her son to the station for a dressing-down by the magistrate for running away from home; a little scare might have a beneficial effect upon the boy's future conduct.

At the station, Bean was questioned by Inspector Penny. Why had he returned home so suspiciously soon after the attempt? He was driven home by hunger, he replied. Penny, convinced that Bean was the assailant, shipped him with Officer Webb in a cab to Gardiner Street. They arrived at midnight. Bean's doppelganger, John Oxman, was still in custody: the resemblance between the two was striking. The Dassetts had to be called in to exonerate Oxman and identify Bean as the one who assaulted the Queen. Charles Dassett and Webb then had the honor of signing the sheet charging Bean with "attempting to shoot at Her Majesty on the Mall in St. James's Park." With an officer to accompany him, then, Bean was placed for the night in the same cell and same bed in which Oxford and Francis had slept.

He awoke Tuesday morning, 4 July, a few minutes after eight, thinking not of his own sorry plight, but of the sorrier one of the neighbor he had seen two or three times around Clerkenwell. "I suppose Cooper is hanging now," he said to his jailer. He was right: William Calcraft had pulled the drop on Thomas Cooper minutes before. Cooper's sullen passivity about his fate had vanished two days before the end, and he quaked as he walked to his death. The last days he had spent in relative privacy, largely freed from the sense of being a public spectacle that his predecessor at the noose, Daniel Good, had endured. The overattended and overexcited last sermon for Good had drawn criticism in both houses of Parliament, so the Court of Aldermen, who had charge of Newgate procedures, had decided to bar outsiders from both Cooper's condemned sermon and his procession to the scaffold. Few inside Newgate, then, were able to witness the helplessness Cooper suffered on the morning of the execution. The poison he had taken on the day of the crime, two months before, had by now paralyzed his hands as well as his feet. Jailers had to dress him; one had to hold a teacup to his lips so that he could drink. His end was quick: he seemed unconscious of the crowd that yelled and groaned at him as he emerged from Newgate, and within a minute he was up the scaffold, hooded and launched, dying, it seems, without pain.

An hour later, while yards away inside Newgate prison John Francis awaited his transportation—and while across town at Gardiner Street John William Bean ate his hearty breakfast—Cooper was cut down, to be buried with Courvoisier and Good inside the prison. At eleven that morning, Bean heard from his cell the patter of one of the many broadsheet sellers hawking the (fictitious) last speech and dying declaration of Thomas Cooper. "So then," Bean observed, "they *have* hanged Cooper."

Just before two that afternoon, to avoid the curious crowds outside the Home Office, Bean was run at a trot within a phalanx of A Division officers through side streets and into a side entrance of Whitehall for his Privy Council examination. Attendance at this examination was fuller and more formidable than the day before: Peel had returned, and a number of members of the government, including the Duke of Wellington, had been recalled from Cambridge, where the Duke of Northumberland was being installed as Chancellor. While both Oxford and Francis had displayed arrogant cockiness during their Privy Council examinations, their exhilaration yet untempered by the dispiriting experience of prison life, Bean came before his august examiners already defeated: he collapsed with agitation on entering the room; after that, he could only watch his accusers sullenly and silently as they connected him with the pistol and positively identified him as the Queen's assailant. Within two hours, Bean was remanded to Tothill Fields Bridewell, to be brought back two days later to the Home Office to be charged. Peel had consulted with his Home

Secretary before the examination, and both absolutely refused to grant Bean the elevated charge of High Treason—which both were now certain was a positive incentive to imitators. They needed some time to decide exactly what to do with the boy. Newgate would have to wait.

He was thus bundled off in a cab with Inspector Hughes to the Bridewell. On the way out, he helpfully told Inspector Martin where he had bought the gun; that evening, Martin, accompanied by Bean's father, confirmed the sale from Mr. Bird. At Tothill Fields, Hughes placed him in the charge of Governor Tracy. He was stripped and bathed, a process open to reporters, who the next day shared with the world the intimate details of the hunchbacked dwarf's twisted body.

While the crowds on the Mall erupted into confusion and hostility, the Queen, Albert, and Leopold heard the service in the Chapel Royal in peace, learning about the attempt only when they returned to the Palace. Victoria was not alarmed or even surprised, writing in her journal "Odd enough to say, only two days ago I remarked to Albert, I felt sure an attempt on us would be shortly repeated." She had basis for this presentiment. She was now certain that the law as it stood would only encourage more attacks. Any desperate and overambitious boy in the kingdom might now attain with a cheap pistol an instant worldwide notoriety granted by the elevated charge of High Treason. Her Prime Minister, she knew, agreed with her. Peel had rushed to London from Kent upon hearing of the attempt, arriving late Sunday night. Early Monday afternoon, he visited Buckingham Palace before Bean's Privy Council examination to consult with Albert about the steps to be taken in the wake of the assault. During this conversation, the Queen entered the room. Peel—according to Albert's first biographer "in public so cold and self-commanding, in reality so full of genuine feeling"— burst into tears. It was a cathartic moment for both Queen and Prime Minister: any sense of a chill between them—a chill that had, three years before, led to a constitutional crisis—was gone, and gone forever.

The public as usual responded to the Queen's preservation with jubilation. Once again, the very thought of losing this monarch drove home to everyone the unprecedented emotional bond between the people and their queen, a bond that seemed to grow stronger with each attempt. "The Queen and People," a commentator in the *Spectator* declared after the attempt, "were drawn into more intimate communion. Compassion for the woman—young, a mother, present to the view in all the most engaging relations of life—thus exposed to senseless perils, from which no general loyalty, no guards, and scarcely any precautions might be able to shield her . . . all these considerations prompted a display of popular feeling that had a deeper seat than mere 'loyalty' or attachment to the office of the Sovereign."

On Sunday and on Monday, crowds of Londoners of every social stripe flocked to the Palace, expecting the usual impromptu royal celebration in the parks. This time, however, Victoria disappointed her public. Her staying in on Sunday could hardly be a surprise, given her earlier excursion to the Chapel Royal. On Monday, however, all of London, it seemed, were certain she would come out: thousands filled Hyde Park, and thousands more gathered before and around the Palace and lined Constitution Hill. While they waited, Victoria and Albert walked privately behind the walls of the palace gardens. Many conjectured about her absence. One rumor held that her ministers commanded her to remain while they gathered more information. But Francis's attempts had made clear that Victoria's ministers did not have that power over her; besides, Bean had already been captured and presented no threat to her. Another rumor was that the Queen was "deeply affected" by the news of the attempt. Perhaps. But Victoria had shown before that she simply refused to give in to that fear. While it is true she did not ride this Monday, the Duchess of Kent did, accompanied by her brother Leopold and his wife. Even more tellingly, Victoria and

Albert allowed the 1½-year-old Princess Royal and the 8-month-old Prince of Wales to take an airing in the parks in an open carriage with Lady Lyttelton. The royal couple's restraint was much more likely rational than emotional, born of concern that any attention given to the attacks might encourage copycat assailants—as Francis's attempt, it seemed, only encouraged Bean's. Whatever the reason, the royal couple remained at Buckingham Palace while outside it the public thronged until late Monday evening, when carriages arriving for a royal dinner party finally convinced the crowd that the Queen would not be coming out, and they dispersed.

The newspapers and the public excoriated young John Bean, finding in his physical deformity evidence of moral ugliness. He was a "deformed, decrepit, miserable looking dwarf," "that crooked piece of malignity," a "hunchbacked little miscreant," and a "miserable and contemptible-looking wretch." In a letter to his father, Prince Albert referred to him as a "hunchbacked wretch," Home Secretary Graham described him as "an hump-backed boy of an idiotic appearance," and Peel told the Queen that Bean was "the most miserable object he ever saw."

But while Bean might be unique, his crime was not: three young men had now assailed the Queen, and it would seem that the evidence of three attempts should provide ample material to discern some sense of a motivation. Some commentators remained as baffled as ever. The *Morning Chronicle* held that "these repeated attempts on the life of our beloved Sovereign are utterly incomprehensible. We do not know what to make of this union of itiotcy [sic], depravity, and crime. Intelligible motive there is none." Others, however, began to make connections.

Victoria had not been alone these last few years in facing would–be assassins. Across the channel, Louis-Philippe, the Citizen King of France, had already faced five attempts since coming to the throne after the revolution of 1830, and would face two more before his deposition in the revolution of 1848. Immediately after

Bean's attempt, one French newspaper deplored that "the savage and impotent monomania, which has emigrated from France to England, is one of the gravest symptoms of the profound disorders which agitated modern societies." Elizabeth Barrett, writing to a friend, noted the connection as well, but was perplexed as to cause or cure: "What is this strange mania of queen-shooting? What is the motive? & what end? In the meanwhile the despots of the earth sit safe . . . & nobody thinks of even smoking a tobacco pipe at them, much less of shooting it. It is only citizen Kings, & liberal queens that their people address themselves to shooting. I am very angry—angry & sorry & ashamed."

The comparison between Victoria's assailants and Louis-Philippe's, however, only went so far. Men, not boys, shot at Louis-Philippe. While all of them, it seems, were, like Oxford, Francis, and Bean, tormented by their own inner demons, they all—unlike those three—were avowedly political, either active in the republican movement that thrived throughout Louis-Philippe's reign, or politically driven lone wolves. There was no question whatsoever that their weapons were loaded, and that they shot to kill, expecting to effect a revolution with a bullet. Many in France believed that the French monarchy would disappear if Louis-Philippe died. The King's most recent assailant, Marius Darmés, might have best articulated the ideological fanaticism of Louis-Philippe's assailants (mixed in his case with more than a *soupçon* of madness). "If I had killed the tyrant," he maintained after his attempt in 1840, "we would have conquered the universe and all the despots." The King's third assailant, Louis Alibaud, went to his execution in 1836 crying "I die for Liberty!" He meant it. Victoria never was to experience anything like the terror and carnage caused by Louis-Philippe's second would-be assassin,* Giuseppe Fieschi, who

---

* Fieschi is usually considered the first of Louis-Philippe's would-be assassins. But three years before, in November 1832, the King was shot at and the shooter never found.

on 28 July 1835 unleashed his "infernal machine" on Louis-Philippe as the King was riding through Paris to review the National Guard. The hail of bullets from this primitive machine-gun—twenty-five loaded gun barrels on a wooden frame—instantly created "a void around the King," killing eighteen, seriously wounding twenty-two, and blowing half of Fieschi's own face off. Remarkably, the King and his sons were able to escape this bloodbath safely, the King proving himself Victoria's equal for courage under fire, continuing along the route and reviewing the troops at the Place Vendôme as scheduled.

Fieschi was a republican conspirator who went to the guillotine with two others, all of them believing they would have brought down a king and a political system if one of their twenty-five bullets had found its mark. No sane person in Britain in the early 1840s—and certainly not Oxford, Francis, or Bean—believed the monarchy would collapse if the Queen died. Whatever motives the Queen's assailants had, political fanaticism was not among them. This did not prevent partisan commentators from seeing the attempts as indirectly political, speculating that these boys were unwitting tools of the opposing political faction, imbibing from the newspapers of the other side a disrespect for the Queen that gave them license to shoot at her. The Whigs and the Chartists blamed the Tories; the Tories blamed the Chartists. The essayist and Victorian sage Thomas Carlyle, always one to spy a cosmic significance in any human action, understood the three attempts to be symptoms of an inarticulate working-class discontent with their government, writing to his mother "Are not these strange times? The people are sick of their misgovernment, and the blackguards among them shoot at the poor Queen: as a man that wanted the steeple pulled down might at least fling a stone at the gilt weathercock."

But given what the public learned and was learning about these three boys, these political explanations were drowned out by a growing groundswell of opinion that the attempts had little to do with the Queen's stature and everything to do with the boys' own.

Variations on a phrase first coined after Francis's attempt became ubiquitous in press and public after Bean's: they were all driven by a "morbid craving after notoriety." And the law as it stood gave them that notoriety: a quick trip from the streets to Whitehall's corridors of power and a widely reported examination by the great men of the Privy Council, while huge crowds gathered outside, hoping to catch just a glimpse of them; the newspapers scrambling to scoop one another with new details about their lives; a starring role in a state trial for High Treason, and, if it came to that, a glorious execution before thousands.

With a growing awareness of the disease came a new certainty about the cure. These attempts would not stop until their perpetrators were degraded rather than elevated. The charge of High Treason only encouraged them; another charge would have to be created to deal with them. And the incentive of the scaffold had to go as well, to be replaced by a punishment that would appeal to their sense of shame rather than vainglory. Two days after Bean's attempt, the *Times* led the charge for a new punishment for the miscreants. If "we would make up our minds to flog them in the sight of their companions, as heartily and as often as should be judged appropriate to the gravity of the offence, these coxcombs would leave off their villainous anglings for notoriety." The Queen's assailants were errant children; let them be treated as such.

Robert Peel and his Home Secretary, James Graham, needed no persuading; they had already come to the same conclusion. John William Bean would not be charged with High Treason. On the day after Bean's first Privy Council examination, Graham met with the two commissioners of the police and with George Maule, who as Treasury Solicitor was for the third time responsible for putting together a case for the prosecution against an assailant of the Queen. Bean, Graham made clear, would be charged not with High Treason but with common assault. It would mean that he would, if convicted, face a shorter sentence than Oxford and Francis. And while the government surely concurred with the writer for the *Times* and a host of other commentators that Bean deserved a good whipping, that was out of the question: the law for assault as it stood did not provide for corporal punishment. A new law would need to be created to humiliate the Queen's assailants. That is the task that Robert Peel immediately took upon himself.

On the next day—6 July—John Bean, discernibly sunk into a depressed torpor, was brought from Tothill Fields for a final examination before Peel and the Privy Council. It would be the last time any of Victoria's assailants came before that body. He was charged with a misdemeanor and sent back to Tothill Fields for the night, to be brought to Newgate the next day to await trial. The lesser charge meant that Bean could return home if he could make bail—but that bail, two sureties of 250 pounds each, was far too much for his family to raise. Only a small crowd had assembled outside the Home Office to see him back to prison, and their "contempt and ridicule," according to a reporter, "was quite enough to act as an effectual antidote against the morbid craving after notoriety to which alone such an insane attempt could be attributed."

Bean's examination took place on the same day that John Francis, having tearfully taken leave of his family forever on Monday the fourth (the day of Cooper's execution), was removed to Gosport outside Portsmouth and to the convict ship *Marquis of Hastings*. The two would-be regicides missed meeting in Newgate by one day.

In less than a week, Peel had created his Act Providing for the Further Security and Protection of Her Majesty's Person. On 12 July, as John William Bean in Newgate observed his eighteenth birthday, the Prime Minister submitted his bill to Commons. Peel had no intention of modifying existing laws of treason, he made clear: rather, he was introducing a new charge altogether to deal with what amounted to a new offense: not attempts to kill the Queen, but attempts to disturb her—and by disturbing her, to disturb the public peace. Any threatening of the Queen, with guns, explosives, or any projectile, was prosecutable as a

High Misdemeanor. The charge skirted the nagging issue of both Oxford's and Francis's trials—whether the pistols were loaded or not—by making threatening the monarch with either loaded or unloaded weapons a prosecutable offense.* Offenders under the Act could be sentenced to as much as seven years' transportation, or three years' imprisonment at hard labor. Moreover, they could expect to face repeated humiliation by being "publicly or privately whipped, as often and in such Manner and Form as the said Court shall order and direct, not exceeding Thrice."

It was the promise of a good whipping for the next miscreant who dared assault the Queen that roused the entire House into enthusiastic cheering. Every single member was for this measure and was zealous to demonstrate his absolute loyalty to Victoria. "These are the offences of base and degraded beings," Lord John Russell claimed in assenting to the measure. "It is right that a degrading species of punishment should be applied to them." Daniel O'Connell agreed, holding that the Irish people in particular would be grateful for a law to "brand . . . with contemptuous execration" any future assailant.

Only one member disturbed the spirit of unanimity. The next day, before the third reading of the Bill, Joseph Hume, radical member for Montrose, decided to use the occasion to contrast the Queen's welfare with the welfare of her poorest subjects. Industrial distress and sheer hunger had only increased as the summer of 1842 progressed; spontaneous disturbances were erupting throughout the countryside north of London. Before Peel presented this bill, debate in Commons had been consumed with the issue of growing popular distress and discontent. And yet, Hume maintained—echoing the complaint of the Chartist petition—while the people's sufferings increased, the Queen and her court lived in comfort: obscene comfort, by contrast. A civil expenditure of £325,000 was

---

* It was under this Act in 1981 that Marcus Sergeant was prosecuted for firing six blanks at Victoria's great-great-granddaughter Elizabeth.

wasted on the "useless parade" of court life. "If anything could be more dissatisfactory to the great mass of the people than another," Hume declaimed, "it was to see outside of the palace squalid poverty, misery, and wretchedness, in all their painful variety, and to behold with inside the palace nothing but extravagance, gorgeous grandeur, and expensive finery." Peel, Hume insisted, should without hesitation recommend to the Queen to drop half of her "monstrous expenditure." His speech could not have been more badly timed. Only one other member cheered him—and was berated for it, by a member who lambasted Hume for his obvious slight on the Queen. Peel joked that Hume must be mistaken about the nature of the motion before the House: this was a bill to protect the Queen, not an economic measure. Hume quickly realized his mistake. "There was no individual in that House who had more regard for the Sovereign than himself," he said, chastened, "or would be more happy to see her Majesty protected." The bill passed without a dissenting vote. On Thursday and Friday, Wellington steered it unanimously through the Lords, and on Saturday Victoria gave the bill her royal assent. It was too late to apply the law to John William Bean. Peel wished instead to reach the would-be Beans or Francises or Oxfords contemplating their own turn at having a "pop" at the Queen. "Let it be known to the world," Peel told an enthusiastic House, that "for these contemptible acts they shall receive the degrading punishment of personal chastisement." If the prospect of death or transportation would not deter them, perhaps a healthy dose of shame would.

In spite of the lesser charge, John William Bean was a celebrity in Newgate, visited by the Lord Mayor, the sheriffs, and a number of aldermen. He was placed in a cell near Reverend Carver, and was attended day and night by a turnkey who surely saw part of his task as guarding the unshakably melancholy boy from killing himself. His trial was set for 25 August—seven weeks, and a long time by Central Criminal Court standards—and he spent his time sadly and studiously poring over the religious material provided him: tracts, the Bible, *Pilgrim's Progress*. He repeated the same story to all his visitors: he never intended harm to the Queen, pointing his pistol at the ground and not her carriage; his only intention was to be arrested and free himself from his miserable freedom. He was tired of life.

Outside Newgate, there was a great deal happening to distract public attention from the hunchbacked dwarf. The summer of 1842 saw the most widespread and sustained civil disturbance of the Queen's long reign. To extend Thomas Carlyle's analogy, if Francis and Bean were throwing stones at the gilt weathercocks, it seemed that the masses were attempting to tear the building down. Drastic reductions of wages, and industrial slowdowns, led to a rash of strikes and demonstrations, beginning in June in the collieries of Staffordshire, spreading throughout the Midlands and the North, and intensifying as June became July and July became August. The enlightened Luddism of the strikers—removing the plugs from industrial machines, draining their boilers, and thus disabling without destroying them—gave the disturbances a name: the Plug Plot Riots. By the second week in August, the disturbances reached a crescendo, as strikers and rioters refused to relent until the People's Charter was law. Two policemen were killed in Manchester; two rioters were shot dead by soldiers in Preston. Parliament was prorogued on 12 August, but neither Prime Minister Peel nor Home Secretary Graham were allowed a moment's respite: the next day, Peel called the Privy Council to meet and issue a royal proclamation warning all subjects to avoid any riotous meetings and disruptive acts, and the cabinet agreed to dispatch a battalion of troops north by train that evening. "I have not had a spare moment since the close of the session," Graham wrote four days before Bean's trial. "My time has been occupied with odious business arising from the mad insurrection of the working classes. . . ." Peel worked closely with Graham as the growing disorder began to threaten him personally. His country home in Drayton, Staffordshire, lay in a particularly disturbed area, and his wife readied their home for a siege, writing to him on 21 August "our arrangements were quickly and vigorously made and should have been equal to an attack from two or three hundred till assistance had come. But then we expected three or four thousand. I am confident, however, that no men actually attacking doors and windows here would have left this place alive." A week before, Peel had been able to travel to Drayton for a couple days, only to be terrified by rumors that the violence had reached the Queen at Windsor: he got word that Victoria had been assassinated. He was not disabused of the rumor until the next train came through. He promptly ordered Graham to step up the Queen's security.

In the meantime, Victoria and Albert were planning a state visit to Scotland, the beginning of what would become a great love affair between the royal couple and that country. The prospect of royal travel during this summer of disruption—disruption in Scotland as well as England—did not please Peel, but he did acknowledge to Graham (on the day of Bean's trial) that the Queen would face no more danger there than in England. To avoid traveling through the riotous north, the couple would go by sea on the yacht *Royal George*. In Edinburgh, expectation for the visit had "superseded all other topics of the day," and in London the public scrambled to obtain choice seats on steamers to see the royal party escorted by the navy from Woolwich to the Channel.

Not surprisingly, then, John William Bean's trial on 25 August did not attract the crowds that Oxford's or Francis's had, and the Old Bailey was no busier than usual when Bean was placed in the dock. His head just cleared the bar, and so he could just see the three judges looking sternly upon him: Baron Abinger presiding, with Mr. Justice Williams and Baron Rolfe. Lord Abinger in his younger days (when he was James Scarlett) had been the most successful advocate in England, with a single-minded partisanship that won cases. His greatest strength as a lawyer, however, became his greatest weakness as a judge. He was not to take Bean's side.

Bean was charged on four counts: the first, third, and fourth accused him of various forms of assault; the second accused him of attempting to fire a pistol with the intent of harassing and alarming the Queen and terrorizing her subjects. The prosecution team consisted of the same formidable five who had established Francis's guilt two months before, led by Attorney General Pollock and Solicitor General Follett. Their strategy to prove Bean's guilt was diametrically opposed to their strategy to prove Francis's. To convict Francis of High Treason, they took great pains to convince the jury that he intended to kill Victoria, and that the contents of his pistol—even if they consisted only of wadding and powder—were lethal. This time, to establish the lesser charge of assault, they would attempt to demonstrate that the contents of the pistol were *not* lethal: that Bean intended to annoy and alarm the Queen and the public, not to kill her. Thus they ignored the curious bits of clay pipe that Inspector Martin found in the pistol, maintaining that only a minute amount of coarse gunpowder was in the pistol, with wadding—wadding that this time could not do the Queen serious harm. They brought forward witnesses—including the Dassett brothers and their uncle—to establish Bean's actions on the Sunday, as well as his connection with the pistol, and his apprehension at home that night.

In his cross-examinations, Bean's barrister Sidney Calder Horry* attempted to present the incident as benign—a few minutes' harmless amusement, with Charles Dassett playing the clown. "Was not there a good deal of laughing going on?" he asked Charles Dassett. "No," Dassett replied. "The people did not laugh that I remember—some might have laughed, I cannot say—there was a great noise after it happened. . . ." Horry's defense of Bean was two-pronged. First, in a breathtakingly risky manoeuvre, he argued that if Bean had indeed assaulted the Queen, he was chargeable with High Treason. And since he was not charged with that crime, he risked being tried a second time for the same offense,

---

* Horry was Thomas Cooper's attorney as well.

"contrary to all the principles of English law." The first, third, and fourth counts (which accused Bean of assault) thus could not stand. As for the second count—harassing and alarming the Queen and the public: Horry held that Bean had harassed and alarmed no one. Only Charles Dassett had seen Bean present the pistol, and Charles Dassett was wrong; the defense had two witnesses to testify that Bean had never pointed the gun. Moreover, the Queen experienced no alarm, being completely unaware of Bean's act, and the public were amused, certainly not alarmed, by the situation, their amusement strengthened by Charles Dassett's clowning with the pistol: even the police on the scene had thought the whole thing a joke.

The two witnesses Horry brought forward to contradict Dassett's testimony that Bean had presented his pistol at the Queen turned out to be of dubious value. The first, Henry Hawkes, testified that if anyone had presented a pistol, "it is probable I must have seen it," but then admitted that he was unaware of the existence of either Bean or Dassett until after the carriages had passed and Dassett was heading across the Mall with Bean in tow. The second witness, Thomas Vosper,* startled the court by claiming that he had stood behind Bean for at least fifteen minutes until the Queen approached, staring at the pistol Bean held by his side—but never lifted. Baron Abinger was mystified by this testimony, asking Vosper several times how he could have simply stood there while Bean waited with a gun for the Queen. Vosper only repeated the same answer: "I wanted to see the result."

> Lord Abinger.—If you saw the prisoner for ten minutes, standing amongst the crowd with a pistol in his hand, waiting to see the result, and knowing that Her Majesty was coming, why did you not take him into custody? Now explain that to the jury.

---

* "Bospher" in the *Proceedings of the Old Bailey*.

I can only say that I merely waited to watch the result.

In summing up, Abinger pointed out that if Vosper had acted as he said he had, he was guilty of misprision of treason. His testimony indeed contradicted Charles Dassett's—but the jury could decide how much credence to accord a criminal by his own admission.

Horry's other witnesses—Bean's former employers and family acquaintances—testified to his good character. When his father took the stand to plead to his son's "mild, peaceable, and inoffensive" conduct, Bean wept bitterly.

By the time of his summing up, Judge Abinger had greatly assisted the prosecution in puncturing the basis of Horry's defense. As for his claim that any assault on the Queen must be High Treason, he responded that this was not so: persons might insult or behave rudely to her. He cited as evidence the curious case where a man had once been indicted for *grinning* at George III. And in response to Horry's claim that an assault cannot be said to take place if the victim is unaware of it, he noted "Is it not an assault to point a loaded gun at a man when he is asleep? I think it is, but Mr. Horry contends the contrary."

It was in the end a simple case for the jury. They consulted for a moment, and gave their verdict: guilty on the second count—harassing and alarming the Queen and the public. Bean heard the verdict without emotion.

Abinger found himself in a frustrating position. He wanted to impose a harsh sentence upon the boy—wanted, indeed, to follow the public consensus and humiliate him. But the old law made no provision for whipping. After consulting briefly with his fellow judges, he tore into Bean: "I know of no misdemeanour more affecting the public peace of the kingdom, of greater magnitude or deserving more serious punishment, than that of which you have just been pronounced guilty." He wished that the punishment he could impose was equal to the offense, but he knew it was not. He thus satisfied himself with a warning to any future miscreants: if they aren't convicted of High Treason and thus forfeit their lives, they will "gain another species of notoriety, by being publicly whipped at a cart's tail through any street in the metropolis." As it was, Abinger imposed the harshest sentence he thought he could: eighteen months at hard labor at Millbank Penitentiary.

John William Bean, tired of his life and by now surely tired to death of the scornful scrutiny of the public, was taken from the bar.

thirteen

TORY SPIES

Four days after John William Bean's trial, on Monday 29 August, the *Royal George* set out of Woolwich in the pouring rain, towed by two steamships. Victoria and Albert were off to Scotland in spite of—and now in part because of—the disturbances across Britain. Besides a short visit by George IV in 1822, no British monarch had set foot in Scotland since the mid-1600s; indeed, Victoria would be the first reigning Queen of Scotland to be there since Mary Queen of Scots. The royal couple planned to put into practice the lessons John Conroy had taught Princess Victoria, enhancing the Queen's prestige through two grueling weeks of processionals between and within the cities of southern Scotland, mingling with all social classes: with cheering crowds by day, and with the elite by night as they stayed at their castles and estates.

The voyage began inauspiciously as bad weather forced the steamships to tow the yacht most of the way up the coast, the royal couple spending much of the time belowdecks, ill. (The fact that Victoria was unknowingly three weeks pregnant with her third child could not have helped.) They arrived off Edinburgh a day after they were expected, letting down the thousands who had the day before trooped from miles around into the city, cramming the scaffolding along the planned procession route in vain expectation of seeing the Queen. Early the next morning, the royal procession shot through the city on the way to Dalkeith Palace, without sufficient warning to the public and before city dignitaries had assembled. Edinburgh's enthusiasm soured into disappointment. The town council and the royal party quickly improvised another procession through the city the next day. It was a rousing success— the first of many. "Scotland has rarely seen a prouder day—perhaps never," wrote the *Times*. Massive crowds showered adulation upon the royal couple. Robert Peel rode in the carriage behind, fretting about the complete lack of security. "The crowds of persons were beyond description," he wrote to his wife. "The mob was close to the carriage, from the narrowness of the streets, and every window in every house looking down into the carriages." The Chartists who ran hooting and groaning beside him added to his anxiety.

Peel had every reason to worry. Somewhere on this route—or in the crowd for one or more of the next fortnight's processions—a man with an overwhelming urge to kill was watching and awaiting his opportunity. He had been for much of the last two years living in London, but he was a native of Glasgow, and had returned home ahead of the royal visit. At the beginning of August, in Paisley— incidentally one of Britain's worst-suffering towns, that hungry summer—he had bought two mismatched percussion-cap pistols. His target would be prominent within the royal processions. But the first carriage, the open phaeton behind the six mounted Royal Dragoons clearing the path, the one carrying Victoria and Albert, was only a distraction to him. It was a carriage further behind this that he was looking for—one clearly marked with the crest of two lions holding a shield marked "Industria": Robert Peel's carriage.

Daniel McNaughtan saw the carriage, saw one man in it—and committed that man's face to memory.

The face, however, did not belong to Robert Peel. During the Edinburgh procession, and on many more during the next fortnight, Peel rode directly behind the royal couple in the carriage of his Foreign Minister, Lord Aberdeen. He left his secretary, Edward Drummond, to ride by himself in the Peel family carriage. Drummond later joked about his being taken for "a great man" in Scotland. He didn't look like Peel, but the two were roughly the same age. Because the illustrated press was in its infancy, images of even highly public figures such as Peel were rare. It was an easy mistake to make. Daniel McNaughtan made it.

Daniel McNaughtan knew that he could find release from his torment only by destroying Peel. The oppressive persecution he suffered had grown for years. It began, he was sure, with the priests of the local Catholic chapel, who tormented him with the assistance of a parcel of Jesuits. But then, he knew, the Tories joined in and soon became his chief tormentors. Their enmity toward him should perhaps not have been surprising, given his enmity toward them. Until 1841, he had been a very successful craftsman, amassing a small fortune as a wood-turner in Glasgow, and politics were a part of his life; as it happens, one of Glasgow's leading Chartists worked as a journeyman in his shop. But at some point—after he voted publicly against them, he claimed—the personal enmity that the Tories of Glasgow bore toward him alone grew to cosmic proportions. Day and night, Tory spies followed him. On the street, they glowered and laughed at him, furiously shaking their fists and their walking sticks in his face. One man repeatedly threw straw at him. His enemies never talked to him, instead communicating with signs. He knew what the straw meant: they intended to reduce him to sleeping on straw in an asylum. They inserted beastly, atrocious libels about him in the *Glasgow Herald* and the London *Times;* they poisoned his food. When he went to bed, they followed him and would not let him sleep. They intended to destroy his peace of mind, drive him to consumption; they would not stop until he was dead.

His enemies were inhabitants of Glasgow, and so he repeatedly sought relief from the authorities of that city. When his father could not help him, he went in turn to the sheriff, the Procurator-Fiscal (or Glasgow's public prosecutor), the Commissioner of Police, the Lord Provost, and even to his Member of Parliament. All of them considered him delusional—and could do nothing to help him. When McNaughtan tracked down his M.P., Alexander Johnson, in London, Johnson fended him off with a curt note sent from the Reform Club: "I can do nothing for you. I fear you are labouring under an aberration of mind." When civil authority failed him, he looked to the divine, begging his father's minister Rev. Mr. Turner for help. The Reverend could do nothing except what the Lord Provost had done—call upon McNaughtan's father and advise him to put his lunatic son in restraints. But Daniel McNaughtan Senior refused, thinking that his son's delusions would pass.

McNaughtan realized that he would have to act for himself. He fled Scotland for London, but to his great dismay his persecutors followed him. He twice fled abroad, but it was no use: the instant he set foot on the quay at Boulogne, he could see one of them scowling at him from behind the custom-house watchbox. Flight was impossible. He would have to stop his tormentors by killing their leader. And so he returned to Scotland and waited for his opportunity to kill the man as he toured the country with the Queen. For some reason, he did not shoot at the man in Peel's carriage. Accordingly, two or three weeks after the Queen's Scottish tour, McNaughtan followed Peel to London, taking the steamship *Fire King* from Glasgow to Liverpool—where the ubiquitous spies beset him particularly mercilessly. In London, McNaughtan tried for a couple months to find a living in spite of the Tories, seeking work and seeking a partner with whom to invest the £750 he had earned from his wood-turning business. At the beginning of 1843, however, the oppression reached the breaking point; he gave up all else in order to stalk his arch-oppressor, Peel.

He took up his post in the heart of Tory darkness: the streets outside of Whitehall, standing all day for two weeks on the steps leading to the Privy Council office. Two recruiters from the army saw him there and asked if he'd like to enlist. No, he told them: he was simply waiting to see a gentleman. Two policemen from A Division—including P.C. Partridge*—took note of him; one told him that those inside the Privy Council office did not like his loitering there. "Tell them their property is quite safe," he replied.

His obsessive urge to kill was matched by an obsessive need to kill the right man. The Prime Minister's official residence was, then as now, 10 Downing Street, but Robert Peel actually resided in his London mansion, Whitehall Gardens, conveniently located directly across from Downing Street, and observable from McNaughtan's position. Edward Drummond had rooms at 10 Downing Street, and his business took him back and forth between the residences, often several times a day. McNaughtan watched him come and go—the man *had to be* Peel. To be absolutely sure, he twice pointed Drummond out to a police constable, asking if that man was Robert Peel. Both times, the constable said yes, thinking McNaughtan was pointing to the man then walking *next* to Drummond: Robert Peel.

On the twentieth of January, McNaughtan, aware of the growing alarm he was causing the Tories and the police around him, came down the steps and shadowed Drummond, who walked from Downing Street to Charing Cross and entered Drummond's bank. (It belonged to his brother.) A few minutes later, Drummond emerged and walked back toward Downing Street. McNaughtan followed. Between the Admiralty and the Horse Guards, McNaughtan walked up to Drummond's back, pulled one of his pistols from the breast of his coat and fired, so close to his victim that Drummond's

---

* The same James Partridge who had put Oxford in a cell and had arrested Charles Dassett after Bean's attempt.

jacket caught fire. He thrust the pistol back into his coat and reached for the other one. Constable James Silver, standing next to the two, was upon McNaughtan an instant after the first shot. The two struggled violently before Silver knocked up McNaughtan's arm and kicked his legs from beneath him. McNaughtan fired the second pistol into the air.

Drummond, clutching at his back, staggered back into his brother's bank. Although the bullet had nearly traveled through his body, he seemed relatively uninjured; initial reports of his condition were extremely optimistic. An apothecary was sent for and deemed him fit to travel to the family house on Grosvenor Street, where doctors were called in, and the bullet was removed. Drummond lingered for five days, while the best doctors in town finished what the bullet had started, leeching and bleeding him relentlessly as his wound grew more infected. On 25 January, he died.

P.C. Silver marched McNaughtan to the Gardiner Lane station house. On the way there McNaughtan muttered that "he" or "she" (Silver could not tell which) "shall not break my peace of mind any longer." Placed in the same cell that Oxford, Francis, and Bean had occupied before him, he spent several hours certain that he had wounded if not killed Sir Robert Peel. It was not until eight or nine the next morning that Inspector John Tierney, interviewing him, realized that McNaughtan had shot the wrong man. "I suppose you are aware who the gentleman is you shot at?" Tierney asked him. "It is Sir *Robert Peel*, is it not?" McNaughtan replied, growing agitated. "No," the inspector at first replied, but then, not wanting to force a confession, said "we don't exactly know who the gentleman is yet." Later that day, at his examination at Bow Street, McNaughtan learned the truth: to his great horror, his persecutors had triumphed.

"The evidence of his mental delusion is strong," Peel wrote to Victoria of McNaughtan on the day Drummond died, and it soon became clear that he would plead insanity. The prospect of an acquittal for insanity pleased no one, certainly not the Queen. McNaughtan, like Edward Oxford, had acted with such deliberation: how could he not be held responsible for his act? "There is and should be," she wrote to Peel, "a difference between that madness which is such that a man knows not what he does, and madness which does not prevent a man from purposely buying pistols, and then with determined purpose watching and shooting a person." Deliberation, in other words, demonstrates awareness, and awareness implies guilt.

More than this, an acquittal of any kind would completely remove any deterrent value from the sentence. The connection between the three attempts upon the Queen and the murder of Drummond was by now obvious to all. "Who can doubt but that Bellingham was as insane as Oxford?" exclaimed a writer in the *Times*, thinking back to the quick execution of Spencer Perceval's assassin in 1812. "But, after the execution of the former, he had no imitators: would that we could say as much after the pardon of the latter!" An insanity acquittal would only perpetuate the outrages and the Queen would remain in danger. Home Secretary Graham, preparing the case against McNaughtan, was adamant that he be convicted. "Every preparation is in progress to meet this vague and dangerous excuse," he wrote Victoria. He had grounds for hope: word had reached him from Scotland that a case could be made that he was a coldhearted, violent Chartist. That lead petered out, however, and no evidence of this kind was presented at McNaughtan's trial.

On the second of February, McNaughtan was brought to the bar of the Old Bailey to enter his plea. His counsel pleaded for more time to set up an insanity defense: McNaughtan's barristers planned to call witnesses from Scotland, and perhaps France. The Attorney General did not object—the government did not want another Bellingham on its hands, found guilty and executed before witnesses to his insanity could be brought forward. The judge, Baron Abinger, gave the defense a month to prepare. Moreover, he granted counsel's request that McNaughtan be allowed access to his bank account: £750 to fund his defense. And if McNaughtan's trial was to prove nothing else, it certainly proved that in 1843, £750 could buy a defense nothing short of magnificent.

It bought the services of Alexander Cockburn, Q.C., for one thing—a highly paid, high-profile barrister (and later Lord Chief Justice). Cockburn was assisted by three others, including William Clarkson, who had defended Francis, and William Henry Bodkin, who assisted in Oxford's defense. Moreover, McNaughtan's money bought the expertise of no fewer than five medical experts, including Edward Monro, Principal Physician at Bethlem, and two doctors brought down from Glasgow. The three London doctors examined McNaughtan several times in company with two doctors retained by the prosecution. When those last two doctors concluded with the others that McNaughtan was indeed insane, the government knew that their case was in trouble before it began.

At 10:00 on 3 March 1843, an excited Daniel McNaughtan was again brought to the bar of the Old Bailey, before Chief Justice Tindal, Justice Williams, and Justice Coleridge. He pleaded not guilty; a chair was brought for him, and he instantly seemed to doze off, ignoring Solicitor General Follett's opening. (He would perk up when the witnesses testified.) The Solicitor General rather than Attorney General Pollock led the prosecution because Pollock was on this day in Lancaster, conducting the government's case against Chartist leader Feargus O'Connor and fifty-eight others for their roles in the Plug Plot Riots. Follett was assisted by the same lawyers who had prosecuted Francis and Bean. They faced the unenviable task of fighting an insanity acquittal while offering nothing to counter the overwhelming evidence that McNaughtan was delusive. Their strategy was to set the legal bar for an insanity acquittal as high as possible, arguing that while McNaughtan might be partially mad, he was still morally aware and thus criminally responsible.

In his opening, therefore, Follett freely admitted that McNaughtan might be suffering from a "morbid affection of the mind." That should not in itself earn him an acquittal, however: public safety required that "this defense should not be too readily listened to." More than this, few crimes—and certainly few crimes as horrendous as this one—are committed by persons *not* laboring under some sort of morbid affection. Follett ignored the most recent and British examples of would-be assassins—Oxford, Francis, and Bean—and pointed instead to Louis-Philippe's. "What motive had they? We know of none but that of an ill-regulated mind, worked upon by morbid political feeling." The great seventeenth-century jurist Matthew Hale—the hallowed setter of precedent in the English insanity defense—had noted the connection between criminality and partial insanity, and held that such "melancholy distempers" cannot absolve a man of criminal responsibility. To be acquitted on the grounds of insanity, that insanity must be total, negating any sense of moral awareness. "If there be thought and design," Follett proclaimed, citing a 1760 formulation of Hale's ideas, "a faculty to distinguish the nature of actions, to discern the difference between moral good and evil; then, upon the fact of the offence proved, the judgment of the law must take place." Two hundred years of precedent (which Follett diligently cited) established moral understanding as the key test of criminal responsibility. And everything about Daniel McNaughtan—his conduct, his habits, and his careful management of his financial affairs—suggested rationality: social and moral awareness. The witnesses called by the prosecution, therefore, both established that McNaughtan indeed shot Drummond down, and testified to his overall possession of reason. "I never thought him unsettled in his mind," claimed his London landlady. "I did not have any idea that his mind was disordered," said an acquaintance who knew him both in Glasgow and in London. Several others said much the same, and several documented his financial acumen, his studious reading habits, and his frequent attendance at the Glasgow Mechanics' Institution. With that, the prosecution rested, and the trial was adjourned for the night, the jurors sequestered in a local coffee house.

The next day, Cockburn demolished the prosecution, eloquently dismissing two hundred years of legal precedence as so much superstitious hogwash. What could be more absurd, he argued, than relying on seventeenth-century jurists' pronouncements on insanity, when modern science alone has succeeded in penetrating the mysteries of madness? "It is but as yesterday," he claimed, "that darkness and solitude—cut off from the rest of mankind like the lepers of old—the dismal cell, the bed of straw, the iron chain, and the inhuman scourge, were the fearful lot of those who were best entitled to human pity and to human sympathy, as being the victims of the most dreadful of all mortal calamities." No one could come to rational conclusions about madness when the mad were rendered raving lunatics by horrendous, unenlightened treatment. True insight into madness lies not in the past, but in the present: to contemporary specialists in the science of the mind. To these, and not to Hale, "the greatest deference should be paid." Modern science completely debunked Solicitor General Follett's claim that total insanity was necessary for an acquittal. Any one of a human being's mental faculties—"the perception, the judgment, the reason, the sentiments, the affections, the propensities, the passions"—might become diseased, and render a man a "victim of the most fearful delusions, the slave of uncontrollable impulses": a state lacking "self-control and dominion, without which the knowledge of right and wrong would become vague and useless." Cockburn essentially posited two grounds for acquittal because of insanity. First, if one, at the moment of committing an act, cannot understand the rightness or wrongness of that act, one cannot be criminally responsible for it. This is not the same as Follett's claim of abstract moral awareness: according to Cockburn, one could understand the difference between right and wrong and still not be aware of the morality of one's own action. The question, Cockburn argued, quoting the "profound and scientific" Scottish jurist, Baron Hume, is not whether one understands evil, but "did he at that moment understand the evil of what he did?" Second, one who is impelled to act by an impulse beyond human control cannot be held responsible for that act; in such a case moral knowledge becomes "vague and useless." The defense would suggest that McNaughtan was not liable in both of these ways.

Cockburn then laid out McNaughtan's history, portraying a man whose delusions had grown a frightening degree over the past two years, until he was indeed their slave—in the words of the French doctor Charles Chrétien Henry Marc, a victim of "homicidal monomania." And the defense spent much of McNaughtan's £750 in backing up that claim—transporting a host of witnesses from Glasgow to London to illustrate his derangement. McNaughtan's father, as well as all of the Glasgow officials who for years could not help him, now took the stand to establish that he was a man in serious need of help.

After these witnesses, the defense called an astounding nine medical specialists to the stand—and apparently had more in reserve. The unmistakable effect of their testimony was to suggest that the medical community was unanimous in holding the man in the dock to be hopelessly insane. And, unlike the medical experts in Edward Oxford's trial, their testimony was remarkably uniform. Edward Thomas Monro, the chief physician at Bethlem, had no doubt: there existed in McNaughtan "the presence of insanity sufficient to deprive the prisoner of all self-control." The four other doctors hired by the defense agreed, William Hutcheson, of the Glasgow Royal Lunatic Asylum, holding that "the delusion was so strong that nothing but a physical impediment could have prevented him from committing the act." All of them were rendering judgments about McNaughtan's state of mind, and, remarkably, not once did any judge or prosecuting counsel question their right to do that. The tension between science and the law, so palpable during Edward Oxford's trial, did not exist in this trial.

After these five hired specialists testified, Cockburn called to the stand doctors whom the defense had not retained, neutral observers whose testimony dovetailed perfectly. The first of these had examined McNaughtan before the trial, but the last two had not, basing their testimony entirely upon their reading of depositions and hearing the testimony in this trial. Astoundingly, the judges and the prosecution let them testify. When a ninth specialist—B. Philips of Westminster Hospital—took the stand, Judge Tindal stopped the trial and turned to the Solicitor General.

> Mr. Solicitor General, are you prepared . . . with any evidence to combat this testimony?
>
> No, my Lord.
>
> We feel the evidence, especially that of the last two medical gentlemen who have been examined, and who are strangers to both sides and only observers of the case, to be very strong, and sufficient to induce my learned brothers and myself to stop the case.

With that, Follett surrendered. He apologized to the jury for bringing the case before them, citing the need for public safety. But he would not now press for a verdict against the prisoner.

Tindal then gave the case to the jury, but in effect directed their verdict: "I cannot help remarking, in common with my learned brethren, that the whole of the medical evidence is on one side, and that there is no part of it which leaves any doubt on the mind."

The jury immediately pronounced McNaughtan not guilty on the ground of insanity.

McNaughtan was returned to Newgate, to await Home Secretary Graham's order for his removal to Bethlem. It was some time in coming. Nine days later, on 13 March, McNaughtan followed Oxford's path from Newgate to Southwark in a cab with Governor Cope. He would walk the criminal wing with Oxford until 1864, when that wing was razed to the ground and both men were transferred to Broadmoor; there, the next year, he died and was buried in an unmarked grave. McNaughtan thus had twenty-two agitated years to consider his utter defeat and the triumph of his enemies.

The tormenting man with the straw had been right: McNaughtan spent the rest of his life in asylums.

The public, already convinced that Oxford's verdict had been a travesty, and certain that the McNaughtan decision offered any degenerate the means to kill with impunity, responded to McNaughtan's acquittal with alarm, outrage—and derision. One bitter wit, writing to the *Times*, captured all these feelings:

> Sir,—I have in contemplation the accomplishment of a certain pet project, which unfortunately involves some degree of violence in its attainment; I mean, however, to retain beforehand some of the most eminent medical men of the day as witnesses in proof of my monomaniacal possession, and in the mean time I hope, through the assistance of your journal, to ascertain when the public (who I understand considers itself rather outraged by the acquittal of my friend Mr. M'Naughten) are sufficiently tranquillized to render it safe and expedient for a British court of justice and a British jury to reward my perseverance with a comfortable and permanent abode in Bethlehem Hospital at the expense of the nation. I confess this latter consideration has much weight with me, as I am at present out of work, and have the much more disagreeable alternative of a union workhouse staring me in the face.
>
> I have the honour to remain,
> Your very insane servant (pro hac vice [for the occasion]),
> KILLING NO MURDER.

The royal family were in residence at Claremont, Uncle Leopold's Surrey estate, on the day of the verdict. Robert Peel sent

Victoria the news with a letter expressing his own disappointment. The three judges in the case, he told her, were certain that the evidence of insanity was too strong to allow anything but an acquittal. Peel had his doubts, however, that anyone who showed as much premeditation as McNaughtan had could be that insane: "It is a lamentable reflection," he wrote her, "that a man may be at the same time so insane as to be reckless of his own life and the lives of others, and to be pronounced free from moral responsibility, and yet capable of preparing for the commission of murder with the utmost caution and deliberation, and of taking every step which shall enable him to commit it with certainty."

Victoria had no doubts whatsoever about the matter: McNaughtan was as guilty as sin, and his verdict was botched. She believed it before the trial, and she believed it now: premeditation signified reason, which proved guilt. The recent trials whose results defied this simple logic were flawed, and Victoria blamed the judges, and their propensity for unorthodox instructions to their juries. "The law may be perfect," she wrote to Peel a week later,

> but how is that whenever a case for its application arises, it proves to be of no avail? We have seen the trials of Oxford and MacNaghten conducted by the ablest lawyers of the day—Lord Denman, Chief Justice Tindal, and Sir Wm. Follett,—and *they allow* and *advise* the Jury to pronounce the verdict of *Not Guilty* on account of *Insanity*,—whilst *everybody* is morally *convinced* that both malefactors were perfectly conscious and aware of what they did! It appears from this, that the force of the law is entirely put into the Judge's hands, and that it depends merely upon his charge whether the law is to be applied or not. Could not the Legislature lay down that rule which the Lord Chancellor does in his paper, and which Chief Justice Mansfield did in the case of Bellingham; and why could

not the Judges be *bound* to interpret the law in *this* and *no other* sense in their charges to the Juries?

The paper to which she referred contained the notes of the speech that the Lord Chancellor, Lord Lyndhurst, planned to give at the House of Lords about the current state of the insanity defense. Lyndhurst proposed convening the judges of the Supreme Court of Judicature in order to codify and promulgate a clear rule to apply in insanity cases—and stated that in his mind, the grounds for an insanity acquittal were clear: no one was criminally liable of a crime when he "is under the influence of delusion and insanity, so as not to know right from wrong, so as not to know what he is doing." In wishing that Parliament lay down this rule, she obviously did not realize that her notion of criminal liability did not quite dovetail with Lyndhurst's. Victoria considered simple awareness of the act enough for guilt; Lyndhurst considered *moral* awareness the standard.

The Lords met the next day and submitted five questions to the Law Lords—the key one being the second: "What are the proper questions to be submitted to the jury when a person, alleged to be afflicted with insane delusion respecting one or more particular subjects or persons, is charged with the commission of a crime . . . and insanity is set up as a defence?" Eleven of the twelve judges agreed upon their response, as set out six weeks later by Chief Justice Tindal (who had of course presided over the McNaughtan trial). That response became the McNaughtan Rules, which set the standard for the insanity defense in courtrooms across five continents. In Tindal's words, "to establish a defence on the ground of insanity, it must be clearly proved, that, at the time of committing of the act, the party accused was labouring under such a defect of reason, from disease of the mind, as not to know the nature and quality of the act he was doing, or if he did know it, that he did not know he was doing what was wrong."

Tindal's standard did not repudiate the precedent of McNaughtan's trial—but it did not wholly vindicate it, either. McNaughtan's inability to understand the wrongness of his action had indeed been a part of his defense—but moral awareness was a minor matter compared to the aspect of his insanity that every one of the medical witnesses had agreed upon—the fact that he was compelled to kill by an urge he had no control over. This notion of "irresistible impulse," as it was generally called, had no part in the McNaughtan Rules. The Rules were thus controversial at the moment of their birth, and have generated a great deal of controversy—in England, the United States, Australia, and elsewhere—ever since.

The Rules, moreover, were not what Victoria desired—though it would take some time before she realized it. Her letter to Peel made it clear exactly what she wanted in a verdict against *anyone* who deliberately raised a hand against herself or her servants: sane or insane, that person was guilty. Whether Oxford and McNaughtan would have been found guilty under the McNaughtan Rules is an open question. The assaults upon the Queen to come would raise the question again and again, and in the end, Victoria would find the insanity acquittal wanting. And she would accordingly change it.

Deep in the archives of the Museum of London is perhaps the oddest fashion accessory a British monarch ever owned: a delicate-looking parasol in the style of the early 1840s, of emerald-green silk, with a satin weave pattern at the fringe, and a carved ivory handle and ferrule. Discreetly hidden between layers of silk is a lining of close-linked chain mail.

This curious protection was designed in 1842, likely at the behest of Albert, to protect the Queen from the miscreants plaguing her. As far as ensuring Victoria's comfort during her regular airings, however, the chain-mail parasol could hardly have done the trick: at three and a quarter pounds, it weighs more than a large hammer, and holding it up for the length of an outing would have taken the strength of an Olympian. Much more likely, this chain-mail parasol was custom-made for the unusual occasion when the Queen *expected* to encounter an assailant during her ride, as she did when John Francis made his second attempt. The manufacture of this parasol almost certainly followed hard upon that event. This gift, if it was indeed Albert's gift, was his material counterpart to Peel's legal gift to Victoria: the Security of the Queen's Person Act.

Victoria is never known to have put the parasol to use. Certainly after Francis she never again flushed out an assailant. Indeed, for a time after Bean the assaults ceased altogether—apparent evidence that the prospect of a shameful public whipping actually stopped would-be Oxfords from confronting Victoria. Seven years would pass before the next assailant struck. And by then, Victoria's delicate-looking green chain-mail parasol was no longer in fashion.

Part Three

EXHIBITIONS

fourteen

BIRTHDAY

The fine weather suited Victoria's spirits and the nation's on this day, 19 May 1849, the official day of celebration of her thirtieth birthday. She had celebrated a dozen birthdays as Queen, and over the years the ceremonies of the day were established: just about all that occurred on this day she had seen and done before. The day began with the pealing of church bells across London, and a ubiquitous raising of the royal standard. In the morning, across the three Kingdoms were military reviews, and first among these was the review of the Household troops on the Horse Guards Parade outside Whitehall, conducted not by Victoria but by Albert, accompanied as he usually was by the Commander-in-Chief of the army, the eighty-year-old Duke of Wellington. Observing the spectacle for the first time was the seven-year-old Prince of Wales, from the prime viewpoint of the back garden of 10 Downing Street, then the residence of Victoria's Prime Minister, Lord John Russell.

At one o'clock the artillery in the park and at the Tower of London boomed a salute that was answered by volleys from Woolwich and from military depots across the United Kingdom. An hour later, Victoria and Albert rode in state to St. James to accept the congratulations of the uppermost 1,700 at the traditional birthday drawing room. The royal couple were resplendently dressed—Albert in his field marshal's uniform, encrusted with the heavily jeweled insignia of the Garter, the Bath, St. Patrick's, the Thistle, and the Golden Fleece; Victoria in "the most beautiful dress at the drawing-room": white satin and a train of green and silver silk, trimmed all over with red roses and violets, with a matching headdress of flowers, diamonds, and feathers. The dress, of course, had been woven in Spitalfields; the Queen required dresses of British manufacture at all her drawing rooms. The royal couple had returned from the drawing room, and now prepared for an outing: an impromptu carriage ride among the many who were milling about Green, Hyde, and Regent's Parks on this holiday.

In the evening, her chief ministers and her household officers would toast her at the full-dress dinners they held in her honor, while the rest of London, it seemed, crowded into the West End in slowly snaking queues to ooh and aah at the elaborate illuminations on the façades of the ministerial residences, the clubs on Pall Mall, and the establishments of the Queen's tradesmen: brilliant, variegated gaslight displays of crowns, stars, mottoes, laurel wreaths, English roses and British lions, portraits of the Queen—and a thousand blinding permutations of VR.

None of it was new to her. But this year, more than any other, the cheers, the well-wishing, the *feux de joie* and toasts, the bows and curtsies, must have seemed more appropriate to her than ever before. Life simply was different this year—different than it had been just a year before, or during any of the years of this difficult decade—years of poverty and hunger, class conflict and outright rebellion.

Much had changed as the decade progressed, but for Victoria, there was one constant: Albert. And Victoria had developed one belief, the anchor of all her thinking: Albert's perfection in all things. Since the fall of Melbourne and the departure of Lehzen, Albert had been her sole confidant and her private secretary, reading, summarizing, drafting replies to all her official correspondence, and tirelessly composing memoranda on issues he deemed important. *His* ideas became hers. "It is you who have entirely formed me," she once told him. They met with her ministers together, and spoke as one. When the Whigs returned to political office in 1846, they were amazed at the change since the days of Melbourne: "The Prince is become so identified with the Queen, that they are one person," wrote Charles Greville. "He is King to all intents and purposes."

While never forgetting Victoria was the monarch, and while always subsuming his own interests to hers, Albert embraced the role of a co-ruler, occupying his own throne at openings and closings of Parliament or at the Royal Balls; when the Queen was indisposed—as she was because of pregnancy nine times during the first seventeen years of their marriage—he took her place at government meetings and public functions. Victoria's Hanoverian relatives carped bitterly at his elevation, especially during the early years of their marriage. When Princess Alice was born in 1843 and Albert stood in for his wife at a court levée, the Cambridges absented themselves from the Court in a huff. A month after this, the King of Hanover battled with Albert physically for precedence at Victoria's cousin's wedding. Hanover lost: "I was forced to give him a strong push and drive him down a few steps, where the First Master of Ceremonies led him out of the chapel," Albert wrote his brother. Victoria was livid at any sign of others' blindness to what were in her mind Albert's transcendent merits. Time was on Albert's side in this respect: the original public image of Albert as a penniless foreign interloper had largely shifted to one of selfless public servant—and respectable *paterfamilias*.

Albert repaid Victoria's complete trust in him by giving her the best years of her life. He had convinced her that her true fulfillment was never to be found in the social whirl she had so delighted in during the Melbourne days, and those days were long gone: just a week after Lehzen had left the palace forever, in 1842, Victoria looked upon that time as if it were a strange dream from which she had awoken: "The life I led then was so artificial and superficial and yet I thought I was happy. Thank God! I now know what real happiness means." Albert never overcame his sense of foreignness, and was resistant to the charms of society—notoriously, almost comically resistant in particular to the charms of society women. He—and, before long, Victoria—found pleasure in escaping the aristocratic sparkle of Court life for the bourgeois *gemütlichkeit* of secluded family life. And over the past few years, he had labored mightily to create that life for his wife and their children.

He gave Victoria babies, for one thing. In 1849, there were six: after Vicky and Bertie came Alice (April 1843), and then Alfred ("Affie," August 1844), Helena ("Lenchen," May 1846) and Louise (March 1848) born just as Europe was erupting into revolution. Albert was a naturally loving and doting father—supervising the royal nursery, to which he kept the keys and constantly checked the locks—concerned, especially in the early days, by intrusions such as the Boy Jones's, and by a number of letters received threatening harm to the royal infants. The Queen was more ambivalent about children: she disliked the discomforts of pregnancy and feared the pains of childbirth, thought infants unpleasantly "frog-like," and confessed that she "only very exceptionally" found conversation with her children "either agreeable or easy." None the less, Victoria learned to find her greatest fulfillment among her family. "I am coming more and more convinced," she would later declare, "that the only true happiness in this world is to be found in the domestic circle." Of course Albert, who always took precedence over her children in her affections, was absolutely necessary to complete that happiness.

Albert's reform of the royal households and his management of the royal estates made his wife rich, and made possible the domestic cocoon he created for her. Once he wrested the management of the royal household from Lehzen, he set to work and replaced the bureaucratic anarchy of the three competing household departments by appointing a single master of the household in each royal residence. Fires were lit without confusion, windows were washed, guests were well attended to—and costs went down. More than this, he took control of the royal estates, and they soon began to pay handsomely. In short order he made the monarchy profitable, removing it forever from the chronic indebtedness that had plagued the Queen's royal uncles.

As the family grew, they spent far less time in London, finding seclusion at first at Windsor and Claremont. (The other royal residence, Brighton, set amid the bustle of the city and away from the ocean, they both disliked; they shut the place up and sold it in 1845, using the money to enlarge Buckingham Palace.) By 1843, they wanted even more seclusion—a residence bought with their own funds, and thus free of government administration. By October they had negotiated the purchase of a thousand-acre estate, Osborne House, on the Isle of Wight. And a little over a year before this birthday—at the end of 1847—they solidified their mutual love for the Highlands by leasing "a pretty little Castle in the old Scotch style": Balmoral. No English monarch before Victoria had ever resided so distantly from the capital before this: such a thing would not have been possible before the 1840s and two great technological developments of the decade. Railways were booming and interconnecting the nation, reducing in particular travel time from London to Osborne House (with the help of a steam-powered yacht) to three hours, and to Aberdeen to less than nine. And the telegraph, which had entered into nationwide operation by the end of the decade, gave the Queen the ability to conduct government business from virtually anywhere in the Kingdom.

Seclusion with Albert and her children, of course, meant that her regular airings from Buckingham Palace decreased dramatically. Indeed, even when she was in residence in London, she and

Albert were more likely to walk in the privacy of the palace gardens than ride out together. Would-be Oxfords could no longer assume that Victoria would ride regularly even when she was in residence. The Queen's ever-increasing urge to remove herself and her family from direct public view did nothing to diminish her popularity. She was paradoxically much more in the eyes of her subjects than any of her predecessors, because of the rise of a cheap illustrated press, beginning with the *Illustrated London News* in 1842. Now the royal couple, the royal children, the royal residences, and every royal event were a part of the shared experience of her subjects of all classes. These illustrations were inexpensive enough to adorn the walls of the poorest. Victoria no longer had to travel among her people to be seen by them. Indeed, it was in the public revelations of her private life that she saw as the key to her ever-growing popularity. "The papers . . . are most kind and gratifying," she wrote to Uncle Leopold in 1844; "they say no Sovereign was more loved than I am (I am bold enough to say) and that, from our happy domestic home—which gives such a good example." A new and enduring idea of monarchy had emerged: the royal family as the ideal family.

She owed it all to Albert: Albert had opened her eyes to the key to happiness, and then had given it to her. And yet she could not have been blind to the disjunction between her private happiness and the public turbulence of the 1840s.

Life had indeed improved for most after that dark year 1842. Industry grew by leaps and bounds. The population, employment, exports, and gross national product all shot up. The railways were the most visible manifestation of this reality-shaking growth, tearing up the old cities, revolutionizing trade and mobility, soaking up surplus labor, and making and breaking fortunes. In 1847, to be sure, the speculative bubble burst and a subsequent run on the banks led to a financial crisis. Recovery, however, was swift, and Britain was poised for the great boom of the 1850s.

And yet. Amidst all the growth existed pockets of dire poverty and hunger; the Hungry Forties was a decade that well deserved its name. In spite of the fact that, economically, 1842 was a turning point, and the economy grew dramatically after that, there existed all this time pockets of terrible suffering—suffering that was brought to the attention of an often-sympathetic but often-stymied public, leading to finger-pointing, handwringing, the shedding of a few sentimental tears, and usually little in the way of remedy. In 1843, Elizabeth Barrett Browning caused a sensation with her "Cry of the Children," laying bare the soul-crushed existences of boys and girls denied their youth by the harrowing demands of factory labor. Four months later, in a Christmas issue of *Punch*, Thomas Hood caused an even greater sensation with "The Song of the Shirt," a poem about London's starving piecework seamstresses, living in low-wage slavery so that their employers, London's slop-sellers or cheap clothing dealers, could undercut the competition:

> Oh, Men, with Sisters dear!
> Oh, men, with Mothers and Wives!
> It is not linen you're wearing out,
> But human creatures' lives!
> Stitch—stitch—stitch,
> In poverty, hunger and dirt,
> Sewing at once, with a double thread,
> A Shroud as well as a Shirt.

And later in 1849, Henry Mayhew would begin publishing his evocative exploration of the hidden world of London's working poor in the *Morning Chronicle*. The poorer of the "two nations" to which Benjamin Disraeli referred in his 1845 work *Sybil, or the Two Nations*, had never been more a part of the awareness of the wealthy—but never, at the same time, was poverty more accepted as an unfortunate and unalterable fact of life. Political economy might have been the dismal science, but it was indeed a science in the minds of the best thinkers of the 1840s, its speculations to them dogma. *Laissez-faire* ruled. Even radical reformers opposed attempts by the government to assist the poor: that, according to the science, would only make things worse.

The worst hunger of all, that decade, struck Ireland with a vengeance—and completely by surprise—in 1845. No one knew exactly where the fungal disease *Phytophthora infestans*, or potato blight, came from; the disease had spread across northern Europe, and, in mid-September, reached Ireland: in a month, a third of that country's overwhelmingly predominant crop transmogrified into a stinking, inedible goo. Prime Minister Robert Peel quickly understood the enormity of the crisis and tried to meet it, ordering £100,000 worth of Indian corn bought with government funds and sent from the United States. Moreover, he came to a momentous decision about the Corn Laws, which protected British farmers by regulating foreign grain imports—and which, many argued, kept the price of food artificially high. Support for the Corn Laws had been fundamental Tory doctrine. But Peel decided that the Corn Laws must be repealed.

It was a decision that destroyed Peel politically, as the majority of his own party turned on him ferociously. Peel could only hope to pass repeal of the Corn Laws by resigning and letting Lord John Russell and the Whigs handle the problem, or by introducing the bill himself and splitting his own party irreparably. When a majority of his own cabinet would not support repeal, then, he resigned. The Queen called upon Russell to form a cabinet. He was unable to do so, and Victoria, with a sense of relief—for Peel had in his own way grown as close to Victoria as Melbourne had—then recalled Peel, who promptly formed a cabinet committed to repeal. From that moment, more than half his party turned on him, vowing to bring him down at any cost. Lord Derby in the House of Lords led this Protectionist faction, and Benjamin Disraeli and George Bentinck in the House of Commons took upon themselves the roles of Peel's chief tormentors, ferociously and regularly attacking Peel's character as well as his policy. Disraeli "hacked and mangled Peel with the most unsparing severity, and positively tortured his victim," Charles Greville wrote of a speech that nearly brought Peel to tears. Ultimately, Peel won—and lost: on 25 June 1846, the same night that the Corn Law repeal passed in the House of Lords, the Protectionists in Commons voted against their principles to defeat a coercion bill for turbulent Ireland, in order to bring down Peel's government. Four days later, Peel resigned. Though John Russell and his Whigs were in the minority—and, after a general election, remained in the minority—the cataclysmic split of the Tories, and the support Peel's faction, the "Peelites," gave the Whigs, kept Russell's government securely in power. And Russell's government still ruled three years later when his ministers threw dinners for the Queen's thirtieth birthday. Lord Wellington was bitter about the cause of Peel's fall, grumbling "rotten potatoes have done it all; they put Peel in his damned fright."

Peel's downfall was a personal tragedy, and a greater one for starving Ireland. For while the chief architect of relief for Ireland, Charles Trevelyan, permanent undersecretary of the Treasury, worked under Peel as well as Russell, with the Whigs he found kindred spirits and full support for a grim *laissez-faire* response to Irish hunger. Under the Whigs, Trevelyan insisted that Irish pay for their own relief. He continued importing food, but demanded that local relief committees buy the food at market price. He instituted a program of public works—but insisted that they be paid for locally, with the help of government loans. When it became clear that the blight had utterly destroyed the potato crop of 1846, he allowed public works to continue, but government loans ceased completely. During the unusually bitterly cold winter months of early 1847, as thousands starved and fever ravaged the population, the government decided upon a radical change of policy: they would halt public works altogether, and feed the starving with soup kitchens, paid for largely from private charity. Victoria contributed £2,000 to one of these charities.* In a few months, the soup kitchens closed

---

* Not £5, as a particularly nasty and long-lived myth would have it (Woodham-Smith, *Great Hunger* 169).

and charity dried up. The British were by then frankly tired of this interminable famine, and most were certain that the indolent Irish were responsible for their own plight. "The great evil with which we have to contend," declared Trevelyan at the end of 1846, is "not the physical evil of the famine, but the moral evil of the selfish, perverse and turbulent character of the people." Victoria and Albert, originally deeply sympathetic to the plight of the Irish, concurred with this assessment, Albert writing at around the same time, in a memorandum, "The state of Ireland is most alarming and seems quite hopeless as every attempt on the part of the Government to relieve it, is turned by the Irish themselves to bad account." In June 1847, the British government essentially washed its hands of the problem by reforming the Irish poor law to fix the costs of relieving the poor entirely upon the poor law unions—the workhouses—of Ireland.

And the famine went on. The crop of 1847–8 was healthy but scarce: amid general starvation and destitution, few healthy seed potatoes were to be found, and fewer planted. The crop of 1848–9 was another total failure, and the suffering during the first few months of 1849 was among the worst of all. In the end, one million died: one out of eight of the Irish population. An equal number emigrated: many to the slums of English cities, but most to the United States. Most brought with them undying hatred for the British and a desire for revenge that would in years to come lead to bitter consequences for Britain—would indeed come to threaten Victoria personally.

Indeed, Irish rage had already burst out a year before, in July 1848, in spite of debilitating fever and hunger.

The spark was the February Revolution in Paris, which in two days toppled Louis-Philippe from the throne. (He and his family sought refuge with the Queen; she put him up at Claremont.) The revolutionary fever spread like wildfire; within weeks Prussia had granted a new, liberal constitution, the King of Bavaria abdicated in favor of his son, and in Austria the chancellor Metternich was forced to flee—to England, of course—and the Emperor forced to give concessions. Austria's Italian domains rose up, as did the rest of the country. Victoria's royal palaces became aristocratic refugee camps.

The revolutionary spark took fire in England, where the Chartists, in decline since the hot summer of 1842, burst back to life under the leadership of the movement's fiery and charismatic agitator-in-chief, Feargus O'Connor. Rioting erupted in Glasgow and London in March. That month, the Chartists announced that they planned to march from Kennington Common, south of the river, to present the People's Charter to Parliament for the third time—and planned to accompany the petition with a threatening procession of 200,000 people. The government betrayed the depth of its alarm with the enormity of its response. The troops in the capital were doubled and stationed out of sight at strategic points across the city, concentrating on the bridges over the Thames, upon which artillery was trained. Eighty-five thousand men were sworn in as special constables—a government masterstroke, ensuring that the middle class, unlike the French middle class, would remain squarely with the state. (One of these constables was Louis Napoleon, who had not yet taken advantage of the French revolution to return to his country, get elected president, and then make himself emperor.) On the advice of Russell and the Home Secretary, Victoria and Albert and their family (including 22-day-old Princess Louise) slipped through the pouring rain onto a train at closely guarded Waterloo Station, and decamped to Osborne.

The revolutionary tenth of April turned out to be a complete bust. Though estimates of the crowd differ widely, nowhere near the 400,000 which Feargus O'Connor expected to come actually showed up. O'Connor, alarmed by the military preparations, lost his own fire on this day. Upon his arrival at Kennington Common, he was called into a pub by Commissioner Mayne and told that he could hold his meeting, but that a monster procession to Parliament was out of the question. O'Connor meekly agreed, mounted the rostrum to ask the crowd to disperse, and took the petition to Parliament himself in a cab. The petition itself only earned ridicule as it was found (after a suspiciously quick count) to have less than a third of the six million signatures claimed, and many of those signatures were found to be fraudulent, including the Queen's as "Victoria Rex." Though the movement percolated on through the summer, the threat had passed. "We had our revolution yesterday, and it went up in smoke," Albert wrote to Stockmar.

He added, however, "in Ireland things look still more serious." There, revolution fermented as spring turned to summer. Daniel O'Connell had died in 1847, and his non-violent movement to repeal the Act of Union between Britain and Ireland had been eclipsed by that of Young Ireland, a group who differed from the O'Connellites in their willingness to use physical force to repeal the union. The February revolution in France electrified Young Ireland as it had the Chartists. "The shock awakened mankind," proclaimed the movement's leader, William Smith O'Brien. "Those who believed themselves to be weak now felt themselves to be strong."

Young Ireland began to promote rebellion openly, and formed the Irish Confederation—clubs across the island with the avowed aim of preparing for insurrection. Lord Clarendon, Lord Lieutenant of Ireland, was deeply alarmed by all this activity, sending Cassandra cries to the government, pleading for a suspension of *habeas corpus* in Ireland. When Parliament did just that at the end of July, the leaders of Young Ireland were faced with a stark decision: passivity and arrest, or outright rebellion. Smith O'Brien feared the worst, but felt bound by honor to raise an insurrection. Dublin was a British armed camp; the south was more auspicious for rebellion. Smith O'Brien thus tramped through the southern towns and countryside, finding large crowds of poorly armed but ardent adherents at every turn—and demonstrating at every turn his utter inability to lead a revolution, tenaciously holding to his belief in the sanctity of private property before would-be rebels who had none. When an excited crowd of six thousand began to build barricades in the village of Mullinahone, Smith O'Brien forbade them to fell trees without the permission of the owners of the nearby estates. To another crowd, hungry and ready to despoil in order to eat, Smith O'Brien ordered them instead to return home, provide four days' provisions for themselves, and return the next day. "This announcement gave a death-blow to the entire movement," stated a witness. The crowds melted away as fast as they formed.

Having thus gathered up and dispersed several armies of the poor, on 29 July in the town of Ballingarry, Smith O'Brien and a ragtag group of about 120 men and women confronted fifty or so policemen who, fleeing the crowd, commandeered a widow's house on the edge of town. The widow was out, but her five or six children were there, and the police took them hostage. Smith O'Brien attempted to secure the children's release and was nearly shot for his pains when gunfire erupted on both sides and he was caught in the crossfire. The police were better armed, and after the rebels expended all of their bullets and stones on the house, hurting no police but losing two of their own, the crowd scattered before police reinforcements arrived. Smith O'Brien fled alone. The Irish revolution of 1848 ended with an Irish whimper and a British snicker, the *Times* dismissively immortalizing the event as the "cabbage-patch revolt." Smith O'Brien was arrested within a week, tried, and sentenced with three others to death for Treason. On this day of the Queen's thirtieth birthday, Smith O'Brien was in Richmond Bridewell in Dublin, the sounds of the festivities outside likely echoing through the prison.

The worst of the European revolutionary fervor was over by May 1849. The hemorrhaging of monarchies had stopped with the June 1848 insurrection in France, during which hundreds of radicals died on the barricades and the conservatives took control. After this, the tide in Europe shifted from revolution to reaction. Victoria's aristocratic refugees (save Louis-Philippe and his family) went home. Die-hard Chartists still met and tried to convince each other that they had significance, but their popular support was gone: they certainly would never send the royal family running again. The economy was surging. Ireland was tamed—tamed enough for Victoria and Albert to consider visiting the country, as Ireland's Lord Lieutenant, Lord Clarendon, had been begging them to do for some time.

There was every reason for Victoria to celebrate—every reason to go among her public. She'd taken few rides in London this year. But for the last four days, and with the fine May weather, she'd toured the parks in an open carriage with various combinations of her children, Albert and his equerry riding on horseback beside them. She would ride again today, bringing Alice, Affie, and Lenchen with her.

Outside the Palace gates and up Constitution Hill the crowd grew larger, as the presence of the royal landau at the Palace steps signaled silently and almost supernaturally the Queen's intent to ride. At half past five, nursemaids and footmen helped the children, and then Victoria and her maid of honor Flora MacDonald, into the carriage. Victoria sat at the left rear. Her sergeant-footman, Robert Renwick, clambered up into the rumble seat behind her, and her equerry, Major General William Wemyss, took up his position on horseback, very close to the left side of the carriage. Albert swung onto his horse, and he and his equerry led the carriage out of the gate and into the shouting and cheering public.

fifteen

THE MAN FROM ADARE

As Victoria and Albert held court that afternoon at the Queen's birthday drawing room, William Hamilton sat in a yard at Eccleston Place, Pimlico—a literal stone's throw from the Palace Gardens—manufacturing his own present for the Queen's birthday. He was an Irishman, having left Ireland for London at around the beginning of the famine, one of the first of what became a wave of Irish immigrants who were seen as taking English jobs and ruining good English wages. He was a working man, as his corduroy trousers, fustian jacket, and greasy cap made clear at a glance. He was a working man, that is, when he was employed, but he had seen precious little employment over the last few months and was virtually penniless. His burliness falsely hinted at comfort; only charity had kept him from starvation. He had once been to France, and possibly dabbled with radical politics there. He was deeply discontented, his face a fixed sullen mask.

In short, he epitomized the British fears of the 1840s.

He had been whittling for some time, shaping a chunk of wood into something like the stock of a pistol. He had scavenged the tin spout of a teapot, which—if one ignored the spout's absurd curvature—might look a bit like a pistol barrel. And he had tied the two together with string, creating a primitive dummy of a gun. With some performance on his part, and if the crowd already assembling along Constitution Hill proved to be the right sort of crowd, he might succeed in alarming the Queen and getting himself arrested.

Imprisonment was all he sought: a bed and regular meals at Millbank or Pentonville or Coldbath Fields. That would be better than this dubious life as a free man, owing his life to the kindness of two women. He had actually encouraged his long-suffering landlord, Daniel O'Keefe, upon whom he sponged, to arrest him for debt so that he could "get a billet for the winter season in prison." But O'Keefe refused to do that, millstone around his neck that Hamilton was. Instead, with a touching if misplaced hope, he preferred to farm Hamilton out to work for others, periodically requesting that he repay his debt. It was a strategy that paid poorly, for Hamilton's work was sporadic and consistently awful; O'Keefe had not recouped the bulk of what he was owed.

Daniel O'Keefe would certainly have expelled Hamilton years before—but O'Keefe's wife, Bridget, had influence over him, and she was captivated by Hamilton, who had an odd and compelling charm over women and children. Bridget saw to it that Hamilton had not only shelter but regular nourishment. In this she was assisted by a lodger at Eccleston Place, a woman whose name is lost to history: this woman was in the "milk line," according to Bridget, delivering milk to London's basement kitchens and receiving at times in return "a deal of broken victuals"—leftovers of leftovers that the servants passed on. These she shared with Hamilton. "Between the two of us," said Bridget O'Keefe, "we managed to keep him."

William Hamilton was a stranger in a strange land from the day he was born, and spent his life drifting from one failure to another.

He likely never knew his birthday, and never did know his parents, taking from them only his name and his religion when around 1826 they died or simply abandoned the infant to the Protestant Orphan Society at Cork. He was a real-life Irish Oliver Twist, learning rudimentary skills at the orphanage school until he reached the age at which he could be contracted as an apprentice to whoever would pay for him. In Hamilton's case, this was a Protestant farmer outside of Adare, near Limerick, who put the boy to work in the fields and set him to building walls and digging ditches. Hamilton would always claim Adare to be his home, though few from Adare would admit to knowing him.

When Hamilton was about thirteen, he was again abandoned: his employer sold the farm and emigrated to Canada with his family. Hamilton found a place in Adare, as assistant to a shop-keeper named John Barkman. Hamilton was working there in 1840 when Edward Oxford shot at the Queen. Barkman's wife recalled that the boy approved of the attempt: "it was not right to serve under petticoat government," Hamilton told her. Afterwards, she would often tease him that he still lived under Victoria's—and her own—petticoat government. Keeping shop did not last: Hamilton abandoned the Barkmans, or they abandoned him, and perhaps the Great Famine forced the issue: in 1845 Hamilton left Ireland forever, coming to London hoping, on the strength of the walls he had built as a farmboy, to find a future as a bricklayer's assistant. A mutual acquaintance had given him an introduction to Daniel O'Keefe, himself a bricklayer and originally from Adare, and Hamilton settled in at Eccleston Place.

From that moment on, Daniel O'Keefe was Hamilton's reluctant protector, as Hamilton repeatedly tried and failed to make a living as a bricklayer's assistant. In 1846, he did attempt to set out on his own, joining the armies of workingmen who had spread out across the country and across Europe to build the burgeoning railways. He became, in other words, a navvy, one of that hard-drinking, reckless, and depraved clan who spread terror across the countryside while they laid tracks: they were the ubiquitous bogeymen of the railway boom. Hamilton's limited expertise was with the masonry of bridges, tunnels, and cuttings. He somehow found employment in France, arriving there in May 1846—or, as Hamilton later put it to a policeman, the time "of Prince Louis Napoleon's escape from Ham." His curious method of dating, as well as the fact that Hamilton was actually imprisoned in Paris, led some to suspect that he had political proclivities. But his arrest was not political, but for being out too late one night. And Louis Napoleon's escape to England was hardly the signal for any insurrectionary activity in France. Hamilton came to France to make money, not trouble.

But he did not make money, and by November he was back with the O'Keefes. His natural indolence and second-rate skills meant that in spite of Daniel O'Keefe's best efforts, Hamilton was only a drain on his own earnings. By the time of the Queen's birthday, Hamilton hadn't "worked seven weeks since Christmas," according to Bridget. The shoddy facsimile of a pistol he carved on this day might have been the hardest work he'd done for some time.

Bridget O'Keefe came upon him that afternoon in the back garden. She was mystified by the pitiful-looking object, and mystified when Hamilton told her he was making an actual pistol, and planned "to fire a shot or two" with it. She pointed out the folly of his plan, and he seemed suddenly to have a thought. "Why, Dan has got an old pistol," he said to her. "Lend me it."

And without hesitation she did, returning to her bedroom to ferret it out, and handing it to him through the window. It was a pocket-sized, with a three-inch brass screw-barrel—extremely old, rusty from disuse. Hamilton complained about that rust to Bridget. "It is of no account," she told him: the pistol was only a toy to her, and, she thought, to him.

Soon afterwards, Hamilton sought out the O'Keefe's ten-year-old son Edward, a child as charmed by the man as his mother Bridget was. Giving boy one of his few halfpennies, Hamilton asked him to fetch as much powder as that would buy. Edward rushed off to a shop nearby on Elizabeth Street to procure a quantity of what was "not the best sort of powder." In the meantime, Hamilton worried that the pistol might not work at all. When the boy returned, Hamilton asked him if he happened to have any squibs (a sort of hissing explosive) or crackers. Those, Edward told him, could be obtained from a nearby shop. He'd like a ha'p'orth of them as well, Hamilton told the boy: he wanted to have some fun firing them through the trees. Edward never bought these for him; no fireworks were later found among Hamilton's few possessions. Hamilton soon found he didn't need them: his landlord's rusty flintlock served his purpose well. With the head broken from a clay pipe Hamilton poured gunpowder into the barrel and onto the pan. He shot once, twice, three times successfully, pretending to take aim at something: practicing his stance. Bridget O'Keefe could hear the loud blasts from inside the house.

Shortly after this, Hamilton left the house, the pistol secreted in the inside breast pocket of his jacket. Young Edward O'Keefe had asked him if he could come too, and play, but Hamilton told him no: "you must stop at home." Hamilton gave—or, rather, sold—the boy another toy to play with: his contraption of rudely carved wood, tea spout, and string. The boy had only the halfpenny that Hamilton had given him, but promised to pay a full penny when he had it. All in all, it had been a productive day for Hamilton: he had a working gun and a decent supply of gunpowder—and was a halfpenny ahead on the deal.

Hamilton disappeared into the city for a couple of hours. By six, he was standing near the bottom of Constitution Hill, not far from the Palace gates, joining a now-swelling crowd, all gazing uphill, waiting for the Queen's carriage to return. He stood slightly downhill from where Oxford had made his attempt, and stood behind the palings separating the park from the road. He paced nervously, his left hand jammed in his trousers pocket, his right at the ready—glancing with the crowd to the top of the hill but seeing nothing—nothing, that is, but the monstrous, bulky, and oddly sedentary statue of the Duke of Wellington, which then topped the triumphal arch through which the Queen's carriage would soon pass.*

At around twenty minutes past six, a cheer rose and rippled down the hill. Albert and his equerry were returning from their ride—alone. The Prince had accompanied Victoria and the children through Hyde and into Regent's Park—but from there he decided to spur on his horse and return ahead of them. The two men quickly disappeared through the Palace gate. Hamilton, confused by seeing the Prince without the Queen, asked a woman beside him if Victoria had yet passed. "No," the woman told him, "she has not come yet; but if you wait a little you will see her."

The royal carriage was not far behind. Cheering recommenced up the road, and the Queen's outriders trotted into view. Then, the carriage. Hamilton strode up to the palings and spoke to both the woman and to a muscular man on the other side of the fence. "Is that the Queen?" Both assented and turned to watch the carriage rush past. "All right," Hamilton muttered. He immediately reached into his coat for the pistol, thrust it through the palings alongside the muscular man's face—and fired with a loud roar and a plume of smoke. The man, deafened, felt something whizz past his ear and realized his face was scorched. He believed Hamilton's gun had been loaded with a bullet.

Sergeant-footman Robert Renwick, sitting in a rumble seat behind the Queen, saw Hamilton point the gun—and immediately called out to the postilions to stop the carriage—giving Hamilton a clearer target. Amazingly, they were obeying just as Hamilton fired. Victoria stood up and gazed in the direction of the shot. "Renwick," she said, "what is that?"

---

* The statue was placed there with great fanfare in 1846, positioned adjacent to Apsley House so that the Duke of Wellington could have the honor of seeing his gargantuan self outside his own windows. Many (including the Queen) regarded the statue as an eyesore completely out of proportion to its setting, and it was removed in 1883 to the military garrison at Aldershot.

"Your Majesty has been shot at."

Victoria sat down and ordered the carriage to move on. Her equerry Wemyss excitedly did the same thing, and then reeled his horse about and trotted into the Park to supervise Hamilton's arrest. Victoria, seemingly unperturbed, pacified Alfred, Alice, and Helena—who, from their position, had had an excellent view of the shooting. Within seconds, the carriage disappeared through the palace gates. Albert, who had heard the pistol-crack, agitatedly met his family at the steps of the Palace: "Thank God," he said to Victoria, "you are safe."

As it happens, George Moulder, Green Park's head park-keeper, had been standing just twelve yards from Hamilton as the Queen passed; he had seen everything. He instantly fell upon Hamilton, who was frantically trying to return the pistol to his coat pocket. Moulder grabbed him by the right arm and collar, but feared that he had another pistol and cried out for the man on the other side of the fence—the startled, singed, muscular man, whose name was Daniel Lamb—to seize him as well. Lamb seemed to Moulder to do nothing. Lamb's abnormal strength (he had the quaint occupation—considered unusual even then—of a "running huntsman," actually running barefoot along with the hounds during fox hunts) was useless to him in this situation, as Hamilton stood too far away on the other side of the palings. All Lamb could do was clutch at the fringe of Hamilton's coat. A police constable named Topley, and a private in the Life Guards, then vaulted the palings and secured an agitated but unresisting Hamilton.

While everyone in the crowd had heard the booming gunshot, very few had actually seen that the Queen was unharmed, and the great majority jumped to the conclusion that she had been hit—had been grievously wounded—had even been killed. "Secure him," several shouted, "he has murdered the Queen!" A hostile mass quickly converged upon a now-frightened Hamilton, crying "tear him to pieces!" and chanting "kill him at once; kill him at once!" A middle-aged man raised his fist to him, intent upon "inflicting summary punishment"; the Queen's equerry William Wemyss restrained him. The several police on patrol around the palace who had run up to seize Hamilton suddenly found themselves his protectors, fending off a growing lynch mob. One constable ran to fetch a hackney cab while the others herded Hamilton through a wicket and onto the road. A policeman who had wrestled the pistol away from Hamilton gave it to the Queen's equerry. Wemyss by this time was already certain that there had been no bullet in the pistol—if there had been, he was sure he would have been hit. One sniff at the barrel confirmed that this was the gun that had fired. But he was certain that the sound of a loaded pistol would have been different.

The hackney cab wheeled up and Hamilton was quickly bundled inside; William Walker, inspector on duty at the Palace, and other police climbed in. With Wemyss riding by their side, they brought Hamilton to A Division station house. On the way there, Hamilton betrayed none of the exhilaration that Oxford and Francis had had upon their capture; he endured rather than enjoyed public attention.

When they arrived at the station house, the commissioners were summoned, and Hamilton was soon placed in the police dock to be questioned, along with several witnesses to the shooting, by Mayne as well as Superintendent May. The attention only seemed to depress him, as he leaned on the dock with his head in his hands. In response to questioning, he was momentarily uncommunicative, at first refusing to state his name and address. He soon gave in and spoke, with a thick brogue: his name was William Hamilton[*], aged twenty-four—an Irishman from Adare, County Limerick; he was an out-of-work bricklayer's laborer. He had acted as he did because he was poor. No one else was involved: he had no friends or relatives in this country.

---

[*] In the first accounts, he is named as *John* Hamilton; in time, William was the clear consensus.

Park-keeper Moulder and others then identified him as the man who had shot at the Queen. Whether the gun was loaded or not—whether Hamilton was to be tried for High Treason or for the High Misdemeanour of annoying the public and the Queen—would be left for the Home Office to decide. Hamilton was remanded to be examined in Whitehall the next day, with all the witnesses bound over to appear there. He was then brought to the cell previously inhabited by Oxford, Francis, and Bean.

Inspector Charles Otway (the man who had entrapped Gould, and had been a sergeant in A Division when Oxford was arrested) hurried to Eccleston Place and discovered the depth of Hamilton's penury. There was nothing in his room besides two sheets lent him by his landlady and a few scribbled-upon sheets of paper—with nothing in them about shooting the Queen. Finding nothing material to the case, Otway returned to the station and interviewed Hamilton directly. Hamilton told him about his long bout of unemployment; about his journey to France at the time of Louis Napoleon's escape; about his work on the French railways—and about his motive. His pistol contained only powder and he had not had the slightest intention of hurting the Queen. "He said he did it for the purpose of getting into prison, as he was tired of being out of work."

By this time, the ministers' celebratory dinners for the Queen were in full swing, and messengers were sent from the Palace to interrupt the Home Secretary and the Prime Minister with the news. Home Secretary George Grey sent to the Home Office, arranging for an examination there at two the next day, and sending word to the commissioners to be present. This examination would be more subdued than the previous ones: not a spectacular convening of the Cabinet, but largely limited to the Home Office and the police. That Grey did not schedule an examination that night demonstrates that from the start he was unwilling to accord Hamilton the notoriety accorded Hamilton's predecessors. (He did, however, send word to A Division that Hamilton be placed on suicide watch.) Grey then hurried to the Palace—as did Prime Minister John Russell.

The reaction to the attempt was predictable: the elite hastening in their carriages to the Palace to inquire after the Queen's health, the raucous celebration at the operas and the plays, the swelling crowds surrounding the palace—but this time, the public celebrations took on a greater intensity, growing out of the many celebrations already underway. At the clubs, and at ministerial dinners, the Queen's health was drunk with three times three; outside, on Pall Mall, along Regent Street, and on the Great Mall between St. James's and Buckingham Palace, crowds cried out "Long live the Queen" and spontaneously burst into the national anthem. Jubilation at the Queen's escape only intensified the illuminations later that night. "Altogether," the *Times* reported, "the routine of a Royal birthday received a vast and visible stimulus from the impulse of public sympathy."

The next day, Victoria wrote to her Uncle Leopold that "the indignation, loyalty, and affection this act has called forth is very gratifying and touching"—just as it had been three times before. And yet, the Queen knew, something about Hamilton's attempt was completely different. Hamilton's attempt was, as everyone seemed to realize from the first—not really an attempt at all. His pistol was almost certainly unloaded with any sort of projectile. The police searched the area exhaustively for a bullet and turned up nothing. At the royal stables, the carriage was scrutinized for marks; none were found. The Queen's equerry Wemyss, who was positive that if there had been a bullet, he or his horse would have been hit, was unscathed. And a thorough search of Hamilton produced a small amount of gunpowder, the head of a pipe, and a few halfpence, but no bullet. Much the same had been the case with Oxford, Francis, and Bean. But with the first two there was no question that treason was afoot and the pistols were loaded. Even with Bean those were at first distinct possibilities. In Hamilton's case, on the other hand—after the initial attempt to lynch him by the angry crowd—the idea that he might have intended to injure or kill the queen was universally and repeatedly denied. His was the perfect case to be tried under Robert Peel's Security and Protection of Her Majesty's Person Act, and everyone hoped he'd find his punishment at the wrong end of a whip rather than a rope.

Victoria was certain from the start that Hamilton had had no intention of killing her, writing to Leopold "I hope that you will not have been alarmed by the account of the occurrence which took place on Saturday, and which I can assure you did *not* alarm *me* at all. *This* time it is quite clear that it was a wanton and wicked wish merely to *frighten*, which is very wrong, and will be tried and punished as a *misdemeanour*." In the Sunday newspapers the day after the shooting, Hamilton's attempt was designated an "absurdity," "an exasperating piece of folly," not worthy of consideration as a capital crime: "The man who commits such an act in this country should be flogged at the cart's tail, for hanging would be treating him with too much consideration." On Monday, the *Daily News*, though it acknowledged the wickedness of pointing a pistol at "a person every way so sacred, in domestic as in political life, as that of her Majesty," noted that at least there "will not be found superadded the heinousness of a really murderous motive" to the act. In the House of Commons that same day, Lord John Russell agreed, claiming that "it has been found that there is no reason to accuse the person who discharged the pistol of a treasonable attempt, and that it is a crime more remarkable for its baseness than its atrocity."

Given the extremely turbulent times through which Britain and Europe were passing, the haste at which virtually everyone disregarded Hamilton as a threat seems on the surface surprising. The fact that Hamilton was from Ireland, a country still starving and defeated in May 1849, would appear to provide him with an obvious political motive for striking out against the British government by harming the Queen. But the papers hurried to disabuse readers of this interpretation. "The accident, or the fact, of the man Hamilton's being an Irishman may be made the theme of animadversion, and conclusions may be drawn from it of the international hate or savage vindictiveness of the Celt," wrote the *Daily News*. But "the Irish elements which have contributed to his crime, will probably be found more those of poverty and vanity, than any thing more peculiarly malignant or Celtic."

The Irish newspapers were particularly adamant in asserting that Hamilton had no intention of killing the Queen. One attempted to claim that Hamilton might not be Irish at all. Others scrambled to prove that while he might be Irish, he could not be from *their* corner of the island. The *Limerick Chronicle* investigated and found that though Hamilton claimed to be from Adare, he had no relatives there. A further report allowed that he had worked on a farm near Adare and assisted at a shop in town, but that Cork, not Adare, was responsible for him: "Hamilton was a native of Cork, and no relative of any persons at or near Adare." The *Cork Constitution* quickly responded with a letter from the secretaries of the Cork Orphan Asylum denying that anyone named William Hamilton had passed through there. (They were probably correct, as they were apparently officials of the larger *Catholic* Orphan Asylum, not the smaller Protestant Asylum from which Hamilton came.) "The Corkonians are most anxious to disclaim having reared the fellow who fired at the Queen," wrote a journalist reporting the squabble. In tossing his origins around like a hot potato, the Irish appeared one and all eager to deny any connection between Hamilton and them—and eager to dissociate him from any Irish cause.

Then, there was a second possibility: that Hamilton might be the last gasp of revolutionary activity in England. This was also vehemently denied by both the press and the politicians. One editorialist, wilfully forgetting the recent past, declared absolutely that "fortunately there are no recent event [sic] which could afford political colour or excitement to a crime of this kind. Never was the country more tranquil or the parliamentary session more dull."

At a grand dinner at Mansion House Monday evening, the Lord Mayor, toasting the Queen, deplored Hamilton's act, but denied it could have been political, because such a revolutionary political act was simply impossible in Britain. "At a time when the all the continental nations are struggling in political convulsions," he said, "this country enjoys a complete immunity from any of those dreadful conflicts to which the rest of Europe is subjected."

Hamilton's shooting threatened to resurrect some of the uglier incidents of the recent past. The British collectively refused to let that happen. His was the most quickly forgotten attempt. Before three days had passed, he was already a fading memory to Victoria and Albert as they traveled with the children to their haven at Osborne.

And yet, three-year-old Princess Helena saw it all and knew what must happen next, stating after she witnessed the attempt "Man shot, tried to shoot dear Mamma, must be punished." *How* he would be punished was the question. The day after the shooting—Sunday the twenty-second—he was examined at the Home Office, brought there between Superintendent May and Inspector Otway. At first he appeared affronted to be there, but within seconds was reduced to trembling before Home Secretary Grey. The Attorney General, John Jervis, examined witnesses for three hours until Grey came to the conclusion that everyone had already reached: Hamilton's pistol was not loaded, and he had meant to annoy the Queen, not to kill her. All of the O'Keefes—Daniel, Bridget, and young Edward—testified, but Hamilton's mysterious young protectress in the milk line was nowhere to be seen. Edward O'Keefe could not let his meeting with Hamilton pass without paying his debt: while testifying he displayed the tea-spout bound to the chunk of wood, and, producing a penny, he turned to the prisoner. "Here, Mr. Hamilton, I can pay you the penny now, for I did not have one on Saturday." The record does not show whether Hamilton took it or not, although he was at that moment given the opportunity to speak—and said nothing.

Hamilton was charged under Peel's Security and Protection of Her Majesty's Person Act—the first person ever so charged. He was conveyed from Whitehall to Newgate in a cab, guarded by three policemen. And in Newgate he remained quietly. Nothing like the sort of celebrity coverage accorded to Oxford, Francis, and to a lesser extent Bean was accorded to Hamilton. Hamilton almost certainly preferred it that way—his perpetual sullenness, his inability to delight in his capture or swell up with self-importance during his few moments in the spotlight suggest he viewed his short burst of notoriety as a grim necessity, a prelude to the steady sustenance that prison or transportation would supply him. Sustenance at the Queen's pleasure at Bethlem, on the other hand, seems never to have occurred to him; the newspapers tended to note his complete sanity, and he never planned an insanity defense.

His trial was set for the next sessions at the Central Criminal Court in three weeks' time. The newspapers speculated as to his possible punishment, most aware that Peel's Act included the humiliation of whipping as a part of the punishment. Less known about the act, however, was that if Hamilton earned the strictest sentence, he could not be whipped at all: 5th and 6th Victoria, c. 31 mandated a sentence of seven years transportation *or* up to three years' imprisonment with hard labor, with the additional penalty of public or private whippings. *The Illustrated London News* deplored the discrepancy:

> It is, perhaps, to be regretted that the framers of the bill did not provide that transportation *and* flogging should be the punishment. We have certainly no desire to revive the barbarous punishments of past ages, but we think that a weekly, semi-weekly, or even daily infliction of the cat-o'-nine-tails for three months at the least, prepa-ratory to transportation, would greatly tend to prevent such lunacy as that of the last offender from breaking out into action. . . . Insane as such offenders may be,

they have sanity enough to understand the logic of the
cat-o'-nine-tails. . . .

Hamilton's judges would have to decide whether severity or
humiliation would best serve prisoner and public.

As Hamilton awaited trial, Victoria and Albert formalized their
plans for visiting Ireland, which they both had desired to do as early
as summer 1843, when the steam-powered royal yacht *Victoria and
Albert* replaced the obsolete *Royal George*. But the Repeal movement
was at its height that year. After that, there was famine and revolt.
In 1849, however, all troubles had passed or were passing. Lord Lieutenant of Ireland Clarendon was positive that the time was now ripe:
"Since Her Majesty came to the throne, there has been no period
more politically propitious for her coming here than the present one.
Agitation is extinct, Repeal is forgotten—the seditious associations
are closed,—the priests are frightened and the people are tranquil.
Everything tends to secure for the Queen an enthusiastic reception.
. . ." He might have added that the Irish rebels of 1848 were about
to become a memory, as well: William Smith O'Brien and his colleagues had been in Richmond Bridewell, Dublin, for nine months
after their sentencing to death for treason, hoping to have their con-
victions overturned on a writ of error. In the week before Hamilton's
attempt, the House of Lords had rejected that writ. At the beginning
of June, the government commuted their sentences from death to
transportation for life. The Irish state prisoners refused to accept the
commutation, preferring imprisonment, full pardon, or even mar-
tyrdom to exile. Refusing the Queen's mercy was an unprecedented
act, and the government had to rush through an Act of Parliament
allowing the government to commute a sentence with or without the
prisoner's agreement. On the ninth of July, three weeks before the
Queen's visit, Smith O'Brien and his comrades shipped out on the
Swift for Van Diemen's Land. For the moment, significant organized
resistance to British rule had ceased to exist.

The only obstacle the royal couple faced was financial: impoverished Ireland simply could not bear the cost of a state visit. Accordingly, Albert made clear to the Prime Minister that their visit would not be a state visit at all, but "one having more the character of a yachting excursion." It would, nevertheless, be a trip filled with high ceremony: in Dublin there would be a ball, a levee, a drawing room, and at every stop there would be addresses and processions. The Queen planned to put Conroy's methods to use once again, winning over her Irish subjects simply by placing herself among them.

They planned to leave for Ireland at the beginning of August, immediately after Parliament prorogued, or ended its session. Albert, in the meantime, occupied himself deeply in furthering a project he had been contemplating for some time. On the day of Hamilton's trial, Albert was busy presenting prizes at the well-attended exhibition of manufactures held by the Society of Arts—an organization of which Albert had been president since Victoria's uncle, the Earl of Sussex, the previous president, died in 1843. A member of the Society, Henry Cole, a quintessentially Victorian dynamo of a man, had been promoting a scheme of a national exhibition of arts and manufactures, with prizes: an exhibition similar to national exhibitions held in Belgium and France—similar indeed to an exhibition in Paris from which Cole had just returned. In his remarks on this day, Albert alluded to the Paris exhibition and spoke favorably of a British exhibition that Cole was proposing to take place in 1851. Already, Albert had high ambitions for that exhibition.

Two weeks later, he met privately with Henry Cole to discuss a permanent home for the exhibitions, proposed to take place in 1851 and every five years thereafter. Cole had suggested, a year before, Leicester Square as a site: central, accessible, and, if seedy, affordable. But before they chose a site, they needed to agree on the scope of the coming exhibition. "I asked the Prince," Cole later wrote, "if he had considered if the Exhibition should be a National or an International Exhibition."

Albert thought for a moment. "It must embrace foreign productions," he said, adding emphatically "international, certainly."

In that case, any building in Leicester Square would not be large enough, and the two agreed on another site: Hyde Park.

With his decision, Albert transformed the Exhibition into something unique and truly great: "The Great Exhibition of the Works of Industry of all Nations in 1851," as Albert later devised the title, a celebration of free trade and the material benefits of industrialization: the first world's fair. With the opening of the Great Exhibition, Britain would symbolically take its place as the greatest nation of all, host to the world and the main exhibitor of ten thousand modern marvels, all of them housed in a building that itself was the greatest modern marvel of all. After his meeting with Cole, Albert never looked back: he embraced this project as if it were his life's great work, which is exactly what it turned out to be. In Victoria's eyes, this project would complete her husband's apotheosis.

At ten in the morning of 14 June, William Hamilton, still dressed as a bricklayer in the only clothes he owned—white fustian jacket and trousers—was brought before the bar of the Old Bailey before Chief Justice Wilde and Justices Patteson and Rolfe, to suffer his final moments in the public eye. He was without legal representation. Unlike every other one of Victoria's assailants, William Hamilton had no family to support him, no one to obtain counsel for him. And the fact that he was Irish did not help him at all. His nation had disowned him; no one sought clemency for him. Nor would he have wanted the Queen's mercy, which would only give him the impoverished freedom from which he only wished to escape. He needed no encouragement whatsoever to plead guilty. The government, nevertheless, was taking no chances: Attorney General Jervis was accompanied by four other prosecutors, more than ready to establish his guilt under Peel's law.

The clerk read the charges, and Hamilton quietly pled guilty. He was then asked whether he could see any reason whether the court should not pass judgment upon him. He did not reply.

Chief Justice Wilde then passed sentence, first reviewing Hamilton's life—noting with disgust the fact that he was fully supported by two women—and then the circumstances of the crime, noting especially that all evidence pointed to the fact that Hamilton's pistol was unloaded: Hamilton had obviously not intended to kill the Queen. His true crime, nevertheless, was heinous: not simply alarming the Queen, or her subjects. Worse than this, in shooting at the Queen in public, Hamilton threatened to damage the relationship between the Queen and her subjects. "The Queen might be perfectly assured of her personal safety," Wilde told Hamilton, "from the feelings entertained by her subjects toward her; but it was necessary that her laudable desire to show herself to her people should not be at all interfered with by such acts of insult as that to which you have pleaded guilty, and that the public should also not be deprived of the wholesome and pleasing enjoyment of seeing their Sovereign in public by such proceedings as these."

He then sentenced Hamilton to seven years' transportation. As if to compensate for the fact that this heavier sentence could not include a public whipping or two, Wilde noted that this sentence involved "a very considerable amount of degradation and suffering." Hamilton was removed from the bar, to embark upon on what could accurately be termed a penal odyssey. He had avowedly shot at the Queen to experience prison life, and he got his wish in spades. Two years before, Colonial Secretary Henry Gray had completely reconsidered and revised the government's policy on transportation. Australia was no longer to be the dumping-ground for felons as much as it was a final destination for the reformed and rehabilitated—the place where criminals, after long, grueling years of confinement and hard labor in England, were shipped, no longer convicts but "exiles," given tickets of leave and dispersed as laborers across the countryside and in the outback. The voyage to Australia, then, became to Hamilton more a reward than a punishment; the punishment he would suffer under the grim discipline and with the backbreaking labour in English prisons, and the hulks of Woolwich. After that—after five years of that—Hamilton was finally shipped aboard the convict ship *Ramillies* to Fremantle, Western Australia, the shores of which he surely greeted as the promised land.

In the afternoon after Hamilton was tried, his landlord, Daniel O'Keefe, appeared before the judges at the Old Bailey, requesting to be heard. William Hamilton, he claimed, had taken his pistol from him; he wanted it back. It had become a precious commodity: he had been offered £40 for it. The courtroom exploded in laughter. *Punch* in its next issue ridiculed this profitable trade in criminal artifacts, "this idolatry of the martyrs of crime and saints of the Newgate Calendar": "A bit of Courvoisier's drop would probably fetch more than St. Katherine's own wheel, or one of the veritable arrows that shot St. Sebastian." The court did order O'Keefe's pistol returned to him, and thus O'Keefe had the last laugh; the £40 repaid William Hamilton's debt to him several times over.

On the night of the second of August 1849, the royal yacht *Victoria and Albert*, accompanied by a flotilla of vessels, steamed into Cove Harbor, the first stop on the Queen's tour of Ireland. Victoria, Albert, and their four eldest children had traveled straight from Osborne the day before without stopping, surprising the town's inhabitants, who expected them to arrive the next day. Nonetheless, they set to welcoming the Queen with zeal, setting off fireworks, firing guns in a *feu de joie*, lighting bonfires: the servants of one landowner lost control of their bonfire, and the resulting wildfire consumed fourteen acres and set the harbor alight with a bright orange glow. Victoria was delighted with the effect. The warm glow at Cove was emblematic of her entire visit, which was an unqualified, stunning success. For nine days the Irish fell in love with the Queen—and Victoria returned their feelings in equal measure. As Victoria progressed through the country, the cheering, shrieking crowds growing ever larger, ever more vociferous, ever more captivated by the little woman with the tall husband and the beautiful children. Victoria's charming of the people of Ireland was the greatest test of her genius as a political performer—and was her greatest *coup*.

She landed in Cove the next day, and at the request of local officials, she ordered it renamed Queenstown, as her Uncle George IV had renamed Dublin's harbor town Kingstown twenty-eight years before.* That afternoon, after steaming up the River Lee, the royal family made their first procession, a two-hour ride through Cork. Victoria was delighted with the enthusiasm of her reception: "the crowd is a noisy, excitable, but very good humored one, running and pushing about, and laughing, talking, and shrieking." She was particularly struck by the beauty of Irish women: "such beautiful dark eyes and hair, such fine teeth, nearly every 3rd woman was pretty, some remarkably so."

The raucous but good-willed crowds of Cork were only a prelude to the enormous and seemingly ubiquitous crowds of Dublin, attending to every movement of the royal family, masses that formed instantly even on Victoria's and Albert's improvised trips, when, according to the *Illustrated London News*, "balconies were filled as if by magic—groups were formed instantaneously—and the waving of hats and handkerchiefs, and the loud huzzas that arose ever and anon, testified that at every new point of her progress there was a new burst of feeling." From the moment the Queen, and then the Prince, and then the royal children showed themselves to the roars of the "thousands and thousands" crowding ships and the shores of Kingstown Harbor, the crowds never abated and the excitement of the public grew to a crescendo. The trip was orchestrated carefully so that the Queen could alternatively show herself to the elite, in a levée, a drawing room, a concert, a visit

---

* With Ireland's independence, officials far less smitten by the Queen renamed the town *Cobh*.

to the Duke of Leinster—and to the masses, in processions, in a review of the troops attended by a hundred thousand people, in her public comings and goings.

Her talent lay not in awing the Irish with regal splendor, but in eliminating the distance between herself and the people, in finding ways to establish a human connection with each and every one who came to see her. Her children were invaluable to her in this respect, never failing to charm the people of Dublin. At Kingstown, an old woman cried out "Ah, Queen dear, make one of them Prince Patrick and Ireland will die for you." Within a year, as it happens, Victoria would comply, naming her next son Arthur William Patrick Albert. She traveled among the crowds without fear, not braving them at all, but enjoying them, with an absolute sense of safety in their honesty and good will. She wrote in her journal, with emphasis, "I never saw more *real* enthusiasm." When she and Albert went out on private rides, they went without an escort, a gesture that did much to win Dubliners over: of one such ride, a reporter for the *Illustrated London News* wrote, "no escort of dragoons followed—no troops of any kind were seen—she trusted herself, almost alone, among the people; and this proof of entire confidence was well bestowed, and warmly repaid." When, for example, on one of her tours of the city, a man roared out as loudly as he could "Arrah! Victoria, will you stand up, and let us have a look at you?" She immediately rose and displayed herself. "God bless you for that, my darling," the man cried out. Even Albert, generally more aloof in public, warmed to Irish familiarity, enjoying the calls of a "brawny wag" outside Trinity College, who with "enthusiastic attachment" shouted "Bravo, Albert!"—the crowd then taking up the chant.

The Queen's ease among the Irish crowds appears nothing short of remarkable given the recent rebellion, as well as the fact that an Irishman had shot at her six weeks before. But Hamilton was by now a distant memory, and her enthusiastic reception convinced her that Ireland's troubles were in the past. True, Ireland's poverty was still a fact, and Victoria was too astute an observer not to notice it. "You see more ragged and wretched people here than I ever saw anywhere else," she wrote to Leopold. But to her, the ending of the rebellion and the million evidences of loyalty to the crown were signs of a promising future for the Irish. Her first procession through Dublin was "a never to be forgotten scene, particularly when one reflects on what state the country was in quite lately, in open revolt and under martial law." The one occasion during her visit when the past intruded upon the present hardly marred the sense of amity. While her carriage was driving slowly through the center of town, a workhouse official approached the carriage and respectfully pleaded "Mighty Monarch, pardon Smith O'Brien."*

Amidst the overwhelming and mutual goodwill between Victoria and the Irish, there was apparently a genuine threat to her safety during her stay in Dublin. Members of Dublin secret societies—remnants of the clubs promoted by Young Ireland—came up with a desperate plot to kidnap Victoria, spirit her to a hideout in the Wicklow Mountains, and hold her hostage to the freedom of Smith O'Brien and the State prisoners. One night as the royal family slept in the vice-regal lodge, two hundred men armed with pistols and daggers assembled on the banks of the Grand Canal. They quickly realized that their force was far outnumbered by Dublin's military garrison, and dispersed. Victoria never learned of this feeble attempt, which only highlighted the nadir to which militant Irish nationalism had fallen.

By the time she left on the tenth of August, she had conquered Dublin utterly. Even the shadowy conspirators might have been won over, Lord Lieutenant Clarendon concluding from police reports that "even the ex-Clubbists, who threatened broken heads and windows before the Queen came, are now among the most

---

* Smith O'Brien was at that moment on a convict ship bound for Australia. Before the Queen could reply, Lord Lieutenant Clarendon rode up and pushed the man away.

loyal of her subjects." The nationalist and Tory press, relentlessly hostile to the Queen during the early part of her visit, finally gave in, *Freeman's Journal* noting "the more the citizens of Dublin see Queen Victoria, the more she wins their affections."

The queen sealed the compact with an astounding act of impromptu theatre in Kingstown Harbor. Everyone, it seemed, had turned out to see her go: every possible surface around the harbor occupied by human beings, right down to the edge of the piers, "swarming around their queen like bees." Victoria was on board the royal yacht, chatting with two ladies in waiting, when she suddenly looked up and gazed upon the immense crowd. She then "ran along the deck with the sprightliness of a young girl, and, with the agility of a sailor, ascended the paddle-box, which . . . is a tolerably high one, and was almost at its top before she was observed by Prince Albert." Albert joined her there and Victoria, clutching his arm, vigorously waved her hand, and then her handkerchief, to the cheering multitude. To extend her farewell, she ordered the paddlewheels stopped, so that she drifted slowly out of Kingstown harbor to "the pealing of cannon and the loudest concert of human voices that ever ascended from a people in praise of any Monarch." When she was too far away to be seen, she ordered the ship's royal standard lowered and raised in salute, three, four, five times—a completely unprecedented gesture from a monarch to her subjects. The crowd was ecstatic, the effect electric—and deeply personal. John Bright, the radical MP from Birmingham, was there, and was overcome. "There is not an individual in Dublin that does not take as a personal compliment to himself the Queen's having gone upon the paddle-box and order the royal standard to be lowered," noted Lord Clarendon.

Victoria's popularity in Ireland exceeded the wildest expectations, and raised great hopes within the government and the public that she had turned the tide and that the previously unquiet union between Ireland and Britain would henceforth be peaceful and prosperous. The *Times* declared that the Queen had put an end to

Irish faction and civil discord. "It may very safely be predicted," the *Illustrated London News* trumpeted, "that as long as Queen Victoria lives (may she live to see her great-grandchildren!) there will be no disaffection—no disloyalty in Ireland."

It was not to be. In spite of the wishes of future ministers, Victoria did little to maintain the bond with the Irish that she had so magnificently created on this trip. She did revisit Ireland with Albert in 1853 and 1861, and made the trip alone in 1900. But she never came close to re-establishing the intimacy she felt for them, and they felt for her, during this trip. Moreover, her success, as great as it was, was personal, not national. Victoria did nothing whatsoever to deal with the root causes of Irish resentment against the British. She did little to popularize her government, with its relentless, insensitive practice of treating the Irish like children and responding to Irish anger and agitation with coercion. Irish nationalism, in August 1849 supine with hunger and defeat, would rise again—and would grow, over the next few decades, to a literally explosive intensity.

William Hamilton, the poor, sullen Irishman who lashed out, embodied the spirit of his nation in its defeat. Perhaps Queen and country should not have been so quick to forget the man.

sixteen

CUT AND THRUST

R obert Francis Pate had no need to seek notoriety. He had
already found it.

The gentry and aristocracy of London, promenading in the
gardens outside Kensington Palace, and riding to see and be seen
along Rotten Row, could set their watches by him. The cabmen
and tradesmen on the fringe of the Westminster parks, as well as
the policemen of A Division, all knew him by sight, though very
few knew his name.

At midday, seven days a week, he would leave his well-appointed
apartments on the corner of Piccadilly and Duke Street St. James,
directly above Fortnum and Mason's emporium, for a circuit
around Green Park, Hyde Park, and Kensington Gardens. He always
followed the same path, passing each point on it at exactly the
same time. He always wore the same impeccable suit of clothing,
regardless of the weather: blue frock coat, always open; white
double-breasted waistcoat, buttoned to the throat; blue neckerchief;

tweed trousers; buttoned boots; stylish top hat and cane. The bright colors—so different from the conservative grays, blacks, and browns that more and more men were wearing in 1850—marked him as a dandy; Prince Albert described him that way to Baron Stockmar. But it wasn't Pate's natty clothing that drew double-takes and backward stares from everyone he passed. It was his startling, frenetic manner. He marched through the West End as a man possessed: in step with invisible phalanxes, battling invisible demons. His gait seemed to defy gravity: with his back unnaturally arched so that his open coat draped and sailed behind him, and glaring straight ahead or toward the skies with hat impossibly horizontal, he would kick out each heel as high as he could: a goose-step so extreme that "it was astonishing how he preserved his equilibrium." At the same time, he would flail his arms about and, in his right hand, wield his cane as a sword, lunging and slashing forwards and backwards at the air. An inspector from A Division who saw his performances regularly nicknamed him "cut and thrust."

At times he would break off from his marching and act out pantomimes of fear and estrangement: abruptly stopping in his tracks, gazing about him, and then, as if suddenly aware he was being watched, running off as fast as he could. At other times—on those days when the Queen took an airing in a carriage and four in the parks—he would grovel with an exaggerated obeisance. "I meet him often in the parks," Victoria would later tell her Prime Minster, John Russell, "and he makes a point of bowing more frequently and lower to me than any one else."

Most would pretend not to see him. Husbands would caution their wives not to draw his attention, for fear of violent consequences. Those few that acknowledged him earned from him an angry glare and a spasmodic shake of his stick.

For years, obsessive and eccentric routine was essential to Robert Pate's being. Not long after he first moved to London, he began to follow another ritual, which he followed without fail for a year and a half. When the clock in the nearby tower of St. James's Palace chimed quarter past three, Pate stopped whatever he was doing to take up two piles of coins that his manservant had carefully laid out on the mantel. In the first pile were nine shillings, each queen's head up and each one turned so that every queen gazed in exactly the same direction. In the second pile were a sixpence and an older, larger penny: his servant was well aware that a newer, smaller penny, or two halfpence, would never do. Carefully pocketing these coins, Pate stepped outside to meet the same cabman and climb into the same cab, which set off southeastward, through the town, across the Thames at Putney Bridge, to Putney Heath. There, at exactly the same spot, Pate would descend from the cab, jump over a ditch, and disappear through thick gorse bushes. The cabman would drive to a spot further up the road, from where he could see Pate standing still and staring into a pond. Inevitably, Pate would start up and dash madly back to the cab, often dripping wet. He would shout conflicting commands to the driver: gallop quickly!—slow down to a walking pace!—as they made their way two miles northwest up Roehampton Lane to Barnes Common. The cabman, mystified by his daily customer, would spy on Pate through the trap at his feet, and would see him either in catatonic stupor or in frantic motion: hurling his body from one wall of the cab to the other or leaning out the front of the cab, slashing his cane in a frenzy from side to side. "I did not know what performance it was," the cabman would later testify. "He seemed to be thoughtless, or something of that kind. I suppose some sudden thought caused him to jump and start, as if he did not know what he was about." Passers-by would stop the cabman to ask about the strange man inside: was he mad? The cabman certainly thought so. As deeply alarmed as he was by Pate's mysterious behavior, however, he did nothing to stop it: as far as he was concerned, the steady income was well worth the bother. At Barnes Common, Pate would again leap out and shun every path, plunging instead into the deepest undergrowth. When he had finished whatever he was doing there, he would return to the cab and be driven back to St. James via Hammersmith Bridge.

The sixpence and penny were for tolls at the bridges; the nine shillings were for the cabman—always given to him, he noticed, with Victoria's heads upward, all gazing toward the same point.

After thus providing this cabman with employment every single day from November 1847 to the summer of 1849, Pate abruptly dispensed with his services. One day the cabman arrived to pick him up and met his manservant instead. "Mr. Pate did not want me," he was told, "and if he wanted me he would send for me." Pate never did. Perhaps the expense had become too great. Perhaps Pate aimed to march among higher society: London's elite, after all, did not go to see and be seen on Putney Heath and Barnes Common. To be among that elite—to come in contact with the Queen herself—he would have to change his route; and so, for the next few months, he brought his obsessions to the parks of Westminster.

In a way, Robert Pate was in his element walking in fashionable London. He was the son of an immensely wealthy and self-made man who had groomed his son to take his place among the upper crust. His father, Robert Francis Pate Senior, made his fortune as a corn factor, or grain dealer, in Wisbech, Cambridgeshire—the breadbasket of England—during those heady days for corn factors when the Corn Laws guaranteed high prices. Growing social recognition accompanied Pate's growing wealth. In 1847 he reached his social zenith, appointed by the Queen and her Privy Council High Sheriff of the counties of Cambridge and Huntingdon. It was an appointment that brought him face to face with Victoria and Albert on a memorable, brilliantly hot and sunny day, 5 July 1847, when Pate Senior looked on as Albert was installed as Chancellor of Cambridge University.

The Chancellorship of Cambridge was a position to which Albert was excellently suited—a position that gave him both public recognition and the opportunity to apply his considerable administrative talents. (He never accepted that the position was supposed to be a ceremonial one.) He accepted nomination eagerly, provided the invitation was "the unanimous desire of the University." He soon found out that it was not. A rival, the Second Earl of Powis, had been proposed, and refused to drop out. Albert thus was in the unusual and uncomfortable position of running for election to the position. He consulted Sir Robert Peel—now out of office, but still Albert's closest political confidant—about withdrawing. Peel persuaded him to stay in. He did, refraining completely from campaigning. He won—but it was close: close enough so that he consulted Peel again, about refusing the office. Peel encouraged him to take it. By July 1847, two months later, when Victoria and Albert traveled to Cambridge for his installation, the sour taste of politicking had passed. Cambridge welcomed the two deliriously. Victoria—never happier than when Albert's virtues and talents were recognized by a larger audience—fought breaking into a smile of mingled joy and embarrassment at the "almost absurd" position she found herself in when Albert, speaking for the university, welcomed her. She replied, assuring the university "of my entire *approbation*" of Cambridge's choice of Chancellor, laying particular emphasis on that last word. Albert turned out to be the one of the best Chancellors Cambridge ever had, guiding the university's curriculum into the modern age, strengthening its emphasis on science and technology. And Robert Francis Pate Senior was there to see the beginning, and was on that day introduced to both Prince and Queen. Robert Francis Pate *Junior*, of course, could not make it, having a more pressing engagement that day on Putney Heath and Barnes Common.

Early on, Pate Senior paid so that his son could assume his place in higher society, sending him to be trained as a gentleman at a school in Norwich. When Pate came of age, Pate Senior bought him rank, literally: in 1841, a commission in the British army could be obtained for several hundred pounds, and Pate set his son up in the Queen's service as a cornet in the prestigious 10th Hussars,* then quartered in Ireland. In a little over a year, Pate was promoted to

---

* The 10th Hussars, known as the "Prince of Wales's Own," was the regiment of Victoria's uncle George, and would be that of her son the Prince of Wales.

lieutenant. He was odd from the start, but was at first tolerated and even liked by his fellows. A couple years after his promotion, however, Pate's military colleagues agreed that something terrible had happened, something that changed Pate's behavior irrevocably. Pate was a cavalryman, and his father had fitted him out with three handsome horses; he also owned a Newfoundland dog to which he was very much attached. All four were bitten by a fellow officer's rabid dog. After one horse had become ill, Pate threatened to "make a hole in the river" if his favorite horse died. Eventually all four animals had to be destroyed, and after that Pate sank into an abyss of depression. He avoided mess with his fellows and instead took long and solitary walks. In time he developed a fear of the mess: the cook and the messman, he convinced himself, were trying to poison him.

In 1845, while his regiment marched to Dublin, Pate fled instead to London with little more than the clothes he wore. His friends there persuaded him to go home to his father at Wisbech. To his astonished father, he explained that he was a hunted man: his pursuers followed him around the streets of Dublin; they were at the barracks; they even lurked about London's hotels. His father persuaded Pate to return to Ireland. He was arrested upon his return, but his attempts at explaining himself were so incoherent that his commanding officers refused to prosecute him. Pate returned to duty, more morose and paranoid than ever. The 10th Hussars were preparing to ship out to India, and his colonel, certain that Pate was insane, wanted to be rid of him; he wrote to Pate Senior a letter asking "in as delicate a manner as I could" for him to take his son away. At around the same time, in March 1846, he granted Pate a leave of absence, and Pate hastened not to Wisbech but to London, where for £1800 he quickly sold his lieutenant's commission and set himself up in comfortable apartments in Jermyn Street, St. James—the center of London society. His father visited him there soon after his arrival. By this point, however, a strong feeling of estrangement had arisen between the two, and the elder Pate kept himself largely at Wisbech while his son kept to his own confused affairs.

At the beginning of 1848, however, Pate Senior was forced to assist his son. Though all who knew him agreed that the younger Pate was a man of extremely temperate habits, and obsessively regular in paying his bills, he had somehow run up a debt of hundreds of pounds, and creditors began to apply to his father for payment. When his father showed up in London to handle the matter, he was alarmed by the change that had come over his son: he was now wild, haunted—clearly insane, his father thought. He began to consider committing his son to an asylum and sought medical advice. A doctor in Brighton recommended that he see the most celebrated mad-doctor of all at the time: John Conolly. After a year and a half of unease and confusion about his son—a time about which Pate Senior admitted "I had no control over him," the father met with Conolly.

In the meantime, the younger Robert Pate had managed, awkwardly and reluctantly, to enter London society. His younger sister had moved from Wisbech to London to live with a family friend, the eminent surgeon James Startin; while there, she soon became engaged to Startin's brother William. From the first, Robert would visit his sister there, and it did not take long before James Startin realized that the wild man whose eccentricities in the parks he had often witnessed was his future sister-in-law's brother. The Startins were hosts to a lively circle of literary, political, clerical, and medical friends, and during his several visits to their home at Savile Row* Pate attempted to interact with them. He generally failed: he spoke in a "short choking manner," with wild eyes and expression, and then would lapse into sullen silence. One visitor, the Irish nationalist journalist and then M.P., The O'Gorman Mahon, though he understood Pate to be a maniac from their first conversation, was

---

* The Startins' Savile Row home became, over a century later, Apple Studios, its rooftop the site of the Beatles' final concert.

nevertheless quite happy to speak with him several times more, each interaction simply confirming his original opinion. Startin kept the elder Pate apprised about his son's dire condition.

That is when Pate Senior consulted with Conolly. After hearing of Pate's history since joining the army, Conolly acknowledged that the man was certainly mad—but advised his father to do nothing. His sister now exerted a positive influence upon him; surely with her help he would improve. It would be better, Conolly thought, if he were not introduced to Pate at all: that might irritate the man, he thought, causing him to relapse. Pate Senior followed his advice.

And so, although his family, two of London's leading medical men, and virtually everyone whose path he crossed knew Robert Francis Pate to be mentally ill, nothing was done to treat him, and he continued with his daily marches through the West End. By the twenty-seventh of June 1850—the last day that Pate made this walk—it was clear to those who observed him regularly that Conolly's diagnosis that he was improving was entirely wrong: he was getting worse. James Startin began to fear that he would commit a violent act upon himself or his relatives. The keeper of a livery stable where Pate had once rented horses, and by which Pate passed regularly, noticed that he had changed greatly since the previous May—where he was once friendly, he was now growing ever more irritable. "I told my foreman I had great apprehensions that Captain Pate, as I always called him, was losing his senses," he later testified. A colleague from the army saw him at 3:00 on the afternoon of the twenty-seventh; "I had never seen him so excited as on this day," he claimed. Three hours later, a cleric, Charles Driscoll, who had known Pate from the Startins, happened to catch sight of him on that day from an omnibus trundling down Piccadilly. Pate was standing outside a mansion, across from Green Park. For a moment, Pate was still. Then he abruptly spun about and marched down the street. "There was something peculiar in the manner in which he turned about and walked away, that made me look through the window after him, and take particular notice of him." His gestures—particularly his heel-kicking—were even more excited than usual.

Driscoll rode on to a dinner engagement. He did not realize it, but he had witnessed a sudden and complete breakdown in Pate's daily routine. For Pate had been as usual completing his circuit, heading eastwards at 6:00 to Duke Street—to his apartment, to dinner, and to an early bedtime. A gathering crowd outside the mansion on Piccadilly had compelled him to halt, to turn, to walk *westwards*—and then to spin around, to return excitedly to the crowd, and to push his way to the front. The mansion was Cambridge House, home of Victoria's uncle, the Duke of Cambridge. Just inside the gates was the royal carriage: the Queen was inside, and there would never be a better time to see her, close up, than when her carriage emerged from the gates and made its slow, tight turn onto Piccadilly.

Pate stopped to await her.

It was a time of troubles for the Queen, this last week of June 1850, and she had come to Cambridge House to deal with one of these: her Uncle Aldolphus, the Duke of Cambridge, was dying. The Queen had come accompanied by her Lady in Waiting, Frances Jocelyn, and three of her children—the eight-year-old Prince of Wales, seven-year-old Alice, and five-year-old Alfred. The Duke of Cambridge was seriously ill with "gastric fever"—most likely typhoid. He had little more than a week to live, and his family were already bracing for the worst. Victoria and Albert would feel the loss keenly. The Queen hardly knew Uncle Adolphus as a child, because until she became Queen he had served as Governor-General and Viceroy in Hanover. When he did return (and Uncle Ernest took the throne of Hanover), the relationship between his family and the Queen was at first rocky: there had been, for one thing, the Duke's and Duchess's attempt to foist their son George upon her as a husband—something that neither she nor George desired. And after she married Albert, the Cambridges seemed remarkably reluctant to

cede precedence to the young Prince. In 1840 Victoria was mortified to discover that the Duchess had refused to rise at a dinner
where a toast to Albert was given, and got her revenge by crossing
the entire family off the guest list to her next ball—a very public
rebuke. The turbulence passed, however. Adolphus was George III's
youngest and mildest son, a true friend to a host of charities. Moreover, unlike his brothers, Cambridge managed to get to the end of
his long life without ensnaring himself in party politics and thus
without annoying at least some sector of the public. Both Victoria
and Albert had come to respect and to love the man.

With his death, only two of George III's fifteen children would
remain. Ernest, the most virulently partisan and the least popular
of all George's sons, still lived, but lived, fortunately, in faraway
Hanover. Time and, more significantly, distance, had dispelled
much of his unpopularity. Closer to home and closer to their
hearts was Aunt Mary, Duchess of Gloucester, living down the
street in Gloucester House. She would be to Victoria a "link with
bygone times and generations . . . we all looked upon her as a sort
of grandmother."

The Queen had suffered another wrenching loss six months
before, when the Queen Dowager Adelaide, widow of William
IV, died after a long and painful illness. Adelaide had around the
time of the Victoria's birth done her best to displace her from
the throne by producing an heir of her own, but when all of her
children were stillborn or died in infancy, she never allowed disappointment to come between herself and her niece. Rather she was
always one of Victoria's warmest supporters, especially so during
the dark days of the Conroy ascendancy, when the Princess and
young Queen was desperate for support, finding so little at home.
All of society understood the significance of Victoria's actions at
her wedding, in 1840: embracing and kissing Aunt Adelaide—but
only shaking hands with her mother. The Duchess of Kent and the
Queen Dowager were enemies then, thanks to Conroy, and Victoria
remembered his machinations bitterly, writing, soon after Aunt

Adelaide died, "Much was done to set Mamma against her, but the dear Queen ever forgave this, ever showed love and affection, and for the last eight years their friendship was as great as ever."

Adelaide thus left her friend the Duchess of Kent as one of the last of her generation. With Conroy exiled, and with the influence of Albert, who was both the Duchess's son-in-law and her nephew, and who had a genuine regard for her, the Duchess had regained her position in the family; she had long before subsumed her ambitions into her daughter's, and found her greatest pleasure in being grandmama to her daughter's growing family.

Ten years before, the term "royal family" would have conjured up in British minds the fat, old, generally vicious and usually penurious children of George III. Now, the term brought to mind Victoria's and Albert's bonny boys and girls, reported every day in the "Court Circular" as taking their usual walking and pony exercises in Buckingham Palace Gardens, or on the Slopes at Windsor, or in the park at Osborne. There were seven now; Victoria had borne her third son—her favorite son, as it turned out—just six weeks ago, on the first of May. That day auspiciously was the birthday of the Duke of Wellington, and so Albert and Victoria gave the boy his name, Arthur, and asked the Iron Duke to stand as his godfather. Last Saturday had been the boy's Christening, the 81-year-old Duke standing alongside the infant, a *tableau vivant* of the older generation giving way to the younger.

The old Duke of Wellington was dear to Victoria and Albert both. Completely gone was all the animosity that Victoria had felt for him during her fiercely partisan days as a Whig, or rather as a Melbournian, when, to her, Wellington, Peel, and the Tories seemed put on this earth to thwart all her desires. Albert, who quickly developed a strong affinity for the old man, had done much to reconcile him to the Queen. The old Duke, muscular and upright, had retained much of his iron, in spite of the series of strokes he had suffered, and the deafness that had come with age. While he now played a lesser role in the House of Lords, he still served as

Commander-in-Chief of the army and still kept up a spirited social life. He, at least, would cheat death a little longer.

One more death during the past year had devastated Victoria and even more so Albert. On 8 October 1849, Albert's secretary, George Anson, thirty-seven years old and apparently completely healthy, complained to his wife of a pain over his eye and immediately collapsed; he died within three hours. When news reached the royal couple at Osborne the next day, they both broke down and were, according to Lady Lyttelton, "in floods of tears, and quite shut up . . . so warm a *friend* they can hardly expect to find again." She was absolutely correct, as far as Albert was concerned: he had lost one of his true friends. Their relationship had begun on the worst of footings, with Victoria and Melbourne foisting Anson, then Melbourne's private secretary, upon the Prince in spite of his protests. But Albert quickly found Anson to be an ideal servant, devoted and loyal, just the sort of man he needed in his battle with Lehzen, and in acting behind the scenes to avoid a second bedchamber crisis when Peel came to power in 1841. Trust led to respect, which led to a true friendship, something rare for the Prince, who was still seen as a foreigner, who was still often awkward and aloof in public, and who rarely opened himself up completely to others.

With Anson gone, there were only two men remaining whom Albert could honestly call his friends. There was, first of all, the indispensible Stockmar, still deeply committed to shaping the British monarchy according to his own ideals. Stockmar was, however, back in Germany, where he spent most of his time: liberal enough with advice spooned out in missives and memoranda, but not there to listen, to confide in, to respond to the growing cares of the moment. That left Robert Peel.

Robert Peel was in character and interests much more like the Prince Consort than Albert's father had ever been: he, too, never quite overcame his shyness in public, but was a man of genuine warmth in private life. Moreover, like Albert, he was a man of intellect and wide-ranging cultural interests. Those interests, and a shared political outlook, brought the two together; with Peel, Albert was able to express himself intellectually in a way that he simply could not with Victoria. And Peel was a mentor to the young Prince, providing him with much-appreciated connection to British intellectual figures. Even after Peel's fall from power, Albert turned to him frequently for advice, as he had during his election to the Chancellorship of Cambridge.

Peel lived, thank goodness, for Albert—and Victoria—had much need of his counsel in June 1850; for at that time, for Victoria—and even more so for her husband—things seemed to be falling apart.

For one thing, the political situation was a mess. Their long-troubled relationship with one of the Queen's ministers had suddenly reached a crisis point. Victoria had of course deeply regretted the fall of Peel after the conservatives split in the wake of the repeal of the Corn Laws. But under Albert's influence she had welcomed John Russell's Whig ministry with good grace. Russell quickly proved himself to be a completely different Prime Minister than Peel. Whereas Prime Minister Peel *was* the government, keeping *"all* in his own hands," as Victoria put it, Russell held the reins with a far weaker hand. Toleration was one of his greatest virtues, and one of his greatest flaws: he generally took a *laissez-faire* approach to the doings of his various ministers. Cartoonists in *Punch* and elsewhere depicted Russell as Master Johnny, an errant little boy, both because of the Prime Minister's diminutive stature, and because he never seemed quite up to the task.

In particular, he was completely unable to control his strong-willed Foreign Secretary, Lord Palmerston. Palmerston had been giving the Queen and her Consort fits for years. He ruled the foreign office as his fiefdom, invariably acting pragmatically and often neglecting or refusing to consult with the Queen or the rest of her government. While he was loyal to the idea of constitutional monarchy, and personally liked the Queen, he had little time for the intervention of a woman who was born a dozen years after he was first elected to Parliament, or to her husband, a German and thus, he once told Albert to his face, unable to understand British interests. He regularly neglected to send the Queen dispatches until after he had issued them. He glibly agreed to changes that Victoria—or rather, Albert—made on dispatches, and then ignored them. When Victoria remonstrated with him, he would apologize, and then behave exactly as before.

Making everything worse was the fact that Palmerston and the royal couple disagreed utterly on matters of foreign policy. In the ongoing dispute between Prussia and Denmark, they favored Prussia, and Palmerston Denmark. When the states of Italy rose up against their Austrian rulers, they favored Austria, and Palmerston Italy: he had actually helped arm Garibaldi the year before, without consulting the Queen or even his Cabinet colleagues. To the royal couple, the revolutions of 1848 were a chaotic nightmare, threatening to destroy the ruling families of Europe—among them, of course, their own extended family. Palmerston, on the other hand, had no sympathy with the despots of Europe, and welcomed the revolutions as harbingers of an enlightened and liberal new age. He was a chauvinist and a populist; his promotion of Britain above all angered the courts of Europe (and thus, often, his own), but played well in the British press: he was by far the most beloved member of the present government.

Victoria had complained about Palmerston's cavalier and insensitive political style since the last days of Melbourne's ministry, and little changed in the four years since the coming of the Russell government. Tension built; in September 1848 she told Russell "I felt really I could hardly go on with him, that I had no confidence in him, and that it made me seriously anxious and uneasy for the welfare of the country and the peace of Europe in general, and that I felt very uneasy from one day to another as to what might happen." Lord John increasingly found himself in the role of umpire between the Queen and Palmerston, repeatedly playing up the man's strengths to the Queen and conveying her complaints to Palmerston.

In February 1850, a political firestorm broke out that seemed to make Palmerston's removal inevitable. All of Europe was inflamed by the news of Palmerston's heavy-handed intrusion into the affairs of Greece. Two and a half years before, during Easter 1847, a Greek rabble had seized the occasion of annual anti-Semitic demonstrations to ransack the home of the Jewish Don David Pacifico, terrorize his family, and burn the house to the ground. Pacifico claimed that he had lost the enormous sum of £32,000 in the conflagration: £5,000 in property, as well as papers that proved he was owed £27,000. Don Pacifico's parents were—and perhaps he was—born in Gibraltar, making him a British citizen. When the Greek government failed to recompense him, he turned to the British consul, who brought the matter to Palmerston. Palmerston agreed that Greece owed Pacifico the full amount—plus another £500 for his suffering. There matters stood for two years, when in mid-January 1850, the British Mediterranean fleet stormed into Athens's waters with more ships than Nelson had commanded at the Battle of the Nile. The fleet's admiral had instructions to seize Greek shipping and blockade the harbor until Pacifico's claims and some other British demands were met.

It was Palmerston's quintessential act of gunboat diplomacy. Opinion in Britain was divided as to whether Don Pacifico or Greece was the true victim, and as to whether Britain or Greece was the true bully; the Queen and Albert, as well as the conservatives—both the Protectionists and the Peelites—were decidedly opposed to Palmerston's militant intervention. Elsewhere in Europe there was little dispute: foreign governments were enraged. The French proposed arbitration in London overseen by themselves, while in Athens simultaneous negotiations took place between the British ambassador and the government. In London, a settlement was reached, but that news had not reached Athens when the Greek government capitulated to every British demand. The French considered that their deal took precedence. Palmerston disagreed. The French ambassador promptly returned to France for consultations; the Russians contemplated recalling their own ambassador, and the Queen celebrated her thirty-first birthday amidst serious talk of a European war.

In the House of Lords on 17 June, Lord Stanley, the leader of the Protectionist wing of the Conservatives, moved a censure in the House of Lords on the government for their actions in Greece. That motion carried by thirty-seven votes. Before this debate, Victoria and Albert had insisted that Palmerston leave the Foreign Office, Albert writing to Russell "one conviction grows stronger and stronger with the Queen and myself (if it is possible), viz. that Lord Palmerston is bringing the whole of the hatred which is borne to him . . . by all the Governments of Europe upon England, and that country runs serious danger of having to pay for the consequences." And they had nearly succeeded; as early as March they had negotiated with Russell for his removal. Russell made clear to them that given Palmerston's enormous popularity, dropping him completely from the government was out of the question: if they tried to do that, the government would fall. But Russell was willing to relegate Palmerston to a post in which he could not antagonize the Queen so deeply. He proposed reshuffling the Cabinet completely, moving Palmerston to the Home Office and offering him leadership in the House of Commons. Russell would remain Prime Minister but move to the House of Lords. Albert objected to this, fearing that the strong-willed Palmerston could parlay leadership in Commons into the Prime Ministership. Russell—a poor soothsayer—was sure this would not happen because Palmerston was too old to be Prime Minister. Palmerston, Russell told the royal couple, had agreed to the move—but to avoid any debate, nothing could happen until the end of the current parliamentary session.

Two months later, just as Victoria returned to public life after the birth of Arthur, the royal couple met again with Russell and modified their plans. Russell now agreed with Albert that Palmerston should not be given leadership in Commons. Palmerston would move to the Colonial Office, Lord John would go to the House of Lords, and Sir George Grey—the present Home Secretary—was to become Leader of the House of Commons.

It was the best Victoria and Albert could hope for. But the censure motion in the House of Lords scuttled their plans completely. The government was forced to respond in the House of Commons, or resign. And their response could not simply be about the business in Greece, for the Lords had thrown their entire foreign policy into question. They would have to defend Palmerston's policy—and that amounted to a vote of confidence in Russell's ministry. If the government won, Palmerston would be vindicated, his position stronger than ever: there could be no further talk about shifting him to another office. If the government lost, Russell would be forced to resign, and chaos would likely ensue. What sort of government could be assembled from the hopelessly split Conservatives and the minority Whigs was anybody's guess. "It is impossible to say at this moment what will be the result," Lord John wrote to the Queen days before the debate. He feared the worst, noting that both wings of the Conservative party had united on this issue: "Lord Stanley, Lord Aberdeen, Mr. Gladstone, and Mr. Disraeli appear to be in close concert." (This was surely one of the very last times anyone made such a claim about the last two men.) "We are in a crisis," Victoria wrote to uncle Leopold. "It is most unfortunate, for whatever way it ends, it must do great harm."

The stage was set for one of the most spectacular debates in British parliamentary history. Palmerston himself later claimed he could hardly remember such a "display of intellect, oratory and high and dignified feeling." For four long nights the fate of the government hung in the balance as the leading political lights of Britain—including no fewer than seven once, present, and future

Prime Ministers*—passionately assailed or defended the Foreign Secretary.

On this very day that the Queen visited her dying uncle Adolphus, the debate had reached its midpoint and was the talk of the nation. The previous Monday, radical (and highly nationalist) M.P. John Arthur Roebuck had introduced the motion "that the principles on which the foreign policy of Her Majesty's government has been regulated have been such as were calculated to maintain the honour and dignity of this country." On that night and the next, members dissected into the early hours of the morning Palmerston's role in the Greek affair. His opponents called attention to the unfounded or exaggerated claims of that man of dubious character, Don Pacifico, and decried the loss of British prestige that resulted from the incident; his proponents waxed indignant about iniquitous Greece and its atrocities against Don Pacifico and others: Britain had had no choice but to intervene. One supporter raged about the vast right-wing conspiracy combining English conservatives and European despots, bent on bringing Palmerston and liberalism down: a vote against Palmerston was a vote for "Cossack domination." The last speaker on the first night, James Graham—once Home Secretary in Peel's government—analyzed every major Foreign Office decision of the last four years and concluded that Palmerston's heavy-handed tactics had resulted in fiasco throughout Europe; Palmerston's actions had toppled Louis-Philippe from his throne, led to the failed uprisings of 1848, and were responsible for the current tide of reaction across the continent.

At 9:45 on the second night of the debate, Palmerston rose to defend himself. He gave the speech of his life. Speaking for four and a half hours with few notes and no pause for the water or oranges set beside him, he covered himself rhetorically with the British flag, responding to Graham's attacks country by country, demonstrating

---

* Peel, Russell, Stanley (that is, Lord Derby), Aberdeen, Palmerston, Disraeli, and Gladstone.

that he had spread the light of liberal reform throughout Europe. In doing this, he had simply enforced the will of the British people, and attacking him personally made no sense: "It is like shooting a policeman," Palmerston claimed. "As long as England is England, as long as the English people are animated by the feelings and spirit and opinions which they possess, you may knock down twenty Foreign Ministers one after another, but depend upon it, none will keep the place who does not act upon the same principles." His policy had bettered mankind: advancing civilization, promoting peace, and augmenting prosperity. In his peroration, he whipped up the chamber by appealing to the unparalleled power and greatness of the British empire: ". . . as the Roman, in days of old, held himself free from indignity when he could say *Civis Romanus sum**; so also a British subject, in whatever land he may be, shall feel confident that the watchful eye and the strong arm of England will protect him against injustice and wrong."

He finished to thunderous cheers at 2:20 in the morning. Victoria, reading the speech the next day, could not help but be impressed: "a most brilliant speech," she admitted in her journal. Russell was ecstatic about it—"one of the most masterly ever delivered," he wrote—and was now optimistic that the government would win the vote. He was, however, not sure that his ministry would survive, informing the Queen that they needed a sizeable majority—forty votes—if they were to remain in office. After Palmerston spoke, the debate had adjourned, to recommence this evening; indeed, as Victoria prepared to return to Buckingham Palace from Cambridge House, the House of Commons had already been in session for two hours. The Stranger's Gallery was packed more tightly than ever, would-be spectators spilling out of the chamber. Lord John was still to speak, as were Gladstone, Disraeli, and Peel. The Queen was in the eye of the political storm, and her feelings about her own government were decidedly mixed.

---

* That is, "I am a citizen of Rome."

Prince Albert, meanwhile, was in the midst of his own tempest, suddenly locked in a battle to keep the most important project of his life alive and to keep his reputation intact. His and Henry Cole's idea a year before of a truly international exhibition had now taken on life, largely thanks to Albert, who was now chair of the Royal Commission for the Exhibition. (This afternoon he had chaired a meeting until six, leaving the Queen to set out to the Cambridges without him.) The project had become to him something of far greater magnitude to him than a simple display of manufactures. Last March he had inspired 136 British mayors and 18 foreign ambassadors with his speech at an elaborate dinner at the Lord Mayor's mansion with his elevated vision of the Exhibition. "We are living at a period of the most wonderful transition," he told them, "which tends rapidly to accomplish that great end to which indeed all history points; *the realization of the Unity of mankind!*" The Exhibition was to be nothing less than the manifestation of this millennial moment: "a living picture of the point of development at which the whole of mankind has arrived in this great task, and a new starting point from which all nations will be able to direct their further exertions."

Albert acted as if he carried the world upon his shoulders, devoting an immense amount of time and energy overseeing every aspect of the planning. He "appears to be almost the only person who has considered the subject both as a whole and in its details," wrote Lord Granville, the vice-chair of the Royal Committee. "The whole thing would fall to pieces, if he left it to itself." The strain upon him showed. In January, Victoria wrote to Stockmar "The Prince's sleep is again as bad as ever, and he looks very ill of an evening." And now, at the end of June 1850, opposition had grown to the point that failure seemed imminent.

Nothing about the project seemed to please the public. Funding, for one thing, was not forthcoming: the Exhibition was supposed to be supported by public subscription, and while Albert had given £500 and Victoria £1,000, no one had come along with the truly substantial donation needed to attract others, and the fear arose that the Treasury would have to take up the burden. And then there was the site. Albert had from the first fixed upon Hyde Park for the Exhibition; he had studied the alternatives and was now absolutely committed to that choice: it would be held there or not be held at all. The residents of Knightsbridge adjoining the site raised a stink about the noise, the inevitable invasion of riffraff, the damage to the Park, and the decline in the value of their property. Dismay about the project spread to the rest of the West End, the upper crust bemoaning the certain loss of their favorite airing ground, Rotten Row. When, earlier in the month, the plans of the Exhibition building became public, however, the complainings of the few transformed into a full-throated, universal outcry.

The Building Committee for the Exhibition, in a classic demonstration of the broth-destroying propensity of too many cooks, consisted of three highly celebrated architects (Charles Barry, Charles Robert Cockerell, and Thomas Leverton Donaldson) and three highly celebrated engineers (Robert Stephenson, Isambard Kingdom Brunel, and William Cubitt), as well as two nobles (the Duke of Buccleuch and the Earl of Ellesmere). These eight held a competition for the design of the Exhibition building and netted 245 plans. They scrutinized these, rejected the lot, and produced a plan of their own, for which they "freely"—in both senses of the term—"availed themselves of the most valuable suggestions" of the rejected plans. The committee's design was largely Brunel's, and might have showed his genius as an engineer, but as a work of architecture, it was an ugly mess: a sheet-iron dome 200 feet in diameter and 150 feet high ("a monster balloon in the process of inflation," according to one angry letter-writer) rising above a squat and sprawling warehouse that would take an estimated 19 million bricks to build: a decidedly permanent solution for a building supposed to be temporary.

Attacks upon the site flooded the papers: the building was an eyesore and an impractical and destructive imposition upon Hyde Park. The *Times* took up the chorus, its attacks reaching a crescendo on this very day, 27 June 1850, when the paper contained not one but two letters railing against the committee's design, as well as an editorial proclaiming the plan an "insanity," and threatening Albert personally that his reputation would suffer irreparably if the Commission went ahead with these plans: he "would become associated in the minds of the people not with a benefit, but with an injury; not with an extension of our industry, but with a curtailment of the recreation and an injury to the health of the metropolis."

The outrage was at its height in Parliament as well, and moves were afoot there to scuttle the Exhibition altogether. In the House of Lords, the quixotic Whig-Radical Lord Brougham had for months railed against the Hyde Park site: any building there would be a "tubercle" on "the lungs of this huge metropolis." Brougham found in the House of Commons an unlikely ally in the arch-reactionary and xenophobic Colonel Charles de Laet Waldo Sibthorpe, who warred against anything with the slightest whiff of the modern with such sputtering virulence that he had become *Punch* magazine's favorite figure of fun. He had opposed the 1832 Reform Bill; he was dead set against the railways; he despised Free Trade: and therefore he was naturally opposed to the Exhibition, which he claimed was "one of the greatest humbugs, one of the greatest frauds, one of the greatest absurdities ever known"—a magnet to attract to London the dregs of foreign lands: Papists, thieves, anarchists, and secret societies bent on assassinating the Queen. Usually a strident voice in the wilderness, Sibthorpe must have been amazed to find himself at the spearhead of a popular movement. Both he and Brougham made clear that they intended to have Parliament reconsider the whole idea of the Exhibition.

Albert was frantic. "The Exhibition is now attacked furiously by *The Times*," he wrote to Stockmar, "and the House of Commons is going to drive us out of the Park. There is immense excitement on the subject. If we are driven out of the Park the work is done for!!" He could rely upon only one man to set things right—his one friend in England and his champion in Parliament: Robert Peel.

seventeen

The Most Disgraceful and Cowardly Thing That Has Ever Been Done

R obert Pate had jostled his way nearly to the front of the excited crowd awaiting the Queen's departure; only one man stood between him and the gate, and that man had refused to give way, throwing out his arm every time Pate tried to pass him. No matter; Pate was close enough to the gate to see that the courtyard of Cambridge House had sprung to life, and a small parade was forming to convey Victoria back to the Palace. Two footmen assisted the Queen, Fanny Jocelyn, and the three royal children into the open carriage. Victoria sat at the right rear, and Fanny sat directly across from her. The footmen then clambered up to the rumble seat in the back, Victoria's sergeant-footman Robert Renwick taking his seat directly behind the Queen, where he had been when he had witnessed Hamilton's attempt the year before. Two mounted outriders took up their position before the carriage's four horses. Colonel Charles Grey, who would usually position himself by the Queen's side, realizing that the gate was simply too narrow to allow his horse to pass through with the carriage, instead took up the rear.*

Grey could not be comfortable in this position, and he must have viewed the sizeable crowd on the other side of the gate apprehensively. Usually, one or two policemen assigned to Palace duty would be on hand to control the situation: when alerted that the Queen would be going out, they were under orders to get there first and patrol the area. The Queen had not planned this visit to her ailing uncle, however; no one had alerted the police; he, the outriders, and the footmen were the Queen's only security.

The little procession clattered out of the courtyard, the outriders bisecting the crowd into two cheering clusters. They trotted to the edge of the street and then stopped, awaiting their opportunity to make the turn onto busy Piccadilly. Victoria's carriage halted on the pavement side of the gate, trapping Colonel Grey in the courtyard and leaving the Queen unprotected, and close enough to the nearest in the crowd to touch them. Proximity and immobility rendered her instantly nervous: such a situation, she later wrote, "always makes me think more than usually of the possibility of an attempt being made on me." She surveyed those beside her, and recognized a man she had often seen in the parks: fair hair, a military moustache—and a small stick in his hand: the man who was always bowing so deeply to her.

He did not bow this time. Stepping forward a pace or two, he raised his cane and brought it slashing down on the right side of the Queen's head, bending the wire of her light summer bonnet,

---

* The narrow entry and exit gates still exist outside Cambridge House, now 94 Piccadilly. From 1866 until 1999, Cambridge House housed the Naval and Military Club, familiarly known as the "In and Out Club" because of the markings on these two gates.

the metal ferrule at the cane's tip audibly smacking her forehead. Victoria instinctively raised her hand to her bonnet and recoiled away from Pate, falling into the laps of her alarmed children. For a few moments she was completely disoriented.

Robert Renwick leapt up, leaned forward, and seized Pate by the collar. Those around him grabbed hold of him as well. All had seen him strike the Queen, and their outrage was instant. "They have got the man," Fanny Jocelyn told Victoria as she sat up and touched her forehead: the wound was beginning to swell. To the crowd, it seemed as if the Queen was simply adjusting her bonnet. To reassure them, Victoria stood up and announced "I am not hurt."

Her words did nothing to prevent the crowd from manhandling Pate. One man threw a vicious punch at Pate's face and blood gushed from his nose. Lady Jocelyn burst into tears, and the Prince of Wales's face went red. Unlike Bertie, the other two children, Alice and Alfred, had seen their mother attacked a year before. But none of the three had seen anything like this.

The postilions, looking back and seeing Pate in Renwick's grasp, had kept the horses still. The Queen ordered them to move on. Renwick released his hold on Pate, the postilions spurred their horses, and the carriage sped up Piccadilly, to turn down Constitution Hill and into the Palace. When a space had cleared, Colonel Grey galloped to Victoria's side, catching behind him the sight of the crowd to the left rushing upon Pate. Voices began to call for a lynching.

Across Piccadilly, patrolling the edge of Green Park, Sergeant James Silver of A Division—the same James Silver who had tripped up, disarmed, and captured Daniel McNaughtan seven years before—noticed the seething crowd and heard a voice: "The villain has struck the Queen!" He instantly ran to the spot, plunged into the crowd, and, with some difficulty and with the help of other constables drawn by the commotion, rescued him from the chaotic assault.

In crossing Piccadilly, Sergeant Silver had crossed the border between A and C Police Divisions, and so once he relieved the bloody and disoriented Pate of his cane, he and the other constables hustled their prisoner not to Gardiner Lane but to C Division's headquarters on Vine Street, east up Piccadilly. On the way, they passed Messrs. Fortnum and Mason's emporium, and Pate could steal a look at his elegant rooms above them. He would never enter them again.

Back at Buckingham Palace, Victoria directed her visibly mortified equerry Charles Grey to ride through the parks and find Albert, who upon his return from the Royal Commission meeting had set out on horseback with their guest, the Prince of Prussia. She sent Fanny Jocelyn back to Cambridge House to inform the Duchess what had just happened. She sent for her physician, James Clark, to tend to her wound—which was by now throbbing so painfully that she retired upstairs to treat it herself with arnica.

The news of the attack spread quickly, and crowds as usual began to assemble about the Palace while the nobility and gentry began to call to inquire. Although by this time the all-important debate on Palmerston's foreign policy had recommenced in the House of Commons, Lord John Russell rushed away from there to have an audience with Victoria. Home Secretary George Grey, "greatly distressed and in tears," came to her later that evening—and managed to compose himself enough to return to the Commons and make his own contribution to the debate, defending his colleague Palmerston. After a surprising delay, Sir James Clark arrived and examined the Queen: he found a "considerable tumor" on her brow: Pate's cane had drawn blood. He concluded that Pate's blow had been an extremely violent one.

Victoria, Albert, and Prince Wilhelm of Prussia had made plans to attend the opera that night, Meyerbeer's *Le Prophète* at Covent Garden. As usual, Victoria refused to change her plans in the wake of an attack. When her ladies-in-waiting begged her to stay at home, she told them "Certainly not: if I do not go, it will be thought I am seriously hurt, and people will be distressed and alarmed."

"But you *are* hurt, ma'am."

"Then everyone shall see how little I mind it."

At 9:20, then, the royal party set out. Victoria was by now familiar with the social afterglow that followed attacks upon her: London united in a spontaneous burst of loyalty and concern for her welfare. She savored the enthusiastically cheering crowds lining the streets between the Palace and Covent Garden. "The feeling of *all* classes [is] admirable," she wrote that night in her journal, "the lowest of the low being *most* indignant."

The scene at the opera itself was, according to one reporter, "one of the most magnificent demonstrations of loyalty it has ever been our fortune to witness." The Queen herself had much to do with the depth of the response, playing the crowd with consummate ability. When her party entered the royal box, Albert and the Prince held back and she walked to the front of the box alone and triumphantly acknowledged the deafening cheers, "the mark of the ruffian's violence plainly visible on her forehead." A writer for *Punch* describes the rapturous reception:

> I never heard such shouting. It was the very madness of affection. It was a deafening tumult of love, in which a thousand voices were trying to outvie one another in giving the loudest expression to their sympathy. It was a loyal competition of sound, in which a thousand hearts were thrown, like so many hats, simultaneously into the air, every one of them struggling which could be thrown the highest. Then came *God Save the Queen*, and soothed the angry waters into something like a calm regularity of flow, until the surging voices rose musically together, and formed one loud swelling wave of devotion and enthusiasm.

Albert, the Prince of Prussia, and Fanny Jocelyn advanced to join Victoria as the company's star mezzo and two star sopranos each sang a verse of the national anthem. When Madame Viardot reached the line "Frustrate their knavish tricks," the crowd roared its approval.

The fact that the Queen could appear in public less than three hours after Pate hit her suggested to press and public that he could not have injured her. While the very first reports of his attack, in papers that evening, claimed Victoria had indeed been injured, those of the next morning "corrected" these reports. "The small stick with which the prisoner struck the blow was not thicker than an ordinary goosequill," noted the *Times*; "it measured only two feet two inches in length and weighed less than three ounces. Of course such a weapon as this could not under any circumstances occasion very serious injury." The *Times* was wrong. Pate's cane—a type known as a partridge cane—was longer, heavier, and much thicker than the newspaper claimed, and was stiff, hard, and tipped with a brass or silver ferrule—quite capable of striking a formidable blow. Victoria long remembered the injury Pate had given her: a walnut-sized welt and a scar that lasted ten years. For Victoria, however, the psychological wound was worse than the physical one; she had been deeply insulted, as a woman and as a monarch. "Certainly," she wrote,

> . . . it is very hard and very horrid that I a woman—
> a defenceless young woman and surrounded by my
> children—should be exposed to insults of this kind
> and be unable to go out quietly for a drive. This is by
> far the most disgraceful and cowardly thing that has
> ever been done; for a man to strike any woman is most
> brutal . . .

Of the many attacks upon her, the Queen until the end of her life considered this one the meanest and most ignoble—"far worse," she wrote, "than an attempt to shoot which, wicked as it is, is at least more comprehensible and more courageous."[*] Unlike her previous assailants, Pate had succeeded in breaking through the invisible barrier between Queen and subject, and in actually hurting her. He shook her until-now unshakeable trust in the public. The effect was immediate; she wrote to Uncle Leopold, days after the attack, "I own it makes me nervous out driving, and I start at any person coming near the carriage." In the short term, she absolutely refused to succumb to this fear: indeed, she, Albert, and the Prince of Prussia rode through the parks in an open carriage and four the very next day. But from her childhood—from her Conroy-planned tours of England, as Princess—Victoria had always struggled between her desire for seclusion and her sense of duty, maintaining the prestige of the monarchy with regular forays among her subjects. Pate's attack served to make that duty more onerous and the temptation to seclude herself that much stronger.

At Vine Street station, Pate was searched: nothing found but two keys and a handkerchief. The several witnesses to the assault who came with him to the station were questioned, and Pate was charged with assaulting the Queen. Whether that charge amounted to a High Misdemeanour or to High Treason was for Home Secretary George Grey to decide; an examination before him was scheduled at Whitehall for the next day. Pate, responding to the charge, asserted emphatically "those men cannot prove whether I struck her head or her bonnet," as if a little wire and woven horsehair on the Queen's head somehow prevented him from touching her, and mitigated his offense.

When he learned about Pate, Superintendent Charles Otway must surely have had the uncanny feeling that Victoria's assailants

---

[*] Seventeen years later, Victoria told Home Secretary Gathorne Gathorne-Hardy, after complaining about Pate's attack, "firearms she had not minded, as if they missed there was nothing to trouble you, and a moving carriage prevented a good aim" (Gathorne-Hardy 1:244).

were following him. Ten years before, as Sergeant in A Division and special assistant to Inspector Pearce, he had worked on Oxford's case. As Inspector a year before, he was the one who searched Hamilton's rooms. All of the Queen's assailants had struck in A Division—until now. Otway had just been promoted to Superintendent of C Division, and the offense of queen-attacking seemed to cross Piccadilly just as he did.

Otway obviously took this case very seriously, and he decided to use to the full the resources of the Metropolitan Police. He therefore turned the investigation over not to his own officers in C Division, but rather to Scotland Yard, and to the top officer there: the chief of the Detective Branch, Inspector Charles Frederick Field. Field, already a legend, was very soon to become an even greater one, as his friend and admirer Charles Dickens would make him the most celebrated and recognizable officer of the Metropolitan Police. Within the next year, Dickens would write and publish in his *Household Words* three adulatory essays about the Detective Branch, especially worshipful of Field, and in 1852 Dickens would accord Field a literary immortality of sorts as his chief model for Inspector Bucket in *Bleak House*. Field was known for his roving eye, which caught all in a glance. The detective made the short walk from Scotland Yard to St. James's and 27 Duke Street, and up three floors to Pate's lodgings. He made note of Pate's obsessive neatness. He also confiscated a number of Pate's papers, but what these revealed about Pate Field ultimately kept to himself: he brought them to the Home Office examination the next day, but did not bring them forward.

At some point while he was held at C Division, Pate recognized a familiar face: one of the inspectors there had grown up in Wisbech, Pate's home town. The two talked. Pate could offer no motive for striking the Queen besides claiming "felt very low for some time past," but he did show regret.

"I wish to Heaven I had been at your right hand yesterday, and then this should not have happened," the inspector said to Pate.

"I wish to Heaven you had," Pate emphatically replied.

Pate did not sleep that night. Discernibly restless, unnerved by the shattering of his obsessive routine, he sat up and observed the comings and goings at the station house. He conversed with the officers about the cases of the criminals around him, but not about his own. None from his family visited him that night. They were, however, aware of his plight, and Robert Pate Senior was already taking steps on his son's behalf. Before Pate attended his examination, Pate Senior had instructed the family solicitor, Edward Hardisty, to retain a barrister, and instructed both to represent him at the Home Office.

At 12:15 the next day, Superintendent Otway personally escorted Pate out of the station, through a hooting mob, into a cab, and to Whitehall, and, after a few minutes of fretting in an anteroom, into the presence of George Grey. Pate Senior was not there; he would arrive from Wisbech later that afternoon. Both police commissioners were in attendance: Richard Mayne—now senior Chief Commissioner since the retirement of Charles Rowan earlier in the year—was to read the charge; beside him sat Rowan's replacement, Charles Hay. John Jervis, the Attorney General, was there to examine witnesses. As Pate sat and stared vacantly, Edward Hardisty entered the room with the barrister he had hurriedly retained, John Huddleston. Huddleston then applied to the Attorney General to act on Pate's behalf. Pate knew Hardisty well, but refused to show any sign of recognizing him on this day.

Jervis brought forward just enough witnesses—the equerry Grey, Renwick, Sergeant Silver—to connect Pate with the attack and to justify a remand. Pate, given the opportunity to question these witnesses, refused to break his silence. Then, surprisingly, Jervis requested that the examination be broken off for the present and resumed the next Tuesday. He apparently was deferring to Pate's defense lawyers, who were at least considering the possibility of an insanity plea, which meant assembling witnesses from outside London. John Huddleston wanted more time than that, requesting a postponement until Friday 5 July. Jervis agreed, and Grey allowed it; the witnesses were ordered to attend in a week, and an order to commit Pate to Clerkenwell prison was made out and placed in Superintendent Otway's hands. While this was being done, Pate drew up a list of books he wished transferred from his library at home to Clerkenwell. This, too, was allowed. Otway then led Pate out the front door of the Home Office and directly into an unruly mob, hissing, hooting, and shouting "Scoundrel!" and "Rascal!" Commissioner Hay had positioned a number of police before the Home Office to control the crowd, and these now were forced to rush ahead, extricate Pate, and set him in a cab. Otway jumped in, and they set out north for Clerkenwell.

Pate's attack, just like every attack upon the Queen, became, in the words of *The Times*, the "absorbing topic of conversation" throughout London. But Pate's monopoly on the public attention was short-lived: during this last week of June 1850, all-absorbing topics followed hard upon one another.

There was the continuation of the Don Pacifico debate in the House of Commons: two more nights of engrossing oratory that recommenced even before Pate had struck the Queen. William Gladstone spoke that Thursday evening, attacking Palmerston's brutal nationalism with a visionary appeal to a brotherhood of nations, all holding to principles "consecrated by the universal assent of mankind." He derided Palmerston's analogy between modern Britons and ancient Romans as primitive: the Romans had recognized no civilization besides their own, holding down all other peoples with the "strong arm of power," and according themselves rights that they denied to all others. Gladstone's oration should have been a powerful corrective to Palmerston's self-defense, but the spell Palmerston cast upon the House on Tuesday was strong; Gladstone was interrupted often by Palmerston's enthusiastic supporters, as were all of Palmerston's opponents.

On Friday, the last night of the debate, public excitement reached its peak. Crowds crammed the avenues outside the entrances to the House. Three parliamentary heavyweights were to speak, and John Roebuck noted that "the House and country only wish to hear Peel, Lord John, and Dizzy; all others are only bores." The most exciting and most heartily cheered speech of the night, to the surprise of everyone, was not by any of these three, but by Alexander Cockburn, Queen's Counsel and the successful defender of Daniel McNaughtan seven years before. Cockburn deftly and with legal precision deflected Gladstone's attack, defending item by item Palmerston's actions in Greece and throughout Europe. He sat to vociferous cheers as his colleagues converged to congratulate him. It was the speech of his career. Palmerston himself thought it the best speech he had ever heard. Cockburn's timing could not have been better: the position of Solicitor General had just opened up. If John Russell had been considering Cockburn for the post before this, Cockburn's speech guaranteed he would get it.

Robert Peel, torn between his duty to speak out against Palmerston's reckless aggression and a sincere reluctance to see Russell's government fall, managed to chide Palmerston's policy and yet conciliate the Whig government. Despite his kind words for them, and his praise for Palmerston's speech, he made clear that he had to vote against Roebuck's motion on principle, and thus reiterated the point that he had made so forcefully in abolishing the Corn Laws, four years before: he would always value principle over party.

John Russell, speaking next, had an easy job of it, largely deferring to Palmerston and Cockburn for the factual argument, and pleading with the conservatives to respect his government's foreign policy, as he had always respected theirs in the past. Benjamin Disraeli's speech was the last of the debate. He stood up early Saturday morning, a tired man before an exhausted house—and he failed to impress. In a speech containing little of his trademark wit, he explained why he would vote as Peel did, for the diametrically opposed reason: putting party over principle. He only spoke, he made clear, out of duty to his colleagues the Protectionists; the House of Commons should reject Roebuck's motion approving of the government's foreign policy, he exhorted them, out of respect for the opposing motion in the House of Lords—put forward by Lord Stanley, leader of his party.

After a few words from Roebuck, the House divided: 310 ayes; 264 noes—a majority of 46. Russell's government survived—and Palmerston was more secure in the Foreign Office than ever. He would remain Victoria's and Albert's political *bête noir* for another year and a half. At a celebratory dinner held a few weeks after the debate, 250 supporters would enthusiastically sing the national anthem and cheer vociferously the lines "Confound their politics,/ Frustrate their knavish tricks"—the knaves in this case completely different from the knaves in the minds of Covent Garden opera-goers the night of Pate's attack. Palmerston would resist Victoria's and Albert's attempts to remove him. Albert would make the first of these two weeks after the debate, rather foolishly resurrecting for Lord John Russell a sordid episode from Palmerston's past, when during the morally more relaxed time at Windsor around the time of Albert's arrival in 1840, one of the Queen's ladies in waiting found that an enamored Palmerston had crept into her bedroom one night. As Albert melodramatically put it, he "would have consummated his fiendish scheme by violence had not the miraculous efforts of his victim and such assistance attracted by her screams, saved her." An embarrassed Russell could only point out that this had happened ten years before and that at sixty-five years old, Palmerston would not likely behave that way again. Albert and Victoria, with the help of Stockmar, tried again a month later, setting out in a memo for Palmerston the behavior they expected in a foreign minister. Russell thought the memo so humiliating that Palmerston would have to resign rather than accept it, but Palmerston agreed to it, and met with Albert, tearfully promising him he would mend his ways. He then ignored the Queen's instructions completely. In September, he would embarrass the government by insulting General Haynau, a reactionary Austrian guest to the country. A year later, he would similarly embarrass his government by welcoming the Hungarian revolutionary Lajos Kossuth to England. He finally went too far in December 1851. When in France Louis Napoleon overthrew the French National Assembly in a coup d'état, and the British government committed itself to strict neutrality in the matter, Palmerston warmly congratulated the French Ambassador for Louis Napoleon's actions. Louis Napoleon was hardly a hero in Britain, and Palmerston's behavior for once would hardly earn him popular acclaim. John Russell, realizing this, demanded Palmerston's resignation—and Palmerston was out.* When the House voted in the early hours of 29 June 1850, however, he was invulnerable, and by far the most popular politician in Britain.

Commons adjourned that morning at four, and as John Roebuck walked out of the House and into the sunrise with his friend Sir David Dundas, he saw Peel ahead of them, making his way home to Whitehall Gardens. "I consider that man to be the happiest in England at this moment," Roebuck told Dundas, "for he has just voted with his party, and yet also in accordance with his own feelings and opinions."

Happy Peel might have been, but also tired and preoccupied: this Saturday morning he would devote to the service of Prince Albert and the Great Exhibition. After a short sleep, he breakfasted alone. His wife Julia was feeling unwell and so she remained in bed, reading a newspaper account of his speech. Impressed, she sent down to Peel a note with her congratulations. Peel then left to consult with Lyon Playfair. Playfair, a noted chemist and Peel's protégé of sorts, had been appointed upon Peel's recommendation Special Commissioner for the Exhibition, to serve as a liaison

---

* Within two months, Palmerston had his revenge on Russell, moving to attach an amendment which the government opposed to a bill; the amendment passed and Russell resigned the next day. "I have had my tit-for-tat with John Russell," Palmerston wrote (St. Aubyn 255).

between the Commission and the provincial committees and as a general workhorse and problem-solver. Peel and Playfair discussed ways to overcome the obstacles that suddenly threatened to halt the project altogether. At around 11:00, Peel rode to the Palace of Westminster for a meeting of the Royal Commission. Prince Albert had arrived ahead of him and was showing the Prince of Prussia the not-yet-completed Houses of Parliament. Albert and Peel then joined Russell, Gladstone, and the other members of the Committee for a short but tense meeting. They discussed the mounting opposition to the Hyde Park site, and resolved that they would hold the Exhibition there or nowhere. Peel agreed to champion the site in Parliament and appeared to relish the prospect of applying pressure to his colleagues. "Depend upon it," he said, "the House of Commons is a timid body."

They discussed as well a dramatic alternative to the Building Committee's plans for a building to house the Exhibition. Several weeks before, as opposition to Brunel's plan grew, Joseph Paxton—head gardener of the Duke of Devonshire, designer of the Duke's spectacular greenhouse at Chatsworth, and a self-made press and railway tycoon—approached Henry Cole with a revolutionary idea for the Exhibition building: an enormous structure of glass set on an iron skeleton. Although the competition for a building was over, Cole suggested that he quickly draw up plans and submit them. Three days later, bored in the middle of a railway director's meeting in Derby, Paxton created the most famous doodle in history: the first sketch of his grand design, on blotting paper. Within a week, he had drawn up full plans. He returned with these to London on the twentieth and threw himself into a self-promotional blitz. On the train from Derby he had run into the engineer Robert Stevenson—of the Building Committee—and quickly gained his support. He met with the vice-chairman of the Commission, Earl Granville, who promised to submit the plan to the Commissioners. He met with Albert, and wrote afterwards "I believe nothing can stand against my plans, *everybody* likes them." He also forwarded a set of plans to Peel. Peel warmly approved of the plan, and said so at this meeting. Had the Commission approved of Paxton's plans then and there, they would have, in a stroke, done much to ensure the Exhibition's popularity. They agreed instead that the Building Committee should decide the matter, and they referred Paxton's plans to them.

The Commission adjourned at 1:15. Peel returned home to work in his study. At around 5:00 he kissed his wife good-bye and set off with his groom for his customary ride around the Parks. The horse he mounted was new to him—an eight-year-old which a friend had purchased for him two months before, from Tattersall's. It later transpired that the horse had a long history of unruly behavior. Peel's coachman was suspicious about the horse, and had recommended Peel not ride it, but Peel disregarded him: he had ridden the horse for weeks now with no problem.

Peel and his groom passed through St. James's Park and stopped at Buckingham Palace, where Peel signed the visitor book, adding his name to the hundreds congratulating the Queen for weathering Pate's attack. Peel and his groom then remounted and rode to the top of Constitution Hill. Near Hyde Park Corner, next to the Palace garden wall, Peel stopped to greet two young ladies whom he knew. The ladies' groom rode a skittish mount. Peel's horse, unnerved, shied and then began to kick and buck violently. Peel flew forward over the horse's head and slammed face first onto the ground. Although he instantly lost consciousness, his reins remained wrapped around his hands and he yanked his horse toward him and onto him; one of the horse's knees crashed down upon Peel's shoulders and his back, smashing his collarbone, breaking a rib— and driving it into one of his lungs.

Two passersby ran to Peel and sat him up: his face, ashen and abraded, was unrecognizable. One man ran to the adjacent St. George's Hospital for medical assistance as several more came running up, among them two doctors, one of these Sir James Clark, the Queen's physician.

Peel began to come to. One of the men clustering about him, the Reverend Henry Mackenzie, flagged down an open carriage; the two ladies inside instantly offered it up to carry Peel back home. Peel was lifted into the carriage. The two men who had sat him up, as well as the two doctors, now supported Peel as the carriage slowly trundled down Constitution Hill, through St. James's, and to Whitehall Gardens. During the trip Peel suddenly became agitated and tried to stand up; the others in the carriage restrained him. He then sank into a stupor. At home, he revived again, enough to walk into his house, with assistance. Lady Peel was distraught. Overcome by pain, Peel fainted. He was brought into the downstairs dining-room and placed on a sofa; later, his doctors deciding he should not be moved, a patent hydraulic bed was set up in the same room.

Five doctors assembled to treat him. At 7:00 they released a bulletin: "Sir Robert Peel has met with a severe accident by falling from his horse. There is severe injury of one shoulder, with a fracture of the left-collar-bone. There is great reason to hope that there is no internal injury." They suspected a broken rib, but Peel's extreme pain made it impossible for them to investigate thoroughly.

Word of the fall spread quickly and London soon had a new all-absorbing topic of conversation. Albert and the Prince of Prussia rushed to Whitehall Gardens as soon as they heard of his fall. The next day Victoria, writing to Leopold, acknowledged that Peel's dire injury completely eclipsed Pate's assault upon her: "We have, alas! now another cause of much greater anxiety in the person of our excellent Sir Robert Peel, who, as you will see, has had a most serious fall, and though going on well at first, was very ill last night; thank God! he is better again this morning, but I fear still in great danger." "I cannot bear even to think of losing him," she added.

Peel knew the injury was fatal. Although his doctors were optimistic, Peel told them on the day of the accident that his injury was worse than they realized, and that he would not survive it. He lingered in agony for three days. Friends and colleagues called at the house regularly, among them the Duke of Wellington, as well as Prince George of Cambridge—whose own father, all now knew, was dying. Outside, the carriages of the rich clogged the streets, while, even more touchingly, the poor in great numbers showed that they had not forgotten that Peel was their champion, giving them cheap bread with the repeal of the Corn Laws. They took up a quiet vigil in Whitehall Place, "always there," according to the *Illustrated London News*, "night and day":

> That silent, solemn crowd betokened the unknown depth to which love and reverence for the great practical statesman had sunk in the minds of humble English men and women. Unknowing the significance of their own appearance, these poor folk were, in reality, the guard of honour accorded to the last hours of Sir Robert Peel—by the People.

On the morning of 2 July, Peel felt better. He ate a little and even walked around the room with assistance. In the afternoon, however, his condition worsened considerably. He began to drift in and out of consciousness. In the evening, the doctors gave up all hope. An old friend, the Bishop of Gibraltar, administered extreme unction. Weakening but largely past feeling pain, he held each of his children's hands in turn, and whispered his good-byes to them, the words "God bless you!" scarcely audible. His wife Julia, overwhelmed, was led from the room. At nine he slipped into unconsciousness, and never woke again. Two hours later, he died.

Peel's death, in the words of the diarist Charles Greville, "absorbed every other subject of interest," as everyone, it seemed, rich and poor, conservative, liberal, and radical—"on every side and in all quarters"—felt the loss deeply—surprisingly deeply, given that Peel was in life hated by the bulk of the conservatives and disliked by the Whigs; he had few genuine friends and was famous for his coldness. In death, sectarian bitterness evaporated and his limitations of personality were forgotten: he was remembered as the great man who transcended political party, guided only by the best interests of the British people. All suddenly realized they had lost a statesman without equal. "All persons agree that there has never been an instance of such general gloom and regret," wrote Baroness Bunsen.

Albert was devastated by Peel's death. "He has felt, and feels, Sir Robert's loss *dreadfully*," Victoria wrote Leopold; "he feels he has lost a second father." And he never needed Peel's advice or advocacy more than at that very moment, as the great project which was now inextricably linked with his name, and upon which his reputation now rested, seemed doomed to failure. The crucial vote was to take place on 4 July—two days after Peel's death: Colonel Sibthorp's motion that the Commission's choice of site be referred to a Parliamentary Committee. If the motion passed, the resulting delay would kill the Exhibition. On the morning of the vote, Albert wrote to his brother in despair:

> Now our Exhibition is to be driven from London; the patrons who are afraid, the Radicals who want to show their power over the crown property (the Parks), *The Times*, whose solicitor bought a house near Hyde Park, are abusing and insulting. This evening the decision is to be made. Peel, who had undertaken the defence, is no more, so we shall probably be defeated and have to give up the whole exhibition.

Colonel Sibthorp was in rare bombastic form during the debate that afternoon; if his energy was any indication, the Exhibition was as good as dead. Sibthorp laid into the greatest trash, fraud, and imposition "palmed upon" the people of Britain. The Exhibition would surely flood the country with "cheap and nasty trash" and attract the nation's criminal element to Hyde Park: "That being the case, he would advise persons residing near the park to keep a sharp look out after their silver forks and spoons and serving maids." But while Sibthorp had heretofore spoken for a growing movement, Robert Peel's death had changed everything. Before the debate began, Sir John Russell, his voice choking with emotion, paid tribute to Peel and to the deep love of country that had informed his every action. And in mid-debate Henry Labouchère, a member of the Royal Commission, reminded the House that assenting to the site was the very last public duty performed by Peel, "that eminent man, who never neglected any duty . . . which he considered conducive to the public good." Member after member deplored Sibthorp's fanatical opposition to the very idea of an Exhibition, and in the end Sibthorp's motion was crushed, 46 for and 166 against.* "The feeling of the house was completely altered," Lord John wrote to Albert the next day, "and all parties seemed to agree that Hyde Park was the best site. So it is to be hoped that no further interruption is to take place." Peel had won the day for Albert after all.

But Albert and the Royal Commission were not yet out of the woods. Money to guarantee the Exhibition was slow in coming, and the Building Committee's design was as unpopular as ever. Within days, however, Joseph Paxton succeeded in overcoming all obstacles. His iron-and-glass design had received a cold reception from the Exhibition's Building Committee, especially from Isambard Kingdom Brunel, who jealously defended his own design. And so on 6 July, Paxton went over their heads, appealing to the public by publishing his plan in the *Illustrated London News*. They loved his design as much as they reviled Brunel's. Still the Building Committee resisted, noting in their meeting of 11 July that Paxton's "peculiar" design would cost 10% more than a variation of their

---

* An amendment, moving the abandonment of the Hyde Park site altogether, fell nearly as badly: 47 for and 166 against.

own stripped of Brunel's beloved dome. The next day the matter was all but resolved when Morton Peto, the wealthy building and railway contractor, in a single act put an end to the Exhibition's money troubles by putting up a £50,000 guarantee. That sizeable donation quickly opened the floodgates to others: in days, there was more than enough to guarantee the erection of an exhibition building. As a codicil to his offer, Peto wrote: "Perhaps I might take the liberty of saying that I consider the success of the Exhibition would be considerably increased by the adoption of Mr. Paxton's plan if it is not too costly." His suggestion was too weighty to ignore. On the sixteenth, the Building Committee met with the Royal Commission. Brunel's design was discarded, Paxton's embraced. "In all the matters which I had in hand," Albert was able to write Stockmar four days later from Osborne, "I had triumphant success."

Palmerston's triumph, Peel's death, the squabble about the site of the Exhibition: all had stolen attention from Pate, so that when he returned to complete his Home Office examination on Friday morning, the fifth of July, there was no large crowd outside to hoot or hiss him. Pate came in the company of Otway and Scotland Yard Detective Stephen Thornton. Pate was, as always, well dressed, but looked paler than he had before. His only complaint about his imprisonment—indeed, his only recorded utterance that day—was that his health suffered from lack of walking; cut off from his obsessive perambulations, he had instead spent most of the last week absorbed in his books. For the most part Pate sat with a vacant stare, drawn deeply into himself, largely oblivious to the questioning of the Attorney General or the maneuvers of his own counsel, with whom he hadn't spoken since his arrest.

The examination began at noon, and was largely a reprise of the first examination—several old and new witnesses to reestablish the fact that the Queen was hit, and that Pate was the one hitting her. Only the Queen's physician, James Clark, had anything new to add, speaking to the extent of the Queen's injury: Pate had indeed done damage to the royal forehead, causing swelling and a severe bruise and breaking the skin, causing royal blood to flow. Such an injury was technically enough for a charge of High Treason, but at this point, Attorney General Jervis and the Home Secretary had agreed that Pate would stand trial under Peel's act, for a high misdemeanour. Huddleston, Pate's attorney, said little, remarking that he would reserve his defense for Pate until another time. Given the charge, Pate could have obtained bail—but he did not apply for it. Commitment papers were drawn up, and Otway and Thornton led Pate to a cab bound for Newgate.

Pate's defense was extremely active during this time, setting up—if not quite an insanity defense, then a defense in which insanity would play a role. Hardisty and Huddleston had already procured for expert testimony the two most noted professional witnesses to insanity of the day: Edward Thomas Monro, still chief physician at Bethlem, as he was when he testified at McNaughtan's trial, and John Conolly, who had testified at Oxford's. Monro visited Pate twice at Clerkenwell and three times in Newgate; Conolly likely accompanied him on some of these visits. Both became convinced that Pate was insane.

And during this time it became clear that Robert Pate Senior had indeed obtained the best legal representation for his son that money could buy: Alexander Cockburn, Q.C., architect of McNaughtan's insanity defense. Cockburn had indeed by this time been offered the position of Solicitor General by a grateful government. As it happens, all three principal lawyers in the Pate case looked forward to impending promotion. Because the Lord Chancellor, Lord Cottenham, had retired, a ladder of legal appointments had opened up; Cockburn was to become Solicitor General, Solicitor General John Romilly was to become Attorney General, and Attorney General John Jervis was to become Chief Justice of the Court of Common Pleas. The promotions all around complicated the timing of Pate's trial: in order for Cockburn to be eligible to defend him, or Jervis to prosecute him, they would need to finish before the promotions took effect. Attorney General Jervis, then, was compelled to hurry the trial along, requesting the presiding judge, Baron Alderson, to schedule Pate's trial for the next morning, 11 July. Pate thus came before the bar less than a week after he was charged.

Expecting Pate's trial to be as overcrowded as those of some of his predecessors, the sheriffs instituted the usual ticket system. They needn't have bothered: the courtroom on that morning was full but not crowded.* At 10:00 Pate entered the dock every bit a gentleman, in dress and in manner. With perfect composure he bowed slightly to the justices Alderson, Patteson, and Talfourd. The charge was read, and Pate loudly pleaded not guilty.

For the prosecution—Attorney General Jervis, Solicitor General Romilly, and three others**—the task was an easy one. That Pate had struck the Queen was hardly in question; the only true question was whether Pate was legally insane at the moment of the attack. But an acquittal on the grounds of insanity would in effect net Pate the virtual life sentence of confinement in Bethlem at the Queen's pleasure, a worse penalty on the face of it than the maximum sentence allowed under Peel's 1842 law, seven years' transportation. While confinement for an insanity acquittal might originally have been intended as therapeutic care, not punishment, neither the judges, nor the defense, nor the prosecution looked at it that way, the Attorney General noting to the jury during the trial that the effect of such an acquittal "would be that he would be imprisoned for the rest of his life." The prosecution's strategy, then, was simply to bring forth a few witnesses to connect Pate with the cane, and the cane with the blow to the Queen's forehead, and to do little to contest any evidence that Pate was insane. They had sent no medical experts to interview Pate or counterbalance Monro's or

---

* Yet another distraction of attention from Pate had occurred three days before: the Duke of Cambridge had finally died on 8 July, throwing Court and polite society into full mourning.

** Welsby, Bodkin, and Clark.

Conolly's testimony. The defense witnesses and their testimony, therefore, were all familiar from the Home Office examination: the equerry Grey, Sergeant-Footman Renwick, Sgt. Silver, Samuel Cowling (a bystander when Pate attacked), and James Clark.

Alexander Cockburn and John Huddleston for the defense, on the other hand, were in a fiendishly difficult position. Since they could not contest the fact that Pate had struck Victoria, they could not in effect win their case. If Pate were found guilty, they lost. And if he were found not guilty by reason of insanity, they lost, as he would face what amounted to a life sentence in Bethlem. As they could not win, they could only hope to make the loss as slight as possible. Therefore, Cockburn could not hope to recreate his triumph in McNaughtan's case. In 1843 he had secured McNaughtan's acquittal brilliantly, by redefining the legal definition of insanity altogether and then demonstrating that McNaughtan's state of mind fit that definition. Since McNaughtan faced the death penalty, a lifetime in Bethlem was indeed a victory. For Pate's trial, the legal definition of insanity had been set by the Law Lords in the wake of McNaughtan's trial: if Pate was aware that what he did was wrong, he could not be considered legally insane. Cockburn now did nothing to challenge that definition, and little to establish that Pate was unaware of the morality of his action. Indeed, Cockburn in his opening admitted to the jury that he simply could not prove "that there were certain and safe grounds for believing that the prisoner at the bar was not enabled to discriminate between right and wrong"—and that "he did not entertain very sanguine expectations as to the result" of the coming testimony as to Pate's insanity. Cockburn's hesitation must have confused the jury—and indeed would confuse anyone who did not realize that Cockburn and Huddleston had no intention of obtaining an insanity acquittal for Pate. They *wanted* to lose the case. Cockburn's oratory, the string of witnesses to Pate's bizarre actions, the medical experts—were all for the benefit of the judges and not the jury—not to gain an acquittal, but to gain the lightest sentence possible after a conviction. While the testimony, Cockburn argued,

> . . . might fall short of that degree of proof of insanity which would be necessary to give [Pate] immunity from the penalties of law, still the jury ought to be satisfied and their lordships who tried the case ought to be satisfied of this, that though some degree of intelligence remained to the prisoner, still it was clear that his mind was in a great degree deranged; and that if responsible at all, he was not responsible in the same degree as if he were of perfect sanity.

Under the 1842 law, judges had a great deal of leeway in their sentencing—from a maximum seven years' transportation, to the minimum of the briefest of prison sentences, with or without a whipping. Cockburn and Huddleston attempted to take advantage of this with an extremely risky strategy, appealing to the judges' sense of pity: Pate was not vicious, but "unfortunate," and did not deserve to be visited with the full severity of the law.

The defense presented a host of witnesses to Pate's traumas and idiosyncrasies while in the army: his morbid reaction to the death of his dog and his horses, his growing paranoia about the army cook and messman leagued to poison him, the bricks and stones in his stomach. Several testified as to his obsessive perambulations first at Putney Heath and Barnes Common, and then through the Parks. Pate's valet, Charles Dodman, enumerated what he considered Pate's many personal eccentricities at home: plunging his head into a four-gallon basin of water upon rising; bathing in a mixture of whiskey, camphor, and water; reading nursery rhymes; constantly singing badly and loudly enough to irritate his neighbors (and to amuse their servants). Visitors who met him at Dr. Startin's house testified to his maniacal and antisocial behavior there. Finally, Conolly and Monro agreed that Pate was of unsound mind.

Both the judges and the prosecution responded to this litany of oddity by adhering strictly to the McNaughtan Rules. Any evidence that did not directly address the question of whether Pate could tell right from wrong at the moment of the attack was not relevant to them. When Charles Mahon, better known as the "O'Gorman Mahon," testified that in his opinion Pate was a "maniac . . . the frequent subject of remark amongst myself and [my] companions," one of the judges asked him "you think he would not do a wrong act, because he would know it to be wrong?" "Certainly," Mahon answered, with that word rendering the rest of his evidence useless.

With the two medical witnesses, the Attorney General took pains to demonstrate that their conception of insanity was not at all the legal conception of insanity—that though much of what was wrong with Pate could be construed as mental illness, as long as Pate was aware of the immorality of his action he was criminally responsible for it. When, for example, Dr. Conolly offered a full diagnosis of his mental debility—"he presents an example of what is not at all uncommon to me, of persons who are very devoid of mental power . . . who consequently persevere in no pursuit, have no object, and are unfit for all the ordinary duties of life"—Jervis shifted the focus to Pate's legal responsibility, Conolly admitting in response to his question "If you were to speak of an action that was decidedly right or wrong he would very clearly understand it, as clearly as I should myself." After Monro's assertion that Pate suffered delusions in the past, Jervis asked him "Is he, in your judgment, capable of distinguishing between right and wrong?" "In many things, certainly," Monro replied. Both Conolly and Monro attempted to explain that Pate could distinguish between right and wrong but was still not responsible for his action since he was at that moment a slave to an impulse he could not control. He was "subject to sudden impulses of passion," Conolly claimed; Monro maintained that "it frequently happens with persons of diseased mind that they will perversely do what they know to be wrong." The notion that an irresistible impulse negated criminal responsibility was not new; indeed, it was a pillar of Cockburn's defense of McNaughtan. But it was the pillar that the Law Lords ignored when formulating their rules, and it was clear that it meant little to the judges now.

Both Conolly and Monro had made clear that Pate knew exactly what he was doing; given this fact, their personal opinions of his unsoundness was irrelevant and, worse, inappropriate in a court of law. When Monro stated his judgment of Pate's mental illness, Baron Alderson gave him a tongue-lashing that showed that, in Alderson's mind at least, the status of the expert medical testimony had not changed since Oxford's trial ten years before. "Be so good, Dr. Monro," Alderson snapped at him,

> . . . as not to take upon yourself the functions of the judges and the jury. If you can give us the results of your scientific knowledge upon the point we shall be glad to hear you; but while I am sitting upon the bench I will not permit any medical witness to usurp the functions of both the judge and the jury.

In his closing statement, the Attorney General demonstrated that he was well aware of the defense's attempt to soften Pate's sentence, and he attempted to head it off. Telling the jury—and more importantly, the judges—that the defense was seeking a more lenient sentence because of Pate's mental weakness, he exhorted them not to mitigate Pate's sentence in the least—Pate was a dangerous man, and if he were soon free, probably "unwatched and unrestrained," he would "renew his dangerous and violent proceedings." Either convict him with a full punishment, or acquit him by reason of insanity and thus restrain him from further mischief.

Baron Alderson agreed with Jervis, and made that extremely clear in his summation to the jury. That Pate had struck the Queen, he told them, was indisputable, and they were thus left with a single question: Was Pate of sound mind when he hit her? He argued that Pate might well be insane but still punishable if his insanity had no bearing on the crime itself. As examples, he noted that a man who killed a man under the delusion that that man was trying to kill him was not criminally responsible, while a man who killed another man while suffering the delusion that his own head was made of glass was still responsible for his crime. He then rephrased the single question for the jury: "Did this unfortunate gentleman know it was wrong to strike the Queen on the forehead?" The notion of an irresistible impulse he dismissed out of hand as "one which would never be listened to by any sane jury." "A man might say that he picked a pocket from some uncontrollable impulse," Alderson wryly observed, "and in that case the law would have an uncontrollable impulse to punish him for it."

It was now 3:20 in the afternoon. The jury consulted for a few minutes, and then retired to discuss the case further. Their decision should have been an easy one, as not a shred of evidence suggested that Pate had been unaware that what he did was wrong. But the defense's abundance of evidence as to Pate's strange behaviors and mental deficiencies apparently complicated their deliberations: McNaughtan Rules or not, some of the jurors must have wondered if the man deserved an acquittal on the grounds of insanity. The jury deliberated for nearly four hours—a long time in a Victorian court of law—before agreeing on their verdict: guilty.

In passing judgment, Baron Alderson noted Pate's eccentric habits, his "differing from other men," his mental affliction. Indeed, he opined that "you are as insane as it is possible for a person to be who is capable of distinguishing between right and wrong." For all that, he told Pate, "you are to be pitied." But none of this mitigated the seriousness of the crime: a soldier striking a woman, and worse, the Queen—"a lady entitled to the respect of the whole country by her virtues and her exalted position." Cockburn and Huddleston had erred in considering that the judges might lessen the sentence out of pity for their client. Alderson, rather, threw the book at him, imposing the maximum sentence of seven years' transportation—the longest time he could prevent Pate from doing mischief. Pate would not be subject to the "disgraceful punishment of whipping," Alderson told him, because of "the station of your family and your own position." Alderson's turn of phrase here was unfortunate, leading several who read the trial in the newspapers the next day, including an angry member of Parliament, to conclude that the court had given Pate special treatment because of his social status. This was simply not the case, as the law was clear: whipping could not be added to a sentence of transportation; it could only be a humiliating addition to a shorter term of imprisonment. If whipping had been involved, Alexander Cockburn could have considered himself a winner in this his final case as Queen's Counsel. Instead, he had lost, and had lost badly.

Pate heard the sentence without any emotion, turned, and without the usual embellishment or excitement in his gait, he walked down the tunnel and back to Newgate.

Pate was, on the next day, transferred—as were all prisoners sentenced to transportation—across town to Pimlico, by the Thames, to towering and stinking Millbank Prison—"one of the most successful realizations, on a large scale, of the ugly in architecture," Henry Mayhew said of it. Once Pate was there, all similarities to the circumstances of other transportees ended. For them, Millbank was the starting point of several years of incarceration—a launching point for Pentonville, Portland, or Portsmouth prisons, or to hard labor in the naval dockyards and to confinement in the dreaded prison ships, the Hulks. William Hamilton had passed through Millbank a year before and was still working his way through the system: his ship to Australia would not sail for another four years. Pate, unlike Hamilton, was the son of a rich man, and though father and son had been estranged, after the attack Robert Pate Senior seemed determined to obtain for his son the best that money could buy. Having failed at obtaining a good verdict, he had better luck at buying a gentler imprisonment and an earlier voyage to Van Diemen's Land.

While Pate, given his history of self-seclusion, might not have minded the usual solitary confinement experienced by prisoners in this, their first stage of what the government euphemistically termed "assisted exile," his weeks at Millbank were rather passed in catered comfort, if an irate letter to the *Daily News* is accurate. According to this letter, Pate was given an officer's room and an officer to attend upon him, had access to the governor, and had a separate exercise yard. He fed on mutton chops, and, extraordinarily, was allowed to wear his own linen and was measured for a custom-made uniform by the prison's master tailor. It all sounds like more than even Pate Senior could buy, and perhaps some of it was: according to another account, Pate spent his time at Millbank in the infirmary, placed there after the Home Secretary ordered him examined, consequent to the medical testimony during his trial. "Pate, we are informed, is in a very delicate state of health, and he employs his time by writing letters in different languages." In either case, his introduction to a convict's life was cushioned.

He was quietly removed from the prison on Monday the fifth of August to Portsmouth, where his ship, the convict ship *William Jardine*, awaited him. He sailed on the twelfth. He left behind him a life of delusion, obsession, compulsion, paranoia, disgrace, and heartbreaking loneliness in London. He could only hope for something better in Van Diemen's Land.

And, amazingly enough, he found it.

eighteen

GREAT EXHIBITION

I t was the happiest day of her life. "I wish you *could* have witnessed the 1*st May* 1851," she gushed to Uncle Leopold—"the
greatest day in our history, the *most beautiful* and *imposing*
and *touching* spectacle ever seen, and the triumph of my beloved
Albert." The day began with a birthday celebration: it was her
son Arthur's first. That meant it was the Duke of Wellington's
birthday as well—his eighty-second—and in the afternoon the
old man came to the infant to exchange presents. But the day was
truly Albert's, the day on which by his talent and ingenuity he
transcended his foreign origin to achieve a sort of national apotheosis. Today was the opening day of his great project, the Great
Exhibition. Finally, the world understood his inestimable value as
Victoria always had. "Albert's dearest name is immortalised with
this *great* conception, *his* own," Victoria wrote; "*his* own, and my
own dear country *showed* she was *worthy* of it."

From early in the morning, the crowds began to assemble in numbers simply too great to count, forming a sea of humanity stretching from the east façade of Buckingham Palace, up Constitution Hill, and covering Hyde Park—boats covering the surface of the Serpentine, boys flocking precariously upon the groaning branches of the Park's trees, multitudes crammed into the windows and onto the roofs of Knightsbridge houses. At the center of it all was Paxton's amazing Crystal Palace, 1,851 feet long and 408 feet wide—more than three times the area of the new Houses of Parliament—900,000 shimmering square feet of glass, packed full with treasures from around the world. At nine, the doors opened and twenty-five thousand season ticket holders made a mad scramble for the north transept of the building to vie for space near the great crystal fountain, where a throne and dais had been set up for the opening ceremony. The crowd swept away the barriers there, but a party of Royal Sappers soon restored order, and the thousands more calmly found places throughout the building, the women taking the seats provided for them, the men standing behind; all craning their necks to watch for august arrivals. The Queen and Prince would be arriving, and the ceremony would begin, at noon.

The universal sense of joy and excitement on this day belied the fact that strident criticism of the Exhibition had continued on long after Parliament agreed to the Hyde Park site and Paxton's design had been adopted, a year before. The irrepressible Colonel Sibthorp had been carping at the project ever since, praying for a hailstorm to bring the building down, and raising Cassandra cries about multitudes of foreigners, "thieves and pickpockets and whoremongers" who would, come May, pollute the West End. *John Bull* magazine agreed that foreigners, less emotionally restrained than the British and less hygienic to boot, would bring moral and physical contagion to London: "We have invited the pestilence into our dwellings, and we shall have to submit to its ravages." Albert in particular suffered from these attacks, and he wrote with exhaustion and exasperation to his grandmother in Coburg, two weeks before the opening,

> I am more dead than alive from overwork. The opponents of the Exhibition work with might and main to throw all the old women into panic and drive myself crazy. The strangers, they give out, are certain to commence a thorough revolution here, to murder Victoria and myself and to proclaim the Red Republic in England; the plague is certain to ensue from the confluence of such vast multitudes, and to swallow up those whom the increased price of everything has not already swept away. For all this I am responsible, and against all this I have to make efficient provision.

These fears and rumors flew abroad to the receptive ears of the autocrats of Europe. The Tsar refused to issue passports to the Russian nobility. The King of Prussia hesitated in allowing his brother and heir, the Prince of Prussia, to attend with his family after the King of Hanover wrote him excoriating this "rubbishy" Exhibition. "I am not easily given to panicking," said Hanover, "but I confess to you that I would not like anyone belonging to me exposed to the imminent perils of these times." When the King wrote about these fears to Albert, the Prince replied with annoyed irony, listing all the supposed threats brought on by the Exhibition: the collapse of the building, destroying visitors, a scarcity of food in London, the reappearance of the Black Death, infection by the "scourges of the civilised and uncivilised world," the vengeance of an angry God. "I can give no guarantee against these perils, nor am I in a position to assume responsibility for the possibly menaced lives of your Royal relatives." Frederick William relented; the Prince of Prussia and his family were Victoria's and Albert's special guests at the opening.

Many feared for Victoria's personal safety on this day; the Duchess of Kent was not the only one terrified at the prospect of her daughter going out among the masses. Victoria's government, as well, was nervous. Two weeks before, the Executive Committee of the Exhibition—in consultation with Albert's courtiers—decided that the Queen would open the Exhibition in a small private ceremony; the public would be admitted later in the day. The skittishness of everyone, including the Queen, was understandable, as this sort of intimate contact between public and monarch had never before been tried. This wasn't a levee, drawing room, or court, in which contact was limited to those of high birth. The memory of Pate's attack was still fresh in the minds of the Queen and Albert, as well as their advisers. If the event were to be public, the Queen would be surrounded by those there not by the grace of God but by the price of admission; any man with the 3 guineas (3 pounds, 3 shillings) to buy a season ticket* could take his place quite literally within striking distance of Victoria. The public responded to the plan of a private ceremony with anger. The *Daily News* blasted that the Commissioners could not have come to "a more impolitic, a more absurd, or a more ludicrous resolution." "Surely," stated the *Times*, "Queen Victoria is not Tiberius or Louis XI, that she should be smuggled out of a great glass carriage into a great glass building under cover of the truncheons of the police and the broadswords of the Life Guards? Where most Englishmen are gathered together there the Queen of England is most secure!" In the face of overwhelming public pressure, Victoria and Albert changed their minds, and Victoria herself decided to open the ceremony to all season ticket holders.

And so on this May Day 1851, Victoria and Albert, hand in hand with the Princess Royal and the Prince of Wales, stepped into the ninth and last carriage of the royal cortege, and rode out into the largest crowd by far they had ever seen—as Victoria put it, a "densely crowded mass of human beings, in the highest good humor and most enthusiastic." The carriages were closed,

---

* Or any woman with 2 guineas (2 pounds, 2 shillings).

perhaps in deference to security, but just as likely because of the falling rain. As they approached the Crystal Palace, however, the dark clouds gave way to the proverbial Queen's weather, and the noonday sun glistened upon the Crystal Palace. They stepped out at Rotten Row and entered the Palace as a sapper on the roof raised the royal standard. "The glimpse of the transept through the iron gates," Victoria wrote, "the waving palms, flowers, statues, myriads of people filling the galleries and seats around, with the flourish of trumpets as we entered, gave us a sensation which I can never forget, and I felt much moved."

When the Queen ascended with her family to the throne, two organs burst into the national anthem, sung by six hundred voices—the massed choirs of the Chapel Royal, St. Paul's, Westminster Abbey, and St. George's Chapel, Windsor, among others. Albert then left his wife to join the Commissioners. He approached the dais and presented an address to the Queen. This was unfortunately tedious—to all but Victoria, to whom it was her husband's well-deserved moment in the sun. Victoria made a short reply, and the organ and choir broke into a sublime rendition of Handel's Hallelujah Chorus.

And at that moment, in the middle of the happiest day of the Queen's life, she experienced a happy breach of security and a benign assault. From out of the ranks of the diplomats stepped a Chinese man decked out in full native costume. He walked to the base of the throne and bowed, repeatedly and deeply, obeisance that the Queen acknowledged graciously. He had been standing among the dignitaries for hours, and had been seen earlier in the day kowtowing to the Duke of Wellington. But no one knew who he was: the Chinese had not even sent a delegation to the Exhibition. The Lord Chamberlain, perplexed as to what to do with the man, consulted with Victoria and Albert. They recommended that he join the diplomats who were then forming up for the great procession through the Exhibition. And so he amiably marched as the impromptu Chinese ambassador. After the ceremony his identity was revealed: he was He-Sing, the owner of a Chinese junk moored on the Thames—a "Museum of Curiosities" open to the public for a shilling. His intrusion upon the royal presence, one of the most memorable moments of the ceremony, turned out to be an act of self-promotion nearly as effective as Joseph Paxton's had been.

Victoria held Bertie's hand, Albert held Vicky's, and the four proceeded around the nave and transepts of the Exhibition. The plan had been to keep the public well clear of their route, but everyone advanced to the very edge of the red-carpeted path around the building, and so the royal family walked, hemmed in by thousands, many with tears in their eyes, all cheering deafeningly and waving handkerchiefs. In a cartoon, *Punch* caught the scene of the four royals strolling happily among the joyful public, the cartoon's caption lampooning the groundless fears that the Queen put to rest: "HER MAJESTY, as She Appeared on the FIRST of MAY, Surrounded by 'Horrible Conspirators and Assassins.'"

Besides the multitudes who cheered her, the Queen could see little else: ahead of her the touching sight of the Duke of Wellington and the Marquis of Anglesey, the heroes of Waterloo, walking arm in arm; towering above her, sculptures such as August Kiss's *Amazon*. She would in the months ahead come back repeatedly to view the Koh-i-Noor diamond, the model of Liverpool docks, the eighty-bladed penknife, the massive steam engines, Mr. Colt's newfangled revolver from America, and the Exhibition's thirteen thousand other displays. Today, it was the people she remembered, in this unprecedented mingling—in what could be justly called the first ever royal walkabout. With this procession, Victoria and Albert declared the beginning of a truly modern monarchy, one in which their legitimacy rested upon the goodwill of the people. It was a unique event, Victoria knew, "a thousand times superior" to her coronation.

Half an hour later, the royal family returned to the throne. Albert spoke to the Lord Chamberlain, who in a booming voice declared the Exhibition open, and a hundred cannons roared outside. Albert was visibly emotional, and the Queen noticed her Home Secretary was crying. They then returned through the hundreds of thousands, a ride, the Queen declared, "equally satisfactory,—the crowd enthusiastic, the order perfect." Back at Buckingham Palace, the royal couple inaugurated a new and enduring tradition, walking out for the first time on the royal balcony to greet the shouting masses.*

Victoria knew: she had reached the high point of her co-rulership with Albert. "It was and is a day to live for ever," she wrote in her journal. "God bless my dearest Albert, God bless my dearest country, which has shown itself so great to-day! One felt so grateful to the great God, who seemed to pervade all and to bless all!"

---

* The balcony and the entire east façade of Buckingham Palace had been constructed in an expansion just four years before.

Part Four

TRIUMPH

nineteen

What Does She Do with It?

On 6 November 1871, Charles Wentworth Dilke, second Baronet of that name, then a young Member of Parliament and brimful with confidence, gave a speech to an overflow crowd of working men in a lecture hall in Newcastle-upon-Tyne. His controversial words about Victoria and her family both established him for a time as the people's champion and touched off an impassioned national reaction. He began his speech with a subject that failed to stir the crowd: equal representation for all voters. But when he turned from representation to royalty, the excitement began.

Dilke carefully calculated the cost to maintain British royalty—the privy purse, the household expenses, annuities for the Queen and her nine children, servants' pensions, palaces, the cost of royal protection—and the enormous cost of the royal yachts: it all came to a million a year. And for what? "A vast number of totally useless officials," for one thing, whom Dilke listed to howls of laughter:

"Chamberlains, Controllers, Masters of Ceremonies, Marshals of the Household, Grooms of the Robes, Lords-in-Waiting, Grooms-in-Waiting, Gentlemen Ushers. . . ." Then there were several court painters, no fewer than thirty-two doctors, a High Almoner, a Sub Almoner, a Hereditary Grand Almoner—even a Hereditary Grand Falconer. And the list went on. In short, for their million, the public subsidized a host of unnecessary sinecures, "made use of for political purposes," and thus guaranteeing political corruption. At one time, of course, all of that money had had a visible result, allowing the maintenance of a splendid Court. But now where does the money go, since the Queen lives in seclusion and "there is no Court at all"? "Has there not been," Dilke asked, "a diversion of pubic moneys amounting to malversation?"

He then questioned a claim that the Queen's former Prime Minister, Benjamin Disraeli, had made in defending the Queen before his Hughenden constituents: the Queen's duties were "multifarious," "weighty," and "unceasing"; her days were filled with reading and signing every single dispatch emanating from the government. But, asked Dilke, of what value was that labor? In signing these dispatches, the Queen might either disagree with her Ministers, subverting the will of government, or she might acquiesce to every dispatch, demonstrating no will whatsoever. "If we adopt the latter alternative, it is one little flattering to the intelligence of the Sovereign whose character Mr. Disraeli has described; and if we adopt the former, it affords us a view of Constitutional Monarchy in which it is impossible to distinguish it from the autocracy that all of us condemn." Moreover, the business of sending dispatches to the Queen had become an enormous waste of time and labor, as every dispatch, as well as a member of government in residence, had to be sent to the Queen at her preferred and distant residences, Osborne and Balmoral—rather than to Windsor and Buckingham Palace, palaces "maintained for her at great cost," but which she avoided.

The huge and unnecessary royal expenditure, Dilke argued, was worse than waste—it was mischief, a relic of the power of birth over the power of merit. Perhaps, he suggested in his rousing closing, it was time to put an end to it all:

> . . . we are told that a limited Monarchy works well. I set aside, in this speech, the question of whether a Republic would work better; but I confess freely that I doubt whether, if the charges to which I have to-night alluded are well founded, the monarchy should not set its house in order. (Loud applause.) There is a widespread belief that a Republic here is only a matter of education and time. (Great cheering.) It is said that some day a Commonwealth will be our Government. . . . Well, if you can show me a fair chance that a Republic here will be free from the political corruption that hangs about the Monarchy, I say, for my part—and I believe the middle classes in general will say—let it come. (Cheers.)

Within days, newspapers across the nation reported—and for the most part, reviled—Dilke's speech. Victoria herself was furious, both that such deplorable political sentiments could be uttered in public by a Member of Parliament, and that the government itself—a Liberal government in 1871, to whose policies Dilke, the radical member from Chelsea, largely adhered—did little to nothing to contradict or condemn Dilke's words. Two weeks after the speech, she wrote to her Prime Minister, William Gladstone, deploring the recent spate of "Gross misstatements & fabrications injurious to the credit of the Queen & to the Monarchy" and asking "whether he or at least some of his Colleagues sh^{ld} not take an opportunity of reprobating in very strong terms such language."

Replying solicitously, Gladstone suggested that responding strongly to republican views would lend them a gravity they did not deserve, and would tend "to exasperate and harden such persons as composed the Newcastle Meeting." Nonetheless, he assured the Queen that he considered the matter one of "grave public importance." It certainly was. In 1871, republicanism as an ideology and a movement threatened Victoria's monarchy more than it had at any other time since she took the throne. While it was true that only a minority of her subjects were republicans, "a few years ago," Gladstone reminded the Queen, "that minority (so far as he knows) did not exist," and "the causes . . . that have brought it into existence may lead to its growth." In 1871, republicanism had become "a distemper," as Gladstone put it, and the "Royalty question" was one of the most vexing problems with which his ministry had to deal.

There were many causes for the unpopularity of the monarchy and the growing sense that it might simply be dispensed with. The economy had slumped since 1866, and unemployment was high, particularly in London where it was exacerbated by an influx of migrants from the countryside. The growing trend toward democracy, demonstrated in the landmark Reform Act of 1867, which nearly doubled eligible voters and dipped eligibility down to a much larger segment of the urban working class, created among many an urge for more. The fall of Emperor Louis Napoleon (now in exile in England) and the establishment of a French Republic led to the spontaneous generation of dozens of republican clubs across the nation: ready-made and enthusiastic audiences for republican speakers such as Charles Bradlaugh and trade union leader George Odger.

But much more than Bradlaugh, Odger, or Napoleon III, it was the royal family, and particularly Victoria herself, who had produced this, the strongest surge of republicanism in the nineteenth century. They themselves had done much to make the monarchy appear useless. "To speak in rude and general terms," Gladstone had put it the year before, "the Queen is invisible, and the Prince of Wales is not respected." By 1871, the relationship with the British public, which Victoria had so carefully cultured in the first part of her reign, had been broken—had indeed shattered a decade before, at the end of Victoria's *annus horribilus* of 1861.

Victoria's family was complete then, her ninth and last child, Beatrice, having been born in 1857. And Albert in 1861 was still Victoria's all-in-all—still her best friend, closest adviser, and the unrelenting (though increasingly exhausted) champion of her monarchy. The once-hated Lord Palmerston was their Prime Minister then, but their conflict with him had ceased when he took the reigns of government during the Crimean War and conducted business completely in accord with their views. But the happiest decade of Victoria's life, which began with the Exhibition year of 1851, came to an abrupt end on 16 March 1861, when her mother, the Duchess of Kent, died at Frogmore of cancer. Victoria was plunged immediately into a chasm of grief, and then into a long-lasting depression, from which Albert devoted much of the rest of the year weaning her.

In 1861, the oldest of the royal children were reaching maturity. Vicky, Princess Royal, had in 1858 at seventeen married Frederick William of Prussia. Their first son Willie (the future Kaiser) was born a year later. Bertie, the Prince of Wales, nineteen years old in 1861, had been from early childhood a source of great concern for his parents. From his earliest childhood it had become clear, to their mortification, that any Saxe-Coburg traits—that is, his father's manifold and unparalleled virtues—were absent in the boy, and that he was, rather, utterly a Hanoverian, reflecting the worst of his mother's uncles' vices—sensuality, intemperance, and indolence among them. Albert was determined to train the Hanoverian vices out of his son with a rigorous course of study; any attempts by Bertie to rebel were met by his tutors—with Albert's encouragement—with boxed ears or a rap across the knuckles with a stick. More than this, his parents, having forgotten the misery Victoria had gone through under the restrictive Kensington system, set severe limits on Bertie's social contacts. Bertie spent the first part of 1861 in oversupervised study at Christ's College, Oxford, and for the last part of the year he faced more of the same at Trinity College, Cambridge. During the intervening summer break, however, he enjoyed an element of freedom while training with the Grenadier Guards at Curragh Camp in Ireland, having there what was likely his first sexual experience, as one night some boisterous fellow officers smuggled Nellie Clifden, a young actress, into his quarters. A brief affair ensued.

Under the prevailing double standard of the time, such wild oat-sowing on the part of sons would typically be tolerated by most parents as a (perhaps unfortunate) fact of life. But Bertie was in no way typical—he was the heir to the throne, and the son, as far as his mother was concerned, of the paragon among men. Albert considered Bertie's disgusting liaison to be the crowning one of all of Bertie's disappointments, proof positive that Albert's efforts to train his son away from the excesses of his Hanover uncles had failed. More than this, Albert despairingly considered that all of his life's work of restoring the prestige of the monarchy had been undone by his son virtually overnight. The affair, thanks to Nellie's boasting, had been the talk of all London before it reached Windsor Castle. When Albert learned of and confirmed the story at the beginning of November, he wrote his son an anguished letter "upon a subject which has caused me the greatest pain I have yet felt in this life." Albert accused his son of surrendering the entire reputation of the royal family to an actress. What if Clifden was pregnant? If the Prince of Wales denied paternity, she could take him to court, and "she could be able to give before a greedy multitude disgusting details of your profligacy for the sake of convincing the Jury, yourself cross-examined by a railing indecent attorney and hooted and yelled at by a Lawless Mob! Oh, horrible prospect which this person has in her power, any day to realise! and to break your poor parents' hearts!"

Albert's heartsickness conspired with overwork, many sleepless nights, nervous strain, and almost certainly the effects of a long-lasting illness to undermine his health and sap his will to live. On the twenty-second of November, he traveled to the Royal Military Academy at Sandhurst to inspect buildings in the pouring rain;

three days later, with a cold and feverish and confessing to his diary "bin recht elend" ("I am very wretched"), he traveled to Cambridge to confront his son. Bertie was abjectly contrite, and Albert forgave him. But the Prince Consort returned to Windsor exhausted and ill. His symptoms persisted and worsened; by the end of November he was near collapse, and was soon diagnosed with typhoid fever.

Albert was dutiful until nearly the end, rendering on the first of December perhaps his greatest service to the nation. In early November, a ship of the U.S. Navy had intercepted a British ship, the *Trent*, and forcibly removed two Confederate diplomats and their secretaries from the ship. In response, Palmerston and Foreign Minister John Russell drew up a bellicose communication demanding reparation and an apology—a letter which would virtually guarantee a warlike response from the Americans. Albert revised the letter, softening the accusation and offering Lincoln's government a face-saving way out. In doing so, he quite possibly prevented the American Civil War from flaring up into an Anglo-American war.

The Prince had moments of improvement during the next two weeks, but he knew he was dying. On Friday the thirteenth of December, a telegram brought the Prince of Wales rushing to Windsor from Cambridge. The family gathered around his deathbed, Victoria forcing herself to remain calm in her husband's presence. The next day, he slowly and peacefully faded and died. Victoria immediately collapsed in shock. "I stood up," she wrote, "kissed his dear heavenly forehead & called out in a bitter and agonising cry 'Oh! my dear Darling!' and then dropped on my knees in mute, distracted despair, unable to utter a word or shed a tear!" In that instant, she experienced a soul-crushing grief and the beginning of a nervous breakdown, an affliction from which she never fully recovered during the forty years remaining to her. That unceasing grief became manifest in the state of mourning into which the Court was thrown, mourning that abated with time but never ceased until she herself died. Albert, so intent upon establishing his co-rulership in the early years of his marriage, had succeeded only too well. He had indeed become her all-in-all; without him she had nothing, could do nothing, was in her own mind nothing. She had not realized, she wrote to her daughter Vicky, "how I, who leant on him for all and everything—without whom I did nothing, moved not a finger, arranged not a print or photograph, didn't put on a gown or bonnet if he didn't approve it shall be able to go on, to live, to move, and help myself in difficult moments. . . ." With Albert gone, Victoria's monarchy immediately became a vacuum. Bertie was there for her, of course: telling her, moments after Albert's death, "I will be all I can to you," to which she responded "I am sure, my dear boy, you will," kissing him over and over. But Bertie, she knew, could not hope to be a tenth of the man his father had been. And the Queen was certain that Bertie's behavior had been the cause of his father's illness and death: she admitted to Vicky that she could not look at him without shuddering. She would never allow him the influence or involvement in her government that his father had had.

For the rest of the decade, Victoria became the nation's real-life Miss Havisham, pathologically desiring seclusion from society.* Losing Albert, she told her ministers, had shattered her nerves and destroyed her health, preventing her from public appearances. She adamantly resisted being "dictated to, or teased by public clamour into doing what she physically CANNOT, and she expects Ministers to protect her from such attempts." She was assisted greatly by her physician-extraordinary, William Jenner, who essentially prescribed that Victoria suspend her public duties, and in 1867 warned Prime Minister Lord Derby that "any great departure from her usual"—that is, isolated—"way of life or more than ordinary agitation, might produce insanity." At first, her need for isolation ran so deep that she would not meet face to face with her Privy

* As it happens, Dickens's *Great Expectations* had just completed its serial publication in August 1861.

Council, sitting instead in one room as her councilors stood and shouted their business through the open door of an adjoining room. Her public appearances ceased altogether for a time, and then were rare, usually limited to inspecting or unveiling monuments to dear Albert. London, a place she had once loved, and which Albert had taught her to dislike, she now loathed, with its noises, its crowds, and the relentless demand of the people there that she display herself. She managed to avoid residence at Buckingham Palace altogether for years after 1861, visiting the place only once in the year after Albert's death, in a visit so secret that her own servants did not know she was there. "I saw enough," she wrote to her daughter Vicky, "to feel I never can live there again except for two or three days at a time." And for the next decade she was as good as her word, preferring the briefest of visits to the capital in day trips from Windsor. Her shunning of the metropolis was lost on no one. In 1864, a wry placard was attached to the gates of Buckingham Palace: "These commanding premises to be let or sold, in consequence of the late occupant's declining business."

Whenever she could, Victoria delegated to her older children appearances at State ceremonies, the levées, and drawing rooms. When Bertie married Alix—Alexandra of Denmark—in 1863 (a wedding that the Queen did her best to transform into a funeral), the Princess of Wales substituted for her at presentations at Court. In response to reports in the press in 1864 that she planned again to take up these functions, Victoria took the unprecedented step of writing personally to the *Times*, protesting that duties "higher than those of mere representation"—that is, her dispatches and meeting with her ministers—were as much as her health and strength could bear. "To call upon her to undergo . . . the fatigue of those mere State ceremonies which can be equally well performed by other members of the family is to ask her to run the risk of entirely disabling herself. . . ." She rarely consented to open Parliament, generally (and grudgingly) doing so when annuities or dowries for her children were to be voted upon.

What Court there was in the 1860s was provided by the Prince and Princess of Wales, who maintained a busy public presence in London from Marlborough House, their mansion on Pall Mall. As Bertie tartly wrote to his mother in 1868, "we have certain duties to fulfill here, and your absence from London makes it more necessary that we should do all we can for society, trade, and public matters." But the Prince of Wales had done his own part in creating the "royalty question." Though he had taken over much of his father's committee work, Victoria adamantly opposed his playing any important role in government. The dispatches which kept her so busy were closed to him. He thus appeared to the public—with his balls, country-house visits, frequent trips to the racetrack, and rumors of assignations, to be little more than a royal pleasure-seeker, maintained at the government expense. His reputation was particularly tarnished in 1870 when he was subpoenaed in a divorce case by his friend Sir Charles Mordaunt, accused of being one of several lovers of Mordaunt's wife. Sir Charles's petition failed, but the damage had been done. The Queen, who believed unreservedly in her son's innocence, still maintained "the whole remains a painful lowering thing . . . because his name ought never to have been dragged in the dirt, or mixed up with such people." For months after the case, the Prince and his wife were hissed as they drove in public, in the theatres, at Ascot. Scurrilous stories circulated about Bertie's private life.

Bertie's morals were not the only ones in question as the 1860s progressed. The very lack of knowledge of Victoria's private life encouraged rumor to fill the vacuum, and her, to say the least, unusual relationship with her handsome Highland servant, John Brown, provided perfect grounds for salacious speculation. Brown had served the royal family since 1848, and Albert himself had appointed him Victoria's "particular ghillie." He had ever since been a devoted retainer to the Queen, filling, as she said, "the offices of groom, footman, page and *maid*, I might almost say, as he is so handy about cloaks and shawls." His forward, abrasive, and often well-oiled ways antagonized servants, ministers, and the royal family alike, but he was indispensable to the Queen. Their relationship was not a sexual one. But it is equally true that Brown filled in part the void that Albert's death left in Victoria's life; he, too, became her protector and in return treated her with an assertive familiarity she would not allow anyone else. Dr. Jenner understood the Queen's dependency upon the man, and essentially prescribed in 1864 that, for the Queen's health, Brown be brought from Balmoral to Osborne. In 1865, Victoria appointed him "Queen's Highland Servant," taking orders from no one but her and attending to her both indoors and out. The relationship between the deeply dependent monarch and her deeply indulged favorite became material for cartoons and insinuations in the press. A portrait by Landseer of the Queen on a horse held by the ghillie shown at the 1866 Royal Exhibition became an object of viewers' titters and outright laughter. Victoria was everywhere jokingly referred to as "Mrs. Brown."

The royalty problem was real, and never more intense than it was in 1871, as complaints about Parliamentary grants to the royal children reached a crescendo, and as outrage grew about the absent monarch. William Gladstone, whose staunch support of the monarchy never wavered during his long political journey from right to left, showed himself more willing to promote and strengthen the monarchy than any other prime minister had. Ironically, however, he was finding that to save the monarchy, he would have to battle the monarch herself.

Gladstone had been Victoria's Prime Minister since 1868, and their relationship had been almost entirely cordial. Gladstone, after all, had been the great Peel's lieutenant; he and Albert had been friendly, and when Albert died, Victoria apparently considered Gladstone the most sympathetic of all her ministers. Though their political sensibilities, as they grew older, shifted in completely opposite directions—Victoria's girlhood Whiggism shifting to Albertian neutrality and then to a distinctly conservative outlook, while Gladstone's Toryism had by 1871 given way to liberalism approaching radicalism, until the middle of 1871 this hardly seemed an impediment to the smooth working of the government. In August, that all changed, and a chill that would never thaw crept into their dealings with each other.

It had been a long and difficult session of Parliament for Gladstone; in the face of growing opposition he had had to defend, first, Princess Louise's dowry of £30,000, and then Prince Arthur's annuity of £15,000. The Parliamentary session drew on, and it became clear that it would not end until late August. The Queen, who had to meet with her Privy Council the day before the end—to approve of the speech proroguing Parliament—had already made plans to leave for Balmoral the week before. Gladstone asked her to stay until the end of the session, certain that this would do much to lessen public criticism of her. Victoria, feeling ill from the heat at Osborne and impatient to be north, resisted. No one, she complained to the Lord Chancellor, understood that there were limits to her powers, and the government's demands upon her were likely to kill her:

> What killed her beloved Husband? Overwork & worry—what killed Lord Clarendon? The same. What has broken down Mr. Bright & Mr. Childers & made them retire, but the same; & the Queen, a woman, no longer young is supposed to be proof against all & to be driven & abused till her nerves & health will give way with this worry & agitation and interference in her private life.

She hinted that unless her ministers stopped pressuring her, she would abdicate, self-pityingly imagining that "perhaps then those discontented people may regret that they broke her down when she still might have been of use."

In the end, she left for Balmoral before Parliament prorogued. Then it was Gladstone who lashed out, livid at Victoria's refusal to act in her own interests. "Upon the whole," he wrote to the Queen's secretary, Ponsonby,

> I think it has been the most sickening piece of experi-
> ence which I have had during near forty years of public
> life.
>   *Worse* things may easily be imagined: but smaller
> and meaner cause for the decay of Thrones cannot be
> conceived. It is like the worm which bores the bark of a
> noble oak tree and so breaks the channel of its life.

At Balmoral, the Queen's annoyance at her Prime Minister only grew as it became clear that the illness of which she complained at Osborne—and which he, only too used to the Queen's excuses of bad health, ignored—grew at Balmoral into her worst illness since she had become Queen, a dire combination of prostration, rheumatism, and a nasty abscess on her arm, which the eminent surgeon Joseph Lister was called north to lance. Gladstone's communications with her softened, but the damage had been done. After a week's stay in Balmoral in October, Gladstone wrote to his Foreign Secretary that the Queen's "repellent power which she so well knows how to use has been put in action towards me on this occasion for the first time since the formation of the Government. I have felt myself on a new and different footing with her."

Nonetheless, he was determined to rehabilitate the monarchy. If the Queen was invisible, she would have to *become* visible, in spite of herself. And if the Prince of Wales was not respected, he would have to gain respect by taking on a more important role in royal affairs. Gladstone had been long contemplating just such a role, spinning out a grand plan: the Prince of Wales would replace the Lord-Lieutenant in Ireland, residing and ruling there each winter; summers he would reside in London, taking over many of his mother's duties. Victoria resisted the plan, but Gladstone clung to it tenaciously. In his mind, it was a plan with a double advantage: not only would it go far in resolving the royalty question, but it would, he hoped, do much to accomplish the mission he set for himself when he became Prime Minister—to pacify Ireland. For Ireland, after years of quiescence, had again become inflamed, and had spread terror to England—terror that personally threatened the Queen and her family.

The seething rage that many Irish had nurtured toward Britain during the dark days of the famine had not disappeared; it spread worldwide and smoldered, with the Irish Diaspora. The United States had taken in most of these immigrants, and in the growing American cities, in particular, that hatred and anger festered. In New York in 1857, the society that would soon be known as the Fenians came into being, a group committed from the start to the militant overthrow of British rule and the establishment of an Irish Republic. The next year, the American Fenian leaders exported their society to Dublin, and the Irish Republican Brotherhood—the IRB—was born. In the early 1860s the Fenians grew both in numbers and in military expertise, the American Civil War providing on both sides training for the planned insurrection in Ireland. With the end of the war, expectations soared that an Anglo-Irish war would soon commence: there were thousands of Fenians in Ireland who needed only money, weaponry, and military leadership from the United States in order to rise up. Delay, infiltration by British authorities, betrayal, mass arrests, and lack of military coordination ensured that when the rising did come, in early 1867, it quickly fizzled out. Even so, Irish republican violence in 1867 crossed the Irish Sea in an unprecedented wave of terror.

In February, as a prelude to the general uprising in Ireland, hundreds of Fenians under the command of John McCafferty, an ex-Confederate raider, descended upon Chester, intending to raid the castle, appropriate the weapons in its armory, and ship them to Ireland.* When it became clear that their plans had been betrayed and the Castle was on the alert, the hundreds of young Irish men melted away as quickly as they had come. With the hope of a full-scale military uprising crushed, the Fenians resorted to guerilla operations to free their captured leaders. In September in Manchester, a gang of Fenians waylaid a prison van carrying Captain Thomas Kelly, leader of the IRB, and his aide. The gang quickly routed the police guard and freed Kelly, killing in the process a police sergeant with a bullet in the eye. Kelly and his aide escaped, but several Fenians were arrested for the murder. Of these, five were found guilty, and the three who were hanged immediately joined the pantheon of Irish nationalist heroes as the "Manchester Martyrs." In December, the Fenians struck again, this time in London; they attempted to free another captured leader, Ricard Burke, from Clerkenwell Prison. On Friday the thirteenth, a London Fenian by the name of Jeremiah O'Sullivan wheeled up a barrelful of gunpowder to the wall of the prison, lit a fuse, and ran off. Half a minute later came the deafening explosion, rendering the prison wall a gaping void and obliterating the tenement façades on the other side of the street. Six people lay dead in the ruins; six later died. A hundred and twenty were injured. The plotters only intended to blow a hole in the wall large enough to free Burke, but had completely overestimated the amount of powder needed to do that. The carnage, then, was an accident: the conspirators had no intention of spreading such a shockwave of terror across the nation. But that is exactly what the Clerkenwell bombers did, all Britons concluding after that moment that the Fenians would destroy innocent British lives to achieve their ends. With the

---

* John McCafferty demonstrates that some among the Fenians indeed considered members of the British Royal family to be legitimate targets in achieving political ends: it was he who proposed in 1874 kidnapping the Prince of Wales in order to compel the British government to release all Fenian prisoners (Quinlivan and Rose 24).

mistake of the Clerkenwell outrage, a frightening new form of political terror was born.*

Not surprisingly, rumors flew in 1867 that the Fenians planned to attack Victoria herself. A month after the shooting in Manchester, word from that city arrived in Balmoral that a plot was afoot to waylay the Queen on one of her afternoon drives. The Government dispatched soldiers to the Palace and ordered plainclothed police to keep a close eye upon passengers boarding trains in Perth and Aberdeen. "Too foolish," the Queen thought about the whole affair. Back at Windsor, she refused to allow anyone but John Brown to protect her on her carriage-rides, and so two guards armed with revolvers were set to shadow her at a discreet distance. And at Osborne in December came the greatest alarm of all: Lord Monck, the governor-general of Canada, sent a telegram that two ships had left New York carrying eighty Fenians "sworn to assassinate the Queen." General Grey, Victoria's private secretary, panicked, begging her "on his knees," as he put it, to flee the vulnerable Isle of Wight for the safer Windsor Castle. "Crimes such as these contemplated," he argued, "cannot easily be perpetrated in crowded thoroughfares, or where there is a large population; and the most unsafe places for your Majesty at this moment, are those where the population is most thin and scattered." Her Prime Minister, Lord Derby, concurred, pleading with her to flee Osborne for London or Windsor. Victoria refused to leave, thinking a show of fear "injudicious as well as unnecessary." More than this, Windsor she did not consider *at all safe*," and as for London—filled, she knew, with an immense population of Irish emigrants—"to London

---

* The Metropolitan Police had been warned in detail about the attack the day before, and the then-sole commissioner Richard Mayne, now an old man of seventy-one, did little in response. Mortified by the blast, he offered his resignation. It was refused, but he likely never recovered from the shock and died in 1868. Jeremiah O'Sullivan escaped to the United States, and only one man, Michael Barrett, was found guilty for the explosion. Barrett was hanged outside Newgate on 26 May 1868, the last public execution in England. The elderly William Calcraft was executioner.

nothing will make her go, *till* the present state of affairs is *altered*." And so at Osborne extra police were posted; a pass system put into effect; some warships patrolled offshore while others were sent to intercept the Fenian ships. The Queen was again annoyed by the fuss, considering herself "little better than a State Prisoner." It was all, of course, a false alarm, and the Queen castigated Monck "for ever having credited such an *absurd* and *mad* story."

It was not as if Victoria was blind to the danger the Fenians posed. In the wake of the Clerkenwell outrage, she exhorted her government (unsuccessfully) to suspend *Habeas Corpus*, and when only one of the Clerkenwell bombers was found guilty at trial she wrote her Home Secretary that "one begins to wish that these Fenians should be lynch-lawed and on the spot." She was, however, slow to understand that her position made her a tempting symbolic target to many who might have nothing against her personally. Four months after the Clerkenwell outrage, the lesson was brutally brought home to her. On 25 April, she learned that six weeks before and half-way around the world her son Alfred had been wounded by a would-be assassin. Alfred, a captain in the Royal Navy traveling around the world on the HMS *Galatea*, had put into Sydney. On 12 March 1868 he was presenting a check at a charity picnic when a man suddenly walked up behind him and at two yards' distance leveled a revolver and shot the prince in the back. The bullet ricocheted off of the rear clip of Alfred's suspenders through his ninth rib, missing his spine by an inch. The shooter, Henry James O'Farrell, cried out "I'm a Fenian. God save Ireland" as he was wrestled to the ground and beaten savagely. O'Farrell's attempt led to a witch hunt to root out the Fenians of New South Wales, but none were found; O'Farrell, with a history of mental problems and an obsession with avenging the Manchester Martyrs, had acted alone. He was found guilty of attempted murder and quickly hanged. Alfred's tour was curtailed while he recovered, attended to by two nurses trained by Florence Nightingale, and he returned home that summer. Victoria was baffled by the attack:

"poor dear Affie is so entirely unconnected with anything political or Irish," she wrote in her journal.

Irish disturbances in England abated after 1867, but the prisons of England and Ireland were clogged with Fenians, and a vocal and broad-based movement for their amnesty was in full force at the end of 1871. Gladstone had made amnesty a cornerstone of his Irish pacification policy, and many had been freed—in the face of the stiff opposition of the Queen. Still, many of them—those involved with the Manchester killing, for example—remained in prison, and the government had no intention of freeing them.

As Sir Charles Dilke's republican tour gathered steam, then, Victoria had a host of reasons to seclude herself. If her prime minister was to bring her out again and restore her to public favor, he needed a miracle.

He got two: a bacillus, and an unruly boy.

Salmonella typhi was above class discrimination: it bred in the foul drains of the rich as well as the cesspits of the poor. All agreed that *Salmonella typhi* had killed the Prince Consort ten years before. Then, the bacillus apparently had its origin in the notorious pools of filth under Windsor Castle. The Prince of Wales, on the other hand, traveled north to drink his contaminated water, to the country estate of Lord Jonesborough near Scarborough, which the Prince and Princess visited in early November 1871. Many besides Bertie became ill, several seriously, including the Earl of Chesterfield and one of the Prince's grooms. It took several weeks before it became clear that the illness was serious: on November 22, the royal doctors announced to the world that the Prince was suffering from typhoid fever. They were at first optimistic. But their regular telegraphed reports from Sandringham—published in every newspaper—became increasingly alarming. The health of the Prince quickly became the national obsession, and as he seemingly neared death, he gained an overwhelming and unprecedented public sympathy.

On 29 November, Victoria hurried from Balmoral to Sandringham. Two days later, the Earl of Chesterfield died; Bertie's groom was to die as well. As his fever worsened, Bertie began to babble deliriously. At thirty, the pleasure-loving prince had already accumulated more than his fair share of royal secrets, and his fevered revelations convinced the doctors that his wife had best be kept from the room. When she did come to him, in the audacity of his illness he accused *her* of infidelity. At the beginning of December, he seemed to improve, and Victoria returned to Windsor. Within a week, however, he was worse than ever. In tears she returned to what seemed his deathbed. Sandringham became so overfull with royals that two of Bertie's sisters had to share a bed. Messages of support flooded in from all corners of the kingdom, as well as many prescribing "remedies of the most mad kind." The Queen noticed and was grateful, writing in her journal "The feeling shown by the whole nation is quite marvellous and most touching and striking, showing how really sound and truly loyal the people really are."

On the eleventh, the doctors told Victoria to expect the end that night. But the Prince survived that day in a raving delirium: deluded that he was now king, he began barking royal orders; he whistled, sang, shouted; he hurled pillows across the room. Victoria kept watch over him from behind a screen. The thirteenth was the worst day at all; and at one point on that day, Victoria and her daughter Alice agreed that "there can be no hope." Victoria realized with horror that her eldest son would probably die on December 14, ten years to the very day after his father.

But she was wrong. On the fourteenth the fever abated, and Bertie had periods of quiet rest. The next day, he was able to say to his mother calmly and coherently "Oh! Dear Mama, I am so glad to see you. Have you been here all this time?" Not long after this, he asked for a glass of Bass's beer.

The prince's recovery was a renewal on every level. About Bertie himself, according to his mother, "there is something quite different which I can't exactly express. It is like a new life. . . ." The Princess of Wales was never happier; she and the Prince were inseparable as he recovered. And Victoria's own bond with her son intensified; it was as if she needed his near-death to understand his value to her. He was now her "Beloved Child," without qualifications. And outside the walls of Sandringham, the relationship between the public and the royal family had altered utterly: the spirit of loyalty had become far stronger than it had been in a decade. The republican tide was quickly ebbing.

Charles Wentworth Dilke, second Baronet, became the chief victim of this sea change. In mid-November, as the *Salmonella typhi* bacillus worked quietly upon the Prince, Dilke continued his speaking tour. The great publicity accorded his Newcastle speech guaranteed that he had to deal with hecklers and scuffles during all his subsequent appearances, but in general he was well received. Then the Prince fell seriously ill. A meeting of constituents in Chelsea on 29 November turned into a riotous brawl between supporters and opponents. Two days after that, Dilke's appearance in Bolton precipitated an even worse riot; as he attempted to speak, royalists outside smashed the windows of the hall with bricks and pieces of iron; they soon burst into the hall and laid into the audience with bludgeons. Many were injured, and one man died. After that, Dilke turned down many appearances and made only a few, at which he backpedaled on his republicanism.

If Dilke was blindsided by the Prince's illness and recovery, his prime minister was overjoyed: the Prince had given Gladstone the perfect opportunity to deal with the "royalty question" once and for all. He had heard that the Princess of Wales desired a national day of thanksgiving for her husband's recovery. Gladstone agreed: a grand service at St. Paul's—with, more importantly, a splendid royal procession with Victoria and her son in an open carriage from palace to cathedral and back again—would do more than strengthen the public's newfound affection for Bertie; it would also reintroduce the Queen to her people, and signal the end of her ten-years' seclusion. Armed with a substantial list of precedents—including the Thanksgiving in 1789 when George III recovered from madness—Gladstone visited the Queen at Windsor on 21 December to persuade her to go among her public.

The Queen refused. "Nothing could induce her to be a party to it," Gladstone wrote. Her excuse was that religion should not be mixed with show; "such a display" she considered "false and hollow." She really feared putting *herself* on display, of course. Gladstone gently argued that the Princess of Wales greatly desired a public thanksgiving. Victoria brushed this off: surely Alix would not insist upon it, given the Queen's reasons for refusal. But Alix *did* insist, writing to Victoria "the whole nation has taken such a public share in our sorrow, it has been so entirely one with us in our grief, that it may perhaps feel that it has a kind of claim to join with us now in a public and universal thanksgiving." The Queen then agreed, grudgingly, and for the next few weeks she and her prime minister haggled about the details, Victoria at every turn attempting to minimize the ceremony, and Gladstone working to pull out every stop. She was livid when Gladstone planned to insert an announcement of her plans in the Queen's Speech: "it gives *too much* weight to it," she complained, and ignores the possibility of *"her* being prevented from going by indisposition." She wanted a half-hour service at St. Paul's; Gladstone wanted nothing less than an hour. The Queen wished to progress in "half-state"—without state carriages, state dress, or detachments of guards. Gladstone accepted this, under the conditions that the carriages remain open and the procession move at walking speed, so that the Queen would be well seen by all along the route. They haggled about the number of tickets for admission to the Cathedral, about the carriage in which the Speaker of the House would ride, about whether the Queen and the Prince of Wales would travel in the same or in different carriages, and about the route of the procession. Five days before what Victoria was calling "this dreadful affair at St. Paul's," her annoyance and anxiety burst out in a letter to Gladstone: "The Queen is looking with much alarm to the Ceremony of the 27th—the fatigue & excitement of w^h she fears will be vy great & she has been g^{ty} annoyed at the constant new suggestions w^h are being made.—It is tho' it was to be *merely a show!*"

But the show went on: the scaffolding and flags and bunting and illuminations and flower-decked triumphal arches went up all along the route. London prepared to welcome the Queen home.

At noon on 27 February, a cold, clear day, Napoleon III, ex-emperor of the French, stood with his wife Eugénie at an eastern window of Buckingham Palace; they were special guests of the Queen, their state of exile preventing their attendance at St. Paul's. The two gazed—wistfully, one assumes—upon the ocean of human beings roiling on the other side of the palace gates and stretching down the Mall. Out of the northeast gate of the Palace, a cortége of ten carriages—the last one carrying the Queen and the Prince of Wales*—was slowly plunging into that cheering, seething, screaming mass. It was the greatest gathering on the streets of London in a generation.

Victoria was ecstatic as she passed through what she estimated to be millions, with their "wonderful enthusiasm and astounding affectionate loyalty." The white detailing of her black dress— miniver on her gown, white flowers on her bonnet—suggested the slightest thaw in her decade of mourning. The cheering seemed never to stop, nor did her enthusiastic response. Bertie, sitting across from her and still pale from his illness, felt it too: the energy of the crowd energized them, their reception "so gratifying that one could not feel tired." At Temple Bar, the traditional entry to

---

* And carrying as well the Princess of Wales, Princess Beatrice, Albert Victor (Bertie's oldest son), and of course, on the rumble seat, John Brown in full highland dress.

the City, they stopped for the Lord Mayor's welcome. Victoria took her son's hand, pressed it, and held it up for the crowd. People cried, the Queen said; Bertie cried. Victoria admitted to a lump in her own throat. The service at St. Paul's, attended by the upper ten thousand,[*] was far less exciting for the Queen; it was stiflingly hot, and—though Victoria had won the argument with Gladstone and the service was shortened—still too long. Then there was the triumphant return to the palace by a northern route, past Newgate ("very dreary-looking," wrote the Queen), up Holborn, down Oxford Street, through Hyde Park, where men and boys perched perilously on every available tree branch, as they had twenty years before at the opening of the Great Exhibition— down Constitution Hill—"the deafening cheering never ceasing for a minute"—and again through the northeast gate. Bertie, Alix, and their two sons then took their leave, but Victoria, with her youngest daughter Beatrice and her three other sons, climbed the stairs and stepped out onto the balcony for another round of vociferous cheers. "Could think and talk of little else," she wrote in her journal, "but to-day's wonderful demonstration of loyalty and affection, from the very highest to the lowest. Felt tired by all the emotion, but it is a day that can never be forgotten." What she had forgotten completely was her own abhorrence to ride in the first place, and the strenuous efforts of her prime minister to get her to show herself. She did afterwards write him, glowing about her reception and asking him to convey her gratitude to her subjects. But she could manage not a word of gratitude to Gladstone himself.

Victoria's triumph seemed complete. But there was more to come. The bacillus had done its work; now, it was the unruly boy's turn.

---

[*] The upper 11,876, to be exact, judging from the number of tickets issued. (Kuhn 155n.)

twenty

LEAP DAY

Nine days before the thanksgiving, Arthur O'Connor in a flash of insight realized what he had to do. On that cold mid-February Sunday, the seventeen-year-old was taking his favorite walk in Hyde Park along the banks of the Serpentine—far from his depressing home in the East London slums of Aldgate. His walk skirted that part of the park where the Crystal Palace had once stood—past, in other words, that part of London which had over the past decade become known as Albertopolis—the ever-growing collection of establishments endowed by the proceeds of the Exhibition of 1851, all of them sacred to the memory of the dead Prince Consort. Just south of the boy and visible through the winter trees were the hoardings surrounding what would become the grand, high-neogothic Albert Memorial—scheduled for unveiling in July. Across the road from that was the distinctively elliptical and domed Royal Albert Hall, which Victoria, overwhelmed with emotion, had opened on a bitterly cold day last

March. Adjoining the Hall were the gardens of the Horticultural Society, the southern limit of which was laid out for a new museum of natural history. And across from that was the South Kensington Museum, which would one day be known as the Victoria and Albert Museum. Albertopolis was far from the only monument to the memory of the Prince Consort. Since his death, monuments to him had been erected through the length and breadth of the kingdom; even Dublin had its Albert statue. By Victoria's wishes, her husband had achieved something close to deification.

The boy had every reason to be infuriated by this cult: what, after all, had that German prince done to deserve this worship? Little more, it seems, than to sire nine royal burdens upon the state, and to put on a fair on this spot in 1851. Monuments to the great men of the boy's own family were surely better-deserved: where were they? The boy was convinced, as were his father and grandfather before him, that the blood of the great Kings of Connaught flowed through his veins: hadn't his great-grandfather changed his name from Conner to O'Connor to proclaim that lineage to the world? Where were the monuments to them? And where was the monument to his great-great-uncle and his namesake, Arthur, a diehard Irish republican and a leader of the United Irishmen? Arthur O'Connor went to France in 1796 to negotiate the landing in Ireland of a French army of liberation. After that invasion failed, Arthur and his brother, young Arthur's great-grandfather Roger— another United Irishman—were arrested, imprisoned, and then exiled by the British to France, where Arthur O'Connor had been appointed a general of the French army by the great Napoleon himself: surely he deserved his monument? Where, for that matter, was the monument to the young Arthur's great-uncle, Francis Burdett O'Connor, who in 1819 set out with two hundred Irish volunteers to liberate South America from the imperial Spanish yoke? Did he not become General Francisco Burdett O'Connor, the great Simon Bolívar's chief of staff, and engage in battles for freedom from Peru to Panama?

And where was the recognition due the greatest O'Connor of all—his great-uncle Feargus O'Connor, the great champion of the working-man—the man still remembered as the "Lion of Freedom"? By virtue of his fiery oratory, his unstoppable energy, his undying love for the "fustian jackets, the blistered hands, the unshorn chins," Feargus O'Connor became for fifteen years the sole and undisputed popular leader of Chartism, repeatedly braving the rich and powerful in Parliament: three times he brought before them the people's demand for a Charter establishing their political rights. At Feargus O'Connor's funeral in 1855, people showed up at Kensal Green in numbers too great for that cemetery to contain. They carried banners declaring him to be their savior: "He lived and died for us." Never had the English proletariat had a stronger champion. His enemies—and he had many—might say that Feargus O'Connor died a raving lunatic. Young Arthur O'Connor refused to believe it—committing him to Dr. Tuke's asylum was simply a trick to deny him the reputation he deserved. Where then was the "Feargus Memorial"? Where was the "Royal Feargus Hall"?*

How unfair it must have seemed to young Arthur O'Connor that Albert was covered in glory while his own family had sunk into obscurity and squalor. Just fifty years before, his family had owned substantial lands in Ireland, but that fortune had now dissipated completely. Arthur lived with his family—nine in all—on the verge of starvation in a single room of a dilapidated Aldgate tenement, at the edge of Seven-Step Alley, one of the worst Irish rookeries in London. His father made just enough money taking tickets for the London and Waterman's Steamboat Company to provide his family with the thinnest veneer of respectability. Arthur was their third child, but perhaps the one upon whom the parents pinned their greatest hopes. While their eldest son had enlisted

---

* Actually, there were two monuments to Feargus O'Connor: a Gothic spire at his gravesite at Kensal Green, and a statue in Nottingham, the city he served as a Member of Parliament (Read and Glasgow 144).

in the army and their eldest daughter had trained as a teacher, Arthur, as a clerk, was on the bottom rung of the ladder to middle-class respectability. He had worked for a firm of printers for four years, then for a lawyer. Now, at seventeen, he worked as a junior accountant across the river in Southwark for Livett Franks and Son, a paint manufacturer. He acquitted himself well in all of these positions. But he had since birth been cursed with ill health—a pigeon-breasted, scrofulous rail of a boy; later, a reporter would see in his pitiful body nothing less than evidence of the degeneration of Western civilization: O'Connor was "of the order from whose plentifulness some physiologists forbode a deterioration of the human race in our great towns." Ill health stifled his advancement: raging scrofula had ended his job with the printers', sending him to King's College Hospital, where he had a toe amputated.

His body was a miserable container for what he knew to be a great soul. He could feel within himself the blood and the spirit of the great O'Connors. He was a scholar, a dreamer, a writer—spending night after night in a corner of his crowded room, studying, and composing great works of poetic genius, which he had assured his parents were destined for publication and fame. He was Johnnie Keats and Lord Byron combined: a hypersensitive romantic soul, aching to live and die for a great cause.

And indeed, he had a cause. Though he had lived his entire life in London, he was "passionately Irish," as he later wrote, and devoted to the struggle for Irish freedom. He had likely never even met a Fenian, but his blood and the acts of his forefathers connected him deeply with them. The flower of the movement, he knew, continued to rot in English and Irish jails, and he knew as well that the greatest act of an Irish patriot would be to free those prisoners. And, as he walked the periphery of the Serpentine, Arthur O'Connor understood his destiny in a flash. He would be that man. He would in one act free the Fenian prisoners, restore the reputation of the O'Connors, and join the pantheon of great Irish heroes.

He would kill Queen Victoria.

There would never be a better opportunity to kill the Queen than during the thanksgiving to be held in two weeks, when she would emerge from her long seclusion and show herself at St. Paul's, where England's rich and powerful would all be witnesses to the shooting.

He mulled over the plan for rest of the day. Something about it was not quite right, and he finally acknowledged the flaw. If he killed the Queen, the now-recovering Prince of Wales would replace her: the new king certainly would not free the Fenians. He would have to modify his plan. He would not kill the Queen, but would terrify her: putting a pistol to her head, he would frighten her into signing a declaration freeing the Irish prisoners. If he could succeed in getting close enough to her, he was sure that all around her would be "paralyzed with horror"—powerless to intervene. He knew he would never escape from his assault. He expected he would be bayoneted on the spot; if not, he would certainly be executed for High Treason. So be it: he cared little for his life and knew that with his death would come everlasting fame. But if he was to sacrifice his life for Ireland, he wished to die a hero—not hanged like a common criminal, but shot by a firing squad. He would include a codicil to that effect in his declaration.

During the next fortnight, then, while Victoria bickered with her prime minister about the coming thanksgiving and the minutiae of her role, Arthur O'Connor prepared to play his own. He somehow managed to obtain a clean parchment; carefully lining it with a pencil, he set out the Queen's declaration in his best clerk's hand and best legalese: "I, Victoria, Queen by the grace of God, do make the following declaration. . . ." With an astonishing overestimation of the power of the monarch, he had Victoria declare that she would "grant a free pardon to each and every one of the said men known and celebrated as the Fenian prisoners," "with the consent of my Parliament"—as if her saying it was so would make it so. He then set out carefully, in four clauses, the conditions of absolute freedom she granted the prisoners. In a fifth clause, he tackled the tricky problem of coercion, attempting to head off any attempt to nullify an Act the Queen had been forced to sign:

> . . . notwithstanding the fact of my agreeing to the above conditions only through fear of my life, I will not attempt to depart from any of them on that account, nor upon any other reason, cause, or pretext whatever will I depart, or attempt to depart, from any of them; neither will I listen to any advice which my Ministers may wish to give toward causing me to depart from my word, or toward the violation of anything above stated, but shall adhere strictly to everything. So help me God.

He left there a space for the Queen's signature and, underneath, inserted the codicil which would, he hoped, guarantee him a hero's execution:

> Now I, the said Victoria, Queen of Great Britain and Ireland, do solemnly pledge my Royal word to the effect that if the said Arthur O'Connor be found guilty of death by my judges, after a just and fair trial, he the said Arthur O'Connor shall not be strangled like a common felon, but shall receive that death which is due to him as a Christian, a Republican, and as one who has never harmed a human being—that is to say, he shall be shot, and after death his body shall be delivered to his friends to be buried wheresoever they may choose.

In order to allay the suspicions of his family or his employers, Arthur O'Connor kept to his daily routine until Monday 26 February, the day before the thanksgiving. On that afternoon, after leaving work in Southwark, he obtained his pistol—the cheapest he could find. He had spotted it in the window of a jeweler's near his workplace—a flintlock, a small, decrepit relic of another age. It was missing its flint, and flints were not easy to come by in 1872; the clerk told him he would have to pick up a piece of flint from the road and cut it to proper shape. (And he did.) O'Connor had never handled a gun in his life, and had to ask how it worked. The clerk told him about powder, bullet, and wad. But there is no evidence that Arthur O'Connor bought any of these things; he paid four shillings for the pistol alone, and left. The pistol was intact when he bought it, but did not remain so for long; the same evening, while practicing his shooting style, he broke off the pan and ruined the lock. At some point a greasy red rag found its way into the barrel; inexplicably, for the next few days it would remain there, broadcasting the worthlessness of the weapon.

That night, O'Connor filled his pockets. He helpfully brought pen and ink, thinking to avoid the awkward wait for one of the ten thousand to produce them while he held his pistol to Victoria's temple. He pocketed the pistol, the petition, and, just in case, a long, thin, open knife of his father's. He slipped out of his house for the short walk due west to St. Paul's. It was 11:00 P.M., and the cathedral was abuzz with activity: workmen were preparing seating; seamstresses were decorating the temporary chambers set aside for the refreshment of the Queen and the Princess of Wales—and police were guarding the entrances. When he attempted to slip in, an officer promptly challenged him and turned him away. Nevertheless, somehow he got in—"by a stratagem," he later claimed. He took cover underneath some benches, hoping to hide until the morning.

He was soon found. He had tracked mud on the otherwise clean carpets to his hiding place; a verger discovered him and turned him out. He then tried to hide in a cold, dark space on the cathedral's porch. A police sergeant caught him there with the glaring spotlight of his bull's-eye lantern and ordered him off the property. O'Connor then wandered the streets of the City until 5:30 the next morning, ruminating upon how he could get close to the Queen. He decided to give up entering the cathedral altogether. Instead, he would confront the Queen somewhere on her procession to or from the service. He returned home, put the pistol, the knife, and the declaration under his pillow, and slept until 8:00, when he rose, rearmed himself, and set out again for St. Paul's and the route of the procession. He quickly realized that he had made a serious mistake. The crowds were already massing along the route in numbers too thick to penetrate. He spent hours wandering the route, looking for a place where he could push his way to the front—but could find none. The Queen had her thanksgiving without him, her subjects—as the newspapers had been saying ever since Oxford's attempt upon her—providing her best protection.

Arthur O'Connor returned home that evening. His mother asked him where he had been. To St. Paul's, he said—but he "had not gained his object." He would not tell her what that object was. He slept until the next morning, and, again arming himself with declaration, pistol, and knife, walked across town to the front of Buckingham Palace, joining the crowd assembled there hoping the Queen would emerge. She did emerge that day—twice, for a ride in the parks and for a visit to a sculptor's studio—but somehow O'Connor missed her. He returned home. His chances, he knew, were running out: the Queen left for Windsor in two days, on the first of March.

That night, O'Connor took a break from stalking Victoria and instead celebrated her; he took his nine-year-old brother out to gaze at the brilliant thanksgiving illuminations that stretched from St. Paul's to the Palace.

The next day, Thursday 29 February—Leap Day—he awoke weary and jaded, according to his father. He complained of having no rest, and pains in his head. Equipping himself with declaration, pistol, and knife, but leaving pen and ink behind, he returned to the Palace in the afternoon, arriving after four to hear the cheering and see the Queen's carriage heading up Constitution Hill. Victoria had that afternoon held Court at the Palace, and, as she had done so many times in the past, she afterwards set out for a ride through the parks. She sat on the right side of the carriage, facing the horses. Next to her sat one of her favorite ladies-in-waiting, Lady Jane Churchill, and across from them were Victoria's two youngest sons: on the Queen's side sat twenty-year-old Arthur and next to him Leopold, who at eighteen was barely older than O'Connor. For Prince Arthur, this was a farewell ride with his mother; he would be returning to army service in Dover that evening. Leopold, on the other hand, had nothing to do with the military. He could not: he was a hemophiliac and had suffered from early childhood his mother's stifling overprotection.

Accompanying her on either side were her equerries—she had two now, since Albert's death—Lord Fitzroy and General Hardinge riding on either side of the carriage. Two outriders rode before, two grooms behind. And John Brown sat at the Queen's back.

O'Connor asked a policeman when she would return. Soon, he was told. He succeeded, this time, in pushing himself to the front of the crowd waiting near the northeast gate of the Palace—the gate though which Victoria had emerged and through which she would return. And he waited, while Victoria circumnavigated Hyde and Regent's Parks.

By the time the noise at the top of Constitution Hill signaled the Queen's return, the crowd had grown and had spilled onto the road. The police began to push them back and clear a space for the carriage. At that moment, with the crowd focused upon the Queen, the police focused on the crowd, and the sentry at the gate staring forward, poised to present arms, O'Connor bolted. Running unperceived to the point where the edge of the Palace's eastern fence meets the northern wall, he removed his overcoat and gingerly hung it over a rail. Then, with a litheness and energy that must have surprised him, he scrambled up and over the twelve-foot fence, tumbling into the corner of the Palace forecourt. Somehow, he managed to keep his low-crowned, wide-brimmed wideawake hat on his head. The carriage was approaching now, the gates being opened. O'Connor took cover behind a pillar near the gatekeeper's lodge.

He saw the carriage enter and pass. The gatekeeper, an old man "rather past work," spied him and shouted "what mischief do you want here?" O'Connor simply raced past the sputtering and helpless man and through the gateway the carriage had just entered. It had stopped and the equerries and outriders were dismounting; John Brown had leapt off the rumble and come to the left side to let down the carriage stairs. O'Connor ran around to that side. His presence alarmed no one, but perplexed all who noticed him: they imagined him to be a gardener's boy, not quite in the right place. He ran up to the side of the carriage, brushing against Brown, who pushed him back. One of the equerries, Lord Fitzroy, told him to go away. Instead, he stepped up to the rear panel of the carriage, peered over the edge, raised his pistol, and timidly muttered something about the Fenian prisoners.

Suddenly confused, he fell silent. He was not looking at the Queen but at Lady Jane Churchill. Lady Jane was oblivious to him; the queen sat equally unconscious of him on the other side of the carriage. He ran around the back of the carriage, raised his face over that side—and stared directly into his Queen's eyes. Victoria thought at first that he was a footman come to remove her blanket. O'Connor said something the Queen could not make out; she noticed only the strangeness of his voice. (Arthur heard his words: "Take that from a Fenian.") She then noticed his uplifted hand, but did not see the pistol it held. Leopold and Arthur, however, did see it, Arthur stretching forward to push it away. It clattered to the ground. Victoria then panicked. "Involuntarily, in a terrible fright, I threw myself over Jane C. calling out, 'Save me . . . !'" she later wrote. At that moment John Brown, who had chased O'Connor around the carriage, with one hand grabbed O'Connor's body and with the other clamped the scruff of his neck. Now everyone was alarmed, and the equerries and outriders converged upon Brown's prize, pushing the boy to the ground. Prince Arthur vaulted over the side of the carriage and joined the scrum. (Leopold, wisely, stayed put.) A vague sense that the boy had actually touched the royal person likely encouraged them all to handle him more roughly than simple capture demanded: they yanked off the boy's necktie and gave him a violent throttling. One of the outriders asked O'Connor if he was hiding anything, and O'Connor admitted to having the knife and the declaration. The two equerries, meanwhile, called out for the police. Police Sergeant Jackson—who had closed the gate with O'Connor inside—and several constables came running. Sergeant Jackson removed knife and declaration from O'Connor's pockets. (He handed the latter to one of the equerries, who soon showed it to Victoria: "an extraordinary document," she called it.)

They stood the boy up. O'Connor was more affronted than shaken. He complained about the damage done to his necktie, and demanded his hat be returned to him before he would answer any questions. He was led off. The Queen, standing up in the carriage for a better view, saw him go, and then suffered another shock. Her attendants asked if she had been hurt: "Not at all," she replied. The equerries and Arthur then told her they thought the boy had dropped something. "We looked," Victoria wrote, "but could find nothing, when Canon, the postilion, called out, 'There it is,' and looking down I then did see shining on the ground a small pistol! This filled us with horror. All were white as sheets, Jane C. almost crying, and Leopold looked as if he were going to faint."

Of all of the attempts upon her, O'Connor's—violating the security of her home as well as her personal space—was the one that frightened her the most. Her worst fears about Fenians, the Irish, and the growing dangers that lurked in the metropolis were all confirmed in the puny boy. At the same time, however, what had just happened confirmed all of her *best* thoughts about her devoted Highland servant. Once again, she was certain she had been saved by providence from death;* and to her mind, one man alone was

---

* The fact that O'Connor's pistol was obviously unloaded made little difference to her; she wrote that day in her journal "The pistol had not been loaded, but it easily might have been!" (Victoria *Letters* second series 2:218).

responsible for saving her life. "It is entirely owing to good Brown's great presence of mind and quickness that he was seized," she wrote to Vicky; "Brown alone saw him spring round and suspected him." Her hero, she quickly decided, deserved a medal.

Safe in the palace, Victoria quickly took steps to disseminate an accurate account of the attempt, and of her safety, to scotch the wild rumors that were already spreading. She sent her two young sons to take the news to Bertie; the two strolled arm in arm, out of the front gates of the Palace, through the crowd, and to Marlborough House. The Prince of Wales, bedridden with the bad leg that was a byproduct of his typhoid and that had been aggravated by his activity on the thanksgiving, could not rush to the palace, but his wife could, and Princess Alix, showing full trust in the public, rode there in an open carriage. Victoria sent royal officers to the police station and the Home Office, and sent as well her equerry Arthur Hardinge to Parliament, to speak with Gladstone personally. Hardinge was delayed for some reason, and for the better part of an hour rumors flew in the lobby of the House of Commons, consternation growing to panic, the excitement overwhelming the debate on the Ballot then proceeding in the House. Finally, Hardinge arrived and closeted himself with Gladstone, who, emerging, hurried into the House, interrupted the debate, and, to relieved cheering, set out a generally accurate account of the attempt. In one particular, however, he stretched the truth: the Queen, he claimed, "was not in the slightest degree flurried or alarmed."[*] (Similarly in the House of Lords, Lord Granville announced that "the Queen showed the greatest courage and composure.") Since no one but the Queen, her family, and her household had seen the attempt, there was nothing to prevent the witnesses to the attempt

---

[*] Later, Gladstone ordered O'Connor's pistol brought to the lobby of the House, to show what a harmless relic it was. The swarm of members around the curiosity grew so great that the detective in charge of it had to reclaim the weapon forcibly and flee Parliament (*Glasgow Daily Herald* 1 March 1872, 5).

to preserve and promote an idealized image of the Queen. Victoria might admit her all-too-human, terrified reaction to her private journal, but there was little need to share this with her subjects. Every newspaper account of the attempt dutifully noted Victoria's unflinching coolness and bravery.

O'Connor, meanwhile, was hurried out of the Palace gates, pushed into a cab with Sergeant Jackson, and brought to the destination of all his predecessors but one*—A Division headquarters, now remodeled and known as King Street station. On the way, he repeatedly proclaimed to Jackson his willingness to die in his great cause: "I wish to God I had succeeded; then they could have done with me as they pleased." He acknowledged his gun had been broken, and that he only wished to intimidate Victoria, not kill her. At the station he gave the Superintendent, Mott, a full account of his abortive attempts to threaten the Queen two days before at the thanksgiving. He was then placed in a cell, Superintendent Mott ordering that he be allowed absolutely no visitors. A number of curious Members of Parliament who came to interview the boy were thus turned away; only the Commissioner of Police, Richard Mayne's replacement Sir Edmund Henderson, saw him that night.

That evening, London reacted to O'Connor's attempt as it had acted toward the others—the fashionable flocking to enquire about the Queen's health and to sign the visitor's book at the Palace; addresses and toasts to the Queen across town. Arthur O'Connor's timing could not have been better, as far as killing off republican sentiment in the metropolis went. Those who until recently had avidly promoted an English republic now hastened to denounce the attempt and protest their devotion to Victoria. At a crowded meeting of working men in the Surrey Chapel Mission Hall, in Southwark, a resolution was moved to express indignation about the attempt and affection for the Queen's person; prayers were said

---

* Pate.

for Victoria's "long-continued life and happiness." Across town at the White Horse Tavern off Oxford Street, George Odger, working-class leader and heretofore outspoken republican, declared himself sure "that every man in that room . . . would denounce in the most indignant manner such a dastardly proceeding."

The next morning, A Division's police surgeon and another doctor examined O'Connor in his cell. Both concluded that while he might be a political fanatic with lousy grammar and a shaky hold on current events, he was decidedly sane. Gladstone visited Victoria in the Palace that morning—"dreadfully shocked at what [had] happened"—she noted, and particularly annoyed that the boy had apparently marred the "splendid effect" of the thanksgiving. He reminded her of Peel's 1842 Act, which he thought fit the crime. If it did not, he told her, then the law must be changed. Victoria was not nearly as sure that a misdemeanor charge—and a possible lenient sentence—was appropriate. In any case, she was sure that when O'Connor's sentence had expired, "he ought not to be allowed to remain in the country."

O'Connor's examination, it was decided after some confusion, was to be held not at Whitehall, as all previous such examinations, but in the more down-to-earth setting of the police court at Bow Street. From 11:00, throngs largely composed of the dregs of the nearby slums of St. Giles and Seven Dials besieged the court and packed the tiny courtroom. Soon after 1:00, Arthur O'Connor was brought in and held for an hour in a jailer's room. When he was brought before the bar, hisses ran through the back benches. Harry Bodkin Poland, Solicitor to the Treasury, quickly both established the charge and demolished Arthur O'Connor's fragile ego by demonstrating to the boy that he was a fool and his action an absurdity. Poland read out in full O'Connor's declaration, and the courtroom met his would-be patriotism with howls of laughter, which peaked as Poland read out the codicil giving O'Connor a hero's death: "that death which is due to him as a Christian, a Republican—(laughter), and as one who has never harmed a human being—that is to say, he shall be shot, and after death his body shall be delivered to his friends to be buried wheresoever they may choose (Laughter)." The blood rushed to O'Connor's face, and, according to a reporter, "out of the eye there blazed the light of fanaticism." Poland then twisted the knife: crimes such as O'Connor's hardly deserved death, he proclaimed, but rather imprisonment—accompanied by the degradation of flogging. O'Connor's flush immediately disappeared, he hung his head, his lip trembled, and he began to cry. Poland then called forward witnesses to the assault. Of these, John Brown, with his broad Scottish accent and the "grim jocularity" with which he recounted his easy capture and drubbing of the boy, provided the most entertainment. Prince Leopold also took the stand; Victoria, as protective of him as ever, was loath to let him come at all, and only agreed if he went under the close watch of an equerry and of his tutor. He testified to the important fact that O'Connor had held his pistol less than a foot from the queen's face, and was cheered by the crowd on both arriving and departing. O'Connor was given the opportunity to speak after the witnesses had testified; he could do nothing besides correct them on a couple of trivial details. He was then committed for trial and led through the hissing and hooting multitude into a waiting police van, which set off down Bow Street to the Strand, following the route of Tuesday's procession, and deposited O'Connor at Newgate prison.

At roughly the same time—4:00 in the afternoon—Victoria went forth triumphantly in her carriage amongst the cheering and shouting people of London. This long-planned journey—from Buckingham Palace to Paddington Station, from whence the queen would escape London for the greater privacy of Windsor—was supposed to be routine; O'Connor's attempt guaranteed it was nothing but. A number of MPs and Peers had assembled in the Palace forecourt that O'Connor had penetrated the day before; with the express permission of the Queen, they formed a phalanx of symbolic protection. Victoria stood in her carriage to acknowledge them. In the carriage with her were her children Leopold

and Beatrice, and a fresh lady-in-waiting, Fanny Gainsborough.*
Outside the gates, the crowds nearly matched those of the thanksgiving day in volume and energy. "Immense enthusiasm," Victoria wrote after she arrived at Windsor Castle. "All along the
Serpentine, up to Prince's gate, the carriages were two deep, and
we could hardly pass along." She was delighted with the people of
London who, with a nudge from O'Connor, had turned a one-day
thanksgiving into a delirious four-day celebration of the monarch
and her monarchy. Nevertheless, she was relieved to be back in
Windsor. And although it seemed as if every obstacle to London's
adoration of the Queen had been removed, her own reservations
about the people of London remained. "Strange to say my head
and health have not suffered from this dreadful fright," she wrote
to Vicky, "but I know I shall feel it when I go out as I always have
done in London."

Arthur O'Connor had hoped and expected, in thrusting his pistol
into the Queen's face, to become an instant hero to the Irish. This
of course never happened. From the start, the newspapers presented
him as an imbecile, a "crack-brained youth," the mind-boggling
absurdity of his plan demonstrating the boy's folly. And despite
his stated intention to free the Fenians, no one was fooled that his
attempt was a rational political act. The Irish, and in particular
Irish nationalists, quickly and vociferously dissociated themselves
from O'Connor, claiming his mad act worked against Irish interests.
The Dublin *Irishman*, clearly forgetting about William Hamilton's
attack in claiming that Victoria had never been attacked by an
Irishman, argued that "nothing could be more repugnant, nothing
more odious, nothing more loathsome to the spirit of the Irish
people than a cowardly assault on a defenceless lady." This article

---

* Victoria changed her lady-in-waiting at the beginning of every month. Lady
Jane Churchill, however, obviously shaken by the attempt, wished not to
leave the Queen the day after, and with the Queen's permission followed her
to Windsor, riding with the equerries in the carriage behind.

concluded with the less-than-comforting assertion that "Queen Victoria may rest assured that if she ever fell a victim to unhallowed hate it shall not be by the hand of an Irishman." Besides, Irish newspapers noted, Arthur O'Connor was not Irish at all, but born and bred in London. Nor were his forebears truly Irish: a letter-writer to the Dublin *Freeman's Journal* pointed out quite accurately that O'Connor's ancestors were Conners, not O'Connors, English settlers in Ireland who changed their name desiring "to become more Irish than the Irish themselves."

Press and the government agreed that the best punishment for this over-imaginative halfwit was the one prescribed under Peel's Act: the "ridiculous and slightly degrading" punishment of a flogging, the shame of which would purge him and any would-be imitators of thoughts of vainglory. Gladstone quickly concluded that O'Connor was more a fool than a Fenian, writing to the Queen the evening of the attempt that "folly seems to have been so mixed with depravity in this attempt that Mr. Gladstone is inclined to hope this young man may perhaps not have been wholly master of his senses"; Peel's Act should suit such a "contemptible" crime. Home Secretary Henry Bruce agreed, writing the Queen that O'Connor's palpable terror on being told he might be flogged demonstrated the "wisdom" of Peel's Act: he had looked forward to a trial as a state prisoner, but "shrunk from a degrading punishment, which would make him ridiculous and contemptible."

Victoria disagreed with every one of these judgments about the boy. She was sure he would have murdered her if his ignorance had not prevented him. He was certainly not mad, and the Queen pointedly sent Gladstone an article from the *Lancet* which she thought proved his sanity. And while he may never have set foot in Ireland, he was still an Irishman—and worse, a Fenian. As soon as she arrived in Windsor the day after the attack, Victoria delved into her journals, found her account of William Hamilton's attempt—which, she realized, *"no one* seems to recollect"*—and sent a copy to Gladstone as a reminder of Irish perfidy. Hamilton was bad, she explained to Gladstone, but O'Connor was worse: Hamilton "was also an Irishman but *Fenianism* did *not exist* then." O'Connor's assault upon her had been truly threatening, and should be treated seriously, not contemptuously. "He meant to *frighten* & *this may* be tried again & again & end badly some day," she told Gladstone. She had lost confidence in the efficacy of Peel's Act. "The Queen feels sure that *too gt leniency* or treating it as totally contemptible w^ld not do—& if the Act is *not* strong enough it had better be amended." Peel's Act, she thought, did not treat the assaults upon her as seriously as she considered them to be. Indeed, over time the Act had become more lenient: since transportation had come to an end five years before, replaced as a penalty with penal servitude in a British prison, exiling O'Connor, as Francis, Hamilton, and Pate had been exiled, was no longer a legal option. If a judge could not remove the boy from the country, Victoria considered that her government could: speaking to Gladstone the day after the attack, she insisted that O'Connor be forced to leave England after serving his sentence, whatever that might be.

The genuine fear the Queen felt during O'Connor's attack had quickly morphed to anger. She was angry at the police, who she thought were neither vigilant or numerous enough to protect her—a conclusion with which the police tacitly agreed by adding three officers to the Palace detail. She was angry as well at her government, which from the start saw O'Connor's crime as the contemptible act of a fool, not the serious attempt of a Fenian to do her harm. From Windsor she telegraphed Gladstone commanding that the result of O'Connor's examination be sent her, as well as "all details respecting this man." She had from the start a premonition

---

* She was right. Most press retrospectives of the attempts written in the wake of O'Connor's attempt neglected to mention Hamilton's.

that Gladstone and the Liberals were going to fail her, and if they did she would be ready to respond.

The "Boy O'Connor," as the press dubbed him, was reportedly an exemplary prisoner at Newgate, accepting with good grace the many visits of medical examiners, including the near-daily visits of the prison surgeon. His parents, too, visited him as often as they were allowed. Significantly, however, no solicitor attended to him during his first days in prison. He remained cooperative but unrepentant—stating that he was fully justified in his act, though he remained tight-lipped about his motive.

For a week after his arrest, he was the undisputed celebrity criminal of Newgate. On the afternoon of 6 March, however, he was eclipsed completely, when a man instantly recognizable by his enormous size of 26 stone (or 364 pounds)* drove his own brougham up to the door of Newgate, the Superintendent of the Scotland Yard's Detective Branch by his side. A crowd had gathered outside the door of the prison, and he jovially acknowledged their cheers as he passed by them. Some shouted "Wagga Wagga!" after the town in New South Wales from which he had come. Others called out "Arthur Orton!" and still others "Sir Roger!" Upon entering the prison, he gave his name as Roger Charles Doughty Tichborne. The warrant for his arrest named him as Thomas Castro, and he was entered in the prison books under that name. Exactly who the man was had been the basis of a debate that had raged for the past five years: for that long the Tichborne Claimant, as he is known to history, had riveted and riven the nation.

The overwhelming love of a grieving mother had drawn the Claimant from Australia to England. In 1853, Lady Henriette Felicité Tichborne's restless son Roger had fled England for South America; the next year he boarded a ship, the *Bella*, which sailed

---

* This was his weight as taken at Newgate upon his admission. Other accounts suggest he was heavier.

out of Rio de Janeiro and was never seen again; all passengers were thought lost. Lady Tichborne could never quite accept that her eldest son had died. When Roger's father died in 1862, Lady Tichborne was free to indulge her fantasy of reuniting with her son and began to search for him, publishing at first advertisements in the *Times,* and then in 1865 in a number of Australian newspapers, as rumors surfaced that survivors of the *Bella* might have been picked up and deposited in Melbourne. As the advertisements promised a generous reward for information about Roger's fate, it is surprising that only one claimant came forward, but only one did: a Wagga Wagga butcher who went by the name Thomas Castro, and had been known to boast about his aristocratic connections. An attorney acquaintance of Castro who had seen the advertisement and was certain that the butcher was the baronet, persuaded him to reveal himself. Castro did so, quickly gathering supporters to his claim, including several in Australia who had known Roger Tichborne years before. He brought himself and his claim to England in 1866. Early the next year, he traveled to Paris, his mother's original and present home, to meet Lady Tichborne. She immediately acknowledged him as her son.

The rest of the Tichbornes, with few exceptions, were far less welcoming. They had long doubted the sanity of their French in-law and gave little weight to her acknowledgment. The obese and dour Claimant hardly resembled the scrawny and sensitive Roger they remembered. Roger Tichborne had lived the first sixteen years of his life in France, with French his first language; the Claimant's French was limited to "oui, madame" in an atrocious accent. The Claimant's knowledge of Tichborne's childhood was a mystifying mixture of intimate knowledge and profound gaps. That mystery was perhaps solved by the Claimant himself in a confession he wrote in 1895 and quickly repudiated; in it he claimed that he was a superb listener, able to "suck the brains" of those who knew Sir Roger, collecting the information he used to convince others that he was Tichborne. The Tichbornes, however, would have none of it, fiercely resisting the Claimant's attempt to usurp the present "infant baronet," Roger Titchborne's nephew Henry, the son of Roger's deceased younger brother Alfred. To contest the Claimant, one of the Titchbornes engaged the services of the famous private detective Jonathan Whicher.* Whicher soon uncovered enough evidence to convince him that the Claimant was not Roger Tichborne at all, but Arthur Orton, the youngest son of a poor family from the east London district of Wapping.

The Claimant eventually sued for possession of the Tichborne estates, in what became one of the longest civil trials of the century, lasting with some breaks from May 1871 until March 1872. The trial became a national obsession, the courtroom always packed and readers of all classes avidly poring over newspaper accounts of byzantine evidence gathered from three continents. Public attention was split during November and December, when the bulletins charting the near-demise and recovery of the Prince of Wales similarly enthralled the nation. Sir John Duke Coleridge, a friend of William Gladstone, Solicitor General at the beginning of the trial and Attorney General at its end, became with the Claimant a star of the trial. Coleridge was a passionate orator who used his skills both to catch out the Claimant in cross-examination, and to deliver a month-long opening speech that demolished the Claimant's case. After that opening, Coleridge was prepared to call forward a host of corroborating witnesses. He did not need to; after a few came forward—several of these testifying to a tattoo they had seen on Roger Tichborne's arm, and which did not exist on the Claimant's— the jury announced that they had heard enough. The next day, 6 March 1872, the Claimant's counsel, knowing the case was lost, abandoned it in a non-suit—an automatic decision in favor of the Tichbornes. The Lord Chief Justice immediately ordered that the Claimant be arrested for perjury. The Claimant had not come to

---

* Whicher was one of the first eight officers appointed to the original Detective Branch in 1842.

court; he was arrested at the Waterloo Hotel on Jermyn Street and allowed to make his semi-triumphal entrance into Newgate. His bail was fixed at £10,000.

The Claimant proved like O'Connor to be a model prisoner, "cheerful and far from reserved," spending most of his time reading books. He was because of his weight specially provided with a bed, rather than the hammock that O'Connor and the rest of those in Newgate slept on. He largely kept apart from the rest of the prisoners, electing as a Roman Catholic to avoid the Anglican services on Sundays—something that O'Connor, a Protestant, could not do—and exercising in solitude in the yard, since authorities decided his weight would make it impossible for him to keep up with others. It is therefore more than possible that O'Connor never met the man. But he was certainly aware of the Claimant's proximity—and he could not help but be jealous. For the Claimant had achieved with his acts something that Arthur O'Connor (and, for that matter, Edward Oxford before him) had yearned for, but never achieved: true popularity. He had become the darling of the masses, who saw in his struggles a reflection of their own: he was a true underdog, courageously standing up to the powerful. First the aristocratic Tichbornes, and now the government itself, exerted their immense resources in order to keep a poor man down. The working classes saw the Claimant as one of them—as one who had chosen the ways of common men over those of the titled snobs. The higher classes sneered at the Claimant's uncouth and ignorant ways; to those that valorized him, they were marks of honor.

The Claimant was to remain in Newgate until the end of April, when he posted bail. His trajectory of popular acclaim was to rise before it fell, as he set out on a triumphant, wildly popular speaking tour. At his criminal trial, which began a year later and was another ten-month legal marathon, the Claimant was found guilty and imprisoned for over ten years. When he emerged from prison in 1884, the popular support he had enjoyed a decade before had passed; he spent the rest of his life in poverty and humiliation, forlornly promoting his claims in music halls, circuses, and pubs. With a single lapse in 1895, he never stopped claiming to be Sir Roger Tichborne; when he died in 1898, he was buried with that name inscribed upon his coffin.

When the Claimant's life intersected with O'Connor's, however, he was nearing the height of his fame. Arthur O'Connor, throttled by John Brown, hooted at by the riffraff at Bow Street, despised by the press and denounced by all classes, both in Ireland and in England, could not help but contrast his great unpopularity with the Claimant's great popularity. Something had clearly gone wrong with his grand plan. What could he do to make things right?

Within a week, John Brown had his medal. For the last five months, at least, Victoria had been contemplating instituting a medal for the most faithful and long-serving of her servants, and she had written last October on the subject to her prime minister. Medals are given to Arctic explorers, she told Gladstone; why shouldn't her servants be given them as well? "*What* in fact can be more important . . . than the faithfulness & discretion & *independent* unselfishess of those personal servants . . . ?" Gladstone approved of the idea, but cautioned the Queen against applying on the subject to the House of Commons, which would only interfere with her personal choice of recipients. He was sure the Treasury could afford the small expense. Thus, by Victoria's own design, the silver "Victoria Faithful Service Medal" came into being. By the day John Brown tackled O'Connor, the die was quite literally cast.

As far as the Queen was concerned, however, the Faithful Service Medal was not enough: John Brown's action had, she thought, saved her life, and he deserved recognition above that given any of her other servants. She quickly devised a higher award for him: the "Victoria Devoted Service Medal," struck from the same die as the other medal but in gold rather than silver. On 5 March, she presented Brown with a £25 annuity and the medal "in recognition of his presence of mind and devotion." It was the only Devoted Service Medal she—or any other monarch—was ever to give.[*]

Not surprisingly, the Prince of Wales, Brown's inveterate enemy, thought the reward excessive, especially since several others had taken a hand in restraining O'Connor, including his brother Prince Arthur. But Bertie held his tongue—for a time. When, a week later, he discovered that for his pains, Arthur had received a paltry tie-pin, however, he could no longer be contained. He wrote a letter to his mother from France—where he was recovering from his illness—blasting her for the discrepancy. Victoria was baffled: obviously, Brown deserved more than her son had. Arthur "could *not* do, for his very position, what Brown *did*, who was deservedly rewarded for his presence of mind, and devotion."

No one could tell her that her ghillie was not the paragon among men—living men, that was. Besides, she wrote, "Arthur was *very* amiable and wore his pin *continuously* and repeatedly said *how much* he liked it."

Nineteen days after Arthur O'Connor had pounded the last nail into the coffin of republicanism, Sir Charles Wentworth Dilke stood up in the House of Commons to defend its corpse. The public, eager to witness his comeuppance, filled the galleries. Dilke knew very well that he would lose this debate. But he had repeatedly called for a parliamentary investigation into the Queen's expenditures, and he was now bound by honor to do the same in Parliament. He thus approached his task with a wincing desire to get it over with. Speaking for an hour and a half, he offered none of the fireworks he had in Newcastle, seeking instead to take cover in sheer boredom, larding his speech with innumerable and questionable

---

[*] On the other hand, well over a hundred silver "Faithful Service Medals" have been awarded by Victoria and her successors; they are still awarded today (Cullen 158-59n.).

facts and figures; he was, he admitted, "unutterably dull." Gone were the crowd-pleasing lists of comically useless court officers. Gone was the rousing welcome to the coming republic. Instead was an interminable list of precedents for parliamentary oversight of the Queen's finance, and a dispassionate analysis of the growth in the royal fortune, the impropriety of that fortune reverting to the Privy Purse rather than to the nation, and a vague foreboding about the risk of the great accumulation of wealth in the hands of the monarch. It was a speech calculated to change no one's opinion.

William Gladstone then stood to champion the Queen; in the words of *Punch*, he "went smashingly into the Chelsea baronet as if he had been Chelsea china." Dilke had tried to strip his argument of every vestige of republicanism, presenting the motion as one of economy alone. The stink of his Newcastle speech was still upon him, however, and Gladstone refused to let him forget it. Because of the Newcastle speech, Gladstone angrily charged Dilke, the whole country understood his motion to be both a personal attack on the Queen and a call for a republic. Dilke was in every particular wrong: wrong about the Queen's wealth, wrong that she cost more than her uncles or her grandfather had, wrong that the annuities for her children were unprecedented and improper. Duty toward the Queen "who reigns in the hearts of her people" impelled him to exhort the House to reject Dilke's motion. Gladstone sat down to universal cheering.

The demolition done, the House was ready to vote. But Dilke's courageous if foolhardy colleague, Auberon Herbert, jumped up, seconded Dilke's motion, and prepared to give his own speech in its defense. "A perfect storm," as Gladstone put it, ensued. The House—and particularly the Conservatives—assailed Herbert with cries of "Divide! Divide!" which degenerated into a menagerie of catcalls, cock-crows, and howls. Large groups walked out, hoping to force an adjournment by lack of a quorum. One member only made things worse by demanding that press and strangers in the gallery be expelled, suggesting that the government wished to stifle free

discussion. The anarchy continued until Herbert finally surrendered to the bellowing and sat down. After a couple short speeches
by Dilke's fellow radicals, explaining why they could not possibly
support this motion, the House divided. Two voted for Dilke's
motion; 276 voted against it.* All in all, concluded *Punch*, Dilke's
attack on the Queen "was about as contemptible as that by the lad
who presented the flintless and empty pistol the other day."

Dilke was mightily relieved his short tenure as republican leader
was over for good. It took some time for him to cease to be a social
pariah, and in the eyes of the Queen, the damage was permanent;
she could not forget the injury he had done her when her popularity
was at its nadir. Ten years later, when he was offered a place in Gladstone's ministry, the Queen insisted that he not be given any office
that would place him close to her, and that he publicly renounce his
"earlier crude opinions." And so he did, leaving no doubt that in the
battle of ideologies, Victoria had triumphed completely over him,
Odger, Bradlaugh, and O'Connor: republicanism was dead.

---

* The two who voted for the motion were not Dilke and Herbert, who acted as
tellers, or vote-counters, and did not vote.

twenty-one

OUT OF THE COUNTRY

According to one of the doctors who examined him in Newgate, Arthur O'Connor's great object was "truth at all times." He was known to quarrel with his siblings because they simply could not understand truth as he did. He absolutely refused to understand his assault upon the Queen as anything less than heroic. His parents visited him as often as they could. His mother Catherine's understanding of his plight differed greatly from his father George's. To Catherine, Arthur was still to her a "good lad" and the "best of boys" who had made a horrible mistake; now he had to endure what he had brought upon himself. Her husband George disagreed; the good lad that he had known was gone. Arthur, he believed, had changed greatly since the day in late 1866 when a cab in Chancery Lane had knocked him down, split his head open, and sent him to the hospital. He had never been the same since—had become increasingly irritable and frequently burst out in fits of irrational passion. George O'Connor began telling his friends that his son's brain was affected. The attack on the Queen simply confirmed his worst fears.

George O'Connor had seen insanity in his family before. Back in 1853, two years before his son Arthur was born, he became deeply involved in the care of his uncle Feargus. Feargus O'Connor's behavior had by then been increasingly eccentric for years. When in June 1852 he struck two members in the House of Commons in as many days, he was arrested and examined by four doctors, all of whom deemed him insane—three of them diagnosing his illness as "general paralysis of the insane"—soon (but not yet) understood to result from syphilis. One of these doctors was the celebrated John Conolly; another was his son-in-law, Thomas Harrington Tuke, who agreed to take O'Connor in at his asylum at Chiswick. When in 1853 George's aunt Harriet petitioned to gain control of her brother Feargus's estate and remove him from Tuke's care, citing ill-treatment, George staunchly defended Tuke, successfully applying to have his uncle placed under the protection of the Lord Chancellor, in order to keep his uncle safe at Chiswick and safe from the designs of his aunt. The commission, examining him, found him frantic and incoherent, but able to sing out all of "The Lion of Freedom," the song written in his honor. Feargus O'Connor lived on for another two years in pitiful physical decline, suffering severe epileptic seizures and losing control of his bodily functions. In August 1855, his sister—in opposition to George's wishes—applied successfully to the Court of Chancery for her brother's removal to her house. He died there in agony ten days later. George O'Connor knew what madness looked like; he knew that madness ran in his family; he was sure that physical injury to his son had brought that madness to the fore. And he trusted Dr. Thomas Harrington Tuke.

Therefore, George O'Connor turned not to a solicitor to help Arthur, but to Tuke. A week after his son's imprisonment, he met Tuke in his consulting room and explained his son's case. Tuke cautioned him: if Arthur were deemed insane at his trial, he would be confined at the Queen's pleasure—in effect a harsher sentence than the seven years' imprisonment and two floggings that he incorrectly thought to be the maximum sentence under Peel's Act. George O'Connor understood that. He still wished that Tuke examine his son.

Five days later, on 12 April, Tuke examined Arthur in the company of J. Rowland Gibson, the surgeon of Newgate. The boy's pupils were dilated; his eyes glistened. His head was asymmetrical, with phrenological indications of insanity. He described his many illnesses—spitting blood, bone disease—all of which indicated to Tuke "a fanciful and hypochondriacal state of mind." O'Connor spoke at length of his abortive attempt at St. Paul's and his attempt at the Palace, his narrative clearly indicating that "an occasion of great national excitement had developed in this poor boy a paroxysm of insanity." Tuke could only confirm Arthur's father's fears. He recommended to George that other doctors examine his son. Four others did; three concurred with Tuke. Tuke then advised the O'Connors that Arthur should indeed plead insanity, reasoning that any number of years of medical care at Broadmoor would serve the boy better than any number of years in prison as a convicted criminal. Besides, he suggested, in the event of the boy's recovery, both his previous good character, and the Queen's well-known propensity to clemency, would surely both work to free the boy.

Tuke offered his services to the penurious O'Connors for free. No solicitor would do the same, but a band of George O'Connor's friends contributed enough to hire the firm of Dickson and Lucas, who in turn engaged J. W. Hume-Williams as defending counsel. All agreed that Arthur would plead not guilty by reason of insanity at the coming sessions.

On Tuesday the ninth of April, the grand jury at the Central Criminal Court briefly heard the testimony of two witnesses—Prince Leopold and John Brown—and quickly returned a true bill against O'Connor, for a misdemeanor under Peel's Act. Later that afternoon, O'Connor was brought before the bar. It was known that he now had legal representation, and his trial was scheduled for Thursday. His counsel was not, however, in the room, nor were his parents. The boy appeared at first sheepish before the trappings of the law, but quickly regained his confidence. The Clerk of Arraigns asked him how he pleaded. O'Connor paused. Earlier that day, he had spoken with his mother in his cell. The scales had been removed from his eyes, he told her: he "saw the effects of what he had done." She understood this to mean that he had been mad when he committed the act—the scales were before his eyes—and now was sane, and contrite. Most likely, neither madness nor contrition had anything to do with it. He knew what he had done; he knew that he had broken the law—and as a devoted adherent to the truth, he knew what he had to do.

He pleaded guilty.

Those in the courtroom were visibly startled by the boy's plea, aware that his family, solicitor, and barrister had for some time been working upon a defense; all were expecting a trial on Thursday. Instead, the verdict was recorded, the Deputy Recorder directed that O'Connor be brought up that day for his sentencing, and he was taken away.

George O'Connor, who had been consulting with Dr. Tuke about his son's defense when his son pleaded, did not learn about the plea until the next day, when he read about it in a newspaper. He, Tuke, and O'Connor's barrister J. W. Hume-Williams agreed that the plea must be withdrawn: O'Connor's insanity prevented him from understanding what he was doing. Hume-Williams thus stood before the presiding judge, Baron Cleasby, on Wednesday, claiming he had a "startling amount of evidence" to support the claim of O'Connor's derangement. Cleasby seemed surprised: he had not heard that there was any hint of madness in the boy when he pleaded. Nevertheless, he allowed Hume-Williams to bring up the matter at O'Connor's sentencing the next day.

O'Connor thus had a trial. The courtroom was crowded, particularly with bewigged barristers expecting the setting of new legal precedents. O'Connor was brought to the dock, now neatly dressed and very much aware of his own importance: "he bowed neither to judge nor jury," noted a reporter, "but posed himself as if sitting for his photograph." His legal position was an odd one, for both his barrister and Attorney General Coleridge, appearing for the Crown, claimed to be his true advocate. Hume-Williams adopted Dr. Tuke's argument that if O'Connor were truly insane, medical care at the Queen's pleasure would better suit him than any number of years in an English prison. Coleridge, on the other hand, argued that an acquittal on the grounds of insanity would in effect ensure a worse punishment—a lifetime of confinement. Though a jury was empaneled to consider the question, it was more limited in scope than a full-blown criminal trial, for—as Baron Cleasby, a judge known to be a niggler on points of law, and never quite comfortable in a criminal courtroom, repeatedly made it clear, the hearing focused upon a single question: was Arthur O'Connor sane at the moment he pleaded guilty? Whether he was insane when he assaulted the Queen was not relevant. O'Connor's barrister J. W. Hume-Williams argued that O'Connor's state of mind at the time of the assault was indeed relevant and admissible, since it pointed to a long-term mental illness which endured until the moment O'Connor pled. But Cleasby would have none of it, interrupting Hume-Williams after the second sentence of his opening speech, and relentlessly afterwards, cautioning him to keep to the single question at issue.

Braving Cleasby's objections, Hume-Williams laid out the evidence for insanity—the life of unceasing illness, the head injury, the family predisposition to insanity, the growing "paroxysm of insanity," which peaked during the week of the thanksgiving. He crafted his case in the now well-tried pattern of Hadfield's and Oxford's defenses, bringing forward witnesses to O'Connor's eccentricities, and then calling a number of medical witnesses, in the hopes of demonstrating to the jury that the overwhelming medical consensus was that O'Connor was insane. But despite Hume-Williams's promise of a "startling" amount of evidence, his witness list was small: he brought forth only O'Connor's parents and four doctors. And only half of these witnesses actually helped his case. George O'Connor, Thomas Harrington Tuke, and another doctor, James Thompson Sabben, did testify to the boy's insanity. But the third doctor—Henry Smith, who had amputated O'Connor's toe years before—claimed that the boy's intelligence was above average. And J. Rowland Gibson, surgeon of Newgate, stated that after observing the boy daily since the first of March, he was certain that O'Connor was of sound mind.

Catherine O'Connor proved to harm more than help the defense, testifying that her son was not only sane, but perfectly correct, in pleading guilty: "I had always told him to tell the truth, and I believe he has done so." If Hume-Williams had any reason to call O'Connor's mother to the stand, it was because she was the one most familiar with her son's writings—writings she never could make sense of, but which her son assured her would make him famous someday. O'Connor burned his papers before his attempt at St. Paul's, but had missed some, and Hume-Williams, employing the time-honored tactic of connecting bad poetry with a diseased brain, took advantage of Catherine's testimony to read some of her son's "incoherent" work, until Baron Cleasby interrupted, dismissing the evidence as irrelevant.

Attorney General Coleridge, having recently made his name with his bitter cross-examination of the Tichborne Claimant, seemed to carry his rage into this case, genuinely affronted that George O'Connor, Dr. Tuke, and Hume-Williams sought to impose a worse punishment upon the boy in defending him. He cross-examined George O'Connor with caustic fervor. He revealed O'Connor Senior's deep concern about his son's "paroxysm of madness" as a lie—what else would explain the fact that the man allowed Arthur to take his nine-year-old brother out to view the illuminations the next day? More than this, Coleridge showed O'Connor to be a fool unable to understand his son's best interests:

> Is it your desire that your son should be imprisoned for
> life in a lunatic asylum?—Certainly not.

But you wish that he should be found not guilty on the ground of insanity?—Excuse me, but it is rather a difficult question.

I want to know whether you are aware of what you are about. Is that your wish that he should be kept for life in a lunatic asylum?—Certainly not.

Do you know that follows?—Yes.

Is that what you wish?—It is not what I wish.

Fully understanding that, you elect that the question of his sanity should be tried?—Yes; as regards his sanity when he did the act.

Coleridge's most bitter attack, however, he reserved for Dr. Tuke, whom he presented as the prime mover of this idiotic defense, whose intrusion, if successful, would only make things worse for the boy. Arthur O'Connor was deeply amused by Coleridge's brutal cross-examination, bursting into laughter as he ran rings around Tuke in attacking the logic of Tuke's diagnosis of "reasoning insanity." Coleridge reduced Tuke to silence when he asked him how O'Connor's getting shut up in Broadmoor for life because of Tuke's testimony was more sensible than the boy's throwing himself upon the mercy of the court. And he forced Tuke to admit that O'Connor's pleading guilty was actually a sign that O'Connor's sanity had returned. Tuke stepped from the witness box smarting, and later considered himself to be victim of poor timing, suffering more greatly in Coleridge's cross-examination because "I was his first subject since he had showered vituperation upon the Tichborne Claimant."

After Dr. Gibson testified to O'Connor's complete sanity, the jury had had enough. They stopped the trial and announced through their foreman "that the prisoner was a perfectly sane man when he pleaded to the indictment, and that he was perfectly sane now." Baron Cleasby agreed immediately. Coleridge, in asking for a sentence, could not help but snipe one more time at "the unfortunate course which Dr. Tuke had thought fit to take in the case," but did note that some good had come from the trial: Tuke had forced him to present O'Connor's character in a better light than he otherwise would have. He requested that the judge take this into account in his sentencing.

And Baron Cleasby apparently did just that. In sentencing O'Connor, he weighed the aggravating factors—O'Connor's evil intention, the cunning and manner of the crime, and the occasion on which it was committed—against the mitigating ones: his age, his unfortunate "enthusiasm," which got the better of his mind, and the absurdity of the attempt itself, which suggested that he was not fully in his right mind at the time. His sentence: one year's imprisonment at hard labor. And during that time, one whipping: twenty strokes with a birch rod.

The courtroom was rent with a shriek at the mention of whipping: Arthur's mother Catherine cried out, apparently devastated by two equally unbearable thoughts: that of the rod on her son's tender back, and of the lost honor of the great O'Connors.

Queen Victoria was told of the sentence that evening at Windsor, and immediately lashed out at her prime minister, dividing her anger between O'Connor, the judge who sentenced him so leniently, and the government that could allow this to happen:

> The Queen's object in writing to Mr. Gladstone today is to express her surprise & annoyance at the *extreme leniency* of O'Connor's Sentence (w^h she has just learnt) especially as regards the length of imprisonment, & to remind Mr. Gladstone of his having said to her that if there was not *sufficient protection* from the *Law*, as it *stood at present* it *must* be *amended*. . . .
>
> Her safety & her peace of mind will be in *constant* danger & constantly *disturbed*—thereby making it *almost impossible* for her to go about in public,—or *at*

all in London, if she has *no security* that such miscreants will NOT be allowed to *go about* in this country—ready at any moment to alarm & insult her again. And the Queen *does demand* from the Govt that protection w^h as a Queen & as a Woman she feels she has a *right to expect.*—It ought to be in the Power of the law to have such a man sent out of the country & not to allow him to return except *under surveillance.*

The effect of this short imprisonment will be *vy bad*—both *abroad* & *at home.*

Gladstone did his best to placate her, agreeing with her in deploring the leniency of Cleasby's sentence, which had astonished his entire Cabinet as well as himself. (Dr. Tuke, he noted, had caused "much mischief" through his "gratuitous intervention," but that offered no excuse for Cleasby's dereliction of duty.) As far as changing the law went—it was the judge and not the law at fault, for the law did allow for the harsher penalties of seven years' penal servitude, or three years' imprisonment with three whippings. Still, he offered to do all he could to create a future for the boy more in accordance with the Queen's wishes. The government, of course, could ensure that after he was released, "the eye of the police should continue to rest upon O'Connor." But he believed the government could do more, and in the convoluted and overcautious style he generally adopted in communicating with the Queen, told her

. . . it may be found practicable, even under present circumstances, to do what will be far preferable, namely by commutation, and voluntary inducement to get him out of the country for good. This arrangement would probably be the most satisfactory to Your Majesty under the circumstances and Mr. Gladstone feels himself safe in saying that the government will be most desirous to

give effect to any wishes which Your Majesty is likely
to entertain upon the subject.

In other words, the government hoped, by offering to remove
the penalty of whipping from O'Connor's sentence, to induce him
to stay out of Britain for the rest of Victoria's life.

The Queen declared herself through her Private Secretary to
be placated—almost. She still wished that Judge Cleasby suffer
some sort of censure at the hands of the Lord Chancellor. (Gladstone suggested in return that the "animadversions of the press"
would more effectively "repress these strange aberrations.") And
she begged to differ with Gladstone about the law as it presently
stood: it *did* need changing, for it lacked a provision expatriating
offenders. Surely, in the course of time, Gladstone could consider
amending the law to do that?

Gladstone suggested that his government might indeed consider that change "should an opportunity occur when it might be
obtained with facility." (The opportunity, however, never arrived;
Peel's law was never amended to incorporate exile as a penalty.)
In the meantime, Gladstone happily reported that he foresaw no
problem with getting O'Connor out of the country: Colonel Henderson, the commissioner of police, had told him that "there will
probably be little difficulty in arranging for O'Connor's permanent
removal from the country." In time, Gladstone would discover that
removing O'Connor would not be that easy. And in her premonition that O'Connor's short sentence and proximity to her would
continue to cause her trouble, Victoria was absolutely accurate.

Home Secretary Henry Bruce quickly acted to keep the possibility of O'Connor's exile alive. The day after the boy's sentencing
he wrote the governor of Newgate to suspend the sentence of
whipping there and at any prisons to which he was transferred—
Clerkenwell and Coldbath Fields, as it turned out. And there
the government left matters until November 1872, when Bruce,
who, acting through Governor Colville of Coldbath Fields, gave

O'Connor an inkling of the government's plan to substitute exile for whipping, and encouraged O'Connor to petition for a remission of his punishment. O'Connor—without consulting his parents, the governor made clear—duly submitted a clearly written, contrite plea, denying that he had ever intended to harm the Queen, and claiming not only that had never met a Fenian in his life, but that he deeply deplored their actions. He claimed that when he assaulted the Queen, he was in a state between sanity and madness—"I was not mad, nor was I perfectly sensible"—and that he was "laboring under two of the most wasting and irritating diseases to which the human frame is liable"—which in turn drove him "to phrenzy" and "a condition bordering upon imbecility." If he could be freed from the shame and reproach of a whipping, he was fully prepared to leave England for a "distant & warmer climate," free from any police supervision, until "all suspicion and distrust of me will cease to exist."

The petition was rushed to the Home Office, and Bruce quickly conveyed to O'Connor the specific terms of the government's offer: O'Connor would be freed from prison without the whipping if he would agree to exile in the southern African colony of Natal and not return during the life of the Queen. The terms likely came too quickly to the boy, for he began to understand how desperately the government wanted him gone, and that this gave him leverage. And so he balked. He wished to speak with his parents about the deal; and he certainly could not agree to exile from England for the rest of the Queen's life. The Queen, as far as he knew, was perfectly healthy, and might live for twenty or thirty years. "I can never agree to a condition which would condemn me to almost perpetual exile; & which would be rendered a living death by the knowledge that the dearest of my relations might pass from this life while I thousands of miles away could only cry out against that which withheld me from them at such a moment. . . ."

Governor Colville, in passing O'Connor's letter on to Bruce, suggested that the boy might be content with five years' exile. Though the Home Secretary personally had no problem with this, considering that if O'Connor ever returned "it w^d be as an altered man," he doubted the Queen would be pleased. In his next letter, written on New Year's Eve 1872, O'Connor proved to be even more recalcitrant. He had completely cottoned on to the government's motives, writing incredulously "I conclude that the Home Office believes me to be possessed of a Royal mania or something of the sort & that for H. Majesty's safety and peace of mind they desire me to leave the country." He was willing to leave the country—but would not do so under any conditions whatsoever, going rather as "an independent and unrestrained individual."

"This is vexatious," Bruce wrote his undersecretary the next day. Understanding now that the boy had the upper hand, Bruce directed that Governor Colville impress upon O'Connor the pain and indignity of flogging, and let him know that if he were willing to go abroad, Bruce would agree to set no conditions as to his returning home, "which," he acknowledged, "in fact we have no power to make." At this point, George O'Connor entered into the negotiations, asking that his son be shipped to Tasmania (where the children of George's uncle Roderic—Feargus's half-brother—were prosperous landowners) rather than Natal, and requesting that the boy be allowed a couple of days at home before he set out. Arthur then repeated his father's demands with a haughtiness that exasperated Governor Colville: "he seems to take a higher tone, and to consider himself a person of some importance." Colville suggested to Bruce that they go ahead and let him be whipped.

That Bruce would not do. By mid-January, he acceded to all of the O'Connors' demands. A suitable passage was obtained on the *Lodore*. O'Connor stayed at his parents' house for a fortnight (for which George O'Connor billed the government £10); and on 12 February 1873 he set sail—for Sydney rather than Tasmania, O'Connor's parents probably deciding their Hobart relatives would want nothing to do with the boy. Bruce contacted the Foreign Office, which in turn contacted the Governor of New South Wales, Hercules Robinson, warning of O'Connor's arrival and asking that the police there keep him under surveillance and find him some sort of employment.

O'Connor arrived at Sydney on 20 May 1873 and reported immediately to Governor Robinson's private secretary. He had adopted the alias "George Morton," which he held religiously while in Australia ("the people being very loyal," he later wrote, "I might suffer some annoyance were I to be known"). While O'Connor impressed favorably all who knew him in Sydney, he was himself less than impressed by the place: Sydney, he claimed, simply did not offer a field for a man of his literary talents. He made clear from the start that he wished to return to England as soon as he could. Life was to get even worse for him, though. Governor Robinson, fearing that if O'Connor's past became known, "the matter would be eagerly seized upon and made the ground for an attack on the Ministry," found him a job in the distant town of Morpeth as a butcher's clerk.

While suffering in Morpeth, O'Connor took what he was sure would be a first step toward gaining the literary fame for which he knew he was destined: he wrote a letter to the Queen. He did so, he told Governor Robinson, because the Queen had asked him to. And so he wrote, passing on the letter to Robinson, who duly sent it on to the Colonial Office, which passed it on to Bruce in the Home Office. The letter detailed O'Connor's depressing passage out, as well as his observations of Sydney and his "distasteful" Morpeth job. It also—at some length and in prose of the deepest purple—waxed glorious about his literary abilities and ambitions. He had a poet's mind, and that mind "stands alone, and lives in a glorious solitude, apart from the world; and to its music, the sounds of trade, are death. It is a heavenly blossom, that would spring up into glory, in a desert, but which would die despairingly, amidst the horrors of the Counting house." "I have not the slightest intention of settling out here," he wrote Victoria. "I shall remain only till my health is restored, then return home and strive for literary eminence." And he expected that Victoria would help him achieve those heights. She would be so deeply impressed by this letter, he was sure, that she would see to its publication. And that would be just the start:

> There is a prize toward which I am ever looking. None but a Poet can obtain it, and as yet I think, no Irish poet has held it—Passionately Irish myself, this honor I will bring upon Ireland, poor Ireland, if the highest limit of human striving can obtain success. It comes from the throne, and is now held by a writer yet "not one of the grand old masters"—He is not immortal.

Tennyson be damned: Victoria would one day understand O'Connor's genius and appoint him Poet Laureate.

The letter, of course, made it no further than the Home Office. "The man must be mad," wrote Bruce; "His self-conceit is intolerable. Of course this letter must not go to H. M." This clear proof of O'Connor's insanity sent Home Office officials scurrying to retrieve a record of his terms of exile, in the hopes of doing something to prevent his return. But Bruce remembered: there were no terms, and there was nothing they could do to stop him returning.

And he did return. He threw up his Morpeth job after a few weeks and returned to Sydney, where a more suitable job as a clerk in a firm of solicitors was found for him. The police, realizing his fifteen-shilling-a-week wage, without board, was not enough to live on, supplemented that pay with public funds. Neither that, nor the promise of a substantial raise, could dissuade him from booking passage back to England.

On 25 February 1874, Governor Robinson telegraphed Whitehall: "George Morton sailed for London(derry) today in *Hydaspes*—Ship may be looked for in ninety days." "I had no legal power to detain the youth," Robinson wrote to Richard Cross, Home Secretary of the newly elected Tory ministry. The authorities in England should feel no uneasiness about O'Connor's return,

Robinson added—because all in Sydney were deeply impressed by his intelligence and demeanor.

Cross was hardly reassured and quickly set a police watch on O'Connor when by summer he had returned to his parents' cramped Aldgate home. In July, Chief Inspector George Clarke interviewed O'Connor there. Clarke saw no signs of insanity, except for the fact that "he is of a romantic turn of mind, he has no employment, and spends most of his time at home reading and writing what he calls poetry." Among his writings were more letters to the Queen—letters which almost certainly never reached her. He attributed the worst of motives to her silence, and his letters grew angry, and then threatening. It was likely the last of these letters which proved too dangerous to ignore, and Cross turned for help to the very person whom the Liberals and Attorney General Coleridge considered the most troublesome actor in the O'Connor case, three years before—Dr. Thomas Harrington Tuke. Cross forwarded O'Connor's letters to Tuke and requested that he obtain the assistance of other doctors to ascertain whether O'Connor was insane, and whether he posed a threat to the Queen. He knew, of course, that Tuke already considered O'Connor deeply insane, and knew as well that by the lunacy laws of the time, a certification of insanity by two doctors would safely place O'Connor in an asylum.

Tuke, delighted that the present government, unlike the last one, showed the highest respect for his expertise, was happy to help, and on 4 May he took O'Connor to the consulting room of Dr. William Gull. Tuke could not have chosen a better colleague to evaluate O'Connor. Gull had experience working with the insane, but more importantly he was a royal physician who had attended to the Prince of Wales in his illness, and who immediately after the scare of O'Connor's attempt had been called from Marlborough House to Buckingham Palace to treat Victoria.* Gull's agreement with Tuke would give a royal sanction of sorts to O'Connor's committal.

---

* Gull considered that the Queen would suffer no lasting effects from the fright she suffered.

Realizing that the government's interest in him had escalated greatly, Arthur O'Connor himself brought matters to a head. He knew that on the next day, 5 May, Victoria would make one of her rare appearances in London, holding a drawing room at Buckingham Palace. That afternoon, therefore, O'Connor reappeared outside the northeast gate of the Palace at the same spot he had stood three years before. The police recognized him immediately. They watched him for a time as he oscillated between quiescence and excitement. "I was not excited," O'Connor protested at his subsequent examination; "I was thinking what a wonderful calm reigned in London, and that it was owing to the perfection of government." His intent, he claimed, was not homicide but suicide; he expected the police would kill him before he got near the Queen. He was arrested quietly, and quietly removed; no newspapers that evening or the next day carried any account of his return.

He was brought back to Scotland Yard, where he was examined by another doctor brought into the case by Tuke, Alexander Tweedie. Tweedie agreed with Tuke's and Gull's diagnosis of insanity. O'Connor himself now agreed with the doctors that he should be placed in an asylum, and had assisted Tuke by writing out for him a list of his symptoms:

> Thought continually revolving upon religion. Visions at night of Angels hurling men [over] precipices to die for ever because they had not given up all they loved to go and sell Bibles to the unconverted. Sense that unless I gave up the drama, witty and happy society, and the world generally I should be everlastingly damned. In a word, one unceasing mania concerning Jesus Christ the intellect warring with the mania yet unable to crush it. Sense of utter want of constitution and energy, a feeling as if I were half dead.

The next day, O'Connor was again brought to Bow Street, where in the far less crowded courtroom he was not committed to

Newgate, but, with Tuke's and Tweedie's testimony and certification, committed to Hanwell Asylum as an "imbecile." The Queen was again safe, and, as far as her Home Secretary was concerned, Thomas Harrington Tuke's involvement had prevented her from harm. Cross wrote Tuke a letter of thanks on behalf of himself and the public. Victoria, "surprised & annoyed" by O'Connor's return, must at least have been more pleased by the Conservatives' handling of him than she had been by the Liberals', three years before. "He is evidentially quite unfit to be at large," Ponsonby wrote to her, "and there is no possibility of his being liberated from the Asylum at present."

Thomas Harrington Tuke, who had never stopped smarting from John Coleridge's brutal cross-examination during O'Connor's trial, was exultant at what he saw to be his complete vindication, and within two weeks of O'Connor's committal he couldn't help but share his triumph and rail at Coleridge's "unfortunate" advocacy of O'Connor. "I freely forgive Lord Coleridge for his personal attack upon myself," he wrote magnanimously in *The British Medical Journal*.

> . . . but he must surely now deeply deplore his share in a proceeding which consigned a sick and insane boy to degrading punishment, and to a prison instead of a hospital, thus, perhaps, rendering him a hopeless lunatic; he may also regret that he treated a medical witness with much discourtesy, and ridiculed scientific evidence that has ultimately proved correct; and he must feel deeply that his unfortunate advocacy very nearly resulted in injury or alarm to the Royal Mistress whom it was his special duty to protect and defend.

With his admission to Hanwell, Arthur O'Connor's involvement in Victoria's life came to an end. He was then twenty-one years old, and still had a long journey ahead of him; he would in a year and a half be freed from Hanwell as cured; another voyage to Australia, and more asylums, were in his future. Victoria in 1875 had not quite lived up to the promise of her great coming-out during the thanksgiving week of 1872. She remained deeply suspicious about London and continued to keep her stays there to a minimum. And she had not involved the Prince of Wales any more deeply in political affairs. Gladstone's plans to make him Viceroy of Ireland, for one thing, had come to naught, for Victoria's jealousy of her own prerogatives was simply too strong, as were her doubts about her son's competence: "If only our dear Bertie was fit to replace me!" she wrote Vicky three months after O'Connor's attack. But though she remained largely invisible, and the Prince of Wales remained unable to gain great respect in politics, Victoria's popularity—and, for that matter, her son's—had grown, and would only continue to grow. British republicanism had passed in 1872 like a bad dream—the distant memory of a clever-looking boy with a rusty flintlock.

twenty-two

BLUE

On the afternoon of 2 March 1882, a slouching and miserable-looking man shuffled down the platform of the Great Western Railway Station at Windsor. He paused furtively in a doorway and then slipped through, out of the cold and into the little paradise of the station's first-class waiting room. Roderick Maclean was filthy, either unwilling or unable to wash off the dust of the many roads upon which he had tramped. Grime and weariness conspired to make him appear older than his twenty-eight years. His chin was black with several days' worth of stubble. He wore shabby shoes, a shabby bowler, and an even shabbier overcoat. He had no train ticket. Anyone seeing him would instantly conclude that he did not belong in this room, with its leather armchairs and sofas, ornate gilded mirrors, writing desks, and luxurious carpet. But the room was empty, and Maclean had a pressing need to sit down and write a letter. He decided to chance it.

Besides, Maclean very well knew that he had every right to sit in this room or in any other. God had told him so, and more: much more. God read his thoughts and spoke to him personally, soothing and directing him as he made his troubled way through a dark and ignorant world. God had given him superhuman abilities—had made him a great poet, artist, and prophet. God had given him eternal life. And Almighty God had assured him that he was the chosen one, born to rule over the greatest empire on earth. He was certain that his own claim to the British throne was at least as great as George IV's had been—and was greater than Victoria's.

To him alone God had revealed the great secrets of the universe. The key to all power, he knew, lay in one number—and one color. The number was four. Earth, air, fire, water; north, south, east, west: four signified the earth and everything on it. More than this, four signified man's dominion over all the earth; chaotic nature drawn up, reconstituted, regularized, and employed to serve human ends. Right angles had little place in nature, but they were the hallmark of human creation and the sign of human power. In the thousand towns and cities through which Maclean had frantically wandered, he saw those four fourths expressed a billion times over: in every brick and cut stone, every intersection of streets, every wall, façade, door and window. And between all of these towns and cities roared the trains, the embodiment of Victorian progress and of the juggernaut of civilization, hurtling over countless rectangles of track and tie into infinity. Four was *his number*; God had given it and all it promised to him. Any occurrence of that number—as in 4, 14, 40, 104, 400, 404, 440, 444 and so on—was supposed to be auspicious for him. In a beaten-up notebook that he kept in his pocket, Maclean had set down in large letters a title for a work he knew would be one of genius: "The Fourth Path, a novel by Roderick Maclean." And below that, he had written out a recipe for an elixir: "four drops of sweet nitre and half a tumbler of water."*

The color—*his* color—was blue, the color of the sky, of the ocean—of immensity: of infinity. Blue signified his immortal and superhuman self, and his unique connection to God. And God had decreed blue his color by some sort of cosmic sumptuary law: Maclean knew that wearing blue was forbidden to anyone besides himself alone, and those who wished him well—who could wear his color to signal their affection for, their loyalty toward him.

But despite God's great favor, and all of God's promises, Roderick Maclean knew himself to be the most miserable man on earth, doomed to wander for years without succor or solace among millions of ignorant and petty people who feared him, hated him, and were engaged in a massive conspiracy to torment him and to destroy him if they could. They had appropriated the power of the number four—*his number*—to themselves: all of the matter of the earth were theirs to command, while he, homeless, without possessions or power over the things of this world, was slowly starving. Occurrences of four were now more likely ominous than auspicious to him. His enemies owned the bricks and stones, the façades and doors and windows, from behind which they sneered at him; they owned the streets upon which they brazenly insulted and attacked him. And his enemies had long been driving him to madness by stealing blue—*his color*—from him. He was no fool; he could see that more and more of his enemies wore blue dresses and bonnets and ribbons, blue waistcoats and overcoats, blue neckties, kerchiefs, scarves and shawls. They had done it at first to deceive him into thinking they were his friends when they were not. But now they meant him active harm: they wore blue to cause him

---

* Sweet spirit of nitre—ethyl nitrite suspended in alcohol—was a common medicine at the time as a diuretic, antispasmodic, and soothing agent; it would indeed thus likely have been beneficial to Maclean.

"perplexity and agony," to "injure, annoy, and vex me on every opportunity."

It hadn't always been this way. His childhood, he would later recall, was "as happy as any youthful days could be." His father Charles Maclean had earned a fortune as master-carver and master-guilder to the gentry and nobility. He had employed—auspiciously—forty people. He specialized in picture frames and mirrors, which filled two luxurious showrooms in London, on Fleet Street and Oxford Street. The Queen herself had seen Charles Maclean's work; a massive console table and mirror that he manufactured had been given pride of place in the nave of the Crystal Palace at the Great Exhibition of 1851. Roderick Maclean was born three years after the Exhibition and for his first dozen years lived in luxury in and above his father's wonderful looking-glass worlds, as well as in larger houses in Gloucester Road and then Earl's Court, and at an estate in the suburbs that he remembered as an Eden. He was educated to be a gentleman at a school on Harley Street, and became fluent in French and German. Roderick's father was a literary gentleman of sorts, taking up in 1861 the proprietorship of a new humor magazine, *Fun*, which became in time a highly successful rival to the great *Punch*. Roderick Maclean remembered his childhood homes as great literary salons, and indeed when he was a boy many up-and-coming writers gathered there. Roderick recalled mingling among George Augustus Sala, Tom Hood (son of the great comic poet), W. S. Gilbert in his pre-Sullivan days, and others. Not surprisingly, he began to contemplate a future as a great writer himself.

But the Macleans—and Roderick most forcibly—were cast out of this paradise in the mid-1860s. Though *Fun* later found its legs, it was in its infancy a drain on Charles Maclean's business, and he sold it in 1865. In the next year, Charles apparently lost much of his fortune in the spectacular collapse of the banking firm of Overend and Gurney, and he sold off his business by the end of the decade. During that same year, 1866, twelve-year-old Roderick suffered his own fall, literally, slipping in the doorway of his Gloucester Road house, smashing his head and gashing his scalp open. He was under a doctor's care for over a month, and was never quite the same. His head continually gave off the sensation of a "slight shock from a galvanic battery," and he suffered severe and recurrent headaches. More than this, Maclean claimed, the injury rendered him completely unable to perform manual labor. Apparently God began to speak to him around this time. In any case, his behavior changed alarmingly. He developed morbid fears that his siblings, his mother, and especially his father were trying to kill him, and began to sense that the world was leagued against him. He lashed back, threatening to kill his family and at one time vowing to blow up St. Paul's and Westminster Abbey.

Charles Maclean attempted to solve the serious problem his son suddenly presented by sending him away. Twice he booked Roderick passage for America. Each time Roderick was certain that his father had bribed the sailors to throw him overboard; on the first ship he lay awake in his berth all night clutching a knife, ready to kill the first sailor who touched him. The next morning he demanded to disembark at Gravesend. He refused absolutely to board the second ship. In 1874, when Roderick was twenty, Charles Maclean took steps to have him committed to an asylum, and engaged the services of the two physicians required by Victorian lunacy law to issue a certificate of commitment. The first of these doctors, the renowned psychologist Henry Maudsley (yet another son-in-law, incidentally, of the now-deceased psychologist John Conolly) was happy to comply, and declared Roderick insane. The other doctor, Alfred Godrich, found Roderick highly excitable but not a lunatic, and thus refused to commit him. Thus thwarted, Maclean's father instead exiled Roderick as an apprentice on a farm near Dover. Horrified by the prospect of agricultural labor, Maclean fled, and as he did so he attempted to strike his first blow against the millions who oppressed him. Next to the farm lay tracks of the London, Chatham and Dover Railway, and there Maclean offered a young boy sixpence to derail a coming train with a beam of wood. The boy, unable to lift the beam, was unsuccessful. Nevertheless, Maclean and the boy were caught and tried at Maidstone Assizes. Maclean's barrister argued ingeniously that inciting a person to do what he was unable to do was not an offense. Maclean and the boy were acquitted. This was not the only time that Roderick Maclean struck out at the railways; his father claimed that he attempted to derail trains at least twice more, and £100 was once offered for his apprehension.

For three years after that, he dwelled uneasily with his family. When his father died in 1877 and his mother died around the same time, his brother Charles tried to place him in the home of a family friend, the artist Samuel Stanesby, in what was a harrowing experience for everyone concerned. And after that, Roderick Maclean drifted. His four living siblings worked out a way both to support him and to keep him away from them: every week, one of his sisters would mail him, wherever he was, a postal order for a few shillings. It was never enough. When he could no longer afford the price of a low lodging house, he sought admission to the local workhouse. Once, denied admission to one of these in Somerset, he deliberately smashed a window so that he would spend the night in jail. Occasionally he was able to gain temporary admission to the local lunatic asylum, as he had once done in Dublin.

And at one point in his wanderings Maclean aspired to the patronage of Victoria herself. In 1877, while living at a lodging house in Guildford, Maclean composed a verse for her and sent it to Buckingham Palace. While Maclean may or may not have known that the poem's execrable meter, logic, grammar, and spelling would hardly appeal to the Queen, he must have been sure that its subject would strike a chord, for it was the one closest to her heart: her undying love and lifelong mourning for Albert:

> On your thrown you set and rule us all,
> By justice you make known

All your power, and the people like
To cheer the Queen they call their own,
When your lamented husband left us,
And went were troubles find no share,
How we felt for you and tried too lessen
The sting of bad fate you had to bare,
But God who knows whats for our best
Sent you comfort in your most trying hour,
And made you bare your troubles as a nobly woman
   should,
And the people showed their love, and liked your
   power.
When History tells, of your good reign,
They will think of you and say,
Its the Queen who made her people happy,
By affection and justice thats how she ruled the sway.

Maclean was unable to remain in his Guildford lodging house long enough for a reply, as his landlady, alarmed when Maclean showed her a dagger he carried in his sleeve to "take care of himself," threw him out. Thus he never heard from the Queen, and almost certainly resumed his wanderings with a growing sense that Victoria scorned him as much as everyone else did.*

For more than four years he anxiously walked the length and breadth of Britain, and beyond: to Boulogne, France; throughout Germany: even perhaps to Jamaica, where according to one report he passed as Roderigues Maclean. It did not matter how far away he went, for he endured the same hellish cycle everywhere. He

---

* Actually, there had been a response, after Maclean left—not from the Queen, who almost certainly did not see the poem, but from the wife of her keeper of the privy purse, who returned the poem with a curt note: "Lady Biddulph is obliged to return to Mr. Maclean his verses. The Queen never accepts manuscript poetry" (*Surrey Advertiser and County Times* 11 March 1882, 5; *Times* 6 March 1882, 6).

would enter a new town seeking anonymity and peace, but before long a stranger would recognize him and would flaunt some article of blue clothing in his face. The word then quickly spread, and he was recognized, accosted, despised, and insulted by all. He would flee to another town, and the torture would begin again. In 1880, thus beset in the town of Weston-super-Mare, he reached a breaking point, and he spilled out his anguish in a letter to his sister Annie:

> Dear Annie,—I have no doubt but that you will be somewhat surprised to receive another letter from me, but as the English people have continued to annoy me, I thought I would write, as you should not be surprised if anything unpleasant occurred, as the people being so antagonistically inclined toward me, makes me raving mad. I can hardly contain myself in fact. I mean, if they don't cease wearing blue, I will commit murder. . . . The pain and anguish that I passed the other night I could not describe. Perhaps by the time you receive this I shall be in prison. I really think I cannot prevent myself having revenge on the English people. I don't mind a bit if they hanged me, as now I see things in a different light. They only pretend to be friendly to annoy and cause untold misery. I fear it will be just as bad in Boulogne or else-where. What chance have I to cope with the millions of people who are against me? Not merely against me, I should not mind that, but at open defiance and publicly annoying me on every possible occasion. What a con-founded fool I must have been to say anything about it or wear blue at the time. From your former words I thought the people had a more forgiving nature, but I perceive I was deceived in them all. I intend to carry my determination into effect to-day (Monday), and after it's done, I shall write you a letter. Of course I shall

not remove nor give myself up, but doubtless they will take me into custody the next day. If I cannot commit a murder (I really assure you, Annie, I mean what I write) in one way, I will in another way. All I can add is, if there is more difficulty, there may be more victims.

Annie Maclean and her sister Caroline, deeply alarmed by this letter, telegraphed Roderick begging him to desist, and quickly arranged for a local surgeon to examine him, sign a certificate of lunacy, and commit him to the Bath and Somerset Lunatic Asylum.* He remained there for fourteen months, happier to be in an asylum than anywhere else—but even there fearing contact with perfidious attendants and visitors.

In July 1881, Maclean was discharged from the asylum as cured, and immediately resumed his frantic wandering. Apparently avoiding London altogether—the massive population there, he wrote Annie, made things "a thousand times worse"—he tramped through southern England, preferring the coastal towns, moving from Chichester to Brighton to Eastbourne to Croydon, and back to Brighton, where he spent a month in the local workhouse. While there, he wrote a letter to Annie complaining that horrible pains in his head were driving him insane, and asking her again to get him into an asylum. From her he received no answer; instead, he got a deeply disturbing letter from his brother Hector, who told Roderick that he refused to be his brother's keeper any longer: he had his own three children to look after.

When the workhouse authorities at Brighton threatened to transfer Maclean to Kensington, his home parish workhouse, Maclean fled west to Southsea, outside of Portland. There he found a room in the poorer part of town, in the home of Mrs. Sorrell. Mrs. Sorrell remembered him as quiet at first, but desperate to prove his

---

* Because Maclean was a pauper, only one doctor's signature (and the cooperation of a magistrate) was needed to commit him (Archibold 183).

respectability: he claimed to be a writer and poet employed by the *West Sussex Gazette*. It was not long before his landlady concluded he was a man "with a tile loose." Nonetheless, for the dozen or so days he remained in Southsea, Maclean got on amazingly well with her and with his fellow lodger Edward Hucker. By day he wandered the town or paced the cold and windy beach, where across the blue-gray bay he could see the Isle of Wight, see even the shore of Victoria's Osborne estate. By night he entertained Sorrell and Hucker with a little concertina that he had obtained in Brighton, and with a little ventriloquist routine, pretending to speak with an imaginary sweep in the chimney. He also conversed freely with the two, and Sorrell and Hucker both remembered Maclean as being deeply engaged in the politics of the day. He would lecture them on political economy until they could take it no more. He was a great admirer of Prime Minister Gladstone. In spite of—or perhaps because of—his special relationship with God, he declared himself to be a freethinker. And he was a passionate supporter of the ultra-radical politician Charles Bradlaugh.

Charles Bradlaugh had been elected MP for Northampton in the general election of 1880, which had swept Gladstone and the Liberals back into power. Because, however, he was an outspoken atheist, he was prohibited either from affirming or taking his oath, and thus from taking his seat. For two years he had repeatedly presented himself in the House of Commons to take the oath, but his atheism, his republicanism, and his scandalous advocacy of birth control ensured that a majority of the Commons supported a measure each time to refuse to let him take the oath or his seat. Twice Bradlaugh was forcibly removed from the House of Commons. Once so far, he had been forced to run for reelection to regain his seat. During Maclean's stay in Southsea—on 21 February 1882—Bradlaugh scandalized the nation by attempting to force the issue: since no one would give him the oath, he decided to take it himself. He strode up to the Table of the House and pulled from his pocket a Bible and a piece of paper from which he read the oath. As the House erupted into an uproar, he kissed the Bible, signed the paper, gave it to the Clerk, and took his seat. The House adjourned in confusion. The next day, Bradlaugh was expelled from the House and his parliamentary seat was vacated. He would have to be re-elected a second time to take his seat in the House. (This by-election was taking place on the very day—2 March 1882—that Roderick Maclean had invaded the first-class waiting room of Windsor railway station.)

Bradlaugh was despised and hated by the millions. He was sneered at regularly by the press. He was forced into a relentless battle to prove his legitimacy, and was continually beaten down by the highest political body in the land. Not surprisingly, Roderick Maclean saw him as a kindred spirit.

In his long talks with Sorrell and Hucker, Roderick Maclean spoke as well, at length, about his deteriorating relationship with his family. While at Southsea he received several letters from them. First, he heard from his sister Annie—his only living sister now, his older sister Caroline having very recently died. Annie wrote to warn him that his family's support of him would soon diminish, if not disappear altogether. She was facing her own poverty—was indeed about to take a position as a governess—and her brothers balked at the idea of continuing to support him without her. A letter from one of his brothers didn't help matters: in it his brother offered no financial support, and instead reminded Roderick of his mental weakness, and recommended he seek restraint. Maclean was enraged at the way his family treated him, he told his landlady and fellow lodger. His brothers were wealthy: one had a good business in London, and the other had married into wealth. Over the years, he felt, he had established his right to be supported by his family: they should be giving him more now, not less. He vowed that he would go to London to enforce his rights.

He also engaged in one other topic of conversation while at Mrs. Sorrell's: Queen Victoria. Did she ever come to Portsmouth? he asked them. She did, of course, passing through every time she came to or went from Osborne on the Isle of Wight. Was Victoria nice? If he happened to be sketching when she passed him and he raised his hat to her, would she stop and talk to him? His odd questions confirmed Sorrell's and Hucker's opinion that Maclean was "soft."

One day he returned to Mrs. Sorrell's, angry because he had been to Gosport, where at midday he had requested to inspect the dockyard, and had been turned away. More than likely, this day was Thursday 16 February, and there was the best of reasons for his exclusion from the dockyard: at about 11:30 that morning, Victoria and her daughter Beatrice disembarked in Gosport from the yacht *Alberta*, to board a train bound for Victoria Station and from there to ride to Buckingham Palace. If Maclean had wanted to see the Queen on that day, he was thwarted. In any case, he was unprepared for any meeting. And so on that day, he began to prepare. Around midday Maclean walked into a pawnbroker's on Queen Street, Portsmouth. He had seen a revolver for sale in the window and asked the assistant, John Fuller, the price: five shillings and twopence. He had already shopped for a pistol at a gunsmith's near Mrs. Sorrell's, but he could never afford the eleven shillings they asked. Indeed, he hadn't 5s. 2d., but he might be able to get it. He asked if Fuller would lower the price; he would not. But he would agree to hold the pistol for 2s. until Maclean raised the rest. It was a cheap pistol: a six-shooter of Belgian make, with a pin-firing mechanism which fired bullets by striking a tiny peg at the heel of each bullet. It was an inaccurate and clumsy weapon, but it was formidable-looking enough for witnesses later to mistake it for a Colt revolver. Maclean invented a reason for buying the gun: his name was Campbell, he told the shopkeeper, and he needed the pistol because he was about to join the South African Cap Mounted Rifles. Fuller accordingly wrote out a receipt for Maclean in the name of Campbell.

Maclean had originally intended to remain in Southsea for three weeks, but by the end of the first one he gave Mrs. Sorrell notice. He told her that while he was out he had seen someone he didn't like: his enemies were closing in on him again, and Portsmouth suddenly seemed too big for him. More than this, he had to resolve his money problems. He had come up with another idea for dealing with these: one of his brothers had married the sister of Augustus Harris, the lessee of the Drury Lane Theatre. Maclean knew himself to be a brilliant actor. He would leave on Thursday morning, the twenty-third, to go to London and find employment in Harris's troupe.

On the day before he left, he received another letter from his sister Annie. She was responding to a letter he had written her from Brighton—a letter that convinced her that her brother had again reached a breaking point. She sent him another postoffice order, and pleaded with him to stay where he was and take on any job he could—even take up a broom and sweep street-crossings. Mrs. Sorrell and Mr. Hucker agreed with Annie and advised Maclean to stay. But he was adamant: he would go to London. To provide him with some pocket money for his journey, Mrs. Sorrell gave him a couple of shillings in return for his concertina and a scarf he owned. That day, Maclean returned to the pawnbroker's, paid what he owed for the pistol, and took it away wrapped in an old piece of white linen. He returned as well to the gunsmith's and bought as many pin-fire bullets as he could for a shilling—eighteen or nineteen in all. The proprietor, who later claimed "it occurred to me that a beefsteak would do him more good than cartridges," asked him what he wanted them for: he was going abroad, he replied.

At seven the next morning, he set out. Mrs. Sorrell gave him a final gift of a better hat and pair of shoes than his own. He told them he would walk from Petersfield to Guildford, and from there to London. At first he faithfully kept to that course. The next morning, five miles north of Petersfield in Newton Valence, he was spotted by a clergyman, Archibald Maclachlan, who saw a shabbily dressed man clutching a battered carpetbag staggering up the road, apparently in great pain. Maclean collapsed outside of

Maclachlan's garden gate in what Maclachlan was certain was an epileptic fit. Maclachlan ran to assist him: he was pale, half-starved, unconscious. With Maclachlan's help Maclean came to, wild-eyed. The clergyman offered to let him stay, but Maclean refused: he had to go on. So Maclachlan fed him some bread and butter, and when Maclean tottered off down the road, Maclachlan sent one of his servants to accompany him part of the way. Maclean made it to Guildford that night. The next morning, Maclean changed course. He did not head to London and dramatic fame, as he had assured Sorrell and Hucker. Instead he struck out due north, and at 3:00 on that afternoon—Saturday 25 February—he arrived in Windsor. The Queen was in residence.

Maclean found accommodation at 84 Victoria Cottages—again, in the poorer part of town. He told his landlord, a man named Knight, that he had just been hired as a grocer's assistant in the neighboring town of Eton and would begin work Monday. He also told him that he received a weekly allowance by mail—and that this should arrive on Wednesday. When Mrs. Knight asked him for a week's rent in advance, Maclean balked, since he did not have enough; could he pay a shilling now and the rest later? Mrs. Knight agreed. He proved to be a quiet lodger, leaving the house after breakfast and returning at teatime. He did by one account have a single eccentricity: he refused to remove his overcoat indoors, even when it was very warm, and he had a constant habit of smoothing down its front. With hindsight, the Knights thought that this might have something to do with his pistol, which they never saw.

On Tuesday, the last day of February, Maclean went to the central railway station, to join the crowds who came to see Queen Victoria off on the royal train for a short visit to London, where she was to hold a drawing room. Maclean was too late and missed her, though he did tell Mr. Knight that he saw "Jock Brown" there. The next day, Wednesday, Maclean asked his landlord if he could remain at home during the day. He had a toothache, he claimed. Also he was waiting for his allowance to arrive in the mail. It never came.

That day of wait was the first of March. The next day—the gloomy wet day of 2 March 1882—Roderick Maclean had made sure that he arrived at Windsor Station long before the Queen did—a good forty-five minutes before, at least. No one took much notice of him as he slipped into the station, came slouching around the platform, and sneaked into the first-class waiting room. He sat at a writing desk, fished out of his pockets a stub of a pencil, tore a scrap of paper out of his little notebook, and wrote his note.

> I should not have done this crime had you, as you should have done, paid the 10s. per week instead of offering me the insulting small sum of 6s. per week, and expecting me to live on it. So you perceive the great good a little money would have done, had you not treated me as a fool, and set me more than ever against those bloated aristocrats, led by that old lady Mrs. Vic., who is an accursed robber in all senses.
> —Roderick Maclean March 2, 1882,
> Waiting-room, Great Western Railway.

Back went the pencil and the note into his pocket. Inside the waiting room it was quiet, but Maclean could hear growing commotion outside; the 4:50 train was loading and about to leave the station. The stationmaster, John George Smythe, was on the platform to signal an all-clear to the engineer. Smythe glanced into the first-class waiting room, and the sight of the seedy black-bewhiskered tramp arrested his steps. He burst in and accosted Maclean: "Did you know this is a first-class waiting room—not the place for you? What are you doing here?"

"I am waiting for a train."

"What train?"

"The next train from London; what time does it arrive?"

"5 5 [5:05]: you had better go into the other room and not here."

Roderick Maclean sheepishly complied, walking past Smythe, out the door and back onto the cold platform. He made his way through the bustle and out of the station, skirting on his way the sumptuous little waiting room reserved exclusively for Victoria's use. It was now 4:50 P.M. At 5:25, the Queen's train was scheduled to steam into the station; Victoria would disembark and pass through her little waiting room to the front of the station, where a closed carriage awaited to take her the short drive to the Castle. On the road outside, Maclean turned left and walked to a set of palings marking the station's verge. He stopped there, within a few feet of the road across which Victoria's carriage would pass as it moved out of the station.

He would wait there. In his pocket, readily accessible, was his pistol. While he carried enough cartridges to fill all the pistol's chambers, he had been careful to ensure his good fortune by loading only four of them. One bullet, somewhere, somehow, he had already discharged. That left him with three live rounds for the Queen.

As Maclean waited in the cold, that old lady—that accursed robber Mrs. Vic—sat in the saloon car of her royal train as it gained speed out of Paddington Station, clattered through the northwest suburbs of London and shot into the countryside. By the Queen's side—*always* by her side, these days—sat her youngest daughter Beatrice. Since Albert's death twenty-one years before, one of her daughters had always served as her companion. First had been Alice, but Alice had married Prince Louis of Hesse and moved away to Darmstadt. (She had since died, the first of Victoria's children to predecease her, of diphtheria in 1878, on 14 December, the terrible anniversary of Albert's death.) Then, Helena became her companion until she too married, in 1866. The daughter next in age, Louise, was far too free a spirit for Victoria to consider as a companion, so the position fell to Beatrice: shy, capable, loyal

Beatrice. Beatrice, Victoria expected, would never marry as long as she had her mother to care for.*

Both Victoria and her daughter were tired, and they surely looked forward to their return to Windsor, as well as their upcoming retreat to the French Riviera. London had been, as usual, exhausting, as Victoria again had crammed their schedule in order to be in and out of the metropolis in little more than two days. There had been the upcoming royal wedding to plan for, between her youngest son Leopold and Princess Helen of Waldeck. Princess Helen was in town with her father, and they had to be entertained and introduced to London society; Beatrice had done much of the chaperoning. There had been for the Queen visits to the Duchess of Cambridge and the widowed ex-Empress of France, Eugènie, as well as the obligatory but to Victoria mildly nerve-racking rides in an open carriage through the Parks. And yesterday there had been a Queen's drawing room, where the Queen, with her daughters Helena and Beatrice, as well as her daughters-in-law Alexandra and Maria (Prince Alfred's wife), welcomed the usual enormous queue of young ladies into high society. Victoria dressed for the occasion, as usual, in a black dress trimmed with white. But she wore another color as well, as was also usual on state occasions: the deep blue sash of the Order of the Garter. And she also wore the gem-encrusted star of that Order, with its sapphire-blue garter and its diamond-studded rays—four major ones, and four minor ones. Roderick Maclean, in following the Queen's movements, surely knew that Victoria was tormenting him as everyone else did, appropriating his color and his number.

For two days straight, then, Victoria had performed the role she had learned by 1882 to play to perfection. Her popularity and prestige had never been higher, and would not diminish for

---

* Victoria was wrong; Beatrice would marry Prince Henry of Battenberg in 1885. The Queen at first resisted the marriage, and only agreed on the condition that the couple always live with her, and that Beatrice would continue in her role as her companion (Purdue, "Beatrice").

the rest of her life. Her annual schedule had changed little over the past decade; she still spent most of the year apart from her people, secluded at Balmoral, Osborne, and Windsor. She still avoided London as much as she possibly could. But the grumbling about her absences, which grew in the 1860s and reached a peak in 1871, no longer existed. London had the grandeur and glitter of a court without her, centered on the Prince and Princess of Wales at Marlborough House. Much had changed in the way the public viewed her: then she was a Queen, subject to public standards of behavior for monarchs. Now she was an institution: an Empress and a ruler unlike and surpassing any previous one. The old rules and expectations no longer applied. Before, the Queen's popularity stemmed from her *doing*; now, it stemmed from her simply *being*.

Victoria was sixty-two, now—old, or at least growing old. She was however more vital and healthy at sixty-two than she had been at fifty-two or even forty-two, during that dark decade after Albert's death when she continually wished her own death and continually pleaded broken health to avoid appearing in public. In the years after the thanksgiving she had regained a zest for life, and had taken up her duties with renewed energy: "What nerve! What muscle! What energy!" her Prime Minister, Benjamin Disraeli, had said of her in 1880. But while she might have a greater vigor, she had become venerable in the public eye. She had ruled now for forty-five years, and was therefore the only monarch that most of her subjects could remember having. Through time, fertility, and royal precedence, she had become the grandmother of Europe. When Oxford had shot at her four decades before, she was pregnant with her first child; now she was a great-grandmother. Her own children had married into the royal houses of Russia, Denmark, and Germany, and her many grandchildren were now beginning to marry, carrying her and Albert's bloodline across the continent. Foreign policy, to Victoria, was a family matter; wars were family squabbles. And her own seniority over European royalty reflected and signified her nation's precedence as a world superpower.

For her subjects, life without Victoria was unthinkable. Victoria had given their era its name: they were all Victorians. Every part of their lives—the great scientific discoveries and technological innovations, the abundance of objects with which they surrounded themselves and cluttered their homes, the great and growing cities in which they lived, and the constantly expanding empire over which they had domain: all of it was Victorian, all of it was connected with her, embodied by her. Victoria had become a living monument to her age, and in Victoria Britons saw their own greatness. Even her appearance was monumental. She had with age exchanged her earlier defining characteristic—her diminutive stature—with another: stoutness. She used her weight to her advantage in public appearances, in photographs, and in portraits, always presenting herself with solidity and calmness, as the central, placid, and unshakeable image of Britain. Her public face, too—recreated through lithographic and photographic mass production and hung on millions of walls, public and private, across the nation—radiated zen-like calmness, with a quiet pride and forward-looking confidence. Hers was the face of Empire.

Much of the credit for Victoria's immense popularity was due to the man who literally made her an Empress, and more than this had made her fit that role, by making her *feel* every inch an Empress: Benjamin Disraeli, or the Earl of Beaconsfield, as she elevated him soon after he elevated her. From the moment Disraeli kissed her hand upon taking office in 1874, dropping to one knee and declaring "I plight my troth to the kindest of *Mistresses*," the tenor of their relationship was clear: he would be her zealous devotee, best serving his country by serving his Queen. His merits as a prime minister might be open to debate, but he was without doubt the best courtier Victoria ever had. And in the style of a master courtier, he flattered the Queen ceaselessly and shamelessly, laying it on, as he famously observed, "with a trowel." Victoria, no fool, was well aware of his hyperbole, though she preferred to see him as "full of poetry, romance and chivalry," commodities which her previous and present Prime Minister, William Gladstone, completely lacked. And Disraeli backed up his honeyed words with genuine service. He was a master at converting policy triumphs into personal gifts to his monarch. When the government succeeded in buying up a substantial number of shares in the Suez Canal, he presented the news to the Queen as if he were Sir Francis Drake presenting Spanish gold to Elizabeth the First: "You have it, Madam," he declared to her. More than once he favored and sponsored legislation that she wanted and that his Cabinet did not. In a thousand ways he succeeded in rendering himself the paragon of prime ministers in Victoria's eyes—and in reminding her by contrast that his predecessor and successor, Gladstone, was the worst of them. He was assisted greatly in this project because the Queen was politically on his side from the start, for by the 1870s and in complete disregard of the beloved Albert's prime directive that the monarch must remain above party politics, Victoria had become a diehard conservative. Disraeli, according to Victoria, had "right feelings," and *"very large ideas, and very lofty views* of the position this country should hold." The two agreed that the endless turbulence in Ireland should be met by coercion, not concession. And they believed in the inherent glory of their ever-expanding empire. With Melbourne, Victoria had been a Melbournian; with Peel, she had been a Peelite; with Disraeli she was, and afterwards forever would be, a Disraelite. And with Disraeli's encouragement, Victoria developed the confident sense that her interests were the interests of the nation. She for once experienced the exhilarating sensation of being a ruler who actually ruled, with the assistance of a government that actually served her.

That dream had to have an end, of course; William Gladstone killed it. Victoria's loathing for Gladstone—a sentiment Disraeli did his best to encourage—grew in tandem with her attachment for Disraeli. Disraeli touched on that truth when he noted that Victoria's concern for his own health was dictated "not so much from love of me as dread of somebody else." Victoria had thought when Disraeli became Prime Minister that she had gotten rid of Gladstone for good. After the Liberals were defeated soundly in the 1874 general election, Gladstone retired, ceding leadership to Lord Hartington and retiring to his study of the classics and theology at Hawarden. In two years, however, he was back: a righteous rage against Turkish atrocities in the Balkans reanimated him, forcing him once again into the political spotlight. Disraeli, more concerned with the threat of Russian hegemony over eastern Europe than with the excesses of the weak Ottoman empire, played down the atrocities, and Gladstone's fervent campaign grew into a crusade against "Beaconsfieldism"—against Disraeli, in other words, and all that his government stood for. And in a dramatic departure from tradition, Gladstone made his case against Disraeli not to Parliament, but to the people directly, in rousing orations at mass meetings. Once re-engaged, Gladstone never relented. Fighting for a new Parliamentary seat in Midlothian, he brought unprecedented fire to his campaign, stumping the district in a "pilgrimage of Passion": appearing in his popular appeal to be conducting an American campaign, not a British one. Victoria was disgusted by his attacks on her beloved Prime Minister, and disgusted by Gladstone's destructively democratic behavior: "like an American stumping orator, making most violent speeches." Her anger was mixed with more than a hint of jealousy, for Gladstone gained an immense national popularity by his appeal to the masses, his procession resembling a royal progress: everywhere he went, he was welcomed with addresses and found fireworks, triumphal arches, and eager crowds. He had stolen a play from the Queen's own book.

And worst of all, he won: he converted the election for his own seat into a national campaign, thanks to full newspaper coverage, and the "People's William" sparked a Liberal surge in the polls; he and his party trounced Disraeli and the Conservatives in the 1880 general election. Victoria at first refused outright to have Gladstone back as her prime minister. She would rather abdicate, she wrote her private secretary, "rather than send for or have any *communication* with that *half-mad* firebrand who wd soon ruin everything & be a *Dictator*. Others but herself *may submit* to his democratic rule, but *not the Queen*." Disraeli recommended that she attempt to form a government under the nominal leader of the Liberals, Lord Hartington. But Hartington could only give Victoria a painful reminder of the constitutional limits of her power: Gladstone, he told her, would refuse to serve under anyone else, and a Liberal government without him would be impossible. With a reluctance that amounted to abhorrence, she called on Gladstone to form a ministry.

And so now in 1882, that horrible Mr. Gladstone was her Prime Minister, and she could only look back wistfully to the days of Disraeli's poetry, romance, and chivalry. Her nostalgia was rendered that much more poignant by the fact that Disraeli had died a year before, on 19 April 1881. Now Victoria could not help but feel both a prisoner and an enemy of her own government. Gladstone was no longer a liberal, as far as she was concerned; he had embraced a democratic radicalism that she was certain would bring ruin upon her nation. She kept him, as he noted, at "arm's length," preferring when possible to work with the other ministers in his Cabinet. And Gladstone, in spite of his immense personal respect for the Queen and the institution of monarchy, generally assumed she would be opposed to his policies and would need to be dealt with as a necessary evil, someone to be handled, not served. He spoke to her, she said, as if she were a public meeting. Victoria had feared that the coming Liberal government would be a "calamity for the country and the peace of Europe," and Gladstone had done little to change her mind. Of all her governments, she told Vicky two years later, this one was "the worst I have ever had to do with." Her political life had become largely a matter of bracing herself: waiting for her own government to mess up, and ready to pounce when they did.

The Queen's insecurity with her own government only heightened the general insecurity she felt in 1882. Life in the 1880s, it seemed, had become that much more difficult for rulers. Not one, but two dramatic assassinations that had occurred a year before had forced her to wonder whether she might be next.

Alexander II, Tsar of the Russians—and incidentally her son Alfred's father-in-law—had been the first to die, the victim of an implacable and highly organized band of Nihilists who called themselves the People's Will and who had dedicated themselves exclusively to killing their Tsar. But even before People's Will, Alexander's life had been threatened—three times, always by men with pistols. The first two attempts—the first in a park in St. Petersburg in 1866, and the second on a state visit to Paris in 1867—were thwarted when bystanders jostled the would-be assassins' arms. Alexander himself thwarted the third would-be assassin, a man named Alexander Soloviev, when in 1879 he got within arm's length of the Tsar and drew on him a high-caliber American pistol nicknamed the "Bear Hunter." Alexander saw the pistol, dodged the first shot, and then turned and fled, serpentining to avoid four more, before Soloviev was captured.

Soon after Soloviev's attempt, People's Will formed, holding as its central belief that destroying the autocrat Alexander would spark a national uprising and thus destroy the Russian autocracy. Their weapon of choice was dynamite—a relatively new technology, more easily transportable, more versatile, and much more powerful than gunpowder. And while People's Will targeted only the Tsar, they were not over-particular about injuring or killing the innocent to achieve their goal. They attempted three times in 1879 to blow up the Tsar's train, succeeding, on the third try, in blowing up the wrong train altogether—the one holding Alexander's baggage and entourage. In 1880, using an agent who had infiltrated the Palace as a servant, they tried to kill the royal family as they ate, secreting a good three hundred pounds of dynamite in a trunk below the dining room of the Winter Palace. The explosion destroyed the room and killed or wounded fifty of the palace guard, but the Tsar and his family arrived at dinner late and were unharmed.

A fourth attempt, to mine a bridge over which the Tsar crossed, failed when the conspirators who were to set off the explosion arrived after the Tsar had come and gone.

Finally, People's Will planned an apocalypse from which Alexander would never escape. Sundays in St. Petersburg, Alexander would usually drive a mile from the Winter Palace and back in order to review his troops, and the group plotted to kill him as he traveled the usual route. They rented out a shop, dug a mine under the road, and filled it with explosives. If this did not kill the Tsar, they equipped five agents to finish the job—four with hand-held dynamite and kerosene bombs, and one with a knife. (In the event, the knife-wielder was arrested before the attempt, and one cold-footed bomber did not show up). On Sunday 1 March 1881,* Alexander unknowingly avoided the mine by choosing to return to the Palace by another route, via the Catherine Canal. Learning of this, the three waiting bombers rushed to the canal. There, the first threw his bomb under the Tsar's carriage, and the street erupted in a deafening explosion. The Tsar was unhurt, but one of his Cossacks as well as a passing boy were killed. Alexander stepped out of his carriage to confront the captured bomber, wagging a finger in his face and berating him: "A fine one!" His aide twice pleaded with Alexander to get back into his carriage and move on, but the Tsar wished to survey the damage at the scene. There, a man suddenly turned, raised his arms, and threw his bomb at the Tsar's feet. When the smoke cleared, twenty people lay wounded on the street. The bomber was dead. And Alexander was a mass of wounds from the head down, his legs virtually blown away. He was carried to an open sleigh. The third bomber realized that the Tsar was dying and his bomb was unnecessary, and so with one arm he helped carry Alexander's body while with the other he held the briefcase containing the explosive.

---

* 13 March 1881 by the Western calendar.

"Feel quite shaken and stunned by this awful news," Victoria wrote in her journal on the day Alexander died. Soon afterwards, she sent her private secretary, Henry Ponsonby, to the Home Office to discuss increased security for Buckingham Palace. On the face of it, it seemed absurd that the Queen would see in the danger to the Tsar any danger to herself; Alexander was an autocrat who despite liberating the serfs in 1861 met dissent with repression. The nation was a police state where expectations for reform had been raised and crushed, ensuring widespread social discontent. Russia's jails and cities were full of men and women dedicated to killing the Tsar. Surely nothing like People's Will could exist in Britain?

Surely, Victoria knew, something like People's Will *did* exist in Britain. There was only one other country on earth in which a disciplined organization, using dynamite as its weapon of choice, had in the early 1880s committed itself to terror-bombing, targeting centers of power to effect revolutionary change. And that country was Victoria's own.

The very first true terror-bombing in the modern world—in other words, the first bombing intended to effect political change by destroying for the sake of destruction, thereby spreading terror through the population, rather than a bombing intended to serve another purpose, such as freeing a prisoner or even killing another human being—had taken place the year before, at 5:20 P.M. on 14 January 1881, when a bomb erupted at the army barracks at Salford near Manchester.* The bombers had obviously chosen the site for its symbolic value: Salford was where the Manchester Martyrs had been hanged fourteen years before. While the explosion was intended to destroy property and not people, it nevertheless drew

---

* The Clerkenwell bombing in 1867 had certainly spread terror across Britain. But the bombers' intention was to free Richard O'Sullivan Burke, a Fenian prisoner. The would-be liberators had overfilled their barrel with gunpowder, and the destruction, the maiming and killing, were unintended consequences. The Salford bombers, on the other hand, fully wished to destroy and to wreak havoc.

blood: a butcher's shop was destroyed; three adults were injured, and a seven-year-old boy was killed.

That the explosion was a Fenian attack and the manifestation of Irish rage was obvious, but who exactly was culpable was less so. In actuality, the immense majority of Fenians, both in Ireland and the United States, had nothing to do with the attack, nor did any of the Irish Nationalists in Parliament or their leader, Charles Stewart Parnell. Both the motivation and the money for the attack came from one man: Jeremiah O'Donovan Rossa. Rossa's hatred of the British had been born when his fatherless family was evicted during the worst of the Great Famine and had been hardened by years of rough treatment in British prisons, to which he was sentenced under a treason-felony charge. Exiled to New York, he openly established a "skirmishing fund" for terrorist attacks upon Britain. The British government might protest, but the U.S. government—hungry for Irish votes—did nothing to stop him. Rossa's politics—his refusal in particular to work with Parnell and the parliamentary nationalists—proved too militant for the largest body of the Fenians in the United States, the Clan-na-Gael, and in 1880 Rossa broke with them, formed his own organization, and founded the extremist newspaper *United Irishman*, which redoubled his calls for a terrorist fund. Though the Clan-na-Gael would also eventually enter the dynamite war against the British, the attacks so far had all been by Rossa's agents.

Two months later, Rossa's bombers targeted London, placing a cruder device—fifteen pounds of blasting powder lit by a fuse—in a niche outside Mansion House, the Lord Mayor's residence. An alert constable discovered the package, snuffed out the fuse, and carried the bomb to Bow Street Station. Mansion House was quiet that night: a planned grand dinner had been called off because Alexander II had been assassinated three days before. (It was this would-be outrage, as well as Alexander's death, that heightened Victoria's concerns about the safety of Buckingham Palace.) In May 1881 the skirmishers hit Liverpool—a badly constructed pipe bomb well-placed at Liverpool's main police station exploded but did little damage. A month later, two bombers were captured lighting the fuse of a far more dangerous dynamite bomb outside Liverpool Town Hall. And the discovery by police, three weeks after this, of eight more "infernal machines"—slabs of dynamite with clockwork detonators, shipped from New York in barrels marked "cement"— made it clear that Irish terror had only just begun.

Since last summer, the bombers had been quiescent. But Ireland itself seethed with unrest. Gladstone's government had passed its own Coercion Act, meeting Irish agitation with repression. And under it, in October, three Irish nationalist leaders—Charles Stewart Parnell, John Dillon, and James J. O'Kelly, had been arrested for their agitation for the Land League; they remained imprisoned in Dublin's Kilmainham prison. It was more than likely that Irish frustration would again re-erupt in a dynamite campaign. So far, the royal family had been clearly placed off limits as a target. But Alexander's death had shown the world the dramatic effect of a dynamite bomb upon a world leader, and Victoria now took greater precautions when traveling than ever before. (On her train journey this day, as on all her train journeys nowadays, a pilot train to guard against derailment of the royal train had been sent ahead of her.) How long would Irish terrorists refrain making a target of her— the living monument to British power, British Empire, and British domination of Ireland?

The second victim of assassination in 1881 could hardly have been further removed from Alexander, in terms both of distance and of ideology. Autocrats, it became clear, weren't the only targets for assassination. On 2 July 1881, President James Garfield was shot by Charles Guiteau, a man who thought that by killing the President he was saving the Union. Guiteau, a failed lawyer, evangelist preacher, newspaper editor, lecturer, writer, and insurance salesman—but a moderately successful con artist—decided in 1880 that he would make his fortune in politics, supporting Garfield in that year's presidential election. He made himself a fixture at

New York Republican Party headquarters, relentlessly buttonholing party leaders and offering to give a speech he had written, and actually giving a part of it once. When Garfield won by a razor-thin popular majority, his winning in New York state proving pivotal in his electoral college victory, Guiteau leapt to the conclusion that his speech alone was responsible for Garfield's election, and that he deserved great reward. He preferred to become Minister to Austria; he would be happy with the consul-generalship in Paris; at the very least, he would accept a consulship in Liverpool. Soon after Garfield's inauguration, Guiteau arrived in Washington, D.C. with a single shirt and $5. Flitting from one upscale boarding house to another as the rent became due, Guiteau joined the many other job-seekers in the capital, haunting the White House and the State Department and barraging Garfield and his Secretary of State, James G. Blaine, with righteous demands for his appointment. He managed once to thrust a copy of his speech into Garfield's hands and once to speak to him; another time he slipped into a White House reception and had a conversation with Mrs. Garfield. When he was finally denied access to the White House altogether, and when Secretary Blaine at the State Department shouted at him "Never speak to me again on the Paris consulship as long as you live," Guiteau understood that his due reward would be denied him. As absurd as his expectations and sense of self were, Guiteau had spent enough time in Republican politics to form an accurate assessment of the state of that party after the election. He realized that the Republicans were split deeply into two factions—the Stalwarts, who supported ex-president Ulysses S. Grant, and the Half-breeds, who did not, and who had been largely responsible for Garfield's election. Those factions, Guiteau knew as he pursued his own appointment, were locked in their own battles over a number of political appointments. As he lay in bed one night, the disappointed office-seeker had a burst of inspiration: if he killed Garfield, all would be well: vice-president Chester Arthur—a true Stalwart—would become president and all party factionalism would come to an end. He would be a hero.

Guiteau's certainty over this course grew quickly. Within two weeks, he realized that his inspiration was divinely inspired. God was speaking to him personally, telling him to kill the president. Suddenly, the entire erratic course of his life made sense: he had been born to perform this patriotic act.

And so Guiteau abruptly shifted from job-seeker to stalker. He borrowed $15 from a distant relative and made his way to a gun shop in downtown Washington, where he found a choice of weapons. He favored a $10 pearl-handled revolver, thinking that it would look best on display in a museum after the shooting. But in the end he opted for economy, choosing a $9 wood-handled, .44-caliber five-shot snub-nosed revolver with a powerful kick, stamped "British Bulldog." A novice with a gun, Guiteau spent time the next day practicing shooting on the banks of the Potomac. He followed the president (who eschewed all security), considered shooting him at church and then outside the White House, and finally decided to shoot him in the Washington terminal of the Baltimore and Potomac Railway. On the morning of 2 July 1881, he wrote one of several letters justifying his conduct. This one was addressed to the White House and began:

> The President's tragic death was a sad necessity, but it will unite the Republican Party and save the Republic. Life is a fleeting dream, and it matters little where one goes. A human life is of small value. During the war thousands of brave boys went down without a tear. I presume the President is a Christian, and that he will be happier in Paradise than here.

"I am a Stalwart of the Stalwarts," he wrote. At 8:30 that morning, he took up a position in the ladies' waiting room of the station, through which he knew Garfield would have to pass to get to the platform and his private Pullman coach. Just before 9:30, Garfield entered with Secretary of State Blaine. When they were

ABOVE: William Hamilton's attempt, 19 May 1849. Hamilton, in his bricklayer's outfit, stood on Constitution Hill close to where Oxford and Francis had stood before him, but on the other side of the Green Park palings. He immediately faced the wrath of crowds on both sides of that fence. From the *Illustrated London News*. BELOW: Robert Pate's attempt, 27 June 1850, outside the narrow gates of Cambridge House on Piccadilly, where Victoria had gone to visit her dying uncle, the Duke of Cambridge. From the *Illustrated London News*.

Sir Charles Wentworth Dilke, Second Baronet: his 1871 speaking tour marked the high-water mark of Victorian British Republicanism. Weeks later, the illness and recovery of the Prince of Wales and the failure of Arthur O'Connor's attempt crushed the movement.

"NEW CROWNS FOR OLD ONES!"

(ALADDIN *adapted.*)

Benjamin Disraeli depicted in *Punch* in 1876 as a sorcerer offering Victoria the grand gift of the imperial crown. Disraeli's carefully cultured dedication to serving the Queen made him the ideal prime minister in her eyes, and made his rival Gladstone that much more unpalatable to her.

Victoria and her recovering son Bertie during the thanksgiving procession of 27
February 18, 1872, as depicted in the *Illustrated London News*. John Brown sits on
the back of the carriage, in full Highland dress. Arthur O'Connor tried and failed to
make his attempt on this day; he would have better luck in confronting the Queen
two days later.

ANOTHER EMPTY WEAPON.

Little Charley Dilke. "PLEASE, SIR, THERE'S NOTHIN' IN IT!"
Gladstone, A 1. "NOTHING IN IT, INDEED! I'LL TEACH YOU——!"

Punch depicts the death of British republicanism: Sir Charles Wentworth Dilke presented as Arthur O'Connor failing in his attempt, with William Gladstone as a policeman, arresting the progress of Dilke's republican motion.

Portrait of Roderick Maclean, from the *Graphic*, capturing the man's dazed look if not his dirty and disheveled state on the day of his attack on the Queen.

Roderick Maclean's attempt, 2 March 1882, from the *Graphic*. Chief Superintendent Hayes and James Burnside converge upon him from the left and behind; the Eton boys approach from the right, about to belabor Maclean with their umbrellas. Princess Beatrice is visible in the carriage: Victoria sits invisible to her right. On the back of the carriage is an ailing John Brown.

Victoria, five years after the last attempt on her life, at the time of her Golden Jubilee of 1887: the face of empire. The Jubilee dynamite plot of that year—effectively nipped in the bud by the Metropolitan Police—did little to disturb her equanimity.

a few steps from the doorway to the main waiting room, Guiteau shot twice, the first bullet grazing Garfield's arm and the second plunging into his back, above his waist and four inches from his spine, shattering a rib and passing through a vertebra, and finally lodging below his pancreas. The wound was serious, but not fatal. The fifteen or so doctors who examined him, however, ensured that he would die, searching in vain for the bullet over the next few days by plunging their unwashed fingers into the wound. Garfield lingered in agony until the nineteenth of September before his body, then a 130-pound mass of putrefaction, succumbed. Victoria, who had sent at least six messages expressing her concern during Garfield's long decline and death, immediately ordered her Court to go into mourning for a week—an unprecedented token of respect for an American president.

Guiteau's trial was a sensation in Washington, and it was widely reported in Britain. He mounted an insanity defense: God had directed him, he claimed; the shooting was a divinely inspired uncontrollable impulse. Insanity in Washington, as in Britain, was defined by the MacNaughtan Rules, and Guiteau's defense (in which he acted as co-counsel) roughly followed Hadfield's, Oxford's, and MacNaughtan's, with a number of lay witnesses to his bizarre behavior and a number of doctors to testify to his insanity. The trial was notable for Guiteau's relentless outbursts against the judge and all the attorneys, including his own. He was found guilty, and awaited execution on 30 June, two days before the first anniversary of his shooting.

Guiteau was obviously insane. His extreme grandiosity, his inability to maintain any grip on reality, and his Maclean-like personal connection with God all made that abundantly clear. But Guiteau's act was undoubtedly political as well. He spent months scheming to elect Garfield. He sought recompense, as thousands of others had done, for his political labors. And he genuinely believed that his shooting Garfield would have positive political consequences, healing a party rift and putting into office a more capable man. Guiteau showed that there can be no clear line drawn between the political and the lunatic assassin.

Nevertheless, after this cold day in March, many Britons would try again to draw that line.

The royal train, having flashed through the station at Slough and turned sharply left to rattle through the playing fields of Eton, slowed to cross Brunel's bowstring bridge over the River Thames and slid to a halt at Windsor Station. It was exactly 5:25. Roderick Maclean heard the train come; he watched the door of the royal waiting room, waiting for Victoria to emerge.

twenty-three

Worth Being Shot At

From their saloon car behind the Queen's own, the members of the household—Victoria's private secretary Sir Henry Ponsonby, her two equerries James Carstairs McNeill and Viscount Bridport, her current lady-in-waiting Lady Roxburghe, and her maids of honor—emerged to take up their positions in a miniature royal procession behind the Queen and Beatrice. Ponsonby offered the Queen his arm. The stationmaster had put out a red carpet, roped off from the public on either side, leading from the door of the train to the Queen's waiting room. Just outside there, three royal carriages awaited. After a respectable few minutes' wait, the royal party emerged onto the platform and made their way through the cheering crowd. As the royal party entered the waiting room, the crowd hastened toward the exits in order to reassemble in the station yard and cheer the Queen out of the station. To give them time, the Queen waited another respectable minute before emerging from the street side of the waiting room.

The yard through which the royal party would take only a few steps was well patrolled. A number of constables from Westminster's A Division—assigned to royal protection and therefore traveling wherever the Queen did—were there. Also there were a number of officers of the Windsor Borough Police, keeping the road clear for the royal carriages from station to Castle. Their head, Chief Superintendent Hayes, stood at the verge of the yard, ready to signal to his sergeant at the moment the royal carriages set off, to stop the traffic on the busy street out of the station. While Victoria was well protected, then, the science of royal protection was still far from a perfect one. When she emerged from the station onto the road, every officer in the yard stopped surveying the crowd in order to look upon their Queen.

By her carriage, drawn by two gray ponies, Victoria could see her faithful Highland servant John Brown; he had let down the carriage stairs and was ready to hand her warm wraps for the short journey. Brown had aged visibly since he had earned his gold medal tackling Arthur O'Connor; he was stouter and suffered several chronic illnesses, of which the worst were pain and weakness in his legs and a nasty regular swelling of the face. His heavy drinking as well contributed to his debilitation. He had only a year to live. Ponsonby led Victoria to the door of the carriage, and Brown helped first her, and then Beatrice and Lady Roxburghe, inside. Victoria and Beatrice sat facing the horses, the Queen on the far side; Lady Roxburghe sat facing them. The carriage was closed because of the cold, but there was an open window on the door. Ponsonby left them to join the equerries in the second carriage; the maids of honor occupied the third. Brown put up the carriage steps and clambered, with some difficulty, onto the rumble seat.

The carriage set off as Victoria enjoyed the cheers of the crowd, the shouting of the boys from Eton, she thought, drowning out the rest. Beatrice, looking out of her side of the carriage, could see the boys, and past them, apart from them, about forty feet away from her, a shabby-looking man: he stepped forward, raised a revolver that glimmered even in that gloaming, leveled it in their direction, and fired.

Victoria heard the sharp report; she thought it had come from a train engine. Then she saw commotion. All the crowd instantly turned its attention from the Queen's carriage to the shooter, who stood still, his arm outstretched, looking as if he were about to shoot again. One man in the crowd was stunned to recognize the man: he, the Rev. Mr. Archibald MacLachlan, was the good Samaritan who had revived Maclean, fed him, and sent him on his way a week before. As one, the crowd surged toward Maclean. Chief Superintendent Hayes, who was nine feet away from him, was the first to reach him, shouting "scoundrel!" and grabbing him by the neck. A young man named James Burnside, a Windsor photographer, jumped at Maclean from the other direction, grabbed him by the right wrist, and yanked his pistol hand down until it collided with Burnside's own thigh; he pushed at Maclean's fingers until Maclean released the pistol, and it clattered to the ground. Inspector Fraser and several of his officers ran up and held Maclean while the crowd fell angrily upon him. Two of the Eton boys, armed with umbrellas, belaboured Maclean over his head and shoulders with zeal but indiscriminate aim, smacking in the process at least one of Maclean's captors. Victoria, her carriage now rushing out of the station, had no idea what was going on but "saw people rushing about and a man being violently hustled." Beatrice, who had seen it all, remained silent, not wanting to frighten her mother. Lady Roxburghe, whose perspective allowed her to see little, thought the whole thing a joke. The carriage sped up the hill, the other two carriages following: the men of the household in the second carriage and the ladies in the third all knew Maclean had fired a shot, and they rode on to the Castle fearing the worst.

The crowd—and particularly the Eton boys—wanted to lynch Maclean on the spot. The role of the police instantly shifted from restraining Maclean to protecting him. They dragged the Eton boys away from him as Maclean cringed and cried "Don't hurt me—I will go quietly." Followed by a hooting mass, they dragged Maclean up the road to Thames Street, where Superintendent Hayes sent an officer to the nearest cab stand for conveyance to the Borough police station.

Victoria's carriage in the meantime rushed up Castle Hill and into the yard. John Brown hopped off the rumble and ran to pull open the carriage door; with a "greatly perturbed face" and yet a calm voice, he declared "that man fired at your Majesty's carriage." The equerry, McNeill, leapt from the second carriage and ran up "in a great state," hoping that the Queen was untouched. He told her that the assailant had been caught. Victoria immediately ordered McNeill back to the station to see if anyone had been hurt. In spite of the excitement around her, Victoria was not at all affected by this attempt—nor would she be in the days to come. "Was not shaken or frightened," she wrote in her journal that day—"so different to O'Connor's attempt, though [this] was infinitely more dangerous. That time I was terribly alarmed." (Beatrice, on the other hand, was shaken enough in the coming days to delay the royal journey to the French Riviera.) Victoria, as usual, immediately set out to broadcast her own version of events before rumors began to fly. She hurried to tell her one child in the Castle—Arthur—what had happened. She then took tea with Beatrice while her account was telegraphed to the rest of her children and to other relatives. Ponsonby took it upon himself that evening to send two short telegrams and one longer letter about the shooting to the prime minister.

While the queen's carriage traveled on to the royal mews, to be scrutinized for bullet-marks, McNeill hurried back down the hill and offered up his carriage to transport Maclean to the station house. The police didn't need it; they had already obtained a hansom cab. Into this they thrust Maclean; Superintendent Hayes of the Windsor Police and Inspector Fraser of the Royal Household Police squeezed in on either side. The cab took off to the High Street and to the station house on Sheet Street, the Eton boys running beside them hooting, and Maclean demonstrating visible anxiety the whole way. He had been starving, Maclean told his captors; otherwise, he would not have done this.

All the Queen's men—Ponsonby, Bridport, and McNeill—arrived at the police station at around the same time as Maclean, in order to see him charged. The news of the attack spread through the town quickly, and the Mayor of Windsor and a number of magistrates quickly made their way to the station as well. From the group of Eton boys, the two who had pummeled the captured Maclean with their brollies identified themselves to Ponsonby, and he took down their names. They were to become, to the press and the Queen both, the heroes of this day.

Maclean was talkative with the police at the station, freely stating his name and Windsor address and his place of birth, and he gave some idea about his movements over the past few weeks. Fraser and Hayes examined his gun: two chambers loaded; two recently discharged; two empty. He was searched; among the detritus in his pockets were his notebook, the note he had written in the waiting room, one penny and three farthings, and, wrapped in paper, fourteen live pin-fire cartridges, which fit his pistol. No bullet had been found at the station yet, and the examination of the Queen's carriage showed no bullet marks. Most of the newspapers the next day reported that Maclean likely shot a blank. But the police already had enough evidence to know better than that. Superintendent Hayes detained Maclean for shooting the Queen with intent to do her grievous bodily harm. Maclean seemed unimpressed: "Oh, the Queen," he replied to the charge. His examination was set for the next day, before the mayor and magistrates at the Town Hall. Maclean was forced to wash himself—an action that improved his appearance considerably. In his cell, he gratefully and voraciously fell upon a dinner of tea, bread, and butter. He seemed more relieved and content in jail than he had been while on the streets. A local surgeon,

William Brown Holderness, was brought in to examine him—and quickly pronounced him sane.

Although this was the first assault upon the Queen that had taken place outside the center of London, thanks to the telegraph, news of this attempt spread quickly, reaching London within minutes. As they had done after every other attempt, the gentry set out in their carriages to offer their congratulations to the Queen. *Where* to go, exactly, since the Queen was not in residence in London, was the question. Most dealt with the difficulty by clogging the Mall to leave their regards both at Buckingham Palace and at the Prince of Wales's residence. Several diplomats who attempted to offer up personal congratulations at the Palace were directed to call at Marlborough House instead. (Others made their way by train to Windsor Castle the next day.) The House of Commons churned for a time that evening with a growing consternation as vague reports about the shooting arrived before Ponsonby's official word did; Gladstone and several ministers, on hearing the rumor, consulted and then rushed from the House to learn further details. When one of Ponsonby's telegrams was placed in Gladstone's hands, he quickly passed it around to his colleagues and to the speaker, quelling the stir. The government quickly sent a reply to Windsor expressing their "profound gratification" for the Queen's escape. Gladstone wrote to Ponsonby personally that evening, expressing his earnest desire that Maclean would suffer a much harsher penalty than O'Connor had a decade before: "I hope the matter will not receive the same sort of judicial handling which a similar one as I recollect received from Mr. Justice Cleasby." From the start, Gladstone wanted the Queen to understand that her government would do its best this time to deal with the assailant according to her desires.

The news spread quickly beyond the metropolis as well, its broadcasting helped by the fact that many had collected outside newspaper offices throughout Britain to hear the results of Bradlaugh's bid for re-election in Northampton. (To Maclean's gratification and Victoria's dismay, Bradlaugh had won.) And via an efficient world-wide telegraphic system, the news traveled quickly throughout the world as well—so quickly that one awed newsman posited the lightning dispersal as a sign of miraculous times and the harbinger of a wondrous future:

> I have before me as I write a copy of an evening paper published in San Francisco on March 2nd, and this paper contains a series of telegrams giving full particulars of the attempt to shoot the Queen, which took place at Windsor at half-past five on the afternoon of the same day. The news, it need scarcely be said, had outstripped by many hours the movement of the daylight, and the people of California were actually reading in their printed newspaper all about Maclean's attempt upon the life of the Queen before the hour at which that attempt took place in England. This fact is of itself sufficiently remarkable, and yet I am not without authority for saying that before long other wonders of science still more marvellous will demand the astonished admiration of the world.

As the news spread, messages of sympathy and congratulations returned in an unprecedented flood, jamming the special telegraph wire to the castle: the Queen herself counted 138 telegrams on the Friday, and 68 on the Saturday. Among these was a telegram from the Tsar of Russia, who had been personally informed about the attempt by his brother-in-law Prince Alfred. She received messages as well as from the King of Spain, the Emperor of Germany, and the legislatures in Spain, Greece, Bucharest, and Ottawa. Before two days had passed, several congratulatory messages arrived from Australia. In the United States, several newspapers responded to the attempt by reminding readers about Victoria's heartfelt sympathy to Lucretia Garfield upon the death of her husband—and

Victoria was particularly affected by President Chester Arthur's message to her. And postbags bulging with congratulations soon joined the telegrams. Ironically the Queen, never more secluded from the world in the wake of an attempt, was never more taxed in responding to the world's congratulations. "Telegrams, as well as letters," she wrote in her journal on 3 March, "pouring in to that extent that I literally spent my whole day in opening and reading them." Actually, after four o'clock that day, the Queen managed to break away from her correspondence to walk with Beatrice to the mausoleum at Frogmore, where they knelt by Albert's tomb and offered up prayers of thanksgiving for the Queen's preservation. After that, they rode out in an open carriage, purposefully leaving the usual paths of the Park to ride among the people of Windsor and of Eton where, Victoria wrote, "the boys cheered as we passed . . . and everyone seemed so pleased." The tonic effect upon the Queen of the spontaneous public acclaim after this attempt had not diminished a bit from every earlier attempt. It was after this one that Victoria finally summed up the curious joy she felt after each of the attempts against her: "anything like the enthusiasm, loyalty, sympathy and affection shown me is not to be described," she wrote to her daughter Vicky. "It is worth being shot at to see how much one is loved."

At around 9:00 the morning after the shooting came a discovery that changed everything: the bullet had been found by Inspector Noble of the Great Western Railway, lying in the mud of the rail yard, about thirty yards from the spot where Maclean had stood. It had obviously struck a truck before falling to the ground, taking on a smudge of white paint. That truck had moved on to Reading, but Inspector Noble found it there that afternoon, and concluded that it had struck the white painted number of the truck at a height of 5' 5"—a level shot, one capable of striking the Queen. These discoveries raised one question—how could Maclean have missed the carriage?—the apparent answer to which was that the bullet passed between the rear of the carriage and the rumble seat—between Victoria and John Brown, in other words. Wherever the bullet went, it was now clear that Maclean had fired live ammunition in the general direction of the Queen. The afternoon of the discovery, John Brown interrupted Victoria's enormous task of correspondence by showing her Maclean's pistol; "it could be fired off in rapid succession with the greatest facility," she noted. That, and the news of the missing bullet, surprisingly brought the Queen relief, "for it proves," she wrote, "that the object was not intimidation, but far worse." In other words, as far as she was concerned, Maclean had tried to murder her. She would not have to worry about any misdemeanor charges this time, which might result in Maclean's being given a paltry one-year sentence, as O'Connor had been. Maclean was a traitor and would be tried as one.

At the Borough police station that morning, the discovery of the bullet apparently alarmed Roderick Maclean: after a sleepless but quiet night, soon after the news of the discovery reached the station house, Maclean called Superintendent Hayes to his cell. The realization that he might now face the death penalty concentrated his mind wonderfully. He wished to make a statement, he told Hayes. The Superintendent had pen, ink, and paper brought, and watched as Maclean wrote:

> I am not guilty of the charge of shooting with the intention of causing actual bodily harm. My object was by frightening the Queen to alarm the public, with the result of having my grievances respected—viz., such as the pecuniary straits in which I have been situated. All the circumstances tend to prove this statement. Firstly, had I desired to injure the Queen I should have fired at her when she was quitting the railway carriage. Quite on the contrary, I pointed the pistol on a level with the wheels: but as I felt a slight kick, doubtless the contents may have lodged in one of the doors.

If Her Majesty will accept this explanation, and allow the words "with intent to intimidate her," instead of "with intent to cause grievous bodily harm," to be inserted in that count, I will offer all the assistance in my power to bring the charge herein specified to a speedy issue.

I hope Her Majesty will accept the only consolation I can offer—namely, I had no intention whatever of causing her any injury.

Roderick Maclean

With this promise that he would make things easy for Queen and government in return for a lesser charge, Maclean thought he had worked out a deal. That notion he considered confirmed when he asked Hayes, before he handed him the letter, whether he would be charged with a capital offense.

"Certainly not," Hayes told him.

He was thus a confident man when at 1:30 that afternoon, handcuffed to a plain-clothed officer, he was rushed in an open fly from the station house to Windsor Town Hall. Since the town magistrates had cleverly announced publicly that the examination would take place at least two hours after it actually did, Maclean rode happily unbothered by the now-usual Windsor mob. The police and the Home Office had already been busy putting together a case against him, and the Solicitor to the Treasury, Augustus Stephenson, was present at the Town Hall to examine witnesses.

Stephenson quickly disabused Maclean that he had struck any sort of deal, stating at the start that Maclean was charged with shooting at the Queen with intent to murder her. Then he quickly brought forward three witnesses, enough to justify a remand for a week, as the police had already uncovered evidence pointing to Maclean's serious mental illness. At this examination, however, there was no testimony whatever about that, Stephenson instead questioning the three witnesses simply to establish that Maclean had indeed shot at the Queen. Two of the witnesses—Superintendent Hayes and the photographer James Burnside, who had wrestled away Maclean's gun—both claimed that they had seen Maclean pointing his gun at the Queen's carriage. Burnside's recollection in particular was remarkable for its specificity: "I saw the prisoner with a revolver in his hand. The line of fire was straight from my eye to one of the panels of Her Majesty's carriage."

Maclean, however, saw the flaw in their evidence and energetically exploited it, exercising his right to cross-examine witnesses by subjecting all of them to a thorough and—all agreed—highly intelligent cross-examination, to establish that none of the three had actually seen him shoot; the fact that two of them had seen where his pistol was pointing after the shot offered no proof whatsoever of where it had been pointing before. In cross-examining Hayes, Maclean asked him to give him back his revolver so that he could demonstrate how he held it when he shot. "No, thank you," Hayes replied. So Maclean used his shabby hat instead to demonstrate that he had been pointing downwards. "You do me an injustice if you were to condemn me on such a point as that," Maclean said. He then used Hayes's extensive experience with firearms to debunk the idea that he had necessarily shot at the Queen.

> Have you fired a pistol in your life?—Some hundreds.
>
> Perhaps you are aware that pistols jump?—Yes, that is so.
>
> The pistol might have been in a very different position after I fired it to what it was before?—That is very possible.

"That is a point in my favor," Maclean claimed triumphantly. It might have been. But it made no difference to the magistrates, who considered that they had evidence enough for a remand of a week charging Maclean with intending to murder the Queen. Maclean protested that he had cooperated on the understanding that his charge would be lowered to intimidation, not murder. "We have nothing to do with that," replied the mayor.

And so Maclean returned to the station house sure that the world had wronged him once again, a conclusion strengthened by his rough treatment along the way: during the examination a hostile crowd had gathered outside the Town Hall, and when police escorted Maclean out and into a carriage ringed with constables, some of the crowd rushed at the carriage and battled the police in order to overturn it; Maclean felt the terror of impending death for a couple of minutes, before the police regained control and hurried him away from the chasing and tormenting mob. The next evening, too, Maclean's paranoid delusions appeared to have become reality, as he was transferred to the county jail at Reading to await the completion of his examination. Superintendent Hayes, attempting to avoid confrontation by avoiding Windsor train station altogether, removed Maclean from the station in a closed fly through Eton and to the railway station at Slough. He was recognized there, and a hostile crowd quickly grew. He was kept out of sight in the station's booking office until the train arrived.

Meanwhile, not a full day had passed after the shooting before Victoria and Gladstone bickered. Touched by the overwhelming public and foreign response to her escape, the Queen fully expected her Parliament to follow suit and present her with a joint congratulatory address: anything less, she thought, would have a *"painful effect."* The last Parliamentary joint address had taken place a full forty years before, after Francis's attempts. Robert Peel had put an end to these, of course, for practical reasons, doing his best to minimize the pomp following each attempt in order to discourage imitators. Peel's disciple Gladstone agreed with him then, and agreed with him now. So when Victoria requested that her secretary convey her desire to Gladstone, her prime minister quickly attempted in a response to Ponsonby to pour cold water on the idea:

> As respects an address, the dominant feeling in my mind has been that the whole of these deplorable attempts on the life of the Queen have proceeded from men of weak and morbid minds: that to such minds notoriety is the very highest reward and inducement that can be offered. . . .the best means of dealing with these cases are to keep from them what feeds the vain imagination and to administer sharp judicial sentences.

Gladstone rejected the idea of an address with the best of intentions, wishing only to protect Victoria as Peel had done. But Victoria's relationship with Peel was nothing like her relationship with Gladstone, and she could not help but understand his thinking to be at best insensitive, and at worst mistaken, and typical of his enmity toward her. The discovery of the bullet on this Friday, however, fortunately put an end to their argument before it escalated. That discovery convinced the Attorney General, Henry James, that Maclean's act was that of a traitor, and that he ought to be tried for attempted murder of the Queen, not for the high misdemeanour of annoying her. Knowing this, and believing that this attempt had become in the eyes of the public more serious than previous ones, Gladstone reversed himself, and the Cabinet, meeting on Saturday, agreed to follow the precedents of 1840 and 1842. On the following Monday, Commons and Lords each overwhelmingly approved of the address, and on Friday, a small Parliamentary delegation took the train to Windsor Castle to present it to her in a small ceremony.

Victoria was satisfied with Parliament, and told Gladstone so. Parliament's was not the first address to be presented, however, and likely not the most satisfying one. On Monday the sixth, before Parliament had even voted for their address, the boys of

Eton presented theirs. At 10:30 that morning, the entire school unknowingly appropriated Roderick Maclean's great number: ranked in rows of four, the nearly nine hundred students marched out of the college, across the Thames, and up to Castle Hill, where they formed a ring in the Quadrangle about the Queen's private entrance. At 11:00 they sent up a tremendous cheer as Victoria appeared, flanked by Leopold and Arthur. The address was then read "extremely well," in Victoria's opinion, by the two boys who wrote it—followed by an even louder volley of cheers, one echoed by the public outside of the walls. Victoria, "visibly affected," replied briefly to the address, and then called forth Leslie Robertson and Gordon Chesney Wilson, the two boys who had loyally belabored Maclean with their umbrellas. She shook the hands of her young saviors.

Later that afternoon, Victoria lunched with the beautiful, restless, and peripatetic Empress Elisabeth, wife of Emperor Franz Joseph of Austria. Elisabeth, a devoted huntress, had been riding to the hounds in Cheshire for the past month, and had come on her way back to the Continent to offer Victoria her congratulations and her farewells. Arthur, Leopold, Helena, and Beatrice met her at the station. The Prince and Princess of Wales came up by train from London to Windsor especially for the occasion, and they with Victoria met Elisabeth at the castle's Sovereign's entrance. The two empresses and the royal family then ate for an hour before the younger children saw Elisabeth to the station and off to Paris. The meeting was in hindsight a poignant one. Victoria had encountered the final attempt upon her life; Elisabeth had yet to encounter hers. Sixteen years later, on 10 September 1898 in Geneva, Elisabeth and a lady-in-waiting were hurrying down the promenade before the lake in order to board a steamer bound for Caux when a burly man suddenly lurched at her, knocking her down. The Empress was helped up, boarded the ship, and collapsed. Her lady-in-waiting cut the very tight stays of her corset and discovered blood on her chemise: she had been stabbed. The man who attacked her, Luigi Lucheni, was an Italian anarchist who when caught admitted that he was out to kill the first royal he could lay his hands upon. The fact that Elisabeth was traveling under a transparent incognito and subsequently lacked any security had given Lucheni his chance, and when he lurched at her he plunged into her body a short file sharpened to stiletto fineness, breaking her rib and piercing her lung, pericardium, and heart. The Empress quickly bled to death. The elderly Victoria, then at Balmoral, telegraphed her condolences to the devastated Austrian Emperor.

During the week between Roderick Maclean's two examinations by the magistrates of Windsor, press and police vied with one another to uncover the man's disturbed past. Every day the papers trumpeted new discoveries, all of them suggesting that Maclean was seriously mentally ill. Before a day had passed after the shooting, Inspector Fraser of the Household Police received a telegram reporting Maclean's lengthy sojourn in Bath and Somerset Asylum; that news was widely reported the next day, along with Maclean's stays in a Dublin asylum as well as Weston-super-Mare infirmary. An attorney from Dover, Wollaston Knocker, recognized Maclean from the first reports of the shooting and quickly telegraphed the Mayor of Windsor to describe his defending Maclean eight years before from the charge of attempting to derail the train at Maidstone, and stating his decided opinion that Maclean was at that time insane. A few days later, Knocker's more detailed account of Maclean's earlier, bizarre behavior appeared in newspapers across the country. Reporters acting upon the discovery of a Southsea address in Maclean's pocket when he was searched tracked down Mrs. Sorrell and Mr. Hucker, who happily revealed to the world Maclean's "soft" behavior there. Maclean's homicidal gestures to his family, his paranoid and frantic letters to his sister Annie, tales—both actual and apocryphal—of his eccentric behavior in the several towns through which he had wandered: all of it poured from the press, an ocean of evidence to prove the man was mad.

The police and the government quickly reached the same conclusion. The Home Secretary, William Vernon Harcourt, did consider the possibility that Maclean was a part of a larger political conspiracy, when within hours after the shooting he received a letter claiming a connection between Maclean and Johann Most. Most was a notorious German anarchist living in London, who in his German-language newspaper *Freiheit* had welcomed with joy news of Tsar Alexander's assassination, and called for the assassination of another "crowned ragamuffin" every month. For this he was tried and convicted, and was now serving sixteen months in Clerkenwell Prison. Harcourt ordered Howard Vincent, the head of the Metropolitan Police's Criminal Investigations Department, to investigate the possible connection. Within forty eight hours Vincent, having accumulated an abundance of evidence of Maclean's mental instability, dismissed the possibility outright, informing Harcourt: "the present attempt on the life of Her Majesty the Queen was the work of a lunatic, whose antecedents have been fully ascertained, and is in no shape or form traceable to any English or Foreign political society."

William Gladstone agreed: Maclean was a madman acting alone, not a member of a political conspiracy. When he introduced in Commons his motion for a joint address, he proclaimed as much, and more—claiming that *every* attempt upon the Queen had been one of apolitical madness. The horror one felt at learning the Queen had again been attacked, Gladstone proclaimed, was mitigated by one "remarkable consideration":

> —that whereas in other countries similar execrable attempts have at least been made by men of average, or more than average, sense and intelligence, and whereas there the real, or at any rate the supposed, cause has been private grievances or public mischief, in this country, in the case of Her Majesty, they have been wholly dissociated from grievances, wholly dissociated from

discontent, and upon no occasion has any man of average
sense and average intelligence been found to raise his
hand against the life of Her Majesty. On each occasion
of the kind morbid minds, combined with the narrowest
range of mental gifts, have been the apparent cause by
which persons have been tempted to seek a notoriety
denied to them in every legitimate walk of life.

His implication was clear: the very thought of harming the
Queen was irrational. Other nations with their lesser rulers and
lesser systems suffered political discontent to an extent that the
threat of political assassination was a reality. But not in Britain,
where such extremities of discontent were simply not possible,
and where Victoria's popularity was so solidly established that
only the weak-minded could entertain the notion of harming her.
Gladstone's conclusion, of course, rested upon the absurd premise
that politics—at least British politics—were by definition rational.
Given the example of the recent antics in Parliament with Bradlaugh's attempts to get in and with the attempts of the Irish nationalist MPs to bring business to a standstill, let alone the excesses
on both sides that Fenianism had engendered—or the example in
1872 of Arthur O'Connor's Fenian-inspired lunacy—that premise
could not bear the slightest scrutiny. But no one was in a mood
to scrutinize it, at least when it came to the Queen: in 1882 her
popularity was so solidly established that any attempt to harm
her could only be explained away as madness. No clearer evidence
exists as to the enormous growth of the popularity of the Queen
and the monarchy since the uneasy life and abrupt death of British
republicanism a decade before.

Thus convinced of Maclean's insanity, Gladstone, Harcourt,
and Attorney General Henry James had, long before the man's
second examination, let alone his trial, decided exactly how they
would handle his case. The fact that he actually shot at the Queen
mandated that he be tried for treason. But the evidence of his

insanity was so overwhelming that an insanity defense was sure to succeed—and that would in effect guarantee Maclean permanent imprisonment at Broadmoor, ensuring that, unlike Arthur O'Connor, he could never bother the Queen again. The government, therefore, had no reason to contest an insanity plea. On 9 March, the day before Maclean's second examination, Gladstone wrote Victoria to justify his government's course. "Your Majesty's Law Officers are sensible how important it is that there should be in this case a power of imprisonment without any limit of time." Therefore,

> It is thought by far the most probable . . . that the friends of Maclean will defend him on the ground of insanity. And the Law Officers seem at present not inclined to resist that plea *à l'outrance*. For, if it be admitted, the man may be imprisoned without limit of time; whereas, if it were overthrown, the parties might be driven to another line of defence, and might try to show that the intent was only to alarm. For, if by any chance a jury were to accept this plea, the term of imprisonment would be limited and comparatively short.

Victoria, writing in her journal the next day, seemed to agree with this strategy. Actually, she betrayed a serious misunderstanding of her prime minister's words: "if there should be any fear of his not being convicted for intent to murder," she wrote, "the plea of insanity will be brought forward; this might be accepted in order to ensure his incarceration for life." While Gladstone attempted to inform Victoria that the Attorney General would abandon altogether any serious attempt to convict Maclean, Victoria thought that they would indeed make their best case that he was guilty of High Treason, and only concede insanity if conviction for treason proved to be impossible. She would certainly prefer that the state establish the man's guilt, for while her subjects might find relief in thinking Maclean mad, she adamantly refused to consider him anything but sane—as she had considered all of her assailants. Maclean might have "a horrid, cruel face." He might be the "utterly worthless" offshoot of "respectable relations." But, as the Queen wrote to her daughter Vicky, "The wretched man is strange and wicked but not mad. He had fourteen bullets on him, and the act was clearly premeditated." As far as she was concerned, if he thought the crime through, he was sane, and thus a traitor, and the Queen expected her government to make every effort to establish his guilt. When five days later, on her way to France, she wrote Gladstone "she is glad to hear of this proposed arrangement for the trial of Maclean w^h seems very satisfactory," she only deepened the misunderstanding between them by signaling approval of a course of which she manifestly did not approve. A collision between the two was inevitable.

By his second examination, on 10 March, Roderick Maclean had had a change of heart. Gone was the fire he displayed in his first examination, when he fought to establish a lesser charge. Since then he had resigned himself to an insanity plea and had relinquished the fighting to others. He entered the Town Hall certain he had legal representation, and indeed there were a solicitor and barrister in attendance, engaged by Maclean's brothers. They were not there to defend Maclean, however, but were there to look after Maclean family interests. It was not until after the examination of the first witness that Maclean realized he was unrepresented:

> The Mayor (to the prisoner) Have you any question to put to the witness?
>
> Prisoner—I understand I am represented by a solicitor.
>
> The Mayor—You are not represented by a solicitor. He only represents your family.
>
> Prisoner—I leave the case entirely in their hands.

> Mr. Haynes [the family solicitor]—You reserve your defence?
>
> Prisoner—I reserve my defence.

He was as good as his word, declining to cross-examine a single witness. His silence guaranteed that he would be tried for treason and not for a high misdemeanor, as he left undisputed the highly disputable evidence that he had fired a bullet at the Queen with intent to injure her. Treasury Solicitor Augustus Stephenson again represented the Crown, examining several witnesses to the attack (including the two umbrella-wielding Etonians) and others who established that Maclean had bought the pistol. Stephenson had little to say about Maclean's state of mind besides noting that, as far as he could tell, there was nothing the matter with the man. Maclean was read the charge: high treason. "I reserve my defence," he said, and was led away.

twenty-four

SPECIAL VERDICT

R oderick Maclean's trial was set for the next assizes in Reading—set, specifically, for 19 April, more than five weeks after his second examination. It was to be by Special Commission, so that the Lord Chief Justice, John Coleridge, could preside in company with the judge of the Assize, Baron Huddleston.[*] In the interim Maclean, the Queen, and the public found their own ways to divert themselves.

Maclean, when his time wasn't occupied by the several alienists that both the Crown and his solicitor sent to interview him, wrote an autobiography, which he titled *Yestern: or The Story of My Life and Reminiscences*. He apparently wished this narrative of his idyllic childhood, his disturbed adulthood, and his special

---

[*] Both judges, as attorneys, had had experience with previous assailants: Coleridge, as Attorney General, was the one who browbeat Dr. Tuke and demolished his attempt to establish Arthur O'Connor's insanity; Huddleston had assisted Alexander Cockburn in defending Robert Pate.

relationship with God to help with his defense, as he argued in it both that he had no intention of whatsoever of shooting the Queen, and that he had long been, and still was, insane. He wished more than this, however, if his overblown prose and his later repeated but unsuccessful attempts to get the manuscript published are any indication: he apparently sought to gain with it the literary fame he knew he so greatly deserved.

Victoria's diversion was her first visit to the French Riviera. She left her subjects with a letter published in the newspapers on 14 March "to express from her heart how very deeply touched she is by the outburst of enthusiastic loyalty, affection, and devotion which the painful event of the 2d. inst. has called forth from all classes and from all parts of her vast Empire." The same morning, she and Beatrice rode to the station under greatly increased security, constables sent from London lining the route, and the station itself closed altogether to the public. Similar precautions were taken at Portsmouth. Two days later, Queen and Princess were in Mentone, where security was lighter, and in which the Queen delighted in riding in an open carriage about the countryside, writing to Vicky of "the bright sunshine and the sea, mountains, vegetation and lightness of the air and the brightness and gaiety of everything." Only John Brown marred the otherwise entirely relaxing journey. Rumors that three Fenian terrorists were on their way from Paris to assassinate Victoria had reached the ears of the police who accompanied her, but they dismissed these rumors as spurious. John Brown did not, and drove everyone to distraction by his frantic attempts to discover the assassins. Victoria attributed his hypervigilance not to any actual threat, but to "his increasing *hatred* of being 'abroad' which blinds his admiration of the country even." Victoria and Beatrice returned to Windsor amidst the same heightened security, four days before Maclean's trial.

In the meantime, public attention was absolutely captivated by a drama that had been building for some time, which competed for column inches in the newspapers with Maclean's attempt, and which in the days before Maclean's trial grew into London's *cause célèbre* of 1882: the Jumbo craze. That the simple transfer of an elephant from Regent's Park Zoo to a circus in New York became a sensational international incident should come as no surprise, for Jumbo had a great publicist—the greatest publicist that ever lived: P. T. Barnum. Barnum and his associates, having the year before merged to create a greater "Greatest Show on Earth," had sent agents across America and Europe in search of new, bigger and better exhibits. Their agent in London had negotiated with the Zoological Society of London for a £2,000 sale of the largest living exhibit he found—Jumbo, reputedly the largest African elephant then in captivity. The Zoological Society was relieved to see Jumbo go, for the elephant had reached the age of sexual maturity and had already experienced musth, a condition common to adult male elephants caused by copious hormonal release, and manifesting itself in violently destructive rages; last August, Jumbo had destroyed the zoo's elephant house. A return of that condition—and the possible need to destroy the elephant—was only a matter of time.

Jumbo, however, apparently had his own opinion about leaving the zoo. When in mid-February he was led from his paddock to the crate especially designed to wheel him across London and aboard ship, he balked and refused to enter. When led out the next day to walk the eight miles to Millwall Docks, Jumbo similarly refused, uttering loud cries of distress, sinking to the ground and laying upon his side, grunting. "Shame," onlookers cried out. The press and the public began to take note. At the same time that Roderick Maclean made his way to Windsor and bided his time there, London focused on the elephant's plight, and visits to the zoo skyrocketed. Members of the Society sued to keep Jumbo in London—and many pleaded with Barnum to let Jumbo stay. Barnum did his best to stoke the flames of publicity, on both sides of the Atlantic, making public all of his correspondence, spreading rumors about the elephant, perhaps even manufacturing letters supposedly from

British children, pleading with him to relent. The resulting furor both increased revenues at the zoo and created a fever of anticipation in the United States ensuring for Barnum's circus a wildly successful season. In mid-March, Jumbo fever peaked, as on one day 24,007 people packed the zoo—a dozenfold more than had come on the same day the previous year. Finally, on 22 March, Jumbo deigned to enter the box; with difficulty he was chained, crated, slowly trundled across the metropolis to St. Katharine's Dock, where he was set on a barge and two days later hoisted aboard ship. Two days after that he sailed for New York. Once the elephant had left, Jumbo fever subsided quickly, the British sheepishly realizing that they could go on without Jumbo, as Americans began to think they couldn't. By the date of the trial, then, Barnum and his elephant no longer competed for column inches with Roderick Maclean.

When on 19 April two constables conveyed Maclean up from the subterranean passage and into the dock of the small courtroom at Reading, he appeared dirtier and shabbier than ever, wearing his faded green-gray overcoat with its soiled once-velvet collar left open to reveal a ratty shirt and a frayed black tie. His demeanor was equally pathetic, betraying his sense of terror at being surrounded by the enemies who had packed the courtroom. His hands fidgeted ceaselessly; his eyebrows twitched, as his vacant eyes wandered nervously about the courtroom, from judge to jury to counsel, and upwards to the gallery, where on one side a number of fashionably dressed ladies stared back at him, some through opera glasses. "Few who looked upon him," his barrister later wrote, "had any doubt that insanity had marked him for its own." Maclean's brothers could easily have provided him with a respectable suit for the trial: they had otherwise provided for him well, paying for his meals at Reading Gaol and for the services of their solicitor and two barristers, including one of the most capable and renowned—and expensive—criminal lawyers of the day, Montagu Williams. But family, his counsel, and Maclean himself had agreed he would plead insanity. And Maclean's rags, the regalia of his distraction, served his case best: and so they remained.

From early that morning, there had been a crush at all of the courthouse entrances. Those admitted had apparently been selected for their respectable appearances, one reporter comparing the spectators to a Nonconformist congregation. They were notable, as well, for their overt conservatism. This day, as it happens, was the first anniversary of Benjamin Disraeli's death,* and many in the courtroom both honored his memory and signified their adherence to his principles by carrying bouquets of primroses, Disraeli's favorite flower. The Queen had that morning done the same, sending a primrose wreath to be placed on his grave at Hughenden.** Maclean's agitation could not have been lessened by these symbols of allegiance to another cause—the blue ones in particular.

There had been growing public nervousness about Maclean's trial. This was the first time one of Victoria's assailants was being tried for treason since John Francis, forty years before. All of Robert Peel's reservations then about providing an attention-seeking scoundrel with the elevated trappings of a State Trial—and thus encouraging other addle-brained attention-seekers—poured forth from the press in the days leading up to this trial. "We cannot help regretting," proclaimed *The Times*, "that the accused has been treated so much *au sérieux*, and that, instead of placing Maclean on a sort of pedestal, he could not have been sent to quarter Sessions to be dealt with in a sharp and summary fashion." It was all too much: the presence of the Lord Chief Justice, as well as a large team of prosecutors headed by the Attorney- and Solicitor-Generals;

---

* Besides being a year to the day after Disraeli's death, 19 April 1882 also happened to be the day that Charles Darwin died.

** By amazing coincidence, Disraeli's estate at Hughenden had been sold after his death to Samuel Wilson, the father of Victoria's Etonian defender, Gordon Chesney Wilson. Samuel Wilson later ordered a stained-glass window for Hughenden Church commemorating Victoria's escape from Maclean.

the very charge of High Treason with its awful sentence—it was "like employing a five ton Nasmyth hammer to crack a walnut-shell," according to one newspaper. More than this, there were fears that this trial would repeat the excesses of an insanity trial that had finished just two months before, and thus that was fresh in everyone's minds: Charles Guiteau's trial for the murder of President Garfield, which had been widely reported on both sides of the Atlantic. During the ten-week trial, Guiteau had acted as his own co-counsel, and with his constant interruptions, his badgering and belittling of attorneys on both sides, his vainglorious week-long pontification from the witness stand, and his dogged insistence upon reading long passages from a book he had written, or rather plagiarized, Guiteau had managed to turn the trial into a circus before his guilt was finally established and he was sentenced to hang.

The fears of all were allayed in the course of this day. For both Crown and defense had come to the courtroom believing the trial's outcome to be a foregone conclusion: an acquittal on the basis of insanity. And for weeks both sides had been working toward the common goal of gathering evidence that would support that conclusion. Both sides, for one thing, had instructed medical experts to interview Maclean and ascertain his state of mind. But while ordinarily the prosecution would instruct medical witnesses in an insanity trial in order to rebut an insanity defense, the government from the start expected their witnesses to *confirm* Maclean's madness. In his diary, Lewis Harcourt, son of the Home Secretary, noted this expectation on the part of his father: "As to Maclean there is no doubt of his insanity and so anxious is the H[ome] S[ecretary] to have it proved that he has given orders for Dr. Sheppard to be instructed by the Solicitor to the Treasury Solicitor to go down to Reading Gaol to examine him." While there had been in the weeks leading up to the trial some dickering about who would pay for which doctor, and how much evidence each side would disclose to each other, there was no question of the verdict, and both sides were committed to counteracting the pomp of the trial with celerity, reaching a verdict as efficiently as possible.

Much therefore had happened in the hour before Maclean stepped into the dock: the two judges in their scarlet robes and full-bottomed wigs had taken their seats, the Grand Jury had been empaneled, Chief Justice Coleridge had presented the charge, and the Grand Jury had left and returned with a true bill for treason against Maclean. Maclean was then brought up and the charge read; in a tremulous voice, he denied his guilt. The jury was then sworn without challenge, and the trial proceeded hastily: before lunch, the prosecution had completed and the defense had called its first three witnesses.

In opening for the prosecution, Attorney General Henry James did not wait for the defense to raise the possibility of Maclean's insanity: the man's state of mind, he proclaimed, was a "matter of grave consideration for the jury." While he noted that it was the job of the defense to prove insanity, he made it clear that the Crown would have no problem whatsoever with that conclusion: indeed, he told the jury, "satisfaction would be felt by every subject of the Queen at the thought that it was not from the ranks of those who were sane that a hand had been raised against our gracious Sovereign." James and his three colleagues then quickly established the facts of the shooting, by examining most of the witnesses who had testified at Maclean's two examinations. Maclean's counsel, having no reason to question those facts, remained silent.

In opening Maclean's defense, Montagu Williams set out a strategy that was a variation on the defense in Hadfield's, Oxford's, and McNaughtan's trials: the defense would call both eyewitnesses and medical experts to support overwhelmingly the claim that Maclean was insane. Williams was careful to point out that the evidence would prove Maclean *legally* insane—that is, prove that he was insane according to the McNaughtan Rules. "At the time of committing this act," Williams stated, "he was an irresponsible agent, not knowing the difference between right and wrong."

Non-medical evidence to Maclean's eccentricities was to be limited: Maclean's family, who could have provided volumes of evidence concerning their brother's oddities, had, in their desire to detach themselves from their embarrassing relative, successfully requested that they not be called. (Victoria had similarly requested that her household not have to testify.) Therefore, to provide anecdotal evidence of Maclean's insanity, the defense called the Reverend Maclachlan, who had assisted Maclean on his way from Southsea to Windsor (and who now added little to the defense) and a Maclean family friend, Samuel Stanesby, who detailed twenty years of Maclean's eccentric behavior and introduced the paranoid and homicidal letters Maclean had written to his sister Annie—strong evidence of true past insanity to counter any notion that Maclean could be shamming madness in the present.

The defense's most compelling evidence, however, came from the medical experts. Nine doctors appeared in all, six of them brought in by the defense, and the last three originally instructed by the prosecution. While the first doctor simply bore witness to Maclean's debilitating head injury as a child, the other eight testified with impressive unanimity to his madness in the past and in the present, unanimity unmarred since the one doctor who had examined Maclean and declared him sane—Dr. Holderness of Windsor, who had examined him on the evening of the shooting—had been conveniently forgotten about by both sides. Four doctors testified to Maclean's history of insanity, having previously certified his insanity or treated him in an asylum. The other four—including the three doctors brought in by the prosecution, now released by them to testify for the defense—had examined him in jail, and while all testified he was insane, not all presented his illness as within the purview of the McNaughtan Rules. Indeed the defense's own expert, Dr. Henry Manning, superintendent at Laverstock Asylum at Salisbury, turned out to be the worst witness in this respect. For while Manning spelled out in admirable detail Maclean's paranoia, the voices in his head, and his notions about the color blue and the number four, he insisted, in spite of leading questioning by the Lord Chief Justice and the Attorney General, that while Maclean's shooting was "an absolutely irresistible moral impulse, as strong as if it was physical," he could distinguish between right and wrong, and "decidedly he would know at the time he fired the pistol that he was doing a wrong act."

Two of the prosecution's three witnesses testified more clearly and effectively to Maclean's legal insanity. (The third, Oliver Maurice, the surgeon at Reading Gaol, simply and briefly declared Maclean's unsoundness.) Edgar Sheppard, professor at King's College and for twenty years superintendent at Colney Hatch Asylum, was certain: Maclean was an imbecile, liable to homicidal or delusional mania, and "the real question of right or wrong does not present itself to a man in such a state." William Orange, Medical Superintendent at Broadmoor, agreed: "I do not think he was capable of appreciating the nature and quality of the act he committed," he stated.

In closing, Attorney General Sir Henry James did just about everything in his power to direct the jury to an insanity acquittal. He did not concede the case outright—such a verdict should not be lightly arrived at—but he admitted that "Crown authorities had come to the conclusion that the prisoner's mind was not in a healthy state." And he reassured the jury that an acquittal on the grounds of insanity would effectively protect the Queen from any future attempt, since Maclean would remain safely in custody at the Queen's pleasure. Summing up, Lord Chief Justice Coleridge repeated James's reassurance that an insanity acquittal would protect the Queen, and added that it would be merciful for Maclean himself. He also rose above the disagreements between judge and medical expert which were a feature of most insanity trials, praising every one of the doctors as "men of undoubted ability and large experience, and wholly without any bias in this case, having no other desire in the world but to arrive at a just and true conclusion."

The trial went to the jury at 4:40 that afternoon, the only surprise occurring when the jury actually chose to retire rather than give an immediate verdict. They returned after five or ten minutes later with the foregone conclusion: Roderick Maclean was not guilty on the grounds of insanity, and was to be kept in custody at the Queen's pleasure.

Maclean was hustled down the stairs and back to Reading Gaol. A week later, Home Secretary Harcourt ordered a warrant for his transfer; a week after that, Maclean made the short trip from Reading to Crowthorne and entered Broadmoor Asylum. He would never leave. The Queen's pleasure became her son's, and then her grandson's; Maclean died, disturbed until the end, half a lifetime later.

The newspapers the day after the trial displayed unanimous satisfaction with the verdict, which confirmed the public's consensus that Maclean was hopelessly mad, his life "saturated with insanity and its symptoms"; he had been rightly consigned to an asylum rather than the gallows. The *Daily News* concluded that "the jury took the only course compatible with the medical testimony, which did but itself confirm the impression produced by the bare narrative of the facts" and added "such an end to an affair which has excited so much sympathy and so much indignation will be received with general satisfaction." Satisfying, too, was the brevity and efficiency of the trial, in striking contrast to the painful ordeal Charles Guiteau had inflicted upon the American public. In short, government and prosecution, Maclean's family and his defense, judge and jury were all well pleased with this day's work—and press and public agreed.

Victoria, however, disagreed completely.

"Am greatly surprised & shocked at the verdict on McLean!" she declared, and confided in her journal "it is really too bad." Her initial astonishment at the verdict quickly grew into an imperious, Queen-of-Hearts rage. She had never considered Maclean insane, and the trial had not changed her mind; he did not deserve an acquittal of any kind. And while his confinement in Broadmoor would keep Maclean from her, she did not feel in the least protected by the verdict. On the contrary, Maclean's acquittal signaled to all notoriety-seeking halfwits that they too could shoot at the Queen—and get away with it. "It is Oxford's case over again," she complained to Ponsonby, reminding him that Oxford himself had said that if had been hanged, the attempts that followed his would never have occurred. Now, she thought, it was only a matter of time before new Francises and Beans attacked her. If an assailant such as Maclean "is *not* to be considered *responsible* for his actions," she wrote angrily, "then indeed *no one* is safe any longer!"

She held her own government most responsible for this threat to her safety. "This always happens when a Liberal Government is in!" she told Ponsonby, with greater passion than accuracy. Her Prime Minister, her Home Secretary, her Attorney General—they all should have protected her by exerting themselves to prove Maclean's guilt, but instead they had colluded to disprove it. When the next day her Home Secretary, William Vernon Harcourt, came to Windsor to introduce a congratulatory address to her, she refused to see him privately, claiming to be "much too excited"; she did, however, make her displeasure known to him through Ponsonby: "She was angry at the result of the Maclean trial as she does not understand the verdict of 'Not Guilty' and said to Sir Henry Ponsonby 'I know that Sir William Harcourt and Sir Henry James were determined to make him out mad all along.'" William Gladstone, to whom the Queen fired an incredulous telegram the moment she heard the verdict, was baffled: he was certain that she both knew and approved of the government's strategy. He replied with a ciphered telegram, referring her to the letter he had written her at the beginning of March laying out his reasons for the government's not contesting an insanity plea: "I did not then understand Your Majesty to disapprove," he told her. But it was clear to him that she disapproved now, with a bitter intensity that called for a quick and delicate response. Gladstone, Harcourt, and Foreign Secretary Granville all wrote to her the day after the shooting to placate her and once again to justify the government's course. Maclean's lifetime of confinement was more strongly guaranteed with the insanity verdict than it would have been with a guilty verdict, Harcourt argued. Granville noted the relief of finding Maclean to be a madman, and tried to flatter the Queen, praising her "calm and serene courage, when so highly tried." Gladstone, in his usual maddeningly dispassionate style, both backed away from his government's collusion in bringing about Maclean's insanity verdict and rather weakly attempted to defend the deterrent value of the sentence:

> Mr. Gladstone humbly feels with Your Majesty that when an individual, such as Maclean, has probably been sane in respect to the particular act for which he is tried, an acquittal on the ground of insanity is not a satisfactory form under which to attain the end of at least disabling him from further mischief by the total loss of his personal liberty. He hopes indeed that all who understand that this forfeiture is really a forfeiture for life may perceive the gravity of the consequences following the act.

These convoluted concessions to her point of view were not enough for Victoria. Her government had done her a great disservice, and she now wanted action, not words. Gladstone must now do his best to set things right, and just as importantly—more importantly, to a monarch who had, in her eyes, for the past two years been talked down to or ignored, defied, and endangered by her own government—she simply wished for her prime minister to do her bidding, to treat her as the Empress she was—to *serve her*, as Disraeli had done so well during his ministry.

After O'Connor's attempt a decade before, Gladstone had promised Victoria that if the law under which he was tried was defective, his government would change it. And after O'Connor's paltry one-year sentence had been handed down, Victoria had called upon Gladstone to change that law—Peel's Law—by appending a provision to exile convicted assailants for life. But Gladstone had reneged, blaming weak-willed Judge Cleasby and not the law for the sentence. And when Victoria had insisted that the law was defective, Gladstone had put her off with a vague promise to change the law in the future; and then he had done nothing.* And now Maclean had shot at her, and had been acquitted: obviously, any law that did not acknowledge his guilt must be faulty, and must be changed. Within hours of the verdict, she demanded that Gladstone find a way to remove "not guilty on the grounds of insanity" as a verdict from cases such as Maclean's.

And Gladstone, eager to rehabilitate his ever-more deeply dysfunctional relationship with the Queen, set out quickly to do just that. In his letter to her the day after the shooting, he expressed himself "deeply impressed with the gravity of the subject." While he did say he was unsure whether such a change could be legally made, he promised to consult with the highest legal authorities about the matter. Within the next fortnight he had met with the Attorney General and the Lord Chief Justice. Telling them that he concurred absolutely with Victoria's position that the stigma of guilt would prevent "dangerous misapprehensions in morbid minds," he energetically promoted the change. Lord Chief Justice Coleridge supported altering the law in this way, but only in cases of high treason, and not those of murder. Coleridge would consult with other high court judges; if they agreed, which seemed likely, Gladstone promised Victoria his ministry would see the change through Parliament.

In this way Gladstone and his government built up a little bit of good will with Victoria. But they squandered that good will completely, two weeks after the trial, when Gladstone and his Cabinet made the momentous decision to release Charles Stewart Parnell and the two other Irish nationalist MPs, whom they had ordered

---

* See pp. 454-455, above.

arrested the previous October in the face of growing Irish agitation and agrarian violence. Since the time of Parnell's imprisonment without trial, violence in Ireland had only increased. Coercion, it seemed, was not working, and almost to a man Gladstone's Cabinet now favored a course of conciliation. Through intermediaries they had negotiated with Parnell and had reached an informal deal: if the government would continue with its reforms initiated with its Land Act of the year before, Parnell would support them, and would speak out against the violent outrages plaguing Ireland. Only one member of the Cabinet refused to be a party to the release, and resigned— W. E. Forster, the violently coercionist Chief Secretary for Ireland.

Victoria was a hardline coercionist as well, and Gladstone attempted to break the news to her gently, informing her on the first of May of the Cabinet's decision, arguing that "this measure will tend to peace and security in Ireland"; the next day, he sent Granville on a special train for an audience and to obtain her consent for the release. Granville, she noted, was very nervous, and Victoria was not happy. She *very reluctantly* gave her consent, "but said it was a great mistake." She then wrote to voice her reservations to Gladstone: releasing Parnell would have, she thought, the opposite effect to the one Gladstone expected: "The Queen cannot but feel that it will have the effect of a triumph to Home Rule and of great weakness. She trusts she may be mistaken as to the results of this course, but she much dreads they will not be favourable to the maintenance of authority and respect of law and order."

That day, Parnell and his two colleagues were released. W. E. Forster was replaced by Lord Frederick Cavendish, who happened to be the husband of Gladstone's niece Lucy. Two days later, as Cavendish and the newly appointed Viceroy, Earl Spencer, prepared to cross over to Dublin, Victoria learned to her amazement that her government was making a further, and to her a dangerous, conciliatory move. She shot a telegram to Gladstone: "Is it possible that M. Davitt, known as one of the worst of the treasonable agitators, is also to be released? I cannot believe it." Her government had already done enough to convince her that their radical actions were again doing damage to her Empire.

On 6 May, Earl Spencer and Lord Frederick Cavendish made what was to all appearances a triumphal entry into Dublin—"... certainly the best reception I ever got in Ireland," Earl Spencer wrote to his wife; "The cheering was tremendous at times, and I would see many old friends at windows, etc."

A few hours afterwards, Spencer wrote his wife again: "We are in God's hands. Do not be filled with alarm and fear. . . . I dare not dwell on the horror for I feel I must be unmanned." Lord Frederick Cavendish had decided that evening to walk from his office at Dublin Castle to his residence in Phoenix Park. In the park, a cab crossed his path and stopped; Thomas Henry Burke—for thirteen years permanent Irish undersecretary, and so now Cavendish's assistant—hopped down to walk with him. As the two proceeded arm in arm, seven men approached them, passed, wheeled around, pulled out long, sharp knives, and fell upon Burke. "Ah, you villain!" cried Cavendish, and smacked one of the attackers in the face with his umbrella. They then turned upon him as well. Slashing and hacking at both men, the attackers inflicted gaping wounds upon Burke's and Cavendish's breasts, backs, necks, and arms. The seven attackers then melted away before passersby ran up to see Burke and Cavendish take their last breaths.

That night, Queen Victoria, who earlier had made her own triumphal procession through London in order to open Epping Forest as a park, learned the horrible news via two telegrams—the first reporting Burke dead but Cavendish alive, the second stating "All is over with Lord Frederick." The murders were all she dreaded, clearly the fruits of Gladstone's destructive policies. She angrily laid out cause and effect in her journal: "How could Mr. Gladstone and his violent Radical advisers proceed with such a policy, which inevitably led to all this? Surely his eyes must be open now." It did not matter to Victoria that Gladstone theorized (incorrectly, as it turned out) that the attackers were Irish-Americans and not

Irishmen, that the attackers were, it transpired, attacking Burke and not Cavendish, and that they had originally targeted the coercionist Forster before he left the country, that the murders horrified Parnell and certainly did not serve his interests, and that he both deplored them and quickly sought police protection. The Queen was certain: Phoenix Park proved that Gladstone and his cabinet were not simply aiding the enemy: they *were* the enemy. While Gladstone of course was devastated personally by the death of his niece's husband, the Queen could hardly restrain herself from launching a general attack on her government. At first, she did so through Granville, declaring to him on the day after the assassinations:

> . . . she *cannot withhold* from him that *she* considers *this* horrible event the *direct result* of what she has always considered and has stated to Mr. Gladstone and to Lord Spencer as a most fatal and hazardous step.
>
> She *must hold those* who recommended the release of not only the three Members of Parliament, but of many other suspects, as responsible for the lives of her subjects, and calls on the Government to take such strong measures as may give her and the country security, or at least as much security as possible. . . .

Two days later, and one day after Gladstone, crushed with grief, broke down in tears while speaking in the House of Commons of Cavendish, Victoria turned upon him: "She wishes now to express her *earnest* hope that he will make *no* concession to *those* whose Actions, Speeches & writings, *have produced* the present state of affairs in Ireland & who would be *encouraged* by weak and vacillating action to make *further demands*."

She would find, however, that she could not quite bend her government to her will in this matter. They did introduce and pass a new coercion bill in the wake of the tragedy, but they also continued on the path of conciliation that the Queen deplored. By the end of

May the relationship between the Queen and her government had reached such a low point that Victoria took the most unusual step of enlisting her eldest son to intervene to save her and her nation from the government:

> Dearest Bertie,—The state of affairs—this dreadfully Radical Government which contains many thinly-veiled *Republicans*—and the way in which they have truckled to the Home Rulers—as well as the utter disregard of all my opinions which after 45 years of experience ought to be considered, all make me very miserable, and disgust me with the hard, ungrateful task I have to go through and weigh on my health and spirits. . . . The mischief Mr. Gladstone does is *incalculable*; instead of *stemming* the current and downward course of Radicalism, which he could do *perfectly*, he *heads and encourages it* and alienates all the true Whigs and moderate Liberals from him. Patriotism is nowhere in their ranks. . . . You . . . should *speak* to *those* who *might and ought*, to act *differently* to what they do!

The Prince of Wales, however, could do little; Victoria and Gladstone would remain locked in their bitter relationship for three more years, until in 1885 another brutal killing—of General Gordon, in the Sudan—crippled the Liberal government and led to its fall. And even that was not the end; to Victoria's great dismay, Gladstone would serve as her prime minister twice more.

In the meantime, Gladstone kept to his promise to change the insanity verdict, though the progress of that change had slowed considerably as judges consulted and wording was agreed upon. By September 1882 this was done. Somehow during that time the scope of the proposed special verdict had grown; the change from the verdict not guilty by reason of insanity to "Guilty, but insane" would now apply to every felony, not just treason. The consequence, of course, would remain exactly the same—detainment at the Queen's pleasure; it was the stigma that was new. The government at first attached this measure to a larger bill consolidating a number of criminal law reforms. That bill, introduced early in 1883, came to nothing. They then detached the measure and introduced it as a special bill. It quietly passed at the end of the session, in August 1883.

Life had become, if anything, less secure for Victoria between Maclean's trial and the passage of the Trial of Lunatics Act. At the beginning of 1883, Irish-American dynamitards had relaunched their bombing campaign, again targeting symbolic sites of British power. And in April John Brown had died, plunging the Queen into grief. "He protected me so, was so powerful and strong—that I felt so safe!" Victoria wrote to Vicky. She would be grateful, then, for any measure that protected her. Therefore, while she pointedly did not thank Gladstone for anything else that he had achieved in the busy parliamentary session of 1883, Victoria thanked him for this: "It will be," she wrote, "a great security."

Perhaps it was. Certainly, Victoria was never shot at or assaulted for the rest of her life, and the special verdict of "Guilty, but insane" never had to be applied in any case concerning her. Instead—and for the next eighty-one years—it applied to every poor insane soul who committed a felony. The first person stigmatized by this verdict was a woman with a history of mental disturbance, Johanna Culverwell, who was brought before the bar of the Old Bailey just three weeks after Victoria gave her royal assent to the change in the law.* Culverwell was charged with the death of her six-week-old son, whom she had placed in a pan of water, walked away, and returned to find drowned. After some

---

* Culverwell, as it happens, was prosecuted by Roderick Maclean's defense attorney, Montagu Williams.

confusion as to the existence of the act, and then about the proper way to word the verdict, she was declared guilty, but insane. She, like Maclean, was detained at Victoria's pleasure. But she, unlike Maclean, was considered morally responsible for her action. So was every other mad felon until 1964, when the Trial of Lunatics Act was amended to its original verdict of "not guilty by reason of insanity."

While Maclean's attempt did not lead to any further assaults upon Victoria, as she had feared it would, it certainly did lead to one final act of mayhem: an assault upon the language, perpetrated by the man widely considered to be the worst poet in English, and perhaps all languages: William McGonagall.

McGonagall and Maclean traveled oddly parallel courses in the years leading up to Maclean's attempt. Both heard voices in their heads: for McGonagall, it was his bedraggled and faulty muse, who came to him in a trance and ordered him to "Write! Write!" during the most "startling incident" of his life, in 1877, when he discovered his poetic calling. Both Maclean and McGonagall had grandiose notions about their talents, and both expected the public to marvel at their gifts. The public refused to comply, although McGonagall had the happier nature of the two and generally interpreted public ridicule as acclaim. Soon after his epiphany, McGonagall, like Maclean, submitted some of his verses to Victoria, hoping for patronage, perhaps even expecting to snatch the Poet Laureateship from Lord Tennyson. Like Maclean's, his efforts were rejected—by Keeper of the Privy Purse Lord Biddulph this time, rather than by Lady Biddulph, Maclean's curt correspondent. Biddulph politely thanked McGonagall for his submission, and that was enough to convince McGonagall, with his happier nature, that the Queen loved his work. This was enough in July 1878 to compel him to an epic journey from Dundee to Balmoral to entertain the Queen, who was then in residence. At the gate he was ridiculed and sent on his way, and threatened with arrest if he ever returned. Undismayed, he lived the rest of his life certain of the Queen's patronage; for twenty-five years he played the part of a stealth poet-laureate, outdoing Tennyson in his startlingly prolific output of occasional poetry. He earned an insecure living by badgering patrons for donations and by reciting his poetry in halls, theatres, public houses, and for a time as a circus act, where he read while the audience was permitted to throw eggs, flour, dead fish, and vegetables at him.

Roderick Maclean's attempt provided him with the occasion of one of his best worst poems—and provides us with enough evidence to conclude that McGonagall must by any standard be considered a better bad poet than Maclean himself was.

"Attempted Assassination of the Queen"

God prosper long our noble Queen,
And long may she reign!
Maclean he tried to shoot her,
But it was all in vain.

For God He turned the ball aside
Maclean aimed at her head;
And he felt very angry
Because he didn't shoot her dead.

There's a divinity that hedges a king,
And so it does seem,
And my opinion is, it has hedged
Our most gracious Queen.

Maclean must be a madman,
Which is obvious to be seen,
Or else he wouldn't have tried to shoot
Our most beloved Queen.

Victoria is a good Queen,
Which all her subjects know,
And for that God has protected her
From all her deadly foes.

She is noble and generous,
Her subjects must confess;
There hasn't been her equal
Since the days of good Queen Bess.

Long may she be spared to roam
Among the bonnie Highland floral,
And spend many a happy day
In the palace of Balmoral.

Because she is very kind
To the old women there,
And allows them bread, tea, and sugar,
And each one get a share.

And when they know of her coming,
Their hearts feel overjoy'd,
Because, in general, she finds work
For men that's unemploy'd.

And she also gives the gipsies money
While at Balmoral, I've been told,
And, mind ye, seldom silver,
But very often gold.

I hope God will protect her
By night and by day,
At home and abroad,
When she's far away.

May He be as a hedge around her,
As he's been all along,
And let her live and die in peace
Is the end of my song.*

McGonagall died in 1902, a year after Victoria. He thus lived long enough to see every wish he had for her come true. God indeed hedged her; after Maclean, she lived, and died, in peace.

---

* Yet another poem connected with Maclean's case, and undoubtedly the best of them, made the rounds of the newspapers in the wake of the verdict:
"Two Pronunciations."
Roderick Maclean
He shot at the Queen.
The jury took "reason"
Out of his treason;
So Rod'rick Maclean
Was pronouncéd insane.
(*Manchester Times* 29 April 1882, 8.)

JUBILEE

For the last nineteen years of her life, Victoria never again confronted a would-be assassin.

But because of the lethal power of dynamite and the ever-growing belief among terrorists—Fenian and otherwise—that monarchs and heads of state were legitimate political targets, the threat of assassination only increased during the last decades of the nineteenth century. Victoria's security detail grew; greater and greater precautions were taken when she traveled between her homes or went among her subjects. And in 1887, the year of Victoria's Golden Jubilee, that increased security proved its worth, when the Metropolitan police shut down what could have been the most serious threat against her.

Since their first dynamite campaign in 1881, Irish-American dynamitards had chosen as their targets ever greater symbols of British power. Between 1883 and 1885, they had hit Whitehall and Victoria Railway Station, the London Underground, Scotland Yard, the Tower of London, and the House of Commons. An unexploded bomb had been found in Trafalgar Square next to one of Landseer's lions, at the base of Nelson's Column. One dynamitard was caught with brass cylinder grenades, planning to throw them from the Strangers' Gallery at the full government bench at the House of Commons. But dynamiting ceased altogether in 1885 when some measure of freedom for Ireland seemed achievable by Parliamentary means, and the Clan-na-Gael, now the most popular group of militant Irish nationalists in the United States, agreed to refrain from violence to give Parnell and the nationalist MPs their chance. Hopes soared at the end of the year when William Gladstone converted publicly to the cause of Irish Home Rule. But those hopes were crushed six months later when Gladstone's Home Rule Bill failed and his Liberal party split irrevocably. Those opposed to Home Rule, calling themselves the Liberal Unionists, shifted their allegiance to the Conservatives—permanently, as it turned out. After the general election of July 1886, much to Victoria's delight, Lord Salisbury's conservative government was in—and Gladstone and any possibility of Irish Home Rule were out. A month later, at a conference in Pittsburgh, the extremists of the Clan-na-Gael resolved to recommence terror-bombing with a "display of fireworks" to disrupt the Queen's Jubilee celebrations.

There exists no evidence that Clan-na-Gael leaders specified a target for the renewed campaign. Quite likely they never did. But in that year, one target was feared above all others: Westminster Abbey on 21 June 1887, Jubilee Day, when Victoria, her children and grandchildren, and a critical mass of the royalty of Europe and the world were to gather to give thanks for the Queen's fifty years on the throne. A strategically placed cache of dynamite could destroy them all; no greater blow against monarchy could have been struck anywhere in the world at any time during Victoria's reign.

And yet it all came to nothing. Thanks largely to the efforts of one man—James Monro, Assistant Commissioner and head of the

Criminal Investigations Department—the "Jubilee Plot" was the attempt on Victoria's life that never was.

The threat, however, was certainly real. On 11 June 1887, the ship *City of Chester* steamed out of New York Harbor and past the newly erected Statue of Liberty, bound for Liverpool. On the ship were three men well equipped for a serious sortie in the dynamite war. All carried portmanteaus containing new Smith & Wesson revolvers and fifteen bullets. Also in their bags—or perhaps sewn into their coats—were over a hundred pounds of American-made Atlas A dynamite in slabs, as well as a number of detonators. The three men all traveled under aliases. The dapper and garrulous one of the three—obviously their leader—called himself Joseph Melville. He was actually John J. Moroney, one of the more militant members of the Clan-na-Gael, and a close friend of the Clan's most powerful leader in America, Alexander Sullivan; Sullivan had obviously hand-picked him for this mission. Moroney had himself almost certainly picked the others. Both traveled under the alias of Scott: brothers, supposedly, though they hardly looked it. The youngest, "Harry Scott," was actually Michael Harkins, a sandy-haired thirty-year-old, his broad shoulders muscular from years of labor on the Reading Railroad. He had been a Philadelphia grocer until Moroney enlisted him, and he left behind a pregnant wife and four young children. He had met Moroney when both were loyal members of the Philadelphia branch of the Clan-na-Gael. How Moroney met and recruited the other man for this mission, however, is more of a mystery. For Thomas Callan, who travelled as "Thomas Scott," had little experience of Moroney's usual stomping grounds of New York, Philadelphia, San Francisco, and Chicago; he had lived a quiet life in the factory town of Lowell, Massachusetts, operating stocking-making machinery. He was unmarried, and at forty-seven his hair was already graying. Moroney likely sought him out because of his military skills; when Callan was twenty-two, in 1862, he had enlisted in the Massachusetts 33rd infantry of the Union Army. He had fought at the Civil War battles of

Chancellorsville, Gettysburg, and Lookout Mountain, and marched with General Sherman from Atlanta to the Atlantic. "No better or braver soldier than he served in that noble old regiment," declared one of his officers. Callan, however, like Harkins, was an extremely mild-mannered man; neither fitted the role of a fiery dynamitard. The skills that must have attracted them to Moroney were loyalty and deference: they took orders well. The "Scott brothers" were the foot soldiers in an operation top-heavy with commanders.

All three men had been born in Ireland; all three had brought with them to the United States a hatred of British oppression so deep it was as natural to them as breathing, a hatred created by centuries of Irish subordination and humiliation, amplified by the starvation of the great famine; indeed, Thomas Callan person-ally experienced the horrors of the famine before emigrating as a child to Lowell. Their hatred was fostered in America by family memories, by nationalist newspapers, and by regular meetings of their Clan-na-Gael camps. And now the three made for London to translate their lifelong hatred into explosive violence. They were supported financially, materially, and morally by thousands of Irish-Americans.

Three conspirators in the Jubilee Plot had preceded Moroney, Harkins, and Callan across the Atlantic. In March, "General" Francis Millen, a twenty-year Fenian veteran, was commissioned by the Clan-na-Gael to sail to France and to take from there overall command of the operation. And in May two other conspirators—one with the now-impenetrable alias of Joseph Cohen, and the other not now known by either alias or actual name—shipped to London, probably with their own supply of dynamite, to settle in and await the coming of their three co-conspirators.

Before the *City of Chester* docked in Liverpool, however, the Metropolitan police knew that the dynamitards were coming and were already taking steps to scotch the conspiracy. By 1887, the detective force of the Metropolitan Police had grown since 1842 from a force of eight to one of over six hundred and had become much more specialized. Assistant Commissioner James Monro, head of the Criminal Investigation Department (CID), commanded in 1887 a Special anti-terrorist Branch, formed in 1883 specifically to track down Fenian dynamiters. He commanded as well a separate division called (among other things) Section D: a highly secret national security service established to surveil anarchists and Fenians. Monro, in other words, oversaw both detectives and spies. He used both to destroy the Jubilee Plot.

The secret of the Jubilee Plot was an open one in the United States since at least the beginning of May, when the *New York Times* reported that Irish nationalists planned to disrupt the Queen's Jubilee. On the first day of June, the London *Times* warned of "a pyrotechnic display in honour of the Queen's Jubilee or in other words a series of dynamite and incendiary outrages to startle the nation amid the peaceful rejoicings of the month which opens today." As it happens, the then-anonymous writer of that article knew what he was talking about: he was Assistant Commissioner James Monro's second-in-command, Robert Anderson. Anderson controlled the Metropolitan Police's most valuable asset in the war against Irish-American terror—a British spy by the name of Thomas Beach, who, posing as a Frenchman, Henri Le Caron, had for twenty years penetrated the highest ranks of the Fenian Brotherhood and the Clan-na-Gael. Thanks to Beach, Monro and his detectives knew that Alexander Sullivan and his branch of the Clan were behind the campaign. They knew that Millen had been sent to France to command the operation. But they knew nothing about Moroney, Harkins, or Callan. Indeed, for all they knew, the dynamitards were already in London, plotting their attack.

Monro therefore acted to cut the known conspirator, Millen, away from the unknown ones. He sent several detectives across the Channel to shadow Millen's every move and prevent him from crossing to England; he then sent the Chief Superintendent of the CID to confront him and inform him that they knew about the plot and his role in it. Millen, duly intimidated, only acted in one way that seemed to support the plot: he wrote three letters of introduction for Moroney to three Irish Nationalist members of Parliament, thus providing Moroney with an entry into the House of Commons. While those letters seemed to help Moroney, they more than likely actually helped the police. For there was another reason why Millen proved to be a weak link in the plot: for over twenty years, off and on, Millen had been an informer to the British government. As a double-agent, it is more than likely that he never intended to assist the Jubilee plotters. Copies of the letters of introduction had reached Monro before the originals were given to Moroney, suggesting that Millen almost certainly betrayed his fellows. Those letters of introduction proved crucial in discovering the bombers.

But the letters only came into Monro's possession after 21 June, and so he experienced a harrowing Jubilee Day. He knew on that day that the plot was afoot and had little idea how far it had progressed. For all he knew, Fenians might have succeeded in planting a bomb in the bowels of Westminster Abbey, one the police had been unable to discover when they searched the building the day before. Monro and his family had tickets in the Abbey to view the thanksgiving. He left his children at home, but he and his wife attended. While they were there, and just as Victoria and her family began their procession from Buckingham Palace to the Abbey, Monro was handed a message stating that conspirators had indeed succeeded in planting a bomb in the Abbey. "I was never in a more delicate position in my life," he later wrote. To alert the crowd now would precipitate a deadly panic. In the end, Monro did nothing but pray. Meanwhile Victoria, who had been reassured by her Home Secretary Henry Matthews that all was safe, proceeded without fear to the Abbey. As usual, she reveled in the crowds, later writing in her journal "there was such an extraordinary outburst of enthusiasm as I had hardly ever seen in London before." Alighting at the Abbey, Victoria slowly walked up the nave and choir to take her place on the Coronation Chair, far less concerned with the threat of dynamite than with the pleasing fact that she did not see Mr. Gladstone (although he was there). The service began and ended; Victoria's children, children-in-law, and grandchildren approached and kissed her hand; all proceeded back to the Palace. There was no bomb. Millen had been disabled. Cohen and his comrade were not prepared. Moroney, Harkins, and Callan were not even in London, having that very day stepped off the *City of Chester* in Liverpool.

Monro knew, however, that the threat had not passed. Within a couple days, Moroney, Harkins, and Callan were in London; they took up lodgings all around the metropolis. They all represented themselves as traveling salesmen—a dealer in tea, Thomas Callan told his landlady. Having missed their golden opportunity on Jubilee Day, they began to explore other uses for their dynamite. Thomas Callan was twice sent to Windsor Castle with a stopwatch to time how quickly he could plant a bomb in the State Apartments and escape to the railway station. His timing was bad; the state apartments were closed both times, and Callan never returned for fear he would be recognized. Moroney, using one of the letters of introduction Millen had written for him, with Harkins twice visited the House of Commons, where they were shown around by an Irish member; Callan, too, was observed to lurk about the place. Harkins was later found with a newspaper clipping detailing an upcoming public appearance of the Chief Secretary for Ireland, Arthur Balfour. The dynamiters planned, but did not act—and the Jubilee season passed.

Monro, in the meantime, managed progressively to strangle their operation. When Moroney and Harkins appeared at the House of Commons, detectives were waiting; they lost Harkins but followed Moroney to his lodgings. Monro then quickly applied the same pressure upon Moroney that he had on Millen, setting a police guard upon him and sending a detective to his lodgings to question him "closely." Thus exposed and spooked, Moroney soon fled to Paris, taking most of the dynamiters' funds with him; there he took up with a young American woman named Miss Kennedy, and the two proceeded to spend the Clan-na-Gael funds with abandon. Moroney lost contact with his subordinates completely, even though he returned to London twice during the next few weeks. In September he abandoned the mission altogether, decamping with Miss Kennedy to New York.*

He left behind him a money trail which Monro used to shut down the disintegrating plot completely. Soon after arriving in London in June, Moroney had cashed drafts for over £500 into Bank of England £5 notes. The cashier had carefully noted the numbers of all those bills, and when Monro discovered Moroney's complicity in the plot, he placed a watch at all banks for anyone cashing them. At the beginning of September, Joseph Cohen cashed two of the notes, writing his signature and address on them. He thus led police to his lodgings. Moroney, before fleeing, had entrusted Cohen with the dynamite, in two heavy tin boxes. Days after cashing the £5 notes, however, Cohen collapsed with a serious pulmonary illness, and, fearing exposure, Michael Harkins, with the help of a muscular cabman, moved the dynamite out of Cohen's lodgings. One of the boxes ended up under Thomas Callan's bed. The other disappeared. Cohen's illness quickly worsened; police watched Harkins and Callan come and go repeatedly, nursing the dying man.

In mid-October, Monro exerted pressure again, this time upon Michael Harkins: two police descended on his lodgings demanding he give an account of himself, and discovered his loaded Smith & Wesson pistol as well as his newspaper clipping detailing Irish Secretary Balfour's upcoming public engagement. Harkins, shaken, raced to Cohen's lodgings, where he found that his comrade had just died. The police found Harkins there and arrested him. They

---

* Moroney later married Miss Kennedy, and within a year he was implicated in what was called "the Crime of the Century" in the United States: the assassination of Dr. Patrick Henry Cronin, a Clan-na-Gael rival of his friend Alexander Sullivan.

soon released him for lack of evidence, but Monro established an around-the-clock watch by six officers who moved into his lodgings. Harkins could do nothing but try to run, writing to Philadelphia begging for someone to buy him a passage home.

Harkins's immobilization left at large only Thomas Callan (with his dynamite) and the mysterious fifth plotter. Callan was surprised when, in the days after Harkins's arrest, Harkins did not show up for prearranged meetings. On 26 October, however, all became painfully clear to him when he read in the newspapers accounts of the inquest of Joseph Cohen. Monro appeared personally at the inquest and used the occasion to expose the dynamite plot to the public, revealing all he knew about Millen, Moroney, Cohen, and Harkins to reporters and thus to the world.

Callan panicked. He was holding most of the hard evidence of the plot: he had to dispose of the "tea," as he called it. The detonators he threw into a local pond. But the dynamite was too heavy for that. And so he dragged the slabs to the back garden and into his lodging house's water closet. He flushed away as much as he could, until the pipe was blocked. He dragged the rest to a nearby dustbin, and for some reason threw some of it over the wall, into a neighbor's back garden. (A week later, a boy living there, looking for something with which to line the floor of his pigeon-coop, put some of it in the oven to dry it out: the resulting explosion blew the oven door apart.) Since Moroney had entrusted Callan with none of the funds, Callan was broke, and trapped: he hunkered down in his lodgings, feigning or feeling illness, refusing to leave his bed. He too wrote home, begging for passage back to Massachusetts. And then he waited.

Three weeks later, in mid-November, Callan thought he had found his path to freedom. On the evening of the seventeenth, a stranger came to his lodgings demanding to see him; he was shown up and left ten minutes later. It was almost certainly the mysterious and anonymous fifth conspirator, who handed to Callan four Bank of England £5 notes—some of the money that Moroney had cashed six months before. The man then left the house and vanished from the observation of the police and from history—though for some time he remained in Monro's mind as a potentially dangerous loose end of the Jubilee Plot.

The next day, Callan received even better news: a letter had arrived from Lowell with a draft for more money—and a prepaid passage to Boston on the Cunard Line. Callan emerged from hiding to cash the £5 notes, to buy a new pair of boots, to disguise himself by shaving off his whiskers. Cashing the £5 notes doomed him: his banker noted their numbers and stalled Callan as he summoned an officer of the City Police. That officer shadowed Callan long enough to conclude that he was about to flee, and then arrested him. Monro ordered Harkins arrested as well. Both were at Scotland Yard by evening.

In the end, only Callan and Harkins went to trial; they alone paid the price for the bungling and double-dealing of their commanders. From the back garden of Callan's lodgings, the police were able to collect over twenty-five pounds of sodden dynamite, which police chemists were able to determine to be of American make. Traces of the stuff were found in both their portmanteaus. At trial in February 1888, Harkins and Callan were both found guilty under the Explosive Substances Act of 1883 and sentenced to fifteen years penal servitude each. Never ceasing to maintain his innocence, Harkins was released from prison in 1892, seriously debilitated by tuberculosis, and died the next year in Philadelphia. Callan—according to a chief constable who interviewed him, "the most harmless of all the dynamiters with whom I have been brought into contact"—at first maintained his innocence as well but later confessed, revealing to police among other things his close encounter with the royal residence at Windsor, if not with the royal person. Monro recommended that Callan be given early release, and after he had served five years of his sentence Callan was quickly put aboard ship and returned via New York to Lowell, whose citizens had never stopped believing that "Poor Tommy Callan" had been railroaded by the perfidious British. They greeted him as a hero. Callan did not have long to enjoy his minor celebrity; a year later, he was thrown from a cart, smashed his leg, and died.

The botched plot to disrupt the queen's Golden Jubilee turned out to be the final skirmish in the Irish-American dynamite war. But the threat to the Queen did not disappear. As the danger of Fenian terror bombing receded, that of pan-European anarchism grew. Following Lucheni's assassination of Empress Elisabeth of Austria in 1898, in 1900, Gaetano Bresci killed King Umberto of Italy with four bullets from a .32 revolver. His assassination inspired Leon Czolgosz to kill American President William McKinley a year later.

The anarchist threat hit home on 4 April 1900, when Victoria's son Bertie was for the only time of his life the target of an assassin's bullet. The Boer War was at that time raging, and across Europe British popularity was at a nadir, so low that Bertie and Princess Alexandra chose to forgo their usual trip to Biarritz for a safer place: Alix's native Denmark. They travelled through Belgium, and at the Gare du Nord on the afternoon of the fourth, just as their train was leaving the station, a boy jumped upon the carriage footboard, thrust a pistol through the window, and from six feet away fired two shots at the Prince. He missed. Bertie later enjoyed joking in letters to his friends about the "pauvre fou," and about his relief that anarchists could not shoot straight. Victoria was in Ireland on that day, commencing her final and triumphal carriage rides among the "wildly enthusiastic" crowds of Dublin; Beatrice told her of the attempt. "Was greatly shocked and upset," she wrote in her journal.*

---

* The attempt became the occasion for a mythic and mythical moment in the history of swearing. A multitude of sites on the Internet today state as fact that the Prince of Wales, when shot at, cried out "Fuck it, I've taken a bullet!" No contemporary account of the shooting, however, mentions this utterance. And the fact that the Prince of Wales did *not* take a bullet strongly suggests that this colorful response is apocryphal.

The assailant's name was Jean-Baptiste Sipido. He was only fifteen years old—younger than any of Victoria's assailants. But he was more truly politically inspired than any of them; he was already a fanatical member of an anarchist club. The Prince of Wales asked Belgian authorities not to treat Sipido too severely, but nevertheless he and the British public were surprised and angered two months later when Sipido was, because of his age, found not mentally responsible for his act. He was set free and immediately fled to France. (He was later extradited to Belgium, where he was confined in a penitentiary until he reached the age of twenty-one.)

At the time of this shooting, Bertie was less than a year away from taking the throne himself—not as Albert I, of course, but as Edward VII. His mother, in the last year of her reign, was already suffering the accumulation of ailments and the slow decline of her faculties that would lead to her death at the very commencement of the twentieth century. Her body was giving out; she routinely travelled in a wheelchair, and her eyesight was fading. Her popularity, however, remained undiminished; indeed, if it were possible, it grew with her every appearance. Those appearances continued until nearly the end. As always, these periodic showings of herself were not motivated by any joy she took in them. She *did* take joy in them, but always after suffering fretting, nervous anticipation: the actual pleasure she felt among her people was perpetually a rediscovery to her, as was the fact that she had become an icon—London's greatest attraction. In 1890, for instance, Victoria was surprised that the public would mass simply to get a moment's view of her when she traveled to London for the interment of one of her beloved ladies, the Marchioness of Ely, at Kensal Green Cemetery. Noting the masses at the cemetery gates, Victoria wrote in her journal "there were crowds out, we could not understand why, and thought something must be going [on], but it turned out it was only to see me." She might have been baffled at the time, but achieving the personal popularity illustrated on that day had of course been Victoria's life's work, and by the end of her reign the very legitimacy of the institution depended absolutely upon that popular desire "only to see me."

And it was during the last two decades of Victoria's reign that British royal ceremonial reached its zenith, with the two great showpieces of the prestige of Victoria's monarchy, the Golden Jubilee of 1887 and the Diamond Jubilee of 1897. The first was a celebration of Victoria's primacy among monarchs as the royalty of Europe gathered to pay homage to her. The second, under the direction of the Queen's imperialist Minister for the Colonies, Joseph Chamberlain, celebrated the greatness of the British Empire, a greatness embodied by the small but stout woman who had just surpassed her grandfather George III in having the longest reign of any English monarch. Both occasions entirely depended for their success simply upon Victoria going out among her people in processions. Indeed, the Diamond Jubilee consisted *only* of a procession, as the Queen, in 1897 no longer able to walk into St. Paul's for the Thanksgiving Service, refused to be carried inside, and instead viewed from her carriage a short *Te Deum* on the cathedral steps before continuing back to Buckingham Palace.

Before both Jubilees, Victoria underwent the same emotional turbulence she had before the 1872 thanksgiving procession: with an apprehension growing to trepidation at the prospect of plunging into the enormous crowds drew near. And then she experienced them with an ecstatic joy and a great sense of oneness with her people. "A never-to-be-forgotten day," she wrote on Diamond Jubilee Day, 22 June 1897. "No one ever, I believe, has met with such an ovation as was given to me, passing through those six miles of streets. . . . The crowds were quite undescribable, and their enthusiasm truly marvellous and deeply touching. The cheering was quite deafening, and every face seemed to be filled with real joy."

She was right: no one in London had ever met with such an ovation. Certainly no monarch before her had experienced anything like the sheer popular jubilation of 1851, or 1872, 1887, 1897—and in 1900, the last year of her life, when in March Victoria went forth in her carriage to celebrate the relief of the South African city of Ladysmith. "Everywhere," Victoria wrote, "the same enormous crowds and incessant demonstrations of enthusiasm; if possible, even beyond that of the two Jubilees." That night, she stood before a window in Buckingham Palace with a light placed behind her, so the crowds could see and cheer her. Lord Rosebery, her Prime Minister five years before, was deeply impressed by her actions, writing to her:

> I saw your Majesty three times in the streets and in the Park; and my overpowering feeling was "What a glorious privilege to be able to make millions so happy!" No one who saw London then will ever forget it, or will cease to pray for the prolongation of your Majesty's life, and of your Majesty's priceless and unceasing exertions for your Empire.

Victoria lived for eight months after that. In those months, her eldest son was shot at, and her second son, Alfred, died. In December she was able to make the trip by train and royal yacht one more time to Osborne; there, she lived through one more Christmas, made miserable by the death of one of her favorite ladies, Jane Churchill; there she saw in the new century, dictating to a granddaughter one of her last journal entries: "Another year begun, and I am feeling so weak and unwell that I enter upon it sadly." And there she weakened and took to her deathbed, flickering in and out of consciousness, and probably never realizing on 19 January that she had become the oldest as well as the longest-reigning monarch of Britain.* Her family gathered around her, in a tableau similar to Albert's death nearly forty years before. On the evening of 22 January it was clear that the end was coming.

---

* Victoria lived longer than her grandfather George III by all of five days. Elizabeth II has since exceeded her great-great grandmother's longevity.

Her children each stood before her, identifying themselves and giving their good-byes. She died in the arms of her grandson Kaiser Wilhelm, "a look of radiance on her face." Her oldest son, now King Edward, closed her eyes, and broke down.

She made one more procession—more subdued than any, but also more fully attended: the journey of her body, across the Solent and to London, past a million of her subjects in the metropolis, all of them, for once, eerily silent, to Paddington Station and Windsor and the funeral at St. George's Chapel—and then to Frogmore, and to silence by the side of her husband.

To Victoria's successors, and to the British people of the twentieth and twenty-first centuries, the popular bond between monarch and public, and the primacy of that popular bond to the legitimacy of the monarchy, seems natural and timeless, a part of the very definition of monarchy, codified and sanctified by royal ceremonies that themselves seem timeless. But these ceremonies are not at all timeless. The royal weddings, the Jubilees, the walkabouts and openings, the triumphal appearances upon the royal balcony, are Victorian creations. And the concept that underlies them, the yoking of royal legitimacy and popular will, is a Victorian concept as well—or, to put it more clearly, is Queen Victoria's concept—a redefinition of monarchy that became her life's work. Though Victoria throughout her life feared public appearances, she steeled herself to make them. Though as she grew older she grew more anxious about the hubbub of London and the shot of the next assailant, she continued to ride out, in open carriages, to accept and to return the goodwill of the people. She was helped in redefining the monarchy by John Conroy, who while hateful to her in every other way, did teach her the valuable lesson: the fundamental importance of popular acclaim. She was helped greatly by her beloved Albert, a foreigner who nevertheless understood instinctively and intellectually the importance of his wife's bond with the people, and devoted his life to promoting it, subsuming himself in her elevation. She was helped by her prime ministers—by Peel and Russell and Disraeli and Salisbury and Gladstone—especially by Gladstone—all of whom did their part to answer "the royalty question" in a way beneficial to the institution. And she was greatly helped—more greatly than they would ever know, and than she would ever admit—by her seven assailants, who in deciding to take a pop at the Queen had no intention whatsoever to strengthen the British monarchy, but who nevertheless gave Victoria seven golden opportunities to do exactly that.

All seven of Victoria's assailants, once they had satisfied their "diseased craving" for notoriety and had their few days in the public spotlight, quickly faded from public attention. Of the seven, only one—Arthur O'Connor—made any sort of attempt to return to it. O'Connor's arrest at Buckingham Palace in 1874, after three years' dissatisfaction in Sydney and obscurity in London, went unnoticed by most, and was less an attempt to regain notoriety and more a successful cry for medical help. With this qualified exception, Victoria's seven assailants shunned public attention; they scattered across England and Australia, or more accurately, were scattered by her Majesty's government, which used every means it could to distance them from their queen. All seven lived on for many years after their attempts. Several lived lives of quiet contentment, suggesting that the harsh psychiatric and penal regimens they endured had a therapeutic and rehabilitative effect. Others, however, suffered until the ends of their lives, in confinement, and in quiet— or not so quiet—desperation.

Edward Oxford, though deemed insane by the court, was considered sane by the doctors at Bethlem from the moment he entered the place, and every medical professional with whom he came in contact over the next twenty-seven years concurred. "Reported sane since his reception," his Bethlem case notes state, that opinion restated emphatically with the same entry repeated through the years: "no change." Contrary to the public perception that Oxford had beat the system and procured himself a life of ease and contentment, Oxford found Bethlem excruciating. He deserved a horse-whipping for his actions, he told a reporter in 1850, not indefinite imprisonment. Nevertheless, no one ever put sane confinement in an insane asylum to better use. Bethlem became his university, and in an obsessive course of study he became fluent in French, German, and Italian. He learned some Spanish, Latin, and Greek as well. He drew; he wrote poetry, his one surviving poem consoling Victoria on the death of the Prince Consort. He outshone his fellow patients in everything he undertook: at knitting gloves, at chess and draughts—and as a painter. He developed in particular great skill in graining, or in simulating wood-grain and marble-lines with paint. When, in 1864, Broadmoor Hospital replaced Bethlem as the national repository for the criminally insane, Oxford was one of the very last to make the trip there. He was from the start "the most orderly, most useful, and most trusted of all the inmates" there; his painting skills were in constant demand and allowed him in time to accumulate £50 or £60. Soon after he arrived at Broadmoor, his doctors attempted to correct the anomaly of a sane man in a lunatic asylum, pleading with the government that he be released. In 1864 the government refused to listen, but in 1867 Home Secretary Gathorne Gathorne-Hardy reviewed Oxford's record and made him a deal: Oxford could go free if he moved to one of her Majesty's colonies and agreed never to return to England. Oxford agreed, knowing exactly where he wanted to go— Melbourne, Victoria, Australia. His decision was motivated not because the place yoked together the names of the queen he had shot at and her prime minister at the time, but because the place had over the years become familiar to him. Twenty-four years earlier, George Henry Haydon had come to Bethlem as steward, and Oxford quickly discovered in him a friend. Haydon was Oxford's own age, and as a young man had explored and then published an account of that part of southeast Australia then known as *Australia Felix*, happy Australia, and later known as the area about Melbourne, Victoria. He often lectured to the patients and spoke to

Oxford about the place; *Australia Felix* became symbolic to Oxford as a place of free men.

In November 1867, then, Oxford, adopting the simple and telling alias of John Freeman,* left Broadmoor in the company of an attendant, took a train to Plymouth, and alone boarded the *Suffolk*, which the next March landed at Melbourne. "Whatever has occurred in the past," he wrote to Haydon in leaving England, "in the future no man shall say I am unworthy of the name of an Englishman."

He was as good as his word. Oxford took up as a painter and grainer and became fully engaged in Melbourne's literary community. He was amused to discover that people in Melbourne thought him "cosmopolitan" because of his London origins. He joined and became vice president of the West Melbourne Mutual Improvement Society. He undertook investigative forays into the Melbourne underworld—sometimes in disguise—and published his observations in Melbourne's leading newspaper. He joined the congregation of Melbourne's oldest Anglican church and served for several years as its churchwarden. In 1881 he married a well-off widow and became a stepfather. And in 1888, the year of an International Exhibition in Melbourne, he found a publisher in London for his sketches, *Lights and Shadows of Melbourne Life*. He sent a copy of the book to Haydon, hoping with Haydon's help to pursue a full-blown literary career with the publications of stories and his memoirs. "There are many old friends . . . in England," he wrote to Haydon, "who would be pleased to hear of me again; and I should like a certain illustrious lady to know that one who was a foolish boy half a century ago, is now a respectable, & respected, member of society." Nothing, however, came of his plans, and the true identity of John Freeman remained a secret shared only between Oxford

---

* Perhaps his choice of name was simple symbolism; perhaps it was sentimental: the marriage register of a church in Lambeth shows that on 21 May 1833, one Hannah Oxford married a man named Edward Freeman. Oxford might have been commemorating a long-lost and short-lived stepfather by taking his surname.

and Haydon. "Even my wife," Oxford told Haydon, "the sharer of my joys, and sorrows, is no wiser than the rest of the world." He took his secret to the grave, dying on 23 April 1900, sixty years after his attempt and seventy-eight years of age.

If Edward Oxford's life demonstrates the rehabilitative effects of Bethlem and Broadmoor, John Francis's later life demonstrates the similar effect of years at the hardest of hard labor in Van Diemen's Land. Francis was sent, soon after his arrival in 1842, to the remote penal colony offering the severest level of punishment on the island: Port Arthur. Convicts there experienced eternal vigilance and unceasing, crushing labor. The place was a "purgatorial grinding mill rather than a torture chamber," in the words of the foremost historian of Australian transportation, a preparation for a higher, less demanding, and more trusted position. Francis emerged after four years from that purgatorial fire a better man. Indeed, he emerged triumphantly, earning a six-month remission of his stay there by raising the alarm when a fire broke out. He was transferred to Launceston, and clearly impressed everyone with whom he came in contact there by his good character. Two years later, in 1848, he fell in love with a free sixteen-year-old girl, Martha Clarke, and married her. While still a convict he fathered several children, eventually fathering ten in all. (Francis's descendants in the antipodes are now numerous.) Eight years into his sentence he obtained his ticket of leave, allowing him to seek private employment; he found it with a Launceston builder who was impressed with his industry and sobriety. After ten years, he sought a conditional pardon—the condition, of course, being his never returning to England. Lord Palmerston, Home Secretary at the time, refused to give it. Three years afterwards, Francis tried again, this time supported by the leading citizens of Tasmania; a petition in his support was signed by the mayors of Hobart and Launceston, Launceston's Catholic bishop, and other notables. Palmerston's successor in the Home Office, George Grey, agreed, and in August 1856 Francis was free to travel about Australia and to operate his own business. During the next decade he moved with wife and some of his children across Bass Strait to Melbourne, where he worked as a contractor. Except for an episode in 1869 in Melbourne's insolvency court—his debts, Francis claimed, caused by an illness in the family—he, like Oxford, apparently lived the life of a well-adjusted, productive, fairly-well-off Melbournian. He died in 1885, aged sixty-three.

John William Bean was the only one of the seven whose attempt did not in the end result in his expulsion from London: he lived there his entire life. He served his eighteen months' imprisonment in Millbank penitentiary, on the bank of the Thames and not too far from Buckingham Palace. Because of his weak constitution, his hard-labor sentence was modified to work at tailoring. During his last month of imprisonment, his father died, and so he returned home as the eldest, if the least respected, male in his family. He attempted to take up his father's profession as a jeweler, and listed that as his profession when in 1846 he married a woman by the name of Esther Martin. That marriage did not last, but lasted long enough to produce a son, Samuel Bean. (Samuel Bean predeceased his father—but before he died produced a son, who in turn had children of his own; Bean and John Francis are the only two assailants who are known to have living descendants.)*

By 1851 John William Bean had given up his father's profession, and taken up the one he had earlier found more fitting for his health and talents: he again became a newsvendor. When Hamilton, Pate, and O'Connor made their attempts, therefore, Bean probably sold newspapers reporting on them. Bean was the only one of the seven who had the opportunity to celebrate with other Londoners the Queen's escape from every one of his successors. Considering his deeply depressed nature, which apparently only worsened with

---

* Although there is no record of a divorce (which would have been extremely difficult to obtain at the time), the marriage most certainly ended in separation and not with a death: Esther Bean lived on, dying in 1898 in Greenwich Workhouse. When Bean remarried in 1863, then, he likely became a bigamist.

age, it is unlikely that he did so. He did, however, manage to marry again, in 1863. His depression, likely mixed with thoughts of suicide, led to confinement in an asylum sometime around 1876. The entry in the 1881 Census shows that life had not improved; he is listed there as a "newsagent out of work." When in February 1882 Maclean made his attempt, Bean was likely in a depressive torpor. Five months later, he gave up altogether. A snippet in *Lloyd's Weekly* reveals his state of mind at the end:

OPIUM POISONING AT CAMBERWELL.—On Friday Mr. Carter concluded an inquiry at St. Thomas's hospital, relative to the death of John William Bean, aged 58, a retired newsvendor, lately residing at 3, The Crescent, Southampton-street, Camberwell, who expired from the effects of poison, alleged to have been self-administered, on Wednesday, the 19th July. The deceased was discovered in bed, with a bottle labelled "Poison" near him, on the day mentioned, and died the same evening. A letter was found, in which the deceased, who five years ago was confined in a lunatic asylum, stated that he was an incumbrance [sic] to his wife, and was only too glad to die. To admit of an analysis of the stomach, and an examination of the contents of the bottle, the inquiry was adjourned till Friday. It was now shown by the evidence of Mr. Sutton that the stomach contained a large quantity of opium, and it was to this poison that the death of the deceased was attributable. The jury returned a verdict of "Temporary insanity."

The jury was being merciful, of course; a verdict of insanity rather than suicide allowed Bean a Christian burial.

Of the seven assailants, William Hamilton was the one who most shunned notoriety, wanting only the security of life in prison and the preservation of his anonymity. For better or worse, he got exactly what he wanted. He was sentenced to seven years' transportation just as the concept of that penalty was altering, so that Australia became not the first stage on the road to rehabilitation, as it was for Francis, but the last—freedom in Australia becoming the reward for years of penal servitude and slow rehabilitation elsewhere. Into this new system Hamilton was thrown, and thus experienced the full range of mid-Victorian penal life. He was taken from Newgate to Millbank and then quickly on to Pentonville, the usual first stage for most prisoners sentenced to transportation in the late 1840s and early 1850s. Pentonville was the "model" prison for the many others that practiced the "separate" system— an imprisonment in which prisoners were doomed to unceasing solitude. Each was confined to his own cell and prohibited from speaking with fellow prisoners, or even looking at them: when together, prisoners were compelled to wear caps with masking visors to hide their individuality from one another. This harrowing system—another Victorian purgatory—was intended to cleanse prisoners morally by forcing them to reflect upon their past moral failings; critics, backed by statistics, claimed it was more likely to lead to madness than moral improvement. After six months at Pentonville—a stay shorter than the usual, gestational, nine months—Hamilton moved to the next rehabilitative step, shipping to the public works at the small penal colony at Gibraltar, where prisoners toiled at constructing and strengthening the harborworks and fortifications. In a colony in which unskilled labor was the norm, Hamilton's masonry skills set him apart. He spent four and a half years at Gibraltar, and finally embarked in May 1854 on the *Ramillies* for Australia. By that year, transportation had been restricted to the point that only one colony—Western Australia— still accepted transported convicts. Accordingly, Hamilton, having served the bulk of his sentence, landed at Fremantle and was placed in prison there. After less than a month, in August 1854, he was granted his ticket of leave. His conditional pardon followed a year and a half later. Hamilton walked out of Fremantle prison and into complete obscurity—a position surely very much to his liking. He might have come to the attention of the authorities one more time, nearly twenty years later, when an ex-convict by his name was up before a magistrate in Perth for neglecting to report his arrival to that city, as conditional pardon-holders were required to do. That might have been William Hamilton, but it might not have been—there were other ex-convict William Hamiltons in Western Australia at the time. Where and when he died remains a mystery.

Robert Pate's effrontery in actually touching Victoria, as well perhaps as his military past and his father's wealth, called for a swifter removal from England than Hamilton experienced. Pate bypassed the revised system altogether, shipping less than a month after his conviction on the *William Jardine* to Van Diemen's Land, to serve his entire sentence there. Life aboard ship seems to have had a remarkably positive psychological effect upon the man, a reporter at Hobart noting at his arrival there "we understand that he has shown no symptoms of insanity upon the passage." He was quickly shipped down-island to the remote Cascades Punishment Station, scheduled to work a full year at hard labor on a chain gang. He set to the task with the determination of an ex-officer of the 10th Royal Hussars. His hard work earned him an eighty-day remission of his sentence, so that in just over nine months, in June 1881, he returned to Hobart and was employed at the milder task of clerking for John Abbott, the registrar of births, marriages, and deaths for Van Diemen's Land. Pate acquitted himself well enough to earn Abbott's recommendation for a Conditional Pardon. He obtained his ticket of leave in September 1853, leaving him free to seek private employment. But apparently he sought none: his father's money now allowed him to live as a gentleman, and that is exactly how he designated himself when he applied for a conditional pardon. That pardon was granted at the end of 1855, and a year and a half later his sentence expired, leaving him free to return home. He was, however, in no hurry to do so. As if in celebration of his complete freedom, he got married just as his sentence ended. Announcements of the wedding said nothing of his being a convict and much about being an ex-officer of the 10th Royal Hussars. He and his wife Mary Elizabeth resided among the elite of Hobart, in an eleven-room mansion complete with stables, coach house, and a brewery. Clearly Robert Pate Sr. had been generous—or, more likely, his legacy had been, as the old man had died in 1856, leaving the bulk of his £70,000 fortune to his only son. Pate was a jealous guardian of his property, as was demonstrated in 1858 when he and his wife hauled an eleven-year-old girl into police court for stealing a sixpenny flowerpot from the front of their house.*

In April 1865, the Pates, having sold their mansion, embarked on the *Robert Morrison* for London. Pate traveled to Wisbech to take care of his father's estate and his servants, to whom he was said to be "remarkably kind," setting up each a pension. He then took up life as a country gentleman not in Cambridgeshire but in Croydon, Surrey, in a home ironically not very distant from the building which had been so much in the news at the time of Pate's assault—Paxton's Crystal Palace, dismantled in Hyde Park after the exhibition, remodeled, and rebuilt in Sydenham. Robert Pate lived, apparently happily and free from his previous obsessions, with Mrs. Pate until he died in 1895, leaving his wife over £22,000—a generous amount, but one that suggests that his gentleman's lifestyle chipped away at the bulk of his father's estate.

Four years after Pate's death, and two years before Victoria's, an object reputed to be the cane with which Robert Pate had struck the Queen went up for auction in London. Word of the proposed sale soon reached Osborne, where the queen was staying, and an official communication soon went out from there to the owner of

---

* To be fair to the Pates, Robert did ask the magistrates to be lenient to the girl, and stated he had only brought her in because they had recently experienced a spate of unsolved thefts.

the cane, who immediately withdrew the cane from sale. It was never seen again.

Although Victoria seemed safely protected from Arthur O'Connor after he was arrested in 1875 and committed to Hanwell Asylum, his stay there turned out to be a brief one, and for a time he continued to be a problem to the police and to the government. He was discharged eighteen months after he was committed to Hanwell as fully cured. Because he was not confined at the Queen's pleasure, the government could do nothing to keep him there or keep him from returning to his family in London, which is exactly what he did. For two years he worked as a copying clerk. His father having died, he claimed that his income was the principal support of his entire family. But he lost that job and as his mother slipped deeper into alcoholism, his family sank deeper into penury. By the end of 1880, O'Connor had grown sick of that life; he approached the police to make an offer to the government much like the one he had brokered eight years before: he would be willing to travel to Australia if the government paid his expenses and found him employment. The government agreed. In January, he shipped to Sydney on the *Helenslea*, disembarking on 20 April, again adopting his Australian alias of George Morton. Henry Parkes, Premier of New South Wales, had taken a personal interest in his case and had procured him a clerkship with a prominent Sydney solicitor. But O'Connor never took the position. Soon after his arrival, the Inspector General of Police reported to Augustus Loftus, the Governor, that O'Connor had been arrested for being drunk, that he had lashed out violently while at the police court—that he was insane and belonged in an asylum. "On his first visit he was a thoughtless youth," Parkes told Loftus; "he has now become an unmitigated ruffian." After assaulting a policeman, O'Connor was restrained, examined, and sent to the lunatic asylum at Callan Park.

He spent the rest of his life in a variety of Sydney asylums, his mind cycling between lucidity and confusion. At times he was considered well enough for short furloughs from his hospitals. At other times he was compelled to escape, only to be returned by the police after a day or two, or to return himself. His psychological state deteriorated; certainly, no doctor ever saw fit to recommend his release. The assigned cause of O'Connor's illness—a diagnosis which never changed as he was transferred from one asylum to another over the years—must surely have galled him, the most ambitious and imaginative of Victoria's would-be assassins. The doctors never considered his illness hereditary—something that may have linked him with his heroic great-uncle Feargus. They never saw poetic, or political, or religious overimagination at the heart of his illness: any of these he would have understood and perhaps would have been proud of. Rather, the doctors all believed his illness was caused by what the Inspector General of the Sydney Police first termed in 1881 "habits of self-indulgence." The Inspector General of the New South Wales Lunacy Department quickly concurred, concluding that Morton was "suffering from considerable mental irritation which is fostered by his debased habits." The Callan Park casebook is blunter: the disorder was melancholia, the cause "masturbation." As late as 1912, when O'Connor was fifty-eight years old and his hair was graying, the cause of his madness was listed as "Onanism."

O'Connor's asylum casebooks record instances of voices in his head, delusions of persecution, and wild hallucinations. Once he refused to drink anything for fear of drowning the Virgin Mary inside him. In 1882, soon after Roderick Maclean's attempt, he hallucinated that he saw his own brother point a pistol at the Queen.* At times he was a quiet and cooperative patient; at others hyper-inflated with self-importance; at others sullen and paranoid. In later years he took to writing persons of importance in New South Wales, pleading for a discharge. No one, of course, listened. O'Connor over the years was shifted from hospital to hospital, from Callan Park, to Parramatta, to Rydalmere, to Morriset, and then back to Rydalmere.

---

* One of O'Connor's brothers was named Roderick.

Roderick Maclean lived a similar long life, half a world away. He entered Broadmoor Hospital for the Criminally Insane fifteen years after Edward Oxford had left it, and the doctors knew from the start that he was a different patient altogether than Oxford had been. Not one of them considered Maclean sane or requested that the Home Office consider releasing him. Maclean, who had while free been hell-bent on finding a place in an asylum, was quickly discontented with his confinement at Broadmoor, and within twenty months of his committal he sent out the first of many petitions for his release. Lest Victoria think he was asking too soon, he assured her "you, I am sure are aware in questions of presumed insanity, duration of time of incarceration should not be considered." The petitions flowed from his pen for years, and he adopted several strategies to persuade Victoria to let him go. He tried aggressive innocence: "*I am innocent* of any guilty *intentions toward* the Queen"—his innocence requiring freedom and recompense, the government supporting him as his family once did: "I should require at least one hundred per annum and I should not accept a farthing less whether from relations or strangers. Any arrangements which did not include such an allowance or more would be entirely useless and would be sternly rejected." He tried abject contrition: "No language could express my sorrow for the past." He attempted the strategy that had worked for Oxford and O'Connor, promising to exile himself to a distant place—to Australia, where a brother lived, or, in one petition, to remote Scotland: "If Her Most Gracious Majesty will allow me to go and reside in the isle of my ancestors Mull on the west coast of Scotland as I intend to live a Christians life in sobriety and in quiet retirement from the Madding crowd and the hurly burly of the World hope to find a balm to my troubles and the troubles of those interested in my affairs." None of this had the slightest effect upon the Queen's pleasure. As the years passed, the petitions slowed. In 1894 Maclean made another attempt to reengage with the world, communicating with the editor of *The Sun* about publishing his poetry, or his memoirs. As the years passed, the voices in his head and the paranoia never left him. Victoria died and the Queen's pleasure became her son's; Edward VII died in 1910 and his pleasure became that of his son, George V.

Roderick Maclean and, half a world away, Arthur O'Connor lived on discontentedly while the world outside changed beyond recognition. Outside, the First World War came and went, taking with it the major monarchies of Europe—all except for the one that Victoria had done so much to preserve. The Victorian age passed; O'Connor and Maclean lived on into the age of the airplane, of radio—the age of Einstein, Eisenstein, and Gertrude Stein, of James Joyce and Virginia Woolf, jazz and *surréalisme*. Mussolini's fascism was ascendant in Italy; Hitler's fascism was slowly ascending in Germany. To both Maclean and O'Connor, the world outside would likely have seemed as mad as the world within. Roderick Maclean died on 9 May 1921, apoplexy stated as the cause. The news was reported as a sort of barely remembered bad dream. Arthur O'Connor—or George Morton, as no one called him Arthur O'Connor for the last forty-two years of his life—outlived Maclean by 4½ years, dying 6 December 1925 at the age of seventy, the cause of death listed as a painful abdominal ailment, tubercular peritonitis. O'Connor was buried in Rookwood Anglican Cemetery in Sydney, under his false name. There would be no monument to the last of the great O'Connors.

Citations

PART 1: YOUNG ENGLAND

Chapter 1: Wedding Portrait

3:      ... the "ganglion" of Southwark's twisted streets: Dickens, *Bleak House* 438.

4:      ... gave his neighborhood an unusual air of gentility: Bowers 466.

4:      ... carefully structured world: Andrews *et al.* 449.

5:      The documents showed Young England to be a highly disciplined, insurrectionary organization: Townsend 119.

5:      Captain Oxford had chosen the rather transparent alias of "Oxonian": TNA PRO MEPO 3/17.

5:      ... this manifesto, though signed by a fictitious secretary Smith, was in Oxford's own handwriting: "Edward Oxford."

6:      The sword would come: TNA PRO MEPO 3/17.

7:      Although dueling was technically illegal, the practice was carried on: Holland 223; Bresler 151; Rawlings 169.

7:      ... overpriced, according to one gunmaker, who later valued them at less than 30 shillings: *Times* 18 June 1840, 6.

7:      ... "coarsely and roughly finished," designed more for show than effect: *Times* 13 June 1840, 6; *Morning Chronicle* 11 June 1840, 2.

7:     . . . but they bore no maker's mark—an obvious sign of their shoddi-
       ness: *Morning Chronicle* 12 June 1840, 6.

7:     "Brummagem firearms": Dickens, *Letters* 2:82.

7:     . . . he bargained down the price of the pistols from 2 guineas (or £2
       and 2 shillings) to £2: *Morning Chronicle* 16 June 1840, 3; *Times* 10
       July 1840, 6.

8:     . . . a baker who worked at a local soda-water factory, but was on the
       verge of a major career change: *Morning Chronicle* 11 June 1840, 2;
       15 June 1840, 3.

8:     . . . he would very soon fall into arrears: *Morning Chronicle* 15 June
       1840, 3.

8:     . . . the arm injury he suffered as a boy, nearly blowing himself up
       while playing with fire and gunpowder: *Times* 11 June 1840, 4.

8:     "He said he would allow me half his pay": *Times* 11 July 1840, 7;
       Townsend 129.

9:     "He said nothing was stirring": *Times* 10 July 1840, 7.

9:     "How could you think of laying your money out in such folly!":
       Townsend 129.

9:     He raised one of the pistols and pointed it, cocked, at his mother's
       face: Townsend 129.

11:    "I write to you from here the happiest, happiest Being that ever
       existed": Hibbert, ed. 64-5.

11:    Albert was away, at the Royal Dockyard at Woolwich: *Times* 5 May
       1840, 5.

12:    " . . . my very intelligent factotum": Woodham-Smith, *Queen Vic-
       toria* 49.

12:    . . . the Duke of York resolved to remain unmarried: Woodham-
       Smith, *Queen Victoria* 57.

13:    A later companion forced upon her was the Duchess's Lady-in-
       Waiting, Lady Flora Hastings: Woodham-Smith, *Queen Victoria* 97,
       111.

13:    . . . she slept in a small bed in her mother's room, and could not
       walk down a flight of stairs without taking the hand of another:
       Woodham-Smith, *Queen Victoria* 57; Longford 38.

14:    "Victoria has not written that letter": Woodham-Smith, *Queen Vic-
       toria* 132-3.

14:    . . . and in one case a royal salute by cannon, a practice King William
       quickly put a stop to: Woodham-Smith, *Queen Victoria* 90-1.

14: "We just passed through a town where all coal mines are": Hibbert, ed. 11.

15: " . . . it is of the greatest consequence that you should be seen": Hibbert, *Queen Victoria* 39.

16: William turned venomously upon the Duchess, chastising her publicly for isolating the Princess from him: Woodham-Smith, *Queen Victoria* 126.

16: . . . she did all, as she pointedly notes in her journal, *"alone"*: Woodham-Smith, *Queen Victoria* 139; Charlot 81.

16: . . . she had removed her bed from her mother's room and had dismissed Conroy from her household: Longford 63-4.

17: . . . she looked over to him for cues about her behavior: Woodham-Smith, *Queen Victoria* 139

18: She drank in his adherence to *laissez-faire* economics: Longford 69.

18: Her popularity during this time was unparalleled: Woodham-Smith, *Queen Victoria* 154.

18: "It was a fine day": Hibbert, ed. 34.

19: " . . . the horrid cause of all this is the Monster & Demon Incarnate": Longford 97.

20: Sir Charles Clark "had said that though she is a virgin still that it might be possible": Hibbert, ed. 42.

20: At the end of March, one of Lady Flora's letters . . . appeared in the *Examiner*: Longford 103.

21: "Mrs. Melbourne": Longford 121.

21: . . . she sent her empty carriage to Lady Flora's funeral: some threw rocks at it: Longford 122.

21: Victoria was thrown into a "state of agony, grief and despair": Hibbert, ed. 45.

21: Sir Robert Peel was "stiff" and "close," according to Melbourne: Longford 110.

21: Melbourne . . . did her a great disservice: Longford 109.

22: "Sir Robert said, 'Now, about the Ladies,'": Hibbert, ed. 47.

23: Victoria . . . was cool to the idea of marriage: Longford 125.

23: "It was with some emotion that I beheld Albert—who is *beautiful*": Hibbert, ed. 55.

23: . . . her new object in life was, as she put it, to "strive to make him feel as little as possible the great sacrifice he has made": Hibbert, ed. 57.

23: Over the next three days, she sent encouraging messages to him: Woodham-Smith, *Queen Victoria* 183.

24: Albert quickly took upon himself what had been Lehzen's task of warming the Queen's tiny hands with his own: Longford 134.

24: "I signed some papers and warrants etc.": Hibbert, ed. 58.

25: "Here comes the bridegroom of Victoria's choice": James 89.

25: " . . . vile, confounded, infernal Tories": Hibbert, ed. 62.

25: Albert was far more complacent with the vote: Von Stockmar 2:31.

26: . . . her uncles Cambridge and Sussex at first agreed with her: Longford 136.

26: " . . . this wicked old foolish Duke, these confounded Tories, oh!": Woodham-Smith, *Queen Victoria* 199.

26: "You forget, my dearest Love, that I am the Sovereign, and that business can stop and wait for nothing": Hibbert, ed. 62.

27: "As to your wish about your gentlemen, my dear Albert": Victoria *Letters* (first series) 1:254.

27: "I never saw such crowds of people": Hibbert, ed. 63.

28: "He does look so beautiful in his shirt only": Hibbert, ed. 64.

28: "the husband, not the master of the house": James 104.

Chapter 2: Bravos

30: The elder Edward Oxford's behavior: *Times* 17 June 1840, 6; 11 July 1840, 5-6.

31: "the best workman in Birmingham": Townsend 127.

31: . . . the son or grandson of a black father: *Times* 11 July 1840, 6; *Morning Chronicle* 12 June 1840, 7; *Caledonian Mercury* 18 June 1840, 4.

31: "jumping about like a baboon, and imitating their grimaces": Townsend 127.

32: The superstition is perhaps best remembered today in the celebrated case of Joseph Merrick: Wilson 14.

32: Hannah herself believed her husband's abuse the cause of her son Edward's eccentricity: *Times* 17 June 1840, 6.

32: "my customers complained of his conduct": *Morning Chronicle* 15 June 1840, 3; *Times* 10 July 1840, 7.

33: "He was once taken to the station house for this": *Morning Chronicle* 10 July 1840, 7.

33: Sandon recalled that he constantly beat other children: *Times* 11 July 1840, 6.

33: Edward was "brought up to the bar": *Times* 11 June 1840, 4.

34: . . . he could only laugh and "jeer" at the injuries the man had received: *Times* 11 July 1840, 6.

34: . . . his aunt remembered one time, when she was ill, leaving Edward to run a busy bar: *Times* 11 July 1840, 6.

35: "When not engaged in his business and while sitting down in front of the bar he has been observed by Mr. Minton and the barmaid . . .": *Morning Chronicle* 15 June 1840, 3.

35: Mary Ann Forman, a barwoman at the Shepherd and Flock, recalled his "strange ways": *Times* 11 July 1840, 6.

35: Oxford thus had a suit of clothing that suggested a respectability above his station: "Edward Oxford."

36: "I gave him warning because he was always laughing": *Times* 11 July 1840, 6.

36: . . . he is known to have threatened her with a pistol again: *Times* 10 July 1840.

36: Susanna Phelps became the primary witness to his behavior and the primary object of his torment: *Times* 16 June 1840, 5.

37: . . . a book that suggests Oxford's love of pedestrian sentiment and high melodrama: Zschokke.

37: The protagonist . . . rises to become one of one of the "two greatest men in Venice": Zschokke 217.

38: . . . he copied, according to his sister, passages from the Bible: *Times* 11 July 1840, 6.

38: . . . none is postmarked: *Morning Chronicle* 13 June 1840, 3.

38: "Young England—Sir": for the letters, see "Edward Oxford."

40: Victoria's Uncle Ernest, without question the most wicked, the most feared, and the most reviled of George III's sons: Fulford 230.

41: Mrs. Packman, being extremely hard of hearing, was not disturbed by the shooting: *Morning Chronicle* 15 June 1840, 3.

42: He bought a brace of pistols in May 1800 . . . : Poole 122.

42: "that serenity and firmness of character which belong to a virtuous mind": *Times* 16 May 1800, 2.

42: . . . "it was not over yet—there was a great deal more and worse to be done": Poole 121.

43: ". . . the safety of the community, and of all mankind, requires that this unfortunate man should be taken care of": *Times* 27 June 1800, 3.

44: There he grew old, "grumbling and discontented": "Constant Observer" 161.

44: . . . he asked her to recognize his sanity and his service to the nation and make him a Chelsea Pensioner: Poole 128.

44: . . . having "no desire to again mix with the world": *Weekly Chronicle* 16 December 1838, 8.

45: Upon rising that morning, Lord Russell's housemaid had discovered signs of disorder throughout the house: For the discovery of Russell's body and the initial investigation of the crime, see the *Times* 7 May 1840, 5.

45: . . . oddly finding the man almost fully dressed: *Times* 7 May 1840, 5; 15 May 1840, 5.

45: . . . blood was pooled deeply around his head, and had dripped through in a puddle under the bed: *Times* 8 May 1840, 5; 12 May 1840, 6.

45: . . . a neighbor did claim to hear groans emanating from Lord Williams's room, during the night: *Times* 8 May 1840, 5.

45: . . . the door had been forced from the inside. . . . Moreover, any intruders exiting from this door would have to scale a high wall: *Times* 8 May 1840, 5.

46: . . . he displayed a great deal of anxiety during the search, and continually "kept running and drinking water": *Times* 7 May 1840, 6.

46: . . . larger items of far greater value in Russell's room were, surprisingly, left alone: *Times* 8 May 1840, 5.

47: . . . he was at the end of May committed to Newgate: *Times* 30 May 1840, 6.

47: . . . the *Times* reported that the carriages of the fashionable clogged the area for days: *Times* 9 May 1840, 5; 11 May 1840, 5; 12 May 1840, 6; 16 May 1840, 7.

47: "the excitement produced in high life by the dreadful event is almost unprecedented": *Times* 9 May 1840, 5.

48: Gould . . . as it happens was (unlike Oxford) actually a potboy: *Times* 19 March 1840, 6.

48: Gould had boasted to others that he was about to free himself from poverty by robbing an old man who was known to wave a £50 note about: *Times* 23 March 1840, 6.

48: Mary Ann was Richard Gould's lover: *Times* 21 March 1840, 7; Pelham 558.

48:    . . . brought to trial on 14 April: *Times* 15 April 1840, 6.

49:    Otway confronted Gould not with the warrant, but with an offer: *Times* 11 May 1840, 5.

49:    . . . he was later censured for his action by the courts and by the police: Fido and Skinner 106.

49:    . . . the landlady . . . commented to Mrs. Oxford on her son's want of economy: *Times* 12 June 1840, 7.

49:    The locks of the pistols . . . rubbed so relentlessly against the Gambroon fabric of his trousers as to create a noticeably worn patch within a few weeks: *Times* 11 June 1840, 4.

50:    William Green's "pistol-repository and shooting gallery": Altick, *Shows* 231-2.

50:    He might have spent some of his time at these places flourishing the scimitar-shaped sword he had obtained during these weeks: *Morning Chronicle* 13 June 1840, 3.

50:    His habit, it seems, was to spend a shilling each visit, for a few shots with pistol and with rifle: *Morning Chronicle* 13 June 1840, 3.

50:    . . . he bet that he could hit within six inches of his target—and he lost: *Morning Chronicle* 12 June 1840, 6.

50:    "He was more fit to shoot at a haystack than at the target": *Times* 10 July 1840.

50:    . . . "he associated . . . alternatively with the higher and lower classes of society." *Morning Chronicle* 15 June 1840, 3.

50:    John Lenton: *Times* 10 July 1840, 6.

51:    J. J. Gray: *Times* 10 July 1840, 6.

51:    . . . the proprietor molded him two dozen bullets, and sold him a quarter-pound of gunpowder: TNA PRO MEPO 3/17.

Chapter 3: If It Please Providence, I Shall Escape

52:    . . . some tea from Mr. Twining's shop: "Edward Oxford."

53:    Lovett, the proprietor, saw Oxford sitting there: *Morning Chronicle* 16 June 1840, 3.

53:    Albert had left the Palace in the morning, visiting, as he had a month before, Woolwich Dockyard: *Times* 11 June 1840, 5.

53:    He had chaired, and given his brief speech to, the Anti-Slavery Society nine days before: *Times* 2 June 1840, 6; Weintraub, *Victoria* 105.

54:    Albert made a great success of his trip to Woolwich, as well: *Times* 11 June 1840, 5

54:    He knew who was in the carriage: *Times* 10 July 1840, 6.

54:    . . . his hands inside his jacket: *Times* 11 June 1840, 4; 18 June 1840, 6.

55:    . . . watched Oxford stare at the carriage and "give a nod with his head sneeringly": *Times* 10 July 1840, 6.

55:    . . . only months away from being the youngest student ever accepted to the Royal Academy Schools: Warner.

55:    The boys doffed their caps to the royal couple, and were delighted to see the Queen bow to them in response: Millais 11.

55:    Albert saw a "little mean looking man": James 111-112.

55:    She later told Lehzen that she thought someone was shooting birds in the park: Boykin, ed. 259.

55:    Oxford's "attitude was so affected and theatrical it quite amused me": James 112. Another witness noted the theatricality of Oxford's stance: *Morning Chronicle* 11 June 1840, 2.

56:    " . . . when I fired the first pistol, Albert was about to jump from the carriage": *Times* 12 June 1840, 6.

56:    "I have another here": *Times* 11 June 1840, 4.

56:    . . . thinking to herself "If it please Providence, I shall escape." Boykin, ed. 259.

56:    "Kill him!": Longford, 151.

56:    The Queen spoke to Albert, who called out to the postilions to drive on, and they did: *Times* 11 June 1840, 4.

56:    " . . . to show the public that we had not, on account of what happened, lost all confidence in them": James 112.

57:    " . . . the apprehensions of the bystanders were in some degree relieved by seeing the Royal carriage containing the Queen and Prince Albert return along the drive towards the palace at about 7 o'clock": *Times* 11 June 1840, 4.

58:    Victoria burst into tears: *Times* 12 June 1840, 6.

58:    Albert held her and kissed her repeatedly, "praising her courage and self-possession": Bennett 59.

59:    . . . calling him a "confounded rascal": *Times* 18 June 1840, 6.

59:    "in an instant several persons seized me by the skirts of the coat, some took hold of my trousers, others twisted their hand into my handkerchief, and all within reach of me had me by the collar": *Morning Chronicle* 12 June 1840.

59:    "I had no intention to run away": *Times* 12 June 1840.

59:    . . . an "immense assemblage": *Times* 11 June 1840, 4.

59:    " . . . hooting and execration": *Morning Chronicle* 11 June 1840, 2.

60: "Look out, Albert. I dare say he has some friends": *Times* 10 July 1840, 6.

60: . . . at the station Oxford was asked, before a number of witnesses, whether the guns were loaded, and Oxford admitted that they were: *Times* 10 July 1840.

60: When they reached the station house, P.C. William Smith, not quite sure whether Clayton was a hero or an accomplice, took him as well as Oxford into custody: *Times* 10 July 1840, 6.

60: Oxford was searched: in his pocket were his knife, the key to his box at home, and half a crown: *Times* 10 July 1840, 6.

60: The police also took note of the wear above his trouser pockets: *Times* 11 June 1840, 4.

60: "I have been brought up to the bar": *Times* 11 June 1840, 4.

61: Oxford was apparently delighted to see him, and asked whether the Queen was hurt: *Times* 10 July 1840, 6.

61: Reforms of the year before—1839—under Home Secretary John Russell had led to the elimination of that group: Lock 39.

61: By 1840, however, the two commissioners of the Metropolitan Police had come to look upon A Division as the special division of the force: Browne 114.

62: 90 officers and Superintendent May traveling to Birmingham, for example, to battle militant Chartists in the Bull Ring Riots a year before: Ascoli 114-15.

62: They found the landlady, Mrs. Packman, there with her sister: *Morning Chronicle* 15 June 1840, 3.

62: There, they found all Oxford's evidence of Young England: *Times* 11 June 1840, 4; *Morning Chronicle* 15 June 1840, 3.

63: They tried one of the confiscated bullets in Oxford's pistols; it fit perfectly: *Morning Chronicle* 11 June 1840, 2.

63: He had meant to destroy the papers, he claimed: *Times* 11 June 1840, 4.

63: . . . the information from the third letter that news had arrived from Hanover was released to a reporter, and was in the newspapers the next morning": *Morning Chronicle* 11 June 1840, 2.

63: Oxford after this interview would greet Maule as a particularly close acquaintance: *Times* 8 July 1840, 7.

63: . . . expressing republican sentiments to some; suggesting at one time that he thought it wrong that England was ruled by a woman: *Times* 12 June 1840, 7; *Morning Chronicle* 12 June 1840, 6.

64: At Almack's Assembly Rooms, a venue traditionally limited to the elite of London society, a sense of melancholy prevailed: *Weekly Chronicle* 14 June 1840, 2.

64: "Our theatres begin the thanksgiving," one reporter wrote, "to be completed in our churches": *Morning Chronicle* 12 June 1840, 5.

64: Oxford slept very soundly that night, and the next morning complimented the police on the comfort of their accommodations: *Morning Chronicle* 12 June 1840, 6.

Chapter 4: This Is All I Shall Say at Present

65: William Millais . . . claimed that two bullet marks were clearly visible: Millais 11.

66: . . . a large detail of officers was dispatched to the wall with birch brooms and barrows, to sweep up all the dirt beneath the walls: *Morning Chronicle* 12 June 1840, 7.

66: . . . someone, it seems, was attempting to assist the police by planting evidence against Oxford: *Morning Chronicle* 12 June 1840, 6; *Times* 13 June 1840, 6.

66: . . . from six paces away, according to Albert: James 112.

66: "It seems the pistols were loaded": RA VIC/MAIN/QVJ/1840, 10 June 1840.

67: " . . . there he is!": *Morning Chronicle* 12 June 1840, 6.

67: Edward Marklew, as Hannah's brother, was naturally a publican, landlord of the Ship, in the City: *Morning Chronicle* 13 June 1840, 3.

67: He had tried to obtain legal counsel for his nephew: *Times* 12 June 1840, 6; *Morning Chronicle* 12 June 1840, 7.

67: Hannah received the news badly: *Morning Chronicle* 12 June 1840, 6; 13 June 1840, 3.

68: . . . he had wanted to make a noise: *Times* 8 July 1840, 7.

68: " . . . he paced up and down the room with perfect self-possession": *Times* 12 June 1840, 6

68: . . . they decided upon the Cabinet: Greville 1:251.

68: "He was young . . . and under the middle size"; John Cam Hobhouse 5:272.

69: One witness, however, claimed that the ball "passed directly before my face": *Times* 18 June 1840, 6.

69: . . . punctuated by his uncanny bursts of laughter: *Morning Chronicle* 12 June 1840, 6.

69: Allowed to make a final statement, Oxford reiterated these discrepancies: *Times* 18 June 1840, 6.

69: Home Secretary Normanby drew up a warrant: *Times* 13 June 1840, 6.

70: . . . Inspector Hughes did tell the Cabinet about Oxford's box of secrets: *Times* 18 June 1840, 6.

70: . . . they had gotten it into their heads that the handwriting on all of Oxford's documents was not actually Oxford's: *Morning Chronicle* 13 June 1840, 3.

70: This time, Oxford was able to embrace his sister: *Morning Chronicle* 12 June 1840, 6.

70: . . . laughing and flourishing his hat to some girls in the building's lobby: *Morning Chronicle* 13 June 1840, 3.

70: One of these held that the letters E R were stamped on Oxford's pistols or his pistol case: Holland 186.

71: . . . many (Baron Stockmar and Albert's personal secretary George Anson among them) could not believe that Hanover was directly involved: Woodham-Smith, *Queen Victoria* 213.

71: . . . in a letter addressed to the people of Ireland, O'Connell railed against the "underlings of that Orange-Tory faction which naturally detests the virtues of our beloved Queen": *Morning Chronicle* 23 June 1840.

71: One persistent rumor in support of this theory held that a respectable, older man had stood near Oxford as the Queen's carriage approached, and gave him the signal to fire: *Morning Chronicle* 12 June 1840, 6.

72: The *Northern Star*, the leading Chartist newspaper, attempted energetically to dispel the rumor that "the diabolical deed was a premeditated act of a band of Chartists": *Northern Star* 13 June 1840, 1.

72: . . . he was the "tool" of a "designing villain": *Morning Chronicle* 12 June 1840, 7.

72: "We should have been at this moment the vassals of a now foreign potentate": *Morning Chronicle* 12 June 1840, 5.

73: Theatres altered their programs to honor the Queen: *Weekly Chronicle* 14 June 1840, 2.

73: . . . to have "oracular demonstration of the well-being of their Sovereign": *Weekly Chronicle* 14 June 1840, 2.

74: Constitution Hill was of course thronged, as all there exchanged the latest news and rumors: *Times* 11 June 1840, 4.

74: . . . as everyone (including the Dukes of Cambridge and Wellington) squeezed in between the police officers, still busy seeking, in vain, balls from Oxford's pistols: *Morning Chronicle* 12 June 1840, 6; *Times* 13 June 1840, 6.

74: . . . Victoria and Albert emerged into a deafening sea of humanity that "all but impeded the progress of the royal party": *Weekly Chronicle* 14 June 1840, 2.

75: "The loyalty of the English was never more finely exhibited than it was during the afternoon of yesterday": *Times* 12 June 1840, 6.

75: On the next day, Friday, the Queen and Albert were prevented from riding as both Houses of Parliament paraded from Westminster to the Palace to present a congratulatory address: *Times* 13 June 1840, 6.

76: . . . partisanship the Queen had herself shown months before in wishing to exclude the Tories from her wedding: Longford 141.

76: The crowd outside the Palace, on the other hand, displayed a strong sense of party spirit, showing its hostility to the beleaguered Whig government: *Times* 13 June 1840, 6.

76: On Monday, however, Westminster once again burst into celebration, as Victoria and Albert departed Buckingham Palace by carriage for Windsor: *Morning Chronicle* 16 June 1840, 3.

Chapter 5: Going to See a Man Hanged

78: . . . her family doctor . . . went so far as to claim she was "most eccentric, if not insane": Clarke 196.

79: Hannah spoke with the permanent undersecretary there, Samuel March Phillipps: *Morning Chronicle* 13 June 1840, 3; *Times* 13 June 1840, 6.

79: Oxford was cheerful when he entered Newgate on Thursday evening: *Morning Chronicle* 12 June 1840, 6.

79: . . . when Alderman Laurie asked him whether he had balls in his pistols, Oxford denied it outright: *Morning Chronicle* 16 June 1840, 3.

79: . . . Oxford was left alone with guards who were strictly ordered to discuss nothing with him beyond his immediate needs: *Morning Chronicle* 13 June 1840, 3.

80: . . . reverting to fits of crying, and developing the odd habit of whistling to mask his distress: *Weekly Chronicle* 14 June 1840, 2.

80: . . . he cared little that he had thrown his own life away, but that he was terrified that he had "sacrificed" his mother's life as well: *Times* 13 June 1840, 6.

80: Because of this "extraordinary interference," he refused to have anything to do with Oxford's case: *Times* 16 June 1840, 5; 17 June 1840, 6.

80: . . . Hannah had a "heart-rending" conversation with her son: *Morning Chronicle* 15 June 1840, 3.

80: " . . . there are others in it": *Morning Chronicle* 16 June 1840, 3.

80: His sister Susannah, who had more closely than anyone else watched Oxford's movements over the past month, was certain that there was no Young England: *Times* 16 June 1840, 5.

80: The police . . . busily collected writing samples from the residents of West Place: *Morning Chronicle* 15 June 1840, 3.

81: "The unhappy parent of Oxford states that her husband died about twelve years since": *Morning Chronicle* 13 June 1840, 3.

81: And at Newgate the next day, Hannah spoke with the aldermen who surrounded her son, telling them of her deceased husband's insanity and abuse: *Morning Chronicle* 16 June 1840, 3.

82: . . . as Oxford still refused counsel, governor Cope prevented any meeting: *Times* 17 June 1840, 6.

82: Oxford proposed to Pelham that they defend his action as a foolish lark: *Morning Chronicle* 19 June 1840, 3.

82: Pelham, on the other hand, quickly resolved that the defense would prove a case "if not of positive insanity, at least of monomania, which will entitle him to the merciful consideration of the Court and jury": *Times* 17 June 1840, 6.

82: " . . . the boy is mad. I am not surprised": Clarke 196.

82: . . . J. Sydney Taylor, a highly reputable barrister and well-known journalist, adamant in his opposition to the death penalty: Clarke 196; Taylor; "John Sydney Taylor, Esq." 220-21.

83: Critics claimed that he was able to testify to madness in any situation: Freemon 364.

83: Conolly's reputation made him, to Clarke, the "most important" of the witnesses: Clarke 199.

83: . . . as many as 110 people, from Birmingham and elsewhere: *Times* 8 July 1840, 7.

83: He sent Pelham a letter: *Times* 18 June 1840, 5.

84: . . . the letter suggests "that P[rince] Albt is an ogre and the Q[uee]n an ogress": Disraeli 280.

84: . . . two days before, she and Albert had attended the races at Ascot to immense crowds (many who had come to see her more than the races) and "deafening cheers from every part of the course": *Times* 17 June 1840, 6.

85: . . . "all the world is talking about Courvoisier, and very little of the quasi Regicide. . . ." Disraeli 279-80.

85: For his first couple of days in Newgate, Oxford inhabited an ordinary cell among the general population: *Morning Chronicle* 13 June 1840, 3.

85: These cells were furnished with bench and table so that jailers could comfortably observe, and if necessary prevent the suicide of, condemned prisoners: "Newgate Prison."

85: Gould, with another inmate who had achieved some amount of public attention at the time . . . had, two weeks before, attempted to break out of the prison: *Times* 30 May 1840, 6.

86: Phillips's aggressive cross-examination on the first day of trial of Courvoisier's fellow servant Sarah Manser indicated this intention: "Francois Benjamin Courvoisier."

86: The evening before, a witness, Charlotte Piolaine, came forward with new evidence: *Times* 20 June 1840, 6-7.

86: "Up to this morning I believed most firmly in his innocence, and so did many others as well as myself": Costigan 325.

87: . . . he questioned Inspector Tedman's finding of a pair of bloody gloves in a trunk the police had thoroughly examined days before, finding nothing: "Francois Benjamin Courvoisier."

87: He also attempted to discredit Mme. Piolaine's evidence by suggesting that her hotel was nothing but a sordid gaming-den: *Times* 22 June 1840, 6.

87: There, he immediately attempted to kill himself by forcing a towel down his throat: Burke 473.

87: Oxford could hardly contain himself, and grinned "and with difficulty restrained his propensity to laughter": *Times* 23 June 1840, 6.

88: John Bellingham: *Times* 16 May 1812, 2-3; Pelham 527-549.

89: "did you see how I was noticed!": *Times* 8 July 1840, 7.

89: . . . they proceeded with pomp and solemnity, in the company of over 150 London officials, to Buckingham Palace and to Ingestre House: *Times* 23 June 1840, 3.

90:    . . . the Duke of Brunswick might have been more interested in Richard Gould's case than Oxford's, having attended Gould's earlier examination for burglary: *Times* 14 May 1840, 5.

90:    Gould endeavored this time to do the same thing, without success: his attempts only earned the laughter of the court: *Times* 23 June 1840, 6.

90:    . . . "there to pass the remainder of his existence in hopeless slavery, poverty and misery of the worst description": *Times* 23 June 1840, 6.

91:    Now, though, he sat in chains on the convict ship *Eden*: *Times* 30 June 1840, 6; "Convict Transportation Registers Database."

91:    The first of these . . . set out in very specific detail events surrounding the murder: Burke 473-76.

91:    . . . the overwhelming majority of death sentences—over 95% of them—were commuted to lesser sentences in his day: Gatrell 617.

91:    In his third confession—a spiritual biography of sorts, written in French—he claimed that he had been influenced to the deed by bad reading: Burke 477-80.

92:    . . . compelling Ainsworth to write to the newspapers contradicting "this false and injurious statement": *Times* 7 July 1840, 7; *Morning Chronicle* 7 July 1840.

92:    . . . the resulting furor[,] was enough to kill the subgenre: Altick, *Victorian Studies in Scarlet* 73-74.

93:    Courvoisier spent most of his last days in fervent prayer, often in the company of James Carver, Newgate's chaplain, and M. Baup, the Swiss minister of a nearby French church: Burke 473, 483.

93:    The sheriffs, besieged by applications, gave out tickets and opened a gallery that had been closed for the past fifteen years: *Times* 6 July 1840, 10.

93:    . . . his coffin placed in front of him: Gatrell 43.

93:    . . . he looked up, and around the chapel, with a foolish grin on his face: *Times* 6 July 1840, 10.

93:    Courvoisier . . . plotted to take his own life by binding up an arm with a strip of cloth and cutting a vein with a sharpened fragment of wood: *Times* 7 July 1840, 6.

94:    . . . these were a celebratory bunch, mostly rowdy youths: Gatrell 63.

94:    Thackeray, recording his impressions of the event in his essay "Going to See a Man Hanged," noted the great social and moral diversity of the spectators: Thackeray 152-5.

94:     . . . as many as 1.6 million would be sold: Gatrell 159.

94:     The *Times* conservatively estimated 20,000 were there; Thackeray reported 40,000: *Times* 7 July 1840, 6; Thackeray 156.

94:     Places in the windows of the houses surrounding the scaffold were going for three guineas, and for two sovereigns one could obtain treacherous places on the house-roofs: Mayhew and Binney 609; *Times* 6 July 1840, 6.

95:     Calcraft had been Newgate's executioner since 1829, and was to continue in that position until 1874: Boase, "Calcraft."

95:     He would also be given Courvoisier's hanging-rope and his effects, including his clothing: Boase, "Calcraft."

95:     . . . Courvoisier would soon be a star attraction in Madame's Chamber of Horrors: *Biographical and Descriptive Sketches* 38.

95:     Calcraft drew from a black bag a rope with which he pinioned Courvoisier's arms before him: *Times* 7 July 1840, 7.

95:     Afterwards, they would have a hearty breakfast with Governor Cope: Gatrell 65.

95:     Among this group was the celebrated actor Charles Kean: *Times* 7 July 1840, 7; Adams 341.

95:     " . . . a great murmur arose, more awful, *bizarre,* and indescribable than any sound I had ever before heard": Thackeray 156.

96:     . . . his only agitation, beyond an imploring look around at the immense crowd, was a clasping and unclasping of his bound hands: *Times* 7 July 1840, 6.

96:     William Calcraft was renowned as a bungler: Boase, "Calcraft."

96:     Long drops of several feet, designed to break the neck—drops which could go horribly wrong in their own way—were not a feature of Newgate hangings until the 1880s: Gatrell 54.

96:     "He died without any violent struggle": *Times* 7 July 1840, 6.

96:     . . . "nothing but ribaldry, debauchery, levity, drunkenness, and flaunting vice in fifty other shapes": Collins 226.

97:     "I fully confess that I came away down Snow Hill that morning with a disgust for murder, but it was for *the murder I saw done*": Thackeray 158.

97:     One cast from that mask remained at the Governor's office; another was exhibited at Madame Tussaud's: Gatrell 115.

97:     In the afternoon, Courvoisier's body was buried in a passageway to the Old Bailey: Mayhew and Binney 609.

97: . . . Oxford was visited by an Italian artist from Manchester: *Freeman's Journal* 20 August 1840, 4.

98: The LUNATIC EDWARD OXFORD: *Morning Chronicle* 23 September 1840:2.

98: . . . Clarke and two of his hand-picked team of medical experts . . . took a carriage to Newgate with an order from the Home Secretary in hand, to examine Oxford and decide whether he was insane: Clarke 200.

98: "I cannot believe that the prisoner is responsible for his actions": Clarke 200.

98: At the prison, Governor Cope, still taking his position of gatekeeper very seriously, at first refused the doctors admittance: Clarke 201.

99: Showing no agitation whatsoever convinced at least Dr. Chowne that the boy was missing normal brain function: was, in a word, an imbecile: "Edward Oxford"; *Morning Chronicle* 11 July 1840, 6.

100: "This youth," Conolly told Clarke, "cannot with such a configuration be entirely right": Clarke 202.

100: When told he had committed a great crime, in shooting at the Queen, he seemed not to understand, replying "that he might as well shoot her as any one else": *Times* 11 July 1840, 6.

100: . . . "he had been decapitated in fact a week before, for he had a cast taken of his head": "Edward Oxford."

100: . . . "I told him to get up and walk about the room, and the brisk manner in which he walked proved to me he was not acting a part, for I think if he had been he would not have walked so much at his ease": *Times* 11 July 1840, 6.

100: . . . there were no bullets in his pistols, he stubbornly maintained, even when the doctors suggested to him that there had been: "Edward Oxford."

101: "We held a consultation after the interview," Clarke states, "and we all felt convinced that we could justly uphold the plea of insanity": Clarke 203.

Chapter 6: Guilty, He Being at the Time Insane

102: The sheriffs, however, had just had good practice with handling the crowds: *Times* 10 July 1840, 5.

102: He emerged after a few seconds, at first dejected: *Morning Chronicle* 10 July 1840, 3.

102: . . . the Duke of Brunswick was again a spectator, as were the Earls of Errol, Colchester, and Uxbridge, as well as a Baron and a Count, and a scattering of Lords and Honorables: *Times* 10 July 1840, 5; *Morning Chronicle* 10 July 1840, 3.

103: . . . Fox Maule, Oxford's seeming friend, and his wife were among the first to arrive: *Times* 10 July 1840, 5.

103: . . . "picking, rubbing, and smelling" them for the next two days: *Morning Chronicle* 10 July 1840, 3.

103: These herbs, particularly malodorous rue, had been placed before the dock at every Old Bailey session for ninety years: Lawrence 296.

103: . . . a founding member of the Society for the Abolition of Capital Punishment, and fought passionately for that cause in the columns of the *Morning Herald*: "John Sydney Taylor Esq."

103: . . . he had for some time been battling against a mysterious and malignant disease: John Sydney Taylor xlvii.

103: Campbell, who would handle opening arguments, had a reputation for aggressive advocacy in his writing, his politics, and in the court-room: Jones and Jones, "Campbell, John."

104: Thomas Wilde, who would handle the prosecution's closing, had admitted liabilities in his presentation of a case: Rigg, "Wilde, Thomas."

104: Denman was thought not to have one of the greatest legal minds of his day, but was renowned for his impartiality and courtesy— as the "personification of judicial dignity": Jones and Jones, "Denman, Thomas."

104: . . . the clerk read the charge of High Treason against Oxford: *Morning Chronicle* 10 July 1840, 3.

105: Oxford pleaded not guilty to the charge, in a "distinct and firm tone": *Times* 10 July 1840, 5.

105: In his opening the Attorney General anticipated and countered the defense's two-pronged defense: *Times* 10 July 1840, 5-7; *Morning Chronicle* 10 July 1840, 3-4.

105: . . . "total alienation of the mind, or total madness, excuses the guilt of felony or treason": *Morning Chronicle* 10 July 1840, 3.

106: . . . "it must be shown that at the very time, the particular time, when the offence charged was committed, he was not an accountable being": *Morning Chronicle* 10 July 1840, 3.

106: ". . . rather, he was a capable employee: *Morning Chronicle* 10 July 1840, 4.

107: . . . "the report of the pistol attracted my attention, and I had a distinct whizzing or buzzing before my eyes, between my face and the carriage": "Edward Oxford."

107: ". . . it was the second flash which appeared to come over the Queen's head, and it came close past me; the flash did—it seemed something that whizzed past my ear, as I stood": "Edward Oxford."

108: Charles Aston Key, the surgeon who had declined to examine Oxford with the defense's medical witnesses, was present and offering advice to the prosecution: Clarke 209.

109: In his opening Campbell read Oxford's Young England papers to the jury in full: *Times* 10 July 1840, 6; *Morning Chronicle* 10 July 1840, 3.

109: The prosecution, in other words, introduced the very evidence that Oxford's defense would claim to make the strongest case for his insanity: *Times* 10 July 1840, 7; *Morning Chronicle* 10 July 1840, 4.

109: . . . in his opening, Taylor carefully instructed the jury to keep their decisions separate: *Times* 10 July 1840, 6; *Morning Chronicle* 10 July 1840, 4.

109: . . . "the suggestion of the ball having passed over the wall was negatived by the witnesses; but the evidence which tended to show that it had struck against the walls was perfectly inconclusive": *Morning Chronicle* 10 July 1840, 4.

110: . . . an extension of the vainglory he exhibited in foolishly but harmlessly pointed a bullet-less pistol at the Queen: *Morning Chronicle* 10 July 1840, 4.

110: Taylor then turned to the evidence for Oxford's insanity: *Times* 10 July 1840, 7; *Morning Chronicle* 10 July 1840, 4.

110: . . . the Young England papers, written in Oxford's hand, and the "creations of his own foolish fancy," "furnished the strongest evidence against the prisoner in proof of his insanity": *Times* 10 July 1840, 7.

111: "the mind of Her Majesty would be relieved from the unpleasant impression that any one of her subjects could be found guilty of imagining and compassing her death": *Times* 10 July 1840, 7.

111: Taylor and Bodkin called to the stand twenty-eight witnesses, twenty-six of whom provided evidence as to the derangement of three generations of Oxfords: *Times* 10 July 1840, 7, 11 July 1840, 5-6; *Morning Chronicle* 10 July 1840, 4, 11 July 1840, 6; "Edward Oxford."

111: Oxford's father "delighted in annoying and teasing me": "Edward Oxford."

112: Every oddity, it seemed, of Oxford's life was presented to the jury: *Times* 11 July 1840, 5-6; *Morning Chronicle* 11 July 1840, 6; "Edward Oxford."

113: Fly, postman, with this letter bound,/To a place they call the Pig in the Pound: *Times* 11 July 1840, 6.

113: . . . Oxford broke, bursting into tears and weeping bitterly: *Times* 11 July 1840, 6.

113: Passing judgment on the moral aberration of a defendant was, in the minds of most legal authorities of the time, the province of the jury, not of any witness: judging good or evil behavior was a legal and not a medical issue: Freemon 368, 373.

114: He was in 1840 a leading citizen of Birmingham: magistrate and coroner, as well as a highly respected physician: "Edward Oxford."

114: "Assuming the facts which have been given in evidence to be true": *Times* 11 July 1840, 5.

115: . . . he had every right to "take the opinion of a medical man upon that evidence": *Times* 11 July 1840, 5.

115: "Mr. BODKIN . . .—Supposing a person in the middle of the day, and without any suggested motive . . .": *Times* 11 July 1840, 5.

116: Thomas Hodgkin, the Quaker social activist and specialist in morbid anatomy (and incidentally, the one who first studied the symptoms of the disease that bears his name): Kass.

116: "If all the appearances described were exhibited by the prisoner, and coexisted in him, I should conclude that he was insane": *Times* 11 July 1840, 6.

116: "Lord DENMAN.—Do you consider that a medical man has more means of judging with respect to such a subject than other persons?": *Times* 11 July 1840, 6.

116: "I am a physician to the Hanwell Lunatic Asylum, and have at present 850 patients under my care": *Times* 11 July 1840, 6.

117: According to Chowne, lesion of the will is often a partial insanity, in the sense that sufferers can "perform the duties of life with accuracy": "Edward Oxford."

117: Oxford's madness manifested itself most apparently in his "involuntary laughter, which is seldom found in sane persons": *Times* 11 July 1840, 6.

118: "There was nothing of imbecility about them": *Times* 11 July 1840, 6.

118:   The doctors, he claimed . . . "went to Newgate with minds prepared to see a madman": *Times* 11 July 1840, 6.

118:   "These questions," he told the jury, "are perfectly separate in themselves": *Morning Chronicle* 11 July 1840, 7.

118:   Dr. Conolly, he said, "a gentleman who it must be presumed was familiar with the treatment in cases of insanity, and must be an extremely good judge, has given his opinion, and the jury would give that weight they think due to it": *Morning Chronicle* 11 July 1840, 7.

119:   . . . "they are against me, all of them": "Oxford" 4.

119:   "We find the prisoner, Edward Oxford, guilty of discharging the contents of the two pistols, but whether or not they were loaded with ball has not been satisfactorily proved to us, he being of unsound state of mind at the time": *Times* 11 July 1840, 7; *Morning Chronicle* 11 July 1840, 7; Townsend 149.

119:   He therefore jumped up "with prompt dexterity": Townsend 149.

120:   This Taylor "strenuously denied": Townsend 149.

120:   The jury showed confusion about the first part of the verdict; but they were perfectly clear about the second: *Times* 11 July 1840, 7.

120:   ". . . and in a prosecution of this kind, where the prisoner's life was at stake, it was not fitting on the part of the Attorney General to stand up and endeavour to visit the prisoner with perpetual imprisonment when the jury found him not guilty": *Times* 11 July 1840, 7.

120:   Dr. Clarke, commenting on the trial, considered that if Taylor had pressed the issue, he could have won a full acquittal for his client: Clarke 212.

120:   Chief Justice Denman intervened. "The jury," he said, "were in a mistake": *Times* 11 July 1840, 7.

121:   Campbell thought the prospect "monstrous" that Oxford might be "let loose upon society to endanger the life of Her Majesty or her subjects": *Times* 11 July 1840, 7.

121:   "The construction you contend for would lead to this, that if a man were charged with an offence, and the jury thought that no offence had been committed at all, yet he must be handed over to the mercy of the Crown perhaps for his life": Carrington and Payne 9:550.

122:   "Guilty, he being at the time insane": *Times* 11 July 1840, 7; Morning *Chronicle* 11 July 1840, 7; Townsend 150.

122:   "Mr. Baron ALDERSON.—Then, you find the prisoner guilty but for his insanity": *Times* 11 July 1840, 7.

Chapter 7: Bedlam

123: Oxford remained in custody at Newgate for a week, until an order arrived from the Home Office for his transfer to Bethlem: *Times* 27 July 1840, 5.

123: Oxford "did not betray the slightest emotion" upon hearing that the time had come: *Times* 27 July 1840, 5.

124: Albert would show them to the Queen: Longford 152.

124: The distinctive towering dome of the hospital, still visible today in the truncated building's present incarnation as the Imperial War Museum, was added four years after this: Andrews *et al.* 408.

125: A medical record from 1864 when Oxford was removed from Bethlem to Broadmoor notes that the medical staff "had always considered him sane": Moran, "Punitive" 188.

125: . . . for the first years of his confinement, he was prohibited from reading newspapers: "Young Oxford in Bethlehem Hospital," *Era* 26 December 1841:3.

125: Sir Peter Laurie . . . informed his mother that he had a "repugnance to mingle" with them and refused to leave his room: *Freeman's Journal and Daily Commercial Advertiser* 20 August 1840, 4.

125: One other inmate was notorious for his aloofness, one who had no friends, and "could not be prevailed upon for some years to walk about with or join the other patients": *Freeman's Journal and Daily Commercial Advertiser* 20 August 1840, 4.

125: He had, according to a witness seventeen years before, long since stopped showing any symptoms of insanity: Moran, "Origin" 516n.

125: . . . "the loss of liberty," he claimed, "was worse than death": Moran, "Origin" 516n.

126: Oxford happened to be one of the very last male patients to make the trip, by train, from London to Crowthorne (and Broadmoor). Soon after, Bethlem's criminal buildings were demolished: Andrews *et al.* 503.

127: . . . Melbourne approached the Queen with the delicate issue that had been on the minds of everyone since the shooting: it was quite possible that the Queen could die, leaving an infant child as her heir: Longford 152.

127: A Regency Bill was in order, such as the one created ten years before, when Victoria became heir apparent, and which held her mother, the Duchess of Kent, sole regent in the event of her King William's death: Longford 35.

127: "I don't hide from myself that there will be all manner of objections, such as his youth, his want of acquaintance with the country and its institutions, &c.": Von Stockmar 2:39.

128: Stockmar and Melbourne had no problems convincing both Peel and Wellington that Albert should be sole Regent; both claimed that this was their position exactly: Von Stockmar 2:40, 42.

128: Sussex stood before the House of Lords on 21 July, proclaiming himself to be personally disinterested in the Bill, but to have questions about it: *Times* 22 July 1840, 3.

128: "Three months ago," Melbourne told Victoria, "they would not have done it for him. It is entirely his own character": Woodham-Smith, *Queen Victoria* 216.

128: "I am to be Regent—*alone*—Regent, without a Council": Duff 178.

128: As King Leopold wrote to Albert's private secretary, George Anson, the bill "had helped the Prince immensely": Woodham-Smith, *Queen Victoria* 216.

128: "It's a great pity they couldn't suffocate that boy, master Oxford, and say no more about it": Dickens, *Letters* 2:81-2.

PART 2: THE GAUNTLET

Chapter 8: Most Desperate Offenders

133: . . . the *Times* reported one nobleman, a true connoisseur of hangings, who had attended the last four or five of them: *Times* 24 May 1842, 8.

134: two hundred City and Metropolitan police were stationed between scaffold and spectators: *Times* 24 May 1842, 8.

134: Crowds at public executions could be fickle: Gatrell, 67, 98-100.

134: " . . . you will leave the world unrespected and unpitied by any one": *Times* 14 May 1842, 8.

134: . . . "a good deed done": For the details of Good's murder, see *Times* 8 April 1842, 13, 9 April 1842, 7; *Morning Chronicle* 9 April 1842, 7.

134: Queely (or Quelaz) Shiell, who had made his fortune as the largest slaveholder on the West Indian island of Montserrat: *1841 England census* (incorrectly transcribed as Queeley Thiel); Browne 114; Dodd 64; Shiell and Anderson.

134: There, Good bought on credit a pair of breeches: *Times* 8 April 1842, 13.

135: Good planted his back against the door and refused entry: *Morning Chronicle* 9 April 1842, 7; *Times* 8 April 1842, 13.

135: "My God, what's this?": *Times* 8 April 1842, 13.

135: Daniel Good bolted, slamming the stable door to, locking it, throwing the key and a lantern into a hedge, and lighting out across the fields: *Times* 8 April 1842, 13; 9 April 1842, 7.

136: It had been gutted—sliced in a ghastly cross vertically from sternum to pubis, and horizontally around the top of the pelvis, in a single cut from one side of the backbone around to the other: *Times* 13 April 1842, 14; 22 April 1842, 6.

136: Gardiner sent Samuel Dagnall to the station house in Wandsworth to fetch help, give a description of Good, and raise the alarm: *Times* 9 April 1842, 7; *Morning Chronicle* 9 April 1842, 7.

136: . . . Sergeant Palmer[,] opened the door to the adjoining harness room and was nearly knocked over by the overpowering stench: *Times* 8 May 1842, 13.

137: . . . two bloody fragments of a woman's petticoat, "violently torn asunder": *Times* 22 April 1842, 6.

137: The Sunday before, on Good's orders, an anxious Jane Jones had left the boy to sleep with a neighbor while she went to visit Good in Putney: *Times* 13 April 1842, 14.

137: He saw his father make a gift to the young woman: a gown, a shawl, a fur tippet, a pair of gloves, a pair of boots, and, in a hatbox, a blue bonnet: *Times* 9 April 1842, 7; 13 April 1842, 14.

138: . . . the trousers . . . which the boy swore his father never took: *Times* 13 April 1842, 13.

138: . . . the trunk—which he first thought was the body of a pig: *Times* 13 April 1842, 13.

138: Young Daniel apparently disclosed that address to one of the policemen investigating the stables: *Times* 8 April 1842, 13; Browne 115.

138: The metropolitan police were adept, through an established system of "route-papers," at communicating information about breaking crimes and fleeing criminals to all metropolitan station houses and to all active officers in a matter of hours: Lock 36; Cobb 102, 188.

138: "V division, April 6, 1842.—Absconded, about half-past 9 o'clock, from Mr. Shiell's": *Times* 28 April 1842, 6.

139: . . . according to local legend, he tossed the gatekeeper his coach-man's coat as he flew by: Féret 1:65.

139: . . . a policeman who had at 5 A.M. witnessed Good hailing a cab: *Morning Chronicle* 22 April 1842, 7.

139: Tedman was suspended from the force for several weeks because of this mistake: Cobb 188.

139: . . . he sought out his actual wife, Molly Good, whom he had abandoned a good two decades before: *Times* 11 April 1842, 3.

139: Together, Daniel and Molly pawned and sold most of Jane Jones's worldly goods: *Morning Chronicle* 26 April 1842, 7.

139: The newspapers soon excoriated the police for their lack of diligence in catching the murderer: *Morning Chronicle* 15 April 1842, 6.

139: . . . the *Times* reported the public sense of "unmitigated indignation" against the police: *Times* 15 April 1842, 6.

140: "The conduct of the metropolitan police in the present case . . . is marked with a looseness and want of decision": *Times* 11 April 1842, 3.

140: Typical of the problem was . . . Inspector M'Gill of the Holborn division: Cobb 193-94.

140: "Thus . . . the circumstance soon got circulation through the neighbourhood, and thus the chances of detection were considerably lessened": *Times* 11 April 1842, 3.

140: . . . he was enraged by M'Gill's hamfisted intrusion: Cobb 196.

141: By a remarkable coincidence, Rose had been a constable in V Division: *Morning Chronicle* 18 April 1842, 3.

141: Thomas Cooper, a morose 23-year-old who had an obsession with guns: For details of Cooper's shooting, see *Morning Chronicle* 20 June 1842, 6; *Times* 20 June 1842, 7.

141: The superintendent of this police division . . . had assigned extra officers to patrol the area: *Era* 8 May 1842, 7.

141: . . . Charles Moss, was carefully watching a gentleman ostentatiously exhibiting a heavily ornamented watch chain: *Morning Chronicle* 20 June 1842, 6; *Times* 20 June 1842, 7.

142: . . . both to reload his pistols (using grass instead of wadding to hold his bullets in place), and apparently to gulp down a vial of poison: *Morning Chronicle* 7 May 1842, 7; 20 June 1842, 7; *Times* 7 May 1842, 7.

142: "I don't think those pistols are loaded," he called out: *Morning Chronicle* 20 June 1842, 7.

142: One pursuer took up a brick, and another—probably Mott—a stick: *Times* 20 June 1842, 7.

143: Daly reeled half a circle and fell dead: *Era* 19 June 1842, 7.

143: . . . he was so angry at the treatment of his mother by the arresting officer, Inspector Penny, that Cooper assaulted Penny brutally: *Times* 7 May 1842, 7; 20 May 1842, 8.

143: . . . he only regretted killing Daly instead of Penny: *Morning Chronicle* 20 June 1842, 8.

143: . . . he seemed pleased to have killed a policeman: it served him right: *Times*, 6 May 1842, 6.

143: "I shall never be happy until I am the death of one of them": *Morning Chronicle* 20 June 1842, 8.

144: He stuck to the same story he had blurted out the moment his sentence of death was spoken: *Times* 23 May 1842, 6.

144: "I never touched the body of the woman, alive or dead! So help me God!": *Times* 23 May 1842, 6.

144: He climbed, unassisted, the steps of the scaffold to the thunderous noise of an enraged mob: *Morning Chronicle* 24 May 1842, 7.

144: "Stop! Stop!" Good cried: *Times* 24 May 1842, 8.

145: Hanging "was much too good for such a fellow": *Caledonian Mercury* 4 June 1842, 2.

145: Later this day he was to take a lease on a shop and parlor at 63 Mortimer Street: *Times* 1 June 1842, 7.

146: His parents still lived there with his sisters Mary and Jane: *1841 England Census*; TNA PRO HO 45/3079.

146: He attempted—feebly, it seems—to survive as a journeyman carpenter in the adjoining neighborhood of Paddington: *Times* 1 June 1842, 7.

146: . . . his father mentioned that he came for Sunday dinner: *Morning Chronicle* 2 June 1842, 6.

146: He was too proud to tell them that he was finding few jobs and was almost out of money, having been too poor for the last three months to pay rent for his room: *Caledonian Mercury* 4 June 1842, 2; *Times* 30 May 1842, 5; 1 June 1842, 7.

146: He was a close and long-standing friend of the head machinist, Henry Sloman, who had been a witness to the marriage of John Francis Sr. and Elizabeth, Francis's mother, in 1817: *London, England, Marriages and Banns, 1754-1921*.

146: John Francis Jr. had been born in November 1822: *Caledonian Mercury* 4 June 1842, 2

146: . . . perhaps witnessing as a child the slapstick antics of Grimaldi, the sublime acting of Kean, the dazzling virtuosity of Paganini, or, more recently, the seductive dancing of young Lola Montez: Stott, throughout; Wyndham 47-52, 78, 117-120.

146: . . . the census of 1841 lists John Francis Sr. as a carpenter, and his son as an apprentice carpenter: *1841 England Census.*

147: . . . "one of the Artisans of Your Majesty's Theatre Royal Covent Garden . . . for more than 23 years": TNA PRO HO 45/3079.

147: Victoria and Albert had seen all these shows in the early months of 1842: Rowell 131.

148: They employed well over a hundred men (including twenty-six carpenters) to deal with creating props and machinery: Wyndham 2.317.

148: . . . a "Star of Brunswick" rising out of the ocean, "which opens as it enlarges": *Times* 13 February 1840, 5.

148: . . . the first performance in London in which Mendelssohn's famous music was employed: Planché, *Recollections* 2:51.

148: Madame Vestris, renowned for her beautiful legs and for displaying them without shame in breeches roles, was responsible for that innovation: Bratton; Rowell 40.

148: The play was a hit largely because of its showstopping finale: Haugen 99.

148: . . . John Francis was specifically noted for his cleverness in construction of pantomime tricks: *Caledonian Mercury* 4 June 1842, 2

148: *The Castle of Otranto or, Harlequin and the Giant Helmet*, was arguably the most mechanically laden pantomime of all time—a "machinist's Sabbath," according to one historian, a pantomime possibly even *written* by a Covent Garden machinist, to show off his crew's talents: Haugen 103, 107. Other accounts attribute authorship to Vestris's and Mathew's house-writer, J. R. Planché.

149: The pantomime essentially ditched the frenetic human interaction which, when the clown Joseph Grimaldi ruled the pantomime stage two decades before, was crucial to the genre: Planché, *Castle of Otranto*; Stott.

149: . . . she liked pantomime least—noting in her journal after one that it was "noisy and nonsensical as usual": Rowell 24.

149: . . . after his quarrel with his father at the end of 1841, he turned his back on Covent Garden and on his family: *Caledonian Mercury* 4 June 1842, 2.

149:   . . . a few months after he left, the Vestris-Mathews management had collapsed: Haugen 134.

149:   Charles James Mathews was arrested for debt and had spent the two weeks before Good's execution at Queen's Bench Prison: *Times* 10 May 1842, 5; 23 May 1842, 7.

150:   . . . after extensive renovations, the theatre finally found success opening in 1847 as an opera house: Wyndham 2:179-80.

150:   Robert Gibbs, the proprietor of the Caledonian Coffee House, who had endless opportunities to observe him, considered him "idle and reckless": *Times* 2 June 1842, 5.

150:   . . . he wrote poetry, for one thing, and preferred musing over coffee to seeking work: *Times* 1 June 1842, 7; *Morning Chronicle* 2 June 1842, 6.

150:   Francis was arrested on suspicion of stealing more than thirty-two sovereigns from an 85-year-old man he had met at a coffee house: *Times* 3 June 1842, 8.

150:   Charles Johns, an outfitter of chemists and tobacconists, would in two days, on Wednesday, be delivering a full inventory to Francis's shop, and he would be expecting full payment on delivery: *Examiner* 4 June 1842, 360.

151:   To fill his shop, then, he lied to Johns outright, presenting himself as a young man with great expectations: *Examiner* 4 June 1842, 360.

151:   . . . bundles of Havana cigars (and imitation Havanas), bales of loose Virginia and Middle Eastern tobacco, packages of snuff; clay and meerschaum pipes: *Times* 1 June 1842, 10.

151:   Grimstone's Eye Snuff: *Times* 1 Feb. 1842, 8.

151:   Francis's friends at the coffee house, and the youth he slept next to, William Elam, were startled by Francis's sudden foray into keeping shop: *Morning Chronicle* 2 June 1842, 6.

151:   Charles Johns was the one certain visitor to Francis's shop on this day: *Examiner* 4 June 1842, 360.

151:   Francis fended him off: the executors of his grandmother's will were being difficult, delaying on signing off on his inheritance: *Examiner* 4 June 1842, 360.

152:   . . . he would borrow £10 from "the old man": *Examiner* 4 June 1842, 360.

152:   Francis was, according to those who knew him, "good-tempered" and "inoffensive," a sober lad, patron of coffee houses, not public houses or gin palaces, who came to his meals regularly and did not stay out late at night: *Times* 1 June 1842, 7.

Chapter 9: Royal Theatre

153: Usually, that theatre housed the Italian Opera, just reaching the peak of its season with performances of Donizetti's *Lucia di Lammermoor* and *Lucrezia Borgia*: Rowell 130.

153: Just before 10:30, the carriages drew up to the entrance on Charles Street reserved exclusively for the Queen's use: For details of the Spitalfields ball at Her Majesty's Theatre: *Times* 27 May 1842, 6; *Morning Chronicle* 27 May 1842, 6; *Illustrated London News* 28 May 1842, 43.

153: . . . the Count's four sons, who had emerged from the carriage in front of them: *Caledonian Mercury* 30 May 1842, 4.

154: . . . a "simultaneous sensation of delight" thrilled the audience: *Times* 27 May 1842, 6.

154: . . . a "perfect crush": *Times* 27 May 1842, 6.

154: Admission to this ball had been pricey: *Times* 11 April 1842, 1.

155: Two weeks before this ball, the British nobility had had their own chance to display their wealth when the Queen threw at Buckingham Palace a glorious, invitation-only *bal masque* or costume ball: For details of the Plantagenet Ball, see the *Times* 13 May 1842, 6-7; 14 May 1842, 6; *Illustrated London News* 14 May 1842, 7-9.

155: The latest in Victorian technology—530 jets of naphthalized gas—spotlit the thrones: *Caledonian Mercury* 16 May 1842, 4.

155: The gold lace of Albert's tunic was edged with 1,200 pearls, and Victoria wore a pendant stomacher valued at 60,000 pounds: *Times* 9 May 1842, 6.

156: . . . on 14 May 1842, the *Illustrated London News*—the first fully illustrated newsmagazine—published its very first issue: *Illustrated London News* 14 May 1842, 7-9.

156: . . . the year of the worst industrial recession of the nineteenth century: Hilton 23.

156: A series of bad harvests, dating back to the thirties, had raised food prices and the overall cost of living: T. A. Jenkins 105; Martin 1:75.

156: Crime rates and pauperism skyrocketed: Dodds 84; Cole and Postgate 305.

156: . . . the Chartists had, with banners and bands and great hope, trundled an immense petition through the crowd-lined streets of London to Parliament: Chase 205.

156: . . . 3,317,752—well over a tenth of the entire population of Britain: Chase 205. The population of Britain and Ireland, according to the petition itself, was around 26 million in 1842, a number that almost matches that of the 1841 Census. "The People's Charter—Petition"; Hilton 6.

156: In their petition, the Chartists claimed that the current misery facing working people was the direct consequence of a corrupt Parliament: For details of the Chartist Petition of 1842, see "The People's Charter—Petition."

157: This crushing of hopes, coupled with sheer hunger, bore bitter fruit: by the time the Queen attended the ball at Her Majesty's, riots were already erupting in the Midlands and the North: *Times* 5 May 1842, 6; Chase 211.

157: . . . Parliament released its first report on the employment of children: Children's Employment Commission.

157: The popular satirical magazine *Punch* bitterly contrasted the "purple dress" of the reveling rich with the "cere-cloth" or shroud of the destitute: *Punch* 2:209.

157: "The most detested tyrant whose deeds history hands down to posterity, set fire to Rome": *Northern Star* 4 June 1842, 3.

158: . . . the economic forces unleashed by the Industrial Revolution had strangled their trade nearly to the point of extinction: Veder 266.

158: Charles Dickens a few years later described the under- and unemployed weavers of Spitalfields as "sallow" and "unshorn": Dickens and Willis 25.

159: . . . "the weavers dine for a day or two": Dickens and Willis 25.

159: The organizers of the ball at Her Majesty's Theatre hoped for a more lasting support: *Times* 25 May 1842; Kean 44.

159: As the *Times* put it, the ball at the theatre was an occasion in which the Queen associated "publicly and personally with her subjects in promoting a common object": *Times* 27 May 1842, 6.

160: . . . as one of his first acts as Prime Minister, Peel appointed Albert president of the Fine Arts Commission: Bolitho 121; Hurd 236.

160: Victoria later said that Albert found a "second father" in Peel: St. Aubyn, *Queen Victoria* 157.

160: He once told Victoria "all depends on the urgency of a thing. If a thing is very urgent, you can always find time for it; but if a thing can be put off, well then you put it off": Hibbert, *Queen Victoria* 87.

160: . . . he attended the *bal masque,* dressed as a figure from a van Dyck painting: *Caledonian Mercury* 16 May 1842, 4.

161: It was a budget informed by his growing belief in free trade, calculated not simply to redistribute wealth—but to *create* wealth: Read 146.

161: The crowd, however, watched not the dancers but the royal pavilion, as with "mute up-gazing curiosity" they observed Victoria perform the rituals of state: *Morning Chronicle* 27 May 1842, 6.

162: Five years before, she was accompanied by her mother and attended to by John Conroy and Lady Flora Hastings; her uncle the Duke of Cumberland was seen to be "very constant in his attention" to his Royal niece: *Times* 2 June 1837, 5.

162: Cumberland was now king in Hanover, his despotic ways finding much grater favor among the Hanoverians than among the British: Palmer.

162: . . . Conroy—an exile in Berkshire: Hudson 176-77.

162: . . . his power implicit in the enormous jackboots he wore: *Morning Chronicle* 27 May 1842, 6.

163: By the end of 1841, she regularly used the term "we" in setting out her opinions: St. Aubyn, *Queen Victoria* 151.

163: . . . the Prince hurried from Victoria's side to lead the Privy Council in her stead: St. Aubyn, *Queen Victoria* 152.

163: Victoria found him indispensable in dealing with government business during her confinement and recovery: Woodham-Smith, *Queen Victoria* 217-18.

163: He became, according to his own secretary Anson, "in fact, tho' not in name, Her Majesty's Private Secretary": Woodham-Smith, *Queen Victoria* 218.

163: At both Buckingham Palace and Windsor by this time, their desks were joined so that they could work as one: St. Aubyn, *Queen Victoria* 152.

164: He attended all ministerial meetings, read his wife's correspondence, and conducted an extensive political correspondence of his own: Gill 174.

164: . . . Albert confronted Lehzen, through Anson, about not reporting to him that a certain Captain Childers was stalking the Queen with "mad professions of love": Woodham-Smith, *Queen Victoria* 215. Such lovelorn lunatics stalking the Queen were legion, particularly in the early years of her reign.

164: She was to him *"die Blaste"*—the hag, the "Yellow Lady" (a reference to her jaundice), "a crazy, stupid intriguer, obsessed with the lust of power, who regards herself as a demi-God": Charlot 194; St. Aubyn, *Queen Victoria* 168; Woodham-Smith, *Queen Victoria* 229.

165: Anson noted her "pointing out and exaggerating every little fault of the Prince, constantly misrepresenting him, constantly trying to undermine him in the Queen's affections and making herself appear a martyr": St. Aubyn, *Queen Victoria*, 168.

165:   On the evening of 3 December 1840, palace servants were startled to discover an unkempt young man hiding under a sofa in the Queen's dressing room—a sofa upon which just hours before the Queen had been sitting: Paul Thomas Murphy. Jones, after breaking into the palace three times, was forced to become a sailor; he served in the Royal Navy for at least six years, and then faded into obscurity.

165:   He claimed that he "sat upon the throne, saw the Queen, and heard the Princess Royal . . . squall": *Times* 5 December 1840, 4.

165:   . . . "the absence of system, which leaves the palace without any responsible authority": Von Stockmar 2:125. For a detailed memorandum of the household dysfunction, see Von Stockmar 2:118-25.

166:   . . . servants, for example, regularly sold off the day's unused candles for their own profit: Feuchtwanger 65.

166:   Albert, in going over Palace expenditures, discovered a weekly charge of 35 shillings for guards at Windsor who hadn't actually served since George III's day: Jerrold, *Married Life* 221-22.

166:   . . . she "lets no opportunity of creating mischief and difficulty escape her": Woodham-Smith, *Queen Victoria* 228.

166:   . . . Stockmar called them back; the Princess Royal was seriously ill—thin, pale, and feverish: St. Aubyn, *Queen Victoria* 171; Gill 182.

167:   "All the disagreeableness I suffer," he wrote, "comes from one and the same person." Woodham-Smith, *Queen Victoria* 230.

167:   He and Victoria had the worst argument of their married lives, the Queen accusing Albert of wishing to kill their children, and screaming that she wished they had never married: St. Aubyn, *Queen Victoria* 171; Gill 183.

167:   "Dr. Clark has mismanaged the child and poisoned her with calomel and you have starved her": Woodham-Smith, *Queen Victoria* 230.

167:   " . . . the welfare of my children and Victoria's existence as sovereign are too sacred for me not to die fighting rather than yield them as prey to Lehzen": Woodham-Smith, *Queen Victoria* 229.

167:   One reporter empathized with the fatigue Victoria must feel, when she and her court had to rise, turn, and curtsey with the arrival of every one of her many honored guests: *Morning Chronicle* 27 May 1842, 6.

168:   . . . "amidst loud cheering and clapping of hands" the royal party returned to their carriages and to the Palace": *Morning Chronicle* 27 May 1842.

168: . . . he shut up shop and returned to Titchfield Street, crept up the two flights to his room, and broke open a locked box containing all of his roommate's possessions: *Times* 1 June 1842, 7.

168: "What have you been about?" Foster asked him. "I suppose you know what I have come here for?": *Times* 1 June 1842, 7.

169: . . . flintlocks missing flints, and with rusted screw barrels: *Times* 18 June 1842, 7-8.

169: Francis chose the smaller of the two, one seven inches long: *Morning Chronicle* 31 May 1842, 5.

169: "It appeared to be all he had in the world," Street later told police: TNA PRO MEPO 3/18.

169: The clerk told him they rarely sold flints: *Times* 18 June 1842, 7-8.

170: Francis paid for the flint with two halfpennies: *Morning Chronicle* 18 June 1842, 7.

170: While the police learned about all of these purchases, however, they could never prove that Francis bought a bullet for his pistol: TNA PRO MEPO 3/18.

170: Francis found shelter at yet another coffee-house: *Times* 11 June 1842, 6; *Post Office London Directory, 1841*, 195.

Chapter 10: A Thorough Scamp

171: . . . under the shade of the magnificent elm trees: Heron 443-44.

171: . . . Victoria and Albert attended the sermon of the Bishop of Norwich at the Chapel Royal: *Times* 30 May 1842, 5.

171: Pearson had only recently arrived in London from Suffolk to work at his brother's printing business as a wood engraver: *Times* 1 June 1842, 6.

172: The youth didn't fire: *Times* 18 June 1842, 7.

172: Then John Francis crossed the Mall and disappeared through the gate and into Green Park: *Times* 1 June 1842, 7.

172: . . . wondering whether what he had seen was a joke: *Times* 1 June 1842, 6.

173: Then, he turned and slowly walked away, toward Piccadilly: *Times* 11 June 1842, 6.

173: He then asked the boy for his name and address: Martin 1:121; *Times* 1 June 1842, 6.

173: The gentleman, whoever he was, must have had the questionable pleasure of reading about himself in the newspapers a few days later, when he was excoriated for not raising an alarm or reporting the crime: *Times* 2 June 1842, 5.

173: George's brother, Matthew Flinders Pearson, was a good fifteen years older than he, a respectable businessman in Holborn: *Morning Chronicle* 28 December 1842, 2.

174: Thomas Dousbery, a boot and shoe retailer, dabbled in radical thought and was the secretary of the Cordwainer's benevolent fund; . . . he would know what to do: *Morning Chronicle* 2 June 1842, 6; Dousbery 2:109.

174: Dousbery was sure that Laurie trusted in him, and would not see Pearson's account as a "trumped up tale": *Morning Chronicle* 2 June 1842, 6.

174: He stammered so badly, Laurie wrote in his diary, "that his brother who was with him had to repeat a statement he had made to him when he was not excited or afraid": Laurie 101. Laurie obviously knew Thomas Dousbery less than Dousbery knew him, mistakenly calling him "Dandbury" in his diary.

174: Laurie considered that Pearson should take his account straight to Buckingham Palace: *Times* 1 June 1842, 6.

174: Laurie, a man well known for his egotism: McConnell.

174: . . . Murray had just sat down to dinner at the Queen's table, and could not—"on any pretence"—be spoken with until bed time: *Times* 1 June 1842, 6.

175: He wrote about the assault to his father the next day: Martin 1:121.

175: Victoria later wrote to her Uncle Leopold "Thank God, my angel is also well; but he says that had the man fired on Sunday, he must have been hit in the head": Victoria *Letters* (first series) 1:399.

176: . . . all was quiet; the crowd had dispersed, "satisfied with having seen the Queen": Martin 1:121.

176: Albert, wishing Arbuthnot to maintain "profound secrecy," asked him to communicate what had happened to four people only: Martin 1:121.

176: Upon hearing of the attempt, Peel rushed to the Palace: Aubyn, *Queen Victoria* 162; Martin 1:121; TNA PRO MEPO 3/18. Albert claims the "Head of Police" was the man accompanying Peel, but Col. Rowan, the Commissioner most involved with the case at its early stages, did not meet with Albert directly on this day—and his account suggests that the other Commissioner, Mayne, was not there either.

176: The Queen in the meantime would not present herself as a target by going out in her carriage until she absolutely had to: TNA PRO MEPO 3/18.

177: Rowan thus ordered his detective (in all but name) Inspector Pearce to join the two inspectors assigned to the Palace and patrol Green and St. James's parks in plain clothes, watching for anyone who fit the description Albert had given: TNA PRO MEPO 3/18.

177: This time Murray saw them, and patiently listened to the boy's excruciatingly drawn-out tale: Martin 1:121.

177: Murray, with less of a sense imminent danger than Laurie had shown, or perhaps an awareness of Sir James's work schedule at the Home Office, wrote the three a letter for Graham and told them to call on the Home Secretary that afternoon between two and three: *Times* 2 June 1842, 6.

177: "I was present," Rowan wrote with exasperation, "during a very long Examination of the Lad who saw the pistol presented made tediously long by the impediment in his speech": TNA PRO MEPO 3/18.

178: He ordered his clerks to write up "as many written descriptions of the offender to be made out as there are entrances with St. James Park": TNA PRO MEPO 3/18.

179: She told Albert's secretary, George Anson, that she had had for some time a premonition that such a "mad attempt" would be made: Martin 1:122n.

179: Albert noted that, upon confirmation of Sunday's attempt, "we were naturally very much agitated, Victoria very nervous and unwell": Martin 1:121.

179: He indeed claims that a doctor recommended she deal with her agitation by going out: Martin 1:121.

179: Victoria rode out, she informed her Uncle Leopold, because she honestly felt she had no other option: Victoria *Letters* (first series) 1:398.

180: "I must expose the lives of my gentlemen," she wrote to her uncle, "but I will not those of my ladies": Longford 170.

180: Her lady in waiting, Lady Portman, and her maids of honor, Matilda Paget and Georgiana Liddell, waited in vain that afternoon to be called; Liddell, thus shunned, stalked off to grumble in the palace gardens: Bloomfield 44; Longford 170.

180: . . . they were on the lookout for the assailant, and, as Albert thought, "would seize him on the least imprudence or carelessness on his part": Martin 1:122.

180: The weather was superb that evening: Martin 1:122.

180: Later, Victoria's visiting Uncle Mensdorff helpfully told her "one is sure not to have been hit when one hears the report, as one never hears it when one is hit": Martin 1:122n.

180: "Looking out for such a man was not *des plus agreables*": Victoria *Letters* 1:398.

181: "You may imagine that our minds were not very easy. We looked behind every tree, and I cast my eyes round in search of the rascal's face": Martin 1:122.

181: "I had seen the prisoner half an hour before this," Trounce later told authorities: *Times* 11 June 1842, 6.

181: But Arbuthnot, feeling in his gut that something was wrong as they approached Constitution Hill, rode up to the postilion and demanded he ride even faster until they reached the Palace Gates: *Times* 18 June 1842, 7.

182: He was later to speculate that the speed of the carriage saved the Queen's life: *Times* 18 June 1842, 6.

182: He stood at attention and smartly saluted the Queen as she passed: TNA PRO MEPO 3/18.

182: . . . a "theatrical attitude," according to one of many witnesses: TNA PRO MEPO 3/18.

182: "It was not as if I had seen him fire the Pistol—I could have then laid hold of him sooner, or if I had known he was going to fire it. . . ." he sputtered guiltily in a police report: TNA PRO MEPO 3/18.

182: Wylde meanwhile galloped from Albert's side toward Francis: *Times* 18 June 1842, 7.

182: Allen had seen the flash from the pistol and heard the shot: *Times* 11 June 1842, 6.

183: Other witnesses—Colonel Arbuthnot in particular—agreed that the pistol's report was sharp and loud, the sign "of a pistol well loaded and rammed": TNA PRO TS 11/80.

183: Victoria, on the other hand, was certain that the shot was not loud at all—certainly, less loud than when Oxford had shot at her: Jerrold, *Early Court* 360.

183: Albert was sure Francis aimed low, the bullet going under the carriage; others claimed it went above; one of the Queen's grooms, riding behind her, thought Francis actually aimed not at the Queen, but at the hind wheel of her carriage: Martin 1:122; *Morning Chronicle* 31 May 1842, 5; "John Francis."

183: Trounce handed Russell the pistol; it was warm, suggesting recent discharge: *Times* 11 June 1842, 5.

183: The group marched Francis to the Porter's Lodge of the palace: *Times* 30 May 1842, 5.

183: There, he was searched: a little notebook, a key or two, a penny—and a small amount of gunpowder, screwed up in a piece of paper: enough to recharge his pistol. But he did not have any bullets: *Morning Chronicle* 31 May 1842, 5; *Times* 11 June 1842, 6; 18 June 1842, 7.

183: Wylde observed the quiver in his lips: *Morning Chronicle* 18 June 1842, 7.

183: . . . they led Francis across the palace to the equerries' entrance, bundled him into a cab, drove him to the Gardiner Lane station: *Times* 18 June 1842, 7.

183: Mark Russell . . . provided police with the whereabouts of Francis's father: Accounts differ as to Francis's father's whereabouts: one account says he was found at home, another at the theatre, and a third, Deptford. *Morning Chronicle* 31 May 1842, 5; *Times* 30 May 1842, 5; 1 June 1842, 6; 18 June 1842, 7; *Ipswich Journal* 4 June 1842, 1.

184: Word of Francis's capture was sent around the building to Colonel Rowan, still in the process of giving orders to find the assailant of the day before: TNA PRO MEPO 3/18.

184: In the Lords, the news was brought to the Duke of Wellington: *Times* 31 May 1842, 3.

184: In the Commons, the news could not have come at a more dramatic moment: *Times* 31 May 1842, 4.

184: . . . in a voice in which his "excitement well nigh overpowered his utterance," he informed the House of the attempt: "Attempt to Assassinate the Queen."

184: Francis's examination was attended by members of both parties: *Times* 30 May 1842, 5; *Morning Chronicle* 31 May 1842, 5.

185: "He is not out of his mind, but a thorough scamp": Martin 1:122.

185: . . . a coolness, calmness, and firmness that astonished the Council: *Freeman's Journal* 2 June 1842, 2.

185: To Colonel Arbuthnot, he asked "whether he thought he intended to shoot the queen, or whether it was done in a frolic": *Times* 30 May 1842, 5.

185: After the examination, Francis was bundled out the back entrance and conveyed to Tothill Fields for the night: *Times* 11 June 1842, 6.

185: "Scene-shifter! No, he's a stage carpenter": *Times* 11 June 1842, 6.

185: The next day, he was brought back to Whitehall at noon to finish his examination: *Morning Chronicle* 1 June 1842, 5.

186: . . . the crowd assembled outside the Home Office saw him lean back in the vehicle: *Morning Chronicle* 1 June 1842, 5; *Liverpool Mercury* 3 June 1842, 175.

186: . . . "the all engrossing topic of conversation amongst all classes": *Times* 1 June 1842, 6.

186: . . . the Duchess hurried back with her brother-in-law to the Palace, where, bursting into tears, she fell upon Victoria, who calmly caressed and reassured her: *Times* 1 June 1842, 7; *Ipswich Journal* 4 June 1842, 1.

186: Robert Peel belied his usual coolness in an emotional meeting with the Queen: Bloomfield 44.

186: . . . an excellent rendition, according to a reporter for the *Morning Chronicle*: 31 May 1842, 5.

187: "When her Majesty goes abroad among the people for the purpose of taking recreation or exercise," John Russell said in Parliament that afternoon, "there is not one among her subjects who has less reason to fear an enemy in any single individual of the millions who constitute her subjects": "Attack on Her Majesty."

187: . . . at around 4:30, the gates opened: *Times* 1 June 1842, 6.

188: . . . bursting into applause at the end of every line, and screaming "deafening acclamations" at the song's command "Scatter her enemies": *Times* 1 June 1842, 6.

188: . . . *Elena da Feltre*, called by a critic an "abortion" and "utterly worthless and common-place": *Times* 1 June 1842, 6.

188: . . . "relying with confidence in the generous loyalty of her people with a determination not to be confined as a prisoner in her own palace": "Attack on Her Majesty."

188: . . . "the feeling now was of a deeper cast": Martin 1:121n.

188: . . . speakers at hundreds of congratulatory meetings across the country waxed enthusiastically about Victoria's chivalric heroism: her calmness and resolution; her "kindness . . . consideration . . . generosity": Thus the tea-merchant Richard Twining and a colleague, W. S. Jones, at a meeting of the East India Company; *Times* 4 June 1842, 6.

188: . . . "we feel sure that it is no flattery to say that a finer instance of mingled heroism and generosity than this would be difficult to find": *Morning Chronicle* 1 June 1842, 5.

189: . . . her action he thought "very brave, but imprudent": Greville 2:96.

189: . . . it was his understanding that the queen *would* be prudent and stay at home: TNA PRO MEPO 3/18.

189: The *Globe*, for instance, held that "the Queen's bravery is more impressive when contrasted with the ministers' apathy": quoted in *Morning Chronicle* 3 June 1842, 4.

190: For years Rowan's younger and in effect junior co-commissioner Richard Mayne had favored a detective branch: Cobb 95.

190: . . . Waterloo veteran Charles Rowan, the prime mover behind the military structure of the police when the department was formed in 1829: Gregory.

190: . . . the Commissioners forwarded a memorandum to Graham at the Home Office: For the fullest information on the formation of the detective branch, see Browne 120-122.

190: . . . that omniscient knowledge of crime and criminals that Charles Dickens, who later became most enthusiastic and vocal fan of the detective branch, declared to be one of their strongest assets: Dickens, *Amusements* 265-282; 356-369.

190: Mayne had probably long had a list in mind for this occasion: Cobb 95.

190: Senior Inspector: Ascoli 118-19.

Chapter 11: Powder and Wadding

191: Her precarious state did not prevent the police from searching their Tottenham Court lodgings: *Freeman's Journal* 2 June 1842, 2.

192: . . . "the disagreeable condition of perpetually collecting pewter pots": *Examiner* 11 June 1842, 376.

192: . . . "his only motive could be like Oxford to ensure a situation for life": TNA PRO MEPO 3/18.

192: . . . Oxford himself claimed that "If they had hanged me, there would have been nothing of the kind again": *Times* 4 June 1842, 6; *Morning Chronicle* 20 June 1842, 6.

192: . . . his imitator, Francis: *Morning Chronicle* 13 June 1842, 3.

192: The procedure "flatters the diseased appetite for *éclat* and noto-riety": *Examiner* 11 June 1842.

192: . . . William Clarkson, a hardheaded, "rough, bluff, testy personage": Robinson 75.

194: . . . the "most perfect *sang froid*": *Liverpool Mercury* 3 June 1842, 175.

195: But the sheriffs only admitted those with written orders: *Times* 18 June 1842, 7.

195: "A child's marble—why, gentlemen, the very gravel path he was treading might have furnished him with a stone smooth or angular, quite adequate to the purpose in view": *Times* 18 June 1842, 7. For various (and varying) accounts of the trial, see *Times* 18 June 1842, 7-8; *Morning Chronicle* 18 June 1842, 7; "John Francis."

196: . . . for the last two weeks he had been taken in hand by a creator and purveyor of a treatment for stammering, Thomas Hunt": Boase, "Thomas Hunt" 280; *Times* 25 June 1842, 8.

196: . . . "a piece fired off with ball sounds somewhat sharper than blank cartridge": *Times* 18 June 1842, 7.

196: . . . the powder was "well rammed down": *Times* 18 June 1842, 7.

196: . . . "what I want to know is, whether a pistol fired from the spot where the prisoner stood, if only loaded with wadding, would cause injury to the Queen?": *Times* 18 June 1842, 7.

196: "At seven to nine feet the wadding of the pistol would wound the skin or any exposed part, such as the face, or set fire to the dress": *Morning Chronicle* 18 June 1842, 7.

197: He became "ten times better off than he was before he committed the act": *Times* 18 June 1842, 7.

197: "I know that the books state, and so do my learned friends, that you must give evidence of the pistols being loaded beyond powder and wadding": *Times* 18 June 1842, 8.

197: " . . . though there were no ball or destructive materials," he instructed the jury, "yet there might have been powder and wadding": *Times* 18 June 1842, 8.

198: . . . "we find the prisoner Guilty on the second and third counts": *Times* 18 June 1842, 8.

198: That verdict, according to a court reporter, "rendered Mr. Clarkson's objection immaterial": *Times* 18 June 1842, 8.

198: "John Francis, you stand convicted of high treason: what have you to say why the court should not give you judgment to die according to the law?": *Times* 18 June 1842, 8.

199: . . . a jaded population, which "seems to require stimulants of an extraordinary nature to arouse it. . . . Poor Daly was only shot. *He was not cut up!*": *Morning Chronicle* 20 June 1842, 6.

200: The prosecution's witnesses methodically established all of Cooper's actions on the fifth of May, from his confrontation with Moss to his eventual apprehension: For full (and at times varied) accounts of Cooper's trial, see the *Times* 20 June 1842, 7-8; *Morning Chronicle* 20 June 1842, 6-7; "Thomas Cooper."

200: . . . he "should have his father up out of his grave, as there was no use in his lying there": *Times* 20 June 1842, 8.

200: Cooper's odd behavior had all begun with a bout of "putrid fever": *Times* 20 June 1842, 8.

201: . . . "he once bought a silver watch for 14s., and picked it to pieces. He then sold it for 7s.": *Morning Chronicle* 20 June 1842, 6.

201: . . . the "regimen and restraint" of Newgate had had a deeply therapeutic effect on his client: *Times* 20 June 1842, 8.

201: . . . "every person who had arrived at the age of discretion must be considered sane until he was proved to be otherwise": *Times* 20 June 1842, 8.

202: . . . Cooper was ordered to stand: *Morning Chronicle* 20 June 1842, 7.

202: "You had better listen to me. You had better listen to me, prisoner, instead of shaking your fist at any one there": *Morning Chronicle* 20 June 1842, 7.

202: . . . Cooper burst into a frenzied rage and tried to tear an inkwell out of the bar of the dock: *Morning Chronicle* 20 June 1842, 7.

202: . . . he instead again shook his fist and hurled threats of vengeance against the all witnesses: *Times* 20 June 1842, 8.

202: When returned to his cell after his trial, he collapsed into a seat, moaning and weeping: *Morning Chronicle* 20 June 1842, 6.

203: . . . the *Times* on the next day ran an editorial that predicted, based on Justice Tindal's "grave and solemn" way of passing verdict, that Francis would indeed be executed: *Times* 18 Jun 1842, 6.

203: . . . "there could be no pretence for entertaining a single thought to her prejudice or against her sacred person": *Morning Chronicle* 20 June 1842.

203: The reporter for the *Morning Chronicle* reporting this scene held that Francis was weak-minded and impressionable: *Morning Chronicle* 20 June 1842, 6.

203: Cooper expected no reprieve; he wished death to come as soon as possible: *Times* 1 July 1842, 6.

203: . . . Cooper generally reverted to his natural state of rage, sputtering curses and threats of violence against the Metropolitan Police: *Times* 1 July 1842, 6; *Era* 26 June 1842, 8.

203: His only regret was that he could not hurt them or the witnesses against him: *Era* 26 June 1842, 8.

203: Francis received the news with "heart-rending despair": *Era* 26 June 1842.

204: John Francis Senior sent his petition for clemency to the Queen via Home Secretary Graham: TNA PRO HO 45/3079.

204: Francis's sister Jane wrote her own petition, and sought a different avenue to the Queen: TNA PRO HO 45/3079.

204: At least three other groups drew up petitions to Graham or the Queen: TNA PRO HO 45/3079.

204: Almost certainly against Cooper's wishes, his mother drew up a petition for her son as well: *Era* 26 June 1842, 8.

204: "I am directed to express to you [Graham's] regret that there is no sufficient ground to justify him consistently with his public duty in advising her Majesty to comply with the prayer thereof": *Era* 26 June 1842, 11.

204: It was a scene of "a most distressing character," according to a witness: *Era* 3 July 1842.

205: On Saturday 1 July, Peel reported the decision to Prince Albert: Charlot 221.

205: "Norfolk Island is scarcely safety—prolonged agony it certainly is": Browning and Browning 6:28.

205: . . . "the feeling that he is to be executed is very painful to me," Victoria wrote in her journal. And when she learned of the commutation she wrote "I of course am glad": RA VIC/MAIN/QVJ/1842, 1 July 1842.

205: A convict ship, the *Marquis of Hastings*, had arrived in Portsmouth on 24 June: *Caledonian Mercury* 30 June 1842, 4.

206: Two days later . . . he was clapped in heavy irons and one of Newgate's chief jailers conveyed him by the Southwestern Railway to Gosport: *Examiner* 9 July 1842, 445.

206: On the eighteenth, he embarked: "Convicts and Convict Ships sent to Tasmania."

206: "The opinion is that he will not long survive the hardships consequent on the fulfillment of his sentence," wrote a writer in the *Examiner*: *Examiner* 9 July 1842.

Chapter 12: Hunchbacked Little Miscreant

207:   . . . on either side of the Mall, two or three deep . . . : *Times* 4 July 1842, 4.

207:   He hardly saw himself as a human being: *Ipswich Journal* 16 July 1842, 1, qtd. from the *Globe*.

207:   . . . [he was] tired to death of his life: *Era* 10 July 1842, 7.

208:   His arms were atrophied sticks: *Ipswich Journal* 16 July 1842, 1, qtd. from the *Globe*.

208:   His eyes sunk into his head. His expression was permanently care-worn and weary: *Times* 5 July 1842, 5.

209:   "I shall never be otherwise than I am": *Ipswich Journal* 16 July 1842, 1, qtd. from the *Globe*.

209:   . . . but the painstaking work was simply too exhausting for his pitiful limbs: *Freeman's Journal* 7 July 1842, 3; qtd. from the *Globe*.

209:   . . . his apprenticeship to a cheesemonger resulted in failure, as did a job as an errand boy at Her Majesty's Stationery Office: *Morning Chronicle* 7 July 1842, 5.

209:   Two months before, he had come across in this way several articles on Edward Oxford: TNA MEPO 3/19A; *Morning Chronicle* 6 July 1842, 5; an example of such an article, appearing a month before, appears in the *Weekly Dispatch* 5 June 1842, 271.

210:   But he suffered greatly from the insults and disrespect of his younger brothers: *1841 England Census* (mistranscribed as "John Bonn"); *Examiner* 9 July 1842, 442.

210:   His mother fell ill with worry; his father frantically took a full description of the boy to Clerkenwell police station and pressed them to find him: *Morning Chronicle* 5 July 1842, 3; 7 July 1842, 5.

210:   Four days later, Bean's employer Mr. Hilton spotted him lurking outside his business: *Morning Chronicle* 7 July 1842, 5.

210:   . . . he bought his pistol from a neighbor, Mr. Bird: *Times* 5 July 1842, 5; *Morning Chronicle* 5 July 1842, 3; 6 July 1842, 5.

210:   . . . he had sold off his meager collection of books, including his Bible, to get it: *Times* 5 July 1842, 5.

210:   . . . probably not worth the three shillings he paid: *Annual Register* 84:120; *Times* 5 July 1842, 5.

210:   Bird noticed Bean's "childish glee": *Annual Register* 120.

211:   Bean then brought the pistol to a neighbor to clean it: *Times* 5 July 1842, 5; *Morning Chronicle* 5 July 1842, 3.

211: . . . a few fragments of a clay smoking-pipe: *Morning Chronicle* 26 August 1842, 4; Martin 1:124.

211: He again lived on the streets, sleeping where he could—in abandoned houses, in fields—on the outskirts of Islington: *Times* 5 July 1842, 5.

211: . . . he had survived last week on only eight pence: *Era* 10 July 1842, 7.

211: "Dear Father and Mother": "John William Bean"; *Times* 5 July 1842, 5. Several variations of this letter appeared in the newspapers, but this one is a transcription of the actual letter, read aloud at Bean's trial.

212: The four had come and gone from the palace: *Times* 1 July 1842, 6; 2 July 1842, 6.

212: The carriages were all covered landaus: "John William Bean."

212: Leopold rode with them. *Times* 4 July 1842, 5; Martin 1:123.

212: . . . "genteel-looking," of normal size and stature, and very nattily dressed: *Morning Chronicle* 4 July 1842, 5; TNA PRO MEPO 1/19A.

213: . . . some could see the light blue or maybe pale green bonnet of the Queen: "John William Bean."

213: He clearly saw the hammer drop and heard the click: *Times* 4 July 1842, 4.

213: "Look here, Fred," he exclaimed, "this chap is going to have a pop at the Queen": *Morning Chronicle* 4 July 1842, 5.

214: "He did not walk so fast as my brother wished," said Frederick Dassett: "he *is* a cripple": "John William Bean."

214: Dassett "certainly appeared to me," one member of the crowd later said, "to be disposed to excite the mob": "John William Bean"; TNA PRO MEPO 3/19A.

214: It was a hoax, some shouted—the gun wasn't loaded! Others called out to Dassett to give the boy back his pistol, and to let him go: "John William Bean"; *Morning Chronicle* 26 August 1842, 4.

214: "put it into your pocket and run away with it": *Times* 4 July 1842, 4.

214: Dassett presented pistol and Bean to P.C. Thomas Hearn, explaining what had happened: *Times* 4 July 1842, 4.

214: . . . an officer with much more experience on the force and particularly with guarding the Queen: *Morning Chronicle* 26 August 1842, 4; "John William Bean."

214: . . . "large numbers actually clambered the sharp-pointed railings": *Times* 4 July 1842, 4.

215:   . . . "otherwise my arm would have been broken": *Times* 4 July 1842, 4.

215:   . . . Partridge dismissed Dassett's story of the hunchbacked dwarf as "shamming": Martin 1:124.

215:   . . . joined by Inspector George Martin, who took custody of the pistol: *Morning Chronicle* 26 August 1842, 4.

215:   . . . at least six hundred of the Queen's loyal subjects": *Morning Chronicle*, 4 July 1842, 5.

215:   Three thousand, according to the *Times*: *Times* 4 July 1842, 4.

216:   One of the first there was Daniel O'Connell; *Times* 4 July 1842, 4.

216:   Graham personally complimented him . . . for his meritorious behavior: *Times* 4 July 1842, 4.

216:   Within a day, they were to be dismissed from the force: *Morning Chronicle* 5 July 1842, 3.

217:   "Description of a boy": *Times* 4 July 1842, 4.

217:   . . . a reporter . . . identified the "exceedingly agitated and flushed" boy: *Times* 4 July 1842, 4.

217:   . . . some newspapers the next day were able to report the certain capture of the assailant: *Times* 4 July 1842, 4; *Morning Chronicle* 4 July 1842, 5.

217:   At Smithfield, an inspector was particularly enthusiastic: *Morning Chronicle* 5 July 1842, 3.

218:   . . . a hunchbacked man was walking down the road dividing E and F Divisions, when he was spotted simultaneously by two officers on either side of the street: *Morning Chronicle* 5 July 1842, 3.

218:   " . . . the number of little deformed men 'detained,' to use a mild phrase, was astonishing": *Illustrated London News*, qtd. Lock 73.

218:   *Punch* caught the absurdity of the moment: *Punch* 3 (1842): 23.

218:   . . . P.C. Henry Webb, lingered after muster and reminded Penny that the description in the route paper matched the description a distraught John William Bean Senior had given the police nearly three weeks before of his son: *Morning Chronicle* 5 July 1842, 3.

218:   His state of undress, in Victorian terms—no coat, waistcoat, or cap: *Morning Chronicle* 5 July 1842, 3.

218:   When Webb touched Bean's shoulder, he realized the boy was trembling uncontrollably: *Times* 5 July 1842, 5.

219: As they left the house, Bean's alarmed mother, Sally, came upon them: *Times* 5 July 1842, 5.

219: . . . the resemblance between the two was striking: *Morning Chronicle* 5 July 1842, 3.

219: The Dassetts had to be called in . . . to identify Bean as the one who assaulted the Queen: *Times* 5 July 1842, 5.

219: Charles Dassett and Webb then had the honor of signing the sheet charging Bean with "attempting to shoot at Her Majesty": *Times* 5 July 1842, 5.

219: "I suppose Cooper is hanging now": *Freeman's Journal* 7 July 1842, 3; qtd. from *The Globe* 5 July 1842.

219: Cooper's sullen passivity about his fate had vanished two days before the end, and he quaked as he walked to his death: For accounts of Cooper's execution, see the *Times* 5 July 1842, 6, and the *Morning Chronicle* 5 July 1842, 3.

220: . . . Bean was run at a trot within a phalanx of A Division officers: *Newcastle Courant* 8 July 1842, 3.

220: Attendance at this examination was fuller and more formidable than the day before: *Era* 10 July 1842.

220: . . . he collapsed with agitation on entering the room: *Times* 5 July 1842, 5.

221: . . . he helpfully told Inspector Martin where he had bought the gun; that evening, Martin, accompanied by Bean's father, confirmed the sale: *Morning Chronicle* 5 July 1842, 3; 6 July 1842, 5; *Times* 5 July 1842, 5.

221: He was stripped and bathed, a process open to reporters: *Examiner* 9 July 1842, 442.

221: "I remarked to Albert, I felt sure an attempt on us would be shortly repeated": Charlot 222.

221: Peel—according to Albert's first biographer "in public so cold and self-commanding, in reality so full of genuine feeling"—burst into tears: Martin 1:124.

222: "The Queen and People . . . were drawn into more intimate communion": *Spectator* 4 July 1842, rpt. in Dodds 68.

222: . . . her ministers commanded her to remain while they gathered more information: *Times* 5 July 1842, 5.

222: Another rumor was that the Queen was "deeply affected" by the news of the attempt: *Morning Chronicle* 4 July 1842, 5.

223: He was a "deformed, decrepit, miserable looking dwarf," "that crooked piece of malignity," a "hunchbacked little miscreant," and a "miserable and contemptible-looking wretch": *Newcastle Courant* 8 July 1842, 3; *Illustrated London News* 1:130, 1:134; *Liverpool Mercury* 8 July 1842, 214.

223: Prince Albert referred to him as a "hunchbacked wretch," Home Secretary Graham described him as "an hump-backed boy of an idiotic appearance," and Peel told the Queen that Bean was "the most miserable object he ever saw": Martin 1:123; Gash 342; Charlot 222-23.

223: . . . "these repeated attempts on the life of our beloved Sovereign are utterly incomprehensible": *Morning Chronicle* 4 July 1842, 4.

224: . . . "the savage and impotent monomania, which has emigrated from France to England, is one of the gravest symptoms of the profound disorders which agitated modern societies;" *Messenger*, qtd. *Illustrated London News* 1:130.

224: "What is this strange mania of queen-shooting?": Browning and Browning 6:25.

224: Men, not boys, shot at Louis-Philippe: The fullest treatment of Louis-Philippe's assailants is in Jill Harsin's *Barricades*.

224: "If I had killed the tyrant . . . we would have conquered the universe and all the despots": Harsin 195.

224: "I die for Liberty!": Harsin 172.

225: The hail of bullets from this primitive machine-gun—twenty-five loaded gun barrels on a wooden frame—instantly created "a void around the King": Harsin 147-66.

225: This did not prevent partisan commentators from seeing the attempts as indirectly political: Poole 188-92; *Caledonian Mercury* 11 July 1842.

225: . . . "Are not these strange times?": Thomas Carlyle to Margaret A. Carlyle, 4 July 1842: Carlyle.

226: . . . they were all driven by a "morbid craving after notoriety": Or a "diseased passion for notoriety," or "villainous anglings for notoriety," and so on. *Liverpool Mercury* 3 June 1842, 180; 8 July 1842, 214; *Examiner* 11 June 1842, 369; 9 July 1842, 433; *Times* 5 July 1842, 4; *Morning Chronicle* 5 July 1842, 3; "Security of the Queen's Person" (in a speech by Lord John Russell).

226: If "we would make up our minds to flog them in the sight of their companions": *Times* 5 July 1842, 4.

226: On the day after Bean's first Privy Council examination, Graham met with the two commissioners of the police and with George Maule: *Morning Chronicle* 6 July 1842, 5.

226: Bean . . . would be charged not with High Treason but with common assault: *Morning Chronicle* 7 July 1842, 5.

227: On the next day . . . John Bean, discernibly sunk into a depressed torpor, was brought from Tothill Fields for a final examination before Peel and the Privy Council: *Morning Chronicle* 7 July 1842, 5.

227: He was charged with a misdemeanor and sent back to Tothill Fields for the night, to be brought to Newgate the next day to await trial: *Morning Chronicle* 6 July 1842, qtd. *Liverpool Mercury* 8 July 1842.

227: . . . "contempt and ridicule . . . was quite enough to act as an effectual antidote": *Liverpool Mercury* 8 July 1842, 214, qtd. from *Morning Chronicle* 6 July 1842.

227: John Francis, having tearfully taken leave of his family forever on Monday . . . was removed to Gosport: *Examiner* 9 July 1842, 445.

227: Peel had no intention of modifying existing laws of treason, he made clear: "Security of the Queen's Person."

227: . . . "publicly or privately whipped": "Treason Act 1842."

228: "These are the offences of base and degraded beings": "Security of the Queen's Person."

228: . . . the Irish people in particular would be grateful for a law to "brand . . . with contemptuous execration" any future assailant: "Security of the Queen's Person."

228: "And yet, Hume maintained—echoing the complaint of the Chartist petition—while the people's sufferings increased, the Queen and her court lived in comfort": "Security of the Queen's Person."

228: "If anything could be more dissatisfactory to the great mass of the people than another": "Security of the Queen's Person."

229: . . . "for these contemptible acts they shall receive the degrading punishment of personal chastisement": "Security of the Queen's Person."

229: He was placed in a cell near Reverend Carver: *Ipswich Journal* 16 July 1842, 1.

230: . . . a rash of strikes and demonstrations, beginning in June in the collieries of Staffordshire: Chase 211.

230: Two policemen were killed in Manchester; two rioters were shot dead by soldiers in Preston: Gash 343; Chase 215.

230: Peel called the Privy Council to meet and issue a royal proclamation: Gash 343.

230: "I have not had a spare moment since the close of the session": Parker 1:323.

231: ". . . our arrangements were quickly and vigorously made": Gash 345.

231: . . . he got word that Victoria had been assassinated: Gash 344.

231: . . . he did acknowledge to Graham . . . that the Queen would face no more danger there than in England: Gash 346.

231: In Edinburgh, expectation for the visit had "superseded all other topics of the day": *Examiner* 20 August 1842, 4.

231: . . . in London the public scrambled to obtain choice seats on steamers to see the royal party: *Caledonian Mercury* 27 August 1842.

231: Lord Abinger in his younger days (when he was James Scarlett) had been the most successful advocate in England: Barker.

232: Bean was charged on four counts: For accounts of Bean's trial, see *Morning Chronicle* 26 August 1842, 4; *Times* 26 August 1842, 6-7; "John William Bean."

232: "Was not there a good deal of laughing going on?": "John William Bean."

232: . . . he risked being tried a second time for the same offense, "contrary to all the principles of English law": *Morning Chronicle* 26 August 1842, 4.

233: . . . "it is probable I must have seen it": "John William Bean."

233: "Lord Abinger.—If you saw the prisoner for ten minutes": *Times* 26 August 1842, 6.

234: When his father took the stand to plead to his son's "mild, peaceable, and inoffensive" conduct, Bean wept bitterly: "John William Bean"; *Freeman's Journal* 27 August 1842, 4.

234: He cited as evidence the curious case where a man had once been indicted for *grinning* at George III: *Morning Chronicle* 26 August 1842, 4.

234: Bean heard the verdict without emotion: *Times* 26 August 1842, 7.

234: "I know of no misdemeanour more affecting the public peace of the kingdom, of greater magnitude or deserving more serious punishment": *Times* 26 August 1842, 7.

Chapter 13: Tory Spies

236: . . . bad weather forced the steamships to tow the yacht most of the way up the coast, the royal couple spending much of the time below-decks, ill: Gill 229.

237: Early the next morning, the royal procession shot through the city on the way to Dalkeith Palace, without sufficient warning to the public and before city dignitaries had assembled: *Times* 5 September 1842, 4.

237: "Scotland has rarely seen a prouder day—perhaps never": *Times* 6 September 1842, 4.

237: "The crowds of persons were beyond description": Peel, *Private Letters* 206.

237: . . . a man with an overwhelming urge to kill was watching and awaiting his opportunity: Daniel McNaughten's movements, and his psychological state, are best set out in the accounts of his trial for murdering Edward Drummond: *Times* 4 March 1843 5-6; 6 March 1843, 5-7; West and Walk, eds. 12-73.

237: . . . Paisley—incidentally one of Britain's worst-suffering towns, that hungry summer: Hurd 262.

238: Daniel McNaughtan saw the carriage, saw one man in it—and committed that man's face to memory: Charles Greville, clerk of the Privy Council, diarist, and acquaintance of both Drummond and Peel first made the credible speculation that McNaughtan first mistook Drummond for Peel during the Queen's visit to Scotland: Greville 1:143-4.

238: Drummond later joked about his being taken for "a great man" in Scotland: Greville 1:143-4.

238: Until 1841, he had been a very successful craftsman . . . a wood-turner in Glasgow: Richard Moran, in his study of McNaughtan, *Knowing Right from Wrong*, makes a compelling case that McNaughtan's delusions of persecution "were lodged firmly in the political reality of the day." His further claim that those "alleged" persecutions were nothing of the kind, but the actual malevolent acts of Glasgow's Tories, is far less compelling. Moran, *Knowing* 25-59.

238: One man repeatedly threw straw at him: West and Walk, eds. 59, 66.

239: "I can do nothing for you. I fear you are labouring under an aberration of mind": West and Walk, eds. 64.

239: But Daniel McNaughtan Senior refused, thinking that his son's delusions would pass: West and Walk, eds. 59.

239: . . . the instant he set foot on the quay at Boulogne, he could see one of them scowling at him from behind the custom-house watch box: West and Walk, eds. 65.

240: He took up his post in the heart of Tory darkness: the streets outside of Whitehall, standing all day for two weeks on the steps leading to the Privy Council office: West and Walk, eds. 25-27.

240: Two policemen from A Division—including P.C. Partridge—took note of him: *Times* 4 March 1843, 4.

240: . . . he twice pointed Drummond out to a police constable, asking if that man was Robert Peel: Moran, *Knowing* 38.

240: McNaughtan . . . came down the steps and shadowed Drummond: *Times* 21 January 1843, 5.

240: Drummond's jacket caught fire: *Times* 27 January 1843, 5.

241: Constable James Silver, standing next to the two, was upon McNaughtan an instant after the first shot: *Times* 4 March 1843, 4.

241: An apothecary was sent for: *Times* 4 March 1843, 4.

241: . . . the best doctors in town finished what the bullet had started, leeching and bleeding him relentlessly: *Times* 23 January 1843, 5; 24 January 1843, 5; 25 January 1843, 4; Moran, *Knowing* 7-8.

241: . . . "he" or "she" (Silver could not tell which) "shall not break my peace of mind any longer": *Times* 4 March 1843, 5.

241: "I suppose you are aware who the gentleman is you shot at?" Tierney asked him: *Times* 3 March 1843, 5; West and Walk, eds. 24.

241: "The evidence of his mental delusion is strong": Victoria *Letters* (first series) 1:572.

242: "There is and should be . . . a difference between that madness which is such that a man knows not what he does": Peel, *Sir Robert Peel* 2:553.

242: "Who can doubt but that Bellingham was as insane as Oxford?": *Times* 30 January 1843, 5.

242: "Every preparation is in progress to meet this vague and dangerous excuse": Victoria *Letters* (first series) 1:459.

242: On the second of February, McNaughtan was brought to the bar of the Old Bailey to enter his plea": *Times* 3 February 1843, 7-8.

242: The judge, Baron Abinger, gave the defense a month to prepare. Moreover, he granted counsel's request that McNaughtan be allowed access to his bank account: *Times* 3 February 1843, 7-8.

243: At 10:00 on 3 March 1843, an excited Daniel McNaughtan was again brought to the bar of the Old Bailey: For differing accounts of the

McNaughtan trial, see the *Times* 4 March 1843, 5-6: 6 March 1843, 5; West and Walk, eds. 12-73.

243: . . . Follett freely admitted that McNaughtan might be suffering from a "morbid affection of the mind": West and Walk, eds. 15.

244: "If there be thought and design": The case is that of Lord Ferrers. West and Walk, eds. 16.

244: "I never thought him unsettled in his mind": West and Walk, eds. 27.

244: "I did not have any idea that his mind was disordered": West and Walk, eds. 29.

244: . . . sequestered in a local coffee house: *Times* 4 March 1843, 6.

245: "It is but as yesterday": West and Walk, eds. 34.

245: . . . "the greatest deference should be paid": West and Walk, eds. 33.

245: . . . "the perception, the judgment, the reason, the sentiments, the affections, the propensities, the passions": West and Walk, eds. 42.

245: . . . "profound and scientific" Scottish jurist, Baron Hume: West and Walk, eds. 43.

246: . . . there existed in McNaughtan "the presence of insanity sufficient to deprive the prisoner of all self-control": *Times* 6 March 1843, 6.

246: . . . "the delusion was so strong that nothing but a physical impediment could have prevented him from committing the act": *Times* 6 March 1843, 6.

247: "Mr. Solicitor General, are you prepared . . . with any evidence to combat this testimony?": West and Walk, eds. 71.

247: . . . "the whole of the medical evidence is on one side": West and Walk, eds. 72.

247: . . . McNaughtan followed Oxford's path from Newgate to Southwark in a cab with Governor Cope: Moran, *Knowing* 23-4.

248: . . . "I have in contemplation the accomplishment of a certain pet project": *Times* 7 March 1843, 5.

249: "It is a lamentable reflection . . . that a man may be at the same time so insane as to be reckless of his own life and the lives of others": Victoria *Letters* (first series) 1:586.

249: "The law may be perfect": Victoria *Letters* (first series) 1:587.

250: . . . no one was criminally liable of a crime when he "is under the influence of delusion and insanity": "Insanity and Crime."

250: "What are the proper questions to be submitted to the jury when a person": West and Walk, eds. 74.

250: ". . . at the time of committing of the act, the party accused was labouring under such a defect of reason": West and Walk, eds. 79.

251: This curious protection was designed in 1842: A record in the database of the Museum of London holds that the parasol was "used by Queen Victoria after [an] assassination attempt, possibly 1840 (or 1842)." Logic points to the latter date—and leads one to question whether it was ever used at all.

251: . . . at three and a quarter pounds: Staniland 144.

PART 3: EXHIBITIONS

Chapter 14: Birthday

255: Observing the spectacle for the first time was the seven-year-old Prince of Wales: *Liverpool Mercury*, 22 May 1849, 325.

256: . . . "the most beautiful dress at the drawing-room": *Liverpool Mercury* 22 May 1849, 325.

256: . . . the Queen required dresses of British manufacture at all her drawing rooms: Weintraub, *Victoria* 199.

257: Albert had been her sole confidant and her private secretary: Weintraub, *Victoria* 170.

257: "It is you who have entirely formed me": Weintraub, *Victoria* 170.

257: "The Prince is become so identified with the Queen": Greville 1:323.

257: . . . the Cambridges absented themselves from the Court in a huff: St. Aubyn, *Queen Victoria* 220.

257: "I was forced to give him a strong push and drive him down a few steps": Gill 208.

258: "The life I led then was so artificial and superficial and yet I thought I was happy": Charlot 215.

258: . . . he kept the keys and constantly checked the locks: Jerrold, *Married Life* 85-6.

258: The Queen . . . thought infants unpleasantly "frog-like": St. Aubyn, *Queen Victoria* 167.

258: . . . she "only very exceptionally" found conversation with her children "either agreeable or easy": Hibbert, *Queen Victoria* 184.

258: "I am coming more and more convinced . . . that the only true happiness in this world is to be found in the domestic circle": St. Aubyn, *Queen Victoria* 204.

259: . . . he set to work and replaced the bureaucratic anarchy of the three competing household departments: Gill 197-8.

259: . . . he made the monarchy profitable, removing it forever from the chronic indebtedness that had plagued the Queen's royal uncles: St. Aubyn, *Queen Victoria* 182.

259: By 1843, they wanted even more seclusion—a residence bought with their own funds, and thus free of government administration: St. Aubyn, *Queen Victoria* 185.

259: "a pretty little Castle in the old Scotch style": Victoria, *Leaves* 59.

260: "The papers . . . are most kind and gratifying": Victoria *Letters* (first series) 2:27.

260: The population, employment, exports, and gross national product all shot up: Evans 74.

261: "Oh, Men, with Sisters dear!" *Punch* 5:260 (1843).

262: No one knew exactly where the fungal disease *Phytophthora infestans*, or potato blight, came from: Donnelly 41.

262: . . . in a month, a third of that country's overwhelmingly predominant crop transmogrified into a stinking, inedible goo: Donnelly 41-3; Woodham-Smith, *Great Hunger* 94-102.

262: Disraeli "hacked and mangled Peel with the most unsparing severity": Greville 2:117.

263: Ultimately, Peel won—and lost: Hilton 511-513.

263: . . . "rotten potatoes have done it all": Greville 2:350.

263: He continued importing food, but demanded that local relief committees buy the food at market price: Donnelly 49.

263: . . . he allowed public works to continue, but government loans ceased completely: Woodham-Smith, *Great Hunger* 105.

263: . . . fever ravaged the population: Woodham-Smith, *Great Hunger* 187-188.

264: "The great evil with which we have to contend," declared Trevelyan at the end of 1846, is "not the physical evil of the famine": Woodham-Smith, *Great Hunger* 156.

264: "The state of Ireland is most alarming": James Murphy 61.

264: . . . the suffering during the first few months of 1849 was among the worst of all: Woodham-Smith, *Great Hunger* 377.

264: In the end, one million died: Saville 70.

265: Victoria's royal palaces became aristocratic refugee camps: St. Aubyn, *Queen Victoria* 222.

265: That month, the Chartists announced that they planned to march: Saville 91.

265: The troops in the capital were doubled and stationed out of sight at strategic points across the city, concentrating on the bridges over the Thames, upon which artillery was trained: Chase 300; Saville 109; St. Aubyn, *Queen Victoria* 223.

265: Eighty-five thousand men were sworn in as special constables—a government masterstroke, ensuring that the middle class, unlike the French middle class, would remain squarely with the state: Saville 109, 112, 227.

265: . . . 22-day-old Princess Louise: Jerrold, *Married Life* 205.

265: . . . estimates of the crowd differ widely: Dorothy Thompson, in *The Chartists*, guesses 20,000; Malcolm Chase, in his *Chartism: A New History*, 150,000. Thompson 325, Chase 302.

266: . . . it was found (after a suspiciously quick count) to have less than a third of the six million signatures claimed: Chase 313.

266: "We had our revolution yesterday, and it went up in smoke": Albert, *Letters* 135.

266: . . . Young Ireland, a group who differed from the O'Connellites in their willingness to use physical force repeal the union: Sloan 162.

266: "The shock awakened mankind": Sloan 209.

266: Lord Clarendon, Lord Lieutenant of Ireland, was deeply alarmed by all this activity: Scherer 172-3.

266: . . . an excited crowd of six thousand: Woodham-Smith, *Great Hunger* 353.

267: Smith O'Brien forbade them to fell trees without the permission of the owners of the nearby estates: Sloan 258.

267: "This announcement gave a death-blow to the entire movement": Sloan 258.

267: . . . the *Times* dismissively immortalizing the event as the "cabbage-patch revolt": Sloan 285.

268: She would ride again today, bringing Alice, Affie, and Lenchen with her: All newspaper accounts of this attempt are wrong about which of Victoria's children actually rode with her that day, most of them stating that Vicky, Bertie, and Helena were in the carriage. Victoria is quite clear on the matter, however, in her letter the next day to uncle Leopold: Alice, Affie, and Lenchen were the ones riding with her. Victoria *Letters* (first series) 2:220.

268: . . . the presence of the royal landau at the Palace steps signaled silently and almost supernaturally the Queen's intent to ride: *Morning Chronicle* 21 May 1849, 5.

268: . . . nursemaids and footmen helped the children, and then Victoria and her maid of honor Flora MacDonald, into the carriage: Victoria *Letters* (first series) 2:220.

Chapter 15: The Man from Adare

269: He was an Irishman, having left Ireland for London at around the beginning of the famine: *Morning Chronicle* 26 May 1849, 3.

269: He was a working man, as his corduroy trousers, fustian jacket, and greasy cap made clear at a glance: *Times* 21 May 1849, 5; *Morning Chronicle* 15 June 1849, 7.

270: He had been whittling for some time, shaping a chunk of wood into something like the stock of a pistol: *Times* 21 May 1849, 5.

270: He had actually encouraged his long-suffering landlord, Daniel O'Keefe . . . to arrest him for debt: *Times* 21 May 1849, 5; *Daily News* 21 May 1849, 5.

270: "Between the two of us," said Bridget O'Keefe, "we managed to keep him": *Times* 21 May 1849, 5.

271: . . . around 1826 they died or simply abandoned the infant to the Protestant Orphan Society at Cork: *Morning Chronicle* 26 May 1849, 3. Hamilton's age is variously reported, ranging from 22 to 28 on the day of the attack. Trial records from the Old Bailey state him to be 23 on 11 June 1849. (*Daily News* 21 May 1849, 5; *Morning Chronicle* 15 June 1849, 7; "William Hamilton"; *Morning Chronicle* 26 May 1849, 3.

271: . . . a Protestant farmer outside of Adare, near Limerick: *Morning Chronicle* 26 May 1849, 3.

271: . . . his employer sold the farm and emigrated to Canada with his family: The farmer is identified in the *Morning Chronicle* 26 May 1849, 3 as Phillip Rynard of Graigue, Adare Parish, and as having emigrated to America. Carolyn Heald identifies Philip Raynard, formerly of Graigue, Adare Parish, as an immigrant to Ontario, Canada: Heald 60.

271: . . . "it was not right to serve under petticoat government": *Morning Chronicle* 26 May 1849, 3.

272: . . . the time "of Prince Louis Napoleon's escape from Ham": *Times* 21 May 1849, 5.

272: . . . his arrest was not political, but for being out too late one night: According to a police report the day after his arrest: TNA PRO MEPO 3/19B.

272: Hamilton hadn't "worked seven weeks since Christmas": *Times* 21 May 1849, 5.

272: "Why, Dan has got an old pistol": *Times* 21 May 1849, 5.

272: It was a pocket-sized, with a three-inch brass screw-barrel: *Trewman's Exeter Flying Post* 24 May 1849, 2.

273: ... "not the best sort of powder": *Times* May 1849, 5.

273: ... "you must stop at home": *Times* 21 May 1849, 5.

273: By six, he was standing near the bottom of Constitution Hill: *Times* 21 May 1849, 5.

274: ... "she has not come yet": *Times* 21 May 1849, 5.

274: Hamilton strode up to the palings and spoke to both the woman and to a muscular man on the other side of the fence: *Morning Chronicle* 21 May 1849, 5; *Daily News* 21 May 1849, 5.

274: The man, deafened, felt something whizz past his ear and realized his face was scorched: *Daily News* 21 May 1849, 5.

274: "Renwick," she said, "what is that?": *Times* 21 May 1849, 5.

275: ... "Thank God," he said to Victoria, "you are safe": *Daily News* 21 May 1849, 5.

275: ... George Moulder, Green Park's head park-keeper, had been standing just twelve yards from Hamilton as the Queen passed: *Times* 21 May 1849, 5.

275: A police constable named Topley, and a private in the Life Guards, then vaulted the palings: *Morning Chronicle* 21 May 1849, 5.

275: ... the great majority jumped to the conclusion that she had been hit: *Lloyd's Weekly* 20 May 1849, 7; *Daily News* 21 May 1849, 5.

276: Wemyss by this time was already certain that there had been no bullet in the pistol: *Times* 21 May 1849, 5.

276: ... his name was William Hamilton, aged twenty-four—an Irishman from Adare, County Limerick: *Daily News* 21 May 1849, 5.

276: ... he had no friends or relatives in this country: *Belfast News-Letter* 25 May 1849, 1.

277: There was nothing in his room besides two sheets lent him by his landlady: *Times* 21 May 1849, 5: two *shirts*, according to the *Daily News* 21 May 1849, 5.

277: "He said he did it for the purpose of getting into prison": *Times* 21 May 1849, 5.

277: He did, however, send word to A Division that Hamilton be placed on suicide watch: *Morning Chronicle* 21 May 1849, 5.

278: " . . . the routine of a Royal birthday received a vast and visible stimulus from the impulse of public sympathy": *Times* 21 May 1849, 5.

278: . . . "the indignation, loyalty, and affection this act has called forth is very gratifying and touching": Victoria *Letters* (first series) 2:220.

278: The police searched the area exhaustively for a bullet: *Times* 21 May 1849, 5.

278: The Queen's equerry Wemyss . . . was unscathed: *Daily News* 21 May 1849, 5.

278: And a thorough search of Hamilton produced a small amount of gunpowder: *Times* 21 May 1849, 5.

279: "I hope that you will not have been alarmed by the account of the occurrence which took place on Saturday": Victoria, *Letters* 2:220.

279: Hamilton's attempt was designated an "absurdity," "an exasperating piece of folly": *Era* 20 May 1849, 12; *Times* 21 May 1849, 4.

279: "The man who commits such an act in this country should be flogged at the cart's tail": *Era* 20 May 1840, 12.

279: . . . the *Daily News* . . . acknowledged the wickedness of pointing a pistol at "a person every way so sacred, in domestic as in political life, as that of her Majesty": *Daily News* 21 May 1849, 4.

279: . . . "it has been found that there is no reason to accuse the person who discharged the pistol of a treasonable attempt": "Firing at the Queen."

279: "The accident, or the fact, of the man Hamilton's being an Irishman may be made the theme of animadversion": *Daily News* 21 May 1849, 4.

280: The Irish newspapers were particularly adamant in asserting that Hamilton had no intention of killing the Queen: *Freeman's Journal* 22 May 1849, 2.

280: One attempted to claim that Hamilton might not be Irish at all: *Belfast News-Letter* 25 May 1849, 2.

280: The *Limerick Chronicle* investigated and found that though Hamilton claimed to be from Adare, he had no relatives there. *Limerick Chronicle* 23 May 1849, rpt. in *Freeman's Journal* 25 May 1849, 5.

280: "Hamilton was a native of Cork, and no relative of any persons at or near Adare": *Limerick Chronicle*, rpt. in *Morning Chronicle* 26 May 1849, 3.

280: The *Cork Constitution* quickly responded that the secretaries of the Cork Orphan Asylum denied that anyone named William

Hamilton had passed through there: *Cork Constitution*, rpt. in *Daily News* 2 June 1849, 2.

280: "The Corkonians are most anxious to disclaim having reared the fellow who fired at the Queen": *Daily News* 2 June 1849, 2.

280: ". . . fortunately there are no recent event [sic] which could afford political colour or excitement to a crime of this kind": *Daily News* 21 May 1849, 4.

281: . . . "this country enjoys a complete immunity from any of those dreadful conflicts to which the rest of Europe is subjected": *Illustrated London News* 26 May 1849, 342.

281: "Man shot, tried to shoot dear Mamma, must be punished": Victoria, *Letters* 2:220.

281: The Attorney General, John Jervis, examined witnesses for three hours: *Belfast News-Letter* 25 May 1849, 1.

281: All of the O'Keefes—Daniel, Bridget, and young Edward—testified, but Hamilton's mysterious young protectress in the milk line was nowhere to be seen: *Times* 21 May 1849, 5.

282: "It is, perhaps, to be regretted that the framers of the bill did not provide that transportation *and* flogging should be the punishment": *Illustrated London News* 26 May 1849, 335.

282: Victoria and Albert formalized their plans for visiting Ireland, which they both had desired to do as early as summer 1843: James Murphy 77.

283: "Since Her Majesty came to the throne, there has been no period more politically propitious for her coming here than the present one": Martin 2:192.

284: . . . their visit would not be a state visit at all, but "one having more the character of a yachting excursion": James Murphy 79.

284: . . . similar indeed to an exhibition in Paris from which Cole had just returned: James 195.

284: "I asked the Prince . . . if he had considered if the Exhibition should be a National or an International Exhibition": Henry Cole 1:124-25.

286: Hamilton quietly pled guilty: *Preston Chronicle* 16 June 1849, 6.

286: "The Queen might be perfectly assured of her personal safety": *Morning Chronicle* 15 June 1849, 7.

286: Two years before, Colonial Secretary Henry Gray had completely reconsidered and revised the government's policy on transportation: Hughes 552-53.

287: Hamilton was finally shipped aboard the convict ship *Ramillies* to Fremantle, Western Australia: Convict Transportation Register Database.

287: . . . his landlord, Daniel O'Keefe, appeared before the judges at the Old Bailey: *Examiner* 16 June 1849, 381.

287: . . . "this idolatry of the martyrs of crime and saints of the Newgate Calendar": *Punch* 16:251 (1849).

287: . . . surprising the town's inhabitants, who expected them to arrive the next day: Woodham-Smith, *Great Hunger* 393.

287: . . . the servants of one landowner lost control of their bonfire: Woodham-Smith, *Great Hunger* 393.

288: She landed in Cove the next day, and at the request of local officials, she ordered it renamed Queenstown: James Murphy 88.

288: "the crowd is a noisy, excitable, but very good humored one, running and pushing about, and laughing, talking, and shrieking": Victoria, *Leaves* 161.

288: . . . "balconies were filled as if by magic": *Illustrated London News* 11 August 1849, 88.

288: " . . . thousands and thousands": James Murphy 89.

289: "Ah, Queen dear, make one of them Prince Patrick and Ireland will die for you": Woodham-Smith *Great Hunger* 397.

289: " . . . no escort of dragoons followed": *Illustrated London News* 11 August 1849, 88.

289: "Arrah! Victoria, will you stand up, and let us have a look at you?": *Illustrated London News* 11 August 1849, 89.

289: . . . a "brawny wag" outside Trinity College, who with "enthusiastic attachment" shouted "Bravo, Albert!": *Illustrated London News* 11 August 1849, 87.

290: "You see more ragged and wretched people here than I ever saw anywhere else": Woodham-Smith, *Great Hunger* 397.

290: Her first procession through Dublin was "a never to be forgotten scene": James Murphy 90.

290: "Mighty Monarch, pardon Smith O'Brien": *Illustrated London News* 11 August 1849, 87.

290: Members of Dublin secret societies—remnants of the clubs promoted by Young Ireland—came up with a desperate plot to kidnap Victoria: Woodham-Smith, *Great Hunger* 387.

290: . . . "even the ex-Clubbists, who threatened broken heads and windows before the Queen came, are now among the most loyal of her subjects": Maxwell 1:302.

290: The nationalist and Tory press, relentlessly hostile to the Queen during the early part of her visit, finally gave in: Loughlin 504.

291: . . . "the more the citizens of Dublin see Queen Victoria, the more she wins their affections": Woodham-Smith, *Great Hunger* 399.

291: . . . "swarming around their queen like bees": *Illustrated London News* 18 August 1849, 126.

291: . . . "ran along the deck with the sprightliness of a young girl": *Times* 13 August 1849, 5.

291: " . . . the pealing of cannon and the loudest concert of human voices that ever ascended from a people in praise of any Monarch": *Illustrated London News* 18 August 1849, 126.

291: John Bright, the radical MP from Birmingham, was there, and was overcome: James Murphy 96.

291: "There is not an individual in Dublin that does not take as a personal compliment to himself the Queen's having gone upon the paddle-box and order the royal standard to be lowered": Victoria *Letters* (first series) 2:226.

291: The *Times* declared that the Queen had put an end to Irish faction and civil discord": *Times* 15 August 1849, 4.

291: " . . . as long as Queen Victoria lives (may she live to see her great-grandchildren!) there will be no disaffection—no disloyalty in Ireland." *Illustrated London News* 18 August 1849, 122.

Chapter 16: Cut and Thrust

293: The cabmen and tradesmen on the fringe of the Westminster parks, as well as the policemen of A Division, all knew him by sight: *Times* 12 July 1850, 7.

293: . . . well-appointed apartments on the corner of Piccadilly and Duke Street St. James: *Times* 28 June 1850, 8; 29 June 1850, 8.

293: He always wore the same impeccable suit of clothing: *Times* 29 June 1850, 8; *Morning Chronicle* 12 July 1850, 5.

294: The bright colors . . . marked him as a dandy; Prince Albert described him that way to Baron Stockmar: Martin 2:285.

294: His gait seemed to defy gravity: "Robert Pate."

294: . . . "it was astonishing how he preserved his equilibrium": "Robert Pate."

294: An inspector from A Division . . . nicknamed him "cut and thrust": *Times* 12 July 1850, 7.

294: . . . abruptly stopping in his tracks, gazing about him, and then, as if suddenly aware he was being watched, running off as fast as he could: *Times* 12 July 1850, 7.

294: "I meet him often in the parks": *Era* 7 July 1850, 9.

294: Husbands would caution their wives not to draw his attention, for fear of violent consequences: "Robert Pate."

294: Those few that acknowledged him earned from him an angry glare and a spasmodic shake of his stick: "Robert Pate."

295: When the clock in the tower of St. James's Palace chimed quarter past three, Pate stopped whatever he was doing: *Times* 12 July 1850, 7.

295: In the first pile were nine shillings, each queen's head up: "Robert Pate."

295: There, at exactly the same spot, Pate would descend from the cab, jump over a ditch, and disappear through thick gorse bushes: "Robert Pate."

295: He would shout conflicting commands to the driver: *Times* 12 July 1850, 7.

295: The cabman, mystified by his daily customer, would spy on Pate through the trap at his feet, and would see him either wholly catatonic or in frantic motion: "Robert Pate."

295: "I did not know what performance it was": "Robert Pate."

295: At Barnes Common, Pate would again leap out and shun every path, plunging instead into the deepest undergrowth: *Times* 12 July 1850, 7.

296: The sixpence and penny were for tolls at the bridges: *Times* 12 July 1850, 7; "Robert Pate." The cabman and Pate's manservant differ as to the exact amount.

296: "Mr. Pate did not want me": "Robert Pate."

296: Robert Francis Pate Senior[,] made his fortune as a corn factor, or grain dealer, in Wisbech, Cambridgeshire: *Times* 28 June 1850, 8.

296: He accepted nomination eagerly, provided the invitation was "the unanimous desire of the University": James 173.

297: Peel persuaded him to stay in: James 173-4.

297: Cambridge welcomed the two deliriously: *Times* 6 July 1847, 5.

297: Victoria . . . fought breaking into a smile of mingled joy and embarrassment at the "almost absurd" position she found herself in when Albert . . . welcomed her: Bolitho 182; Bunsen 2:136; Martin 1:396.

297: She replied, assuring the university "of my entire *approbation*" of Cambridge's choice of Chancellor, laying particular emphasis on that last word: *Times* 6 July 1847, 5; Jerrold, *Married Life* 299.

297: Albert turned out to be the one of the best Chancellors Cambridge ever had, guiding the university's curriculum into the modern age: Gill 244.

297: And Robert Francis Pate Senior . . . was on that day introduced to both Prince and Queen: Walford 228.

297: . . . sending him to be trained as a gentleman at a school in Norwich: *Times* 29 June 1850, 8.

297: Pate set his son up in the Queen's service as a cornet in the prestigious 10th Hussars: *Times* 28 June 1850, 8; 12 July 1850, 7.

298: He was odd from the start, but was at first tolerated and even liked by his fellows: *Times* 12 July 1850, 7.

298: . . . Pate threatened to "make a hole in the river": *Times* 12 July 1850, 7.

298: He avoided mess with his fellows and instead took long and solitary walks: *Times* 12 July 1850, 7.

298: . . . the cook and the messman, he convinced himself, were trying to poison him: *Times* 12 July 1850, 7; "Robert Pate."

298: Pate fled instead London with little more than the clothes he wore: *Times* 12 July 1850, 5; *Morning Chronicle* 12 July 1850, 5.

298: To his astonished father, he explained that he was a hunted man: *Times* 12 July 1850, 5.

298: He was arrested upon his return: *Morning Chronicle* 12 July 1850, 5.

298: . . . his attempts at explaining himself were so incoherent that his commanding officers refused to prosecute him: *Times* 12 July 1850, 7.

298: . . . he wrote to Pate Senior a letter asking "in as delicate a manner as I could" for him to take his son away: *Times* 12 July 1850, 7.

298: . . . he granted Pate a leave of absence: *Times* 12 July 1850, 7.

298: . . . for £1800 he quickly sold his Lieutenant's commission and set himself up in comfortable apartments in Jermyn Street: *Reynolds's Weekly* 14 July 1850, 5; "Robert Pate."

299: . . . the younger Pate was a man of extremely temperate habits, and obsessively regular in paying his bills: *Times* 12 July 1850, 7.

299: . . . creditors began to apply to his father for payment: *Times* 12 July 1850, 7; "Robert Pate"; *Reynolds's Weekly* 14 July 1850, 5.

299: . . . he was alarmed by the change that had come over his son: *Times* 12 July 1850, 7; "Robert Pate."

299: A doctor in Brighton recommended that he see the most celebrated mad-doctor of all: "Robert Pate."

299: His younger sister had moved from Wisbech to London to live with a family friend, the eminent surgeon James Startin: *Morning Chronicle* 12 July 1850, 6.

299: . . . it did not take long before James Startin realized that the wild man whose eccentricities in the parks he had often witnessed was his future sister-in-law's brother: *Times* 12 July 1850, 7; "Robert Pate."

299: . . . he spoke in a "short choking manner," with wild eyes and expression, and then would lapse into sullen silence: *Morning Chronicle* 12 July 1850, 6; "Robert Pate"; *Times* 12 July 1850, 7.

299: . . . The O'Gorman Mahon . . . understood Pate to be a maniac from their first conversation: *Reynolds's Weekly* 14 July 1850, 5; *Times* 12 July 1850, 7; *Morning Chronicle* 12 July 1850, 6.

300: . . . Conolly acknowledged that the man was certainly mad—but advised his father to do nothing: *Times* 12 July 1850, "Robert Pate."

300: James Startin began to fear that he would commit a violent act upon himself or his relatives: *Times* 12 July, 7; "Robert Pate."

300: "I told my foreman I had great apprehensions that Captain Pate, as I always called him, was losing his senses": "Robert Pate."

300: "I had never seen him so excited as on this day": *Times* 12 July 1850, 7.

300: "There was something peculiar in the manner in which he turned about and walked away": "Robert Pate."

301: The Duke of Cambridge was seriously ill with "gastric fever"—most likely typhoid: Victoria *Letters* (first series) 2:257.

302: . . . Victoria was mortified to discover that the Duchess had refused to rise at a dinner where a toast to Albert was given: Fulford 309-11.

302: She would be to Victoria a "link with bygone times and generations . . . we all looked upon her as a sort of grandmother": Purdue, "Daughters."

303: . . . "Much was done to set Mamma against her": Victoria *Letters* (first series) 2:273.

303: . . . her third son—her favorite son, as it turned out: Frankland.

304: George Anson, thirty-seven years old and apparently completely healthy, complained to his wife of a pain over his eye and immediately collapsed: Martin 2:230.

304:   . . . they both broke down and were, according to Lady Lyttelton, "in floods of tears, and quite shut up": Lyttelton 393.

305:   And Peel was a mentor to the young Prince: James 151.

305:   . . . she had welcomed John Russell's Whig ministry with good grace: Weintraub, *Victoria* 189.

305:   Peel *was* the government, keeping *"all* in his own hands": Victoria's Journal 2 July 1846, qtd. in Longford 188.

306:   . . . her husband, a German and thus, he once told Albert to his face, unable to understand British interests: St. Aubyn, *Queen Victoria* 245.

306:   He regularly neglected to send the Queen dispatches until after he had issued them: Hibbert, *Queen Victoria* 204; St. Aubyn, *Queen Victoria* 247.

306:   In the ongoing dispute between Prussia and Denmark, they favored Prussia, and Palmerston Denmark. When the states of Italy rose up against their Austrian rulers, they favored Austria, and Palmerston Italy: St. Aubyn, *Queen Victoria* 248.

306:   . . . he had actually helped arm Garibaldi the year before, without consulting the Queen or even his Cabinet colleagues: St. Aubyn, *Queen Victoria* 249; Longford 200.

306:   "I felt really I could hardly go on with him": Victoria *Letters* (first series) 2:195.

307:   Pacifico claimed that he had lost the enormous sum of £32,000 in the conflagration: Ridley 507.

307:   Don Pacifico's parents were—and perhaps he was—born in Gibraltar: Derek Taylor 9, 17.

307:   When the Greek government failed to recompense him, he turned to the British consul, who brought the matter to Palmerston: For details of the Don Pacifico affair, see Ridley 486-528; Derek Taylor throughout.

307:   Palmerston agreed that Greece owed Pacifico the full amount—plus another £500 for his suffering: Ridley 508.

307:   . . . in mid-January 1850, when the British Mediterranean fleet stormed into Athens's waters with more ships than Nelson had commanded at the Battle of the Nile: Martin 2:269.

307:   Opinion in Britain was divided as to whether Don Pacifico or Greece was the true victim: Ridley 515.

308:   The French ambassador promptly returned to France for consultations; the Russians contemplated recalling their own ambassador: Derek Taylor 198.

308: Before this debate, Victoria and Albert had insisted that Palmerston leave the Foreign Office: Victoria *Letters* (first series) 2:235-6.

308: He proposed reshuffling the Cabinet completely: Victoria *Letters* (first series) 2:235-37.

309: Two months later . . . the royal couple met again with Russell and modified their plans: Victoria *Letters* (first series) 2:243-4.

309: "It is impossible to say at this moment what will be the result": Victoria *Letters* (first series) 2:248.

309: "We are in a crisis," Victoria wrote to uncle Leopold: Victoria *Letters* (first series) 2:251.

309: Palmerston himself later claimed he could hardly remember such a "display of intellect, oratory and high and dignified feeling": Ashley 2:161.

310: " . . . the principles on which the foreign policy of Her Majesty's government has been regulated have been such as were calculated to maintain the honour and dignity of this country": Victoria *Letters* (first series) 2:248; *Times* 24 June 1850, 3.

310: . . . a vote against Palmerston was a vote for "Cossack domination": *Times* 26 June 1850, 2.

310: Speaking for four and a half hours with few notes and no pause for the water or oranges set beside him: Roebuck 242; Ridley 522.

311: "It is like shooting a policeman": *Times* 26 June 1850, 4.

311: His policy had bettered mankind: *Times* 26 June 1850, 5.

311: ". . . as the Roman, in days of old, held himself free from indignity when he could say *Civis Romanus sum*": Ridley 524.

311: " . . . a most brilliant speech," she admitted to her journal: Longford 201.

311: Russell was ecstatic about it—"one of the most masterly ever delivered," he wrote: Victoria *Letters* (first series) 2:252.

311: The Stranger's Gallery was packed more tightly than ever: *Times* 27 June 1850, 2.

312: "We are living at a period of the most wonderful transition": Albert, *Addresses* 60.

312: He "appears to be almost the only person who has considered the subject both as a whole and in its details": Martin 2:202.

312: "The Prince's sleep is again as bad as ever, and he looks very ill of an evening": Martin 2:243.

312: . . . Albert had given £500 and Victoria £1,000: ffrench 46.

313: . . . he had studied the alternatives and was now absolutely committed to that choice: Cole 1:166-7.

313: The residents of Knightsbridge adjoining the site raised a stink: ffrench 77; Christopher Hobhouse 18.

313: . . . a classic demonstration of the broth-destroying propensity of too many cooks: Cole 1:163.

313: . . . they "freely"—in both senses of the term—"availed themselves of the most valuable suggestions": *Times* 3 June 1850, 8.

313: . . . a sheet-iron dome 200 feet in diameter and 150 feet high: Christopher Hobhouse 16.

313: . . . "a monster balloon in the process of inflation": *Times* 21 June 1850, 8.

313: . . . a squat and sprawling warehouse that would take an estimated 19 million bricks to build: Cole 1:164; Leapman 52; ffrench 73. Others claim 15 million: Strutt 9; Christopher Hobhouse 16; Auerbach 42.

314: . . . he "would become associated in the minds of the people not with a benefit, but with an injury": *Times* 27 June 1850, 5.

314: . . . a "tubercle" on "the lungs of this huge metropolis": Auerbach 43; *Times* 19 March 1850, 3.

314: He had opposed the 1832 Reform Bill; he was dead set against the railways; he despised Free Trade: Auerbach 43.

314: " . . . one of the greatest humbugs, one of the greatest frauds, one of the greatest absurdities ever known": *Times* 19 June 1850, 4.

314: . . . a magnet to attract to London the dregs of foreign lands: Papists, thieves, anarchists, and secret societies bent on assassinating the Queen: Christopher Hobhouse 20.

314: "The Exhibition is now attacked furiously by *The Times*": Martin 2:235.

Chapter 17: The Most Disgraceful and Cowardly Thing That Has Ever Been Done

315: . . . that man had refused to give way, throwing out his arm every time Pate tried to pass him: *Times* 29 June 1850, 8; 12 July 1850, 7.

316: . . . when alerted that the Queen would be going out, they were under orders to get there first and patrol the area: Geraghty 30.

316: . . . no one had alerted the police: RA VIC/MAIN/QVJ/1850, 27 June 1850.

316: They trotted to the edge of the street and then stopped, awaiting their opportunity to make the tight turn onto busy Piccadilly: *Times* 29 June 1850, 8.

316: . . . such a situation, she later wrote, "always makes me think more than usually of the possibility of an attempt being made on me": Geraghty 30.

316: . . . brought it slashing down on the right side of the Queen's head, bending the wire of her light summer bonnet, the metal ferrule at the cane's tip audibly smacking her forehead: Victoria *Letters* (first series) 2:253; *Times* 28 June 1850, 8.

317: Victoria instinctively raised her hand to her bonnet and recoiled away from Pate, falling into the laps of her alarmed children: *Times* 6 July 1850, 8; *Morning Chronicle* 28 June 1850, 5; Geraghty 30.

317: Robert Renwick leapt up, leaned forward, and seized Pate by the collar: *Times* 29 June 1850, 8.

317: Those around him grabbed hold of him as well: *Times* 28 June 1850, 8.

317: "They have got the man," Fanny Jocelyn told Victoria: Geraghty 30.

317: To the crowd, it seemed as if the Queen was simply adjusting her bonnet: *Morning Chronicle* 28 June 1850, 5.

317: One man threw a vicious punch at Pate's face and blood gushed from his nose: *Times* 28 June 1850, 5.

317: Lady Jocelyn burst into tears, and the Prince of Wales's face went red: Longford 192.

317: . . . Colonel Grey galloped to Victoria's side, catching behind him the sight of the crowd to the left rushing upon Pate: "Robert Pate."

317: Voices began to call for a lynching: *Daily News* 28 June 1850, 4.

317: James Silver of A Division . . . noticed the seething crowd and heard a voice: "The villain has struck the Queen!": *Times* 29 June 1850, 8.

317: He instantly ran to the spot, plunged into the crowd, and, with some difficulty and with the help of other constables drawn by the commotion, rescued him from the chaotic assault: *Times* 29 June 1850, 8.

318: . . . they passed Messrs. Fortnum and Mason's emporium, and Pate could steal a look at his elegant rooms above them: *Morning Chronicle* 28 June 1850, 5.

318: . . . Victoria directed her visibly mortified equerry Charles Grey to ride through the parks and find Albert: Geraghty 31.

318: She sent Fanny Jocelyn back to Cambridge House to inform the Duchess what had just happened: *Leeds Mercury* 29 June 1850, 5.

318: She sent for her physician, James Clark, to tend to her wound—which was by now throbbing so painfully that she retired upstairs to treat it herself with arnica: *Times* 6 July 1850, 8; Geraghty 31.

318: Home Secretary George Grey, "greatly distressed and in tears," came to her later that evening—and managed to compose himself enough to return to Commons and make his own contribution to the debate: Rowell 31; *Times* 28 June 1850, 4.

318: Sir James Clark arrived and examined the Queen: he found a "considerable tumor" on her brow: *Examiner* 6 July 1850, 428; *Times* 12 July 1850, 7.

318: "Certainly not: if I do not go, it will be thought I am seriously hurt, and people will be distressed and alarmed": "The Character of Queen Victoria," 318.

319: "The feeling of *all* classes [is] admirable," she wrote that night in her journal, "the lowest of the low being *most* indignant": Rowell 31.

319: . . . "one of the most magnificent demonstrations of loyalty it has ever been our fortune to witness": *Morning Chronicle* 28 June 1850, 5.

319: . . . "the mark of the ruffian's violence plainly visible on her forehead": *Times* 28 June 1850, 8.

319: "I never heard such shouting": *Punch* 19:18 (1850).

319: When Madame Viardot reached the line "Frustrate their knavish tricks," the crowd roared: *Morning Chronicle* 28 June 1850, 5.

320: "The small stick with which the prisoner struck the blow was not thicker than an ordinary goosequill": *Times* 28 June 1850, 8.

320: Pate's cane—a type known as a partridge cane—was longer, heavier, and much thicker than the newspaper claimed: *Lloyd's Weekly* 7 July 1850, 7; *Times* 29 June 1850, 8.

320: Victoria long remembered the injury Pate had given her: a walnut-sized welt and a scar that lasted ten years: *Lloyd's Weekly Newspaper* 30 June 1850, 12; Gathorne-Hardy 1:244.

320: " . . . it is very hard and very horrid that I a woman": Geraghty 30.

320: . . . the Queen until the end of her life considered this one the meanest and most ignoble—"far worse," she wrote, "than an attempt to shoot": Geraghty 31.

321: "I own it makes me nervous out driving, and I start at any person coming near the carriage": Victoria, *Letters* (first series) 2:253.

321: At Vine Street station, Pate was searched: *Times* 28 June 1850, 8.

321: The several witnesses to the assault who came with him to the station were questioned, and Pate was charged with assaulting the Queen: *Times* 28 June 1850, 8.

321: Pate . . . asserted emphatically "those men cannot prove whether I struck her head or her bonnet": *Morning Chronicle* 28 June 1850, 5.

321: . . . a little wire and woven horsehair: "Robert Pate."

322: Otway had just been promoted to Superintendent of C Division: *Times* 28 June 1850, 8.

322: Field, already a legend, was very soon to become an even greater one: Collins 204, 206-7.

322: Field was known for his roving eye, which caught all in a glance: Dickens, Amusements 357-369.

322: He made note of Pate's obsessive neatness. He also confiscated a number of Pate's papers: *Times* 28 June 1850, 8.

322: . . . he brought them to the Home Office examination the next day, but did not bring them forward: *Reynolds's Weekly News* 30 June 1850, 1.

322: Pate could offer no motive for striking the Queen besides claiming "felt very low for some time past": *Times* 29 June 1850, 8.

322: "I wish to Heaven I had been at your right hand yesterday, and then this should not have happened": *Times* 29 June 1850, 8.

322: . . . he sat up and observed the comings and goings at the station house: *Times* 29 June 1850, 8.

323: At 12:15 the next day, Superintendent Otway personally escorted Pate out of the station: *Lloyd's Weekly Newspaper* 30 June 1850, 12.

323: Pate Senior was not there; he would arrive from Wisbech later that afternoon: *Times* 29 June 1850, 8.

323: Richard Mayne—now senior Chief Commissioner since the retirement of Charles Rowan earlier in the year—was to read the charge: *Times* 29 June 1850, 8; Emsley.

323: . . . Pate sat and stared vacantly: *Reynolds's Weekly* 30 June 1850, 1.

323: Jervis brought forward just enough witnesses . . . to connect Pate with the attack and to justify a remand: *Times* 29 June 1850, 8.

323: John Huddleston requested more time than that, requesting a postponement until Friday 5 July: *Times* 29 June 1850, 8.

324: Pate drew up a list of books he wished transferred from his library at home to Clerkenwell: *Times* 29 June 1850, 8.

324: Otway then led Pate out the front door of the Home Office and directly into an unruly mob: *Times* 29 June 1850, 8.

324: Commissioner Hay had positioned a number of police before the Home Office to control the crowd: *Reynolds's Weekly* 30 June 1850, 1.

324: . . . the "absorbing topic of conversation" throughout London: *Times* 29 June 1850, 8.

324: William Gladstone spoke that Thursday evening, attacking Palmerston's brutal nationalism with a visionary appeal to a brotherhood of nations: *Times* 28 June 1850, 5.

324: Gladstone was interrupted often by Palmerston's enthusiastic supporters, as were all of Palmerston's opponents: Ridley 524.

325: Crowds crammed the avenues outside the entrances to the House: *Times* 29 June 1850, 2.

325: . . . "the House and country only wish to hear Peel, Lord John, and Dizzy; all others are only bores": Roebuck 242.

325: Cockburn deftly and with legal precision deflected Gladstone's attack, defending item by item Palmerston's actions in Greece and throughout Europe: *Times* 29 June 1850, 2-3.

325: Robert Peel . . . managed to chide Palmerston's policy and yet conciliate the Whig government: *Times* 29 June 1850, 4-5.

325: John Russell, speaking next, had an easy job of it: *Times* 29 June 1850, 5.

325: In a speech containing little of his trademark wit, he explained why he would vote as Peel did: *Times* 29 June 1850, 5-6.

326: . . . 250 supporters would enthusiastically sing the national anthem and cheer vociferously the lines "Confound their politics,/Frustrate their knavish tricks": Ridley 525.

326: . . . he "would have consummated his fiendish scheme by violence had not the miraculous efforts of his victim and such assistance attracted by her screams, saved her": Ridley 532.

326: Albert and Victoria, with the help of Stockmar, tried again a month later, setting out in a memo for Palmerston the behavior they expected in a foreign minister: St. Aubyn, *Queen Victoria* 250-1.

326: Russell thought the memo so humiliating that Palmerston would have to resign rather than accept it: Ridley 532.

327: "I consider that man to be the happiest in England at this moment": Roebuck 242.

327: His wife Julia was feeling unwell and so she remained in bed, reading a newspaper account of his speech: Gash 697.

327: Playfair . . . had been appointed upon Peel's recommendation Special Commissioner for the Exhibition: Davis 71; Auerbach 70-1.

328: They discussed the mounting opposition to the Hyde Park site, and resolved that they would hold the Exhibition there or nowhere: RC/8/A, minutes for 29 June 1850, np.

328: "Depend upon it," he said, "the House of Commons is a timid body": Cole Henry 167.

328: Joseph Paxton . . . approached Henry Cole with a revolutionary idea for the Exhibition building: Davis 81.

328: Three days later, bored in the middle of a railway director's meeting in Derby, Paxton created the most famous doodle in history: Christopher Hobhouse 28; Auerbach 48; ffrench 91.

328: On the train from Derby he had run into the engineer Robert Stevenson—of the Building Committee—and quickly gained his support: Auerbach 49; Christopher Hobhouse 32.

328: He met with the vice-chairman of the Commission, Earl Granville, who promised to submit the plan to the Commissioners: Christopher Hobhouse 34.

328: "I believe nothing can stand against my plans, *everybody* likes them": Auerbach 49.

328: He also forwarded a set of plans to Peel: ffrench 97.

329: . . . they referred Paxton's plans to them: Christopher Hobhouse 35.

329: The Commission adjourned at 1:15: according to the "Court Circular": *Times* 1 July 1850, 4; it adjourned at 3:00, according to Norman Gash: Gash 697.

329: . . . he kissed his wife good-bye and set off with his groom for his customary ride around the Parks: Gash 697; *Times* 1 July 1850, 5.

329: The horse he mounted was new to him—an eight-year-old which a friend had purchased for him two months before, from Tattersall's: Gash 697; *Illustrated London News* 17 (1850): 10.

329: Peel's coachman was suspicious about the horse, and had recommended Peel not ride it: Gash 697.

329: Peel and his groom passed through St. James's Park and stopped at Buckingham Palace: For Peel's ride, see Gash 697-701; *Times* 1 July 1850, 5; Daily News 1 July 1850, 5; *Illustrated London News* 17 (1850): 10.

330: The two men who had sat him up, as well as the two doctors, now supported Peel: *Times* 1 July 1850, 5. According to the *Illustrated London News*, a doctor from St. George's Hospital accompanied Peel home: 17 (1850): 10.

330: . . . a patent hydraulic bed was set up in the same room: *Illustrated London News* 17 (1850): 10.

330: "Sir Robert Peel has met with a severe accident by falling from his horse": Gash 698-99.

330: Albert and the Prince of Prussia rushed to Whitehall Gardens as soon as they heard of his fall: *Times* 1 July 1850, 5.

330: "We have, alas! now another cause of much greater anxiety in the person of our excellent Sir Robert Peel": Victoria *Letters* (first series) 2:253.

330: Peel told them on the day of the accident that his injury was worse than they realized, and that he would not survive it: Gash 699.

331: "That silent, solemn crowd betokened the unknown depth to which love and reverence for the great practical statesman had sunk in the minds of humble English men and women": *Illustrated London News* 17 (1850): 3.

331: He ate a little and even walked around the room with assistance: Gash 701.

331: . . . he held each of his children's hands in turn, and whispered his good-byes to them, the words "God bless you!" scarcely audible: *Illustrated London News* 17 (1850): 10.

331: His wife Julia, overwhelmed, was led from the room: Gash 701.

331: Peel's death . . ."absorbed every other subject of interest": Greville 2:458.

332: "All persons agree that there has never been an instance of such general gloom and regret": Bunsen 2:142.

332: "He has felt, and feels, Sir Robert's loss *dreadfully*": Victoria *Letters* (first series) 2:256.

332: "Now our Exhibition is to be driven from London": Albert to Ernst, 4 July 1850, qtd. in Auerbach 46.

332: Sibthorp laid into the greatest trash, fraud, and imposition "palmed upon" the people of Britain: *Times* 5 July 1850, 3.

333: . . . Peel, "that eminent man, who never neglected any duty . . . which he considered conducive to the public good": *Times* 5 July 1850, 4.

333: "The feeling of the house was completely altered": Lord John Russell to Albert, qtd. in Davis 78.

333: His iron-and-glass design had received a cold reception from the Exhibition's Building Committee, especially from Isambard Kingdom Brunel: Auerbach 49.

333: . . . Paxton's "peculiar" design would cost 10% more than a variation of their own: Davis 83.

334: "Perhaps I might take the liberty of saying that I consider the success of the Exhibition would be considerably increased by the adoption of Mr. Paxton's plan": Cole 1:124-25.

334: On the sixteenth, the Building Committee met with the Royal Commission: *Times* 16 July 1850, 8.

334: "In all the matters which I had in hand," Albert was able to write Stockmar four days later from Osborne, "I had triumphant success": Martin 2:247.

334: . . . when he returned to complete his Home Office examination on Friday morning, the fifth of July, there was no large crowd outside to hoot or hiss him: *Examiner* 6 July 1850, 428. (Other newspapers, however, such as *Lloyd's Weekly*—on 7 July 1850, 7—note a larger crowd.)

334: . . . his health suffered from lack of walking: *Times* 6 July 1850, 8; *Examiner* 6 July 1850, 428.

334: . . . he had instead spent most of the last week absorbed in his books: *Manchester Examiner* 6 July 1850, 4.

334: . . . his own counsel, with whom he hadn't spoken since his arrest: *Times* 6 July 1850, 8.

334: Only the Queen's physician, James Clark, had anything new to add: *Times* 6 July 1850, 8; *Examiner* 6 July 1850, 428.

335: Huddleston, Pate's attorney, said little: *Times* 6 July 1850, 8.

335: Monro visited Pate twice at Clerkenwell and three times in Newgate: "Robert Pate."

336: Attorney General Jervis, then, was compelled to hurry the trial along, requesting the presiding judge, Baron Alderson, to schedule Pate's trial for the next morning, 11 July: *Times* 11 July 1850, 7.

336: . . . the courtroom on that morning was full but not crowded: *Times* 12 July 1850, 7.

336: With perfect composure he bowed slightly to the justices: *Times* 12 July 1850, 7.

336: . . . Pate loudly pleaded not guilty: *Times* 12 July 1850, 7.

336: . . . the effect of such an acquittal "would be that he would be imprisoned for the rest of his life": *Times* 12 July 1850, 7.

337: . . . Cockburn in his opening admitted to the jury that he simply could not prove "that there were certain and safe grounds for believing that the prisoner at the bar was not enabled to discriminate between right and wrong": *Morning Chronicle* 12 July 1850, 5.

338: . . . the testimony, Cockburn argued, "might fall short of that degree of proof of insanity which would be necessary to give [Pate] immunity from the penalties of law": *Morning Chronicle* 12 July 1850, 5.

338: Pate was not vicious, but "unfortunate," and did not deserve to be visited with the full severity of the law: *Morning Chronicle* 12 July 1850, 5.

338: The defense presented a host of witnesses to Pate's traumas and idiosyncrasies while in the army: For varied accounts of the testimony in Pate's trial, see *Times* 12 July 1850, 7; "Robert Pate"; *Morning Chronicle* 12 July 1850, 5; *Reynolds's Weekly* 14 July 1850, 5.

338: Pate's valet, Charles Dodman, enumerated Pate's many personal eccentricities at home: *Times* 12 July 1850, 7; "Robert Pate."

339: . . . Charles Mahon, better known as the "O'Gorman Mahon," testified that in his opinion Pate was a "maniac . . . the frequent subject of remark amongst myself and [my] companions": *Reynolds's Weekly* 14 July 1850, 5.

339: . . . "he presents an example of what is not at all uncommon to me, of persons who are very devoid of mental power . . . who consequently persevere in no pursuit, have no object, and are unfit for all the ordinary duties of life": "Robert Pate."

339: . . . "Is he, in your judgment, capable of distinguishing between right and wrong?": "Robert Pate."

339: He was "subject to sudden impulses of passion": *Times* 12 July 1850, 7.

340: "Be so good, Dr. Monro," Alderson snapped at him, "as not to take upon yourself the functions of the judges and the jury": *Times* 12 July 1850, 7.

340: . . . if he were soon free, probably "unwatched and unrestrained," he would "renew his dangerous and violent proceedings": *Times* 12 July 1850, 7.

341: "Did this unfortunate gentleman know it was wrong to strike the Queen on the forehead?": *Morning Chronicle* 12 July 1850, 6.

341: "A man might say that he picked a pocket from some uncontrollable impulse": *Times* 12 July 1850, 7.

341: . . . Alderson noted Pate's eccentric habits, his "differing from other men," his mental affliction": *Times* 12 July 1850, 7.

341: . . . "you are as insane as it is possible for a person to be who is capable of distinguishing between right and wrong": *Morning Chronicle* 12 July 1850, 6.

341: For all that, he told Pate, "you are to be pitied": *Times* 12 July 1850, 7.

342: Pate would not be subject to the "disgraceful punishment of whipping": *Times* 12 July 1850, 7.

342: . . . leading several who read the trial in the newspapers the next day . . . to conclude that the court had given Pate special treatment because of his social status: *Times* 13 July 1850, 3.

342: . . . "one of the most successful realizations, on a large scale, of the ugly in architecture," Henry Mayhew said of it: Mayhew and Binny 234.

343: According to this letter, Pate was given an officer's room and an officer to attend upon him, had access to the governor, and had a separate exercise yard: *Daily News* 9 August 1850, 4.

343: "Pate, we are informed, is in a very delicate state of health, and he employs his time by writing letters in different languages": *Moreton Bay Courier* 18 November 1850, 1.

Chapter 18: Great Exhibition

344: "I wish you *could* have witnessed the 1st *May* 1851": Victoria *Letters* (first series) 2:317.

344: "Albert's dearest name is immortalised with this *great* conception . . . *his* own": Victoria *Letters* (first series) 2:318.

345: From early in the morning, the crowds began to assemble in numbers simply too great to count: *Times* 2 May 1851, 4; one estimate of the numbers was 700,000 (Martin 2:369).

345: . . . a party of Royal Sappers soon restored order: *Times* 2 May 1851, 5.

345: The irrepressible Colonel Sibthorp had been carping at the project ever since: *Times* 5 February 1851, 4; ffrench 141; James 199.

345: "We have invited the pestilence into our dwellings, and we shall have to submit to its ravages": qtd. Leapman 65.

346: "I am more dead than alive from overwork": Martin 2:359.

346: The Tsar refused to issue passports to the Russian nobility: Longford 223.

346: "I am not easily given to panicking . . . but I confess to you that I would not like anyone belonging to me exposed to the imminent perils of these times": qtd. in ffrench 147.

346: "I can give no guarantee against these perils": qtd. in James 199-200.

347: ... the Commissioners could not have come to "a more impolitic, a more absurd, or a more ludicrous resolution": *Daily News* 17 April 1851, qtd. in Davis 117.

347: ... "Queen Victoria is not Tiberius or Louis XI": *Times* 17 April 1851, 5.

347: ... a "densely crowded mass of human beings, in the highest good humor and most enthusiastic": qtd. in Martin 2:365.

348: "The glimpse of the transept through the iron gates . . . gave us a sensation which I can never forget": qtd. in Martin 2:365.

348: When the Queen ascended with her family to the throne, two organs burst into the national anthem: For details of the opening ceremony see the *Times* 2 May 1851, 4-6; Davis 126-8.

348: ... sung by six hundred voices: Weintraub, *Victoria* 219.

348: The Lord Chamberlain, perplexed as to what to do with the man, consulted with Victoria and Albert: Playfair 120.

348: They recommended that he join the diplomats who were then forming up for the great procession through the Exhibition: Martin 367n.

349: The plan had been to keep the public well clear of their route: Martin 2:367.

349: ... and so they walked, hemmed in by thousands, many with tears in their eyes, all cheering deafeningly and waving handkerchiefs: 2:367.

349: "HER MAJESTY, as She Appeared on the FIRST of MAY, Surrounded by 'Horrible Conspirators and Assassins'": *Punch* 20 (1851): 194.

349: Besides the multitudes who cheered her, the Queen could see little else: Martin 2:367-8.

349: It was a unique event, Victoria knew, "a thousand times superior" to her coronation: Martin 2:366.

350: Albert was visibly emotional, and the Queen noticed her Home Secretary was crying: *Times* 2 May 1851, 5; Martin 2:368.

350: "It was and is a day to live for ever": Martin 2:366.

PART 4: TRIUMPH

Chapter 19: What Does She Do with It?

353: His controversial words about Victoria and her family both established him for a time as the people's champion: The same report of Dilke's 6 November 1871 speech, "Representation and Royalty," appears in the *Times* 9 November 1871, 6, and the *Daily News* 10 November 1871, 6. A shorter account appears in the *Newcastle Courant* 10 November 1871, 5.

355: . . . she wrote to her Prime Minister, William Gladstone, deploring the recent spate of "Gross misstatements & fabrications injurious to the credit of the Queen & to the Monarchy": Guedalla 1:309.

355: . . . asking "whether he or at least some of his Colleagues sh^ld not take an opportunity of reprobating in very strong terms such language": Guedalla 1:308.

356: In 1871, republicanism had become "a distemper," as Gladstone put it, and the "Royalty question" was one of the most vexing problems with which his ministry had to deal: Hibbert, *Queen Victoria* 336; Gladstone and Granville 283.

356: The economy had slumped since 1866, and unemployment was high, particularly in London where it was exacerbated by an influx of migrants from the countryside: Nicholls 48.

356: . . . the landmark Reform Act of 1867 . . . nearly doubled eligible voters and dipped eligibility down to a much larger segment of the urban working class: Rubinstein 111.

356: The fall of Emperor Louis Napoleon . . . and the establishment of a French Republic led to the spontaneous generation of dozens of republican clubs across the nation: Rumsey 4-8, 100-106.

356: . . . ready-made and enthusiastic audiences for republican speakers such as Charles Bradlaugh and trade union leader George Odger. Leventhal; Royle.

357: Victoria was plunged immediately into a chasm of grief, and then into a long-lasting depression, from which Albert devoted most of that year weaning her: Hibbert, *Queen Victoria* 266-67; St. Aubyn, *Queen Victoria* 318-19.

357: Albert was determined to train the Hanoverian vices out of his son with a rigorous course of academic study; any attempts by Bertie to rebel were met . . . with boxed ears or a rap across the knuckles with a stick: Hibbert, *Royal Victorians* 16; Magnus 9, 12.

357: . . . he enjoyed an element of freedom while training with the Grenadier Guards at Curragh Camp in Ireland: Hibbert, *Royal Victorians* 45-46; St. Aubyn, *Edward VII* 50-51.

358: The affair, thanks to Nellie's boasting, had been the talk of all London: Magnus 47.

358: ... "upon a subject which has caused me the greatest pain I have yet felt in this life": James 268.

358: ... "she could be able to give before a greedy multitude disgusting details of your profligacy for the sake of convincing the Jury:" James 268.

358: Albert's heartsickness conspired with overwork, many sleepless nights, nervous strain, and almost certainly the effects of a long-lasting illness to undermine his health and sap his will to live: In his biography of Victoria, Giles St. Aubyn disputes the diagnosis that Albert came down with typhoid fever and speculates that he suffered from cancer of the bowels. St. Aubyn, *Queen Victoria* 328; James 268.

358: ... three days later, with a cold and feverish and confessing to his diary "bin recht elend" ("I am very wretched") he traveled to Cambridge to confront his son: James 269-70.

359: Palmerston and Foreign Minister John Russell drew up a bellicose communication demanding reparation and an apology: James 271.

359: On Friday the thirteenth of December, a telegram brought the Prince of Wales rushing to Windsor from Cambridge: James 273.

359: The family gathered around his deathbed, Victoria forcing herself to remain calm in her husband's presence: James 273.

359: "I stood up," she wrote, "kissed his dear heavenly forehead": Woodham-Smith, *Queen Victoria* 429.

360: "I will be all I can to you": Hibbert, *Royal Victorians* 56-57.

360: And the Queen was certain that Bertie's behavior had been the cause of his father's illness and death: she admitted to Vicky that she could not look at him without shuddering: Victoria and Victoria, *Dearest Mama* 30, 40.

360: She adamantly resisted being "dictated to, or teased by public clamour into doing what she physically CANNOT": Victoria *Letters* (second series) 2:443.

360: ... "any great departure from her usual"—that is, isolated—"way of life or more than ordinary agitation, might produce insanity": Derby 313.

360: ... she would not meet face to face with her Privy Council, sitting instead in one room as her councilors stood and shouted their business through the open door of an adjoining room: Hibbert, *Queen Victoria* 298; St. Aubyn, *Queen Victoria* 331.

361: "I saw enough," she told Vicky, "to feel I never can live there again except for two or three days at a time": Victoria and Victoria, *Dearest Mama* 145.

361: "These commanding premises to be let or sold, in consequence of the late occupant's declining business": Longford 321. A contemporary report of this incident, however, suggests that the story is an invention intended to attack the Queen: a joke on paper if not actually upon the gates of the palace: Bellows 19.

361: . . . Victoria took the unprecedented step of writing personally to the *Times*: *Times* 6 April 1864, 9.

362: . . . "we have certain duties to fulfill here": Magnus 99.

362: . . . "the whole remains a painful lowering thing": St. Aubyn, *Edward VII* 162.

362: For months after the case, the Prince and his wife were hissed as they drove in public, in the theatres, at Ascot: Hibbert, *King Edward the Seventh* 109.

362: Brown had served the royal family since 1848, and Albert himself had appointed him Victoria's "particular ghillie": James 183; St. Aubyn, *Queen Victoria* 356.

363: Dr. Jenner understood the Queen's dependency upon the man: Hibbert, *Queen Victoria* 324.

363: In 1865, Victoria appointed him "Queen's Highland Servant," taking orders from no one but her and attending to her both indoors and out: Lamont-Brown 73.

363: A portrait by Landseer of the Queen on a horse held by the ghillie shown at the 1866 Royal Exhibition became an object of viewers' titters and outright laughter: Cullen 91.

363: . . . Victoria apparently considered Gladstone the most sympathetic of all her ministers: Guedalla 1:22.

364: "What killed her beloved Husband? Overwork & worry": Guedalla 1:299-300.

365: "I think it has been the most sickening piece of experience which I have had during near forty years of public life": Guedalla 1:304.

365: . . . a nasty abscess on her arm, which the eminent surgeon Joseph Lister was called north to lance: Victoria *Letters* (second series) 2:157.

365: . . . the Queen's "repellent power which she so well knows how to use has been put in action toward me on this occasion for the first time since the formation of the Government": Roy Jenkins, *Gladstone* 347.

365: Gladstone had been long contemplating just such a role: Magnus 111; St. Aubyn, *Edward VII* 206.

366: In New York in 1857, the society that would soon be known as the Fenians came into being: Ó Brion 1; Nowlan 92-93.

366: The next year, the American Fenian leaders exported their society to Dublin: D'Arcy 12.

366: Chester: For the Chester Castle raid, the attack on the Manchester prison-van, and the Clerkenwell outrage, see Quinlivan and Rose throughout.

367: Six people lay dead in the ruins; six later died. A hundred and twenty were injured. *Times* 22 May 1869, 11.

368: The Government dispatched soldiers to the Palace and ordered plain-clothed police to keep a close eye upon passengers boarding trains in Perth and Aberdeen: St. Aubyn, *Queen Victoria* 373.

368: "Too foolish," the Queen thought about the whole affair: Victoria *Letters* (second series) 2:466.

368: . . . two guards armed with revolvers were set to shadow her at a discreet distance: Stanley 324.

368: Lord Monck, the governor-general of Canada, sent a telegram that two ships had left New York carrying eighty Fenians "sworn to assassinate the Queen": James Murphy 160.

368: "Crimes such as these contemplated . . . cannot easily be perpetrated in crowded thoroughfares": Victoria *Letters* (second series) 1:477-78.

368: Victoria refused to leave, thinking a show of fear "injudicious as well as unnecessary": Victoria *Letters* (second series) 2:479.

369: . . . at Osborne extra police were posted; a pass system put into effect; some warships patrolled offshore while others were sent to intercept the Fenian ships: Hibbert, *Queen Victoria* 425; Longford 361.

369: The Queen was again annoyed by the fuss, considering herself "little better than a State Prisoner": Victoria *Letters* (second series) 2:484.

369: . . . "one begins to wish that these Fenians should be lynch-lawed and on the spot": qtd. Quinlivan and Rose 133.

369: The bullet ricocheted off of the rear clip of Alfred's suspenders through his ninth rib, missing his spine by an inch: Tavers 20. Tavers provides a full history of O'Farrell's attempt on Alfred and its aftermath.

369: O'Farrell's attempt led to a witch hunt to root out the Fenians of New South Wales: Tavers 54-79.

369: O'Farrell, with a history of mental problems and an obsession with avenging the Manchester Martyrs, had acted alone: Lyons and Nairn; Tavers 60.

369: Alfred's tour was curtailed while he recovered, attended to by two nurses trained by Florence Nightingale, and he returned home that summer: Kiste; Tavers 117.

370: . . . "poor dear Affie is so entirely unconnected with anything political or Irish": qtd. James Murphy 168.

370: . . . many had been freed—in the face of the stiff opposition of the Queen: Victoria *Letters* (second series) 1:628.

370: The Prince of Wales, on the other hand, traveled north to drink his contaminated water: For the Prince of Wales's illness from typhoid fever, see Hibbert, *Royal Victorians* 127-31; Magnus 113-14; St. Aubyn, *Edward VII* 214-16.

370: Many besides Bertie became ill: *Times* 1 December 1871, 5.

371: When she did come to him, in the audacity of his illness he accused *her* of infidelity: Hibbert, *Royal Victorians* 128.

371: In tears she returned to what seemed his deathbed: *Times* 9 December 1871, 9.

371: . . . "remedies of the most mad kind": Victoria *Letters* (second series) 2:176.

371: . . . "The feeling shown by the whole nation is quite marvellous and most touching and striking": Victoria *Letters* (second series) 2:176.

371: "Oh! Dear Mama, I am so glad to see you. Have you been here all this time?": Hibbert, *Royal Victorians* 130.

371: About Bertie himself, according to his mother, "there is something quite different": Victoria and Victoria, *Darling Child* 28.

372: . . . he had to deal with hecklers and scuffles during all his subsequent appearances: Nicholls 53.

372: . . . Dilke's appearance in Bolton precipitated an even worse riot: Nicholls 54.

372: He had heard that the Princess of Wales desired a national day of thanksgiving for her husband's recovery: Kuhn 150.

373: "Nothing could induce her to be a party to it": qtd. Herbert John Gladstone 333-34.

373: . . . "such a display" she considered "false and hollow": qtd. Herbert John Gladstone 333.

373: . . . "the whole nation has taken such a public share in our sorrow": Lee 323.

373: " . . . it gives *too much* weight to it," she complained: qtd. Guedalla 1:330.

373: The Queen wished to progress in "half-state": Kuhn 153.

373: They haggled about the number of tickets for admission to the Cathedral: Kuhn 154.

373: . . . "this dreadful affair at St. Paul's": Victoria and Victoria, *Darling Child* 30.

374: "The Queen is looking with much alarm to the Ceremony of the 27th": qtd. Guedalla 1:336.

374: . . . Napoleon III, ex-emperor of the French, stood with his wife Eugénie at an eastern window of Buckingham Palace: Victoria *Letters* (second series) 2:194.

374: . . . their "wonderful enthusiasm and astounding affectionate loyalty": Victoria *Letters* (second series) 2:194.

374: The white detailing of her black dress: *Daily News* 28 February 1872, 5.

374: . . . their reception "so gratifying that one could not feel tired": Victoria and Victoria, *Darling Child* 31.

375: People cried, the queen said; Bertie cried. Victoria admitted to a lump in her own throat: Victoria and Victoria, *Darling Child* 31; Victoria *Letters* (second series) 2:195.

375: The service at St. Paul's, attended by the upper ten thousand, was far less exciting for the Queen: Victoria *Letters* (second series) 2:195.

375: . . . Newgate ("very dreary-looking," wrote the Queen): Victoria *Letters* (second series) 2:196.

375: "Could think and talk of little else": Victoria *Letters* (second series) 2:197.

Chapter 20: Leap Day

376: . . . the distinctively elliptical and domed Royal Albert Hall, which Victoria, overwhelmed with emotion, had opened on a bitterly cold day last March: *Times* 30 March 1871, 9.

377: . . . hadn't his great-grandfather changed his name from Conner to O'Connor to proclaim that lineage to the world?: Livesey.

377: Arthur O'Connor went to France in 1796 to negotiate the landing in Ireland of a French army of liberation: Livesey.

377: . . . Arthur O'Connor had been appointed a general of the French army by the great Napoleon himself: Read and Glasgow 11.

377: Francis Burdett O'Connor . . . in 1819 set out with two hundred Irish volunteers to liberate South America from the imperial Spanish yoke: Dunkerley.

378: . . . the "fustian jackets, the blistered hands, the unshorn chins": Read and Glasgow 62.

378: They carried banners declaring him to be their savior: "He lived and died for us": Read and Glasgow 144.

378: Arthur lived with his family—nine in all—on the verge of starvation in a single room of a dilapidated Aldgate tenement, at the edge of Seven-Step Alley, one of the worst Irish rookeries in London: *Daily News* 1 March 1872, 5.

379: He had worked for a firm of printers for four years: *Daily News* 1 March 1872, 5.

379: . . . a pigeon-breasted, scrofulous rail of a boy: *Daily News* 1 March 1872, 5.

379: O'Connor was "of the order from whose plentifulness some physiologists forbode a deterioration of the human race": *Daily News* 2 March 1872, 5.

379: . . . sending him to King's College Hospital, where he had a toe amputated: *Times* 12 April 1872, 11; *Daily News* 1 March 1872, 5.

379: . . . he was "passionately Irish," as he later wrote: Arthur O'Connor, letter to Queen Victoria 11 June 1873, TNA PRO HO 144/3/10963.

379: He would kill Queen Victoria: *Times* 12 April 1872, 11. According to Thomas Harrington Tuke, who examined O'Connor in prison, killing Victoria was the original plan. O'Connor himself later denied this (TNA PRO HO 144/3/10963).

380: . . . he finally acknowledged the flaw: *Times* 12 April 1872, 11.

380: . . . he was sure that all around her would be "paralyzed with horror": *Times* 12 April 1872, 11.

380: "I, Victoria, Queen by the grace of God, do make the following declaration": O'Connor's declaration, in full, appears in the *Times* 2 March 1872, 9-10.

381: He had spotted it in the window of a jeweler's near his workplace—a flintlock: *Times* 2 March 1872, 10.

382: . . . the clerk told him he would have to pick up a piece of flint from the road and cut it to proper shape. *Times* 2 March 1872, 10.

382: At some point a greasy red rag found its way into the barrel: *Times* 1 March 1872, 9.

382: He helpfully brought pen and ink: *Daily News* 2 March 1872, 5.

382: He pocketed . . . a long, thin, open knife of his father's: *Manchester Weekly Times* 2 March 1872, 5; *Times* 12 April 1872, 11.

382: . . . the cathedral was abuzz with activity: *Daily News* 28 February 1872, 8.

382: Nevertheless, somehow he got in—"by a stratagem": *Times* 12 April 1872, 11.

382: He had tracked mud on the otherwise clean carpets to his hiding place; a verger discovered him and turned him out: *Daily News* 12 April 1872, 6; Geary 125.

383: He returned home, put the pistol, the knife, and the declaration under his pillow, and slept until 8:00: For O'Connor's movements between 27 and 29 February, see the *Times* 12 April 1872, 11.

383: His mother asked him where he had been. To St. Paul's, he said—but he "had not gained his object": *Times* 12 April 1872, 11.

383: . . . he took his nine-year-old brother out to gaze at the brilliant thanksgiving illuminations: *Pall Mall Gazette* 11 April 1872, 8-9.

383: . . . he awoke weary and jaded, according to his father: *Times* 12 April 1872, 11.

384: . . . he was a hemophiliac and had suffered from early childhood his mother's stifling overprotection: Rigg, "Leopold."

384: . . . the sentry at the gate staring forward, poised to present arms, O'Connor bolted[, r]unnning unperceived to the point where the edge of the Palace's eastern fence meets the northern wall: *Daily News* 1 March 1872, 6; *Times* 2 March 1872, 10.

384: Somehow, he managed to keep his low-crowned, wide-brimmed wideawake hat on his head: *Belfast News-Letter* 1 March 1872, 3; *Birmingham Daily Post* 1 March 1872, 5. The wideawake was a style worn by nineteenth-century Quakers, and remembered today as the headgear of the Quaker Oats man.

384: O'Connor took cover behind a pillar near the gatekeeper's lodge: *Leeds Mercury* 2 March 1872, 8, qtd. *Evening Telegraph*.

385: The gatekeeper, an old man "rather past work," spied him and shouted "what mischief do you want here?" *Victoria and Victoria, Darling Child* 33; *Bristol Mercury* 2 March 1872, 8; *Glasgow Daily Herald* 1 March 1872, 5.

385: . . . they imagined him to be a gardener's boy: *Times* 2 March 1872, 9.

385: . . . he . . . timidly muttered something about the Fenian prisoners: According to the *Glasgow Daily Herald*, 1 March 1872, 5, he said "I demand the release of the Fenian prisoners, or I will . . ."

385: Victoria thought at first that he was a footman come to remove her blanket: Victoria *Letters* (second series) 2:197.

385: Arthur heard his words: "Take that from a Fenian": RA VIC/MAIN/QVJ/1872, 29 February 1872.

385: "Involuntarily, in a terrible fright, I threw myself over Jane C.": Victoria *Letters* (second series) 2:197.

385: . . . John Brown, who had chased O'Connor around the carriage, with one hand grabbed O'Connor's body and with the other clamped the scruff of his neck: *Times* 2 March 1879, 10.

386: . . . they yanked off the boy's necktie and gave him a violent throttling: *Leeds Mercury* 2 March 1872, 8.

386: Sergeant Jackson removed knife and declaration from O'Connor's pockets: *Times* 12 April 1872, 11.

386: "an extraordinary document," she called it: Victoria *Letters* (second series) 2:198.

386: He complained about the damage done to his necktie, and demanded his hat be returned to him before he would answer any questions: *Leeds Mercury* 2 March 1872, 8; *Birmingham Daily Post* 2 March 1872, 5.

386: "Not at all," she replied: Victoria *Letters* (second series) 2:198.

386: "We looked," Victoria wrote, "but could find nothing": Victoria *Letters* (second series) 2:198.

387: ". . . it is entirely owing to good Brown's great presence of mind and quickness that he was seized": Victoria and Victoria, *Darling Child* 33.

387: . . . the two strolled arm in arm, out of the front gates of the Palace, through the crowd, and to Marlborough House: *Bristol Mercury* 2 March 1872, 8.

387: . . . the Queen, he claimed, "was not in the slightest degree flurried or alarmed": "Outrage on the Queen" (Commons).

387: . . . "the Queen showed the greatest courage and composure": "Outrage on the Queen" (Lords).

388: Every newspaper account of the attempt dutifully noted Victoria's unflinching coolness and bravery: For example, the *Pall Mall Gazette* (1 March 1872, 8) calls Victoria "perhaps the calmest person in the thrilling group, who drew herself up at sight of the pistol, and with the greatest presence of mind leaned back within the frame of the carriage."

388: "I wish to God I had succeeded; then they could have done with me as they pleased": *Daily News* 2 March 1872, 5.

388: At a crowded meeting of working men in the Surrey Chapel Mission Hall, in Southwark, a resolution was moved to express indignation about the attempt and affection for the Queen's person: *Times* 1 March 1872, 9.

389: . . . George Odger, working-class leader and heretofore outspoken republican, declared himself sure "that every man in that room . . . would denounce in the most indignant manner such a dastardly proceeding": *Times* 1 March 1872, 9.

389: A Division's police surgeon and another medical man examined O'Connor in his cell: *Lancet* 13 April 1872, 515.

389: Gladstone visited Victoria in the Palace that morning—"dreadfully shocked at what [had] happened": Victoria *Letters* (second series) 2:199.

389: . . . throngs largely composed of the dregs of the nearby slums of St. Giles and Seven Dials besieged the court and packed the tiny courtroom: *Pall Mall Gazette* 1 March 1872, 8.

389: When he was brought to the bar, hisses ran through the back benches: *Daily News* 2 March 1872, 5.

389: " . . . that death which is due to him as a Christian, a Republican— (laughter)": *Daily News* 2 March 1872, 5.

390: The blood rushed to O'Connor's face, and, according to a reporter, "out of the eye there blazed the light of fanaticism": *Daily News* 2 March 1872, 5.

390: . . . John Brown, with his broad Scottish accent and the "grim jocularity" with which he recounted the easy capture and drubbing of the boy, provided the most entertainment: *Times* 2 March 1872, 10.

390: Victoria, as protective of him as ever, was loath to let him come at all, and only agreed if he went under the close watch of an equerry and of his tutor: Victoria *Letters* (second series) 2:199.

390: A number of MPs and Peers had assembled in the Palace forecourt that O'Connor had penetrated the day before: *Times* 2 March 1872, 9.

391: "Strange to say my head and health have not suffered from this dreadful fright": Victoria and Victoria, *Darling Child* 33.

391: . . . the newspapers presented him as an imbecile, a "crack-brained youth": *Times* 4 March 1872, 8; 2 March 1872, 9.

391: The Dublin *Irishman* . . . argued that "nothing could be more repugnant, nothing more odious, nothing more loathsome to the spirit of the Irish people than a cowardly assault on a defenceless lady": qtd. in *Times* 4 March 1872, 8.

392: . . . a letter-writer to the Dublin *Freeman's Journal* pointed out quite accurately that O'Connor's ancestors were Conners, not O'Connors: *Freeman's Journal* 5 March 1872, 3.

392: . . . the best punishment for this over-imaginative halfwit was the one prescribed under Peel's Act: the "ridiculous and slightly degrading" punishment of a flogging: *Spectator*, qtd. in *Pall Mall Gazette* 2 March 1872, 1.

392: ". . . folly seems to have been so mixed with depravity in this attempt that Mr. Gladstone is inclined to hope this young man may perhaps not have been wholly master of his senses": Guedalla 1:338-39.

392: . . . he had looked forward to a trial as a state prisoner, but "shrunk from a degrading punishment": Victoria *Letters* (second series) 2:201.

392: She was sure he would have murdered her if his ignorance had not prevented him: Victoria and Victoria, *Darling Child* 33.

392: . . . the Queen pointedly sent Gladstone an article from the *Lancet* which she thought proved his sanity: Guedalla 1:340.

393: Hamilton "was also an Irishman but *Fenianism* did *not exist* then": Guedalla 1:339.

393: "He meant to *frighten* & *this may* be tried again & again & end badly some day": Guedalla 1:339.

393: . . . transportation had come to an end five years before: Hughes 180.

393: . . . she insisted that O'Connor be forced to leave England after serving his sentence: Victoria *Letters* (second series) 2:199.

393: She was angry at the police, who she thought were neither vigilant or numerous enough to protect her: Victoria and Victoria, *Darling Child* 33-34.

394: The "Boy O'Connor," as the press dubbed him, was reportedly an exemplary prisoner at Newgate: *Times* 8 April 1872, 13.

394: . . . no solicitor attended to him during his first days in prison: *Daily News* 12 April 1872, 6; *Birmingham Daily Post* 11 March 1872, 8.

394: . . . a man instantly recognizable by his enormous size of 26 stone (or 364 pounds), drove his own brougham up to the door of New-gate: *Times* 7 March 1872, 12.

395: . . . Lady Tichborne was free to indulge her fantasy of reuniting with her son and began to search for him: Gilbert 33-34.

395: . . . as rumors surfaced that survivors of the *Bella* might have been picked up and deposited in Melbourne: Woodruff 32.

395: An attorney acquaintance of Castro who had seen the advertisement and was certain that the butcher was the baronet, persuaded him to reveal himself: Woodruff 40.

395: . . . the Claimant's French was limited to "oui, madame" in an atrocious accent: Woodruff 80; Atlay 214.

395: That mystery was perhaps solved by the Claimant himself in a confession he wrote in 1895 and quickly repudiated: Orton 31.

396: Whicher soon uncovered enough evidence to convince him that the Claimant was not Roger Tichborne at all, but Arthur Orton: Summerscale 264-65.

396: Coleridge was a passionate orator who used his skills both to catch out the Claimant in cross-examination, and to deliver a month-long opening speech that demolished the Claimant's case: Gilbert 153-54, 180.

397: The Claimant proved like O'Connor to be a model prisoner, "cheerful and far from reserved": *Times* 8 March 1872, 12.

397: He largely kept apart from the rest of the prisoners, electing as a Roman Catholic to avoid the Anglican services on Sundays: *Times* 11 March 1872, 12.

397: . . . exercising in solitude in the yard: *Times* 9 March 1872, 11.

397: . . . he spent the rest of his life in poverty and humiliation, forlornly promoting his claims in music halls, circuses, and pubs: McWilliam.

398: . . . when he died in 1898, he was buried with that name inscribed upon his coffin: McWilliam.

398: "*What* in fact can be more important . . . than the faithfulness & discretion & *independent* unselfishess of those personal servants . . . ?": Guedalla 1:305.

398: On 5 March, she presented Brown with a £25 annuity and the medal . . .: *Daily News* 6 March 1872, 4.

399: Arthur "could *not* do, for his very position, what Brown *did*, who was deservedly rewarded for his presence of mind, and devotion": McClintock 148. The Queen wrote these words to Arthur's governor, Howard Elphinstone, hoping that he would contact the Prince of Wales and set him straight about the propriety of Brown's and Arthur's rewards.

399: . . . "Arthur was *very* amiable": McClintock 148.

399: The public, eager to witness his comeuppance, filled the galleries: *Punch* 30 March 1872, 130.

400: . . . he was, he admitted, "unutterably dull": Nicholls 55.

400: . . . . he "went smashingly into the Chelsea baronet as if he had been Chelsea china": *Punch* 30 March 1872, 130.

400: "A perfect storm," as Gladstone put it, ensued: Guedalla 1:342.

401: Dilke's attack on the Queen "was about as contemptible as that by the lad who presented the flintless and empty pistol the other day": *Punch* 30 March 1872, 130.

401: It took some time for him to cease to be a social pariah: Roy Jenkins, "Dilke"; Nicholls 59.

401: . . . the Queen insisted that he not be given any office that would place him close to her, and that he publicly renounce his "earlier crude opinions": Nicholls 111-12.

Chapter 21: Out of the Country

402: According to one of the doctors who examined him in Newgate, Arthur O'Connor's great object was "truth at all times": *Times* 12 April 1872, 11.

402: To Catherine, Arthur was still to her a "good lad" and the "best of boys": *Times* 12 April 1872, 11.

402: . . . he had to endure what he had brought upon himself: *Daily News* 12 April 1872, 6.

402: Arthur, he believed, had changed greatly since the day in late 1866 when a cab in Chancery Lane had knocked him down, split his head open, and sent him to the hospital: *Times* 12 April 1872, 11.

402: He had never been the same since—had become increasingly irritable and frequently burst out in fits of irrational passion: *Lancet* 27 April 1872.

403: Back in 1853, two years before his son Arthur was born, he became deeply involved in the care of his uncle Feargus: For Feargus O'Connor's insanity, and Thomas Harrington Tuke's and George Roger O'Connor's involvement, see Geary 127-36. In the accounts of 1853, Feargus's son is invariably referred to as Roger, but the accounts of 1872 make clear that *George* Roger is the nephew connected with Tuke and with his uncle Feargus's last days. In the *Lancet* 27 April 1872, Tuke identifies George O'Connor as the nephew with which he was acquainted.

403: " . . . general paralysis of the insane"—soon (but not yet) understood to result from syphilis: Geary 132.

403: The commission, examining him, found him frantic and incoherent: *Times* 13 April 1853, 8.

403: Feargus O'Connor lived on for another two years in pitiful physical decline, suffering severe epileptic seizures and losing control of his bodily functions: Geary 135.

403: A week after his son's imprisonment, he met Tuke in his consulting room: *Lancet* 27 April 1872, 571.

404: . . . all of which indicated to Tuke "a fanciful and hypochondriacal state of mind": *Lancet* 27 April 1872, 571.

404: He recommended to George that other doctors examine his son. Four others did; three concurred with Tuke: *Lancet* 27 April 1872, 572.

404: Besides, he suggested, in the event of the boy's recovery, both his previous good character, and the Queen's well-known propensity to clemency, would surely both work to free the boy: Tuke 673.

404: On Tuesday the 9th of April, the grand jury at the Central Criminal Court briefly heard the testimony of two witnesses—Prince Leopold and John Brown—and quickly returned a true bill against O'Connor, for a misdemeanor under Peel's Act: *Daily News* 10 April 1872, 6; *Times* 10 April 1872, 11.

405: . . . he "saw the effects of what he had done": *Times* 12 April 1872, 11. The *Daily News* 12 April 1872, 6 reports him as saying that he "saw the *evil* of what he had done."

405: Those in the courtroom were visibly startled by the boy's plea: *Times* 12 April 1872, 11.

405: George O'Connor . . . did not learn about the plea until the next day: *Daily News* 12 April 1872, 6.

405: The courtroom was crowded, particularly with bewigged barristers expecting the setting of new legal precedents: Transcripts of O'Connor's trial appear in the *Daily News* 12 April 1872, 5-6, and the *Times* 12 April 1872, 11.

406: . . . "he bowed neither to judge nor jury," noted a reporter, "but posed himself as if sitting for his photograph": *Daily News* 12 April 1872, 5.

406: . . . Baron Cleasby, a judge known to be a niggler on points of law, and never quite comfortable in a criminal courtroom: Boase, "Cleasby."

406: But Cleasby would have none of it, interrupting Hume-Williams after the second sentence of his opening speech: *Daily News* 12 April 1872, 5.

407: "I had always told him to tell the truth, and I believe he has done so": *Daily News* 12 April 1872, 6.

407: "Is it your desire that your son should be imprisoned for life in a lunatic asylum?": *Daily News* 12 April 1872, 6.

408: Coleridge reduced Tuke to silence: *Times* 12 April 1872, 11.

408: "I was his first subject since he had showered vituperation upon the Tichborne Claimant": Tuke 672.

408: They stopped the trial and announced through their foreman "that the prisoner was a perfectly sane man when he pleaded to the indictment, and that he was perfectly sane now": *Times* 12 April 1872, 11.

409: "The Queen's object in writing to Mr. Gladstone today is to express her surprise & annoyance at the *extreme leniency* of O'Connor's Sentence": Guedalla 1:344-45.

410: . . . "the eye of the police should continue to rest upon O'Connor": Guedalla 1:346.

411: Gladstone suggested in return that the "animadversions of the press" would more effectively "repress these strange aberrations": Guedalla 1:348.

411: The day after the boy's sentencing he wrote the governor of Newgate to suspend the sentence of whipping: TNA PRO HO 144/3/10963.

412: "I was not mad, nor was I perfectly sensible": TNA PRO HO 144/3/10963.

412: "I can never agree to a condition which would condemn me to almost perpetual exile": TNA PRO HO 144/3/10963.

413: . . . if O'Connor ever returned "it w^d be as an altered man": TNA PRO HO 144/3/10963.

413: "This is vexatious": TNA PRO HO 144/3/10963.

413: Tasmania . . . where the children of George's uncle Roderic—Feargus's half-brother—were prosperous landowners: Hughes 394; Read and Glasgow 14.

413: . . . "he seems to take a higher tone, and to consider himself a person of some importance": TNA HO 144/3.

414: . . . "the people being very loyal," he later wrote, "I might suffer some annoyance were I to be known": TNA PRO HO 144/3/10963.

414: He had a poet's mind, and that mind "stands alone, and lives in a glorious solitude, apart from the world": TNA PRO HO 144/3/10963.

415: "The man must be mad": TNA PRO HO 144/3/10963.

415: "I had no legal power to detain the youth": TNA PRO HO 140/3/10963.

416: . . . "he is of a romantic turn of mind, he has no employment, and spends most of his time at home reading and writing what he calls poetry": TNA PRO HO 140/3/10963.

416: Gull had experience working with the insane: Hervey.

417: "I was thinking what a wonderful calm reigned in London, and that it was owing to the perfection of government": TNA PRO HO 144/3/10963.

417: "Thought continually revolving upon religion": TNA PRO HO 144/3/10963.

418: . . . committed to Hanwell Asylum as an "imbecile": Tuke 673.

418: " . . . surprised & annoyed" by O'Connor's return: RA VIC/MAIN/L/13/191, May 1875.

418: "He is evidentially quite unfit to be at large": RA VIC/MAIN/28/10, 22 May 1875.

418: ". . . but he must surely now deeply deplore his share in a proceeding which consigned a sick and insane boy to degrading punishment": Tuke 673.

419: "If only our dear Bertie was fit to replace me!": Victoria and Victoria, *Darling Child* 47.

Chapter 22: Blue

420: Roderick Maclean was filthy, either unwilling or unable to wash off the dust of the many roads upon which he had tramped: *Glasgow Daily Herald* 4 March 1882, 5.

420: . . . his twenty-eight years: *Daily News* 4 March 1882, 5.

421: God read his thoughts: *Reynolds's Weekly* 23 April 1882, 1 summarizes Maclean's autobiography on this subject; see also the psychological evidence given at his trial, in *Times* 20 April 1882, 11.

421: God had given him eternal life: *Leeds Mercury* 7 March 1882, 8.

421: He was certain that his own claim to the British throne was at least as great as George IV's had been: *Times* 20 April 1882, 11.

421: The number was four: *Reynolds's Weekly* 23 April 1882, 1.

421: "The Fourth Path, a novel by Roderick Maclean": *Daily News* 5 March 1882, 5.

422: The color—*his* color—was blue: *Times* 20 April 1882, 11; *Daily News* 20 April 1882, 3.

422: Maclean knew that wearing blue was forbidden to anyone besides himself alone: *Times* 20 April 1882, 11.

422: Occurrences of four were now more likely ominous than auspicious to him: "He had, he said, a mysterious connection with no. 4, and this numeral in any combination of figures was always disastrous to him": testimony of Dr. Sheppard at Maclean's trial, *Times* 20 April 1882, 11.

422: . . . they wore blue to cause him "perplexity and agony," to "injure, annoy, and vex me on every opportunity": From a letter Maclean sent to his sister Annie, *Times* 20 April 1882, 11.

423: His childhood, he would later recall, was "as happy as any youthful days could be": Maclean wrote this in his (now lost) autobiography; rpt. *Reynolds's Weekly* 23 April 1882, 1.

423: His father Charles Maclean had earned a fortune as master-carver and master-guilder to the gentry and nobility. He had employed— auspiciously—forty people: *1851 England Census* [database on-line]. Provo, UT, USA: Ancestry.com Operations Inc., 2005.

423: . . . a massive console table and mirror that he manufactured had been given pride of place in the nave of the Crystal Palace: Auerbach 96-7.

423: Roderick Maclean was born three years after the Exhibition: *Daily News* 4 March 1882, 5, notes "He gave his age as 28, and his birthday occurred during his stay at Southsea"; if this is true, Maclean was born sometime between 9 February and 23 February 1854; the Berkshire Records Office (Broadmoor Hospital) file (BRO D/H14/02/2/1/1095) gives Maclean's exact birth date as 10 February 1854.

423: . . . an estate in the suburbs that he remembered as an Eden: Maclean's lost autobiography, qtd. Sims 69.

423: He was educated to be a gentleman at a school on Harley Street: *Reynolds's Weekly* 23 April 1882, 1.

423: Roderick's father was a literary gentleman of sorts, taking up in 1861 the proprietorship of a new humor magazine, *Fun*: Lauterbach 4.

423: Roderick recalled mingling among George Augustus Sala, Tom Hood (son of the great comic poet), and W. S. Gilbert in his pre-Sullivan days, and others: Lauterbach 5, Sims 69.

423: . . . he sold it in 1865: Lauterbach 11.

423: . . . Charles apparently lost much of his fortune in the spectacular collapse of the banking firm of Overend and Gurney: White 66n.; *Leeds Mercury* 7 March 1882, 8; a classified advertisement in *The*

Times, 23 January 1868, notes "late Charles Maclean" about what had once been his operation, the Commercial Plate Glass Company.

423: . . . Roderick suffered his own fall, literally, slipping in the doorway of his Gloucester Road house, smashing his head and gashing his scalp open: *Reynolds's Weekly* 23 April 1882, 1; *Times* 20 April 1882, 11.

424: His head continued to give off the sensation of a "slight shock from a galvanic battery": *Reynolds's Weekly* 23 April 1882, 1.

424: He developed morbid fears that his siblings, his mother, and especially his father were trying to kill him: *Leeds Mercury* 7 March 1882, 8.

424: He lashed back, threatening to kill his family and at one time vowing to blow up St. Paul's and Westminster Abbey: *Leeds Mercury* 7 March 1882, 8.

424: Twice he booked Roderick passage for America: *Leeds Mercury* 7 March 1882, 8.

424: In 1874, when Roderick was twenty, Charles Maclean took steps to have him committed to an asylum: *Daily News* 20 April 1882, 3.

424: . . . the renowned psychologist Henry Maudsley . . . was happy to comply, and declared Roderick insane: *Times* 20 April 1882, 11.

424: The other doctor, Alfred Godrich, found Roderick highly excitable but not a lunatic: *Daily News* 20 April 1882, 3.

424: . . . Maclean's father instead exiled Roderick as an apprentice on a farm near Dover: *Leeds Mercury* 7 March 1882, 8. According to the dates given by the attorney Wollaston Knocker, Maclean could have been at this farm earlier, at age eighteen (or about 1872). Newspaper reports of his trial make clear that he left the farm in August 1874.

424: . . . Maclean offered a young boy sixpence to derail a coming train with a beam of wood: *Leeds Mercury* 7 March 1882, 8.

425: Maclean and the boy were acquitted: *Dover, Folkestone, and Deal Guide.*

425: . . . his father claimed that he attempted to derail trains at least twice more: *Leeds Mercury* 7 March 1882, 8.

425: . . . his brother Charles tried to place him in the home of a family friend, the artist Samuel Stanesby: *Times* 20 April 1882, 11.

425: . . . one of his sisters would mail him, wherever he was, a postal order for a few shillings: *Hampshire Telegraph* 4 March 1882, 8.

425: Once, denied admission to one of these in Somerset, he deliberately smashed a window so that he would spend the night in jail: *Daily News* 4 March 1882, 5.

425: Occasionally he was able to gain temporary admission to the local lunatic asylum, as he had once done in Dublin: *Daily News* 4 March 1882, 5; *Bristol Mercury* 4 March 1882, 8.

425: "On your thrown you set and rule us all": *Surrey Advertiser and County Times* 11 March 1882, 5.

426: . . . Maclean showed her a dagger he carried in his sleeve to "take care of himself": *Surrey Advertiser and County Times* 11 March 1882, 5.

426: . . . to Boulogne, France; throughout Germany: even perhaps to Jamaica, where according to one report he passed as Roderigues Maclean: *Times* 6 March 1882, 6; 20 April 1882, 11; *Daily News* 4 March 1882, 5. A long list of his residences between 1874 and 1882, which Maclean submitted at Broadmoor in an attempt to ascertain which parish should support his stay there, lists Boulogne—but not Germany or Jamaica.

427: "Dear Annie,—I have no doubt but that you will be somewhat surprised to receive another letter from me": The first of two letters to Annie introduced at Maclean's trial: *Times* 20 April 1882, 11.

428: . . . quickly arranged for a local surgeon to examine him, sign a certificate of lunacy, and commit him to the Bath and Somerset Lunatic Asylum: *Times* 20 April 1882, 11; *Bristol Mercury* 6 March 1882, 8; *British Medical Journal* 11 March 1882, 355.

428: He remained there for fourteen months, happier to be in an asylum than anywhere else—but even there fearing contact with perfidious attendants and visitors: *Times* 20 April 1882, 11.

428: . . . the massive population there, he wrote Annie, made things "a thousand times worse": *Times* 20 April 1882, 11. Some reports did, however, place Maclean in London at this time: for example, *Manchester Times* 18 March 1882, 6.

428: . . . Brighton, where he spent a month in the local workhouse: *Daily News* 4 March 1882, 5.

428: While there, he wrote a letter to Annie: *Reynolds's Weekly* 23 April 1882, 1.

428: . . . he got a deeply disturbing letter from his brother Hector: *Daily News* 4 March 1882, 5, which does not name the brother who sent this letter; that it was Hector Maclean is suggested by the entry for Hector Maclean (with three children) in the 1881 census: *1881 England Census* [database on-line]. Provo, UT, USA: Ancestry.com Operations Inc., 2004.

428: . . . the workhouse authorities at Brighton threatened to transfer Maclean to Kensington, his home parish workhouse: *Daily News* 4 March 1882, 5.

428: There he found a room in the poorer part of town, in the home of Mrs. Sorrell: The *Hampshire Telegraph* 4 March 1882, 8, published in Portsmouth, has the clearest and fullest account of Maclean's stay in Southsea. See also *Times* 4 March 1882, 10, which like most accounts mistakes Mrs. Sorrell for "Mrs. Hucker."

429: . . . he claimed to be a writer and poet employed by the *West Sussex Gazette*: *Daily News* 4 March 1882, 5; *Birmingham Daily Post* 4 March 1882, 5.

429: It was not long before his landlady concluded he was a man "with a tile loose": *Daily News* 4 March 1882, 5.

429: By night he entertained Sorrell and Hucker with a little concertina that he had obtained in Brighton, and with a little ventriloquist routine: *Hampshire Telegraph* 4 March 1882, 8; Bayes.

429: He would lecture them on political economy until they could take it no more. He was a great admirer of Prime Minister Gladstone: *Hampshire Telegraph* 4 March 1882, 8.

429: And he was a passionate supporter of the ultra-radical politician Charles Bradlaugh: *Daily News* 4 March 1882, 5.

429: . . . his atheism, his republicanism, and his scandalous advocacy of birth control ensured that a majority of the Commons supported a measure each time to refuse to let him take the oath or his seat: Royle; Tribe 197, 210.

429: . . . since no one would give him the oath, he decided to take it himself: Tribe 214-15.

430: . . . his older sister Caroline having very recently died: *Lloyd's Weekly* 19 March 1882, 8.

430: Annie wrote to warn him that his family's support of him would soon diminish: *Birmingham Daily Post* 4 March 1882, 5; *Hampshire Telegraph* 4 March 1882, 8.

430: . . . his brother offered no financial support, and instead reminded Roderick of his mental weakness, and recommended he seek restraint: *Reynolds's Weekly* 23 April 1882, 1.

430: His brothers were wealthy: one had a good business in London, and the other had married into wealth: *Daily News* 4 March 1882, 5.

430: He vowed that he would go to London to enforce his rights: *Hampshire Telegraph* 4 March 1882, 8.

430: He also engaged in another topic of conversation while at Mrs. Sorrell's: Queen Victoria: *Hampshire Telegraph* 4 March 1882, 8.

431: His odd questions confirmed Sorrell's and Hucker's opinion that Maclean was "soft": *Hampshire Telegraph* 4 March 1882, 8.

431: Around midday, Maclean walked into a pawnbroker's on Queen Street, Portsmouth: For details about Maclean's purchase of a pistol, see *Times* 20 April 1882, 11.

431: It was a cheap pistol: a six-shooter of Belgian make: *Times* 20 April 1882, 11; *Leeds Mercury* 20 April 1882, 7; *Birmingham Daily Post* 4 March 1882, 5.

431: . . . it was formidable-looking enough for witnesses later to mistake it for a Colt revolver: *Times* 3 March 1882, 5.

431: . . . his name was Campbell, he told the shopkeeper, and he needed the pistol because he was about to join the South African Cap Mounted Rifles: *Times* 20 April 1882, 11.

431: . . . by the end of the first one he gave Mrs. Sorrell notice: *Daily News* 4 March 1882, 5.

432: Maclean knew himself to be a brilliant actor: *Times* 20 April 1882, 11.

432: He would leave on Thursday morning, the twenty-third, to go to London and find employment in Harris's troupe: *Times* 4 March 1882, 10.

432: She sent him another postoffice order, and pleaded with him to stay where he was and take on any job he could—even take up a broom and sweep street-crossings: *Daily News* 4 March 1882, 5; *Times* 4 March 1882, 10.

432: Mrs. Sorrell gave him a couple shillings in return for his concertina and a scarf he owned: *Glasgow Herald* 4 March 1882, 5.

432: That day, Maclean returned to the pawnbroker's, paid the remainder on the pistol, and took it away wrapped in an old piece of white linen: *Reynolds's Weekly* 23 April 1882, 1.

432: He returned as well to the gunsmith's and bought as many pin-fire bullets as he could for a shilling: *Times* 20 April 1882, 11.

432: Mrs. Sorrell gave him a final gift of a better hat and pair of shoes than his own: *Daily News* 4 March 1882, 5.

432: Maclean collapsed outside of Maclachlan's garden gate in what Maclachlan was certain was an epileptic fit: *Times* 20 April 1882, 11.

433: . . . at 3:00 on that afternoon—Saturday 25 February—he arrived in Windsor: *Reynolds's Weekly*, 23 April 1882, 1.

433: Maclean found accommodation at 84 Victoria Cottages: *Daily News*, 4 March 1882, 5.

433: He did by one account have a single eccentricity: *Daily News* 4 March 1882, 5.

434: "I should not have done this crime": *Times* 4 March 1882, 10.

434: "Did you know this is a first-class waiting room—not the place for you?": *Times* 20 April 1882, 11.

435: . . . he had been careful to ensure his good fortune by loading only four of them: *Daily News* 3 March 1882, 5; *Times* 3 March 1882, 5.

435: The daughter next in age, Louise, was far too free a spirit for Victoria to consider as a companion: Hibbert, *Queen Victoria* 394.

436: . . . Beatrice had done much of the chaperoning: *Times* 1 March 1882, 3.

436: But she wore another color as well, as was also usual on state occasions: *Times* 2 March 1882, 8.

437: "What nerve! What muscle! What energy!": St. Aubyn, *Queen Victoria* 428.

438: . . . "I plight my troth to the kindest of *mistresses*": Weintraub, *Disraeli* 521.

438: . . . he flattered the Queen ceaselessly and shamelessly, laying it on, as he famously observed, "with a trowel": St. Aubyn, *Queen Victoria* 427.

438: . . . she preferred to see him as "full of poetry, romance and chivalry": Matthew and Reynolds.

439: "You have it, Madam," he declared to her: Weintraub, *Disraeli* 544.

439: More than once he favored and sponsored legislation that she wanted and his Cabinet did not: Most notably the Public Worship and Regulation Act of 1874 and the Royal Titles Act of 1876. Weintraub, *Disraeli* 529, 550.

439: Disraeli, according to Victoria, had "right feelings," and *"very large ideas,* and *very lofty views* of the position this country should hold": Matthew and Reynolds; Weintraub, *Disraeli* 547.

439: . . . Victoria's concern for his own health was dictated "not so much from love of me as dread of somebody else": Guedalla 2:7.

440: . . . a righteous rage against Turkish atrocities in the Balkans reanimated him, forcing him once again into the political spotlight: Matthew.

440: . . . Gladstone made his case against Disraeli not to Parliament, but to the people directly, in rousing orations at mass meetings: Matthew.

440: . . . "like an American stumping orator, making most violent speeches": St. Aubyn, *Queen Victoria* 442.

440: Her anger was mixed with more than a hint of jealousy: Hibbert, *Queen Victoria* 487; St. Aubyn, *Queen Victoria* 442.

440: She would rather abdicate, she wrote her private secretary, "rather than send for or have any *communication* with that *half-mad* fire-brand": Weintraub, *Disraeli* 625.

441: She kept him, as he noted, at "arm's length": Guedalla 2:39.

441: He spoke to her, she said, as if she were a public meeting: St. Aubyn, *Queen Victoria* 384.

441: Victoria had feared that the coming Liberal government would be a "calamity for the country and the peace of Europe": Victoria *Letters* (second series) 3:73.

441: Of all her governments, she told Vicky two years later, this one was "the worst I have ever had to do with": Hibbert, *Queen Victoria* 369.

442: The first two attempts . . . were thwarted when bystanders jostled the would-be assassins' arms: Burleigh 34; Radzinsky 177, 199.

442: Alexander himself thwarted the third would-be assassin, a man named Alexander Soloviev: Burleigh 45.

442: . . . they tried to kill the royal family as they ate, secreting a good three hundred pounds of dynamite in a trunk below the dining room of the Winter Palace: Radzinsky 332-33.

443: Finally, People's Will planned an apocalypse from which Alexander would never escape: For accounts of Alexander II's assassination, see Burleigh 50-51; Radzinsky 411-16.

443: Sundays in St. Petersburg, Alexander would usually drive a mile from the Winter Palace and back in order to review his troops: Hingley 113.

443: "A fine one!": Radzinsky 414.

443: . . . with one arm he helped carry Alexander's body while with the other he held the briefcase containing the explosive: Radzinsky 416.

444: "Feel quite shaken and stunned by this awful news": Victoria, *Letters* (second series) 3:202.

444: The bombers had obviously chosen the site for its symbolic value: Short, 50; K R M Short offers a fully-detailed study of the Fenian bombing campaigns in his *The Dynamite War.*

445: Rossa's hatred of the British had been born when his fatherless family was evicted during the worst of the Great Famine: Edwards.

445: The British government might protest, but the U.S. government—hungry for Irish votes—did nothing to stop him: Burleigh 3-4.

445: Rossa's politics—his refusal in particular to work with Parnell and the parliamentary nationalists—proved too militant for the largest body of the Fenians in the United States, the Clan-na-Gael: Gantt 132.

445: . . . Rossa's bombers targeted London, placing a cruder device—fifteen pounds of blasting powder lit by a fuse—in a niche outside Mansion House: Short 55.

446: . . . the discovery by police . . . of eight more "infernal machines"—slabs of dynamite with clockwork detonators: Short 69.

446: Guiteau, a failed lawyer, evangelist preacher, newspaper editor, lecturer, writer, and insurance salesman: Clark 1-2, 11, 18-19; Ackerman 134-5.

447: . . . Guiteau leapt to the conclusion that his speech alone was responsible for Garfield's election: Clark 38.

447: He preferred to become Minister to Austria; he would be happy with the consul-generalship in Paris; at the very least, he would accept a consulship in Liverpool: Clark 40.

447: Soon after Garfield's inauguration, Guiteau arrived in Washington, D.C. with a single shirt and five dollars: Clark 37.

447: He managed once to thrust a copy of his speech into Garfield's hands and once to speak to him; another time he slipped into a White House reception and had a conversation with Mrs. Garfield: Clark 37, 41-2; Ackerman 268.

447: . . . "Never speak to me again on the Paris consulship as long as you live": Ackerman 338.

447: As he lay in bed one night, the disappointed office-seeker had a burst of inspiration: Ackerman 346-47.

448: Within two weeks, he realized that his inspiration was divinely inspired: Ackerman 346.

448: But in the end he opted for economy, choosing a $9 wood-handled, .44-caliber five-shot snub-nosed revolver with a powerful kick, stamped "British Bulldog": Ellman 165-66 supports his claim that the handles were wood with a photograph; Clark 49, and Ackerman 355, claim that he actually bought the pearl-handled model. Despite its name, the pistol was probably not British, but a cheap American knockoff of the well-known pistol produced by the British firm Webley: Ellman 165-66.

448: A novice with a gun, Guiteau spent time the next day practicing shooting on the banks of the Potomac: Ackerman 355.

448: "The President's tragic death was a sad necessity": Ackerman 374.

448: At 8:30 that morning, he took up a position in the ladies' waiting room of the station: For accounts of Garfield's assassination, see Clark 56-63; Ackerman 375-380.

448: . . . Guiteau shot twice, the first bullet grazing Garfield's arm and the second plunging into his back, above his waist and four inches from his spine: Clark 58, 110.

448: The fifteen or so doctors who examined him, however, ensured that he would die: Clark 69.

449: Victoria, who had sent at least six messages expressing her concern during Garfield's long decline and death, immediately ordered her Court to go into mourning for a week: King, ed. 417-18.

Chapter 23: Worth Being Shot At

451: From their saloon car behind the Queen's own, the members of the household—Victoria's private secretary Sir Henry Ponsonby, her two equerries James Carstairs McNeill and Viscount Bridport, her current lady-in-waiting Lady Roxburghe, and her maids of honor—emerged: *Illustrated London News* 11 March 1882, 228.

451: Ponsonby offered the Queen his arm: *Pall Mall Gazette* 3 March 1882, 8.

452: Their head, Chief Superintendent Hayes, stood at the verge of the yard, ready to signal to his sergeant: *Times* 4 March 1882, 10.

452: . . . he had let down the carriage stairs and was ready to hand her warm wraps for the short journey: *Daily News* 4 March 1882, 5.

452: . . . he was stouter and suffered several chronic illnesses: Cullen 165-8.

452: . . . Victoria enjoyed the cheers of the crowd, the shouting of the boys from Eton, she thought, drowning out the rest: Victoria *Letters* (second series) 3:265.

453: . . . about forty feet away from her: *Times* 20 April 1882, 11.

453: Victoria heard the sharp report; she thought it had come from a train engine: Victoria *Letters* (second series) 3:265.

453: Chief Superintendent Hayes, who was nine feet away from him, was the first to reach him, shouting "scoundrel!" and grabbing him by the neck: *Times* 4 March 1882, 10; 20 April 1882, 11.

453: Two of the Eton boys, armed with umbrellas, belabored Maclean over his head and shoulders with zeal but indiscriminate aim, smacking in the process at least one of Maclean's captors: *Times* 20 April 1882, 11.

453: Victoria . . . "saw people rushing about and a man being violently hustled": Victoria *Letters* (second series) 3:265.

453: The carriage sped up the hill, the other two carriages following: According to more than one account, Ponsonby and the equerries, about to enter the second carriage, dashed to the spot where Victoria's carriage had been, and reassured themselves she was uninjured before continuing on to the Castle. How they could possibly ascertain Victoria's state by examining the place she had vacated, however, is left unexplained: *Daily News* 3 March 1882, 5; *Times* 3 March 1882, 5.

453: The crowd—and particularly the Eton boys—wanted to lynch Maclean on the spot: *Aberdeen Journal* 3 March 1882, 4.

454: . . . "Don't hurt me; I will go quietly": *Times* 4 March 1882, 10.

454: . . . he declared "that man fired at your Majesty's carriage": Victoria *Letters* (second series) 3:266.

454: Victoria immediately ordered McNeill back to the station to see if anyone had been hurt: *Times* 3 March 1882, 5.

454: "Was not shaken or frightened," she wrote: Victoria *Letters* (second series) 3:266-67.

454: She hurried to tell her one child in the Castle—Arthur—what had happened: Victoria *Letters* (second series) 3:267.

454: She then took tea with Beatrice while her account was telegraphed to the rest of her children and to other relatives: Victoria *Letters* (second series) 3:267.

455: . . . the Eton boys running beside them hooting, and Maclean demonstrating visible anxiety the whole way: *Daily News* 3 March 1882, 3.

455: From the group of Eton boys, the two who had pummeled the captured Maclean with their brollies identified themselves: *Times* 12 March 1936, 10.

455: Fraser and Hayes examined his gun: two chambers loaded; two recently discharged; two empty: *Daily News* 3 March 1882, 5.

455: Superintendent Hayes detained Maclean for shooting the Queen with intent to do her grievous bodily harm: *Times* 3 March 1882, 5.

455: "Oh, the Queen": *Times* 4 March 1882, 10.

455: Maclean was forced to wash himself: *Reynolds's Weekly* 5 March 1882, 1.

455: A local surgeon, William Brown Holderness, was brought in to examine him: *Daily News* 3 March 1882, 5. Other early accounts claim that Victoria's doctor, James Reid, also examined Maclean and pronounced him sane, but later denials suggest this to be unlikely.

456: Several diplomats who wished to offer up personal congratulations at the Palace were directed to call at Marlborough House: *Belfast News-Letter* 3 March 1882, 5.

456: Others made their way by train to Windsor Castle on the next day: *Pall Mall Gazette* 3 March 1882, 8.

456: The House of Commons churned for a time that evening with a growing consternation: *Times* 3 March 1882, 5.

456: "I hope the matter will not receive the same sort of judicial handling which a similar one as I recollect received from Mr. Justice Cleasby": Guedalla 2:179.

456: . . . many had collected outside newspaper offices throughout Britain to hear the results of Bradlaugh's bid for re-election in Northampton: *Bristol Mercury* 3 March 1882, 8.

457: I have before me as I write a copy of an evening paper published in San Francisco on March 2nd: *Leeds Mercury* 25 March 1882, 5.

457: . . . jamming the special telegraph wire to the Castle: *Pall Mall Gazette* 3 March 1882, 8; *Graphic* 11 March 1882, 227.

457: She received messages: *Times* 3 March 1882, 5; *Pall Mall Gazette* 3 March 1882, 8; *Daily News* 6 March 1882, 6; *Times* 6 March 1882, 6.

458: . . . Victoria was particularly affected by President Chester Arthur's message to her: *Aberdeen Journal* 6 March 1882, 3.

458: And postbags bulging with congratulations soon joined telegrams: *Aberdeen Journal* 8 March 1882, 5. One newspaper reports that five hundred telegrams poured in by 6 March, another two thousand telegrams by the seventeenth. *Bristol Mercury* 6 March 1882, 8; *Newcastle Courant* 17 March 1882, 8; White 41.

458: "Telegrams, as well as letters," she wrote in her journal on 3 March, "pouring in": Victoria *Letters* (second series) 3:267.

458: . . . "the boys cheered as we passed . . . and everyone seemed so pleased": Victoria *Letters* (second series) 3:267.

458: . . . "anything like the enthusiasm, loyalty, sympathy and affection shown me is not to be described": Victoria and Victoria, *Beloved Mama* 116.

458: . . . the bullet had been found by Inspector Noble of the Great Western Railway: *Times* 4 March 1882, 10.

458: That truck had moved on to Reading, but Inspector Noble found it there that afternoon: *Daily News* 4 March 1882, 5.

458: . . . the apparent answer to which was that the bullet passed between the rear of the carriage and the rumble seat—between Victoria and John Brown: *Illustrated London News* 11 March 1882, 230.

459: . . . "for it proves," she wrote, "that the object was not intimidation, but far worse": Victoria *Letters* (second series) 3:267.

459: I am not guilty of the charge of shooting with the intention of causing actual bodily harm: *Times* 4 March 1882, 10.

460: He was thus a confident man when at 1:30 that afternoon, hand-cuffed to a plain-clothed officer, he was rushed in an open fly from the station house to Windsor Town Hall: *Daily News* 4 March 1882, 5.

461: "I saw the prisoner with a revolver in his hand. The line of fire was straight from my eye to one of the panels of Her Majesty's carriage": *Times* 4 March 1882, 10.

461: "Have you fired a pistol in your life?": *Daily News* 4 March 1882, 6.

461: "That is a point in my favor": *Glasgow Herald* 4 March 1882, 5.

462: "We have nothing to do with that": *Daily News* 4 March 1882, 6.

462: . . . some of the crowd rushed at the carriage: *Daily News* 4 March 1882, 5; *Times* 4 March 1882, 5.

462: Superintendent Hayes, attempting to avoid confrontation by avoiding Windsor train station altogether, removed Maclean from the station in a closed fly through Eton and to the railway station at Slough: *Times* 6 March 1882, 6.

462: . . . anything less, she thought, would have a *"painful effect"*: Guedalla 2:181.

463: . . . "the dominant feeling in my mind has been that the whole of these deplorable attempts on the life of the Queen have proceeded from men of weak and morbid minds": Guedalla 2:180.

463: . . . Gladstone reversed himself, and the Cabinet, meeting on Saturday, agreed to follow the precedents of 1840 and 1842: Guedalla 2:180.

463: Victoria was satisfied with Parliament, and told Gladstone so: Guedalla 2:181.

464: The address was then read "extremely well": Victoria and Victoria, *Beloved Mama* 116.

464: Victoria, "visibly affected," replied briefly to the address: *Leeds Mercury* 7 March 1882, 8.

464: She shook the hands of her young saviors: *Leeds Mercury* 7 March 1882, 8. By some accounts Victoria promised the boys a commission in the army. With or without this incentive, one of the boys, Gordon Chesney Wilson, grew up to become a true son of the Empire: he served as aide-de-camp to Baden-Powell at the siege of Mafeking, married the daughter of the Seventh Duke of Marlborough and thus became an uncle to Winston Churchill, died in battle in Ypres in the first months of the First World War, and was buried in a Flanders field (Clutterbuck and Dooner 448-49).

464: Elisabeth, a devoted huntress, had been riding to the hounds in Cheshire for the past month, and had come . . . to offer Victoria her congratulations and her farewells: *Times* 4 February 1882, 9; 7 March 1882, 10.

464: Luigi Lucheni[,] was an Italian anarchist who when caught admitted that he was out to kill the first royal he could lay his hands upon: Sinclair 174.

465: . . . he plunged into her body a short file sharpened to stiletto fineness, breaking her rib and piercing her lung, pericardium, and heart: Sinclair 177.

465: . . . that news was widely reported the next day, along with Maclean's stays in a Dublin asylum as well as Weston-super-Mare infirmary: *Daily News* 4 March 1882, 5; *Birmingham Daily Post* 4 March 1882, 5; *Leeds Mercury* 4 March 1882, 3.

465: . . . Wollaston Knocker[,] recognized Maclean from the first reports of the shooting and quickly telegraphed the Mayor of Windsor: *Daily News* 4 March 1882, 5.

465: A few days later, Knocker's more detailed account of Maclean's earlier, bizarre behavior appeared in newspapers across the country: *Leeds Mercury* 7 March 1882, 8.

466: The Home Secretary, William Vernon Harcourt, did consider the possibility that Maclean was a part of a larger political conspiracy: TNA PRO HO 144/95/A14281.

466: Most . . . called for the assassination of another "crowned ragamuffin" every month: *Times* 26 May 1881, 11.

466: . . . "the present attempt on the life of Her Majesty the Queen was the work of a lunatic": TNA PRO HO 144/95/A14281.

466: The horror one felt at learning the Queen had again been attacked, Gladstone proclaimed, was mitigated by one "remarkable consideration": "Attempt on the Life of Her Majesty."

468: "Your Majesty's Law Officers are sensible how important it is that there should be in this case a power of imprisonment without any limit of time": RA VIC/MAIN/L/14/116.

468: . . . "if there should be any fear of his not being convicted for intent to murder . . . the plea of insanity will be brought forward": RA VIC/MAIN/QVJ/1882, 10 March 1882.

469: Maclean might have "a horrid, cruel face": RA VIC/MAIN/L/14/115.

469: He might be the "utterly worthless" offshoot of "respectable relations": Victoria and Victoria, *Beloved Mama* 116.

469: . . . she wrote Gladstone "she is glad to hear of this proposed arrangement for the trial of Maclean w^h seems very satisfactory": Guedalla 2:181-82.

469: "The Mayor (to the prisoner) Have you any question to put to the witness?": *Daily News* 11 March 1882, 3.

470: Stephenson had little to say about Maclean's state of mind besides noting that, as far as he could tell, there was nothing the matter with the man: *Times* 11 March 1882, 10.

Chapter 24: Special Verdict

472: . . . he argued in it both that he had no intention of whatsoever of shooting the Queen, and that he had long been, and still was, insane: *Reynolds's Weekly* 23 April 1882, 1.

472: . . . if his overblown prose and his later repeated but unsuccessful attempts to get the manuscript published are any indication: he apparently sought to gain with it the literary fame he knew he so greatly deserved: *Reynolds's Weekly* 23 April 1882, 1; Sims 67-70; White 56. Maclean's memoirs have disappeared, but fragments from and summaries of them appear in *Reynolds's Weekly* following his trial, and in writer George R. Sims's own memoirs, *My Life: Sixty Years' Recollections of Bohemian London*.

472: . . . "to express from her heart how very deeply touched she is by the outburst of enthusiastic loyalty, affection, and devotion which the painful event of the 2d. inst. has called forth from all classes and from all parts of her vast Empire": *Times* 14 March 1882, 10.

472: . . . "the bright sunshine and the sea, mountains, vegetation and lightness of the air and the brightness and gaiety of everything": Victoria and Victoria, *Beloved Mama* 117.

472: Rumors that three Fenian terrorists were on their way from Paris to assassinate Victoria had reached the ears of the police who accompanied her: Nelson 35; Lamont-Brown 132.

472: John Brown did not, and drove everyone to distraction by his frantic attempts to discover the assassins: Cullen 190.

472: Victoria attributed his hypervigilance not to any actual threat, but to "his increasing *hatred* of being 'abroad'": Nelson 35.

472: Victoria and Beatrice returned to Windsor amidst the same heightened security, four days before Maclean's trial: *Daily News* 15 April 1882, 5.

473: London's *cause célèbre* of 1882: the Jumbo craze: For the Jumbo craze, see Chambers 116-164.

473: . . . last August, Jumbo had destroyed the zoo's elephant house: Chambers 109-110.

473: When led out the next day to walk the eight miles to Millwall Docks, Jumbo similarly refused: Chambers 125.

474: In mid-March, Jumbo fever peaked, as on one day 24,007 people packed the zoo: Chambers 146.

474: . . . Jumbo fever subsided quickly, the British sheepishly realizing that they could go on without Jumbo: Chambers 196.

474: When on 19 April two constables conveyed Maclean up from the subterranean passage and into the dock of the small courtroom at Reading, he appeared dirtier and shabbier than ever: Williams 115; *Illustrated London News* 22 April 1882.

474: . . . a number of fashionably dressed ladies stared back at him, some through opera glasses: *Pall Mall Gazette* 19 April 1882, 8.

474: . . . "Few who looked upon him . . . had any doubt that insanity had marked him for its own": Williams 115.

474: . . . they had otherwise provided for him well, paying for his meals at Reading Gaol: *Times* 13 April 1882, 9.

475: . . . one reporter comparing the spectators to a Nonconformist congregation: *Pall Mall Gazette* 19 April 1882, 8.

475: The Queen had that morning done the same, sending a primrose wreath to be placed on his grave at Hughenden: *Daily News* 20 April 1882, 5.

475: "We cannot help regretting," proclaimed *The Times*, "that the accused has been treated so much *au sérieux*": *Times* 19 April 1882, 11.

475: "like employing a five ton Nasmyth hammer to crack a walnut-shell": *Reynolds's Weekly* 23 April 1882, 4.

476: Guiteau had managed to turn the trial into a circus: Clark 125-39.

476: "As to Maclean there is no doubt of his insanity": Journal of Lewis Harcourt, rpt. White 52.

477: Much therefore had happened in the hour before Maclean stepped into the dock: *Times* 20 April 1882, 11; *Pall Mall Gazette* 19 April 1882, 8.

477: The jury was then sworn without challenge: *Pall Mall Gazette* 19 April 1882.

477: . . . a "matter of grave consideration for the jury": *Times* 20 April 1882, 11.

477: . . . "satisfaction would be felt by every subject of the Queen at the thought that it was not from the ranks of those who were sane that a hand had been raised against our gracious Sovereign": *Times* 20 April 1882, 11.

477: "At the time of committing this act," Williams stated, "he was an irresponsible agent": *Daily News* 20 April 1882, 3.

478: Maclean's family, who could have provided volumes of evidence as to their brother's oddities, had, in their desire to detach them-selves from their embarrassing relative, successfully requested that they not be called: TNA PRO HO 144/95/A14281.

479: . . . "an absolutely irresistible moral impulse, as strong as if it was physical": *Times* 20 April 1882, 11.

479: . . . "decidedly he would know at the time he fired the pistol that he was doing a wrong act": *Daily News* 20 April 1882, 3.

479: . . . "the real question of right or wrong does not present itself to a man in such a state": *Daily News* 20 April 1882, 3.

479: "I do not think he was capable of appreciating the nature and quality of the act he committed": *Daily News* 20 April 1882, 3.

479: "Crown authorities had come to the conclusion that the prisoner's mind was not in a healthy state": *Times* 20 April 1882, 11.

479: . . . "men of undoubted ability and large experience": *Daily News* 20 April 1882, 3.

480: A week later, Home Secretary Harcourt ordered a warrant for his transfer; a week after that, Maclean made the short trip from Reading to Crowthorne and entered Broadmoor Asylum: TNA PRO HO 144/95/A14281; BRO D/H14/02/2/1/1095.

480: . . . his life "saturated with insanity and its symptoms" *Times* 20 April 1882, 9.

480: . . . "the jury took the only course compatible with the medical testimony, which did but itself confirm the impression produced by the bare narrative of the facts": *Daily News* 20 April 1882, 4-5.

480: . . . in striking contrast to the painful ordeal Charles Guiteau had inflicted upon the American public: *Birmingham Daily Post* 20 April 1882, 4.

480: "Am greatly surprised & shocked at the verdict on McLean!" she declared, confiding in her journal "it is really too bad": RA VIC/MAIN/L/14/131; RA VIC/MAIN/QVJ/1882 19 April 1882.

481: "It is Oxford's case over again": RA VIC/MAIN/L/14/133, 134; rpt. White 61.

481: If an assailant such as Maclean "is *not* to be considered *responsible* for his actions," she wrote angrily, "then indeed *no one* is safe any longer!": RA VIC/MAIN/L/14/133.

481: "This always happens when a Liberal Government is in!": RA VIC/MAIN/L/14/134.

481: "She was angry at the result of the Maclean trial as she does not understand the verdict of 'Not Guilty'": Journal of Lewis Harcourt 20 April 1882, rpt. White 61.

481: William Gladstone, to whom the Queen fired an incredulous telegram the moment she heard the verdict, was baffled: Hamilton 1:254.

481: "I did not then understand Your Majesty to disapprove": RA VIC/MAIN/L/14/132.

481: Maclean's lifetime of confinement was more strongly guaranteed with the insanity verdict than it would have been with a guilty verdict, Harcourt argued: RA VIC/MAIN/L/14/139.

482: Granville noted the relief of finding Maclean to be a madman, and tried to flatter the Queen, praising her "calm and serene courage, when so highly tried": RA VIC/MAIN/L/14/138.

482: "Mr. Gladstone humbly feels with Your Majesty that when an individual, such as Maclean, has probably been sane in respect to the particular act for which he is tried": Guedalla 2:186-87.

483: . . . he expressed himself "deeply impressed with the gravity of the subject": Guedalla 2:187.

483: . . . he concurred absolutely with Victoria's position that the stigma of guilt would prevent "dangerous misapprehensions in morbid minds": Victoria *Letters* (second series) 3:278-79.

484: She *"very reluctantly"* gave her consent, "but said it was a great mistake": Victoria *Letters* (second series) 3:276.

484: "The Queen cannot but feel that it will have the effect of a triumph to Home Rule and of great weakness": Guedalla 2:188.

484: "Is it possible that M. Davitt, known as one of the worst of the treasonable agitators, is also to be released?": Guedalla 2:189.

485: . . . "certainly the best reception I ever got in Ireland": Spencer 1:189.

485: "We are in God's hands. Do not be filled with alarm and fear. . . . I dare not dwell on the horror for I feel I must be unmanned": Spencer 1:189.

485: Lord Frederick Cavendish had decided that evening to walk from his office at Dublin Castle to his residence in Phoenix Park: For details of the Phoenix Park assassination, see Molony 20-27.

485: . . . the two proceeded arm in arm: Spencer 1:190.

485: "Ah, you villain!" cried Cavendish: Molony 27.

485: That night, Queen Victoria, who earlier had made her own triumphal procession through London in order to open Epping Forest as a park, learned the horrible news via two telegrams: Victoria *Letters* (second series) 3:282-83.

485: "How could Mr. Gladstone and his violent Radical advisers proceed with such a policy, which inevitably led to all this? Surely his eyes must be open now": Victoria *Letters* (second series) 3:283.

485: It did not matter to Victoria that Gladstone theorized (incorrectly, as it turned out) that the attackers were Irish-Americans and not Irishmen . . . : Victoria *Letters* (second series) 3:287.

486: . . . "she *cannot withhold* from him that *she* considers *this* horrible event the *direct result* of what she has always considered and has stated to Mr. Gladstone and to Lord Spencer as a most fatal and hazardous step": Victoria *Letters* (second series) 3:285.

486: . . . one day after Gladstone, crushed with grief, broke down in tears while speaking in the House of Commons of Cavendish: Molony 59.

486: "She wishes now to express her *earnest* hope that he will make *no* concession to *those* whose Actions, Speeches & writings, *have produced* the present state of affairs in Ireland & who would be *encour-*

aged by weak and vacillating action to make *further demands*": Guedalla 2:194-95.

487: "Dearest Bertie": Victoria *Letters* (second series) 3:298-99.

487: In the meantime, Gladstone kept to his promise to change the insanity verdict: For the progress of the Trial of Lunatics Act, see White 63-67.

488: "He protected me so, was so powerful and strong—that I felt so safe!": Victoria and Victoria, *Beloved Mama* 137.

488: . . . she pointedly did not thank Gladstone for anything else that he had achieved in the busy parliamentary session of 1883: "The Queen, before she took herself off to Scotland yesterday, treated Mr. Gladstone to a characteristic letter . . . referring with satisfaction to the amendment of the Criminal Lunacy Law alone out of all the measures passed this year!" Hamilton 2:475.

488: "It will be," she wrote, "a great security": Victoria *Letters* (second series) 3:439.

488: The first person stigmatized by this verdict was a woman with a history of mental disturbance, Johanna Culverwell: For the Culverwell trial, see "Johanna Culverwell."

489: . . . it was his bedraggled and faulty muse, who came to him in a trance and ordered him to "Write! Write!" during the most "startling incident" of his life, in 1877: McGonagall *Autobiography* 3.

489: . . . his efforts were rejected—by Keeper of the Privy Purse Lord Biddulph this time: McGonagall *Autobiography* 9.

489: At the gate he was ridiculed and sent on his way, and threatened with arrest if he ever returned: McGonagall *Autobiography* 2.

490: he read while the audience was permitted to throw eggs, flour, dead fish, and vegetables at him: Hunt viii.

490: McGonagall, "Attempted Assasination."

Epilogue: Jubilee

494: One dynamitard was caught with brass cylinder grenades, planning to throw them from the Strangers' Gallery at the full government bench at the House of Commons: Short 180. For the other dynamite targets, see Short 50-208.

494: . . . the Clan-na-Gael . . . agreed to refrain from violence to allow Parnell and the nationalist MPs their chance: Le Caron 246-47.

494: A month later, at a conference in Pittsburgh, the extremists of the Clan-na-Gael resolved to recommence terror-bombing: Le Caron 247-48; Funchion 97; TNA PRO HO 144/1537.

495: . . . the "Jubilee Plot" was the attempt on Victoria's life that never was: Christy Campbell provides a full-length history of the Jubilee Plot in his tantalizingly but not quite accurately titled *Fenian Fire: The British Government Plot to Assassinate Queen Victoria.*

495: Also in their bags—or perhaps sewn into their coats—were over a hundred pounds of American-made Atlas A dynamite in slabs, and a number of detonators.: TNA PRO HO 144/209/A48131; "Report from the Select Committee" 30; Campbell 236-37.

495: . . . he was actually John J. Moroney, one of the more militant members of the Clan-na-Gael, and a close friend of the Clan's most powerful leader in America, Alexander Sullivan: Le Caron 253; Campbell 322, 373.

495: . . . Michael Harkins, a sandy-haired thirty-year-old, his broad shoulders muscular from years of labor on the Reading Railroad: *Times* 22 November 1887, 12; 4 February 1888, 5.

495: . . . he had lived a quiet life in the factory town of Lowell, Massachusetts, operating stocking-making machinery: *Times* 22 November 1887, 12.

495: He was unmarried, and at forty-seven his hair was already graying: *U.S. Naturalization Record Indexes*; "Thomas Callan, Michael Harkins."

495: He had fought at the Civil War battles of Chancellorsville, Gettysburg, and Lookout Mountain, and marched with General Sherman from Atlanta to the Atlantic: Historical Data Systems.

496: "No better or braver soldier than he served in that noble old regiment": TNA PRO HO 144/209/A48131.

496: In March, "General" Francis Millen, a twenty-year Fenian veteran, was commissioned by the Clan-na-Gael to sail to France: Campbell 218.

496: . . . in May two other conspirators . . . shipped to London: "Report from the Select Committee" 30.

497: . . . James Monro . . . commanded in 1877 a Special anti-terrorist Branch, formed in 1883 specifically to track down Fenian dynamiters: Allason 4.

497: The secret of the Jubilee Plot was an open one in the United States since at least the beginning of May: *New York Times* 4 May 1887, rpt. in Campbell 226.

497: . . . "a pyrotechnic display in honour of the Queen's Jubilee or in other words a series of dynamite and incendiary outrages": *Times* 1 June 1887, 8.

497: . . . he then sent the Chief Superintendent of the CID to confront him and inform him that they knew about the plot and his role in it: Campbell 270-71.

498: . . . for over twenty years, off and on, Millen had been an informer to the British government: Christy Campbell documents Millen's decades of double-dealing in his *Fenian Fire*.

498: . . . they searched the building the day before: Lant 74.

498: "I was never in a more delicate position in my life": Campbell 240.

498: . . . Victoria . . . had been reassured by her Home Secretary . . . that all was safe: Lant 74.

498: . . . "there was such an extraordinary outburst of enthusiasm as I had hardly ever seen in London before": Victoria, *Letters* (third series) 1:321.

499: Victoria's children, children-in-law, and grandchildren approached and kissed her hand: Victoria, *Letters* (third series) 1:324.

499: They all represented themselves as traveling salesmen—a dealer in tea, Thomas Callan told his landlady: "Thomas Callan, Michael Harkins"; TNA PRO CRIM 1/27/3.

499: Thomas Callan was twice sent to Windsor Castle with a stopwatch: "Report of the Select Committee," 31; TNA PRO HO 144/209/A48131.

499: Callan, too, was observed to lurk about the place: "Thomas Callan, Michael Harkins."

499: Harkins was later found with a newspaper clipping detailing an upcoming public appearance of the Chief Secretary for Ireland, Arthur Balfour: TNA PRO CRIM 1/27/3.

499: Monro then quickly applied the same pressure upon Moroney that he had on Millen, setting a police guard upon him and sending a detective to his lodgings to question him "closely": TNA PRO HO 144/1537.

500: At the beginning of September, Joseph Cohen cashed two of the notes, writing his signature and address on them: TNA PRO CRIM 1/27/3.

500: . . . Michael Harkins, with the help of a muscular cabman, moved the dynamite out of Cohen's lodgings: *Times* 2 February 1888, 10.

500: . . . two police descended on his lodgings demanding he give an account of himself: TNA PRO CRIM 1/27/3; "Thomas Callan, Michael Harkins."

501: They soon released him for lack of evidence, but Monro set upon him an around-the-clock watch by six officers who moved into his lodgings: "Thomas Callan, Michael Harkins."

501: Monro appeared personally at the inquest and used the occasion to expose the dynamite plot to the public: *Times* 27 October 1887, 12.

501: The detonators he threw into a local pond: TNA PRO HO 144/209/A48131.

501: . . . he dragged the slabs into the back garden and into the lodging house's water closet: TNA PRO HO 144/209/A48131.

501: On the evening of the seventeenth, a stranger came to his lodgings: TNA PRO CRIM 1/27/3.

502: . . . for some time he remained in Monro's mind as a potentially dangerous loose end of the Jubilee Plot: HO 144/1537/2.

502: . . . a letter had arrived from Lowell with a draft for more money— and a prepaid passage to Boston on the Cunard Line: TNA PRO CRIM 1/27/3.

502: From the back garden of Callan's lodgings, the police were able to collect over twenty-five pounds of sodden dynamite, which police chemists were able to determine to be of American make: TNA PRO CRIM 1/27/3; "Thomas Callan, Michael Harkins."

502: He was released in 1892: TNA PRO HO 144/209/A48131.

502: . . . "the most harmless of all the dynamiters with whom I have been brought into contact": TNA PRO HO 144/209/A48131.

502: "Poor Tommy Callan": "Poor Tommy Callan."

503: . . . he was thrown from a cart, smashed his leg, and died: "Poor Tommy Callan."

503: His assassination inspired Leon Czolgosz to kill American President William McKinley a year later: Laucella 85.

503: Bertie and Princess Alexandra chose to forgo their usual trip to Biarritz: St. Aubyn, *Edward VII* 302.

503: . . . a boy jumped upon the carriage footboard, thrust a pistol through the window, and from six feet away fired two shots at the Prince: *Times* 5 April 1900, 6.

503: Bertie later enjoyed joking in letters to his friends about the "pauvre fou": St. Aubyn, *Edward VII* 302.

503: he was already a fanatical member of an anarchist club: Magnus 265; Brust 49.

504: The Prince of Wales asked Belgian authorities not to treat Sipido too severely: Brust 50.

504: He was later extradited to Belgium, where he was confined in a penitentiary until he reached the age of twenty-one: *Times* 22 November 1900, 5; 30 December 1905, 5.

504: . . . "there were crowds out, we could not understand why, and thought something must be going [on], but it turned out it was only to see me": Weintraub, *Queen Victoria* 514.

505: The second, under the direction of the Queen's imperialist Minister for the Colonies, Joseph Chamberlain, celebrated the greatness of the British Empire: Lant 219.

505: . . . the Queen, in 1897 no longer able to walk into St. Paul's for the Thanksgiving Service, refused to be carried inside, and instead viewed from her carriage a short *Te Deum* on the cathedral steps: Lant 223-24, 244-45; Matthew and Reynolds.

505: "No one ever, I believe, has met with such an ovation as was given to me, passing through those six miles of streets": Hibbert, *Queen Victoria* 457.

506: "Everywhere," Victoria wrote, "the same enormous crowds and incessant demonstrations of enthusiasm": Hibbert, ed. 343.

506: "I saw your Majesty three times in the streets and in the Park": Rennell 41.

506: Victoria lived for eight months after that: For Victoria's last days, see Tony Rennell's *Last Days of Glory: The Death of Queen Victoria*.

506: "Another year begun, and I am feeling so weak and unwell that I enter upon it sadly": Rennell 57.

507: She died in the arms of her grandson Kaiser William, "a look of radiance on her face": Rennell 137-38.

507: . . . past a million of her subjects in the metropolis: Rennell 247.

508: "Reported sane since his reception," his Bethlem case notes state, that opinion restated emphatically with the same entry repeated through the years: "no change": Bethlehem Royal Hospital. The statement that Oxford was perfectly sane was repeated, and reasserted, in his Broadmoor records held in the Berkshire Record Office, BRO D/H14/D2/1/1/1.

509: He deserved a horse-whipping for his actions: Warren 571.

509: Bethlem became his university: Oxford's achievements are set out in both his Bethlem and his Broadmoor case notes.

509: He was from the start "the most orderly, most useful, and most trusted of all the inmates" there: *Times* 13 January 1865, 10.

509: . . . his painting skills were in constant demand and allowed him in time to accumulate £50 or £60: *Times* 13 January 1865, 10.

509: . . . in 1876 Home Secretary Gathorne Gathorne-Hardy reviewed Oxford's record and made him a deal: BRO D/H14/D2/2/1/96.

509: 24 years earlier, George Henry Haydon had come to Bethlem as steward, and Oxford quickly discovered in him a friend: F. B. Smith 467.

510: . . . the *Suffolk*, which the next March landed at Melbourne: *Assisted and Unassisted Passenger Lists*.

510: . . . "in the future no man shall say I am unworthy of the name of an Englishman": Freeman.

510: Oxford took up as a painter and grainer: *Argus* 28 January 1870, 1.

510: He was amused to discover that people in Melbourne thought him "cosmopolitan" because of his London origins: Freeman.

510: He joined and became vice president of the West Melbourne Mutual Improvement Society: *Argus* 28 February 1887, 4.

510: He . . . published his observations in Melbourne's leading newspaper: *Argus* 28 March 1874, 4; 4 July 1874, 4; 22 May 1875, 9.

510: He joined the congregation of Melbourne's oldest Anglican church and served for several years as its churchwarden: *Argus* 3 January 1889, 10; 22 February 1896, 8.

510: In 1881 he married a well-off widow and became a stepfather: *Argus* 21 March 1881, 1.

510: "There are many old friends . . . in England," he wrote to Haydon, "who would be pleased to hear of me again": Freeman.

510: "Even my wife," Oxford told Haydon, "the sharer of my joys, and sorrows, is no wiser than the rest of the world": Freeman.

510: He took his secret to a grave, dying on 23 April 1900: F. B. Smith 472.

511: The place was a "purgatorial grinding mill rather than a torture chamber": Hughes 400.

511: . . . he emerged triumphantly, earning a six-month remission of his stay there by raising the alarm when a fire broke out: TNA PRO HO 45/3079.

511: Two years later . . . he fell in love with a free sixteen-year-old girl, Martha Clarke, and married her: Archives Office of Tasmania CON 51/1/3.

511: . . . he found it with a Launceston builder who was impressed with his industry and sobriety: TNA PRO HO 45/3079.

511: . . . a petition in his support was signed by the mayors of Hobart and Launceston, Launceston's Catholic bishop, and other notables: TNA PRO HO 45/3079.

512: . . . an episode in 1869 in Melbourne's insolvency court: *Argus* 21 January 1869, 5; 29 May 1869, 6.

512: He died in 1885, aged sixty-three: *Australia Death Index.*

512: . . . his hard-labor sentence was modified to work at tailoring: *Examiner* 15 October 1842.

512: During his last month of imprisonment, his father died: *London, England, Deaths and Burials.*

512: He attempted to take up his father's profession as a jeweler: London Metropolitan Archives, St. James, Clerkenwell, *Register of Banns of marriage.*

512: By 1851 John William Bean had given up his father's profession: *1851 England Census.*

512: He did, however, manage to marry again, in 1863: *England & Wales, Free BMD Marriage Index.*

513: . . . he is listed there as a "newsagent out of work": *1881 England Census.*

513: OPIUM POISONING AT CAMBERWELL: *Lloyd's Weekly* 30 July 1882.

514: He was taken from Newgate to Millbank and then quickly on to Pentonville: TNA PRO PCOM 2/211; TNA PRO HO 24/16.

514: . . . critics, backed by statistics, claimed it was more likely to lead to madness than moral improvement: Mayhew and Binny 102-04n.

514: . . . Hamilton moved to the next rehabilitative step, shipping to the public works at the small penal colony at Gibraltar: TNA PRO HO 8/102; TNA PRO HO PCOM 2/137.

514: . . . in August 1854, he was granted his ticket of leave: "Convict Database."

515: He might have come to the attention of the authorities one more time, nearly twenty years later: *West Australian Chronicle* 8 September 1885, 3.

515: ". . . we understand that he has shown no symptoms of insanity upon the passage": *Cornwall Chronicle* 16 November 1850, 808.

515: His hard work earned him an eighty-day remission of his sentence: Bolam 14.

515: Pate acquitted himself well enough to earn Abbott's recommendation for a Conditional Pardon: TNA HO 45/3079.

515: He obtained his ticket of leave in September 1853: Archives Office of Tasmania CON 33/1/98.

515: That pardon was granted at the end of 1855: Bolam 14.

515: Announcements of the wedding said nothing of his being a convict and much about being an ex-officer of the 10th Royal Hussars: *Courier*, 26 August 1852, 2.

515: He and his wife Mary Elizabeth resided among the elite of Hobart, in an eleven-room mansion: *Mercury* 11 April 1863, 4.

516: . . . the old man had died in 1856, leaving the bulk of his £70,000 fortune to his only son: *Times* 12 August 1856, 1; *Morning Chronicle* 12 November 1856, 3.

516: In April 1865, the Pates, having sold their mansion, embarked on the *Robert Morrison* for London: *Launceston Examiner* 29 April 1865, 4.

516: Pate traveled to Wisbech to take care of his father's estate and his servants, to whom he was said to be "remarkably kind": Gardiner 330.

516: . . . he died in 1895, leaving his wife over £22,000: *England & Wales, National Probate Calendar.*

516: . . . an object reputed to be the cane with which Robert Pate struck the Queen went up for auction in London: *Lloyd's Weekly* 1 January 1899, 17; *Times* (New York) 15 January 1899.

517: He was discharged eighteen months after he was committed to Hanwell as fully cured: Geary 142.

517: His father having died, he claimed that his income was the principal support of his entire family: TNA HO 144/3/10963.

517: . . . he would be willing to travel to Australia if the government paid his expenses and found him employment: TNA HO 144/3/10963.

517: Henry Parkes, Premier of New South Wales, had taken a personal interest in his case and had procured him a clerkship with a prominent Sydney solicitor: TNA HO 144/3/10963.

517: O'Connor had been arrested for being drunk: TNA HO 144/3/10963.

517: "On his first visit he was a thoughtless youth": TNA HO 144/3/10963.

517: At other times he was compelled to escape: Callan Park Hospital, Medical case book.

518: . . . the doctors all believed his illness was caused by what the Inspector General of the Sydney Police first termed in 1881 "habits of self-indulgence": TNA PRO HO 144/3/10963.

518: . . . Morton was "suffering from considerable mental irritation which is fostered by his debased habits": TNA PRO HO 144/3/10963.

518: . . . the disorder was melancholia, the cause "masturbation": Callan Park, Medical case book.

518: . . . the cause of his madness was listed as "Onanism": Rydalmere Hospital Medical File.

518: O'Connor's asylum casebooks record instances of voices in his head, delusions of persecution, and wild hallucinations: Callan Park, Medical Case Book; Rydalmere Hospital Medical file.

518: In later years he took to writing persons of importance in New South Wales, pleading for a discharge: Rydalmere Hospital Legal Files.

519: . . . "you, I am sure are aware in questions of presumed insanity, duration of time of incarceration should not be considered": TNA PRO HO 144/95/A14281.

519: *I am innocent* of any guilty *intentions toward* the Queen": BRO D/H14/D2/2/1/1905—in an undated petition, but dateable by internal evidence to c. April 1886.

519: "I should require at least one hundred per annum and I should not accept a farthing less whether from relations or strangers": BRO D/H14/D2/2/1/1905.

519: "No language could express my sorrow for the past": BRO D/H14/D2/2/1/1905, petition dated 18 June 1885.

519: "If Her Most Gracious Majesty will allow me to go and reside in the isle of my ancestors Mull on the west coast of Scotland": BRO D/H14/D2/2/1/1905, petition dated 4 December 1885.

519: In 1894 Maclean made another attempt to reengage with the world: BRO D/H14/D2/2/1/1905, letter dated 5 August 1894.

520: Roderick Maclean died on 9 May 1921, apoplexy stated as the cause: BRO D/H14/D2/2/1/1905.

520: The news was reported as a sort of barely remembered bad dream: *Times* 10 June 1921, 7.

520: . . . the cause of death listed as a painful abdominal ailment, tubercular peritonitis: Rydalmere Hospital Medical File.

WORKS CITED

ARCHIVAL SOURCES

Archives Office of Tasmania. CON 33/1/98 (Conduct Record for convicts).

Archives Office of Tasmania. CON 51/1/3 (Convict Applications for Permissions to Marry 1829-1857).

Bethlem Royal Hospital. *Criminal Lunatics 1816-1850*.

BRO D/H14/A1/2/4/1. Berkshire Record Office, letters from the board and doctors of Broadmoor Hospital requesting release of Edward Oxford.

BRO D/H14/D2/1/1/1. Berkshire Record Office, case notes on Edward Oxford from Broadmoor Hospital.

BRO D/H14/D2/2/1/96. Berkshire Record Office, correspondence regarding release of Edward Oxford from Broadmoor Hospital.

BRO D/H14/D2/2/1/1095: Berkshire Record Office, Roderick Maclean file.

Callan Park Hospital, Sydney. Medical case book.

"Convict Database." Fremantle Prison [online.]

"Convict Transportation Registers Database." *State Library of Queensland Online*.

"Convicts and Convict Ships sent to Tasmania." *Convicts to Australia* [online.]

Freeman, John [Edward Oxford]. Papers, 1862-1889 [manuscript]. National Library of Australia MS 243.

RA VIC/MAIN/: Royal Archives, Correspondence and Journals of Queen Victoria.

RC/8/A: Archives for the Royal Commission for the Exhibition of 1851: Royal Commission minutes.

Rydalmere Hospital. Medical File 1890-1950.

Rydalmere Hospital. Legal Files 1855-1950.

State Library of Tasmania Records, CON 51/1/3: Convict Applications for Permissions to Marry 1829-1857.

TNA (The National Archives) PRO CRIM 1/27/3 (Central Criminal Court Depositions in the case of Thomas Callan and Michael Harkins).

TNA (The National Archives) PRO HO 8/102 (Attested list of the Convict Hulks at Gibraltar).

TNA (The National Archives) PRO HO 24/16 (Pentonville prison register).

TNA (The National Archives) PRO HO 45/3079 (Home Office papers concerning John Francis and Robert Pate).

TNA (The National Archives) PRO HO 144/3/10963 (Home Office papers concerning Arthur O'Connor).

TNA (The National Archives) PRO MEPO 3/19A (Metropolitan Police files concerning John William Bean).

TNA (The National Archives) PRO HO 144/209/A48131 (Documents concerning the conditional pardon of Thomas Callan).

TNA (The National Archives) PRO HO 144/1537 (Report by James Monro on the Jubilee Plot).

TNA (The National Archives) PRO MEPO 3/17 (Metropolitan Police files concerning Edward Oxford).

TNA (The National Archives) PRO MEPO 3/18 (Metropolitan Police files concerning John Francis).

TNA (The National Archives) PRO HO 144/95/14281 (Home Office papers concerning Roderick Maclean).

TNA (The National Archives) PRO MEPO 3/19B (Metropolitan Police files concerning William Hamilton).

TNA (The National Archives) PRO PCOM 2/211 (Newgate prison register).

TNA (The National Archives) PRO PCOM 2/137: (Ships' Prisoners' Register: Europa at Gibraltar, 1840-1855).

TNA (The National Archives) PRO TS 11/80 (Treasury Solicitor's transcript of the trial of John Francis).

NEWSPAPERS

Aberdeen Journal.

Argus (Melbourne, Victoria, Australia).

Belfast News-Letter.

Birmingham Daily Post.

Bristol Mercury.

British Medical Journal.

Caledonian Mercury (Edinburgh).

Cornwall Chronicle (Launceston, Tasmania, Australia).

Courier (Hobart, Tasmania, Australia).

Daily News (London).

Era.

Examiner.

Evening Telegraph.

Freeman's Journal and Daily Commercial Advertiser (Dublin).

Glasgow Daily Herald.

Graphic.

Hampshire Telegraph (Portsmouth).

Illustrated London News.

Ipswich Journal.

Lancet.

Launceston Examiner (Launceston, Tasmania, Australia).

Leeds Mercury.

Liverpool Mercury.

Lloyd's Weekly.

Lowell Sun (Lowell MA).

Manchester Examiner.

Mercury (Hobart, Tasmania, Australia).

Moreton Bay Courier (Brisbane, Queensland, Australia).

Morning Chronicle.

Newcastle Courant.

Northern Star.

Pall Mall Gazette.

Preston Chronicle.

Punch.

Reynolds's Weekly.

Spectator.

Surrey Advertiser and County Times (Guildford).

The Times (London).

The Times (New York).

Trewman's Exeter Flying Post.

Weekly Chronicle.

Weekly Dispatch.

West Australian Chronicle (Perth, Western Australia, Australia).

SECONDARY SOURCES

1841 England Census [database on-line]. Provo, UT, USA: Ancestry.com Operations Inc., 2006.

1851 England Census [database on-line]. Provo, UT, USA: Ancestry.com Operations Inc., 2006.

1881 England Census [database on-line]. Provo, UT, USA: Ancestry.com Operations Inc., 2004.

Ackerman, Kenneth D. *Dark Horse: The Surprise Election and Political Murder of President James A. Garfield.* New York: Carroll & Graf, 2003.

Adams, W. H. Davenport. *A Book about London.* London: Henry & Co., 1890.

Albert, Prince Consort. *Letters of the Prince Consort 1831-1861.* Ed. Kurt Jagow. New York: Dutton, 1938.

——. *Addresses Delivered on Different Public Occasions by His Royal Highness the Prince Albert.* London: Society of Arts, 1857.

Allason, Rupert. *The Branch: A History of the Metropolitan Police Special Branch 1883-1893.* London: Secker & Warburg, 1983.

Altick, Richard. *The Shows of London.* Cambridge, MA: Belknap, 1978.

——. *Victorian Studies in Scarlet.* New York: Norton, 1970.

Andrews, Jonathan, Asa Briggs, Roy Porter, Penny Tucker, and Keir Waddington. *The History of Bethlem.* London and New York: Routledge, 1997.

Annual Register . . . of the Year 1842. London: various publishers, 1842.

Archibold, John Frederick. *The New Statutes Relating to Lunacy.* London: Shaw and Sons, 1854.

Ascoli, David. *The Queen's Peace: the Origins and Development of the Metropolitan Police 1879-1979*. London: Hamish Hamilton, 1979.

Ashley, Evelyn. *The Life and Correspondence of Henry John Temple, Viscount Palmerston*. London: Bentley & Son, 1879. 2 vols.

Assisted and Unassisted Passenger Lists 1839-1923 [database on line]. Provo, UT, USA: Ancestry.com Operations Inc., 2009.

Atlay, J. B. *Famous Trials of the Century*. London: Grant Richards, 1899.

"Attack on Her Majesty." *Hansard 1803-2005* [Online], 31 May 1842.

"Attempt on the Life of Her Majesty." *Hansard 1803-2005* [Online], 6 March 1882.

"Attempt to Assassinate the Queen." *Hansard 1803-2005* [Online], 30 May 1842.

Auerbach, Jeffery A. *The Great Exhibition of 1851: A Nation on Display*. New Haven: Yale University Press, 1999.

Australia Death Index, 1787-1985 [database on-line]. Provo, UT, USA: Ancestry.com Operations, Inc., 2010.

Barker, G. F. R. "Scarlett, James, first Baron Abinger (1769–1844)," rev. Elisabeth A. Cawthon, *Oxford Dictionary of National Biography*. Online ed. Ed. Lawrence Goldman. Oxford: Oxford University Press.

Bayes, James. "The Bullet from his Gun (Bought in Portsmouth) Sped toward the Queen he Revered." *Evening News* (Portsmouth), 29 November 1963, p. 12.

Bellows, John. *Remarks on Certain Anonymous Articles Designed to Render Queen Victoria Unpopular, with Exposure of Their Authorship*. Gloucester, UK: John Bellows, 1864.

Bennett, Daphne. *King without a Crown*. Philadelphia and New York: J. B. Lippincott, 1977.

Biographical and Descriptive Sketches of the Distinguished Characters Which Compose the Unrivalled Exhibition and Historical Gallery of Madame Tussaud and Sons. London: G. Cole, 1866.

The Black Pirate, or the Phantom Ship. London: William Emans, 1839.

Bloomfield, Georgiana [Baroness]. *Reminiscences of Court and Diplomatic Life*. London: Kegan, Paul, Trench, & Co., 1883.

Boase, G. C. "Calcraft, William (1800–1879)." Rev. J. Gilliland. *Oxford Dictionary of National Biography*. Online ed. Ed. Lawrence Goldman. Oxford: Oxford University Press.

——. "Cleasby, Sir Anthony (1804–1879)." Rev. Hugh Mooney. *Oxford Dictionary of National Biography*. Online ed. Ed. Lawrence Goldman. Oxford: Oxford University Press.

———. "Thomas Hunt." *Dictionary of National Biography.* Ed. Sidney Lee. Vol. 28. London: Smith, Elder, 1891, p. 280.

Bolam, Valentine. "Robert Pate: neither drunk, nor mad." *Annual Report of the Wisbech Society* 60 (1999), pp. 9-16.

Bolitho, Hector. *Albert the Good.* New York: D. Appleton & Co., 1932.

Bowers, Robert Woodger. *Sketches of Southwark Old and New.* London: William Wesley and Son, 1902.

Boykin, Edward, ed. *Victoria, Albert, and Mrs. Stevenson.* New York: Rinehart & Co., 1957.

Bratton, Jacky. "Vestris, Lucia Elizabeth (1797-1856)." *Oxford Dictionary of National Biography.* Online ed. Ed. Lawrence Goldman. Oxford: Oxford University Press.

Bresler, Fenton. *Napoleon III: A Life.* New York: Carroll & Graf, 1999.

Browne, Douglas G. *The Rise of Scotland Yard.* London: George G. Harrap, 1956.

Browning, Elizabeth Barrett, and Robert Browning. *The Browning Correspondence.* Ed. Philip Kelly and Ronald Hudson. Winfield, KS: Wedgestone Press, 1988.

Brust, Harold. *I Guarded Kings: The Memoirs of a Political Police Officer.* New York: Hillman-Curl, 1936.

Bunsen, Frances Baroness. *A Memoir of Baron Bunsen.* London: Longmans, Green & Co, 1868. 2 vols.

Burke, Peter. *Celebrated Trials Connected with the Aristocracy in the Relations of Private Life.* London: William Benning, 1849.

Burleigh, Michael. *Blood and Rage: A Cultural History of Terrorism.* New York: HarperCollins, 2009.

Campbell, Christy. *Fenian Fire: The British Government Plot to Assassinate Queen Victoria.* London: HarperCollins, 2002.

Carlyle, Thomas, and Jane Welsh Carlyle. *The Carlyle Letters Online [CLO].* 2007.

Carrington, F. A., and J. Payne. *Reports of Cases Argued and Ruled at Nisi Prius, in the Courts of King's Bench, Common Pleas, & Exchequer.* Volume 9. London: S. Sweet, 1841.

Chambers, Paul. *Jumbo: The Greatest Elephant in the World*: Hanover, NH: Steerforth, 2008.

"The Character of Queen Victoria." *Quarterly Review* 193:386 (April 1901), pp. 301-337.

Charlot, Monica. *Victoria: The Young Queen.* Oxford: Blackwell, 1991.

Chase, Malcolm. *Chartism: A New History*. Manchester: Manchester University Press, 2007.

Children's Employment Commission. *First Report of the Commissioners. Mines*. London: Her Majesty's Stationery Office, 1842.

"Chronicle." *Annual Register* 84 (1843): pp. 1-199.

Clark, James C. *The Murder of James A. Garfield*. Jefferson, NC: McFarland, 1993.

Clarke, J. F. *Autobiographical Recollections of the Medical Profession*. London: J & A Churchill, 1874.

Clutterbuck, Lewis Augustus, and William Toke Dooner. *The Bond of Sacrifice*. Volume 1. London: Anglo-African Publishing Contractors, 1914.

Cobb, Belton. *The First Detectives*. London: Faber and Faber, 1957.

Cole, G. D. H., and Raymond Postgate. *The Common People: 1746-1946*. London: Methuen, 1961 [1938].

Cole, Henry. *Fifty Years of Public Work*. London: Bell, 1884. 2 vols.

Collins, Philip. *Dickens and Crime*. New York: St. Martin's, 1994. Third edition.

"Constant Observer." *Sketches in Bedlam*. London: Sherwood, Jones & Co., 1823.

Costigan, George P. *Cases and Other Authorities on Legal Ethics*. St. Paul: West, 1917.

Cullen, Tom. *The Empress Brown*. Boston: Houghton Mifflin, 1969.

D'Arcy, William. *The Fenian Movement in the United States: 1858-1866*. Washington, D.C.: Catholic University of America Press, 1947.

Davis, John R. *The Great Exhibition*. Thrupp, Stroud, Gloucestershire: Sutton, 1999.

Derby, Edward Henry Stanley, Earl of. *Disraeli, Derby, and the Conservative Party*. New York: Barnes & Noble, 1978.

Dickens, Charles. *Bleak House* [1853]. Harmondsworth: Penguin, 1972.

——. *The Letters of Charles Dickens*. Ed. Madeline House and Graham Storey. Volume 2. Oxford: Clarendon, 1969.

——. *The Old Curiosity Shop*. Harmondsworth: Penguin, 1972 [1841].

——. *The Amusements of the People and Other papers: Reports, Essays and Reviews 1834-1841*. The Dent Uniform Edition of Dickens' Journalism, vol. 2. London: J. M. Dent, 1996.

Dickens, Charles, and W. H. Wills. "Spitalfields." *Household Words* 3.54 (5 April 1851) 25-30.

Disraeli, Benjamin. *Letters: 1838-1841*. Toronto: University of Toronto Press, 1987.

Dodds, John W. *The Age of Paradox*. New York: Rinehart & Co, 1952.

Donnelly, James S. *The Great Irish Potato Famine*. Thrupp, Stroud, Gloucestershire: Sutton, 2001.

Dousbery, Thomas. Letter to the Editor. *The Crisis*. Ed. Robert Owen and Robert Dale Owen. 2:109.

Dover, Folkestone, and Deal Guide. Dover, Dover Chronicle, 1875

Duff, David. *Victoria and Albert*. New York: Taplinger, 1972.

Dunkerley, James. "O'Connor, Francisco Burdett (1791–1871)." *Oxford Dictionary of National Biography*. Online ed. Ed. Lawrence Goldman. Oxford: Oxford University Press.

"Edward Oxford." *The Proceedings of the Old Bailey* [Online].

Edwards, Owen Dudley. "Rossa, Jeremiah O'Donovan (*bap.* 1831, *d.* 1915)." *Oxford Dictionary of National Biography*. Online ed. Ed. Lawrence Goldman. Oxford: Oxford University Press.

Eigen, Joel Peter. "Hadfield, James (1771/2-1841)." *Oxford Dictionary of National Biography*. Online ed. Ed. Lawrence Goldman. Oxford: Oxford University Press.

Ellman, Robert. *Fired in Anger: The Personal Handguns of American Heroes and Villains*. New York: Doubleday, 1968.

Emsley, Clive. "Mayne, Sir Richard (1796-1868)." *Oxford Dictionary of National Biography*. Online ed. Ed. Lawrence Goldman. Oxford: Oxford University Press.

England & Wales, FreeBMD Marriage Index: 1837-1915 [database on-line]. Provo, UT, USA: Ancestry.com Operations Inc., 2006.

England & Wales, National Probate Calendar (Index of Wills and Administrations), 1861-1941 [database on-line]. Provo, UT, USA: Ancestry.com Operations Inc., 2010.

Evans, R. J. *The Victorian Age 1815-1914*. 2nd ed. New York: St. Martin's, 1968.

Féret, Charles James. *Fulham Old and New*. London: Leadenhall Press, 1900. 3 vols.

Feuchtwanger, Edgar. *Albert and Victoria: the Rise and Fall of the House of Saxe-Coburg-Gotha*. London: Hambledon Continuum, 2006.

ffrench, Yvonne. *The Great Exhibition: 1851*. London: Harvill, 1950.

Fido, Martin, and Keith Skinner. *The Official Encyclopedia of Scotland Yard*. London: Virgin, 1999.

"Firing at the Queen." *Hansard 1803-2005* [Online], 21 May 1849.

"Francis Benjamin Courvoisier." *The Proceedings of the Old Bailey* [Online].

Frankland, Noble. "Arthur, Prince, first duke of Connaught and Strath-earn." *Oxford Dictionary of National Biography*. Online ed. Ed. Lawrence Goldman. Oxford: Oxford University Press.

Freemon, Frank R. "The Origin of the Medical Expert Witness: The Insanity of Edward Oxford." *The Journal of Legal Medicine* 22 (2001): 349-373.

Fulford, Roger. *Royal Dukes: The Father and Uncles of Queen Victoria*. London: Gerald Duckworth, 1937.

Funchion, Michael F. *Chicago's Irish Nationalists 1881-1890*. New York: Arno Press, 1976.

Gantt, Jonathan. *Irish Terrorism in the Atlantic Community, 1865-1922*. London: Palgrave MacMillan, 2010.

Gardiner, Frederic John. *History of Wisbech and Neighborhood, during the Last Fifty Years 1848-1898*. Wisbech: Gardiner & Co., 1898.

Garrison, Wendell Phillips, and Francis Jackson Garrison. *William Lloyd Garrison 1805-1879*. New York: Century, 1885. 4 vols.

Gash, Norman. *Sir Robert Peel*. London: Longman, 1986 [1972].

Gathorne-Hardy, Alfred E. *Gathorne Hardy: First Earl of Cranbrook: A Memoir*. London: Longmans, Green and Co., 1910. 2 vols.

Gatrell, V. A. C. *The Hanging Tree*. Oxford: Oxford University Press, 1994.

Geary, Laurence M. "O'Connorite Bedlam: Feargus and His Grand-Nephew, Arthur." *Medical History* 34 (1990): 125-143.

Geraghty, Tony. *The Bullet-Catchers: Bodyguards and the World of Close Protection*. London: Grafton, 1988.

Gilbert, Michael. *The Claimant*. London: Constable, 1957.

Gill, Gillian. *We Two*. New York: Ballantine, 2009.

Gladstone, Herbert John. *After 30 Years*. London: Macmillan, 1928.

Gladstone, William Ewart. *The Gladstone Diaries 1881-1883*. Oxford: Clarendon, 1990.

Gladstone, William Ewart, and Granville Leveson Gower, 2nd Earl Gran-ville. *The Gladstone-Granville Correspondence*. Ed. Agatha Ramm. Cambridge, UK: Cambridge University Press, 1998.

Green, E. R. R. "The Fenians Abroad." *Secret Societies in Ireland*. Ed. T. Desmond Williams. Dublin: Gill and Macmillan, 1973.

Gregory, F. E. C. "Rowan, Sir Charles (1782?–1852)." *Oxford Dictionary of National Biography*. Online ed. Ed. Lawrence Goldman.

Greville, Charles. *The Greville Memoirs (Second Part): A Journal of the Reign of Queen Victoria from 1837 to 1852*. London: Longmans, Green & Co., 1885. 2 vols.

Guedalla, Philip. *The Queen and Mr. Gladstone*. London: Hodder and Stoughton, 1933. 2 vols.

Hamilton, Walter Edward. *The Diary of Sir Edward Walter Hamilton: 1880-1885*. Oxford: Clarendon, 1972. 2 vols.

Harsin, Jill. *Barricades*. New York: Palgrave, 2002.

Haugen, Claire Oliver. *Covent Garden and the Lyceum Theatre under the Charles J. Mathewses*. Unpublished dissertation, 1968.

Heald, Carolyn. *The Irish Palatines in Ontario*. Milton, Ontario: Global Heritage Press, 2009.

Heron, Mark. "The Elm in London." *Gentleman's Magazine* 260 (1886): 437-50.

Hervey, Nick. "Gull, Sir William Withey, first baronet (1816-1890)." *Oxford Dictionary of National Biography*. Online ed. Ed. Lawrence Goldman. Oxford: Oxford University Press.

Hibbert, Christopher. *The Royal Victorians*. Philadelphia: J. B. Lippincott, 1976.

——. *Queen Victoria: A Personal History*. New York: Basic Books, 2000.

——, ed. *Queen Victoria in her Letters and Journals*. New York: Viking, 1985.

Hilton, Boyd. *A Mad, Bad, and Dangerous People?* Oxford: Clarendon, 2006.

Hingley, Ronald. *Nihilists*. New York: Delacorte, 1967.

Historical Data Systems, comp. *American Civil War Regiments* [database on-line]. Provo, UT, USA: Ancestry.com Operations Inc., 1999.

Hobhouse, Christopher. *1851 and the Crystal Palace*. London: John Murray, 1950. Revised edition.

Hobhouse, John Cam. *Recollections of a Long Life*. London: John Murray, 1909-11. 6 vols.

Holland, Barbara. *Gentlemen's Blood*. New York: Bloomsbury USA, 2004.

Hudson, Katherine. *A Royal Conflict*. London: Hodder & Stoughton, 1994.

Hughes, Robert. *The Fatal Shore*. New York: Vintage, 1986.

Hunt, Chris. "Introduction." In *Collected Poems*, by William McGonagall. Edinburgh: Birlinn, 2006.

Hurd, Douglas. *Robert Peel: A Biography*. London: Wiedenfeld & Nicholson, 2007.

"Insanity and Crime." *Hansard 1803-2005* [Online], 13 March 1883.

James, Robert Rhodes. *Prince Albert: A Biography*. New York: Alfred A. Knopf, 1984.

Jenkins, Roy. "Dilke, Sir Charles Wentworth, second baronet (1843-1911)." In *Oxford Dictionary of National Biography*. Online ed. Ed. Lawrence Goldman. Oxford: Oxford University Press.

——. *Gladstone*. New York: Random House, 1997.

Jenkins, T. A. *Sir Robert Peel*. Houndmillis, Basingstoke, Hampshire: MacMillan, 1999.

Jerrold, Clare. *The Early Court of Queen Victoria*. New York: G. P. Putnam's Sons, 1912.

——. *The Married Life of Queen Victoria*. New York: G. P. Putnam's Sons, 1913.

"Johanna Culverwell." *Proceedings of the Old Bailey* [Online].

"John Francis." *Proceedings of the Old Bailey* [Online].

"John Sydney Taylor, Esq." (Obituary). *Gentleman's Magazine*, 1822, 220-21.

"John William Bean." *Proceedings of the Old Bailey* [Online].

Jones, Gareth H., and Vivienne Jones. "Campbell, John, first Baron Campbell of St. Andrews (1779–1861)." *Oxford Dictionary of National Biography*. Online ed. Ed. Lawrence Goldman. Oxford: Oxford University Press.

——, "Denman, Thomas, first Baron Denman (1779-1854)." *Oxford Dictionary of National Biography*. Online ed. Ed. Lawrence Goldman. Oxford: Oxford University Press.

Kass, Amalie M. "Hodgkin, Thomas (1798–1866)." *Oxford Dictionary of National Biography*. Online ed. Ed. Lawrence Goldman. Oxford: Oxford University Press.

Kean, Hilda. "The Silk Weavers of Spitalfields." *Family History Monthly* 67.4 (Apr. 2001): 44-47.

King, Horatio Collins, ed. *Turning on the Light*. Philadelphia: J.P. Lippincott, 1895.

Kiste, John Van der. "Alfred, Prince, duke of Edinburgh (1844–1900)." *Oxford Dictionary of National Biography*. Online ed. Ed. Lawrence Goldman. Oxford: Oxford University Press.

Kuhn, William M. "Ceremony and Politics: The British Monarchy, 1871-1872." *Journal of British Studies* 26 (1987): 133-162.

Lamont-Brown, Raymond. *John Brown: Queen Victoria's Highland Servant*. Thrupp, Stroud, Gloucestershire: Sutton, 2000.

Lant, Jeffrey L. *Insubstantial Pageant: Ceremony and Confusion at Queen Victoria's Court*. New York: Taplinger, 1980.

Laucella, Linda. *Assassination: the Politics of Murder*. Los Angeles: Lowell House, 1998.

Laurie, Sir Peter. *The Journal of Sir Peter Laurie*. London: Costello, with the Saddlers' Co., 1985.

Lauterbach, Edward. *Fun and Its Contributors: A Victorian Humor Magazine*. Unpublished dissertation, University of Illinois [Urbana-Champaign], 1961.

Lawrence, Frederick. *The Life of Henry Fielding*. Hall, Virtue and Co., 1855.

Leapman, Michael. *The World for a Shilling*. London: Review, 2002 [2001].

Le Caron, Henry [Thomas Beach]. *Twenty-five Years in the Secret Service*. 16th ed. London: William Heinemann, 1893.

Lee, Sidney. *King Edward VII: A Biography*. London: MacMillan, 1925. 2 vols.

Leventhal, F. M. "Odger, George (1813-1877)." *Oxford Dictionary of National Biography*. Online ed. Ed. Lawrence Goldman. Oxford: Oxford University Press.

Livesey, James. "O'Connor, Arthur (1763-1852)." *Oxford Dictionary of National Biography*. Online ed. Ed. Lawrence Goldman. Oxford: Oxford University Press.

Lock, Joan. *Dreadful Deeds and Awful Murders: Scotland Yard's First Detectives 1829-1878*. Taunton, Somerset, UK: Barn Owl Books, 1990.

London, England, Deaths and Burials, 1813-1980 [database on-line]. Provo, UT, USA: Ancestry.com Operations, Inc., 2010.

London, England, Marriages and Banns, 1754-1921 [database on-line]. Provo, UT, USA: Ancestry.com Operations, Inc., 2010.

London Metropolitan Archives, Saint James, Clerkenwell, *Register of Banns of marriage* [database on-line]. Provo, UT, USA: Ancestry.com Operations, Inc., 2010.

Longford, Elizabeth. *Queen Victoria: Born to Succeed*. New York: Harper & Row, 1964.

Loughlin, James. "Alliance and Illusion: Queen Victoria's Irish Visit of 1849." *History* 87: 288.

Lyons, Mark, and Bede Nairn. "O'Farrell, Henry James (1833-1868). *Australian Dictionary of Biography*, Volume 5. Melbourne: Melbourne University Press, 1974, 356-357. Online ed.

Lyttelton, Sara Spencer. *Correspondence of Sarah Spencer Lady Lyttelton 1787-1870*. New York: Scribner, 1912.

Martin, Theodore. *The Life of His Royal Highness the Prince Consort*. New York: Appleton and Company, 1875.

Matthew, H. C. G. "Gladstone, William Ewart (1809–1898)." *Oxford Dictionary of National Biography*. Online ed. Ed. Lawrence Goldman. Oxford: Oxford University Press.

Matthew, H. C. G., and K. D. Reynolds. "Victoria (1819–1901)." *Oxford Dictionary of National Biography.* Online ed. Ed. Lawrence Goldman. Oxford: Oxford University Press.

Maxwell, Herbert. *The Life and Letters of George William Frederick Fourth Earl of Clarendon.* London: Edward Arnold, 1913.

Mayhew, Henry, and John Binny. *The Criminal Prisons of London* [1862]. London: Frank Cass, 1968.

McClintock, Mary Howard. *The Queen Thanks Sir Howard.* London: John Murray, 1945.

McConnell, Anita. "Laurie, Sir Peter (1778–1861)." *Oxford Dictionary of National Biography.* Online ed. Ed. Lawrence Goldman. Oxford: Oxford University Press.

McGonagall, William. "Attempted Assassination of the Queen." *McGonagall Online.*

———. *The Autobiography of Sir William Topaz McGonagall.* Part 2. *McGonagall Online.*

McWilliam, Rohan. "Tichborne Claimant (*d.* 1898)." *Oxford Dictionary of National Biography.* Online ed. Ed. Lawrence Goldman. Oxford: Oxford University Press.

Millais, John Guillie. *The Life and Letters of John Everett Millais.* London: Methuen, 1905.

Molony, Senan. *The Phoenix Park Murders.* Cork: Mercier Press, 2006.

Moran, Richard. *Knowing Right from Wrong.* New York: Free Press, 1981.

———. "The Origin of Insanity as a Special Verdict: The Trial for Treason of James Hadfield (1800)." *Law & Society Review,* 19 (1985): 487-519.

———. "The Punitive Uses of the Insanity Defense: The Trial for Treason of Edward Oxford." *International Journal of Law and Psychiatry,* 9 (1986): 171-90.

Murphy, James. *Abject Loyalty: Nationalism and Monarchy in Ireland during the Reign of Queen Victoria.* Washington, D.C.: Catholic University of America Press, 2001.

Murphy, Paul Thomas. "Jones, Edward [the Boy Jones] *b.* 1824." *Oxford Dictionary of National Biography.* Online ed. Ed. Lawrence Goldman. Oxford: Oxford University Press.

Nelson, Michael. *Queen Victoria and the Discovery of the Riviera.* London: I. B. Taurus, 2001.

"Newgate Prison." In *Capital Punishment UK* [Online].

Nicholls, David. *The Lost Prime Minister.* London: Hambledon, 1995.

Nowlan, Kevin B. "The Fenians at Home." *Secret Societies in Ireland*. Ed. T. Desmond Williams. Dublin: Gill and Macmillan, 1973.

Ó Brion, Leon. *Fenian Fever: An Anglo-American Dilemma*. New York: New York University Press, 1971.

Orton, Arthur. *The Entire Life and Full Confession of Arthur Orton, the Tichbome Claimant (Written by Himself)*. Reprinted from *The People*. [London]: n. p, [1895].

"Outrage on the Queen" (Commons). *Hansard 1803-2005* [Online]. 29 February 1872.

"Outrage on the Queen" (Lords). *Hansard 1803-2005* [Online]. 29 February 1872.

"Oxford," *North Wales Chronicle* 28 July 1840, 4.

Palmer, Alan. "Ernest Augustus (1771–1851)." *Oxford Dictionary of National Biography*. Online ed. Ed. Lawrence Goldman. Oxford: Oxford University Press.

Parker, Charles Stuart. *The Life and Letters of Sir James Graham*. London: John Murray, 1907. 2 vols.

Peel, Robert. *The Private Letters of Sir Robert Peel*. Ed. George Peel. London: John Murray, 1920.

——. *Sir Robert Peel: from His Private Papers*. Ed. Charles Stuart Parker. London: Murray, 1899. 3 vols.

Pelham, Camden. *The Chronicles of Crime, or the New Newgate Calendar*. London: Thomas Tegg, 1841. 2 vols.

"The People's Charter—Petition." *Hansard 1803-2005* [Online]. 2 May 1842.

Planché, James Robinson. *The Castle of Otranto, or Harlequin and the Giant Helmet*. Unpublished MS.

——. *Recollections and Reflections of J. R. Planché*. London: Tinsley Brothers, 1872. 2 vols.

Playfair, Lyon. *Memoirs and Correspondence of Lyon Playfair*. Ed. Wemyss Reid. London: Cassell, 1899.

Poole, Steve. *The Politics of Regicide in England, 1760-1850: Troublesome Subjects*. Manchester and New York: Manchester University Press, 2000.

"Poor Tommy Callan." *Lowell Sun* 28 May 1894, 1.

Post Office London Directory, 1841. London: Kelly, 1841.

"Protection of her Majesty's Person." *Hansard 1803-2005* [Online], 13 July 1842.

"Punch's Dream." *Punch* 2:209 (1842).

Purdue, A. W. "Beatrice, Princess (1857–1944)." *Oxford Dictionary of National Biography.* Online ed. Ed. Lawrence Goldman. Oxford: Oxford University Press.

———. "Daughters of George III." *Oxford Dictionary of National Biography.* Online ed. Ed. Lawrence Goldman. Oxford: Oxford University Press.

Quinlivan, Patrick, and Paul Rose. *The Fenians in England 1865-1872: A Sense of Insecurity.* London: John Calder, 1982.

Radzinsky, Edvard. *Alexander II: the Last Great Tsar.* New York: Free Press, 2005.

Rawlings, Philip. *Policing: A Short History.* Cullompton, Devon, UK: Willan, 2005.

Read, Donald. *Peel and the Victorians.* Oxford: Basil Blackwell, 1987.

Read, Donald, and Eric Glasgow. *Feargus O'Connor: Irishman and Chartist.* London: Edward Arnold, 1961.

Rennell, Tony. *Last Days of Glory: The Death of Queen Victoria.* New York: St. Martin's, 2000.

"Report from the Select Committee of the House of Commons (Admission of Strangers)." 19 April 1888 Session. *EPPI (Enhanced British Parliamentary Papers On Ireland).*

Ridley, Jasper. *Lord Palmerston.* London: Panther, 1970.

Rigg, J. M. "Leopold, Prince, first duke of Albany (1853–1884)." Rev. K. D. Reynolds. *Oxford Dictionary of National Biography.* Online ed. Ed. Lawrence Goldman. Oxford: Oxford University Press.

———. "Wilde, Thomas, first Baron Truro (1782–1855)." Rev. T. G. Watkin. *Oxford Dictionary of National Biography.* Online ed. Ed. Lawrence Goldman. Oxford: Oxford University Press.

"Robert Pate." *Proceedings of the Old Bailey* [Online].

Robinson, Benjamin Coulson. *Bench and Bar.* 2nd. Ed. London: Hurst and Blackett, 1889.

Roebuck, John Arthur. *Life and Letters of John Arthur Roebuck.* Ed. Robert Eadon Leader. London: Edward Arnold, 1897.

Rowell, George. *Queen Victoria Goes to the Theatre.* London: Paul Elek, 1978.

Royle, Edward. "Bradlaugh, Charles (1833-1891)." *Oxford Dictionary of National Biography.* Online ed. Ed. Lawrence Goldman.

Rubinstein, W. D. *Britain's Century: A Political and Social History 1815-1905.* London: Arnold, 1998.

Rumsey, Christopher. *The Rise and Fall of British Republican Clubs 1871-1874.* Oswestry, Shropshire: Quinta, 2000.

Saville, John. *1848*. Cambridge: Cambridge University Press, 1987.

Scherer, Paul. *Lord John Russell: A Biography*. Selinsgrove, PA: Susquehanna University Press, 1999.

"Security of the Queen's Person." *Hansard 1803-2005* [Online], 12 July 1842.

Shiell, Richard, and Dorothy Anderson. "Queely Shiell (1755-1847)" [Online] 2005. 20 Sep. 2010.

Short, K. R. M. *The Dynamite War*. Atlantic Highlands, NJ: Humanities Press, 1979.

Sims, George R. *My Life: Sixty Years' Recollections of Bohemian London*. London: Everleigh Nash & Co., 1917.

Sinclair, Andrew. *Death by Fame: A Life of Elisabeth, Empress of Austria*. New York: St. Martin's, 1998.

Sloan, Robert. *William Smith O'Brien and the Young Ireland Rebellion of 1848*. Dublin: Four Courts Press, 2000.

Smith, F. B. "Lights and Shadows in the Life of John Freeman." *Victorian Studies* 30.4 (1987): 459-73.

Spencer, John Poyntz, Fifth Earl Spencer. *The Red Earl: The Papers of the Fifth Earl Spencer 1835-1910*. Publications of the Northamptonshire Record Society, vol. xxxi. Northampton: Northamptonshire Record Society, 1981. 2 vols.

Staniland, Kay. *In Royal Fashion*. London: Museum of London, 1997.

Stanley, Edward Henry, Lord. *Disraeli, Derby and the Conservative Party: Journals and Memoirs of Edward Henry, Lord Stanley 1849-1869*. Ed. John Vincent. New York: Barnes & Noble, 1978.

St. Aubyn, Giles. *Edward VII: Prince and King*. New York: Atheneum, 1979.

——. *Queen Victoria: A Portrait*. New York: Atheneum, 1992.

Stott, Andrew McConnell. *The Pantomime Life of Joseph Grimaldi*. Edinburgh: Canongate, 2009.

Strutt, Jacob George. *Tallis's History & Description of the Crystal Palace and the Exhibition of the World's Industry in 1851*. London: J. Tallis & Co., 1852.

Summerscale, Kate. *The Suspicions of Mr. Whicher*. New York: Walker, 2008.

Tavers, Robert. *The Phantom Fenians of New South Wales*. Kenthurst, New South Wales: Kangaroo Press, 1986.

Taylor, Derek. *Don Pacifico*. London: Valentine Mitchell, 2008.

Taylor, John Sydney. *The Writings of the Late J. Sydney Taylor*. London: C. Gilpin, 1843.

Thackeray, William Makepeace. "Going to See a Man Hanged." *Fraser's Magazine* 22 (1840): 150-58.

"Thomas Callan, Michael Harkins." *The Proceedings of the Old Bailey* [Online].

"Thomas Cooper." *Proceedings of the Old Bailey* [Online].

Thompson, Dorothy. *The Chartists.* New York: Pantheon, 1984.

Townsend, William C. *Modern State Trials.* London: Longman, Brown, Green & Longman, 1850.

"Treason Act 1842." Legislation.gov.uk [Online].

Tribe, David. *President Charles Bradlaugh, M.P.* Hamden, CT: Archon Books, 1971.

Tuke, Thomas Harrington. "The Case of Arthur O'Connor." *British Medical Journal* 22 May 1875, 672-73.

U.S. Naturalization Record Indexes, 1791-1992 (Indexed in World Archives Project) [database on-line]. Provo, UT, USA: Ancestry.com Operations, Inc., 2010.

Veder, Robin. "Flowers in the Slums: Weaver's Floristry in the Age of Spitalfields' Decline." *Journal of Victorian Culture* 14:2 (2009), 261-81.

Victoria. *Leaves from the Journal of Our Life in the Highlands.* London: Smith, Elder & Co, 1868.

——. *The Letters of Queen Victoria.* First Series. Eds. Arthur Christopher Benson and Reginald Baliol Brett Esher. London: John Murray, 1908. 3 vols.

——. *The Letters of Queen Victoria.* Second Series (1862-1878). Ed. George Earle Buckle. New York: Longmans, Green & Co., 1926-28. 3 vols.

——. *The Letters of Queen Victoria.* Third Series (1886-1901). Ed. George Earle Buckle. London: John Murray, 1930. 3 vols.

Victoria and Victoria [Crown Princess of Prussia]: *Beloved Mama.* Ed. Roger Fulford. London: Evans Brothers, 1981.

——. *Darling Mama.* Ed. Roger Fulford. New York: Holt, Rinehart and Winston, 1969.

——. *Dearest Child.* Ed. Roger Fulford. London: Evans Brothers, 1976.

Von Stockmar, E. *Memoirs of Baron Stockmar.* London: Longmans, Green, & Co., 1873. 2 vols.

Walford, Edward. *Hardwicke's Annual Biography for 1857.* London: Robert Hardwicke, 1857.

Warren, Samuel. "Modern State Trials." *Blackwoods* 68 (1850): 545-72.

Warner, Malcolm. Millais, Sir John Everett, first baronet (1829-1896). *Oxford Dictionary of National Biography*, Online ed. Ed. Lawrence Goldman. Oxford: Oxford University Press.

Weintraub, Stanley. *Disraeli: A Biography*. New York: Dutton, 1987.

——. *Victoria: An Intimate Biography*. New York: Truman Talley, 1987.

West, D. L., and Alexander Walk. *Daniel McNaughton: His Trial and the Aftermath*. London: Gaskell, 1977.

White, Stephen. *What Queen Victoria Saw: Roderick Maclean and the Trial of Lunatics Act, 1883*. Chichester, England: Barry Rose Law Publishers, 2000.

"William Hamilton." *Proceedings of the Old Bailey* [Online].

Williams, Montagu. *Later Leaves*. London: MacMillan, 1891.

Wilson, Philip K. "Eighteenth-Century 'Monsters' and Nineteenth-Century 'Freaks': Reading the Maternally marked Child." *Literature and Medicine* 21 (2002): 1-25.

Woodham-Smith, Cecil. *The Great Hunger*. New York: Harper & Row, 1962.

——. *Queen Victoria*. New York: Knopf, 1972.

Woodruff, Douglas. *The Tichborne Claimant*. London: Hollis & Carter, 1957.

Wyndham, H. Saxe. *Annals of Covent Garden Theatre*. London: Chatto and Windus, 1906. 2 vols.

"Young Oxford in Bethlehem Hospital." *Era* 26 December 1841, 3.

Zschokke. *The Bravo of Venice* [1804]. New York: Arno, 1972.

INDEX

A

Abbott, John, 515

Aberdeen, Lord, 238, 309

Abinger, Lord, 231, 233–35

Adelaide, Queen Dowager, 12, 15, 53,
  161–62, 212, 302–3

Ainsworth, William Harrison, 37, 92

Albert of Saxe-Coburg
  betrothal of, 23–28
  children of, 163–67, 257–58, 265,
    268, 275, 281, 317, 357, 384–85,
    435–36
  death of, 359–60
  marriage of, 10, 27–29, 53–54
  role of, 28–29, 53–54, 162–65
  royal balls and, 153–62

Alderson, Baron, 336, 340–42

Alexander II, Tsar, 442–43, 445–46,
  466

Alexandra of Denmark, 361

Alibaud, Louis, 224

Allen, Henry, 182, 196

Anderson, Robert, 497

Anne, Queen, 25

Anson, George, 27, 71, 129, 159–60,
  163–66, 179, 188, 304

Arbuthnot, Colonel, 176, 180, 182–
  83, 185, 196

Arthur, Chester, 447, 458

assassination attempts
  by Arthur O'Connor, 385–86
  by Edward Oxford, 54–64
  by John Francis, 181–83, 186
  by John William Bean, Jr., 212–16
  on King George III, 42–43
  on King Louis-Philippe, 223–25
  on Prince of Wales, 503–4
  on Queen Victoria, 54–64, 181–
    83, 212–16, 274–81, 315–17,
    385–86, 452–54
  by Robert Francis Pate, 315–17
  on Robert Peel, 237–41
  by Roderick Maclean, 452–54
  by William Hamilton, 274–81

"Attempted Assassination of the
  Queen," 490–92
Augustus, Duke of Sussex, 10, 128

B
Bailey, Samuel, 85
Balfour, Arthur, 499–500
Barkman, John, 271
Barnaby Rudge, 129
Barnum, P. T., 473–74
Barrett, Elizabeth, 223, 261
Barrett, Michael, 368
Barry, Charles, 313
Bartley, George, 150
Baup, Monsieur, 93–94
Beach, Thomas, 497
Bean, Esther, 512
Bean, John William, Jr.
  arrest of, 218–19
  assassination attempt by, 212–16
  defense of, 232–34
  early years of, 207–11
  escape by, 215
  examination of, 217–21, 226
  imprisonment of, 220–21, 227–31,
    512
  last years of, 512–13
  sentencing, 234–35
  trial of, 231–35
Bean, John William, Sr., 209, 234
Bean, Sally, 219
Bean, Samuel, 512
Bedchamber Crisis, 22, 27, 57, 159,
  304
Bellingham, John, 88–89
Bentinck, George, 262
Bicknell, Thomas, 136, 138–39
Biddulph, Lord, 489
Bird, Mr., 210–11, 221
Black Death, 346
Black Pirate, 37
Blaine, James G., 447–48

Bleak House, 322
Bodkin, William Henry, 199, 243
Bolívar, Simon, 377
bombings, 442–46, 493–503
Bow Street Runners, 61–62
Bradlaugh, Charles, 356, 401, 429–30,
  457
Bravo of Venice, The, 37
Bresci, Gaetano, 503
Bridport, Viscount, 451–52, 455
Brougham, Lord, 314
Brown, George, 59, 60
Brown, John, 362–63, 368, 374,
  384–87, 390, 398–99, 404, 452,
  459, 472, 489
Browning, Elizabeth Barrett, 261
Bruce, Henry, 392, 411–13, 415
Brunel, Isambard Kingdom, 313, 328,
  333–34
Bull Ring Riots, 62
Bunsen, Baroness, 332
Burke, Richard, 367
Burke, Thomas Henry, 485–86
Burnside, James, 453, 461
Butcher, Susan, 134, 137–38, 144

C
Calcraft, William, 95–96, 144, 219,
  368
Callan, Thomas, 495–503
Campbell, Sir John, 88
Carlyle, Thomas, 230
Carroll, Sir George, 79
Carver, James, 80, 93, 95, 144, 202–3,
  229
Castro, Thomas, 394–96
Cavendish, Lord Frederick, 484–86
Chamberlain, Joseph, 505
Chowne, Dr., 83, 98–100
Churchill, Lady Jane, 384–85, 391,
  506
Cibber, Colley, 42

Claimant, Tichborne, 394–98
Clarendon, Lord, 266–67
Clark, Dr., 120, 167, 179
Clark, Sir Charles, 20
Clark, Sir James, 20, 318, 329, 334, 337
Clarke, George, 416
Clarke, James Fernandez, 78, 82–83,
  98, 100–101
Clarke, Martha, 511
Clarkson, William, 193–98, 243
Claxton, William, 214, 216
Clayton, William, 59–60, 105
Cleasby, Baron, 405–11, 456, 483
Clifden, Nellie, 358
Cockburn, Alexander, 243–45, 325,
  335–42
Cockerell, Charles Robert, 313
Cohen, Joseph, 496, 500–501
Cole, Henry, 284, 312, 328
Coleridge, John Duke, 396, 406–8,
  416–18, 471, 477, 483
Coleridge, Justice, 243
Colville, Governor, 412–13
Conolly, Dr. John, 83, 98–100, 299–
  300, 335–39, 403, 424
Conroy, Sir John, 12–17, 19, 22–23,
  162, 236, 284, 302–3, 507
convict ships, 91, 205, 227, 287, 290,
  343
Cooper, Isabella, 201
Cooper, James Fenimore, 37
Cooper, Thomas
  arrest of, 143
  capture of, 142–43
  crimes by, 141–42
  hanging of, 219–20
  imprisonment of, 143–44, 192,
    202–24
  sentencing, 202–4
  trial of, 199–202
Cope, Governor, 70, 80, 82, 97–99,
  123–24, 144, 201, 247

Corn Laws, 156, 262–63, 296, 305,
  325, 331
coronation, 10, 16–19, 77, 349
costume balls, 153–62
Cottenham, Lord, 335
Courvoisier, François Benjamin,
  45–46, 62, 67, 85–88, 91–93,
  96–97, 100, 133
Cowling, Samuel, 337
Cronin, Dr. Patrick Henry, 500
Cross, Richard, 415–16, 418
"Cry of the Children," 261
Crystal Palace, 345, 348, 376, 423
Cubitt, William, 313
Culverwell, Johanna, 488
Czolgosz, Leon, 503

D
Dagnall, Samuel, 134, 135
Daly, Timothy, 142–43, 199–200
Darmés, Marius, 223
Darwin, Charles, 475
Dassett, Charles Edward, 213–16,
  219, 232–33
Dassett, Frederick, 214, 216, 232–33
Davis, John Birt, 83
Davitt, Mr., 484
Denman, Chief Justice, 134, 145
Derby, Lord, 368
Diamond Jubilee, 505
Dickens, Charles, 3, 7, 37, 94, 96–97,
  129, 158–59, 190, 208, 322, 360
Dilke, Charles Wentworth, 353–55,
  370, 372, 399–401
Dillon, John, 446
Disraeli, Benjamin, 5, 84–85, 261–62,
  309, 311, 325, 354, 437–41, 475,
  508
Dodman, Charles, 338
Donaldson, Thomas Leverton, 313
Dousbery, Thomas, 174, 177
Driscoll, Charles, 300

Drummond, Edward, 238, 240–41, 244

Drury, Edward, 200

Duchess of Cambridge, 57, 436

Duchess of Gloucester, 302

Duchess of Kent, 10, 12–17, 21, 57, 90, 127–28, 154, 222, 302–3, 346, 357

Duke of Brunswick, 89–90

Duke of Buccleuch, 313

Duke of Cambridge, 74, 127, 161, 301, 336

Duke of Clarence, 12

Duke of Cumberland, 18, 40, 127, 162, 302

Duke of Devonshire, 328

Duke of Kent, 12

Duke of Sussex, 127–28, 161, 284

Duke of Wellington, 26, 74, 76, 161, 184–85, 255, 263, 303, 331, 344, 348

Duke of York, 12, 41–42

Dundas, Sir David, 327

dynamite bomb, 442–46, 493–503

E

Earl of Beaconsfield, 438, 440

Earl of Chesterfield, 370–71

Earl of Ellesmere, 313

Edward VII, 166, 504, 507, 520

Elam, William, 145–46, 151–52, 168

Elephant Man, 32

Elisabeth of Austria, 464, 503

Elizabeth II, 506

Erskine, Thomas, 43

Exhibition. *See* Great Exhibition

F

famine, 262–64

February Revolution, 264–68

Field, Charles Frederick, 322

Fieschi, Giuseppe, 224–25

Fisher, Mr., 201

Fitzclarence, Adolphus, 16

Fitzroy, Lord, 384, 385

Follett, William Webb, 193, 232, 243–45

Forman, Mary Ann, 35

Forster, W. E., 484

Foster, James, 146, 168–69

Foster, John, 129

Francis, Elizabeth, 146

Francis, Jane, 204

Francis, John
  arrest of, 183–86, 191
  assassination attempt by, 181–83, 186
  assassination preparations by, 133–70
  on convict ship, 205, 227
  examination of, 184–85
  exile of, 205–6, 511
  imprisonment of, 185–86, 188, 191, 194–95, 202–6
  last years of, 511–12
  motive of, 192, 197
  sentencing, 198–99, 203–6
  trial of, 192–98

Francis, John, Sr., 146–47, 184, 191, 204

Fraser, Inspector, 453–54

Frederick William of Prussia, 357

Freeman, Edward, 510

Freeman, John, 510

Fuller, John, 431

G

Gainsborough, Fanny, 391

Gardiner, William, 135–36

Garfield, James, 446–49, 457, 476

Garfield, Lucretia, 457

Garrison, William Lloyd, 68

George II, 25

George III, 11, 14, 25, 40–43, 302–3, 505–6

George IV, 12, 14, 25, 236
George V, 520
Gibbs, Robert, 150
Gibson, J. Rowland, 404, 407–8
Gilbert, W. S., 423
Gladstone, William, 309, 311, 324, 328, 355–56, 363–66, 370–73, 387, 389, 392–94, 400–401, 409–11, 419, 429, 439–41, 456, 462–63, 466–69, 481–87, 494, 508
Godrich, Alfred, 424
"Going to See a Man Hanged," 94
Golden Jubilee, 493–503, 505
Good, Daniel, 133–50, 219
Good, Jane, 137–41
Good, Molly, 139, 140
Goodman, Mr., 170
Gordon, General, 487
Gould, Richard, 48–49, 67, 85, 90–91, 97
Graham, James, 174, 176, 189–90, 204, 215–16, 223, 226, 230, 242, 247
Grant, Ulysses S., 447
Granville, Lord, 312, 387, 481–84
Gray, Henry, 286
Gray, J. J., 51
Great Exhibition, 54, 284–85, 312–14, 327–33, 344–50, 375, 423, 510
Great Expectations, 360
Greville, Charles, 189, 257, 262, 331
Grey, Charles, 316, 318
Grey, George, 277, 281, 309, 318, 321, 323, 337, 368, 511
Grimaldi, Joseph, 149
Guiteau, Charles
  assassination of Garfield, 446–49
  trial of, 449–50, 476, 480
Gull, Dr. William, 416, 417
Gurney, Judge, 199

H
Hadfield, James, 41–44, 70, 105–14, 119, 125–26, 199–200
Haining, William, 217
Hamilton, William
  arrest of, 275–76
  assassination attempt by, 274–81, 391–92
  early years of, 269–74
  exile of, 286–87, 514
  imprisonment of, 276–77, 342
  last years of, 513–15
  sentencing, 286–87
  trial of, 282–86
hangings, 94–96, 133–34, 143–45
Harcourt, Lewis, 476, 480
Harcourt, William Vernon, 465–67, 481
Hardinge, Arthur, 384, 387
Hardisty, Edward, 323, 335
Harkins, Michael, 495–97, 499–503
Harmer, James, 79
Hartington, Lord, 440
Hastings, Flora, 13, 19–21, 57, 162
Hawkes, Henry, 233
Hay, Charles, 323–24
Haydon, George Henry, 509–10
Hayes, Superintendent, 453–54, 459–62
Haynau, General, 327
Haynes, John, 190
Hayter, George, 9–10
Hearn, Thomas, 214, 216
Henderson, Sir Edmund, 388, 411
Herbert, Auberon, 400
He-Sing, 348–49
Hilton, Mr., 209
Hobhouse, John Cam, 68
Hodgkin, Dr. Thomas, 98, 116
Holderness, Dr. William Brown, 456, 478
Home Rule Bill, 484, 494

"homicidal monomania," 246

Hood, Thomas, 261, 423

Horry, Sidney Calder, 199–200, 232–34

Houghton, Thomas, 135–36

Household Words, 322

Hucker, Edward, 429, 430–33

Huddleston, John, 323, 335, 337, 341, 471

Hughes, Inspector, 62–63, 67, 70, 221

Hume, Joseph, 228–29, 245

Hume-Williams, J. W., 404–7

Humphreys, William Corne, 79–81

Hungry Forties, 156, 260–61

Hutcheson, William, 246

I

Industrial Revolution, 158

insanity defense
    in Cooper case, 201
    in Francis case, 193–94
    in Guiteau case, 449–50
    in Hadfield case, 43
    in Hamilton case, 282
    in Maclean case, 468–69, 476–80
    in McNaughtan case, 242–44, 250
    in O'Connor case, 406–7
    in Oxford case, 105–8, 112, 117
    in Pate case, 335

J

Jack Sheppard, 37, 92

Jackson, Sergeant, 386

James, Sir Henry, 463, 467, 477, 479, 481

Jarvis, John, 48–49

Jarvis, Mary Ann, 48–49

Jenner, Dr. William, 360, 363

Jervis, John, 281, 285, 323–24, 335–40

Jocelyn, Fanny, 315, 317–19

Johns, Charles, 150–52, 168–69

Johnson, Alexander, 239

Jones, Edward, 165

Jones, Jane, 137–41, 144

Joseph, Elisabeth, 464, 503

Joseph, Franz, 464

Jubilee Day celebrations, 493–503

"Jubilee Plot," 493–503

K

Kean, Charles, 95, 146

Kean, Edmund, 95

Kelly, Thomas, 367

Kennedy, Miss, 500

Kensington System, 13–16, 19, 357

Kenyon, Chief Justice, 43

Key, Charles Aston, 99

Kiss, August, 349

Knight, Mrs., 433

Knocker, Wollaston, 465–66

Kossuth, Lajos, 327

L

Labouchère, Henry, 333

Lamb, Daniel, 275

Laurie, Sir Peter, 79, 85, 125, 174

Law Lords, 250, 337, 340

Lawrence, Thomas, 51

Le Caron, Henri, 497

Lehzen, Baroness, 13, 16–20, 23–25, 28, 55, 129, 163–67, 204, 304

Lenton, John, 50

Léon, Comte, 7, 62

Leopold, Prince, 10–12, 16, 25, 129, 175, 179, 212, 221–22, 260, 278–79, 290, 309, 329–32, 344, 384–86, 390, 404, 436, 464

Liddell, Georgiana, 180

Lights and Shadows of Melbourne Life, 510

Lincoln, Abraham, 359

Loftus, Augustus, 517

London Labour and the London Poor, 34

Louis Napoleon, Prince, 7, 57, 62, 265, 272, 277, 327, 356

Louis XVI, 41–42

Louis-Philippe, King, 223–25, 244, 264, 267

Lovett, Mr., 53

Lowe, Albert, 59–60

Lowe, Joshua, 59–60

Lucheni, Luigi, 464, 503

Lyndhurst, Lord, 250

Lyttelton, Lady, 187, 223, 304

M

MacDonald, Flora, 268

MacLachlan, Archibald, 432–33, 453, 478

Maclean, Annie, 427–28, 430, 432, 478

Maclean, Caroline, 428, 430

Maclean, Charles, 423–25

Maclean, Inspector, 150

Maclean, Roderick
arrest of, 453–54
assassination attempt by, 452–54
assassination preparations by, 434–36, 450
defense of, 477–78
early years of, 420–25
examination of, 456–62, 465–69
imprisonment of, 461, 474–76, 480
last years of, 519–20
trial of, 471–72, 474–81

Macready, William Charles, 147

Mahon, Charles, 299, 339

Manning, Dr. Henry, 478

Manser, Sarah, 86

Marc, Charles Chrétien Henry, 246

Marchioness of Ely, 504

Marklew, Edward, 33, 67, 79, 82

Marquis of Anglesey, 349

Marryat, Captain, 8

Martin, Esther, 512

Martin, George, 215, 221, 232

Mary Queen of Scots, 236

Mathews, Charles James, 148–50

Matthews, Henry, 498

Maudsley, Henry, 424

Maule, Fox, 63, 68–69, 89

Maule, George, 99, 226

Maurice, Oliver, 479

May, Superintendent, 276, 281

Mayhew, Henry, 34, 342

Mayne, Commissioner Richard, 62, 140, 143, 190, 276, 323, 368, 388

McCafferty, John, 366, 367

McGonagall, William, 489–90, 492

McKinley, William, 503

McNaughtan, Daniel
arrest of, 241
assassination attempt by, 237–41
defense of, 243, 325, 337
examination of, 243
imprisonment of, 245–47
motive of, 244
sentencing, 247
trial of, 242–47

McNaughtan Rules, 250–51, 339, 341, 449, 477–78

McNeill, James Carstairs, 451, 454–55

Melbourne, Lord, 16–17, 22–28, 54, 58, 67, 127, 160–64, 304, 439

Melville, Joseph, 495–96

Mensdorff-Pouilly, Count, 153, 180, 186–87

Merrick, Joseph, 32

M'Gill, Inspector, 140

Millais, John Everett, 55, 65, 66

Millais, William, 65, 66

Millen, Francis, 496–501

Minton, Mr., 35, 38

miscreants, 179, 207, 216, 223–28, 235, 251, 410
Mitford, John, 43
monomania, 82, 224, 246–48
Monro, Edward, 243, 246, 335–39
Monro, James, 497–503
Montez, Lola, 146
Mordaunt, Sir Charles, 362
Moroney, John J., 495–502
Morton, George, 414–15, 517, 520.
    See also O'Connor, Arthur
Moss, Charles, 141, 199–200
Most, Johann, 465–66
Mott, Charles, 142–43, 199
Mott, Superintendent James 388
Moulder, George, 275, 277
Murray, Charles Augustus, 174–75

N
Napoleon, Louis, 57, 62, 272, 277, 327, 356
Napoleon III, 356, 374
"Newgate novels," 37, 92, 113
Nightingale, Florence, 369
Noble, Inspector, 458
Normanby, Lord, 58, 68, 70, 83, 98

O
O'Connell, Daniel, 71, 216, 228, 266
O'Connor, Arthur
    arrest of, 388–89, 417
    assassination attempt by, 385–86
    assassination preparations by, 379–84
    confinement of, 417–18
    early years of, 376–79, 391–92
    examination of, 389–90, 402–4
    exile of, 414–16
    imprisonment of, 390–94, 397–98, 402–4
    last years of, 508, 517–18, 520
    sentencing, 409–14

trial of, 404–9
O'Connor, Catherine, 402, 407, 409
O'Connor, Feargus, 243, 265–66, 378, 403, 518
O'Connor, Francis Burdett, 377
O'Connor, George, 402–4, 407, 413
Odger, George, 356, 389, 401
O'Farrell, Henry James, 369
O'Gorman Mahon, Charles, 299, 339
O'Keefe, Bridget, 270, 272–73, 281
O'Keefe, Daniel, 270–73, 281, 287
O'Keefe, Edward, 272–73, 281
O'Kelly, James J., 446
Old Curiosity Shop, The, 208, 209
Oliver Twist, 37
Orton, Arthur, 396
O'Sullivan, Jeremiah, 367, 368
Otway, Charles, 47–49, 62–63, 67, 90, 277, 281, 321, 324, 334
Oxford, Edward
    arrest of, 61, 65–66
    assassination attempt by, 54–64
    assassination preparations by, 49–54
    confinement of, 123–29, 509
    defense of, 79–86
    early years of, 3–9, 30–44
    examination of, 65–70, 82–84, 98–101
    imprisonment of, 70–87, 97
    last years of, 508–11
    motive of, 70, 192, 197
    sentencing, 122
    trial of, 100–122
Oxford, Edward, Sr., 30–32
Oxford, Hannah, 8–9, 30–32, 36, 41, 67, 78, 80–83, 88, 97, 510
Oxford, Susannah, 8. *See also* Phelps, Susannah
Oxman, John, 218, 219
Oxonian, Captain, 5, 7, 9, 113. *See*

also Oxford, Edward

P

Pacifico, Don David, 307, 310, 324

Packman, Mrs., 8, 41, 62

Paget, Matilda, 180

Palmer, Sergeant, 136, 138

Palmerston, Lord, 67, 305–11, 324–27, 357, 359, 511

Parke, Baron James, 90

Parkes, Henry, 517

Parnell, Charles Stewart, 445–46, 483–84, 494

Partridge, James, 60, 214–15, 240

Partridge, William Henry, 83

Pate, Mary Elizabeth, 516

Pate, Robert Francis
  arrest of, 317, 321–22
  assassination attempt by, 315–17
  defense of, 335–41
  examination of, 323–24, 334–35
  exile of, 343, 515
  imprisonment of, 322–23, 342–43
  last years of, 515–17
  in London society, 299–300
  mysterious behavior of, 293–99
  sentencing, 341–42
  trial of, 335–41

Pate, Robert Francis, Sr., 296–300, 323, 335, 342–43, 516

Patteson, Judge, 199, 201–2, 285, 336

Paxton, Joseph, 328–29, 333–34, 345, 349, 516

Pearce, Nicholas, 62, 67, 70, 140, 178, 184, 322

Pearson, George, 171–75, 177–78, 185, 195–96

Pearson, Matthew Flinders, 173–74, 177

Peel, Julia, 327, 330–31

Peel, Sir Robert, 21–22, 25, 58, 61, 76, 159–60, 164, 176, 184, 186, 205, 215, 223, 226–30, 237–41, 248–49, 262–64, 304–5, 311, 314, 325–31, 439, 462–63, 475

Peel's Security and Protection Act, 227, 252, 279, 281–82, 335, 389, 392–93, 404

Pelham, Jabez, 81–83, 88–89

Penny, Inspector, 143, 201–2, 218–19

Perceval, Spencer, 88–89, 242

Perks, Samuel, 107

Peto, Morton, 334

Phelps, Susannah, 8, 36, 41, 52, 62, 67, 70, 80, 113

Phelps, William, 8, 70

Phillipps, Samuel March, 68, 79

Phillips, Charles, 86, 87

Pilot, The, 37

Piolaine, Charlotte, 86, 87

Playfair, Lyon, 327–28

Plug Plot Riots, 230, 243

Poland, Harry Bodkin, 389–90

Pollock, Frederick, 193, 195–97, 232

Ponsonby, Henry, 365, 418, 444, 451–52, 455, 463, 481

Portman, Lady, 180, 188

potato blight, 262–64

poverty concerns, 157–59, 256, 260–61, 280

"powder and wadding," 52, 191, 193, 197–98

Powell, Clarinda, 33–34

Prince Alfred, 436, 457, 506

Prince Arthur, 384–85

Prince Henry of Battenberg, 436

Prince Louis of Hesse, 435

Prince of Prussia, 318–19, 321, 328, 330, 346, 357

Prince of Wales, 166, 187, 223, 255, 297, 301, 317, 347, 356–62, 365, 370–74, 387, 419, 437, 464, 503–4

Princess Beatrice, 374, 451–53

Princess of Wales, 361–62, 372–74, 387, 437, 464

R

recessions, 156–59, 260–61
Reform Act of 1867, 356
Reform Bill of 1832, 14, 40, 160, 314
Regency Bill, 127–28, 162–63
Renwick, Robert, 268, 274, 317, 323, 337
Rex, Ernestus, 71, 72
Robertson, Leslie, 464
Robinson, Hercules, 413–15
Robinson, Mr., 36, 40, 113
Roebuck, John Arthur, 310, 325–27
Rolfe, Baron, 231, 285
Romilly, John, 335, 336
Rose, Thomas, 141
Rosebery, Lord, 506
Rossa, Jeremiah O'Donovan, 445
Rowan, Commissioner Charles, 140, 143, 176–78, 184, 189–90, 215, 323
Roxburghe, Lady, 451–52
royal balls, 153–62
Russell, James, 183
Russell, Lord John, 45–47, 58, 61, 67, 184, 187, 228, 255, 262, 278, 305–9, 318, 325–28, 333, 359, 508
Russell, Lord William, 45–46, 64, 86, 91
Russell, Mark, 183–84

S

Sabben, James Thompson, 407
Sala, George Augustus, 423
Salic Law, 18
Salisbury, Lord, 494, 508
Sandon, George, 33
"scamp," 171, 185
Scarlett, James, 231
Scott, Harry, 495–96
Scott, Thomas, 495–96

Security and Protection of Her Majesty's Person Act, 227, 252, 279, 281–82, 335, 389, 392–93, 404
Sergeant, Marcus, 228
Shakespeare plays, 147–49
She Would and She Would Not, 42
Sheppard, Dr. Edgar, 476, 479
Sheridan, Richard Brinsley, 42
Shiell, Queely, 134
Sibthorp, Charles, 314, 332–33, 345
Silver, James, 241, 317–18, 323, 337
Sipido, Jean-Baptiste, 504
Sloman, Henry, 146
Smith, A. W., 38–39
Smith, Charles, 59
Smith, Henry, 407
Smith, William, 59
Smith O'Brien, William, 266–67, 283, 290
Smythe, John George, 434
"Song of the Shirt, The," 261
Sorrell, Mrs., 428, 430–33
Speed, Robert, 135–36
Spencer, Earl, 484–85
Stanesby, Samuel, 425, 478
Stanley, Lord, 308, 309, 310, 326
Startin, James, 299–300, 338
Startin, William, 299
Stephenson, Augustus, 460–61, 470
Stephenson, Robert, 313, 328
Stockmar, Baron, 16, 71, 167, 304, 312, 326
Sullivan, Alexander, 495, 497, 500
Sybil, or the Two Nations, 261

T

Talfourd, Justice, 336
Taylor, Sydney, 88, 193
Tedman, John, 35, 46–47, 87, 139
Templeman, John, 48–49
Tennyson, Lord, 489
terror bombings, 444–46, 493–503

Thackeray, William Makepeace, 94–96
Thistlewood, Arthur, 95
Thornton, Stephen, 190, 334
"thorough scamp," 171, 185
Tichborne, Henriette Felicité, 394–95
Tichborne, Roger Charles Doughty, 394–98
Tierney, John, 241
Tindal, Chief Justice Nicholas, 89, 195–99, 203, 243, 247–50
Tory opposition, 104, 127–28
Tory spies, 236–39
Tracy, Governor, 221
Trevelyan, Charles, 263–64
Trial of Lunatics Act, 488–89
Trounce, William, 181–82, 189
Truelock, Bannister, 42
Tuke, Dr. Thomas Harrington, 403–10, 416–18
Turner, Reverend, 239
Tussaud, Madame, 95, 97–98
Tweedie, Alexander, 417–18
Twining, Mr., 52
"Two Pronunciations," 492
typhoid fever, 301, 359, 370–71, 387

U
Umberto, King, 503
unemployment concerns, 157–59, 260–61, 356
Uxbridge, Lord, 61, 63, 103

V
Vestris, Lucia, 148–50
Vicky, Princess Royal, 163, 165, 167, 187, 223, 357, 360–61
Victoria, Queen
    assassination attempts on, 54–64, 181–83, 212–16, 274–81,

315–17, 385–86, 452–54
    betrothal of, 23–28
    birthday celebration for, 255–68
    children of, 163–67, 257–58, 265, 268, 275, 281, 317, 357, 384–85, 435–36
    coronation of, 10, 16–19
    death of, 506–7
    early years of, 9–19
    last years of, 493–520
    marriage of, 10, 27–29, 53–54
    royal balls for, 153–62
Victoria of Saxe-Coburg, 10, 12–19, 21, 57, 90, 127–28
Victorian age, 127, 438, 507, 520
Vosper, Thomas, 233–34

W
Walker, William, 276
Walpole, Horace, 149
Webb, Henry, 218–19
Wemyss, William, 268, 276
Whicher, Jonathan, 396
Whig opposition, 17, 27
Wilde, Chief Justice, 285–86
William, Kaiser, 507
William IV, King, 12–16, 18, 40, 162, 302
Williams, Justice, 231, 243
Williams, Montagu, 475, 477
Wilson, Gordon Chesney, 464, 475
Wilson, Samuel, 475
Wylde, Colonel, 172, 180, 182–83, 196

Y
Yestern: or The Story of My Life and Reminiscences, 471